Oyer and Allied Families

Their History and Genealogy

by

Phyllis Smith Oyer

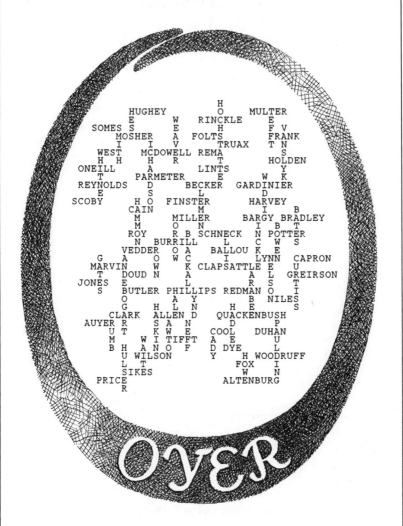

Rochester, New York
1988

ISBN: 0-9620297-0-x

Heart of the Lakes Publishing
Interlaken, New York 14847

DEDICATION

This book is fondly dedicated to mother-in-law

ROSE DUHAN OYER

for her endless aid and encouragement;

RALPH PETER AUYER

for his family archives, interest and research;

and husband

WALTER CHARLES OYER

for his unbounded patience, trust and support.

APOLOGIA

When at the first I took my pen in hand
Thus for to write, I did not understand
That I at all should make a little book
In such a mode; nay, I had undertook
To make another; which, when almost done,
Before I was aware I this begun.

And thus it was: I, writing of the way
And race of saints in this our gospel-day,
Fell suddenly into an allegory
About their journey, and the way to glory,
In more than twenty things which I set down
This done, I twenty more had in my crown,
And they again began to multiply,
Like sparks that from the coals of fire do fly.
Nay, then, thought I, if that you breed so fast,
I'll put you by yourselves, lest you at last
Should prove ad infinitum, and eat out
The book that I already am about.
Well, so I did; but yet I did not think
To show to all the world my pen and ink
In such a mode; I only thought to make
I knew not what: nor did I undertake
Thereby to please my neighbor; no, not I;
I did it my own self to gratify...

From <u>Pilgrim's Progress</u>' Author's
Apology for his Book,--John Bunyan

Walter and Phyllis Oyer

Phyllis Smith Oyer
Sept. 1991

CONTENTS

ACKNOWLEDGMENTS......................................i
PREFACE...iii
    Variant Spellings of the Oyer Name...........v
1 HISTORICAL OYER INORMATION.........................1
2 HISTORICAL AND RELIGIOUS BACKGROUND...............7
3 ERNEST KRAUSS RESEARCH...........................13
4 RELIGIOUS CHANGE IN AMERICA......................21
5 FIRST GENERATION.................................31
6 SECOND GENERATION - ALLIED FAMILIES: Finster-
    Clemens-Schneck-Miller-Ellis-Ballou..........51
7 SECOND GENERATION................................59
    Allied Families - Becker/Bekker: 63; Hochstatter-
    Rema-Bargy-Widrig-Rinckle: 65; Clark: 76
8 THIRD GENERATION.................................79
    Allied - Frank-Clapsattle-Folts-Hess: 84;
      Lints: 89; Van Slyke: 91; Scoby: 94; Childs:
      94; Harvey: 96; Hammond: 97; Morrow: 98;
      Hufstater: 100; Frank: 102; Cain/Kane: 106;
      Burrill: 108; Wemple: 111; Clemens: 112
9 FOURTH GENERATION...............................113
    Allied - Vedder-Gardinier-Van de Bogart-Truax:
      116; Spaulding: 122; Nelson: 124; Crumb: 124;
      Schell: 126; Bowen 126; Frank: 127; Miller:
      128; Quackenbush: 131; Altenburg: 133; Cady:
      134; Larabee: 138; Tefft: 141; Holden: 145
10 FIFTH GENERATION...............................165
    Allied - Brown-Doud-Phillips-Senter: 170;
      Nelson: 175; Beach: 177; Goodemote: 179;
      Woodruff: 180; Fox: 186; Wm Clark: 186;
      Hughey: 188
11 SIXTH GENERATION...............................203
    Allied - Capron: 203; Lougee: 204; Duhan-Lynd-
      Blackall: 210; Reynolds: 216; Waite: 216;
      Hadley: 220; Goodemote: 226; Fox: 231
12 SEVENTH GENERATION.............................245
    Allied - Webster: 249; McFeeley: 251; Learn:
      252; Smith-King-Palmer-Hale: 256; Wise: 259;
      Bishop: 261
13 EIGHTH GENERATION.............................305
14 UNPLACED OYERS................................334
APPENDICES
  i Additional Hanseclever Data....................335
 ii Other Oyers in America.........................337
iii Coats of Arms Details..........................341
 iv Autobiography of Raymond Elbert Oyer............343
  v The Holland Land Company and the Erie Canal......347
    ABBREVIATIONS, ABBREVIATED FORMS AND SOURCES...355
    INDEX...361

ILLUSTRATIONS

Page

Walter[7] and Phyllis (Smith) Oyer
A New York Oyer and a New Orleans Oyer: Leland and Jacob   5
Peter Hasenclever and his book   12
Ringwood, N.J. Ironworks and workmen's buildings   15,16
Martin Luther hymn/psalm book - 1745   22
Palatine church   23
Fort Herkimer church   30
Oriskany Monument and map   41
F. C. Yohn painting of Gen. Herkimer; cannon description   42
Revolutionary soldier's arms   43
Fort Dayton and bicentennial news clipppings   44
Portions of John Finster will   50
Portion of Peter[2] Oyer inventory   52
Frederick[2] and Elizabeth Oyer gravestone and marker   58
Chart of Peter[2] Oyer family   74
Gravestones - Peter[2] and Elizabeth Oyer   75
Town of Ashford, N.Y. - 1900   78
Oyer Mountain, Town of Great Valley, N.Y.   83
Jacob P.[3] Oyer's account book - 1823   104,105
Solomon and Christina (Redman) Oyer gravestones   110
Daniel[3] and Mary (Lints) Oyer; Ida Auyer graveplate   112
Portions: Clark[5] Oyer letter from Lookout Valley, Tenn. -
   Civil War; Eliza Nelson letter telling of Charles[5]
   Oyer's death   115
Eva (Oyer) Crumb, Jacob[4] Oyer and wife Amanda Spaulding   121
Betsy (Curtiss) Auyer family group   148
Foster Jacob[4] Auyer   154
Julia Auyer and husband Edwin McDowell   159
Gravestones: Elizabeth[4] (Oyer) and John Hulser; sons
   Irving and Ezra; Oyer marker, MRC, E. Schuyler, N.Y.   162
Gravestone Oscar[4] and Anna Oyer, MRC, E. Schuyler, N.Y.   164
David Smith[5] Oyer (inset) and Sheldon Brown home   169
Top: Clarence[6] Oyer. Bottom: Nellie[6] and Wallace[6] Oyer   202
World War II grouping - Wallace[6] Oyer family   206-207
Civilian Conservation Corps camp - Allegany State Park   209
Howard[6] and Johanna (Foppes) Oyer; (left) Clarice and
   son Clarence; (right) Clarence and son Ralph   234
Leland[7], Edith (Brougham) and Raymond[8] Oyer   244
Georgia (Lougee) Webster family group   249
WWII letter from Paul Oyer to grandmother; news clippings 304
Johann Adam Eyer vorschrift   338
Eyer/Oyer coats of arms   342
Holland Purchase   345
Erie Canal commerce   346
Lockport, N.Y.'s ten locks   347
Rochester, N.Y.'s aqueduct; packet boat and passengers   350
Miscellaneous documents   Rear

MAPS
In Order of Appearance

Canton of Valais (Wallis)
The Brig/Sion Area of Switzerland
The Rhine Basin With Locations of Oyers and Allied Families
The Rhine Valley around Neuwied and Bendorf, Germany
The Frankfurt-on-the-Main area of the Rhine Valley, Germany
Colonial America
Province of New York - 1771
Pre-revolutionary Mohawk Valley, New York State
New York State With County Lines 1790 - 1900
Herkimer County, New York State
Town of Sandy Creek, Oswego County, New York State
Onondaga County, New York State
Cattaraugus County, New York State
Town of Ashford, Cattaraugus County, New York State
Town of East Otto, Cattaraugus County, New York State
Town of Great Valley, Cattaraugus County, New York State
Town of Concord, Erie County, New York State
Canals of New York State - 1855

NOTE: "Town" is the correct name for the areas that counties are divided into in New York State. The only areas designated "townships" are under military jurisdiction, not civil. There are places where the term "township" has been used erroneously in this book.

Valais, stretching from the Matterhorn to
Mont Blanc and from the Rhone Glacier to
Lake Geneva, bisects Europe's main north-
south trading route. The Valais welcomed
the transient visitor centuries before becoming a world-renowned holiday region.

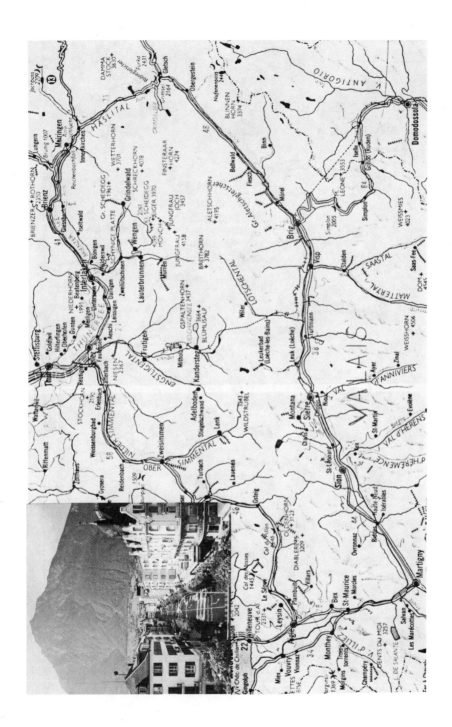

The Rhine Basin showing the Rhine River route to
Rotterdam and some places Oyers and their allied
families settled.

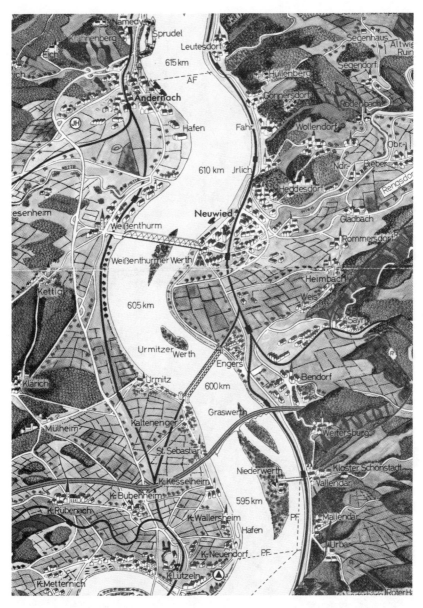

The Neuwied/Bendorf area of the Rhine Valley from
where Johann Jacob Faesch was chosen to be the manager of the Peter Hasenclever proposed iron works in
America. Neuwied is the District capital, flourish-
ing in the 17th century through the establishment
of a large variety of religious denominations.

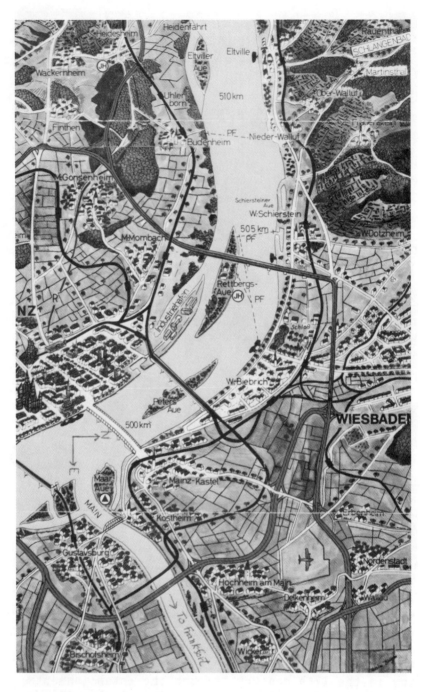

The Frankfurt, Germany area of the Rhine Valley.

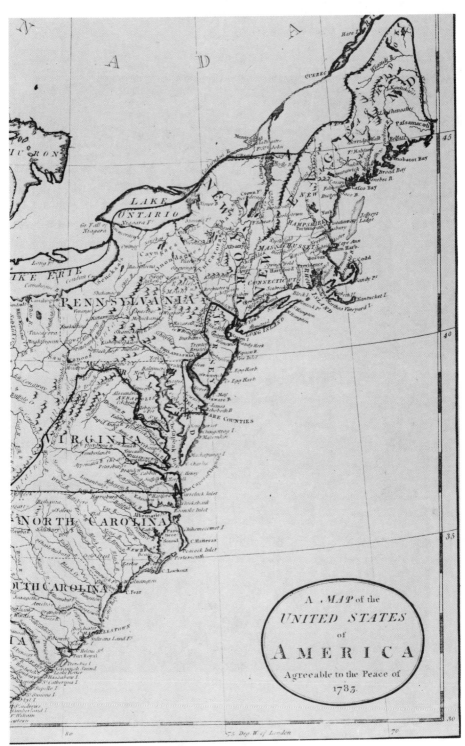

Colonial America

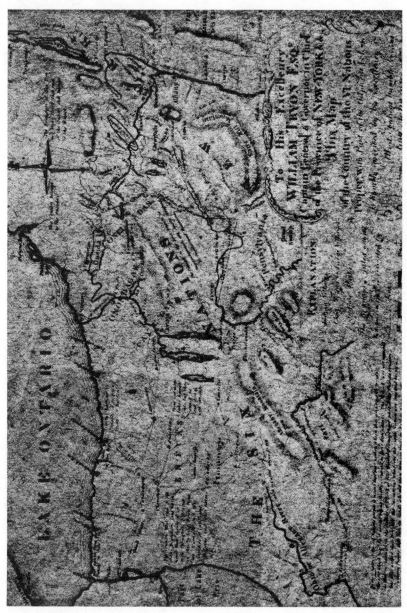

This 1771 map of the VI Nations of New York was presented to William Tryon by Guy Johnson.

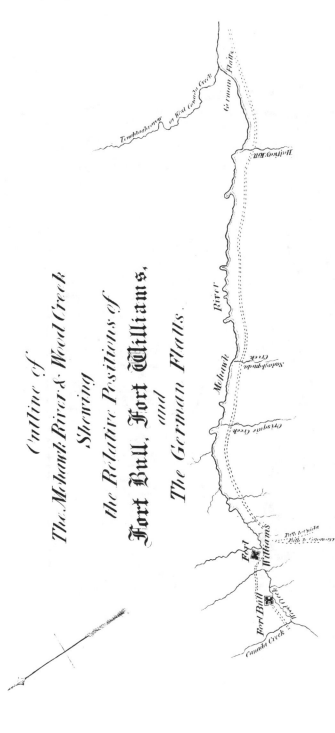

Outline of
The Mohawk River & Wood Creek
Showing
the Relative Positions of
Fort Bull, Fort Williams,
and
The German Flatts.

Pre-revolutionary Mohawk Valley, NYS, showing Fort Bull and Fort William. Fort Bull is the site of Rome, Oneida County, located between the Mohawk River and Wood Creek. It was known as De-o-wain-sta, "a place for carrying canoes." As a portage of about a mile was necessary, a canal was built. It quickly became a great thoroughfare, the Erie Canal later following this route.

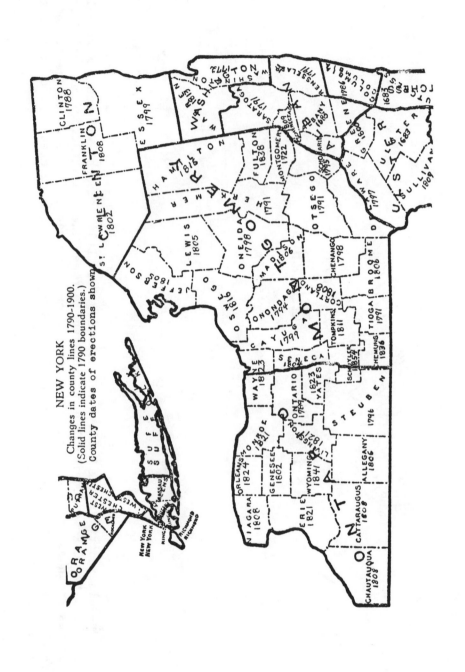

NEW YORK

Changes in county lines 1790-1900.
(Solid lines indicate 1790 boundaries.)
County dates of erections shown

Herkimer County

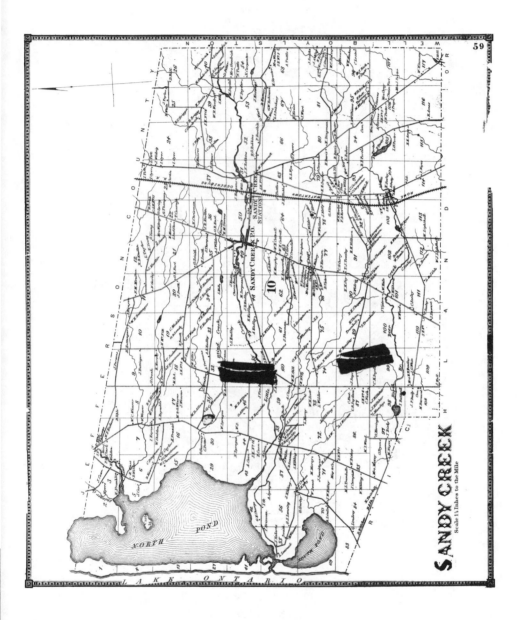

SANDY CREEK
Scale 1½ Inches to the Mile

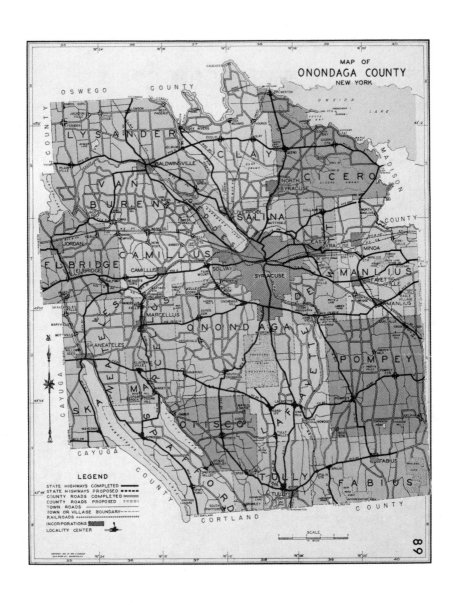

MAP OF
ONONDAGA COUNTY
NEW YORK

LEGEND

STATE HIGHWAYS COMPLETED
STATE HIGHWAYS PROPOSED
COUNTY ROADS COMPLETED
COUNTY ROADS PROPOSED
TOWN ROADS
TOWN OR VILLAGE BOUNDARY
RAILROADS
INCORPORATIONS
LOCALITY CENTER

SCALE
IN MILES

69

CATTARAUGUS Cº

Scale 3¹⁄₃ Miles to the Inch.

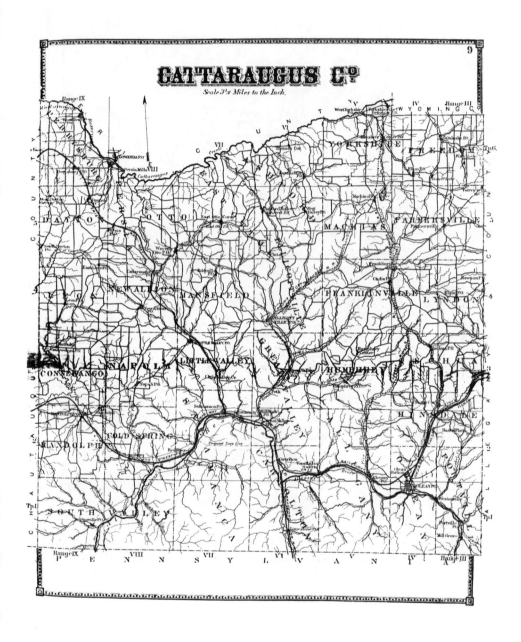

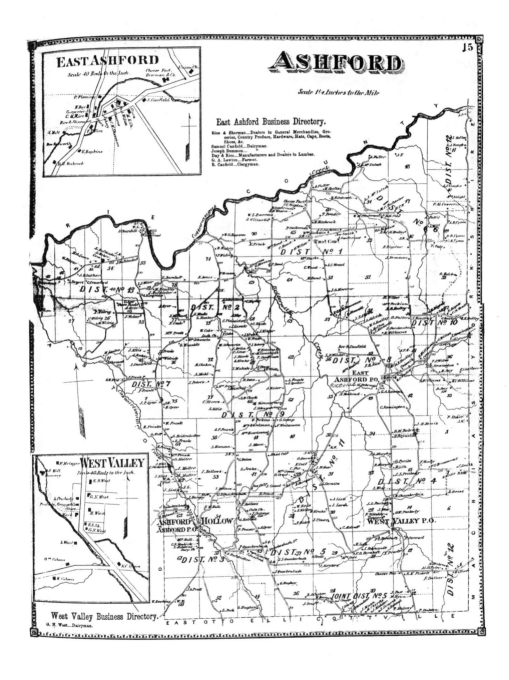

ASHFORD

Scale 1¼ Inches to the Mile

EAST ASHFORD

Scale 40 Rods to the Inch.

East Ashford Business Directory.

Rice & Sherman...Dealers in General Merchandise, Groceries, Country Produce, Hardware, Hats, Caps, Boots, Shoes, &c.
Samuel Canfield...Dairyman.
Joseph Demmon...
Day & Rice...Manufacturers and Dealers in Lumber.
G. A. Lawton...Farmer.
R. Canfield...Clergyman.

WEST VALLEY

Scale 40 Rods to the Inch.

West Valley Business Directory.

G. N. West...Dairyman.

EAST OTTO CORNERS.

Scale 30 Rods to the Inch.

East Otto Corners Business Directory.

Merchants.

J. Laing & Son...Dealers in Dry Goods, Groceries, Hardware, Queensware and Country Produce.
Wm. Bonsteel & Son...Dealers in Dry Goods, Groceries, Flour, Seeds, and Fancy Articles.

Manufacturers.

H. Safford...Manufacturer of Cheese, and Proprietor of Factory at East Otto Corners.
S. Tefft...Manufacturer of Cheese, and Proprietor of Tefft's Factory.
Wm. C. Rannals...Manufacturer of Cheese, at the Union Factory.
A. L. Whiting...Manufacturer of Cheese, at H. Safford's Branch.
N. J. Brace...Manufacturer of Carriages and Wagons.

Miscellaneous.

N. N. Tefft...Surveyor, Justice of the Peace and Farmer.
Clark Burchard...Farmer, Carpenter and Joiner.

EAST OTTO

Scale 1½ Inches to the Mile.

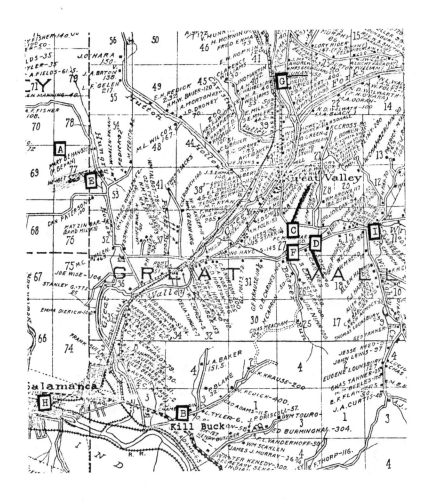

Town of Great Valley and surroundings, Cattaraugus Co, NY.

A Oyer Mountain
B Wallace Oyer homestead
C David S.[5] Oyer homestead
D Clarence Oyer homestead
E Walter Oyer home
F Paul Oyer home
G Felix Duhan homestead
H Phyllis S. Oyer homestead
I Charles Lougee homestead

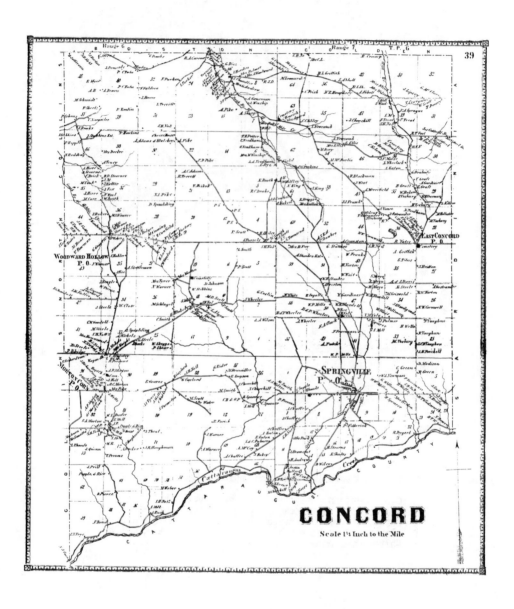

CONCORD

Scale 1¼ Inch to the Mile

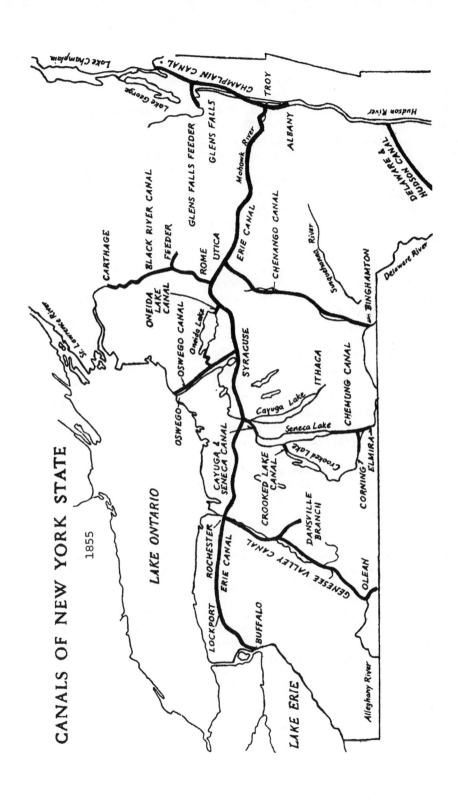

CANALS OF NEW YORK STATE

1855

LAKE ONTARIO

LAKE ERIE

Lake Champlain

Lake George

St. Lawrence River

CARTHAGE

BLACK RIVER CANAL

GLENS FALLS FEEDER

GLENS FALLS

FEEDER

ROME

UTICA

ERIE CANAL

CHAMPLAIN CANAL

TROY

ALBANY

Mohawk River

Hudson River

DELAWARE & HUDSON CANAL

CHENANGO CANAL

Susquehanna River

BINGHAMTON

Delaware River

ONEIDA LAKE CANAL

OSWEGO CANAL

Oneida Lake

SYRACUSE

Cayuga Lake

ITHACA

CHEMUNG CANAL

OSWEGO

Seneca Lake

Crooked Lake

CAYUGA & SENECA CANAL

CROOKED LAKE CANAL

CORNING

ELMIRA

ROCHESTER

ERIE CANAL

GENESEE VALLEY CANAL

DANSVILLE BRANCH

OLEAN

LOCKPORT

BUFFALO

Allegheny River

ACKNOWLEDGMENTS

This project, brought about by the many additions gathered since the publication of the first book in 1977, Frederick Oyer and His Descendants, was begun in 1985 when A. Hawley Arnold of Jordan, New York (#278iii) agreed to collaborate with me in its writing. Hawley and I worked for many months researching and otherwise correlating material from our notes and data supplied to us by family members and others. The pressure of other committments forced his withdrawal from the undertaking in early 1987. Without his many hours of researching, sorting, typing and organizing this book would not have been written.

There are many sources of information that we are incorporating in this book. Our libraries are gems. Wayne Arnold and his staff in Local History at the Rochester Public Library have been obliging in answering many queries. Other libraries' and historical societies' personnel, family members, curators, interested researchers—all have contributed greatly. The town clerks, historians and other officials of many counties, especially Cattaraugus, Onondaga, Montgomery, Steuben, Herkimer, Monroe, Erie, all in New York State, have rendered much information—their painstaking efforts invaluable. Through many family members' efforts we trust names and numbers will come alive for our readers, combining statistics with personification. Regrettably there are some we did not reach; some have not responded. The length of the biographies varies; we hope our readers will understand.

For Oyer historical background, we are indebted to Darrell Oyer of Alexandria, Virginia; Verle and Margaret Oyer of Gibson City; their son Gordon of Champaign, all in Illinois; Dr. Delbert Gratz, librarian/genealogist/European tour conductor at Bluffton College, Bluffton, Ohio (whose help has been extended in advising, writing and editing as well); Dr. John S. Oyer of the faculty of Goshen College, Goshen, Indiana; Hermann Guth and Dr. Hermann of Saarbrucken, Germany; Hubert Eyer of Naters, Switzerland; David D. Eyer of Ligionier, Pennsylvania; Paul Anthon Nielson of Worblaufen, Switzerland; C. E. Prol of Hagen, Germany; and, through his writings, the acknowledged Oyer expert in Switzerland, Paul Heldner of Glis. For the research in northeastern New Jersey we are indebted to Elbert Prol and Jack Chard of Ringwood Manor, Ringwood, New Jersey.

There are many researchers whose unpublished works have been been located and used. We are grateful for permission to publish from many sources.

We need to give special recognition to Ernest Krauss, deceased, of Waldwick, New Jersey. Born in Frankfurt, Germany in 1914, his family migrated to the United States in 1924. He developed an

interest in other German immigrants and their contributions to
this country. Having worked for years with metals, when he came
upon an abandoned ironworks while hiking in the mountains near
his home, he became very interested in researching it.   He
learned that two unheralded Germans were involved, and thus
began his more than twenty year quest to document them and
their accomplishments. He made lengthy stays in Germany and
Switzerland researching Peter Hasenclever and Ringwood's iron-
master, Johann Jacob Faesch. His rich legacy of works is now at
Ringwood Manor. We were originally referred to him by Rutgers
University, founded under the name of Queens College in New
Jersey by leaders of the Dutch Reformed Church in 1766. Hasenclever and the Provincial Governor of New Jersey were two of the
signers of the royal charter from George III.

Letters made available to us by Elbert Hadley (#250) late in
1987 have provided more "flesh and bones" to our people.

It is this wealth of bits and pieces that we are putting together.
As this has been processed by computer, our indebtedness to Dr.
Stanley Ames of Rochester is most gratefully extended: he led a
complete novice through the intricacies of composing a genealogy book. Ruth Metzler of Rochester has helped in advising and
editing. Our son Ron is my basic computer mentor: "Did you have
to start out by writing a genealogy book?!" Our granddaughter
Beth put in many hours the summer of 1987 at the computer, pro-
pelling the work along. Her interest provided a needed boost.

Some of the formats are not the usual ones--we are including
the women in our numbering in the same manner usually reserved
for the men. In addition to putting surnames other than Oyer
right along in the text, it also complicates the generationals. Our
choice to put the allied families where they enter the family is
another deviant. Italics is used for them in all cases except for
Chapter 6. In this way we trust they may be satisfactorily sort-
ed out.

Our copious use of numerals and abbreviations is justified we
trust by squeezing in as much data as we can. The ".1," ".2,"
etc. affixed to a few family numbers were used when a new family
"surfaced"--it has no pedigree significance. It enabled us to
avoid re-numbering everyone.

We have tried hard to avoid errors, although accuracy in all
things has been the top priority. Your corrections, additions and
other comments will be gratefully accepted and put in our records, but another book is not planned.

Our sincerest appreciation is proffered to one and all. We do
hope that our efforts provide a satisfactory tribute to all who
have helped in any way, and that it aids in promoting a worth-
while knowledge of history, religion and family. And may future
scholars find more of the missing pieces!

PREFACE

This book updates and extends greatly the 1977 book, <u>Frederick</u> <u>Oyer</u> <u>and</u> <u>His</u> <u>Descendants</u>, continuing the historical research of Johann Friederich Eyerer (Frederick Oyer) who came to America in 1764 from the Kingdom of Wuerttemberg with many other workmen and their families, the first of them arriving at New York City about the first of October. Many of the families became allied with the Oyers.

These skilled workmen were recruited by Peter Hasenclever, an enterprising German merchant from Remscheid-Ehringhausen who became a British subject. They came from areas that include the River Lahn and Sieg; Ronsdorf in the Wuppertal area of Germany, many places in Alsace and Lorraine, and Saarbrucken.

To our knowledge, no good emigration records of these workmen exist. At first the workmen were not considered important enough. This, though, was the best iron and steel producing area in all Europe. Therefore, when the authorities finally realized they were being stripped of their best tradesmen: carpenters, forgemen, colliers, masons, miners, founders, etc., they objected to their removal. After that they were transported stealthily--no ships' lists; no passengers' lists. The first contingent consisted of about 200 persons for whom quarters and sustenance had to be provided as called for in the agreement. Hasenclever had arrived at New York in June of that year, and quickly purchased a run-down ironworks at Ringwood, in what is now Passaic County, New Jersey, where the men went to work.

There are reasons to believe that Frederick Oyer was first at Ringwood, arriving later in what was to become Herkimer County, New York in 1765. Our research has encompassed many Oyers and allied families, not only of Frederick's line, but others from "his" area of Europe. We therefore are going into some historical detail as we feel the resultant information is not only intriguing, but holds much for the history and/or genealogical researcher.

As with many ethnic groups, the Germans, Dutch and Swiss have certain spelling and naming characteristics that can confuse or assist the genealogist. There are many consonant variations, for instance, resulting in many spelling variations. By far the most common is the interchanging of letters, such as "F" and "V," as in Fischer/Visscher; Folts/Vols. Another: "C" and "K", even using "G", as in Clock/Glock/Klock.

Addressing the question of how to present the Germanic names of people and places, we are copying the example of the authors of <u>The</u> <u>Wuerttemberg</u> <u>Emigration</u> <u>Index</u>, Vol. 1, Trudy Schenk, Ruth Froelke, and Inge Bork [Salt Lake City, Utah 1986]. Therein they state, "German names that carry an 'Umlaut' ...have been changed to their English equivalents (i.e. using the vowel with an "e" added--such as "Wuerttemberg"). Surnames composed of two or more distinct words have been alphabetized under the final word. Thus, von Vogel is found as Vogel von." [p x] Surnames are likewise anglicized.

There are many other problems for the genealogical researcher. Variants, nicknames, "known as"--all are stumbling blocks. "Jr." and "Sr." do not always mean Jr. was the son of Sr. It often denoted someone younger than another of the same name who also resided in the same small community. From 1780 to at least 1860 that the middle initial in a three-part name usually meant the first letter of the given name of that person's father, applying possibly only to New York State Dutch and German families. [Jones, 1:xxv]

Intermarriages between the Dutch and Germans occurred in early New York State families in the 18th century especially, the Palatines and other Lutherans settling where the Dutch had been settled for years.

There is another common habit--dropping the first of two given names: Mary Elizabeth becoming Elizabeth; Anna Margaretha becoming Margaretha; Johann Friederich becoming Friederich.

There are many name conversions: Charity became Gertrude; Melchior became Michael; Dabold/Theobald became David; and Mary was so often Polly.

We also want to reinforce Jones' statements on "family traditions." "Although well-intentioned [they] can be very misleading." [1:xxvi] Previous wars, especially World Wars I and II caused Germanic peoples to mask their heritage. In the 17th and 18th centuries, Rotterdam was the point of departure for so many, departures often delayed for extended periods of time. The awaiting emigrants were treated favorably and had no reservations considering themselves as Dutch, having children born while there. There was also confusion over accents, speech, and hard-to-read writing; consider "Deutsch" vs. "Dutch" as one example. On the other hand, these same reasons apply for some who chose to be considered German, regardless of their ancestors' country of origin. We have learned that the Alsace-Lorraine area has often been cited because it can be considered German or French. Thus we can see that the normal migratory patterns of any peoples should enable us to minimize the importance of a person's ethnic background.

In addition to the Oyer families, many families allied with the Oyers went from Montgomery and Herkimer Counties to settle in Western New York. The county histories produced for our country's centennial did a commendable job of tracing these settlers' histories. We have found that there is often a gap between the generations, or a finality in following a family, their families being lost track of as a result of emigrating. With the help of many people and additional books, we have been fortunate to have been able to fill in many of these gaps, coming close to it in other instances, and "finding" many uncounted descendants. We are therefore presenting the results of our research by including sizable segments on the allied families. It is fascinating to look over the Beers' Herkimer and Montgomery county histories and see name after name appearing there as founding fathers or pioneers-- names that subsequently appear in the same manner as they moved west, especially in Cattaraugus and Erie Counties.

> Pages could easily be filled with worthy names of those who here had homes, those whose brawny arms helped to level forests, and bring into productiveness and beauty the primitive wilderness. The...Quackenbosses (sic), Ellises, Herricks, Cadys, Schuylers, Vedders, Veeders, Wemple,...-- many of these lived brave, noble lives, and left spotless names as an inheritance for their children.

> Names here so oft recurring are known no more in all the region.

> [Beers' Mont]

We can add others: Altenburg, Bargy, Bekker, Cain, Clark, Clemens, Gardinier, Folts, Frank, Hale, Hess, Hochstetter, King, Larabee, Lints, Miller, Multer, Neff, Palmer, Petrie, Redman, Rima(h), Tefft, Widrig... We take a great deal of pleasure bringing them back into the fold and shedding some light on their continuing stories.

VARIANT SPELLINGS OF THE OYER NAME

As all genealogical researchers learn, the spelling of names is one of the biggest obstacles. The following list exemplifies this. The earliest spellings, dated 1767: AYRER and EYERER.

SPELLING   LOCATION AND REMARKS

Aiyer   1.   Beers' History of Herkimer County
         2.   Benton's History of Herkimer County- seems

		to "echo" Beers
Auver	1.	descendants of Peter Oyer (#4), from an old family chart
	2.	some of their current family members
Auer		found only in the New Orleans Oyer lines
Avarer		undated military record, Bellinger's Reg't, Staring Co. – National Archives
Aver	1.	cross reference, original DAR record 1908, and on that DAR application
	2.	Hardin's History of Herkimer County
	3.	MacWethy's The Book of Names, Tryon County Militia, Bellinger's Regiment, Enlisted Men
	4.	Beers' History of Montgomery and Fulton Counties
Ayre		none substantiated
Ayrer	1.	on an early list of Hasenclever workmen
	2.	on a list of men in "Capt. Marx Petry Companie," 1767 of the Annual Report of the State Historian
	3.	on petition to New York State for provision: signature of Elizabeth Ayrer
	4.	naturalization record, 1773
Eierer		baptismal record at birth of Lorentz – the "Johann" was dropped from Friedrich – 1776
Eigher		on a DAR application of a Finster family member
Eirer	1.	baptismal record at birth of daughter Catharina 1777
	2.	1790 marriage of son: Jacob Eirer
Euer		signature on inventory of executor
Eyer	1.	as shown in Swiss family name encyclopedias detailing origin of name
	2.	correct German spelling per Penn. German expert, Rev. Frederick S. Weiser
	3.	variant spelling on DAR application along with Ayer
	4.	as shown on the top section of the Oriskany monument
	5.	1789 marriage of son: Friedrich Eyer
	6.	most common variant
Eyerer	1.	baptismal record at birth of Johann Jacob – 1767
Eyre		federal census 1790, showing Elizabeth and son Frederick
Irer		certification, Bellinger's Regiment: "Frederick Irer has been a corporal in my command..." as shown on the bottom section of the Oriskany monument

Preface

Irer		given as variant spelling in both Beers and Benton histories of Herkimer County
Iser		listing under corporal in Tryon County Militia in MacWethy's book of names
Iver		Hardin's <u>History</u> <u>of</u> <u>Herkimer</u> <u>County</u>: "He spelled his name "'Iver.'"
Our		first land records of the New Orleans Oyers
Oyer	1.	Beers' and Benton's preferred spelling
	2.	1767 militia list: "Johann Friedrich Oyer"
	3.	1780 list of Indian captives Jacob and George
	4.	censuses beginning 1800
	5.	heading of Frederick's son Peter Oyer's chart
	6.	common usage since early years in America

As the families' stories unfold, keep in mind that early America lived off of the land, succeeding because all the energies and abilities of each family member were combined toward that end. America was a nation of farmers. It was a life of manual labor that never ended, only changed with the seasons. For the man, field and forest; for the woman, kitchen and child-rearing.

In 1775 life-expectancy was 34 for the males; 36 for the females. Women married very young; husbands scarcely older. Remarrying after the loss of a spouse was requisite.

Group spirit extended far beyond the village. In winter everyone was expected to help plow the roads. There were numerous bees (gatherings to work communally on a project), barn raisings, tree undercuttings, and log rollings.

Women's education usually consisted of learning to read, and perhaps write their name. Ink was known to freeze as it was being used.

Living through times of privations, poverty, depressions, disease, epidemics and wars, our pioneering ancestors deserve our utmost appreciation and gratitude.

Phyllis Smith Oyer

CHAPTER 1

HISTORICAL OYER INFORMATION

The first historical reference of the Eyer/Oyer name was in the
14th century shown with a listing of the names of families that
settled in Naters in the Canton of Valais (Wallis), Switzerland:
"Eyer (in der Oye, 1440 Oyer, 1480 Eyer)." [Schweiz FN]
     The following is an excellent translation of information
regarding the Oyer name and coats of arms [Valaisan WB]:

EYER

This family first called itself In der Oeye, In der
Oeyen, then Oeyer, Oyer, Hoyer, often also Eier, Aier,
after the district named Eya, which means a little island
in the plains of the Rhone river, and has no relation to
a hen house or a chicken coop. This family, which
since the 14th century, was very well known in Naters
spread itself out to Birgisch, Mund, Brigerberg, Glis,
Baltschieder and Sitten/Sion. (Hildebrand, Priest, acted
as a witness in the testament of Bishop Wilhelm III von
Raron.) Another Hildebrand was Lord Standard Bearer
(Bannerherr) 1473-1490 of the former Zenden Naters,
1478 Grosskastlan; Jakob, Standard Bearer 1495-1502;
Johann, Standard Bearer 1508-1509, District messenger
1510, a follower of Schiner; Peter, Grosskastlan 1513.
Hans, Son of Martin, Citizen of Sitten, is mentioned in
1510. Because of the repressive politics of Schiner, he
had entered into the service of the king of France.
Today this family resides in Naters, Birgisch, Ried-Brig
and Termen. A branch of this family appears in the
18th century (quite likely through marriage) under the
name of Eyer or Albert. (Compare this name.)

Details of the various Eyer coats of arms included in the book
are to be found in Appendix iii. Switzerland does not give official
status to coats of arms.
     The following is from Schweiz HB:

Eyer (in der Oye, Oyer, Hoyer) other spellings Naters in
14th century and spread over Birgisch, Mund,
Brigerberg. Switzerland 1. Hylprand, von Naters,
Kastlan 1478, Bannerherr von Brig 1473-1490. Jakob,
von Naters 1499-1508, Bannerherr, Kastlan von Brig
1505. 3. Johann, von Naters, Bannerherr, von Brig und

1510.   BWGIK-Imesch: Wall Landratsabsch I. Lok.
Archive.

This then confirms some information in the previous translation.
The English and German translation of the Swiss canton Valais
is "Wallis", which interestingly shows up as the given name in a
family of the New York Oyers. Oyers' and allied families' points
of origin as well as current residences include places in the
Alsace-Lorraine area, ownership of which alternated between
Germany and France. Niederhoff is where Ferme de la
Neuf-Grange (New Barn) is located, the home from where the 1830
migration began. Verle's son Gordon has visited there. It is west
of Landau and Strasburg in the Palatinate, not far from Pirmasens.
In Niederhoff are several registrations for the families of Joseph
and Jacob Oyer, with parents, grandparents and children. Other
places include Saarbraucken; Kerpraich-au Bois in Lorraine;
Repaux, Colmar, Caen, Nancy and Bayeux, France; Homberg and
Munich, Germany; Feltbach in Lower Alsace; Milhausen, Kingdom
of Prussia; Emmen, Switzerland (as well as those mentioned in
the translation above). Another note states Termen--no country
noted.

David Eyer of Ligonier, Pennsylvania who researched in
Switzerland in 1985 learned that in certain areas in Switzerland
from 1615-20 to 1900 the Eyer name was very common--there were
more Eyer births than all but one other. Sometimes the ratio was
2:1. His ancestor John Martin Eyer arrived in Philadelphia in 1749
from Alsace, one of but two that we know of, that predates the
arrival of "our" Frederick. [For details, see Appendix ii] To his
dismay he learned the records from 1641-49 are gone. David spent
a day with Paul Heldner, the Oyer expert. He speaks no English;
German should be used in writing him.

Data from Hermann Guth of Saarbrucken states:

> ...there must have been the old Hans Oyer (as a
> witness of the birth record of his granddaughter
> Susanna in 1808 - at this occasion his age is given as
> 56 years) whose maiden name was ...Regle, English:
> Regle, Negle, or Reple. She dies on 25 March, 1820 in
> Niederhoff...
>
> ...At Kutzenhausen we could state one branch of the
> Palatine- Alsatian Eyer family. Another branch can be
> found at Wingen in Alsace, well researched by Mr. Erich
> Wegner, Huttenstr. 7, 673 Neustadt, Weinstr., West
> Germany. Both branches were reformed resp. Catholics
> and not related to the Mennonite Eyers who resided at
> Schweighouse, Alsace.   However, they came from
> Switzerland according to a [confirmable] opinion.

Actually we decline to the view (but we already changed it several times!) that as well the Mennonite Oyers as the Mennonite Eyers could lead back to an Anabaptist Hans Ayer, mentioned about 1700 at St. Marie-aux-Mines (Markirch) in Alsace. But we have no evidence so far.

...Dr. Fritz Eyer, the too early died archivist of the Nancy Departemental archives, who was a specialist in Eyer family history, had the opinion that the Eyers came from Naters near Brig in the Valais, Switzerland. If in fact the proposition of a relationship of the Mennonite Eyer to the St. Marie-aux-Mines Anabaptist Hans Ayer could be proven, the town AYER in the Valais would be the original place for this family.

Darrrell Oyer has noted the areas in America where Oyers are located and their countries of origin. His booklet, Oyer's in America, prepared in 1982, adds Rumania, Sweden, Norway and Ireland to the list of countries of origin for Oyers.

There are interesting connections with other Oyers in the United States. We have concluded that there is a strong likelihood of common ancestry with at least some of them; for this and for pertinent historical reasons we are including information about them.

There was a large group of Oyer emigrees that arrived in 1830 aboard the ship Superior, arriving from LeHavre, France at New Orleans, Louisiana. All twenty-three of them, representing but a few families and ages ranging from 1 to 85, were of the Amish belief, and stated their country as "Suisse" (Switzerland), although they had lived in France. It is pointed out in Chapter 2 that an area of Switzerland, the Canton of Valais (Wallis) is where history's first recorded Oyers were located. This canton for a time was part of France, from 1810 to the middle of the 19th century. This could account for the belief that the Oyer name is French. However, Dr. Gratz states that when a person was once a Swiss citizen, he was always thereafter considered to be a Swiss citizen. Pennsylvania German Society expert, the Reverend Frederick S. Weiser whose work is cited in Appendix ii, states that OYER is the pronunciation spelling; EYER is the correct German. Confusion and/or differences of opinion are very understandable and acceptable.

Families named Eyer/Oyer and Fenster/Finster are both of Swiss origin. [Brumbaugh & Faust]

It should be noted that, although there are many subsequent authenticated spellings of the Oyer name, sometimes changing from one to another within the same family as well within the same generation, we are assuming the origin of the name as Eyer, found

in several reference books.   Our informants have found it is
usually not spelled Oyer in Europe.   The extensive records of the
Church of the Latter Day Saints (LDS) show about twelve pages
of Eyers in Thurnen, Switzerland in the 1670-1700 era.   The
spelling was Eyer in the Lower Alsace Archives that David Eyer
viewed in Strasburg, France.   The Oyer spelling was not used by
the Catholic Eyer family in Brig/Naters, Switzerland.

Verle and Margaret's research found that in one U.S. census,
the name was spelled "Eyer;" ten years later the same family
became "Oyer."   They believe the family originated in Switz.,
reasons for which may be seen in the following data they found.

The New Orleans Oyers, as we shall refer to them, have many
descendants in the areas of Illinois, Indiana, and Ohio, as well as
other midwest states.   Many of them are Mennonites of Amish
descent.   [We will cover the religious aspects of emigration in
Chapter 2.]   There are a number of Mennonite colleges in that
area, with not only Oyer personnel, but with very interested
knowledgeable people who have contributed to this work.

The New Orleans Oyers' progenitor, John Oyer, was 85 at the
time of arrival.   This puts his birth within about two years of our
Frederick, said to be 1747; and hence the strong association with
them begins.

Verle's great-grandfather Peter was the oldest son of fourteen;
twelve were on the ship Superior.   Peter was born in Nancy,
France per his naturalization papers.   An old conversation noted
that this was near the French border, and that perhaps Switzerland was the ancestral home.

According to Margaret Oyer a ninety-two year old cousin living
in the 19th century had said that "one of the brothers had gone
up into Germany and been lost track of."

As these families peopled the midwest we find the same family
names allied with them as with the New York Oyers.   In fact,
Margaret's maiden name is Birkey, that being just one of the
several variant spellings of the name Bargy (Birchi).   Others
include Clemens, Hochstetler (Hochsteder, Hufstader), Muller
(Miller), and Witterrich (Wittrig, Widrig).   To climax this
association, when Margaret's husband Verle compared the facial
features and characteristics of the photographs in Frederick Oyer
and His Descendants, the author's first book [Oyer, 1977], he
noted and described in detail a number of very distinct similarities
to his family members!   Pursuing this information, we now have
acquired photographs that strongly support common ancestry. [See
next page]

Leland[7] Oyer - New York Oyer   Jacob Oyer - New Orleans Oyer

Translations have proven problematic at times. For example, one translator, Jackie Smith of Chatham, Ontario, Canada, indicated she could not literally translate "der eine Insel in der Rhoneebene bezeichnet" as "a little island in the plains of the Rhone River." This has subsequently been explained by information from Dr. John S. Oyer of Goshen College, Goshen, Indiana. He located an elderly parish priest while researching in the village of Eyholz in Switzerland in 1983. In that valley there were a number of people of the name Eyer. "Eya" is a dialect word in the Naters area of the Rhone Valley of Switzerland to designate a plot of land rescued from flooding during the spring snow-melting run-off by dyking the river. Such work is done, then, by an "eyer." The "holz" in the village name of Eyholz means "wood."

Furthering this premise, a letter from the University of Bern in March 1987 to Dr. Gratz explains in detail the family name "Ramseier," which follows in part (note the suffix of the name is "eier"):

...As for our family-name: The Eggiwil - Ramseier write their family-name with -i-. ...Since the 14th century my ancestors have written "Ramseyer" with -y-.
The second part of the name "-ey-" is the same as German "die Aue" 'a fertile plain near the water, mostly on a river'. "Ram-" ...is an old German first name...in English "raven"... The whole name means 'a fertile plain on a river in possession of a man, named raven.' Ramseier/Ramsey<u>er</u> marks the inhabitants of the Ramsey.

[For more detailed information concerning other Oyers in America see Appendix ii.]

CHAPTER 2

HISTORICAL AND RELIGIOUS BACKGROUND

As the likelihood grows that our Oyer family originated in Switzerland, let us examine its early history. Early tribes first established their primitive settlements along the shores of Lake Lucerne, their patron saint being Saint Leodegar. Lucerne/Luzern is the cradle of the Swiss Confederation, dating from 1291.

During the Middle Ages after the defeat of the Habsburg army (1315), Lucerne exemplified friendly relations with the confederates, a historic turn of events. There were three original cantons: Uri, Schwyz and Unterwalden. Bern is the federal capital. The University of Basel was founded by Pope Pius II in 1460 and was the principal center of learning. Erasmus taught there.

The Naters-Birgisch-Mund-Brigerberg-Glis-Sitten area, all in the Canton of Valais, may very well be the place of origin for the hundreds of Oyer families we find today.

The Reformation began in the 16th century. The forerunners of the Mennonites, known as "Anabaptists" to others and referring to themselves as "Swiss Brethren," organized in Zurich, Switzerland in 1525. The name "Mennonite" was taken from Menno Simons, a former Roman Catholic priest who led the Anabaptists in the Netherlands and northern Germany in the 1530's. They believed in the separation of church and state, feeling the Reformation leaders up to that time had not gone far enough in that respect.

They later split into groups, of which the Amish are one, breaking away under Jacob Ammann in the 1690's, (hence the name Amish). Their doctrine was stricter. The Canton of Valais was Roman Catholic, whose capital is Sion (Sitten), which has been a bishopric for hundreds of years. There is a 9th-century cathedral there.

There was little contact between the Swiss and Dutch Anabaptists, who had separate origins, until the 17th century. The Mennonites were expelled from the Canton of Bern in this era.

Often throughout history Valais is shown as a separate entity from Switzerland. From 1291-1513 it was part of the Swiss Confederation. From 1560-1618, it was Roman Catholic, the rest of Switzerland mostly Protestant. In 1810 Valais became part of France. In 1814-15 it was still separate, but Swiss. Gradually the Swiss confederation assumed the structure of today, with both Catholic and Protestant faiths accepted by 13 member states--7 remaining faithful to the Church of Rome.

Alsace-Lorraine is Switzerland's neighboring area. Several Oyer progenitors, including "ours," name that as their place of origin.

As we all are aware, religious problems were a prime reason for emigration; not only from one country to another within Europe, but on to colonial America. Information about these peoples is cited because their travails could have included our Frederick's parents or grandparents; they may have arrived at Frankfurt-on-the-Main as a result of these religious upheavals. Frederick's wife's first husband's name, Finster, has Swiss derivations also: Fenster, Finsterer, Finsterle, Finsterbach, and Finsterwald, found in the cantons of Basel and Vaud. [Schweiz FN]

There is a very detailed account of those times, giving what name detail is available. [Brumbaugh & Faust, pp 84-95] The official list of recruited emigrants has not been preserved. It states that many left without the knowledge of the authorities. Interesting detail is told of even a Northern Italian family emigrating via Geneva, Bern and Rotterdam to America in the 1730's. The emigrants from Switzerland are referred to as "German Swiss" in correspondence. [That may be a good term for us to use!] Family names include Auer, Egger, Burgi, Hans (John) Martin, Mosimann, and Muller/Miller.

An emigration tax of ten per cent was imposed. Many Anabaptists emigrated in 1754, partly because of "lively propaganda." They were "skillful farmers and prosperous." Brumbaugh correlates Anabaptists with Mennonites.

We quote from the book, page 84:

> ...there are any number of cases where persons are recorded as absent without any indication of where they had gone...there was perhaps no cause to make an official record of it....had in 1772 so little definite knowledge of the number of emigrants who had left within a few years...estimated about 500 or at most 600.

The city of Basel, Switzerland is situated on the Rhine River, often called the main artery of Western Europe. It forms the boundary line between Switzerland, Germany and France, taking its waters from the snow-capped peaks and glaciers of the Swiss Alps. Flowing west from within Switzerland, it turns sharply to the north at Basel, flowing through Germany past Rotterdam in Holland and on to the North Sea. Rotterdam thus became the debarkation point for thousands during the early 18th century.

From the maps you will note how close to this area are all the points of origin of the various Oyers known to us. From Basel to Rotterdam is but about 300 miles. From Neuwied to Wuppertal is about 100 miles.

Holland welcomed the Huguenots from France and the Pilgrims from England. However, the Dutch Mennonites moved to northern Germany and Prussia in the 1600's and to the Russian Ukraine in the 1700's. In 1874, many moved from Russia to Canada and to Kansas, Nebraska, and nearby states. Swiss Mennonites settled in southern Germany and France. Some moved to Penn. in 1683 after William Penn offered them religious liberty. They are considered part of the Penn. Dutch, as are the Amish.

Some people made their way quite directly, with help, to America. Some became ill and were taken in by sympathetic peoples; some perished. Some were released (as many were actual captives) by friendly people along the Rhine River. History tells of one Mennonite circa 1711, a Birchi/Bargy who was tied to the mast of a vessel and set adrift down the Rhine. He was taken in at Cleve in Holland, and there "treated well." [PSO]

The first Mennonites came to America in 1683 settling at Germantown, Penn,, near Philadelphia. The first Amish came to America in 1723; the New Orleans Oyers were all Amish, arriving in 1830. [See Chapter 1]

Some of these early arrivals later separated from the stricter Amish, and became Amish-Mennonite. In modern times they have merged with the Mennonite Church, again becoming "Mennonite." There is more of a distinction between the Mennonites and Amish in modern times than in times past. There still are the conservative Amish whose productivity is so well known. In Lancaster Co., Penn. alone there are 1,200 Amish farms. They are thriving doing things in the ways of their forefathers. In recent years many of those families have moved to the Keuka Lake, Yates Co. area of central N.Y.

It is likely that some of the progenitors of these Penn. Amish could be Christian or John Martin Oyer who are shown in Appendix ii. However, we have not found a connection with the New York Oyers.

Brumbaugh's book goes on to explain in detail variations in the spelling of family and women's names:

> ...Most common is the change between Hans
> and Johannes and Joggi and Jacob, and Hans
> and Anna or sometimes prefixed to other
> Christian names, but now and then omitted.

There is much fascinating detail in this book.

Reference is made of the Mennonites in Knittle's book. They were known as Anabaptists in England. Passage was granted to a group that included "60 Switzers under one 'Mitchell' (Franz Louis Michael)", a former citizen of Bern, Switzerland. They were able to lease land there for either three lives or 99 years. [The derivation of the 99-year lease?]

Michael enlisted Christoph von Graffenried of an aristocratic family of Bern to escort the above group. They left secretly in

1708 supported by the Swiss government, anxious for their removal. A small party of miners were to follow him. The first group got as far as England and were delayed. England pushed to get them on their way to America, leaving in September 1709. The Palatines wanted to go to North Carolina with the Swiss. [We researched briefly in New Bern, North Carolina in 1984 but found no Oyers or allied families.] The British government was very involved, including financially, with this Palatine emigration.

Von Graffenried's second group never reached America. It has been noted above that some were taken in by sympathetic citizens of the countries through which they passed; some died enroute; a few are said to have gotten to Virginia, where an ironworks was built near Fredericksburg.

A history of the Graffenried Family covering 1191 AD to 1925 AD by Thomas de Graffenried, published by the author in New York City in 1925 [Vail-Ballou Press, Binghamton, New York] states that "much literature of America was distributed in Switzerland around 1708." Through a plan developed with Charles II of England who supported Roman Catholicism, peoples were to go to England for two years. As a result over 10,000 souls from Germany and England, all under the name "Palatines" were gathered, including many "Switzers." Many were sent to America.

Von Graffenried goes on to state that "the affairs became hopeless," undoubtedly due to his attempts to aid the Swiss Palatines (who were destitute) under his charge and to reimburse them for their losses. Over 20,000 people overran Switzerland and England. Every well-to-do Swiss had one or more refugees quartered on them by order of the government. He noted that in Switzerland the George Ritter Company was in charge of transporting.

Our only other clue is that there was a packet boat captain, Alex Guillot, but that may have referred to the flat bottomed boats in which the Hasenclever men were said to have come up the Hudson River.

There is a paper prepared by Lillian F. Wood (deceased) for the North Carolina Society of the Descendants of the Palatines at a meeting in Kingston, North Carolina 11 April 1956, Palatine Settlers on the Neuse River and Trent River 1710. We have been unable to examine it. We know though that in it the author states that many were orphans; von Graffenried returned to England in 1713; 50 or more got to Virginia; we find the names "Franck" and "Isler" mentioned.

Referring once more to Knittle's book, we first find reference to Oyer allied names. A number of Bekkers are listed, including Michel, Simon, Mighel, Antony and Johan/John Peter, most with families. They embarked June, 1709; Johan Bekker returned to

Holland in 1709.   The closest we can come to "Oyer" is Peter
Eygner, wife Anna Margaretha and 2 children.

Beckers include Conrad; Friederich; sister Anna Elizabeth; Jacob,
wife and children; Johann Jacob, wife Maria Elizabeth; Peter, wife
Elizabeth.   Here too is found Roche, a Palatine.   [This is an old
Irish name which is found in the ancestry of Walter Oyer's
mother, Rose Duhan Oyer.]   The Miller name is also on the North
Carolina list.

Let us now take a look at the history of the Province of New
York where Frederick eventually settled.

The Dutch had originally settled the area, and were well established, with homes, churches, and governing bodies.   The Reformed Church in America is the country's oldest continuous denomination, although its membership is but 350,000, whose representatives hold annual governing synods.

The English won over the territory in the latter part of the
17th century.   A main body of Palatines, 2,500 of them, arrived in
colonial New York from the 1709 group in 1710.   Disease-laden,
nearly 500 had died either enroute or soon after their arrival.
Families were broken up.   Children were apprenticed.   Subsistence
was hard to come by.   Troubles kept mounting, politically and
financially; settlement agreements were a problem.

Six thousand acres were obtained along the Hudson River, where
it was hoped that manufacture of naval stores would be accomplished.   Some of these Palatines remained in New York City; some
went into N.J.

Although work progressed--clearing ground, building huts--their
subservient status was deplorable.   Dissatisfied with their lot, an
unsuccessful rebellion took place.   A change in the governing body
of England from Whigs to Tories caused the loss of what meager
financial support there had been.   The Palatines were abandoned,
but their resourcefulness, determination and ingenuity enabled
them to survive.   In 1712, a number of them went to the Schoharie Valley, where they bought land from the Indians.   Litigation abounded.   Having been unable to bring their tools, they
fashioned their own.   Eventually seven villages were settled.   In a
few years' time they were well-entrenched in this frontier area of
colonial New York.

Lutheran congregations were begun with the help of the Dutch,
which were already well established.   [See Chapter 4]   Though
conquered by the English in 1664, very few English had settled in
the region, choosing rather to send in groups under their control.
In this era began the intermarriages of the Dutch and Germans,
accelerated by the arrival in 1765 to the area, expanded to be
known as the Mohawk Valley, of the Hasenclever workmen and
their families.

Original house built at Ringwood by and for workmen;
picture taken 1983. It has since been badly burned.

Pre-revolutionary stucco country store at Ringwood, New Jersey;
it is currently being restored.

CHAPTER 3

ERNEST KRAUSS RESEARCH

Basel, Switzerland with its strategic location attracted the great minds of Western Europe, and those seeking to improve their fortune. About 1404 two Vaesch/Faesch men settled there, their place of origin not known. [As noted in the Preface, changing "F's" to "V's" happens frequently.] They and their families after them became goldsmiths and stonemasons; during the 17th and 18th centuries they were mostly lawyers, diplomats, and officers in the Swiss Mercenary Armies. Their history is fascinating, but for our purposes, we note that Johann Jacob Faesch was born in 1726. His father died in the 1750's.

In nearby Germany was the Bendorf-Neuwied [noy-veed] highly-industrialized area. Neuwied was founded by Count Frederick of Wied in 1653. An earlier village on that site had been completely destroyed during the Thirty Years' War and the entire countryside had been completely de-populated. In order to re-populate his Duchy, he invited numerous settlers without distinction to race, religion or class. Thus it brought in Jews, Protestants and Catholics. There schools were founded. A gristmill was built on the River Wied to help the economy. This river flows through Neuwied to the Rhine. The mill was converted in 1700 to the production of black powder. In 1739 it became an iron forge and furnace, the Rasselstein Mill, which is still in existence today [early 1970's], known as the "Steel Works and Rolling Mill Rasselstein/Andernach. A. G." It is one of the foremost producers of strip steel in Germany.

Neuwied and Isenburg, two of the prime German regions of origin for many New Yorkers, had atmospheres of religious toleration in the late 1500's. Henry Z. Jones, Jr. whose extensive Palatine research has resulted in his two-volume work, The Palatine Families of New York 1710, (Universal City, Calif. 1985), offers this as a possible explanation for the "theologically flexible viewpoint of many of the 1709ers." (p iv)]

What follows now is quoted extensively from the works of Ernest Krauss, noted in our Preface. He wrote an article, "Johann Jacob Faesch, Morris County Iron Master" in the early 1970's, printed in The North Jersey Highlander, Vol. XV, No. 3, Issue No. 56, Fall 1979.

Jacob Remy, a French Huguenot from the Lorraine, came to Neuwied at the end of the 16th century. A descendant, Johan Heinrich Remy leased the Count of Wied's iron works in 1760. He came from his brother's ironworks in Bendorf. He was an uncle of Faesch's. Faesch, who had left Basel to work with his uncle in Bendorf, accepted an offer from Remy to join him when he went to Neuwied, apparently having learned the trade well enough to become its manager.

Let us read what follows in Krauss' own words:

> ...In the years 1763/1764 a German merchant, Peter Hasenclever of Remscheid-Ehringhausen, had formed a Company in London, England, to exploit the abundant resources and raw materials for the manufacture of iron in the American Colonies. He himself setting out for America in June of 1764 to acquire the necessary properties, he had earlier in that year entrusted his nephew Francis Caspar Hasenclever with the task of procuring the skilled workmen necessary for the successful operation of the proposed Ironworks in America.

The posting of the Hasenclever notices recruiting people to accompany him to America took place in Ronsdorf. In Hermann Kellenbenz's 4th volume of "Rheinischen Lebensbilder" is a long article [pages 79-99] concerning Peter Hasenclever. On page 85 it states that the "male cousin of Franz Caspar Hasenclever has a business in Rotterdam, and in the spring of 1764 in the registers (small places) of Amtern, Beyenburg, Elberfeld (like sister cities) in Ronsdorf (now Ruhrgebiet) he placed an ad for steel specialists, also iron; forgers; carpenters and coal miners,and their families." These places are suburbs or parts of the City of Wuppertal.

[It is interesting to find ship's lists with their manifests showing points of origin and places of stopovers in this era. For instance in 1749, prior to this time, we find the Ship Ann arriving 28 Sept 1749 "from Rotterdam and last from Cowes in England" with passengers from Basil, Wirtemburg, Zweybrecht and Darmstad. If only the Hasenclever families were on ships' lists!]

Krauss' article continues:

> Francis Caspar Hasenclever seems to have made his headquarters at NeuWied. One of his agents there was a Carl Casar. This Carl Casar appears to be the link in a family relationship between the Faesch and Hasenclever families, because he refers to both Francis Caspar Hasenclever and Johann Jacob Faesch as his cousins.

> Workmen were hired selectively from Iron Works on the River Lahn and Sieg in Germany, and as far away as Alsace Lorraine in the neighborhoods of Saarbrucken, Saar Louis, and Deux Ponts. Johann Jacob Faesch

Alsace Lorraine in the neighborhoods of Saarbrucken, Saar Louis, and Deux Ponts.   Johann Jacob Faesch

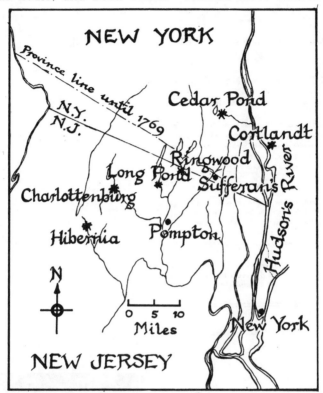

Area first settled by Hasenclever workmen - 1764 - northeast New Jersey.

THE

REMARKABLE CASE

OF

PETER HASENCLEVER,

MERCHANT,

Formerly one of the Proprietors of the IRON WORKS
POT-ASH Manufactory, &c. established, and successfully carried on under his Direction, in the Provinces
of NEW YORK, and NEW JERSEY, in NORTH
AMERICA, 'till November 1766.

IN WHICH

The Conduct of the TRUSTEES of that Undertaking,
in the Dismission of the said PETER HASENCLEVER,
and their unprecedented Proceedings against him in
AMERICA, and in the COURT of CHANCERY,
since his Return to ENGLAND, are exposed.

This CASE is humbly submitted to the Consideration of the
KING, and both HOUSES of PARLIAMENT, to
whom the much-injured Complainant looks up for Redress.

LONDON:

Printed in the Year 1773.

Peter Hasenclever and the book he wrote in his defense, with map and
details of the workmen and their families.

himself was hired and put under contract in the capacity of Chief Manager of the proposed Iron Works in
the Colonies.

Faesch, who was born in the Canton of Basel, Switzerland
according to the inscription in his family Bible, was hired from
the ironworks at Neuweid. We have found numerous families of
Swiss heritage among the workmen.
Some of these, such as Hochstadter/Hufstatter, Burghy/Birkey/
Bargy/Birchi and Witterich/Wuttrich/Widrig, still reside in the
upper northeast New Jersey area where Ringwood (Passaic Co.) is
located. These names are associated with the Oyers throughout
these many generations, both in New York State and among the
New Orleans Oyers.

[Attempts to correspond with families still in northeast New
Jersey brought information from Alan Hochstetler of Glen Rock
about two large genealogies written on the Hochstetlers.
[Hostetler Gen 1; Hostetler Gen 2] tells their stories during the
same era our Frederick was in the Mohawk Valley. We do not
know of a direct connection with "our" Hochstatterrs at this time,
their families being associated with the New Orleans Oyers. See
additional details from these volumes included under our allied
family, the Hochstatters, Chapter 7.]

Faesch was to have had the use of a "comfortable house and
enough acreage to support up to four cows."
The workmen and their families were to be provided transportation and sustenance for a period of five years, no small
undertaking. Although reports state that there were over 500 in
all, Krauss considered this to be an exaggeration, now thought to
be about 350.

> ...It would seem that Faesch was approached with the
> offer to be Manager of the Iron Works in the American
> Colonies late in   1763...

We are quoting extensively now for the express purpose of
transporting you back to those times, as there is so much detail
that can be equated with those who accompanied Faesch, our
Hasenclever workmen. It provides us with such a unique picture
of the days in which our Friederich, his wife and four year old
stepson Johannes Finster made the decision to come to America.
These are excerpts from letters of Faesch's family to him in
early 1764:

> I confirm receipt of yours of the second (Feb.), since
> then received day before yesterday yours of the 9th
> instant, which has set your mother, grandfather and all
> your relatives to wondering why your establishment in

that country should come to pass so suddenly. The reason for this decision we cannot see or guess at... I cannot say anything but advise, that if your friends and your wife are agreeable to this American Journey, then you should take care and see that your contract is signed by the highest of authorities... May God lend you and your wife continuous good health and grant a successful trip to you and your companions. It is unnecessary to remind you how you must conduct yourself in such a position of Honor as that of Chief Manager; the eyes of all subordinates will be upon you and they will guide themselves by your conduct. It would be well if there is nothing to reproach yourself with, for if you have your employees' due respect, you will be able at all times to impose your will upon them. Beware of unwholesome food and drink, one must become accustomed to the climate and decide upon moderation in all things, for we all must consider that our bodies are not made of iron, but to the contrary are very fragile, and, unless a little foresight is used in new as well as old habits of eating and drinking, one could very well invite one's death... Upon your Mother's commission, the requested Cloth for the shirts will be sent tomorrow by Stagecoach to your address at Neuwied, but the Cheeses will be sent next week either by wagon or water, so that everything will reach you in ample time.

Quoting further from Krauss' article:

...No doubt Faesch was getting ready for the trip to America by acquiring the Cheese.

In April a letter confirms the forwarding of four good old Emmenthaler Cheeses, weighing a total of 230 lbs. Also a Merian Bible, edged with copper. Round wheels of Emmenthaler Swiss Cheese were meant for provisions which each passenger had to bring for his use on board ship. [This is widely exported yet today.] Passengers on board 18th century sailing ships going to North America usually brought a sufficient amount of hard tack, smoked and pickled meat, butter salted down in crocks, dried peas and dried apples. etc., to last from six to eight weeks, all foods which are easily kept and do not easily spoil under ordinary conditions.

Faesch probably started his journey to America by leaving Neuwied in April 1764 where mail was addressed to "Madame Faesch nee Hegeman presently at Rotterdam". Excerpts from letters from Faesch's mother are included as they portray poignant thoughts that must have been shared by the families that accompanied him. Mr. Krauss' report goes on:

The mother writes, dated Basel April 23, 1764:

"Dear beloved Son!
As we have seen from your letter your impending journey will go forward in God's name. I, therefore, wish for you the very best and beg the gracious God for His Blessing to all of your projects. May he bring you and your dear wife to that far away place well and hearty....much luck on your journey. I am pleased to hear that you have acquired a Bible, as this indicates to me that you are not only concerned with worldly things, but with the spiritual as well, for it is said, 'in the first place be concerned with the Kingdom of God and His Righteousness and everything will come to you as a matter of course.'"

She goes on and laments the fact that she "will never see again her dearest son in her lifetime."

Krauss relates that tragedy struck Faesch while in Rotterdam--his wife died. This no doubt delayed the departure. Peter Hasenclever, who hired Faesch, embarked for America at Falmouth, England on April 20, 1764, arriving in New York on 4 June 1764.

As previously stated, a contingent of German workers arrived in New York about the first of October of that year. Faesch was probably with this contingent; and as it is the only group arriving in 1764, we believe Frederick Oyer also. Faesch and his workmen began to repair and modernize the Ringwood Iron Works, producing their first iron by November!

The next year some of the workmen were sent from Ringwood to the Mohawk Valley to build and organize Hdasenclever's proposed "pot and pearl ashery," and to grow hemp and flax.

From a paper, "Notice of Peter Hasenclever, an Early Iron-Manufacturer," by Henry A. Homes, LL.D. (1874), we learn that between the time the workmen and Faesch arrived in Nov. 1764 until Nov. 1766 they had succeeded in having in operation four furnaces and seven forges in New Jersey and New York, and a pot and pearl ash factory on the Mohawk River. They had also built stores, workshops and dwelling houses numbering 235. In addition they had built dams for thirteen mill ponds and ten bridges, with many miles of roads.

At New Petersburg, a settlement about five miles above the Town of Herkimer in Herkimer County, was built one saw mill, two frame houses, thirty-four log houses (indicating thirty-four workmen according to Krauss), one stable, one barn, one pond, as well as the pot and pearl ashery.

[There is a booklet prepared by Jack Chard, for the North Jersey Highlands Historical Society of Newfoundland New Jersey (07435), illustrating just how 18th-century ironmaking was done, along with samples of the raw materials.]

Faesch continued his work very successfully, going from Ringwood to "Charlottenburg," Bergen Co., New Jersey, as it is shown
on an early map. He remained loyal during the Revolution and his
ironworks contributed greatly to the war effort, including the
chain that was put across the Hudson preventing the English navy
from proceeding up it. He also supplied much ammunition. To do
so he was supplied with about 300 prisoners of war, mostly Hessians, nearly all of whom settled afterward in New Jersey. He
served as a delegate to the New Jersey convention in December
1787 and signed the ratification of the federal Constitution. He
died May 1799. His Family Bible is at Rutgers University.
Through his story may we feel a "tie that binds."

CHAPTER 4

RELIGIOUS CHANGE IN AMERICA

Religion greatly influenced our forefathers, as it did countless others throughout recorded history. An examination of our religious backgrounds and various other religious aspects is of interest.

As the first church affiliation in America of the New York Oyers was the Dutch Reformed Church, let us examine its history. The Church of the Reformation began in the Netherlands in the 16th century. (The Reformation dates from 1517.) The Protestants on the continent divided into two groups: Lutherans and Reformed. In Scotland it was known as Presbyterian. In America, Reformed. The Church of the Reformation in America was under the control of the Netherlands until 1772, when it became autonomous.

The church in the Ringwood, New Jersey area as early as 1764 is the Pompton Plains Reformed Church, which celebrated its 250th anniversary in 1986. A search of its records of that era was negative--no sign of Oyer or the other Hasenclever families, its members plainly being of Dutch descent. However, we did locate current families in the area of Bergen and Passaic Counties that not only have the same names as the allied workmen, but even retain the "original" spelling: Clemons, Hochstetter, Witterich. We are currently attempting to establish correspondence with them. One, Alan R. Hochsteder of Glen Rock traces his ancestry to an allied family of the New Orleans Oyers as noted in a family book dated 1912. [Hostetler Gen 1,2]

The first known church records in America of the New York Oyers are found in the Dutch Reformed Church at German Flats, Herkimer County, N.Y. The church established in Basel, Switzerland in the 1735 period was also the Reformed. In Germany it was the Lutheran. A Lutheran psalm/hymn book (thought by the descendants all these years to be a bible) dated 1745 is in the possession of Mark Oyer (#340). It undoubtedly came with the emigrants. [See Illus p 22]

Let us try to picture the religious situation in the 17th and early 18th century in the Mohawk Valley. It was at that time the frontier of the colonies. New Netherland, controlled by the Dutch West India Company, had established their Dutch Reformed Church in the young colony as early as 1628. The first known Lutherans arrived 1637/39. As the West India Company had decreed in 1624 that the Reformed religion should be the only religion practiced publicly, it was years before Lutheranism developed to any extent. A pastorate was established after a second petition was sent to the New Netherland headquarters.

Psalm and hymn book, published Marburg, 1745. A meaning—not—
literal translation: A song book for the exercise of God's
holiness in 615 Christian and belief—enriching psalms and
songs, collected by Misters D. Martin Luther and other holy
teachers, in twelve parts. (This has been passed down,
thought to be a bible, from generation to generation with
the following message, written by LeGrand L. Oyer, West
Valley, N.Y. 2 May, 1930: "This Bible has been in the Oyer
family for several generations. The plan is that it shall be
so kept for ever and that the oldest boy in each generation
shall be the Custodian. Kindly pass it on. Note the
scorched condition; tradition tells us that at sometime in
the past the Indians burned the log house of the Oyer family,
which is the cause of this scorched appearance." This is in
the possession of W. Mark⁶ Oyer. Also extant is a pre—
revolutionary pewter teapot.)

Old Palatine church. This was also the military training ground of the
militia for many years after the Revolution. It is located on the Mohawk
Valley Turnpike, three miles east of St. Johnsville.

A prominent Lutheran pastor, the Reverend Wilhelm C. Berkenmeyer, was responsible in the mid-18th century for Lutheranism to be practiced and extended, growing from New York City up the Hudson River and on to the Mohawk Valley. Even early 17th century growth proceeded despite religious intolerance (intolerance abated surprisingly by the emergence of the English, victorious over the Dutch in 1662).

Constitution problems, the acquiring and/or construction of church buildings, incompatibility of the settlers, divergent beliefs, lack of pastors, the use of unordained and otherwise unsatisfactory ministers, lack of money, non-believers, intermittent warrings, rude behavior, language preferences (Dutch versus German), shortage of hymnals, bibles and school books--all of these were tremendous problems during the latter half of the 17th and the first half of the 18th century. The German (Lutheran) newcomers were settling among the better established Dutch (Reformed) inhabitants. [Interestingly, the books needed were sent for in Switzerland, arriving by way of Holland.]

Pastor Berkenmeyer who served from 1722 to 1750 has provided a rich legacy of the day by day life of the church, ending abruptly at the same time the church was beset by a further language dispute between the Dutch and Germans, just one of many differences causing problems between the Lutherans and the Reformed.

The congregations at times merged, and inter-marriages helped lessen their conflicts and problems, a story to be repeated so often throughout history. The first Lutheran catechism was written in Dutch and printed in New York City in 1708. Joint church services and preaching in both languages took place, but not peaceably or satisfactorily.

Churches of that time were houses made of logs; or, if high, put together with boards and covered with plaster. Farm huts and barns were sometimes used, services being cancelled occasionally due to lack of room. Even a former brewery was transformed into a church. Only the Lutheran church in New York City was made of stone.

Despairing Lutheran pastors wrote of the impending "death" of their religion, and thereby of their children if help from the ministerium in Hamburg, Germany was not forthcoming. Miles and miles were covered by the pastors on horseback, as inhabitants numbering 10,000 came to settle in the Hudson-Mohawk River Valleys. This included the area to which our Frederick Oyer and his co-settlers came.

Reunion attempts were many and the strife bitter. By 1745 the Germans were granted "one service in their language every other Sunday on condition that they did not neglect the Dutch services; which, however, they afterward did, in that they came very rarely to the Dutch services." [Hart and Kreider, p 393]

Referring to Knittle's book we find for the first time reference to allied names. [See Chapter II] Knittle goes on to tell of John Conrad Weiser, a magistrate in old Wuertemburg, who was an early Palatine. He was very influential in the Schoharie–Schnectady area in the early 18th century. The royal governor of New York and New Jersey, Robert Hunter, gave permission for the Palatines to move anywhere. Many settled in Schoharie. Land was purchased from the Indians, who were known to sell the same land to various purchasers. Gov. Hunter then changed his mind, but land was acquired regardless. The people were extremely poor; food was scarce, and necessities in very short supply.

The peoples of Schnectady and Albany helped in many ways. Lutheran services were held in the Dutch Reformed Church. [Walter Oyer's Vedder line (see #25) goes back to these early Dutch settlers in Schenectady and Albany, whose influence was so great in our nation's early years.]

In 1710 some Mennonites (Palatines though) settled toward the Susquehanna River, which rises in central New York State.

1725 marks the time of the Burnetsfield Patent. 100 acre lots were acquired by ninety people. Among the settlements were German Flatts, Schoharie, and Herkimer, so prominent in our Oyer history.

By 1727 more immigrants seeking freedom from religious persecution arrived at Philadelphia. Many left Schoharie because of the harsh treatment and ensuing problems and went to Pennsylvania. Knittle notes that our frontiers were pushed forward by Palatines from the Schoharie and Mohawk Valleys (as our genealogical data shows).

Mention is made of the "Switzers" in various parts of Ireland. [Could this account for the Marcus Oyer who came from Ireland in about 1872 per Darrell Oyer's "Oyers in America?"] We know from Knittle that there were Palatine settlements in Ireland in the early 18th century, just south of the Shannon River, for one, and as late as 1758. John Wesley visited there and helped revitalize the area. The Irish women were impressed with the "industry of the women [Palatine]" and improved their (the Irish) ways through their encouragement. Huguenots were found in various parts of Ireland. They were French followers of John Calvin. Fascinating is the fact that the Palatines taught the Irish better potato cultivation. Palatine numbers remained quite constant; loss of the German language came about 1860. By 1935 all prejudice between the Irish and Palatines had vanished.

Another early prominent American Lutheran minister was Pastor Knoll. He preached his services in Dutch, until in 1742 the Germans requested German. He then preached in both Dutch and German. Stubbornness exhibited by members of the church council who tried to prevent German from being used were a result of some leaders of the German party "exhibiting some exceedingly rude behavior." [Kreider, pp 331-485]

In the Mohawk Valley, records of both the German Flats and Stone Arabia Dutch Reformed Church were kept by Pastor Rosencrantz, keeping them in the latter book. Although the German Flat's records were later copied by him to a separate register, it was never finished...some gaps from 1767 to 1775. Baptisms for German Flats up to 1772 are in the Stone Arabia register.

In 1813 this pastor deplored the fact that so few were willing to have births recorded; this though was partly because of the cost--2 shillings, and also because "certain 'fanatics' think that baptism is an absolute senseless act."

The Baptist records of the Fort Herkimer church begin 1763, but some pages from them are lost. [Dailey, p 15, 16]

We found records of these allied families in records of the Lutheran Trinity Church: Schenck, Miller, Frank, Bekker, Finster, and Hockstedter, but no Oyers. We did find "Eachers."

In Stone Arabia we found: Vedder, Vrooman, Witterich, Gardinier, Finster, Fischer, and Quackenbush.

We must rely on the actual churches' records, which are excellent for certain years, lapses occurring as noted and because of the chaotic circumstances of the tumultuous years that followed the Revolution.

The Reverend Frederick Weiser of New Oxford, Penn. is currently his state's Lutheran expert. He was unable to aid us in New York's Lutheran history except to say that the New York State Library has records. A reply from them in December 1986 states they have copies of the records of the Reformed Church of German Flats (Baptisms, 1765-1795, 1811-1848; marriages, 1781-1796, 1813-1814), but of course these are not Lutheran. Further research at the Herkimer County Historical Society in Herkimer would be helpful.

These is a diversity of religions among the Oyer families. Among those we know of are Lutherans, Methodists, Presbyterians, Roman Catholics, United Methodists, Episcopalians. You will note as you read the biographical notes many are involved extensively in religion.

In the early 19th century there were Free-Will Baptists; ancestors were in on the formation of their Society. We do not know of any of Frederick's line that have followed either the Amish or Mennonite religion. Other early descendant church affiliations have included "Methodist Protestant," Free Methodist, Baptist and Presbyterian, in addition to the Dutch Reformed and Lutheran. We have not attempted to determine religious background of the 20th century families. and therefore cannot write knowledgably about such affiliations.

America's religious history, unlike Europe's, has been remarkably ordered and placid. "We have bridled human passion with the judicious exercise of the art of compromise" [Barzun and Graff]

These authors note also that Christianity in the United States is not the result of special creation, but of evolution. Our American history does not begin with the Declaration of Independence, or even with the settlements of Jamestown and Plymouth; rather it descends in unbroken continuity from the beginning of the Reformation. Quoting from The Rules of Sociological Method, an 1894 work reprinted 1950 in Glencoe, Ill., p. 107, "The determining cause of a [religious] fact should be sought among the [religious] facts preceding it, and not among the state of the individual consciousness."

It is interesting to note that by the time of the Revolution, most of the colonies had "state" religions.

Our era is indeed extremely fortunate in that we not only have religious freedom, but live in a time when ecumenism is so alive and well, having had its birth early this century and having "burst into flame in the 1960's, exhilarating even the most casual of church-goers." [Religion editor John Dash, in Rochester's Democrat and Chronicle, 31 Jan. 1987] We are becoming more aware that there is but one God; religions are more in communion with one another than ever before. Fortunate indeed are those who have not experienced the effects of religious intolerance. How very meaningful is the acceptance of one another's religion, on both a personal and social level.

Here are some cases in point:

Early in 1987 a plan was worked out for a television channel in Louisville, Ky. to allow various segments of their religious community to broadcast on the same channel. Christians and Jews are cooperating together to work out details of this "Faith Channel." This it can be predicted will be a model for other cities.

In 1987 Roman Catholicism's chief ambassador to other Christians is underscoring his church's "passion for unity" and acceptance of other denominations as partner churches. He is Cardinal Johannes Willebrands, head of the Vatican's Secretariat for Christian Unity. He visited several eastern U.S. cities in May emphasizing "substantial progress" toward that goal and Rome's commitment to it.

In Washington, D.C. Willebrands encouraged continued interchurch theological talks, as past mutual distortions and misunderstandings are dissipating, and stated that all the churches can learn from each other. He noted that the historic Vatican II council of 1962-65 brought many reforms in his church, including its full-fledged entry into ecumenical efforts. Vatican representatives are meeting with Russian and Greek Orthodox leaders,

Willebrands states, "There has been a great evolution, not only theologically, but in the mentality of the people," with attitudes changed from mutual ignorance and distrust tomutual love and caring.

A conference in Atlanta drew 475 ministers and lay people concerned about Christian unity, with representatives of Episcopalians, Presbyterians, Methodists, Baptists, United Church of Christ and Christian Church (Disciples of Christ) participating.

In New York, Willebrands was presented a unity award; lunched and lectured among the Interchurch Council's key church officials.

At the Rochester Institute of Technology, Rochester, New York there is a campus ministry program with no fewer than fifteen chaplains and adjunct chaplains. The main groups served are Roman Catholic, Lutheran, Episcopalian, both cultural and religious Jews, United Methodists, American Baptists, Mormons, members of the Assembly of God and black Christians. In addition prayer rooms are provided for Moslems. There is space for religious clubs and prayer groups.

There is intensive cooperation among the ministers. For the past three years there has been great growth in solidifying goals and developing good relations.

For the past eight years an Ecumenical Task Force has been working in Western New York to address the toxic waste crises in our country. They are pioneering ways to help victims of such human-made disasters as Love Canal in Niagara Falls, New York. The executive director is Sr. Margreen Hoffmann, OSF (the Roman Catholic Franciscan order). The work of the ETF is being propelled by support from various additional denominations: Methodists, Presbyterians, Episcopalians. Why the churches? Sr. Hoffmann's reply is, "The church must be the voice of conscience, consoling, compassionate, but also confrontive." The ETF speaks not only with victims, but also with the governor, scientists, industrialists, and acedemics. They are learning what needs to be done, and letting people know through their booklet, Earthcare: Lessons From Love Canal. [ETF, 259 4th St., Niagara Falls, New York 14303]

A "spiritual survey" made by *Better Homes and Gardens* and published in their Jan. 1988 issue reveals a startling fact. An expected response of 30,000 brought instead 80,000. More than 50 percent said they believe spirituality is gaining influence here.

It is said America has had three spiritual awakenings: the first in 1800; the second in the 1850's; the last in 1905. All were precipitated by a sense of need after a downturn of morals, or a dividing issue such as slavery. The various denominations put aside their theological differences for the common good, often joining together for prayer. The awakenings, rather than being sparked by politicians or charismatic preachers, came from the by politicians or charismatic preachers, came from the people. Today there is a resurgence of families returning to organized religion.

On 7 Feb. 1988 "an extraordinary ecumenical event" took place in Rochester, N.Y. A priest of the Episcopal Diocese, the Reverend Robert Wainwright of St. Paul's Church, and a Lutheran pastor, the Reverend Ralph Anderson of the Lutheran Church of the Incarnate Word exchanged pulpits: each celebrated the Eucharist according to the other church's rites. This is believed to be the first in the area, if not the nation. In the same article [John Dash, Rochester Democrat & Chronicle, 7 Feb 1988, p 9A] tells of clergy of various denominations attending the installation that same day of the first bishop of the Upstate New York Synod of the Evangelical Lutheran Church in America, formed in 1987 by a merger. Roman Catholic Bishop Matthew Clark was present.

At the same time, we find some mainline churches are losing members, but at a slower rate than before. Counteracting that, there is rapid growth within conservative denominations, some of which are labeled fundamentalist. The two largest church bodies report a slight increase: the Roman Catholics a .71 percent increase to 52,654,908; the Southern Baptist Convention, a .95 percent increase to 14,477,364. Those showing decreases: the Episcopal Church, down 1.3 percent to 2,739,422; the United Methodist, down .48 percent to 9,266,853 (counting 37,483 members for the first time); the Lutheran Church in America down .42 percent to 2,898,202; the American Lutheran Chruch, down .33 percent to 2,332,316; the Christian and Missionary Alliance, a conservative denomination, down 2.27 percent to 227,846. This moderating change eases the enormous losses in the mainline churches since the 1960's.

Among those showing increases are: Jehovah's Witnesses, up 4.7 percent to 730,441; The Assemblies of God, up 2.28 percent to 2,082,878; Seventh-day Adventists, up 2.04 percent to 651,954; Church of the Nazarene, up 1.17 percent to 522,082; and the Lutheran Church--Missouri Synod, up .38 percent to 2,638,164.

[Source: Jim Castelli of Gannett News Service in the Rochester Democrat & Chronicle, 20 June 1987.]

For those who decry the calamities of centuries past that religions have caused, we must realize that they occurred "not because men and women practiced Christianity, but because they failed to [practice it wisely]. Bad as it was with religion, mankind would be infinitely worse off without it. ... Through grace, God illuminates our minds and gives us the power of belief and the ability to see him." [Paul Johnson, "Why I Must Believe in God," Reader's Digest, June 1985, pp. 124-127.]

We should gauge religion by all the relevant variables, and be aware of the duty to make individual judgments, and of our right to affirm those judgments, utilizing the stockpile of available evidence.

We conclude by quoting Francis Bacon who said more than 350 years ago in his essay, "Of Atheism:" "They that deny a God, destroy man's nobility: for certainly man is of kin to the beasts by his body; and if he be not of kin to God by his spirit, he is a base and ignoble creature."

Historic Fort Herkimer church.

Soon after General Herkimer left his home for Fort Dayton, he passed the Fort Herkimer Church. Near the Church was the cabin his father built when he first settled in Herkimer County (about 1723), and where Nicholas was born. The original cabin had been replaced by a large stone house in 1740. This is where Nicholas, his four brothers and eight sisters grew up. It was here that Sir William Johnson decided a fort should be built in 1756 to protect the important military river route during the French and Indian War. It was at Fort Herkimer in 1758 that young Lieutenant Nicholas Herkimer, in command of the troops, met the enemy in a raid on the settlement. The Church was outside the walls around Johan Jost Herkimer's house but did provide protection from the enemy.

The building of the church began about 1753. Above the doorway on the north side are Johan Jost Herkimer's initials and the date 1767, giving us the name of the chief builder and the date of completion. The second story was added in 1812. A successful restoration project in 1976, with remodelling of the interior, has put the church back in use.

The church was an important part of the German community in which Herkimer lived. The General's father and grandfather were among those who left Germany in 1710 to find religious and economic freedom in the new world. After living briefly in the Schoharie and Hudson River settlements, they came with 92 others, to settle in what is today Herkimer County.

CHAPTER 5

FIRST GENERATION

1.   JOHANN FRIEDERICH[1] EYERER (FREDERICK OYER), born probably Germany 17 Apr. 1747 (D.A.R. #55358); died Oriskany Battlefield, Herkimer County, (hereafter Herk. Co.), 6 Aug. 1777. He married in Germany as her 2nd husband ELISABETHA _____, born possibly Wuerttemberg, perhaps ca. 1740; died Schuyler Twp., (hereafter Schuy.), Herk. Co., after 1810.

Our research has failed to establish with certainty a place and date for the birth of the immigrant ancestor, Johann Friedrich Eyerer (Frederick Oyer.) The Preface and Chapter 4 detail research on the ancestry of others in this country who bear the surname Oyer. Although there are several strong associations with them as noted, a common ancestry has not been proven. Similarly, research in the areas from where Frederick's contemporaries originated has failed to offer any clues as to the parentage of Frederick or his wife.

Beers' Herk, [p. 146] states that Johannes/John Finster, the step-son, "was born in the Kingdom of Wurtemberg in 1760, and came to this country with his step-father, Frederick Oyer, in 1764." On p. 141 it shows the name as Oyer, adding in parentheses "formerly written Aiyer and Irer."

There is unsubstantiated family tradition that wife Elizabetha and her son John Finster were with him when they emigrated in 1764, but it seems most likely.

According to obituary notices, Frederick came to America from Germany, of which Wuerttemberg was a portion. The obituary of grandson James Auyer (#20) states that his grandfather was of German descent, "having come from Frankfort-on-the-Main before the revolution, and settled in the Mohawk Valley." Great-grandson Ira Oyer's (#67) obituary notice states: "The ancestor...came to the Mohawk Valley from Frankfort-on-the-Main, capital of the Holy Roman Empire and the seat of great wealth and learning."

Replies from family informants and statements from the Peter Oyer families (#25) state Alsace-Lorraine as their point of origin, one family going so far as to say the name is French.

Frederick came to America with a group of workmen and their families who were brought to this country by Peter Hasenclever, who was an industrialist with interests obtained in New Jersey and New York, beginning with the Ringwood Iron Works, Ringwood, Passaic Co., New Jersey, in 1764.

[A number of the allied family names who were also Hasenclever

workmen as well as the Oyer family name had origins in
Switzerland. See Chapters 1 and 2.]

It is very possible that Frederick was at Ringwood prior to his
coming to the Mohawk Valley, as we have found with other Hasenclever workmen. [See Chapter 3 for many details.]

The first substantiated evidence of Frederick in America is
found in the baptismal record of his son Johann Jacob 29 Apr.
1767. [GF DRC] He was then located at Hasenclever's Mohawk
Valley settlement of New Petersburg/Germantown, and was just
west of German Flats bordering the Schuy. area of Herk. Co.
"The German settlers came up the Hudson and Mohawk Rivers in
flat-bottomed boats as roads were hardly known at that period."
[Beers' Herk., p. 142]

Hasenclever contracted for a tract of 24,755 acres north of the
Mohawk River in Albany/Herk. Co. While his other "manufacto-
ries" were iron works, the New Petersburg project was involved in
manufacturing potash and pearlash, and the growing of hemp, flax
and madder. (Pearlash is impure carbonate of potash.)

Between 1 May 1765 and Nov. 1766 Hasenclever had built at New
Petersburg a saw mill, 2 frame houses, 34 log houses, a stable,
barn, pond, and 1 pot- and pearlash factory. Without a doubt
Frederick Oyer was one of the workers on this construction, as
we learned from the Ringwood curator that a number of the
workmen who had been at Ringwood were sent from there to the
Mohawk Valley site. This gives rise to their speculation that
Frederick may have been a carpenter. In view of the innumerable
Oyer artisans descended from him, we can envision him as an all-
around craftsman.

In addition to establishing the village, fields were cleared, and
Hasenclever induced the workmen to establish farms of their own.
Extant is a deed between him and Lorenz Rinckel (Wrenckle), a
friend of Frederick's and sponsor for 2 of his children. We believe this to be similar to that which Frederick and the other
heads of families agreed:

> THIS INDENTURE made the eighth day of July in the
> year of our Lord One Thousand Seven Hundred Sixty
> Six, Between Peter Hassenclever, of London, Esquire, of
> the one part and Laurence Renekel, the other part;
> Witnesseth; That the said Peter Hassenclever, for the
> consideration of Five Shillings, Lawful Money of New
> York, to him now paid and by the said Laurence
> Renckel, His Heirs, Executors and assigns forever; by
> him confessed and confirmed and by these presents he
> doth hereby Bargain and Sell, Alien, Release and
> Confirm unto the said Laurence Renckel in his actual
> Possession, and being by Indenture to him made and to

his Heirs and Assigns All that certain Tract of Land, situated in the county of Albany, there being One Hundred and Twenty-five acres, Bounded as follows, to wit...

Together with the rights, Edifices, Advantages and Heredataments to the said Tract hereby granted, Appertaining and also the Reversions Remainders of the same And All the Estate, Right, Title, Interest, Property, Claim, Demand whatsoever both in Law and Equity. The same Peter Hassenclever, of, in and to the same or any poart thereof, TO HAVE AND TO HOLD the said Tract of land and premises hereby granted with the Appurtenances unto the said Laurence Renckel, his heirs and Assigns, to his and their only proper use and Behoeff, FOR EVER. AND the said Peter Hassenclever Doth hereby Promise and Grant for himself and his heirs, to and with the said Laurence Renckel, his heirs and assigns, that the said Laurence Renckel his heirs and assigns shall and may at all times hereafter peacably possess and enjoy the said tract of land above granted, with the appurtenances, without the let, hindrances or interruption of him the said Peter Hassenclever his heirs and assigns; and of all and every other person and persons and freed and discharged of and from all other wills, intails, fines, post fines, issues, amerclaments, seizures, bonds, annuities, writings, obligatory, statutes merchant and of the staple, recognizances, extents, judgements, dowers, executions, rents and arrearages of rents and of and from all other charges, estates, rights, titles, troubles and encumbrances whatsoever had, made, committed, done or suffered to be had, made committed, done or suffered by said Peter Hasenclever or any other persons whatsoever, claiming or to claim by, from or under him, them or any of them. And also, That he the said Peter Hassenclever, and his heirs, the said tract of land and premises hereby granted, with their appurtenances unto the said Laurence Rinckel, his heirs and assigns, against him the said Peter Hassenclever and his heirs or any other person or persons lawfully claiming the same under him or them, shall and will WARRANT AND FOREVER DEFEND by these Presents, Provided always, and by those Presents and upon this express Condition That the above named Laurence Rinckel, his heirs and assigns shall yearly and every year forever hereafter, raise upon every Five and Twenty acres of the said tract of land above granted, one ton of good

merchantable hemp, fit for exportation and deliver the
same to the said Peter Hassenclever, his heirs and
assigns at the customary landing place. Provided
likewise that the said Laurence Rinckel his heirs and
assigns do at any time hereafter sell any hemp by him
or them raised on said tract to any person other than
the said Peter Hassenclever his heirs and assigns. That
then the said Laurence Rinckel his heirs and assigns,
for every time that he or they shall so sell any
quantity to any person other than the said Peter
Hassenclever his heirs and assigns, shall forfeit five
hundred pounds of live merchantable hemp to be by
him or them delivered to the said Peter Hassenclever,
his heirs or assigns at the place above mentioned; but
nevertheless it shall and may be lawful for the said
Laurence Rinckel his heirs and assigns, at any time
hereafter to sell and dispose of any other produce from
the said tract of land to any person whatsoever, having
first offered the same for sale to the said Peter
Hassenclever, his heirs and assigns; provided also and
these presents are upon this further express
CONDITION, that if the said Laurence Rinckel, his heirs
and assigns shall make default in raising and delivering
the said one ton of hemp for every five and twenty
acres of the said tract of land at the place above
mentioned in manner aforesaid, then the said Peter
Hassenclever his heirs and assigns provided also, and
these presents be utterly void to all intents and
purposes whatsoever. And the said Peter Hassenclever,
for himself, his heirs and assigns, doth covenant and
grant to and with the said Laurence Rinckel, his heirs
and assigns that the said Peter Hassenclever his heirs
and assigns shall and will advance immediately after the
execution hereof to the said Laurence Rinckel. his
heirs and assigns a sum of money sufficient to pay for
his passage from Germany to America; and also pay and
discharge all the reasonable costs and charges which he
may be put to until he shall be settled on the said tract
of land above mentioned. And also, that the said Peter
Hasenclever's heirs and assigns shall and will provide
the same Laurence Rinckel, heirs and assigns, with a
sufficient log house and provisions, during one year;
and also with necessary implements for agriculture,
horses and other cattle; And likewise that he, the
said Peter Hassenclever, his heirs and assigns upon the
delivery of the hemp in the manner as by the said
Laurence Rinckel, his heirs and assigns as above

covenated, shall and will pay to the said Laurence
Rinckel, his heirs and assigns for the same at the rate
of Twenty pounds for every ton; and for every ton of
the like merchantable hemp that shall at any time
hereafter be raised on the same tract of land by the
said Laurence Rinckel, his heirs and assigns and be by
him delivered to the said Peter Hassenclever, his heirs
and assigns in the manner above mentioned, at the rate
of thirty pounds, like money, for every ton. And the
said Laurence Rickel, for himself, his heirs and assigns,
Doth COVENANT by and with the said Peter Hassenclever, his heirs and assigns, that he the said Laurence
Rinckely, his heirs and assigns shall and will before the
first day of January in the year of our Lord One Thousand Seven Hundred and seventy repay unto the said
Peter Hassenclever the sum and sums of money as he or
they shall advance to the said Laurence Rinckel, his
heirs and assigns for the payment of his passage from
Germany to America or for any other expenses till he
the said Laurence Rinckel, his heirs and assigns shall be
settled on the same.

IN WITNESS whereof the parties to these presents
have hereunto interchangeably set their hands and seals
the day and the year above written.

Peter Hassenclever (L.S.)   Laurence Rinckel
(L.S.)

Contracts differed apparently; one reference states that their
contract was still to run until June 1776: three years and four
months. The clothes provided included soldier's jackets, black
with red cuffs.

With the deeding of individual farms to the workers, a sense of
proprietorship was kindled; these men had probably never owned
land in Germany. With ownership of land came the necessity of
protecting it. New Petersburg was located at the very
westernmost area of settlement in the Province of New York: a
wild and dangerous area. The settlers of New Petersburg joined
with the local militia to defend their homes and property. A
"Liste of Cap. Marx Petry Companyie," dated at "Bornets Field
May the 9th 1767," shows the name of "Friederik Ayrer," as well
as others including Michael Widrig, Dabold Bekker, and Johannes
Rema, descendants of all of whom married into the Oyer family.

Hasenclever had purposely picked the lands adjoining German
Flats because of the fertility of the soil. Hemp, flax, and madder,
the crops Hasenclever designed that his New Petersburg families

grow, required "good and strong lands, as flax and particularly hemp are prodigious impoverishers of land, and the farmers have not yet cattle enough to make manure, and when once the land is exhausted, it will bear no grain." [Hasenclever, Remarkable Case.]

Klock writes [p 5] that Hasenclever "expected his tenants to cut the trees from their lands, burn them and deliver the ashes to his ashery to be manufactured into Pot and Pearl ash; afterward plant the cleared land to flax and hemp to sell him their products. These he was to ship by flat boat down the Mohawk River to Albany and bring back supplies on the return trips to sell to the settlers thru his store at New Petersburg." Klock figures that Hasenclever got the better part of the deal, and it is quite probable that the settlers felt that way too.

But if the New Petersburg families were less than happy with the arrangements, Hasenclever himself had grievances that he outlined in 1773, which follows in part:

> The refractory disposition of the people was also a troublesome affair; they had been engaged in Germany to be found in provisions; they were not to be satisfied; the Country People put many chimeras in their heads, and made them believe, that they were not obliged to stand to the contract and agreements, made with them in Germany; they pretended to have their wages raised, which I refused. They made bad work; I complained, and reprimanded them,; they told me, they could not make better work at such low wages; and, if they did not please me, I might dismiss them. I was, therefore, obliged to submit, for it had cost a prodigious expence to transport them from Germany; and, had I dismissed them, I must have lost these disbursements, and could get no good workmen in their stead. The desertion, sickness, and death of many of the people, and of two of my first managers, was not only a great loss and trouble, but also a terrible disappointment, which occasioned many things to be neglected; but, particularly, made me behindhand with my accounts. In a word, it would be too tedious a talk to mention the several accidents that happened.

The importance of pearlash in these pioneering days was because of multiple uses for it. After the first burning down, lye was produced from which to make soap. The next burning produced fertilizer; the third, leavening. The later successful "black salts" industry near Buffalo in the early 19th century created good commerce for that area, the Erie Canal providing transportation so essential. Only the terminology was changed.

Hasenclever detailed his cost of producing two tons of pearlash at his "manufactory" on the Mohawk in Oct. 1767:

	£	s	d
To make 2 tons of pearl-ash would require 800 bushel of wood-ashes, at 1s. N.Y. c. per bushel	40	0	0
Firewood to boil the lyes for 2 ton of Pearl-ashes	3	0	0
Three men for a week at 3s. wages per day	2	14	0
Barrels and packing at 16s. per ton	1	12	0
Salaries, utensils and reparation of buildings, at 1£. 15s. per ton	3	10	0
Transport to New York, and shipping, at 4£. per ton	8	0	0
Two ton of pearl-ashes rendered on board the ship at New York, cost N.Y. c.	58	16	0
58£. 16s. reduced at 180 per cent. is 32£. 13s. 4d. per ton, sterl.	16	6	8
Freight from New York to London, and commission, insurance and charges	4	19	4
	21	6	0
A ton of pearl-ashes sold 1764, on an average, at 40£. per ton. Profit per ton	19	14	0
	40	0	0

Account of the Expences to raise a Ton of Flax in America fit for Exportation, which requires 10 Acres of Land.

	£	s	d
Plowing 10 acres twice, at 5s. per acre	5	0	0
20 bushels of feed at 4s. 6d. per bushel	14	10	0
Harrowing 10 acres at 5s. per acre	2	10	0
Pulling flax on 10 acres, at 7s. per acre	3	10	0
Watering and drying flax from 10 acres, at 7s. per acre	3	10	0
Breaking and swindling, supposing each acre produces 224 lb. swindled flax, at 3d. per lb. is per ton	28	0	0
Transport from the Mohawk river to New York, and shipping	4	0	0
	51	0	0
A ton of swindled flax rendered on board the ship at New York at 180 per cent. cost sterl.	28	6	8
Freight from America to London, and commission, insurance, and charges in London	4	19	4
	33	6	0
A ton of swindled flax is sold in London at	40	0	0
Profit	6	14	0
An acre produces, on an average, 6 bushels of flax-seed, amounts on 10 acres, 60 bushels, at 4s. 6d. per bushel , is 13l£. 10s. N.Y. c &c. sterl.	7	10	0
Bounty in London per ton	6	0	0
At the exorbitant high American wages renders a ton, Profit	20	4	0

Other examples, including costs of production in Europe, are given.   He makes the statement that a "gentleman farmer in America has but a small advantage by cultivating wheat."

The production of flax and hemp requried much labor, depleted the soil, and was particularly susceptible to spring-time freshets. The settlers preferred to grow Indian corn or wheat.

Apparently neither Hasenclever nor his workmen were entirely satisfied with one another.   Hasenclever himself was having difficulties, particularly with his iron works. By 1769 he was in deep financial troubles. "Poor Peter Hasenclever who has buried in the last 5 years the better part of an hundred thousand pounds in this country...," one man wrote in September of that year. Hasenclever returned to London to try to redeem his good name, never to return to America. Hasenclever's New Petersburg lands went into the hands of the Ellises of England. The settlers paid the Ellis' agents, the Bleeckers of Albany, rent in wheat which they drew by teams to Albany. Flax and hemp production ceased, but state censuses of 1825 and 1835 show considerable linen cloth production by the families of Schuyler Township.   Frederick's farm was located on high ground to the north of New Petersburg (also known as Germantown and presently East Schuyler). The high area became known as Stone Arabia, though the "Yankees" of the area called it the "Dutch (Deutsch) Settlement" because of the number of Germans residing therein.

During the early 1770's Frederick was occupied in building his farm and raising his family. (Life expectancy was 34 for males; 36 for females! Most deaths occurred before the age of 10; for those who survived to 20, men could expect to reach 54; women 56.) Stepson John Finster was apprenticed to a weaver, with all helping to clear the land and farm.

"Fredrick Ayrer" was among those who on 8 Mar 1773, "Have by their Petitions pesented to the General Assembly desired that they may be naturalized and become his Majesty's liege Subjects within this Colony."   Having paid 10s. to the Speaker of the General Assembly, 6s to the Judge, 3s. to the Clerk, and taken the oath of allegiance, his British citizenship was granted. Many of Frederick's neighbors were similarly naturalized on that day. On a "a List of the inhabitants & freeholders of Kingsland & German flats District" signed "the 22d of May 1775" the name of "Frederick Ayrer" is listed, along with many of his neighbors. Frederick's allegiance to the British crown was to be short-lived. As tensions between Great Britain and her American colonies increased, the German settlers of New Petersburg smypathized with the patriotic cause. The Tories and their Indian allies soon became a very real threat; any undecided people, fearing the Indians, espoused the cause of the mother country. For those who remained strong to the patriotic cause, the fear of ravaging Indians was met by one

Nicholas Herkimer, leader of the local militia. Herkimer was the grandson of Palatine immigrant George Herkimer, who was on the N.Y. Palatine subsistence list in 1710. George drew lot #44 on the 1723 Burnetsfield Patent. Nicholas, his father, had fought in the French and Indian War. In 1776 he was appointed brigadier general by the Tryon County Committee of Safety. This commission was formed at a town meeting to protect the frontier area (which this was at that time) from marauding Indians, and to provide for a militia to fight in the on-rushing revolution.

On July 17, 1777 General Herkimer issued this proclamation:

> Whereas, it appears certain that the enemy, of about 2,000 strong, Christians and savages, are arrived at Oswego, with the intention to invade our frontiers, I think it proper and most necessary for the defence of our country, and it shall be ordered by me, as soon as the enemy approaches, that every male person, being in health, from sixteen to sixty years of age, in this our county, shall, as he is in duty bound, repair immediately, with arms and accoutrements, to the place to be appointed in my orders, and will then march to oppose the enemy with vigor, as true patriots, for the just defence of our country.
>
> But concerning the disaffected, and who will not directly obey such orders, they shall be taken, along with their arms, secured under guard, to join the main body.
>
> And as such invasion regards every friend to the country in general, but of this county in particular, to show his zeal and well affected spirit in actual defence of the same, all the members of the committee, as well as all those who, by former commissions or otherwise, have been exempted from any other military duty, are requested to repair also, when called, to such place as shall be appointed and join to repulse our foes.
>
> Not doubting that the Almighty Power, upon our humble prayers, and sincere trust in Him, will then graciously succor our arms in battle for our just cause, and victory can not fail on our side.

Frederick, who had defended his home in Capt. Petry's Company in 1767 under the British crown, was now drilling as a member of the Fourth Regiment of the Tryon County Militia, under Col. Peter Bellinger. Beside him was stepson John Finster, 16 years of age. As the Indian raids became a reality for the German settlers of New Petersburg, a piece of ground on a slight rise (at or near the site of Hasenclever's ashery) and a spring were appropriated.

Encircled with pickets 10 or 12 feet high, it was called the "Fort."
"Three or four log houses were built in this 'fort' and for some
time the families of New Petersburg lived there, during the day
time working some of the adjacent land, and at night gathering
within the pickets for safety." [Beers' Herk. p. 141]   The valley
was deeply divided between the forces of revolution and the tug
of loyalty, fertile ground for the Tory uprising that the English
had long hoped would quench the rebellion. Those in the militia
were said to be without uniforms, undisciplined, badly trained,
poorly armed, but very good with guns.

On 2 Aug. 1777, St. Leger's forces at Ft. Stanwix (present site
of Rome) confidently lay siege to this fort, the last serious
obstacle on the route to Albany. Meanwhile, Gen. Herkimer
having received this news, called forth the militia to relieve the
besieged fort.   800 (some say 850) men and boys responded,
including Frederick and John Finster.   Also in the group were
many whose families were or would become allied with the Oyers:
Bercki (Bargy), Bekker, Clapsattle, Clemens, Eeisemann, Folts,
Frank, Hess, Hochstetter, Lentz (Lints), Miller, Multer, Petrie,
Riema (Rima), Renckel, Sneck, Van Slyck, Wents, and Widrig.

Along with 400 ox carts laden with supplies, the militia left
Fort Dayton at Herkimer on 4 Aug. 1777. The British commander,
St. Leger, learning of Herkimer's advance, had sent 400 Indians
under Joseph Brant and an auxiliary of about 70 Tories to
intercept them. They set up an ambush at a wooded ravine near
the Village of Oriskany, about 6 miles from Fort Schuyler, and
waited.   On 6 Aug. Herkimer was ten miles from Ft. Schuyler.
He wanted to wait for a prearranged signal from Col. Peter
Gansevoort's sortie sent out from Ft. Stanwix--he was to fire
three cannon as a signal for Herkimer to advance. However, his
officers were restless and confident, and he succumbed
reluctantly to their persuasion and recommenced the march.
(Some questioned his loyalty as his younger brother, John Jost
Herkimer, Jr., had joined the British forces.)

The route they followed was the military road, which went
through the ravine and crossed a narrow bridge. The unsuspecting
militia descended the hill into the ravine from the east and were
beginning to climb the western bank when the ambush began.

Gen. Herkimer was quickly wounded, but sat under a tree
attended by Capt. Petry, continuing to lead his men.   Col.
Bellinger and his soldiers who had not yet crossed the causeway
were ordered to retake the hill. The fighting was bitter--swinging
blows from clubbed muskets effective in such close quarters.
When the hill was retaken, one of two known orders were
given--form the men into circles.

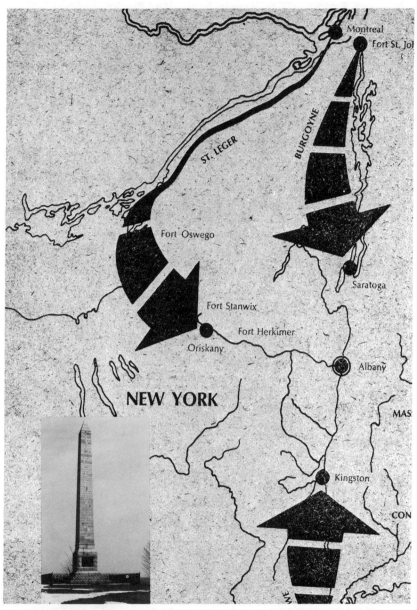

Oriskany Monument. There are 2 separate nameplate groupings,
the second one erected as more names became known. Frieder-
ich/Frederick Oyer is on both, with the name spelled "Eyer"
in one location; "Irer" on the other.

Gen. Nicholas Herkimer (1728-1777) leading a force of 800 militiamen to the
relief of beseiged Ft. Stanwix. Seriously wounded, he continued to direct
his men. His leg was amputated, but he succumbed to his wounds. This
painting by F. C. Yohn was the model for a 1977 commemorative Bicentennial
stamp honoring the 200th anniversary of the battle.

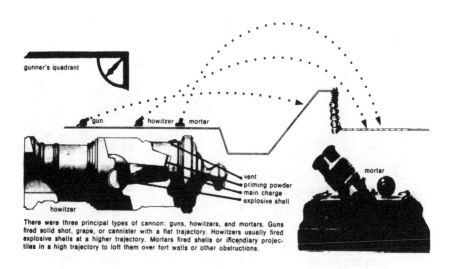

There were three principal types of cannon: guns, howitzers, and mortars. Guns
fired solid shot, grape, or cannister with a flat trajectory. Howitzers usually fired
explosive shells at a higher trajectory. Mortars fired shells or incendiary projec-
tiles in a high trajectory to loft them over fort walls or other obstructions.

Weapons

The flintlock musket was the basic arm of the Continental infantryman, and commanders on both sides planned their tactics around its capabilities. A smoothbore firing a loose-fitting ball, it was not accurate but it loaded fast and was reasonably dependable. A trained soldier could hit an enemy at 80 to 100 yards. He could load and fire four a minute if he didn't stop to aim closely, and with his bayonet fixed he could fight hand-to-hand when there was no time to load.

The two main types of muskets in general use were the British musket (the "Brown Bess") or an American copy of it, and, after 1777, the French musket. Some Continentals carried the American long rifle, but used it mostly for skirmishing and long-range work.

Flintlock

flint   frizzen

pan

The flintlock produced its spark by striking flint against steel. These sparks ignited the priming powder in the pan, which flashed through the touch hole and set off the main charge inside.

Loading a Musket

A musketeer loaded and fired by command. These are the main steps in loading.

A pick and brush, attached to the shoulder strap of the cartridge bag, were used to clean the pan and touch hole of the musket.

French Musket

After 1777 the French musket of .69 caliber with iron mounts became the most popular long arm of the Continentals. Stronger and lighter than the British musket, it served as the pattern for American muskets after the war.

American Long Rifle

The rifle was accurate but not an effective arm in formal battle. It was slow to load, and lacked a bayonet, and in battle riflemen needed the protection of the musketeer with his bayonet. In the hands of a good shot, it could hit targets at astonishing ranges, striking officers and harassing troops who thought themselves safe.

1 He opened the pan of his musket (1), bit off the end of the cartridge, and poured some of the powder into the pan for priming.

2 Then he poured the rest of the powder down the barrel (2).

3 He inserted the ball (still wrapped in paper), and rammed it all down the barrel with the ramrod (3).

He pulled the cock back to the full-cock position, and the musket was ready to shoot.

Cartridge Box

The soldier carried his cartridges in a leather box. The cartridges fitted into holes bored in a wooden block, and the flap (not shown here) protected the cartridge from the weather.

Cartridge

A ball and charge of powder were wrapped in paper to form a cartridge. Sometimes three buckshot were added for extra effect.

The Turning Point

This replica of Fort Dayton was built in 1976 by 600 Boy Scouts of General Herkimer Council at Exit 30 of the New York State Thruway. In 1977 this Bicentennial Project was awarded the George Washington Medal by the Freedoms Foundation at Valley Forge.

The original Fort was built in July and August of 1776 by the Third New Jersey Regiment of Continental Troops. Today the site is covered by private homes, the Herkimer County Historical Society (1884), the County Courthouse (1873) and Jail (1834) and the Reformed Church (1823). One of the wells believed to have been dug within the Fort still exists on North Main Street.

Fort Dayton was named after Col. Elias Dayton, commander of the 3rd New Jersey Regiment, by Capt. Joseph Bloomfield, the office in charge of construction. George Washington and the Continental Congress ordered fortifications built along the Mohawk by General Philip Schuyler, commander of the Northern Department. As German Flatts (today's Herkimer) was the most western settlement, it seemed a logical site for a fortification.

Throughout the War, Fort Dayton was garrisoned by Continental and Militia troops. From this fort on August 4, 1777, General Herkimer led the 800 men on their fateful march to relieve Fort Stanwix. When Fort Stanwix was destroyed by fire and flooded in May, 1781, Fort Dayton became the western Fort protecting the frontier.

This was bloody ground 200 years ago. Blunder and brilliance on both sides made it so.

Distant from the passions of 1777, a grateful community begins its own Bicentennial celebration, for what happened here helped decide the fate of a nation.

Conflict in the Mohawk Valley was as much a civil war as it was a military contest. Control of 90-miles of rich river land was the prize.

Formal warfare between His Majesty's forces and Continental troops lasted three weeks on this frontier. Twentyone days of glory.

But the bitter struggle between former neighbors who were divided by old suspicions and new hatreds went on and on.

Even as the war shifted south, the white and Indian raiders struck the settlements with such frequency and ferocity that the earth seemed charred and bleeding.

The British strategy was to divide New York and separate rebellious New England from the rest of the colonies.

Three armies were to converge on Albany. Forces commanded by Sir William Howe were to sweep up the Hudson from their stronghold in New York City. A grand army under Gen. John Burgoyne would march south from Montreal through the Champlain Valley. The third force was ordered to storm down the Mohawk.

The campaign failed for several reasons. Lord Howe sailed south rather than march north as planned. Burgoyne chose to hack a road through the tangled wilderness instead of using a faster water route and was snared at Saratoga.

But the first reverses to the invasion came where victory had been thought certain. The turning point in the War of Independence began at Fort Stanwix and Oriskany.

A mid-morning cloudburst halted the battle for some time, during which Herkimer reorganized his men. Then came the order to put 2 men behind each tree. This enabled one to fire while the other reloaded, thus effectively preventing tomahawking. Thwarted in losing the advantage of quick, savage attacks, the Indians grew tired of the extended close range fighting and returned to their camps. There they found they had been stripped bare by Americans under Col. Marinus Willet. About that time St. Leger was told that Benedict Arnold was coming with a troop of Regulars and he withdrew. The battle was won.

The Indians fought on both the British and American sides. Most of those who fought with the British were Senecas; it is said 60 friendly Oneidas were with Herkimer's militia.

Gen. Herkimer succumbed to his wounds, after the amputation of his leg. The famous painting of the battle by Frederick C. Yohn which hangs in the Utica Public Library has been memoralized by the issuance of a commemorative stamp issued at the time of the bicentennial celebration and reenactment of the battle in 1977. It shows the wounded general under a tree talking with Col. Bellinger, directing the militia. They each are credited with having given the orders that won the battle.

Frederick lost his life at Oriskany, as did a Petry, Clapsaddle, Lents, and Renckel, along with over 400 others. Finster survived, as did Michael Widrig, although the latter was wounded, as were many of the others listed. Jacob Widrig was made a prisoner of war, as were 200 others. Oriskany ranked high in per cent of casualties, with approximately 800 taking part, of whom 150 returned safely. Other estimates vary with these figures.

The battle, along with St. Leger's defeat at Fort Stanwix, ended the campaign from Oswego. It also ended Burgoyne's hopes for reinforcements from the west. Instead the opposing armies would receive aid he had schemed so long to prevent. From then on, however, the Senecas sided with the British. Revenge would bring strife for the area for 7 years, continuing nearly 2 years after Cornwallis' surrender.

On a raid in Sept. 1778 Johann Jacob and Georg Oyer were captured, taken away, and kept prisoner for several years. [See #2] The Indians destroyed every house not occupied by a Tory. Their leader, Joseph Brant, desolated German Flats. One rainy night the settlers, warned of Brant's impending approach, fled to safety. By morning the Indians had burned all the dwellings, enraged that the people had gone.

The Indian raids were regular events. Destructive ones occurred in 1779 and 1780; in 1781 at the time of the Ross and Butler incursion there was nothing left to destroy; the area was once more a wilderness.

Elisabetha found herself a widow with children ranging from 10 years to 1 month. The farm which her husband had established was abandoned for the most part, her family seeking refuge in the "Fort." Her son John Finster who had been apprenticed to a weaver before the hostilities had set up a loom in his stepfather's house. The house was later burned. [See Chapter 6]

Fort Dayton, August the 3rd

This is to certify that Frederick Irer has been a corporal in my compagnie, Col. Peter Bellinger's reg't of militia, he being killed in General Herkimer's battle the 6th of August, 1777. [Source: AHA]

In Beers' history [pg 141] is the following:

While the fort was occupied, the inhabitants were harassed by raids of Indians and Tories, in which several were killed or taken prisoners. At one time a small party were at work in the field on land now [1879] owned by Mrs. Duane Richardson, and were surprised by the Indians and several taken prisoners. One of the younger boys hid and the Indians ordered their prisoners to call him. They called in the German language, "Peter, bleib wo du bist!" (stay where you are) and Peter Rima was not taken captive.

The widow Oyer and her children suffered much during the 1780's. Families without support were granted food amounting to 1 pound of bread and of beef per day for those over 16 years; half a pound of bread and of beef per day for those under 16 years. The children grew up knowing want of food and clothing. It is no wonder that Peter Oyer never received education enough to be able to do more than sign his name. [Source: AHA]

Records of Elisabetha's attempts to obtain a pension reveal this document, seeking help along with other petitioners from the State Legislature:

To the Honerable the Legislature of the State of New York our humble petition sheweth:

We the subscribers humbly beg to take in consideration our poor circumstances, it has been pleased to grant ten of the poor widows occasioned by the enemy, the legislature by the session of last spring, some provision where Peter Tygert, Esq., should have the charge of, we never have got anything yet until this moment, and have apended the chief parts of our clothes and effects for the maintenance of our familys.

We therefore humbly beg to order this provision to be issued to us by Peter Tygert, Esq., to be forwarded so that we may in our distress be supported. Then further, since the petition of us has been grant four other families have shared the same fate with us and Catherine Demood, Anna Colsh, Catharine Reigel and Anna Lents, where two of their husbands had been killed and two taken prisoner.

So we humbly beg to grant us some support wherefore we shall ever pray and call ourselfs your honours' most obedient humble servants.

Fort Dayton.   March 3d, 1787.

Elizabeth Ayrer,	Catharine Rinkill,
Catharine Demood,	Sybila Dinis,
Eva Keeler,	Anna Colsh,
Gertrand Steinway,	Margareth Clementz,
Catharine Reigel,	Maria Skiff,
Susan Oyd,	Anna Lentz,
Margareth Brown,	Magdalen Snek.

"General Herkimer's battle" as some referred to it was one of the bloodiest conflicts of the American Revolution; the toll it took upon the Mohawk Valley families is hard to conceive.

Each family had its vacant chair and many a widow with a flock of little ones or crippled survivors to care for, unable to escape, faced the winter not only in sorrow and dread of Indian torture and scalping but faced starvation as well, for their crops were largely unharvested and no help at hand or likely to come. [Nellis]

The American Revolution was able to sustain itself largely because of those who had gone out with the steadily extending frontier. They had fought the forest and the Indian. They learned what liberty was. [McGill]

[Oriskany] enabled the militia to hasten back to Saratoga and reinforce Gen. Gates; rendered useless the British–Iroquois alliance; fired the hearts of the people...; and was a victory most needed [Johnson]

If the Revolutionary movement, in its immediate origin, began in colonial seaports and was chiefly a protest of merchants and townsmen against British oppression, it drew its strength from the men who tilled the soil.

Without their aid Great Britian would have remained
sovereign in America. [Miller]

It was largely Mohawk farmers who made up the force
to meet St. Leger...The story of Oriskany is well
known, but every descendant, indeed every American,
should read it over and over again. [Snell]

The fight at Oriskany insured the surrender of
Burgoyne. Burgoyne's surrender insured the French
alliance. The French fleet insured the surrender of
Yorktown. Oriskany made possible the birth of the
new nation. [Reid]

When hostilities ended, the families of NP began rebuilding their
homes and farms. John Finster and the 3 sons rebuilt their father's home. In 1789 Frederick[2] married and set off on his own;
in 1790 Jacob followed suit. They both built in the vicinity of the
original farm, as did Finster, who had married in 1785. [See Chap
6]

In 1790 we find Elisabetha with a family of 4 persons: 1 male
over 16 years of age, and 3 females, in Herk. Twp., Mont. Co.

In the early 19th century the number of baptisms fell off. It
cost two shillings to record a baptism. As many could not afford
this, they failed to do so, making researching for genealogical
purposes more difficult.

Territorial designations changed rapidly in the years just before
and after the Revolution. When Frederick first settled in the
Mohawk Valley, the land had been part of Albany County. In
1772 Tryon and Charlotte Counties were formed from it. Tryon
was named for the colonial governor of New York, William Tryon,
who actually espoused the cause of the King of England. In 1784
Tryon was therefore renamed for Gen. Richard Montgomery, an
Irish-born British army soldier who in 1772 sold his British
commission and joined the Continental Army. He replaced Philip
J. Schuyler as commander of the Montreal expedition. Charlotte
Co. became Washington Co. [Col Ency p 1822] GF was incorpor-
ated as a district of Tryon Co. 24 Mar 1772; it became Kingsland
Dist. 8 Mar 1773, and was formed as a township 7 Mar. 1778.
Herk. Twp. was formed from it 7 Mar 1788, and Schuy. Twp. was
formed therefrom 10 Apr. 1792.

John Finster was the patriarch of the family for some years,
responsible for several transactions, resulting in land ownership
for 3 of his stepbrothers. [See Chapter 6]

In 1799 Peter Oyer married and took over as head of the family
from John Finster. He and his wife made their home on his
father's farm and rebuilt the homestead. In 1800 Peter's family is

listed as consisting of four persons; one of them, a female aged 45 years and upwards, was undoubtedly Elisabetha. It is quite probable the same is true in the 1810 census. After that date we lose track of her--no death record or gravestone can be found.

Ch (OYER), all b NP, Herk Co:

2.   i.   JOHANN JACOB², b 25 Apr 1767

3.   ii. JOHANN FRIEDRICH (FREDERICK) Sr, b 29 Feb 1968

        iii. ELISABETH, b ca 1770; d Schuy after 1855. Elisabeth was a deaf mute and is so indicated in the censuses of 1840, 1850, and 1855. She lived at the old homestead with her brother Peter and (after his death) nephew Daniel.

4.   iv. PETER, b 5 Dec 1777

        v.   JOHANN GEORGE, b ca 1772; d poss y. He was captured by the Indians (as was brother Jacob above) in Sept 1778. Possibly he is the same as the George J Oyer in Warren Twp, Herk Co in the 1810 census (aged over 45 yrs with a female 16 to 26 yrs of age). We find no conclusive evidence to prove him to be a son of Frederick.

        vi. LORENZ, b 15 June 1776; d prob 1780-1790. The bp of "Lorentz," son of Friedrich Eierer und Elizabeth," [rec GF DRC, Dom. Abraham Rosencrantz, pastor] was on 23 June 1776, "Lorentz Rinckel und Catharina" sp. We find no other record of him.

        vii. CATHARINA, b 3 July 1777; d possibly after 1790. Catharina's bp is also rec at the GF DRC 13 July 1777, "Lorentz Rinckel und Catharina" again as sp. The 1790 census lists 3 females in the household of Elisabetha "Eyre," undoubtedly the mother; dau Elisabeth; and quite possibly this Catharina, who would then have been 13. She cannot be placed in later Oyer family census listings, but by then may have been married.

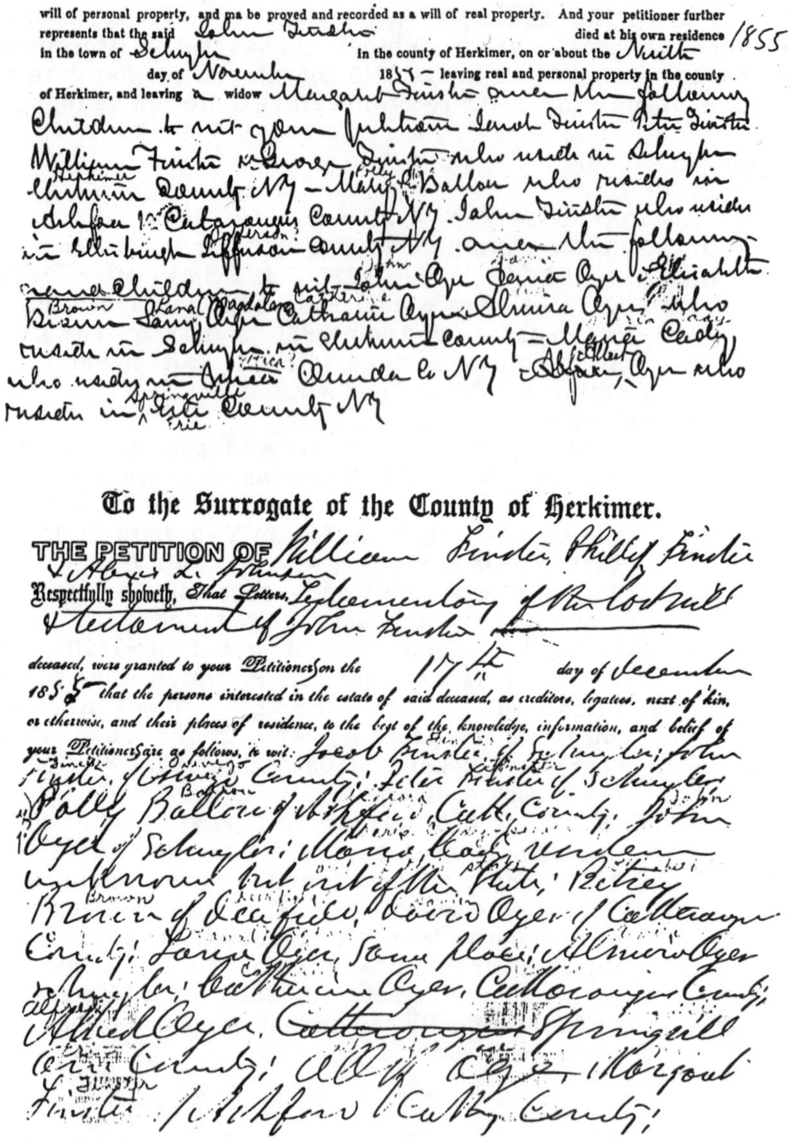
will of personal property, and ma be proved and recorded as a will of real property. And your petitioner further represents that the said John Finster died at his own residence 1855 in the town of Schuyler in the county of Herkimer, on or about the Ninth day of November 1855 — leaving real and personal property in the county of Herkimer, and leaving a widow Margaret Finster and the following Children to wit Jacob Finster Peter Finster William Finster & George Finster who reside in Schuyler Herkimer County NY — Mary (Polly) Ballou who resides in Ashford in Cattaraugus County NY John Finster who resides in Ellenburgh Jefferson County NY and the following grandchildren to wit John Oyer Jonas Oyer Elizabeth Brown Sarah Oyer Magdalena Catharine Oyer Almira Oyer who reside in Schuyler in Herkimer County — Maria Cady who resides in Utica Oneida Co NY — Alfred Oyer who resides in Springville Erie County NY

To the Surrogate of the County of Herkimer.

THE PETITION OF William Finster, Philip Finster & Abner L. Johnson

Respectfully showeth, That Letters Testamentary of the last will & testament of John Finster deceased, were granted to your Petitioners on the 17th day of December 1855 that the persons interested in the estate of said deceased, as creditors, legatees, next of kin, or otherwise, and their places of residence, to the best of the knowledge, information, and belief of your Petitioners are as follows, to wit: Jacob Finster of Schuyler; John Finster, of Oswego County; Peter Finster of Schuyler; Polly Ballou of Ashford, Catt. County; John Oyer of Schuyler; Maria Cady residence unknown but out of the State; Betsey Brown of Deerfield; David Oyer of Cattaraugus County; Lana Oyer, same place; Almira Oyer Schuyler; Catherine Oyer, Cattaraugus County; Alfred Oyer, ~~Cattaraugus~~ Springville Erie County; All of age; Margaret Finster, Ashford, Catt. County;

Portion of Herkimer Co. surrogate record of John Finster listing many Oyer descendants, the basis for much of our early research.

CHAPTER 6

SECOND GENERATION ALLIED FAMILIES

* THE FINSTER-CLEMENS-SCHNECK-MILLER-ELLIS-BALLOU FAMILIES *

During this second generation, so many of the Schuyler/German Flats/Stone Arabia/New Petersburg families intermarried we will devote this section to some of them, as well as paying tribute to the importance of JOHN FINSTER in the lives of the Oyers.

Johann/John Finster, born Wuertemberg, Germany 23 Apr 1760; came to America with mother Elizabeth and stepfather Frederick Oyer 1764; died 9 Nov. 1855; married Herkimer County (hereafter Herk. Co.) 1st MARY (MARIA) FREDERICKA SCHNECK, born ca. 1766; died ca. 1816; probably daughter of George and Barbara Schneck, Jr; m 2nd MARGARETHA (BEKKER) OYER, widow of JACOB OYER. [See #2]

John Finster was the patriarch of the Oyer family after his stepfather's death, figuring prominently in his stepbrothers' lives. Recent information states that John could have "drawn a pension if he had been willing to give up his property." [Ellis Inf 1] Ellis Inf 2 states she was told by her father to be proud of her middle name (Finster) as her Finster ancestor had fought in the Revolutionary War and when offered a pension, refused it, saying the government needed the money more than he did. [See Ellis family data below.]

It is said that there are Finster families in the "north country" of New York State.

John Finster who had been apprenticed to a weaver before the hostilities had set up a loom in his stepfather's house. He usually spent time there weaving during the day, returning to the safety of the fort at night. After finishing one day, "he rolled his harness and reed in his cloth and prepared to go to the fort. But upon going out of the house he fancied he smelled Indians, and fearing the house might be burned during the night he took the loom apart and threw piece after piece down a bank among the bushes to save it from the expected fire. That night the house was burned; but the precious loom was saved to do good service in after years when peace was restored." [Beers' Herk. pg. 141] John held several town offices and built 2 saw mills, one of the first in town. "He acquired and retained the respect of his townsmen...died at the advanced age of ninety-five years and eight months."

[Since reporting this in the first Oyer book we learned from W. Mark Oyer (#340) that he has a singed Lutheran hymn book

To One woollen under jacket		50
To another woollen under jacket	1	
To One woollen short coat	1	50
To another short woollen coat	3	
To another blue short coat	3	
To One old blue great coat		50
To One old short woollen coat		50
To One fur hat		25
To four chairs at 37, 5 mills each	1	50
To One chair at 18¾ cents		
To One Table	2	
To One blue chest	2	
To One grindstone		
To One Iron shod slay		
To One span of Horses	100	
To One Waggon	40	
To One set of harness or horse tackling	21	
To One fanning mill	14	
To One dung hook and fork	1	
To One Log chain	2	
To One bush ax		75
To One Iron bar	1	
To One pick ax	1	
To One saddle	5	
To One year old colt	21	
To One three year old heifer	18	
To One Cow	15	
To three calves at 3 dolls a piece	9	
To two sheep at 1, 75 cts a piece	2	

Valentine Meller   } Appraisers   { Jacob Zimmers
Peter Roma   Peter Euer   } Executor

Portion of Peter F.[3] Oyer will.

thought throughout the years to be a bible) that survived this fire. Also extant is a pewter teapot dating from revolutionary days.]

Military records show John to have been a member of Bellinger's Reg't from Nov. 1779 to April 1787. He was in the Battle of Brandywine as well as Oriskany. After the war John built a log house; then a frame one, one of if not the first in his district. "Soon after his marriage he bought the 'five hundred tract' about which there had been much litigation... Of this tract Finster retained one-fifth and sold three-fifths to his step-brothers, Jacob, Frederick and Peter, and the balance to Jacob Clemens." [Beer's Herk, p 146] Two of Clemens' sons married daughters of Peter Oyer, (#4), and Clemens' daughter Mary married Jacob Finster, John's son.

In addition to being a successful farmer, John held several town offices and built 2 saw mills, so essential in those times. His will, proved in Herk. Co. in 1855 and a prime source for our earliest research, shows many Oyer grandchildren, several of them being from his second marriage. He died at age 95. Margaret removed to Cattaraugus Co. (hereafter Catt. Co.), and is bur AHC. [See #2]

Ch (FINSTER):

    i.   JOHN, b Schuyler 1786; m Nancy Shead, Ellenburg, Jefferson Co, d 17
        a) ABRAM B, b Deerfield, Oneida Co, 1828; to Schuyler 1842; m Mary Robbins b 1837

    ii. PETER, b GF 2 May 1791 (sp Peter Eier, Marg Beyer); m Katy Rima. An obituary with a byline of Dutchtown 1905 in Jacob Oyer's account book tells of an eldest dau of Peter's, Mary, marrying 1 Jan 1833 Alexis Lockling Johnson. Their ch: Horace M, of Frankfort; Seymour P, Hiram, and Frederica M (Mrs Widrig), Mary d 1887. We are assuming it is this Peter's dau.

    iii. JACOB, b _____, m MARY MARGARET CLEMENS

    iv. PHILLIP, b GF 4 Dec 1793; m BETSEY RIMA

9.   v.   CATHERINE, b Schuy 3 Dec 1795; m PETER F OYER (#9); d 30 Jan 1855

    vi. MARY/POLLY, b _____, m (1) WILLIAM ELLIS, b ca 1800, d 1841; (2) DAVID BALLOU (BLUE), b Vt, (his 1st w Eliza Barrett) res Ash, bur AHC, Catt Co. She d_____

    vii. WILHELM (WILLIAM), b GF 1 Jan 1801; m NANCY LINTS

viii. GEORGE, b _____ , deaf mute, unm

   The CLEMENS family history dates back to early times, but
"our" JACOB, father and son, came with the Hasenclever group in
1765. One of the few with specific points of origin, the son was
born in Saarbrucken, Germany. The son Jacob's wife was Eva
Catherine Steinwax, dau. of Arnold and Gertraud. Arnold was
killed at Oriskany. Jacob died Alder Cr, Oneida Co, 1840. Eva d
1835 in Schuy. [There is conflicting data in the Genealogy, a
Weekly Journal of American Ancestry, Volume 1, No. 26, New
York, 29 June, 1912. It states that Jacob and Philip Clemens came
from Germany and settled in Frankfort in 1749. Philip was killed
by Indians at Ft Schuyler; Jacob had sons Michael, Jacob and
Philip. This journal has much additional Clemens data, dating from
the 17th century. Our records are mainly from Klock.
   The earlier Clemens, Gerhart, born ca. 1681 [no connection at
this time] married Anna Reiff in Holland Aug 1702. Her step-
father, Hans Stauffer, and family fled Switzerland because of persecution of the Mennonites, settling near Mains, Germany. There
is a diary giving an account of the journey down the Rhine,
written by him. Anna was born in Holland 1680; died ca. 1745,
having come to America in 1709. A Jacob was Gerhart's father!
Gerhart was a linen and cloth weaver.

     Ch Jacob and Eva Clemens:

          i.   Mary Margaret, m Jacob Finster [Barker says Eliz
               Miller, she b 1810--perhaps a later Jacob.]
          ii. Michael, m Catherine Lints, dau of Peter Lints
               a) JACOB, b Schuyler 14 Feb 1811, m NANCY
                  OYER, dau of PETER and ELIZABETH, b
                  Schuyler 26 Nov 1816
23.   b) MICHAEL, b Schuyler 14 Feb 1814, m RACHEL
                  OYER, dau of PETER and ELIZABETH, b
                  Schuyler 27 Feb 1821
               There may be other children of Michael and
               Catherine.
          iii. Abram, m Abbis Caldwell
22.   iv. CATHERINE, b Schuyler 27 June 1817; m HENRY
               OYER
   There is more data in #4, xi regarding church records. Jacob
(wife Eva) was in the Battle of Oriskany.

   John Finster's wife, MARY FREDERICKA SCHNECK, is prob. the
dau. of George and Barbara (_____) Schneck, born ca. 1766,
whose grandparents then would be George and Lena (_____)

Schnek. George, Sr. born ca. 1710 to 1725; was among the Hasenclever men; and in 1769 in the GF militia in Bellinger's Reg't. [Barker, p. 313]

Hiram Finster married Huldah Miller, dau. of Valentine and Sarah (Witrig) Miller; Valentine b 1755. Sarah was dau. of Michael and Elizabeth Witrig, she born 1791; died 1856. Also Huldah's bro. Michael married a Philinda Finster; her sister Elisabeth, born Schuy. 8 Apr 1810, bp. Herk June 1810, married a Jacob Finster.

We don't know the original parentage, but Valentine could be an ancestor of a PETER MILLER who married ELIZABETH ANN OYER (#33); MARY/POLLY MILLER who married GEORGE3 OYER (#10); or MARY ROXANNE MILLER who married ANSON5 OYER (#155). Peter Miller's parents were John and Mary (_____) Miller; Mary's could have been George Mathew and Catherine (Bekker [m. rec. has Baker]) Miller. Barker's book has no further data on John and Mary/Polly Miller, which is so often the case when they leave the area. If this is the right Miller family, they descend from yet another Hasenclever workman, Valentine [see above] who married Sarah Witrig. Barker's data comes from The Valentine Miller Papers by Reuben M. Brockway. Valentine's point of origin is Hettingen, Germany, born 10 Mar 1740, son of Andreas and Eva Muller. This once more leads us to Switzerland where some Mullers have originated. Interestingly the papers relate that he paid 71 pounds, 7 shilling and 6 pence (New York money) for passage with the group. This differs from what the majority of the workmen did, as they were to work out their passage and sustenance. [see #1] Valentine was also in Bellinger's Reg't. Finsters, Widrigs, Bekkers and Dygerts allied with them. For Miller families, see #'s 10, 33, and 155.

WILLIAM ELLIS, who m MARY/POLLY FINSTER went to Catt Co. His father was a "Yankee," one of but a few in the Schuy. area then. He was born ca. 1800, dying at ae. 41 in 1841, bur. AHC.

Ch (ELLIS):

    i.   SALLY, b Schuy 5 May 1826, d 31 Dec 1914; m
          _____ Multer, d Ash 27 Jan 1915
    ii. PETER, b 26 May 1829, d 18 June 1896, m Mary
          Frank, b 25 Feb 1836 d 25 Jan 1915
          a) Nancy A b ca 1854, d 4 Nov 1917 (flu epidemic era)
          b) Albert E, b ca 1857, d 1872
          c) Mary F, b ca 1861
          d) William, b 26 June 1864

iii. JOHN, b 3 Apr 1836, d 12 May 1907, m Cornelia
      _____, b ca 1841
      a) Inez L, b ca 1859; m James B Weber of Ash
      1) James Weber
      b) May, b ca 1865, m R G Holden of Roch
         1) Helen May Holden b NYC 27 Nov 1893, d Roch,
            m Vincent Bennett, b 16 Apr 1891, ch (Bennett):
            Robert H, b 28 Jan 1913, 3 sons; Jane Stewart
            Bennett, b Roch 7 Mar 1917, m Robert H Morris,
            b Roch 14 Feb 1918, res Pittsford, Monroe Co.
            ch (Morris); Robert T, unm; Betsy Holden, unm;
            John Bennett, twin, 2 sons, 1 dau; Richard
            Bennett, twin, unm, like his gr uncle, lacked
            feeding instinct, had to be force-fed. Helen &
            Vincent's 3rd ch: Richard Gordon Bennett, b
            Roch 18 Mar 1919,has 2 sons, 1 dau; Helen &
            Vincent'sr 4th ch: (Bennett) John Lansing, b
            Roch 24 Sept 1924, 1 son, 2 adopted, a boy & a
            girl.
         2) Hazel Holden, m Lawrence Bickford; 3 ch: Jack,
            Mary Jane, Lawrence, Jr
         3) Lois Holden, twin, m Leicester Mengins, res Fla,
            1 son & 1 dau
         4) Ellis Holden, twin, called Pete, drowned ae 21
         5) Harold Holden, twin, m Ruth Given 2 ch: James.
            Douglas. Harold d 1986
         6) Grant Holden, twin, d y; lacked feeding instinct

[For more Holden detail, see Holden Allied line.]

      c) Clayton J, b ca 1871 per 1870 census, rec: 31 Jan
          1876, m Madge Trevett; common law wife.
          Geraldine (Holland) Misner, d 7 May 1941, bur
          MWC, res WV, Sprvl. Madge d Sprvl 1945+;
          Geraldine b 17 July 1897, dau of Bert and Maude
          (Phillips) Holland, d 2 Oct 1939, bur MWC. Ch
          (Ellis):
          1) Robert Misner, b Hamburg 8 June 1922, m
              Niagara Falls 13 Oct 1945 Virginia Rougeaux;
              res Sprvl. Their ch (Ellis): Robert Clayton, b
              Hamburg, Erie Co 8 Aug 1948, m Liverpool.
              Onon Co 19 June 1972 Sylvia Essig, res
              Valrico, Fla. 2 sons: Robert J, b Sprvl 29 Sept
              1979 & Richard C, b Tampa, Fla 3 Aug 1981;
              Richard James, b 30 Oct 1951. m 18 Sept 1977
              Balboa Is, Calif Carol Crump, res Orlando. Fla.

2 ch, both b Orlando, Fla: Stephen L, b 10
June 1982; Katherine V, b 3 May 1984.
2) Sally Misner, b WV 18 Jan 1930, m Sprvl 21 Dec
1957 John Joseph Dwyer, res Victor. John is
election comm for Ontario Co, Canandaigua; Sally
employed there. Their ch (Dwyer): James
Patrick, b 24 Sept 1958, res Deerfield Beach, Fla,
hotel management; Thomas Edward, b 16 June
1961, m Weddington, NC 22 Sept 1984 Marisa
Suzanne Konrad, packaging industry rep, dau
Nicole Lauren, b 20 July 1985; Robert John, b
Sprvl 29 Apr 1966, res with parents, student
SUNY Geneseo. Sally is a helpful informant.
d) John C, b near Sprvl 13 Feb 1874, d NYC 11 May
1908, bur MWC, Sprvl, m Lorinia/Vinny/Beatrice
_____. John, known as "dapper Uncle Jack",
was a dentist.
e) Claude, b 1882, d 1952, m Ruby Prior, b MWC,
Sprvl
1) John, b 1913, m 1941 Lorraine Joslin
ch: Carolyn, b 1942; David, b 1953? Carolyn
res Cleveland, Oh
2) Faith Finster, b 1916, m 1941 Edward Spas, he
d 1974, res Sprvl, Faith and Edward's ch
(Spas): Claudette, b 1942, m J Wells, res
Syracuse; April b 1950, m Joseph Gongal, div'd,
m 1985 Kris Burkardt, res Minneapolis, Minn;
Andy, b 1951, m 1983 Li Nordstrom, res
Sweden; Thomas, b 1957, m Rosa Rojas, res
Miami. [Source: Faith Spas]
iv.   Mary, b 16 Apr 1842

Two other boys born d y.

William Ellis, born ca. 1800 and husband of Polly Finster, had 4
bro, "one a doctor, and Samuel, Murray and James, 4 sisters--
Phoebe, Eliza, Polly, and Sarah. His father William farmed sev-
eral years on a 125 acre tract just north of Finster's 500 acres.
The father moved later to Jeff. Co. where he held the office of
Justice of the Peace a long time in "Ellisburg." This comes from
an Ellis informant and "fits" with our data that Margaret Oyer,
dau. of Peter (#4) married 2nd a ROSWELL MURRAY ELLIS, born
Schuy. 7 Dec 1797. (See #18)   And "Ellisburg" could be the
"Ellenburg" shown in records of John Finster's son John's family.

[Sources: Ellis Inf 1,2,3,4; Adams' Catt; Botsford.   For more
Ellis-Oyer marriages, see #78 through #81.]

William's wife Mary married "Charles F. Ballou's father" after the early death of William. This was David Ballou (Blue), and it was his 2nd marriage, 1st wife Eliza Barrett. They were natives of Vermont. Our data comes partly from Adams' Catt. It states the Ballou family in America is of Huguenot descent and early settled in Rhode Island with Roger William's colony.

William Ballou, born Richmond, Cheshire Co., New Hampshire 26 Dec 1792, went to Rutland Co., Vermont; then to Zoar in Collins, Erie Co. in 1817, one of the first settlers there. He was in Sprvl. 1844-66. He married in Vermont Eunice Cook, dau. of Wm. Cook. He died 1853; he and his wife were born in the same town on the same day! They had 8 ch. William was a jeweler; went on to De-Kalb, Illinois.

A Charles Ballou, born in E. Otto in 1840, was a cooper; taught school; served in Co. I, 44th NY Vols; severely wounded; discharged a cripple 1863; finally a grocer in Ellicottville (hereafter Ellvl). Living nearby in early Ash. was a James M. Ballou. Charles' brother Herbert Eugene Ballou served in Co. A, 100th N.Y. Vols, serving three years during the Civil War. He married CHARITY VEDDER, dau. of CORNELIUS and ADELINE (OYER) VEDDER. [See #62] He married 2nd Matie Fox.

There was a John Ballou who married Mary _____. Mary was born Clarendon, Vermont 1827; died Springville (hereafter Sprvl.), Erie Co. 24 Mar 1925, its oldest resident at the time, bur MWC. She spent all her years there except for a few in St. Charles, Illinois. They had sons John and Spencer, grdau. Lillian of Springville, and grdau. Marion, married _____ Armstrong, resided Armington, Mont. Her husband was 84 when he died.

Plot marker and gravestone: Frederick[2] and Elizabeth Oyer, Elderkin Cemetery, Ashford, just south of the Town of Concord, N.Y.

CHAPTER 7

SECOND GENERATION

2. JOHANN <u>JACOB</u>[2] OYER (*Frederick*[1]), born New Petersburg,
now East Schuyler, Herkimer County, (hereafter NP, Herk. Co.) 26
Mar. 1767 and baptized [rec. GF DRC] 29 Apr. 1767 with "Joh:
Georg Schnek Jun. and Barbara" sponsors; died Schuyler, (hereafter
Schuy.),   Sept. 1815.   He married [rec. GF DRC] 2 Feb. 1790
MARGARETHA/E BEKKER, prob. daughter of Dabold Bekker and
Elizabeth _____, born NP, poss. 1 Jan. 1770 and baptized
[rec. SA DRC], poss. the unnamed daughter of "Theobald" Bekker
and Elizabeth, with sponsors Elizabeth Heinrich, Barbara Schnek
and Christian Hochstatter; died Ashford Township (hereafter Ash.
Twp.) 13 Apr. 1860; buried AHC.

Jacob was left fatherless at the age of 10 in an area particularly hard hit by the recurring ravages of war. On 3 April 1780
when 13 years old he was taken prisoner by Indians. The prisoners were taken to Canada, walking all the way. The following is
a letter Gov. Clinton wrote to Gov. Haldeman of Canada 27 Mar.
1781: [Clinton Papers, VI:723-726, document #3599]

> Sir,   While I entertain too high an opinion of your
> character as a gentleman to suppose you inclined to add
> to the miseries of by involving in it the Captivity of
> helpless women and Children, permit me to assure you
> it has always been my Desire from motives of humanity,
> to afford them whether connected with friends or ene-
> mies, any relief that their situation required and cir-
> cumstances would admit. ...I directed Coll: Gansevoort
> last fall to forward to Major Carlton, who was then in
> the vicinity of Crown Point, upwards of one hundred
> women & Children whose husbands and parents were
> then in Canada.
> I now inclose your Excellency a list of the names of
> sundry women & Children, who at different periods have
> been taken by arties in the British service in their
> ravaging incursions on the frontiers of the State over
> which I have the Honor to preside, and have to request,
> that your Excellency will order them to be liberated, and
> furnished with the necessary means to return to their
> families. It becomes at the same time my duty to inform
> your Excellency that unless the inhuman & unmilitary
> practice of capturing women & Children ceases, I shall be
> reduced to the disagreeable necessity of detaining &
> treating the remaining families of those who have gone

into the British Lines as objects of Exchange, and thus involuntarily increase the Distresses of many whom the Fate of War have separated from their nearest Connections. I have the Honor to be with Sentiments of personal respect your Excellency's most Obed't Serv't.
                    [G. C.]
Since writing the above I have rec'd the original List of the women & Children sent last Fall to Canada ...; their No. is 159.

Some of interest under listing of "Colo. Benninger's Regt. Militia, Tryon County" are Lieut. Tibalt Becker, Jacob Van Slyck, Lawrence Frank, "taken Sep'r 1778 not in arms," Jacob Wydrig, Tibalt Steinwax, Jacob Ayrer, "taken 3d Apl. 1780 not in arms," George Ayrer, Stephen Easeman, John Frank, "taken 8 June 1778 not in arms." A further listing includes Jacobus and Gerard Van Slyck, taken 3d April 1780, not in arms.

[The reference, "not in arms" shows that they were not soldiers and therefore children, or women.]

When he was returned to his family 3 years later, undoubtedly wearing Indian clothing, he returned to the farm north of the old settlement of NP (Germantown) on land which had been cleared by his father before the Revolution. The house had been burned during an Indian raid but he and his bride settled on a portion of the family's land and were listed as living there in the 1800 census. No clear title to the land existed until 19 Mar. 1805 when John and Mary (Schneck) Finster, Jacob's half brother and wife quit claimed it for $10, a tract of 100 acres. This farm seems to have been the only land in Herk. Co. that Jacob owned, although there is record of his co-owning with James W. Nutt a tract of 138 acres in Onon. Co. which they sold in 1798 to Lawrence Rinkle, Jr. This land was later purchased by Jacob's brother Peter.

Jacob built up a sizeable estate during his 48 years. Appraised by Valentine Miller and Peter Rima, it was valued at 378.705 pounds; the inventory filed at Herk. Co. 29 Oct. 1815 shows many kitchen utensils, pewter ware, blacksmith tools, farm tools, carpentry tools, weaving utensils (including a loom), clothing, furniture, wagons, harnesses, and livestock (a 1 year old colt, a 3 year old heifer, a cow, 3 calves, 4 sheep, 2 yearling heifers and a yearling steer.) Other property was specifically bequeathed to his heirs.

His will is as follows:

In the name of God amen I Jacob Oyer of the Town of Schuyler and County of Herkimer and State of New

York being of perfect mind and memory blessed be God
for the same therefore on this eighteenth day of July
one thousand eight hundred and fifteen make and
publish this my last will and testament in manner &
form following (that is to say) first of all I commend
my soul unto the hands of Almighty God who gave it
and my body to the Earth from whence it was taken in
hopes of a joy full Resurection through the merits of
my Saviour *Jesus Christ.* and as for my worldly Estate
wherewith it hath pleased God to bless me with in this
world I dispose thereof as follows   First I Give and
bequeath to my beloved wife Margaret Oyer after my
death the equal third part of my real Estate for her to
enjoy during her life time in the same manner and
form as the law would allow her in case of dowry and I
also give unto her and her heirs and assigns one horse
one sow and ten sheep and also give unto my s^d wife
all the full management of my farm so long as she
remains my widow or untill my sons shall one by one
become of age _____?_____.   Secondly I Give and
bequeath unto my three sons namely Theobald John and
Jacob and unto their respective heirs and assigns
forever all my farm whereon I now live in the town of
Schuyler and county of Herkimer, together with all and
singular and _____?_____ and any other privilege there
unto belonging to be eaqually divided amongst them or
their heirs.   Thirdly I Give and bequeath to my daughter Mary Oyer or unto her heirs the sum of three
hundred dollars to be paid by my three sons eaqually
eight years after my death without interest _____?_____
Fourthly I give and Bequeath unto my son Jacob Oyer
my Span together with all the equippage thereunto belonging _____?_____.   Fifthly I give unto my two sons
John and Jacob and unto their heirs after they become
of age each one of them one horse one cow and two
sheep which shall be reserved out of my personal property _____?_____.   Sixthly it is also my will and desire
that all my personall property that remain after my
children _____?_____ their shares shall be eaqually
divided amongst my four Children and my wife Margaret.   Seventhly it is also my express will and desire that
all my just debts which my come against me together
with all funeral charges shall be paid out of my personal Estate _____?_____   Lastly I do nominate consti-
tute and appoint my trusty and well beloved friends
Jacob Clemens and Peter Oyer as Executors of this my
last will and testament hoping they will see the same

Executed according to the true intent and meaning thereof   In witness whereof I the said Jacob Oyer have hereunto set my head and seal the day and year first above written-- signed sealed published & acclaimed by the said testator as and for his last will and testament in his presence who at his request and in his presence and in the presence of each other have subscribed our names in witness hereunto

                              Jacob "X" Oyer
     David Clemens
     Jacob "X" Clemens

[Herk. Co. surr. rec.]

Margarethe, his widow, stayed on the Oyer farm for a few years, later marrying Jacob's half brother John Finster, whose first wife had died in 1815. Finster's farm was located near the Oyer farm, which she undoubtedly left to her son Theobald and his brothers; it was later sold to Philip Finster.   After John Finster's death in 1855 she went to Ash. Twp., Catt. Co., where her husband's daughter Polly Ballou lived. She went to live with Polly and died there. She was buried at the Ellis-Ballou plot at AHC: "MARGARETT,/ wife of/ JOHN FINSTER/ DIED/ APR. 13, 1860/ Aged 90 Y'rs."

        Ch (OYER), all born in Schuy Twp:

5.   i.   THEOBALD/DAVID[3], b 17 Jan 1791
         ii.   CHRISTIAN, b 15 Feb 1791; prob d y. B and bp [rec
               GF DRC] both on 15 Feb 1791 (Christian Hoch-
               statter, sp). We can find no explanation for the
               conflicting dates of Theobald's and Christian's
               births.
6.   iii. MARY/POLLY, b 1 May 1794
7.   iv. JOHN, b 16 Oct 1798
8.   v.   JACOB J, b ca 1805; d after 1850; m ELIZABETH
               ELIZA _____, b ca 1807; d after 1850. On date
               of 16 Feb 1816 Jacob Clements and Theobald Oyer
               "are held firmly bound unto Jacob Oyer, an
               infant... in the sum of two hundred dollars."
               On 28 May 1830 he was located at Scriba Twp,
               Oswego Co, where he on that date purchased 66
               acres of land; he sold this 24 Dec 1832 and
               removed to Potter Twp, Yates Co, where he is
               listed in 1850 as farmer with his wife. The

censuses of 1830, 1840 and 1850 indicate he had no children.

*** THE BEKKER/BECKER FAMILY ***

We believe MARGARTHE A to be the dau of DABOLD BEKKER. There is a possibility he is another of the Hasenclever workmen. The earliest record we have found of him is on the list of Capt. Marx Petry's Company in 1767 of the local British militia where we find so many who came to be associated with the Oyers. This list was made by localities.

Dabold survived the Rev., and is listed in church records as sponsor at baptisms on two occasions. We feel he is the "David Baker" listed in the 1790 census with a family of six: two males over 45 yrs; one male under 45 yrs; three females. He appears to have married twice; 1st Elizabeth _____ and 2nd (by 1786), Catherine _____.

While we have a great many other Bekker family records, we are unable to associate them with Margarethe. However, the Becker/Bekker spellings are interchangeable. Therefore the Dutch Becker family of Jan Jurrianse, 17th century settler shown in Pearson's Alb. could be Margarethe's ancestors. Other Becker sources include Cuyler Reynolds' volumes, and SA DRC Records, Vol. VI. Reynolds' work states Beckers came from Meisenheim and Wuertemburg, Germany; it also states Beckers came from Holland. [pp 628 and 1648]. Vosburgh's CR is another good source.

Ch (OYER):

2.　　 i.　 MARGARETHE[2]
　　　 ii.　 MARIA. m 17 Mar 1795 JOHANN FRIEDRICH RIMA
　　　 iii.　 ANNA CATHERINE. m 4 Oct 1801 GEORGE MATTHEW MILLER

3. FREDERICK[2] OYER, Sr. (Frederick[1]),born Schuy., Herk. Co. 29 Feb. 1768, bp. 17 Apr. 1768 [rec SA DRC], sp. Johann Georg Schnek and Barbara his wife; died Ash. Twp., Catt. Co. ca. 1825, buried prob. EldC.　 He married [rec. GF DRC] 29 Dec. 1789 ELIZABETH HOCHSTATTER, dau. of Christian and Maria Catharine (Widrig) Hochstatter, born Schuy. ca 1767; died E. Otto Twp. 31 Jan. 1866; buried EldC.

Like his brothers. Frederick Oyer built his home and farm and raised his family on land that had been settled by his father. He acquired clear title to it March 1805 from his half brother John Finster.　 Klock writes that he "lived first in a log house on the upper end of his farm, which he rebuilt into a frame house prior to 1800 where he kept a tavern; and in a 'leanto' a store. The leanto was soon removed."

By the early 1820's a large contingent of friends and family from Schuy. had migrated to Ash. Twp., Catt. Co. A number of Oyer and Hochstatter kin had removed there and in 1823 Frederick's son George emigrated. Undoubtedly influenced by his family, Frederick decided to move himself and his remaining family west, so on 28 Apr. 1824 he sold his farm to Francis Pryne of Schuy. Frederick came to Ash. Twp., beginning "at what is now called New Ashford, coming in by marked trees over corduroy roads and pole bridges. [For description of corduroy, see Appendix v] The nearest gristmill was at Springville in Erie County, whither they went in summer with a wood-shod sled drawn by oxen." [Everts' Catt.] Frederick was a farmer in his new home.

Frederick's early death occurred probably in 1825, though no record of it can be found. One of two small footstones inscribed with the initials "F.O." at the EldC. on Henrietta Rd., Ash. Twp., might mark his grave.

In 1830 Elizabeth, Frederick's widow, was found as head of a household of five in Otto (now E. Otto) Twp., living near her brother Michael Hufstader and her children George, Michael and Frederick, Jr. In later years [1840 and 1850 census] she was living with son William's family, though he may possibly have simply taken over as head of the household. In 1854 she went to live with her son John, also in E. Otto Twp. She died at a very advanced age and was buried at the EldC., where her gravestone still stands: "ELIZABETH,/ WIFE OF/ FREDERICK OYER/ DIED/ JAN. 31, 1866, IN THE 99, Y'R/ OF HER AGE."

Ch (OYER), all b in Schuy:

8.	i.	FREDERICK[3] Jr, b ca 1791
9.	ii.	PETER F, b 20 Feb 1793
10.	iii.	GEORGE, b 15 Mar 1797
11.	iv.	JACOB, b 30 Jan 1799
12.	v.	MICHAEL, b ca 1802
13.	vi.	JOHN F, b ca 1810
14.	vii.	WILLIAM, b Dec 1812
15.	viii.	ROXANNA, b ca 1813

[Sources: AHA; GF DRC; censuses; Ash cem rec;l Elderkin cem. The Federal censuses of 1800, 1810 and 1820 seem to indicate a family with a total of thirteen children. The five unnamed children are a male, b betw 1800 and 1805; a male b betw 1805 and 1810; a female b betw 1805 and 1810; a male b betw 1815 and

1820; and a female b betw 1815 and 1820. All of these children presumably d y.]

*** THE HOCHSTATTER-WIDRIG-RINCKLE-BARGY-REMA FAMILIES ***

The Hochstatter-Huffstater-Hochstetter-Hocstetter-Hockstetter name is one of several found with the Oyer families of other than our Frederick's line. [See Preface and Chapter 3] Marrying into this family are the familiar names of BARGY, BEKKER, FRANK, RIMA and WITRIG and BREITENBACKER, with many variant spellings. "Hoch" means "high," and with "stetter" indicates a family from a high place (mountainous).

ELIZABETH HOCHSTATTER, wife of Frederick Oyer (#3) is the dau of CHRISTIAN HOCHSTATTER, who came with the Hasen-clever workmen in 1764. His first wife d enroute to America. After settling in NP he md MARIA CATHARINE WIDRIG, dau of MICHAEL and MAGDALENA (_____) WIDRIG. Christian served in Col Bellinger's Reg't of the Tryon Co militia, enlisting in 1777. He received a pension for his services.

Christian farmed in Schuy near the Oyers. In 1830 he was living with his son David. He d there 14 Jan 1834, just before reaching 100 years.

This Hochstatter family is not to be confused with the Hoch-stetler families whose family history consists of two volumes, written by the Rev. Harvey Hostetler. [Hostetler] The first volume has a "Historical Introduction" by Wm F Hochstetler (1912). We are relating some of that history with good reason.

Our book makes periodic reference to ill fortune falling to many of the frontier people at the hands of Indians. [Treatment of the Indians that precipitated reprisals is not often publicized.] In the very same year that Indians were on a rampage in the Mohawk Valley raids were taking place in Penn where these other Hoch-stetlers settled.

What came to be known as the Hochstetler Massacre occurred 19 Sept 1757. A plaque commemorating the event is to be found on the north side of US Route 78 near Shartlesville, Penn. The Indians attacked after a gathering of neighbors held for the purpose of paring and slicing apples for drying, after which the young folks had a "social or frolic." Jacob, his wife and a third man were killed, and 3 children taken captive. Two of the sons were Jacob and Christian.

The several years' struggle with the Indians is related, but the point we want to establish is this: In November 1764 200 captives were returned; in the spring, 100 more. We quote from p 45 of the first volume:

*...Many of the captives had been taken when young, and
did not remember their names...notice given...[so] that
those who had lost relatives might have a chance to
find them. Many touching scenes occurred [at Carlisle
where they had been assembled]...*

*There has been much misapprehension of the treatment,
...many have thought it strange that [they] could be
satisfied with their Indian associations. A writer in the
Pennsylvania Gazette of July 25, 1765 speaking of the
kindness of the Indians toward their prisoners, says:
"Cruel and unmerciful as they are, by habit and long
example in war, yet...they exercise virtues which Christians need not blush to imitate... Among those who had
lived long with the Indians it is not expected that any
marks of joy would appear on being restored to their
parents or relatives. Having been accustomed to look
upon the Indians as the only connections they had, and
having been tenderly treated by and speaking their
language, it is no wonder they considered their new
fate in the light of a captivity and parted from the
savages in tears.*

The same kindly ideas are brought out in the speech of a Shawnee chief in the council with Col. Bouquet, on surrendering his
captives. "Fathers, we have brought your flesh and blood to you:
they have all been united to us by adoption and though we now
deliver them, we will always look upon them as our relations,
whenever the Great Spirit is pleased that we visit them. We have
taken as much care of them as if they were our own flesh and
blood. They are now become unacquainted with your customs and
manners: and therefore we request you will use them tenderly and
kindly, which will induce them to live contentedly with you."

It goes on to relate how mutual attachments caused difficulty
with some in deciding to return to the whites and how habits thus
acquired never fully left them.

Back to "our" Hochstaters: Christian Hochstatter's ch, all b NP:

3.   i.   *Elizabeth Hochstatter, m FREDERICK OYER, Sr*
       ii.   *Johann Heinrich Hochstatter, b 5 Aug 1770, [sp
             Henrich Bekker and Elisabeth Frank]*
      iii.   *Maria Catharine Hochstatter, b 3 Jan 1776, d
             Schuy 23 Feb 1840, m Peter L Rema (see #17)*
       iv.   *Jacob Hochstatter, b 27 Dec 1779, d Ashford 19
             Oct 1859, m Catharine N Rema (see #15 and 38)
             Listed with them in Ash 1850 census: Jeremiah*

> *Hufstater, 29; Jane, 19; Peter, 26, Geo Ward, 26
> and Esther Hufstater, 2/12. In Ash 1870 Jeremiah
> 45, is listed with Ella, 16; Esther, 15; Emma, 12,
> Abba, 9; Clara, 7; and Henry H. 3.   Son Andrew,
> b Frkf,1812, m MARY ANN OYER*

v.   *Christian Hochstatter, b 28 Jan 1782. A Christian
is shown in Ash 1835 St census with 2 males and
6 females, 1 male old enough to vote.*

vi.   *Johann George Hochstatter, b 15 Oct 1784, res
Oswego Co*

vii.   *Michael Hochstatter, b 11 Dec 1787, d Ashford 6
June/July 1860, m Elizabeth _____, b ca 1788;
farmed Ash*

viii.   *Theobald/David Hochstatter, b 7 Mar 1790, m
Margaret _____*

ix.   *Maria Hochstatter, b 15 Nov 1792, d y*

x.   *Maria/Polly Hochstatter, b 2 Mar 1795, m Peter
Bargy, Jr*

*Henry Arrison <sic> Hufstater was b 10 Apr 1840 at Otto, en-
listed May 1861, 100th Inf; d soon after discharge Feb. 1863; bur
Ash. He was in the 7 days battle before Richmond [Vol. 6 pg.
194 PSO]*

*ELIZABETH's bro Jacob Hufstater went to Ash in 1818; he sold
out to Henry Frank in 1825, settling nearby. He may be the Jacob
in Erie Co whose will was probated in Feb 1890 with James as executor. Another bro Michael moved to and from Frkf, Herk Co;
finally settled in Ash. Michael C, b Jan 1809, Elizabeth's
nephew, md Sadie/Sally Ann Dygert, dau of Abram Dygert of Frkf;
b 11 Apr 1812; d 26 Mar 1880; bur MWC. On the same monument
"Christian, mother and son, d in his 5(?) year; Abraham Dygert, 64
y 2 m 1 d, died 20 Feb 1852; Hannah, his wife, 77 y 4 m 19 d,
died 8 May 1867." In same plot is Mary, dau of Lucretia Dygert,
d ae 3. This Michael went to Ash from Frkf in 1822, making the
journey on foot and carrying his provisions on his back. Michael
d 23 June 1900; bur MWC. Their ch: Willard of Salem, Ore;
Michael, d before 1893; Hannah C, m George O Fox (Fuchs?), res
Ash; Mary E, m John Holland; Abram, b ca 1849, d 17 Nov 1930,
bur Pine Hill Cem, Gowanda, Catt Co, m Alice Reynolds, (ch: Fred
of Lake Geneva, Wis; Edwin of Gowanda; Alson of Kenmore,) and
Sadie, b June 1853, m Edverdo Hughey, of Ash,, son of James
Hughey, b June 1854. Michael C. Hufstater is with wife and
family in the Ash 1900 census; ch: Cornelius, b Dec 1875; Edna, b
June 1878. Also in 1900: Abraham, b 1850; w Alace, b July 1850.
Next listing: Ferdinand, b 1874; Jennie, b Nov 1878; two bros of
Ferdinand, Edwin, b Oct 1879 and Alon, b Oct 1889. Nearby:*

Mary, widow b Dec 1840, sons Walter, b Jan 1871 and Herbert, b Dec 1873.

Several other Oyers md Hufstater, as it came to be spelled by the Catt Co families, one being Andrew who m Mary Oyer. Other families: Rufus Hufstater [Concord, Erie Co 1880] with family and mother (she b Hamburg, Erie Co); Amos E Hufstater with wife Sally Ann, ch: Willard, Hannah, Mary E and Polly Rowland, 34 and Peter Folts, 19 [census Ash 1850]; Ezra Hufstater [census Ash 1870] with wife MARY and ch; James Hufstater [census E Otto 1870], wife Hellen, b Apr 1841, and ch. In census Concord 1900 we learn James b Feb 1838; w b England; 3 ch, 1 alive: Lillian Green b Dec 1864, Case Green b May 1862, son-in-law.

E Otto 1860 census shows David Hufstater, 51; Eliza, 40; Francis, 15; Almira, 14; Charles, 12; Oscar, 9.

In a cemetery on a hill above the village of E Otto, Catt Co are buried these Hufstaters: Francis, 1844-1891; Temperance, 1844-1919; Oscar, b July 1851, d 1936; and Ophelia, b July 1856/7, d 1936. In the 1900 census E Otto, shows ch: Vida M., b Nov 1876 and Fred C, b Dec 1881. Surrogate rec for Francis, above, shows his widow Temperance in the Town of Little Valley with these other heirs: Eliza (Vedder?), mother and bro Charles, Yorkshire Center, Catt Co; bro OSCAR, E Otto, Catt Co; sis Mrs Geo Sacket, Mrs Geo Lincoln, and Mrs H K Armstrong, all of E Otto; Eugene Travers, nephew of Kalamazoo, Mich; and Earl Travis, Sherwood, Mich.(?)

In E Otto 1900: Oscar, 48, m 25 yr; Ophelia, 42; Vida M, 23; Fred C, 18. All the following Ash 1900 in addition to Charles Hufstader, (#38iii): Seneca Hufstader, 40, m 14 y; Jane, 30; Lottie, 13; Matie, 8; 1 dec; Mary, widow, 67, 1 ch. With the Edverdo Hughy family, w Sadie, ae 45 & 46, is Michael C Huffstader, f, b Jan 1809. Nearby is Abraham Huffstader, b 1850, m 27 yr; Alace, b 1850, 3 ch.

MICHAEL (WEIDERICK/WIDRICK/WEDDRICK) WIDRIG, Christian's 2nd wife's father, was also a Hasenclever workman. Two of his descendants md Oyers in the 4th generation. (See #35 and 36) He came from Germany with at least 4 of his children, who were b in Germany: Maria Catherine, b ca 1750; Michael, Jr, b Wuertemberg, Germany ca 1785; Capt Jacob W, b "Elthes" (Alsace), Germany, m Catherine Elisabetha Rinkle/Rinckel Jan 1785; and Col George W, b 1740. [DAR record]. 5 other children were born in America: Maria Sybilla, b 21 Oct 1779; Eva Catherine, b Jan 1771; and possibly Conrad, (although a Conrad was b to George and Maria Elisabeth Witrig 28 July 1790); Elizabeth, b 15 Mar 1783; and Philip, b ca 1775. On 21 Feb 1802 Conrad, son of Michael Wiederich, Schuylertown, and Maria, dau of George Steele of "Germanflats, were md in the church built of stone... Nicholas

*Steele and George Steele, brothers, being present." "Feb 14, 1804
- Michael, Michael Wiederich's son, of Germantown, married Susanna, dau of George Lones of Osquewak..." [Both of these are
in rec of Herk DRC. There are many records in the GF DRC and
at least 1 in SA DRC. It is to be noted that the GF rec skip
from 1795 to 1811. Some of this data comes from Klock, available
at the Herk Co Hist Society.]*

*A Michael was b 12 Nov 1780 in GF to "Michael & Elizabeth
Wiederichs."*

*Michael Widrig in 1790 at Ft. Herkimer "was pulled into Court
for non-payment of his liquor bill." In 1793 Jacob Widrig was
granted permission to sell strong liquor in Schuy. [Rec supplied
by Lois Blotner]*

The early Widrigs were German Lutherans.

*The descent of the Widrigs marrying Oyers in Catt Co is Mi-
chael[1], Michael[2], Michael[3], Lavina[4], (see #35); and Conrad4, (see
#36). We will list the family of Michael3, he b Schuy 2 Feb 1812,
son of Michael & Catherine Lentz. He was a farmer in Herk Co;
d Ash 14 Sept 1860, bur Ash Cem; m Sarah _____, b 1817.*

Ch (WIDRIG), the 1st 7 b in Herk Co; others, Catt Co:

    i.   *Mary, b 1836, m Russell Bulter (sp?)*
   ii.   *Catherine, b 1838*
  iii.   *Nancy, b 1839, m Henry Chapman*
          a) 5th child: Phoebe Ann m Michael Blotner

*[The Blotners are grandparents of Lyle Blotner, whose wife
Lois of Amarillo, Tex is an informant.]*

   iv.   *John Simon, b 1841, m ca 1864 Mary Shiffner, whose
          last born Maytie m _____ Blotner. Lyle is
          their son.*
    v.   *George, b 1842*
   vi.   *CONRAD, b 1844 (see #36)*
  vii.   *LAVINA, b 1846 (see #35)*
 viii.   *William, b 1849*
   ix.   *Hannah?, b 1852*
    x.   *Jacob, b 1854*
   xi.   *Louise, b 1859*

*There are numerous other Widrigs. Here are some of the census
rec of Catt:*

ASHFORD 1850

Conrad Widrig	49	Peter Widrig	29	George Widrig	70
Barbara "	48	Alzina "	32	Elizabeth "	66
Elizabeth "	27	Albert "	7	Mary E "	47
Jacob "	26	Mary "	4	Harriet Johnson	8
Nancy "	24	Rosette "	2		
John "	21	Melissa "	9/12	Jacob Widrig	24
Catherine "	19			Lucy "	23
Clark "	4	Henry Widrig	43	James	1
		Eliza Ann "	26		
Michael "	38	Wm H "	4	George G Widrig	46
Sarah "	33	Elida N "	2	Eveline "	45
Mary "	14			Catherine "	17
Catherine "	12			Hellen "	15
Nancy "	11			Ezra "	13
John Simon "	9			William	12
George "	8				
Conrad "	6	(see #36)			
Lavina "	4	(see #35)			
William "	1				
Michael Widrig	41				
Elizabeth "	44				
Hall "	17				
Charles "	15				
Julia Ann "	12				
Meron (sp?)"	6				

*LORENTZ RINGKEL (Rinckle), another Hasenclever workman,
said to be b in Holland in 1747 [DAR #55358 per Barker], was
killed at Oriskany. Klock's records which we feel are correct
states he came form Elsas, Germany, this being another spelling of
Alsace. The Indians captured his widow and son Lorentz. She
was released. When he was returned to his mother after 7 years
he did not know her, and ran from her. There were also 3 daus:
Catherine, b ca 1764; m 1784 Johannes Jukker; Catherine Elisabeth,
b ca 1766; m 31 Jan 1786 Jacob Witrig; and Maria Sybille b 14 Nov
1770; m Philip Lentz. Lorentz was b 8 Dec 1777; m by 1812
Catherine Youcker. [Barker, p 310. There appears to be a
discrepancy in DAR #'s as that is the same as Frederick Oyer's.]*

*The BARGY (Bircky-Birkey) family is found prominently with
both the New York Oyers and the New Orleans Oyers (see Preface
and Appendix ii). Many of these families: the Rinckles, Remas,*

Hochstetters, Birkeys, Clemens, Steinwax, Millers, Finsters, all are found to have Swiss origins and associations there as far back as the 17th century. There is reason to believe that Peter may have traveled with Frederick Oyer from Europe as another of the Hasenclever workmen. He is shown on the 1800 census as over 45 with 3 sons under 10; 3 daus under 10; 1 female 16-26; 1 female 26-45; and res adjacent to Oyers. In 1810 they are neighbors, as are the Clements, Finsters, Huffstatters, Widrigs, and others of these groupings. In 1830 Peter is in Frkf, perhaps his son Peter.

The Bargy families of Catt Co have been and still are neighbors of the Oyer family. This spelling of the name found in Catt Co is not the usual spelling.

The first Oyer association is found when Jacob Bargy, son of Peter Bircky, m Dorothea/Dorothy Ann Frank, who was the sister (or possibly aunt) of Mary Elizabeth Frank who m DAVID3 OYER (see #5). There is confusion regarding the ancestors. A Jacob and Peter are shown in Bellinger's Regiment of the Tryon Co Militia. MacWethy [BOOK OF NAMES] feels that these are the same men, there being a Peter Sr in addition. Barker feels this Peter was b ca 1720 to 1740, with Jacob b ca 1745, m Anna (prob Lentz). Peter owned land where Hiram Finster was; sold it to John Finster. Such land deals were common when so many set out for Catt Co. He had son Peter, b ca 1765, md 1790 Elizabeth Young (Jung). Their son Jacob, b GF 8 Jul 1792 is the one who m Dorothy Ann Frank, dau of Henry and Gertraud (Clapsattle) Frank.

This Jacob served at Sackett's Harbor in the War of 1812, where he was poisoned by water from wells, as were other soldiers. After working shares on David3 Oyer's farm in Ash, he settled on Lot 62 there. He served as a Justice of the Peace.

Jacob and Dorothy Ann's dau Mary md John Quackenbush, b 16 Apr 1818 in Montgomery Co. [See #40 for Quackenbush details.]

Peter and Elizabeth had these ch (BARGY):

    i.   *Peter, m 1st Polly Hochstetter; she d ca 1825; son Lawrence who d in Va. He m 2nd Polly Folts, who had a son Warner. Warner's son Charles was progenitor of the Frkf Twp, Catt Co line.*

    ii. *Garrett, m Nancy Lints, dau John and Anna (_____) Lints. They had dau Catherine who m _____ Helmer.*

    iii. *Jacob, m Dorothy Ann Frank [see Frank Family data] Jacob's son, Michael Bargy was b 16 May 1833 served in the 154th in 1864 (Civil War); was discharged June 1865. Another son Jacob m*

Catherine Ha_____. dau of Wilhel_____ and
wife Elizabeth Miller.

iv.   Polly. m Lawrence Widrick [see Widrig Family data]
v.   dau. _____, m Sanford Barber; had son Ira
vi.   Nancy/Nancey. b ca 1804, d 30 Mar 1865; m as his
      2nd wife Sidney Valentine, b ca 1795; d 24 Aug
      1865
vii. Barbara, m Conrad Widrick, son of Jacob and
      Catherine (Rinkle) Widrig, bro of Barbara's
      sister Polly's husb Lawrence

A James J Bargy owned land in Ash early.

The RIMAH/RIEMA/REMA/RIMA family is another of the Hasenclever families. JOHANNES/JOHN. the progenitor. thought to be
b in Germany ca 1715 to 1735, m Catherine _____. The families
that m into the Rima families are very numerous, covering several generations. We are not of the opinion that there is a relationship to the Riemensneider families, who were in the Bush settlement north of Little Falls, Herk Co, although it is a possibility.
Early Riemas who could be his children include Elisabeth (Romar) b say 1748; m by 1765 Jacob Hiller; John, Jr. b say 1752 and
George, b say 1756 both were in Bellinger's Regiment, Tryon Co
Militia; Jacob; b say 1760; Frederick, b say 1765, m 1795 Maria
Bekker; Christian, b SAR 14 Aug 1767, m by 1789 Margaret...;
Margaret, b say 1769, m Jan 1788 Peter Lentz; Deobald/Theobald/
David b SAR 2 Dec 1770, m 1795 Margaret Breitenbacher; Peter,
b NP 18 Apr 1772, d Schuy 22 Mar 1844, m 29 Dec 1793 Maria
Catherine Hochstatter, dau of Christian and Maria Catharine
(Widrig) Hochstatter (she b 29 Dec 1775, d 23 Feb 1840); poss
Catherine, b say 1774; living in 1794. [Some data from Barker]
Peter Rimah, b 1772, who farmed in W Schuy had these ch:

        i.   Catharine, b 6 May 1794, d 21 Nov 1862, m Peter
              Finster
       ii.   Mary Margaret. b 3 Mar 1796, d Sandy Creek Oswego
              Co 22 Aug 1877, m Jacob Widrig
19.   iii.   Frederick m ELIZABETH OYER
       iv.   Elizabeth, b 9 Sep 1800, d 17 Apr 1878, m Philip
              Finster
17.   v.   Mary, m JACOB P OYER
       vi.   George, b 30 Apr 1805
      vii.   Eve, b 10 Aug 1807, d Parish, Oswego Co 24 Oct
              1891, m Daniel Klock
     viii.   Lany, b 20 Mar 1810, d 11 Aug 1814
       ix.   Sophronia, b 22 May 1812, m James Widrick

    x. Peter, Jr, b 28 May 1814, m Lydia Farmer
    xi. Philinda, b 15 June 1816, d Cambria Twp, Mich 5 Jan
    1902, m Lyman B Ouderkirk
    xii. Anna, b 25 July 1820, d 26 Sept 842

The families intertwined extensively. The Maria Bekker that a Frederick m was a dau of DIEBOLD BECKER, whose dau Margaretha m JACOB² OYER (see #2). Peter's son FREDERICK m ELIZABETH OYER (see #19). Peter's dau MARY md JACOB P OYER (see #17).

[Sources: censuses, data extracted mostly by LM; Hochstetler; Adams' Catt; Everts' Catt, Barker; Catt & Erie Co Surr Rec; Jones; CCHS; AHA; cem rec]

4. PETER² OYER *(Frederick¹)*, born Schuy. 5 Dec. 1771; died Schuy. 6 June 1853, ae. 83 years. He married 9 Feb. 1799 ELIZABETH CLARK, dau. of Cornelius and Margaret (_____) Clark, born Northeast Twp. ("Nine Partners"), Dutchess Co. 9 Dec. 1782; died Schuy. 14 Jan. 1853, ae. 70 yr; both buried MRC.

Left fatherless at the age of 5, "Peter Euer" (as he signed his name) grew up in and around the fort of New Petersburg and on the farm cleared by his father before the Revolution. He apparently retained the old homestead farm and lived there with his mother and unmarried sisters. He brought his wife there and raised a large family, though he did not acquire clear title to his 100 acre farm from his half brother John Finster until March of 1805. His land occupied the upper 100 acres of Finster's 500 acre tract.

Peter acquired land in other counties. 28 Aug. 1816 he purchased 138.5 acres in Onon. Co., which later became the farms of sons James and Solomon. 18 Mar. 1818 Peter purchased from his brother Frederick 7 acres adjoining his own land; son Jacob occupied this land for a time. 4 Feb. 1831 he purchased a farm in Boyleston Twp., Oswego Co., that was for a time owned by grandson John F. Cain.

In 1825 Peter is listed farming 100 acres, owning 16 cattle, 11 horses, 25 sheep and 14 hogs and producing fulled and flannel cloth.

The 1850 census lists Peter Oyer, farmer, owning real estate worth $3,000. Living with him were his wife Elizabeth, sister Elizabeth (deaf mute), son Daniel, dau. Hannah Clemens and son-in-law Jacob Clemens, laborer.

Peter Oyer then replaced John Finster as the patriarch of the Oyer family. Surviving his elder brothers by many years and

Chart of Peter[2] Oyer family.

retaining the family homestead, he naturally fitted into the role of family head. He was well-to do and lent money locally. The inventory of his estate shows indebtedness to his estate of over $4,000; most of his loans were to family and neighbors. The inventory reveals some interesting things about his life. He owned at the time of his death much lumber, carpenter's tools, several wagons and sleighs, a weaving loom, shoe making tools, farm tools, kitchen items and livestock including horses, cows and a bull. His farm was retained by his youngest son, Daniel Auyer. You will note how Peter's line changed the spelling of Oyer to Auyer. Many families continue this spelling.

Peter Oyer and his wife were not buried in the old burying grounds near his farm, but instead in the new Miller Rural Cemetery, a short distance away.

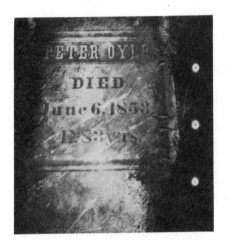 

Gravestones of Peter[2] and Elizabeth Oyer, located MRC, E. Schuyler, Herkimer Co., N.Y.

Ch. all b in Schuy:

16.	i.	JOHN P³ OYER, b 14 July 1799
17.	ii.	JACOB P OYER, b 14 Mar 1801
18.	iii.	MARGARET OYER, b 14 Oct 1802
19.	iv.	ELIZABETH OYER, b 14 Oct 1804
20.	v.	JAMES AUYER, b 10 Apr 1806
21.	vi.	SOLOMON OYER, b 24 Dec 1808
22.	vii.	HENRY OYER, b 3 Aug 1809

viii. EVE OYER, b 17 June 1810; d Schuy Twp, 29 June 1810; bur. poss in an unmarked grave in the abandoned burying grounds near her father's farm. "This privilege of burying was given by Peter Oyer, without price; the ground was never fenced. No graves have been opened there since 1848" when MRC opened.

22.1   ix.   CATHARINE OYER, b 29 Aug 1811

x. PETER OYER, Jr, b 23 Oct 1814; d Schuy Twp 9 Apr 1821

xi. HANNAH/NANCY OYER, b 26 Nov 1816; d after 1853; m Herk Co 9 Sept 1838 JACOB CLEMENS. 2nd son of Michael Clemens and Catharine Lents. b Schuy Twp 14 Feb 1811. "Joanne Lentz and Catharina Clemens, sing" sp. [The marriage entry in the Herk DRC records is: "married by me in my office Jacob M Clemens fil: leg: Michaelis Clemens & Catharinae Lentz uxoris farmers ex Shyler to Anna Oyer fil: leg: Petri Oyer & Elisabeth Clerk uxoris farmers copulanti sunt in presence of Daniel Oyer fratre et Margareth Clemens caelibus ibidem."] Jacob's bro Michael and sister Catharine m Hannah's sister Rachel and bro Henry respectively. Jacob was a farmer. In 1850 he and Hannah were living with her parents in Schuy Twp; later they removed to Oneida Co.

23.	xii.	RACHEL OYER, b 14 Mar 1819
24.	xiii.	DANIEL AUYER, b 21/27 Feb 1821

[Sources: GF DRC; Herk Co LR; VR; surr rec; Beers' Herk]

*** THE CLARK FAMILY ***

Elizabeth Clark's father was CORNELIUS CLARK. one of the earliest "Yankee" settlers in the Schuy area. coming to Herk Co prior to 1800 from Dutchess Co. We believe him to be the Cornelius Clark listed in the town of Northeast. formerly N E

Precinct, Dutchess Co, in the area where there were many other
Clarks, as we find a dau Elizabeth b to a Cornelius there. Some
of the settlers there supported the Revolution; some were Loyalists. In 1775 Cornelius was a non-signer of the Association
(taking the American side), and served in the Revolutionary War.
The 1790 census shows a Cornelius in "Northeast Town," located
along the Conn border, with a family of 7, apparently including 5
children. That census lists a Cornelius in Duanesburgh Twp,
Albany Co and one in Bedford Twp, Westchester Co as well. The
1800 census lists 4 Corneliuses, "ours" in Herk Co, living in the
Oyer vicinity of Herk Twp with a family of 5. Nearby is his son
Andrew. We have been unsuccessful in connecting him to other
Clark families, although we have much Clark data. [Efforts to
learn MARY CLARK's parentage, she being the first wife of
PETER D OYER (#25) have been unsuccessful. The land rec shows
her as "Fanny."]

Ch (CLARK, Cornelius):

i.   Andrew, res in Schuy Twp; m Elisabeth Shno(?)
ii.   Elizabeth, m PETER OYER
iii. Cornelius

Other early Clarks in Herk Co are Sanford, Jeremy (Schuyler),
David and Simon, both in GF. [1800 census] About 1803 an
Alexander Clark of Florida, Mont Co, d intestate, a Benjamin of
Florida Twp a grantee.

We find many Clarks in Catt Co early also. In the 1835 St
census in Ash we find Cornelius A Clark. This could be iii. above.
He was b 8 Jan 1802; m Malinda _____, b Wyoming Co 5 Mar
1809. They had a large family and moved to Illinois; both d in
Warren Lake Co, Illinois in Aug 1881.

Among the other Clarks found in Catt Co before 1865 are Frederick A in Ash; m Corinna _____ (10 chill); Augusta, Homer
and Thankful Biggs, all bur Franklinville (hereafter Frklnv); Wm
and Caroline, both b Mass, he f of Wells Clark, Ellvl; J T Clark,
lawyer at Versailles, went to Calif in 1848; Wm who was in the
Rev, b ca 1790 in Leon, Catt Co, had dau Mary. There's a Henry
S of Humphrey, Great Valley Twp (hereafter GrV), b Chatham,
Conn; his f was Hiram. He had a dau Mary. There was a Francis
G Clark, town clerk and justice of the peace in Frklnv 1840–1853.
He had sisters who could be of Mary/Fanny (Clark) Oyer's age,
but we don't know the names.

[Sources: Clark Inf 1 and 2; Barker; Col Co VR; Herk Co LR,
VR, SR]

Town of Ashford, Cattaraugus Co., N.Y. circa 1900.

Chapter 8

THIRD GENERATION

5. THEOBALD/DABOLD/<u>DAVID</u>[3] OYER (*Jacob*[2], *Frederick*[1]), born Schuyler Twp., Herkimer Co. (hereafter Schuy., Herk. Co.), 17 Jan. 1791; bp. "Johann Dieterich Eirer" 22 Jan. 1791 [rec. GF DRC]; sp. Clem McGnot and wife Elisabeth Barbara; died Springville, Erie Co. (hereafter Sprvl.) 2 Mar. 1878, buried Maplewood Cem. (hereafter MWC), married MARY ELISABETH FRANK, dau. Johann Heinrich/Henry and Gertraud (Clapsaddle) Frank, born Frkf, Herk. Co. 28 Apr. 1790; bp. Maria Catharina Franck 5 May 1790 [rec. GF DRC]; sp. Wilhelm and Maria Klepsattel; died E. Otto, Cattaraugus Co. (hereafter Catt. Co.) 17 Mar. 1884; buried Ashford Hollow Cem. (hereafter AHC).

In 1816 David contracted with the Holland Land Company, whose holdings covered all of Western New York east to the Phelps-Gorham purchase, for a 100 acre parcel, Lot 56, in the township of Olean/Ischua/Ashford (hereafter Ash.), Catt. Co. [See Appendix v]

It was reported that others were strongly influenced to emigrate by Jacob Frank, a boatman on the soon-to-be-opened Erie Canal. In-laws Henry, Andrew and Jacob Frank had similarly acquired land there, settling in Ash. Hollow in 1817, becoming the earliest settlers in the area.

Remaining for a time on his father's farm in Schuy., Herk. Co., in the spring of 1818 "Dabold Oyer and Mary Elizabeth his wife" joined their Frank relatives in Ash. Hollow. There were roads as far as Sprvl. in Erie Co.; the last 8 miles through the wilderness included crossing the spectacular Zoar Valley Gorge, through which flows Cattaraugus Creek, which later became the dividing line between Erie and Catt. Counties.

[We learn the following details from a booklet prepared in 1978 for the sesquicentennial celebration of the Town of Ash., the historical notes taken from records of Roy Conrad by Cecelia Schumacher. The booklet was compiled by the Ash. Historical Society.]

Catt. Co. was set off from Genesee Co. in 1808 to become the immense town of Olean. In 1812 that was split to from the towns of Olean and Ischua. On 16 Apr. 1824 Ash. was separated from Ischua to become a township. On 13 Apr. 1835 the Town of Otto was split to become Towns of Otto and E. Otto. It was at that time a part of E. Otto was transferred to Ash., adding nearly 34,000 acres.

The first residents settled along Cattaraugus Creek and extended southward through Franktown and Thomas Corners.

From early town meetings we find David Oyer was named a highway supervisor, collector, constable and overseer of the poor. At one the sum of $250 was voted to be raised for the support of roads and bridges; $25 for support of the poor, $50 for the support of common schools, $20 to purchase blank book and ballot boxes for the town; no money for destruction of wolves; and hogs were to be free commoners in the town.

Other early items: all horned cattle be free commoners; fences shall be 4'6" high; brush fences and all others well erected; all rams found running at large between Sept. 1 and Nov. 1 shall forfeit the sum of $5 to be applied to the poor fund; horses and sheep shall not run at large, horned cattle may. By 1859, cattle may not be allowed to run on public highways.

George West, a supervisor of the Town of Ash., was elected to the State Assembly, and the village of West Valley was named in his honor.

Ellicottville was the county seat of Cattaraugus Co. from 1817 until May 17, 1869, when it was moved to Little Valley.

About 1900 Ash. Hollow had 1 hotel, 1 church, 2 stores, 1 school, 1 saw mill, 1 harness shop, 2 wagon shops, 1 furniture store and 1 physician. Population was 150.

WV had 1 hotel, 3 churches, 7 stores, 1 school, 1 furniture store, 2 blacksmith shops, 1 woodworking shop, 1 harness shop, 1 saw and shingle mill, 1 physician and several societies and Orders. Population was 200.

E. Ash. (Riceville) had 2 churches, 2 stores, 1 blacksmith shop, and 1 saw mill. Population was 75.

David quickly improved his land and increased his holdings. By 1822 he owned Lots 47, 63 and 66 in Ellicottville Twp., (hereafter Ellvl). His saw mill, as noted below the first in Ash. Twp., was built in 1826.

The following is quoted from Briggs' Concord, p. 251-2:

A BEAR STORY

The following bear story is related by the late David Oyer, father of Jacob Oyer, of Springville: "It was some 60 or more years ago since I went to the town of Ashford. Only a few settlers were there at that time, and the few cows they possessed were suffered to roam through the woods. The few settlers would take turns in looking them up at milking time. The evening in question it fell to my lot to bring the cows home, and it being Sunday I did not take my gun along, as was customary with me, but I coaxed all the dogs in the settlement to accompany me, and I started out in an easterly direction, and it was not long before I could hear the tinkling of the bells. All at once the dogs set up a terrible outcry in the direction that I was going, and I quickened my footsteps and soon came up with dogs, who had a bear at bay. He sat upright upon his haunches with his back to a large tree, and whenever a dog got within his reach it received a terrible blow from Bruin's paw, and whenever he turned and attempted to climb the tree the dogs would seize him and haul him back. What was to be done? My only arms was a pocket-knife, but this stood me well in hand; with it I cut a heavy cudgel (short thick stick), and by keeping the tree between myself and the bear, I was able to approach near enough, and by stepping to one side I dealt him a stunning blow across the nose, and a few more over the head finished him. That bear was dressed and divided up among the settlers, who enjoyed a feast.

The first letters of guardianship in Catt. Co. were issued to David Oyer as guardian of Michael Hufstader.

David was one of the founding members of the First Free-Will Baptist Society, their first meeting being held at his father-in-law Henry Frank's home in 1821. Jacob Hufstater, Jacob Frank and Augustus Van Slyke were also members.

The 1835 state census shows him owning 20 cattle, 3 horses, 32 sheep, and 15 hogs. An 1843 map of Ash. shows David owning land on Lots 48, 55, 62, and 63 of township 5, range 6. In 1850 his real estate was worth $304; listed as a farmer in successive censuses.

By 1860 David and Mary Elizabeth had moved to Ellvl. Twp. In Feb. 1865 they moved to E. Otto Twp., near daughter Margaret and her husband Chauncey Crumb. In 1870 his property was worth $1,000; his house was 3 doors from theirs.

As they aged, they alternated living with son Jacob and daughter Margaret. On 21 Aug. 1876 they moved in with Jacob in Sprvl. There they had separate bed and sitting rooms, built for them by Jacob, boarding with the family. David was able to work in the garden from time to time, and would occasionally go fishing, of which he was fond, until the last several months of his life. The last 3 months he was helpless and confined to bed. Various members of the Oyer and Crumb families would take care of and sit up with him.

Buried in Jacob's plot in Maplewood Cem. in Sprvl., his inscription reads: "DAVID OYER/ BORN IN HERKIMER CO, N.Y./ JAN 17, 1791,/ PIONEER SETTLER IN ASHFORD, N.Y. 1818/ DIED IN SPRINGVILLE, N.Y./ MARCH 2, 1878."

David's will left instructions to provide for Mary Elizabeth "her comfortable support and maintenance" out of the estate. Living at Jacob's when her husband died, by 1880 she was back with Margaret in E. Otto. A disagreement over the handling of the estate in fulfilling the request for her care and assigning a value on the care of David during his final years comprises two large packets of transcripts, minutes, affidavits, etc. on file at Catt. Co. Surrogate's Court in Little Valley. A New York Supreme Court judge's ruling eventually decried the wasting of the money on interminable court costs--not what David would have wanted.

In 1979 David was honored by having a mountain in the town of GrV named Oyer Mountain. This was arranged by the family of Walter Oyer. The news item announcing it follows in part:

LANDMARKS NAMED FOR AREA SETTLERS

Three mountains in Hungry Hollow have been named in honor of early settlers in this area, including one of Salamanca's first physicians.

Names for the three nearby "geographic features of Cattaraugus County" have been approved by the United States Board on Geographic names...published in Decision List 7093. The approved names were proposed by Mrs. Diane O. Quagliana of Dublin, Ohio, a descendant of two of the three. The idea for doing so was in celebration of her parents', Walter and Phyllis Oyer, fortieth wedding anniversary.

..."Oyer Mountain" at an elevation of 2,128 feet and four and one half miles north of Salamanca in the towns of Little Valley and Great Valley, is named for the late David Oyer, who settled in the Town of Ashford in 1819, "traveling the last eight miles through the wilderness from Springville." His great great grandson, Walter Oyer of Rochester...now owns a home and many acres of farm and woodlands in Hungry Hollow Road, which runs between the two mountains. [The other one, Smith Mountain, was named for Phyllis Oyer's paternal grandfather, Dr. Julian G. Smith, one of Salamanca's first physicians.]

...He was supervisor in 1830-31...Cattaraugus County is peopled with many of his descendants, including numerous area residents.

--Salamanca Republican Press, Dec. 1979

Ch (OYER), the first 2 b in Schuy, the last 2 b in Ash:

25.	i.	PETER D[4], b 1811
	ii.	ELIZABETH, b ca 1817; d y. She came with parents and brother to Catt Co and d there.
26.	iii.	JACOB, b 31 Mar 1823
27.	iv.	MARGARET EVE/<u>EVA</u>, b 7 Apr 1827

Oyer Mountain, Great Valley, Cattaraugus Co., N.Y., named in 1982; located on Hungry Hollow Road; elevation, over 2,000 feet.

*** THE FRANK-CLAPSATTLE-FOLTS-HESS FAMILIES ***

There are conflicting records regarding MARY ELIZABETH FRANK. Everts' 1879 history states that she was the dau of AN-DREW FRANK. Our research indicates otherwise. However, all attempts to sort out the early Franks completely accurately are apt to fail. Suffice it to say their history alone is a fascinating one.

Mary Elizabeth is but one of several FRANK connections with the Oyers, all of whom come from the family of HENRICH/HENRY FRANK, immigrant, who arrived at Philadelphia, Penn. with his wife Catharine _____ and brother Christopher before the French and Indian War. They came from Germany and stayed in Penn for a number of years before moving to the area of Frkf, Herk Co. In the 1757 raid of German Flats during the French and Indian War, Catharine, five of her daughters, and her 18-month old son were taken captive by the Indians and taken to Montreal. The mother had to carry the boy to keep up with the rest, or have him tomahawked. Some were released in 1760 and 1761.

Henry, Sr served in Capt Conrad Frank's militia company in 1767, as did Henry, Jr. [It is believed Conrad is the only early Palatine Frank in Herk Co. However, the DAR records show Conrad as Henry's father. It could be Henry emigrated after other Franks.]

Henry, Sr.'s ch (FRANK):

  i.   *Maria, b ca 1743 (twin), m 1766 John Myer(s), an early settler in Carrolton Twp, Catt Co*
       a) *1 son we know of: John Myers*
  ii. *Eva, b ca 1743 (twin), m 1766 Johann/John Stephen Frank [Researchers believe this Stephen to be of the Conrad Frank line.]*
  iii. *Elizabeth, m Frederick Philip Stahring, d 1835*
  iv. *Johann Henrich/Henry [see below]*
  v.   *Lawrence, b Frankfort, Oct 1749, m Mary Myers (b Germany 1753, came when young with parents to Frkf, Herk Co: d Busti Twp, Chau Co, 1831). Lawrence was captured by Indians in 1777 and kept in captivity over 3 yrs. He lived in Frkf, later became a pioneer settler in the town of Busti, where he d 13 Apr 1813.*

       Lawrence's ch: Lawrence, Jr (d in Frkf), Margaret, Elizabeth, Peter, Henry L, John L, Michael, Joseph and Matthew. Margaret m Stephen Frank, d Oh; Elizabeth never went to Chau Co; Peter d

Oh; Henry m Margaret Damoot, moving to Kirt-
land, Oh where both d.
vi.   Margaret
vii. Jacob, b say 1756; d in Revolution.

The twin sisters were among the 6 children captured by the
Indians at the time of the "French war." They were kept 3 and
4 years respectively; 3 others were drowned while in flight from
the Indians.

HENRY FRANK, iv. above, was b in Penn ca 1745, m 20 Nov
1769 Gertraut Clapsaddle/Klebbsattel, dau of the immigrant Andrew Clapsaddle, he ca 1750. Henry lived in GF, Herk Co; later
in Frkf. In Apr 1777 he enlisted, serving in Capt Tare Putnam's
Company and Col Willett's New York Reg't; he was in the Battle
of Oriskany and many other skirmishes. He served in Col Bellinger's New York Reg't; in 1779 he guarded the frontiers of
Herk Co. He served as a scout in the Rev.

Henry's ch (FRANK):

i.   child, b ca 1770, drowned in flight from Indians 1780
ii.   Henry H Frank (Henry Frank, Jr), b 1772, m
       Mary/Polly) Clapsaddle; to Ash 1825, buying out
       Jacob Hufstater; d Ash 2 July 1830
              a) one of his sons, Frederick, settled Ash 1824
iii.   John H Frank, b 1775, m 20 Dec 1795 Anna Margaret
       Gerlach, b 1775. Farmed in the Franktown area of
       Ash; dau CHARITY m JOHN P OYER (see #16)
iv.   Jacob Frank, b 21 Oct 1777, drowned 1780
v.   child, b ca 1779, drowned 1780
vi.   Gertraut Frank, b 27 Jan 1782, m Michael Weaver, (b 7
       Aug 1774; d Sprvl, Erie Co, 1842), d 13 Dec 1869
vii.   Anna Eva/Nancy Eve Frank, b 5 Mar 1786, d 9 Nov
       1867, m Augustus Van Slyke (see John Oyer, #7)
viii. Elisabeth Frank, b 1 Dec 1787, bp 17 Dec 1787
ix.   Maria Catherine/Elizabeth, m DAVID OYER (see #5)
x.   Andries/Andrew Frank, bp 20 Feb 1792, m Catharine
       Bircky/Bargy, prob dau of Jacob Bargy, b ca 1745
       (see #3). Andrew was in the War of 1812. He was
       one of the first settlers in Ash, Catt Co (1816, then
       Ischua), where his dau Phebe's death 30 Aug 1818
       was the first death there.
xi.   Dorothea/Dorothy Ann Frank, b 9 Dec 1794, bp 10
       Mar 1795, m 26 Feb 1811 Jacob P Bargy, b 1790 (see
       #3).
xii.   Jacob H Frank, b Frankfort 1798; to Ash 1817; m 1st
       Margaret (Maria?) Weber (1797-1843). They had 11

children; m 2nd Mary (Maria?) _____. (See
#32) Jacob d Camden, Hillsdale Co, Mich , bur Berg
Cem 1873. Jacob is the Erie Canal boatman whose
influence brought about the migration of many to
Catt Co from Herk Co.

Ash VR show Andrew P Frank, Mont Co b 10 Sept 1817, son of
Peter A and Elizabeth (Ferncrook) Frank, both b Mont Co; a re-
tired blacksmith; d 2 Feb 1915, ae 97 y, 4 m, 23 d; bur Bellows
Cem, Ash; [inf: J O Frank, W Virginia]
Among the Franks bur in Ash with their year of death are:
Henry, 1876; Henry, 1840; Lawrence, 1867; Peter A, ae 71, 1868;
Helen E, wife of Lawrence and later Ernest, 1901; Henry Jr, 1830;
Robert, 1907; Welthy, his wife, 1918; Jeremiah, d 1866?); Manley J,
1971; Eva M, 1976; Lyman B, 1919; Julia M, 1913; Frederick F,
1904; Annie M, 1916; Mrs Betsy, 1918 (b 1836); Lyman B, d 1919,
son of Lawrence and Liddy (Multer) Frank of Ash, he b Frkf.
We have much additional Frank data. There is a Frank
cemetery in the Ash area known as Franktown. Early families
that can be found in Catt and Erie Counties include Robert
(Concord, Erie); Jacob, Reuben, Daniel, Jacob H, Peter, Andrew
P, John, another Peter, Henry, Lawrence, Frederick, all in Ash
1850 census. The 1865 St census of Ash lists 28 Franks.

[Interesting Frank information is in Young's Chau. We found a
copy of it at the Ellvl Historical Society. Other sources: Adams'
Catt; Everts' Catt; LV Hist; LM; Ash VR; Ash cem rec.]

There were said to be 3 CLAPSATTLE/Klepsattle brothers who
immigrated, with 2 moving to the Mohawk Valley and 1 staying
in Penn. An Andreas arrived at Philadelphia, Penn 27 Aug 1735,
being naturalized in 1737. This is likely Gertraud's father, he b
ca 1713. Her sister Catherine, b ca 1748 m Joseph Meyer; a bro
Andrew b ca 1755 m Maria Dygert, dau of William and Maria
Elisabeth (Ecker) Dygert. He later md the step-sister of Maria's,
Margaret Dygert. A third wife was the widow Phoebe Rollin.
There were 3 Clapsattels in Tryon Co Militia, Col Bellinger's
Reg't: Andrew, William and Jacob, the latter being engaged at
Oriskany.
There are other Clapsattle liaisons: Augustinus/Tinus who some
say was killed at Oriskany was a pension applicant. His son
Augustinus b 1774 m by 1803 Elizabeth Frank, the dau of Law-
rence Frank, b Oct 1749. Elisabeth, b 1790, dau of Col William
and Mariae (Haener) Clapsaddle, b 1758 and ca 1758 resp, m Jo-
seph Conrad Folts, b 9 Feb 1782.

The *FOLTS/VOLTS/VOLS/FOLS/VOLTZ* family stems from 2 brothers who came to "lower New York" in the early part of the 17th century. They received a grant from the King of England. Because of given name similarities and the repeated use of the same names by brothers of their siblings it is difficult to sort out the Folts without error. Metchum and Melchior may be brothers; we are combining the spellings as though one person as various records show alternate spellings.

In 1711 METCHEM/Metchum/Melchert/Melchior Volts (1676-1759) with company of neighbors came to the Mohawk Valley. Metchum m 1st Anna Eva _____; 2nd, Margaretha _____; 3rd Anna Catherine. One of Metchum's several sons, JACOB MELCHIOR, served as a lieut in the GF militia, and fought in the French and Indian War. He was wounded at the Battle of Oriskany 6 Aug, 1777. Other Folts/Vols were also in the militia.

JACOB m'd Anna Catherine Petrie (1714-1799), dau of Johan Jost and Cordelis (Demuth) Petrie. Ch: Anna Maria, Ann Margret, Jacob, Elizabeth, Catherine (who m John Klock), a second Anna Maria, CONRAD, Anna, Delia and Dorothea. Jacob was blind from his 80th yr and "spent his last years in second childhood." [Beers' Herk, p 246-8]

Jacob Melchior Folts' son CONRAD J(1747-1793) was a capt in the GF militia. Conrad was wounded at the Battle of Oriskany. He m Anna Dygert, dau of Warner and Magdalena (Herkimer) Dygert. Conrad drowned in the Mohawk River at Frkf in June 1793; his widow m 2nd Timothy Frank, son of Conrad Frank. Ch: Jacob C, Warner, Mary, JOSEPH, Severenus/Sylvanus (m Dorothy Dygert), Johannes, Catharina, Abraham and Daniel.

JOSEPH FOLTS, b Herk 1782, m Elizabeth/Betsy Claptsadle (she b 14 Apr 1790, d 22 Feb 1871). Joseph bought land from Jacob Over in 1825, and brought his family to Ash, Catt Co in 1828 at the age of 20. He learned blacksmithing, and became a skillful mechanic. [One source says he was 20; this could be a different Joseph. There was a Joseph, b ca 1808. He came to Ash in 1832 from Herk Co and was an axemaker by trade, and Adams' Catt says he md Elizabeth Clapsaddle. The FOLTS had large families, and they are allied with several of the families with whom Oyers are allied: VAN SLYKE, FRANK, MULTER and QUACKENBUSH. Barker's book has done a remarkable job detailing the families, and we refer the interested reader to his book. The problem there is that Barker "loses" them after they left Herk Co.]

JOSEPH and Betsy's sons were Timothy, b 10 June 1808 who m Mary E Frank, dau of John Frank of Ash; William, b 1 Feb 1810 of Mansfield, Catt Co who m Caroline Riddle; Hiram, b 25 Dec 1813; Joseph, b 10 Feb 1821; Oliver (Ash), b 18 Aug 1833. Dau: Sally, b 16 Oct 1812 (widow of John Van Slyke); Elizabeth, b 7 June 1829 who md Justin Munger of LV, Catt Co; Mary, b 15 Oct

1816; Maria, b 17 Jan 1819; and Margaret, b 7 June 1829 were deceased by 1893.

William's sons were Charles, Morris and George Luman; daus Mary, m Geo Tinkcom; Sarah, d 1883-; Elizabeth, m Charles Goss; and Ida, m John Hughey.   Timothy's sons were Frank, Allen, Joseph and Newton; Hiram had none; Oliver had Ernest; Joseph had Luke.   There may have been daus.

Sylvanus' children: Henry, b Frkf ca 1812, m Mary E Hess, b ca 1818, to Ash 1840; Matthew; and William.

[We believe Barker's information on "Severenus" #2847 (p 83) to be Sylvanus, above.]

Henry (b 1812) and Mary's children: David H, b 1841; Wm H, b 1845; Harriette, b ca 1848; Mariette, b 1850, m C G Miller.

A Dr D V Folts, in Concord 1883-, removed to Boston, Mass.

Henry's wife MARY HESS was the dau of GEORGE HESS, whose f was "Capt HONYOST H HESS," a captain for 8 years in the war of the Rev...b in Herk Co 18 Dec 1788, and served in the War of 1812. He came to Ash in 1841 and settled on the farm now owned [1893] by Andrew Frank." [Adams' Catt, p 697]   There were 6 Hesses in the Tryon Co Militia, Bellinger's Reg't, one being Augustinus who was killed near Ft Herkimer 15 July 1782. This may be the explanation of the discrepancy regarding Augustinus Clapsaddle, mentioned above.

George Hess m MARY CLAPSADDLE and had Joseph, Mary E (Mrs Henry Folts), Nancy (Mrs. Jedediah Walker), Michael E, George W, b 1833 Columbia Co, enlisted 1861, 154th, Cpl; in 11 engagements, discharged when age 31; and Elias Hanen, b 1825, Herk Co, enl Mar 1865, 65th Inf, discharged June 1865.

The Hess family trace their ancestry to JOHN HESS who came from Hesse Cassel, Germany in 1710, settling in Palatine. Honyost was b 3 Nov 1758; m CATHERINE EDIC, and had children Nancy, George, Catharine, Elizabeth, Polly, and Margaret.   Other Hess genealogical data shows a Johannes that could be "Honyost." Johannes came from Bleichenbach Hanau, Germany in 1710 and was on the NY Palatine subsistence list in 1710 and 1712.

[Sources: Adams' Catt; Barker; Everts' Catt; Beers' Herk; LV LR, surr rec, Hist, VR; Young's CHAU; LM; Briggs;Folts Reunion at Allen Folts, August 17, 1905, pamphlet; Frank Inf 1.   Barker's book has much Hess data.]

6. MARY/POLLY³ OYER (*Jacob²*, *Frederick¹*), born Schuy. Twp., Herk. Co. 31 May 1794; died Schuy. Twp. 16 Nov. 1879, buried MRC.   She married JOHN LINTS, 2nd son of Philip and Mary (Rinkle) Lints, born Schuy. Twp. 29 July 1793 and baptized [rec

GF DRC] 4 Aug. 1793, sp. Jacob and Catharina Elisabeth Widrig; died Schuy. Twp. 16 May 1870, buried MRC.

John and Mary Lints resided in Schuy. near the Oyers. He purchased a farm from Peter and Elizabeth Bargy 12 Sept. 1827 about the time of their marriage. In 1830 they lived between David Hofstader <sic> and Peter F. Oyer. By 1835 they were farming 50 acres, with cattle, horses, sheep and hogs. His real estate was valued at $3,000 in 1850. Their son-in-law Duane Jackson and wife moved in with the parents toward the latter part of their lives and Jackson took over the Lints farm.

Child (LINTS):

28.   i.   MARGARET⁴,   b Mar 1831

*** THE LINTS FAMILY ***

JOHN LINTS, 2nd is a grandson of JOHN LINTS, Sr, who was b in Pfalz (Palatinate), Germany in 1710; emigrated to New Jersey where he m ANNA _____.

He later came to NP with Hasenclever's group. This gives further credence to the belief that Frederick Oyer, too, could have been in the group that was first in the Ringwood, NJ area, as suggested in Chapter 5.

John, Sr was killed in action in the Revolution. John, 2nd was killed by a man 6 Oct 1780 while working in a field near Mohawk, Herk Co.

John Lints, Sr's Ch:

   *i.   Jacob, b Philadelphia, Pa 14 Nov 1754, d Frkf, NY
          1841; m (1) Catherine _____; m (2) Elizabeth
          Rema; m (3) Elizabeth Bender*
   *ii.   John, Jr. b ca 1758, POW in 1780; killed by
          Indians.*
   iii. Elizabeth, b ca 1760, m MICHAEL WIDRIG [see Chpt 7]
   iv.   Catharine, b 1761, d 1847, m 1783 Conrad Folts, Jr
   v.   Nancy, b ca 1762, m Peter Bargy
   vi.   Margaret, b _____, m Jacob Rema
   vii. Peter, b before 1772, m Jan 1788 Margaret Rema
   viii. Sarah, b ca 1768, m Christian Rema
   ix.   Philip, b ca 1772, m GF 1791 Maria Rinckel
          Their son John is subject covered (#6), above.

John, Sr and Jr, Peter and Jacob Lentz were in Bellinger's Reg't. [MacWethy]. It is difficult to differentiate between the 3 successive John Lints. Jacob Lints lived near Henry Frank and

Andrew Bell in GF. Other Lints marriages were with Breiten-
bachers, Baumans and Meyers.

In Ash in 1855 we find these additional Lints: Philip Lints, b
Herk Co., 48 years old, in Catt Co only 5 mo; Polly, b Herk, 44;
Martha, 12; Catherine, 11; Jane, 9; Philip, 1, all ch b in Oneida
Co. Also: John Lints, b Herk Co, age 32; Mary, b Herk Co, age
30; Lister, b Catt Co, 8/12. In 1870, John and Mary, ages 43 and
40; ch Duane, 26; Jane A, 16. In Concord 1900: John b Aug 1822
m 56 years; Harry b Sept 1824, 3 ch: 0 alive.

[Sources: Censuses; Herk and Catt SR & LR; Barker; GF DRC]

7. JOHN³ OYER *(Jacob², Frederick¹)*, born Schuy. Twp., Herk.
Co. 16 Oct. 1798; died E. Otto Twp., Catt. Co. 5 Mar 1867, ae. 68
y., 4 m. 17 d.; buried AHC. He married MARY ANN/POLLY VAN
SLYKE, dau. of Augustus and Nancy Eva (Frank) Van Slyke, born
Frkf., Herk. Co. ca. 1803; died 1880+.

John was raised under the supervision of his brother David and
uncle, Peter Oyer. He accompanied his brother David to Catt. Co.
in about 1818 and helped clear his farm. He also soon established
himself as a landowner. By 1822 he had acquired Lot 55 in the
Ellvl. Twp. and was listed as farmer in 1823. He was also a
miller.

In the 1830's John and his family moved from Ash. Hollow to E.
Otto Twp. where he farmed. In 1860 his real estate was worth
$3,170 and his personal property was worth $1,280.

After John's death Polly lived with her son Augustus on the E.
Otto farm; later in the village of Sprvl., Erie Co., on N. Bflo. St.

Ch (OYER); first 5 b Ash Twp; last 4 b E Otto:

	i.	DAVID⁴, b 1822; d after 1880, unmarried; lived with his parents and later his brother Augustus in Ash, E Otto and Sprvl. He is indicated as an invalid in some censuses, but may have done light farming when able.
29.	ii.	JACOB J, b Nov 1824
30.	iii.	MARGARET E, b 24 June 1826
31.	iv.	JOHN, Jr, b 24 Sept 1828
32.	v.	MARY E, b 1832
33.	vi.	ELIZABETH ANN, b 1833
34.	vii.	AUGUSTUS/GUST V, b Sept 1840
35.	viii.	ANDREW J, b 26 May 1843
36.	ix.	HARRIET CATHARINE, b 24 Apr 1847

*** THE VAN SLYKE FAMILY ***

MARY ANN/POLLY VAN SLYKE's father, AUGUSTUS, was another early settler of Ash Twp. He was b 22 May 1777 and lived in Frkf, Herk Co for many years before coming to Catt Co in 1819 with his wife and 2 children. She was Anna Nancy Eva Frank, dau of Johann Heinrich (Henry) and Gertraud (Clapsaddle) Frank, b 5 Mar 1786. Augustus settled on Lot 47 and was a prominent early farmer and resident of Ash Hollow. He was instrumental in the establishment of the first church (Baptist) in the township. He d 21 Nov. 1861; his wife d 9 Nov 1867; both bur at AHC.

The Van Slyck emigrant Dutch ancestors were early settlers of Beverwyck, later Schenectady, and their history is told in Pearson's Schenec Gen. Van Slykes married Vedders and Bratts/ Pratts and Fischers/Visschers, Veeders, Vroomans, Wemples and Folts, all allied with Oyers.

We do not know who Augustus' ancestors were. A John Van Slyke was in the War of 1812. A Van Slyke from Mt. Jewett, Penn. was a doctor in WWI. Morris Van Slyke owned a farm in Wyoming Co. with a relative adjacent. Annie Scott Baxter published some Van Slyke data in the 1920-30 period. She wrote some for an Erie, Penn newspaper.

[Sources: Beers' Mont; Beers' Herk; GF DRC, Herk LR; Catt LR; Everts' Catt; Pearson Schenec; Rutherford]

8.   FREDERICK³ OYER, Jr. (*Frederick²⁻¹*), born Herk./Schuy. Twp., Herk. Co. ca. 1791; died Otto/E. Otto Twp., Catt. Co., between 1830-1835; buried poss. EldC., Ash., Catt. Co. He married NANCY _____, born Herk. Co. ca. 1785; died Allegany, Catt. Co. June 1869.

Frederick purchased 68 acres in Schuy. from his brother George on 28 Feb. 1823, the same land that George had purchased from their father. On 22 Dec. 1825, Frederick Oyer, Jr., farmer, Nancy his wife and others sold land which had belonged to his father to Edward Ellis of London. At about this time Frederick, Jr. moved to E. Otto.

Although no record of Frederick's death can be found, he is listed as head of a household in the 1830 census of Otto. Five years later his wife Nancy is listed as head of the household, so we assume his death occured between those years. One of two small stones inscribed "F.O." might mark his grave at EldC., Ash. Twp. where in 1986 his mother's gravestone still stands.

Nancy is listed as farming 8 acres in 1835 with 3 cattle, a

horse, 4 sheep and 4 hogs. By 1840 she and her family had
moved to Ash. where she farmed. In 1850 Nancy is listed
with real estate worth $150 and residing next door to her son
Robert. She is listed as living in Ash. in 1860 and 1865 with the
family of John Quackenbush whose wife was Mary, born Herk. Co.
Soon after, she went to live with her dau. Sarah Altenburg in
Allegany Twp., Catt. Co., where she died. Her will bequested: 1)
to Sarah, all real estate, 1 bed and bedding; 2) to Ann Quackenbush, a black silk shawl; 3) to the 3 daughters equally divided, the
remainder of her property.

Ch (OYER) first 4 b in Schuy; last 3 b in E Otto:

| 37. | i. | JOHN H⁴, b ca 1816 |

37.   i.   JOHN H^4, b ca 1816
38.   ii.   MARY, b ca 1819
39.   iii.   ROBERT, b ca 1822
       iv.   REUBEN , b ca 1824, date of death unknown; m
              Dilect _____In 1850 they res in Little Valley,
              Catt Co.   In 1869 their whereabouts were
              unknown.
40.   v.   ANN, b 11 Feb 1828
       vi.   ADELIA, b ca 1830; d perhaps Ash before 1869, list-
              listed as living with her mother in 1850 and 27
              Aug 1850 she and her mother deeded land to An-
              derson Rowland. She is not listed with her moth-
              er in 1860 or 1865 and is not included in the list
              of her mother's heirs.
41.   vii.   SALLY/SARAH, b 13 Aug 1831

9.   PETER F.^{3} OYER (*Frederick*$^{2-1}$), born Schuy. Twp., Herk.
Co. 20 Feb. 1793 and baptized [rec. GF DRC] 25 Feb. 1793 with
sp. "Pieter Rimaah u. Catharina Hochstaed.;" died Schuy. 25 Feb.
1854. He married CATHARINE FINSTER, dau. of John and Maria
Fredericke (Schnek) Finster born Schuy. 3 Dec. 1795; died Schuy
30 Jan. 1855; both buried MRC.
      Peter fought in the War of 1812 in the local militia. He resided
in the Oyer neighborhood on a farm deeded from John and Margarethe Finster to Peter F. and Catharine Oyer for $600 18 Sept.
1823.
      In 1825 Peter is listed farming 30 acres, owning 9 cattle, 5
horses, 19 sheep, 4 hogs, and producing 115 yards of fulled,
flannel and linen cloth. In 1835 he was farming 45 acres of improved land, owning 6 cattle, 5 horses, 22 sheep, 4 hogs and pro-
oducing 74 yards of fulled, flannel and linen cloth. In 1850 Peter
owned real estate worth $2,000, and was residing next door to
son-in-law Ebenezer Cady.

Peter's will is dated 29 Sept. 1853 and bequests; 1) to David, 30 acres from the west side of the farm, the till mare, a double wagon harness and sleigh and all farm utensils, half of the horn cattle and sheep. David should pay all debts except a $225 loan (payment of which should be made by each child paying $25 except David who should pay $50) on which David should pay interest; David should provide a home for his 3 unmarried sisters (Magdalena, Almira and Catharine); 2) to his wife Catharine, one third of the land, in lieu of dower, on the east side of the above mentioned 30 acres, half of the horses, cattle and sheep, the old mare "we call pone", all household furniture for use during her lifetime (though she may sell it if she wishes) and then to be divided equally among the children. It appoints Catharine (wife) and David executors and was witnessed by Daniel Auyer and William P. Pruyn, both of Schuy. A codicil, dated 4 Feb. 1854, mentions expectation of money from the government "for services in the last war"; this pension to be divided between David and widow Catharine. [Herk Co SR]

Ch (OYER) b Schuy Twp, Herk Co:

42.	i.	JOHN[4], b 5 May 1815
43.	ii.	MARIA, b 3 Mar 1817
44.	iii.	ELIZABETH, b 25 Feb 1819
	iv.	DAVID, b 9 Feb 1821; d Sprvl 16 Aug 1890; unm. He was a farmer or farm laborer in Schuy and later in Sprvl. His estate was inherited by his family of numerous sisters, nieces and nephews.
	v.	MAGDALENA, b 8 Dec 1823; d after 1890; m 23 Feb 1864, Peter W S Pratt, son of Peter and Olive (Short) Pratt, b Erie Co, ca 1815. Magdelena/Delana/Laney was Peter's 3rd wife. In 1870 they res in E Otto where he was a farmer with real estate worth $2,700 and personal property worth $1,000. In 1890 she was res in Sprvl. We find no rec of ch.
	vi.	ALBERT, b 4 Apr 1825; d Sprvl 20 Feb 1879; m Sept 1855/6 EMMA JANE SCOBY, dau of Alexander and Serepta (Boss) Scoby, b 30 Sept 1835; d 17 Aug 1865; both bur MWC. Albert is listed as a blacksmith in Concord 1883-.

[We are inserting Scoby data here as we find no ch.]

*** THE SCOBY FAMILY ***

*Alexander went to Otto from Herk Co in 1824, settling on lot 6,
E Otto; m 1827; in 1829 went to Ash; d Sandusky, Freedom Twp,
Catt Co 24 June 1880, ae 73 y, 11 d; Serepta d 30 June 1874; both
bur Ash.   He bought the grist-mills of Peabody, 2 1/2 miles
southwest of Sprvl, known as Scoby Mills, Ash.   He rebuilt the
grist-mill and saw-mill dam and sold to Loveland & Daggets in
1864. He built bridges, including an 182 foot one across the Catt
Creek; was pres of Catt Agricultural Society; was on the Board of
Supervisors.   Other ch of Alexander: Madison, b Ash 1829/30, m
Agnes Bensley, had 7 ch, res Kansas, to Chicago in 1868 where he
was a co-partner in Bensley Bros--livestock; Maryette, m Thomas
Pierce, res Sprvl; Emeline E, m E Smith, d 1870; Wm G, m Frances
A Eddy, res Mansfield; Louisa A, m W F Lincoln, E Otto; Adaline
L,m Wm H Warner, Sprvl; Herbert D, m Sophia Bensley, res Ft
Scott, Kans; Marshall D, m Addella Thomas, res Sprvl. Sam (1779-
1872) and Marshall D Scobey (1848-1912) are bur Ash.*

[Sources: Briggs, p 451; Everts' Catt, p 339; Ash VR; cem rec]

      vii.   ADALINE, b 31 Aug 1827; d Schuy Twp 12 Jan 1831.
               Her death was caused by cancer.
45.   viii. ALMIRA, b 7 May 1829
      ix.   CATHARINE, b 3 Oct 1833; d Sprvl, 6 May 1891; m
               as his 3rd wife Sprvl [Presbyterian Ch] 11 Mar
               1875 Isaac B Childs, b Concord, Erie Co 13 Oct
               1823. They had no ch.

*** THE CHILDS FAMILY ***

*Issac's 1st wife: Marsha A Brown, d 22 Nov 1861; ch: Ellen, b
21 Mar 1850, wife of B Baker; Charles F, b 18 June 1854. Isaac's
2nd wife: Mary Ann Jones, d 12 Mar 1866, no ch. Isaac's parents
were Lewis and Deborah (Starks) Childs, Lewis removing from
Deerfield, Mass 1832, settling nw of Sprvl. He did coopering and
had a stone quarry, furnishing stone for a large number of the
buildings in the area. Lewis d Sprvl 1853; Deborah, who was dau
of Jedediah, d 5 July 1873.*

*[Sources: Briggs; LM; CCHM; Herk LR & SR; Erie Co SR;
censuses]*

10.   GEORGE³ OYER (*Frederick²⁻¹*), born Schuy. Twp., Herk. Co. 16 Mar. 1797; died Concord Twp., Erie Co. 10 July 1875, ae. 78 yrs, 3 mos, 25 days.   He married MARY/<u>POLLY</u> MILLER, born Herk. Co. 18 Sept 1798; died Ash. Twp., Catt. Co. 10 July 1860; both buried FrktC.   We do not know who her parents were.

George and Polly made their home in Schuy. after their marriage; 1 July 1820 his father sold them for $262.15, 68 acres in the Oyer tract, bound by Jacob Widrig (east) and, Peter Oyer (south and west) and William Ellis (north).   They occupied the farm for only a short time for it was already in brother Frederick's possession when the latter purchased it for $2,000, 28 Feb 1823. At this time George and his family moved to Ash. Twp.   In 1835 he is listed farming 30 acres with 12 cattle, two horses, 5 sheep and 8 hogs.   In 1840, 1850 and 1860 George is listed as farmer and landowner (in 1860 he owned real estate worth $3,500 and personal property worth $300).

After his wife's death in 1860, George removed to Concord Twp., Erie Co.   In June of 1875 he was boarding with Augustus V. Oyer. He died intestate in Concord, leaving an estate valued at $6,000. Son Simon was appointed administrator.

Ch (OYER):

46.   i.   LEVI⁴, b 5 May 1820
       ii.   ADAM, b Schuy 12 June 1823; d Ash Twp 13 Apr 1901; bur. FrktC; unm.   He resided with his parents in Ash listed in 1860 as farm laborer with real estate ($700) and personal property ($2,100). In 1860 he was living with brother Davis, farming; in 1875 he is listed in Ash farming, owning 145 acres.
       iii.   DAVIS, b Ash 12 Apr 1827; d Ash 9 Aug 1909; bur FrktC; unm; listed as owning real estate ($1,700) and personal property ($100).   He was living with brother Adam in Ash in 1865.   In 1874 he owned 97 acres; in 1880 he was living with Jeremiah Hufstader; he is next door to Chas & Mary Tefft in 1905.
47.   iv.   SIMON, b 5 Nov 1831

[Sources: CCHM; censuses; Catt SR & LR; LM; Herk Co LR]

11.   JACOB³ OYER (Frederick²⁻¹), born Schuy. Twp., Herk. Co. 30 Jan. 1799; died West Monroe Twp., Oswego Co. 19 Aug. 1854, ae. 55 y. 6 m. 20 d.   He married ELIZABETH HARVEY, dau. of Elijah and Betsey (_____) Harvey, born Herk. 8 Oct. 1803;

died West Monroe Twp. 3 May 1822, ae. 78 y. 6 m. 25 d.; both buried West Monroe Cem.

This family's first home was in Herk. Twp. near her father's. On 26 June 1832 Edward Lynch of New York City sold to Elijah Harvey, Jr., and Jacob Oyer, 100 acres (Lot 2 in a subdivision of Great Lot 3). 12 July 1832 "Elijah and Delilah" Harvey sold their share to Jacob for $350 (in 1836 Elijah and several brothers moved to Mansfield Twp., Catt. Co).

In 1846 Jacob and family moved to West Monroe Twp., Oswego Co. 1 Apr. 1847 Martin and Thankful Owen of West Monroe sold to Jacob for $2,000 the half of Lot 93 containing 75 acres. In 1850 Jacob's real estate was worth $3,000.

Jacob's will bequests: 1) to "beloved wife Elizabeth", all real estate in West Monroe and all personal property as long as she remains my widow, and than to the 4 children, the farm going to the sons and they to pay their sisters half of the real estate value, $100 per year to Almeda, and $100 to Catherine when she reaches 21 years and $100 per year until paid. It appoints Elizabeth sole executrix.

In 1855, Elizabeth, farmer, is listed in West Monroe with her children; next door is dau. Almeda and family. She continued to occupy the farm during her lifetime.

Ch (OYER) all b Herk Co:

48.   i.   ALMEDA L[4], b 1830
49.   ii.   WILLIAM H, b 1831
         iii. SARAH JANE, b 1833; d W Monroe 19 Oct 1851; bur
               W Monroe Cem, Oswego Co
         iv.   ELIJAH, b 1839
         v.   CATHARINE ELIZABETH, b ca 1843

[Sources: Censuses; Herk LR & SR; Onon LR & SR; family rec; cem rec]

*** THE HARVEY FAMILY ***

In 1836 ELIZABETH (HARVEY) OYER's brothers Charles, Elijah Jr, Isaac H and Gates (Erastus) all settled in Mansfield Twp, Catt Co. Families are listed 1855 St census. Birthplaces include Washington, Onon and Herk counties. Elijah Sr, Elizabeth's father, died Herk Co 21 June 1850.

[Sources: LM; more found in Everts Catt]

12.   MICHAEL[3] OYER (Frederick[2-1]) born Schuy. Twp., Herk.
Co. ca. 1802; died E. Otto Twp., Catt. Co. 17 Dec. 1847. He
married BETSEY HAMMOND, dau. of Joseph and Sarah (Middaugh)
Hammond, born 10 Oct. 1812; died Ash. 2 Apr. 1874, ae. 61 yrs, 5
mos, 22 days; buried TCC. Michael accompanied his father to
Ash./E. Ash., "coming in by marked trees over corduroy roads and
pole bridges. The nearest grist-mill was at Springville in Erie
County, whether they went in summer with a wood-shod sled
drawn by oxen. Frederick Oyer resided there until his death."
[Adams' Catt, p 598] Five years later he removed to a partly
cleared farm in E. Otto. In 1830 he was living near his brothers
George and Frederick, his mother, and his uncle Michael Hufstader. In 1835 he is listed as farming 20 acres with 3 cattle, 3
horses, 5 sheep and 7 hogs.
      Michael died intestate, leaving an estate worth $200. The
articles kept for his widow and children were: 2 spinning wheels,
1 loom and utensils, a Bible, books, photographs, 10 sheep, 1 cow,
4 bedspreads, beds and bedding, 1 stove, kettles, 1 table, 6 chairs,
knives, forks and plates. Administrator of his estate was John G.
Morrow, who had resided near the Oyer farm. He became Betsey's
second husband.
      There was said to be 6 daus.; we find but 5.

      Ch (OYER), all b E Otto:

50.   i.   ROXANNE[4], b ca 1831
51.   ii.   JOSEPH, b 1832
52.   iii. SARAH JANE, b ca 1834
53.   iv.   MARY ELIZABETH, b 14 Nov 1835
54.   v.   CATHERINE, b 1837
55.   vi.   ANGELINE, b ca 1840

      [Sources: CCHM; LM; LV LR & SR; Erie Co LR & SR; Adams'
Catt; Herk LR]

                *** THE HAMMOND FAMILY ***

      BETSY HAMMOND was the third of 11 ch of JOSEPH and
SARAH (MIDDAUGH) HAMMOND. Joseph came from near the Sus-
quehanna River in northern Pennsylvania to Concord in 1818, lo-
cating near the "Big Spring" north of Sprvl. He d in Kane Co,
Illinois 1883-. The ch: John (d Kane Co, Ill 1883-); Samuel; Betsy;
Joseph; Abram (settled early in Concord); Robert (d Iowa 1883-);
Clinton. (b Concord 2 Apr 1819; Washington; Napoleon; Louise;
Cordelia (m Wm White, d Collins, Erie Co 1883-).

Henry C Hammond was killed in the second battle of Bull Run in the Civil War.

Clinton Hammond was a hotel-keeper, farmer and drover and held office in Concord, Erie Co. Enlisting in Aug 1862, he was a Second Lieut. of Co F 116th New York Vols, resigning because of ill health in that Dec. He m Sophia Ballou. Ch: Ursula, b 6 Apr 1844; m Norman Crandall; Josephine, b 30 May 1846, m Henry Deet, d 1883-; Eunice, b 2 Nov 1848, m Frank Chase; Ella, b 13 Dec 1815, m Charles Odell; Clinton, Jr. born July 1853, d 1883-; William, b 5 Aug 1856; Agnes, b 1 Nov 1858.

Another Joseph Hammond came to E Otto in 1823; m Mary Folts in 1832. Son Samuel b ca 1810; son William b 7 Nov 1834, m Jan 1857 Mary E Scott, dau of Justus J and Catherine (Bullis) Scott of E Otto. Their ch: Sarah E m Elmer D Williams; William S. David Hammond Jr was in N Albion, Catt Co in 1818. John Hammond was in Dayton, Catt. Co. in 1833.

In Briggs' Concord, early settlers were listed and included Samuel, Joseph and Abram Hammond.

There are 4 Hammonds bur in Riceville Cem, Ash: Frederick, wife Electa; Lovinia; and an infant.

*** THE MORROW FAMILY ***

JOHN G MORROW, BETSY's 2nd husband, had dau Jenette, b ca 1835; Mary, b ca 1841, m _____ Prince; and Lafayette, b ca 1843 by his 1st wife. John, b 14 May 1806, was the son of James Morrow; John d Machias, Catt Co, 1 Mar 1873. John is bur next to Betsey at TCC.

Ch by Betsy Hammond Oyer Morrow: EUDORA, b ca 1849, m _____ STARKS, and AVA who m _____ BOND.

13. JOHN F.³ OYER (*Frederick²⁻¹*), born Schuy. Twp., Herk. Co. ca. 1810; died after 1860. He married HARRIET M. _____, born Onon. Co. ca. 1818. John was a farmer residing in E. Otto Twp. In 1850 he is listed with real estate worth $1,560. Also living with the family in that year was nephew Joseph Oyer, son of John's late brother Michael Oyer. Joseph helped with farm work. In 1860 John F. and family are listed in E. Otto, with real estate worth $3,250 and personal property worth $800. Listed as farm laborer in that year was 32 year old "David" Oyer, probably nephew Davis Oyer, son of George Oyer.

Ch (OYER):

    i.   JULIUS C[4], b Ash ca 1842; d E Otto 21(?) Apr 1860,
        ae 18 y 9 m 18 d; bur Brooklyn Cem, Ash. Julius
        was a farmer and was killed by a horse.
   ii.   FRANCES F, b E Otto ca 1856

[Sources: censuses; Herk SR; LM; CCHM; Onon VR]

14. WILLIAM[3] OYER (*Frederick[2-1]*), born Schuy. Twp., Herk.
Co. Dec. 1812; died E. Otto Twp., Catt. Co. 17 July 1871; buried
EldC., Ash. Twp. He married JERUSHA PARMETER, born ca. 1818.
William was a farmer. In 1830 he is listed living in Otto Twp.
with a family of five. In 1850 he is listed living in Ash. as
farmer owning real estate worth $1,110, with his wife, 2 children
and mother. In 1860 William Oyer, farmer, was listed in E. Otto
Twp. with real estate worth $4,000 and personal property worth
$800. His household included his wife, son, mother (aged 90
years) and a farm hand. The only Parmeter data noted: Martha
Parmenter of Norwalk and Florida (NYS), is shown as next of kin
of Jacob Hufstater, apparently #15ii, below. [Bflo SR 10849]

Ch (OYER), both b E Otto:

56.   i.   NELSON[4], b 28 Feb 1838
       ii.   CATHARINE, b ca 1841

[Sources: censuses; LM; CCHM; family rec]

15. ROXANNA[3] OYER (*Frederick[2-1]*), born Schuy. Twp., Herk.
Co. ca. 1813; died Sprvl. Erie Co. 8 June 1890. She married
JACOB HUFSTADER, Jr., son of Jacob and Catharine (Rema) Hochstatter, born Herk. Co. 4 Dec. 1806; died Sprvl. 25 Dec. 1876, ae.
70 y. 21 d.; buried Elderkin Cem. She signed her name Roxana.
    Jacob Hufstader was a farmer, making his home in E. Otto Twp.
In about 1847 the family moved to Ash. Twp., where the family
lived for several years. In 1850 he is listed as farmer, owning
real estate worth $2,625. In 1855 Jacob is listed in Ash. as
farmer; assisting him were his three sons: Ezra, William and James,
all listed as farmers. By 1865 the family was reduced to just the
youngest child, dau. Ada. Jacob and Roxanna moved to Concord
Twp., Erie Co. where Jacob is listed as retired farmer in 1875. In
1880 the widowed Roxanna is listed as living alone on Mill Street
in Sprvl.

James was executor of his estate, with all property given to the one who took care of Roxanna. Otherwise, Jacob wanted the family to agree Mrs. Cook and husband would do the work and have the income or interest from it.

Ch (Hufstader), 1st 6 b in E Otto; the 7th b in Ash:

57.   i.   EZRA⁴, b 1832

       ii.   LAMARTHA (twin), b ca 1834; m _____ Evans; res Norwalk; apparently md 2nd _____Parmenter

     iii.   LAMANTHA (twin), b ca 1834; m _____ Cook; res Alden, Erie Co

     iv.   WILLIAM O, b ca 1837; res Shell Rock, Butler Co., Iowa

5.   v.   JAMES, b Feb 1838

     vi.   HENRY HARRISON, b 10 Apr 1840; d Ash Twp Feb 1863; m _____; enlisted 1861 100th Inf, d soon after discharge. He was in the 7 days battle before Richmond.

    vii.   ADA E, b 1852; m _____ EVERHART; res Concord Twp, Erie Co. and Cleveland, Ore, 1890

[Sources: LM; Erie LR & SR 10849; GF DRC]

*** THE HUFSTADERS ***

ROXANNA OYER's husband was her first cousin, Jacob Hufstader, Jr. His father, JACOB Sr, was a farmer who came from Herk Co to Ash in 1818, an early settler. He later sold his farm (in 1825) to Henry Frank (son of Henry Frank, Sr and brother of David Oyer's wife). He settled on another farm in Ash, where he remained. He d aged 82 years, 19 Oct 1859, and was bur at AHC. Catharine, Jacob's wife, was a dau of Johannes Rema, and related to many Oyer spouses. She d 6 Feb 1855, aged 77 years and is also bur in AHC.

[For more Hufstader detail see Chapter 7]

16.   JOHN P.³ OYER (*Peter²*, *Frederick¹*), born Schuy., Herk. Co. 14 July 1799; died Ash. Twp., Catt. Co. 3 Sept. 1872, ae. 74 y. 1 m. 14 d. He married CHARITY FRANK, dau of John H. and Margaret (Gerlach) Frank, born Frkf., Herk. Co. Sept. 1802; died Ash. 14 Mar. 1881, ae. 78 y. 9 m.; both buried FrktC.

John P. made his home on his father's land in Schuy. when they were first married. By 1825 he is next door to Peter Finster with a family of 6 farming 30 acres of improved land, owning 10 cattle, 6 horses, 11 sheep and 10 hogs.

About 1827 the family moved to Ash. settling in the northern part of the town in the Frkt. area. On 12 Oct. 1829 Henry Frank and his wife sold him 100 acres. In 1835 he was listed farming 30 acres of improved land, owning 16 cattle, 4 horses, 25 sheep and 11 hogs.

John lived the remainder of his life on that farm, adding parcels of land to his holdings from time to time. In 1870 his real estate was valued at $8,840 and he had personal property worth $2,000.

John's will, dated 23 Nov. 1865, bequests: 1) to wife Charity: part of Lot 1 (east middle) in township 6 in the 7th range and Lot 25 (west middle) in township 6 in 6th range, totaling 100 acres (the same conveyed by Henry Frank in 1829), during her natural life and at her death the land should be divided into two parts; the land on the west side of the highway from Ellvl to Sprvl to go to Frederick and Charity Smith (and in the event of their deaths to Hiram and Arley Frank); land on the west of the highway to go to Hiram Oyer; also to Charity, all personal property, she to pay to each of Rachel Vedder's children, upon their reaching the age of 21 years, $100 from that property. Also to Charity, a quarter acre (conveyed by John Ellis and wife), in lieu of dower; 2) to Philinda Holden: part of Lot 1 in township 7 of the 6th range (22 acres, conveyed by J. Fox and wife, 10 Oct. 1853); 3) to Mary Tefft, Betsey Vedder, Adaline Vedder, two parcels of land. His wife's nephew Frederick Frank, Jr., was appointed executor; witnesses were Henry Frank and David Boss, both of Ash.

In Ash. St. Census of 1855 we find with John P. and Charity: Sally Frank, 33, b Herk. Co.; Aaron Oyer, 19, son b Catt. Co.; Clarissa Frank, 9, Hiram Frank, 7; Olive Frank, 2; grandchildren; William O. and Philinda Holden, Charles O. Holden, 4.

In 1874, Charity is listed owning 100 acres in Catt. Co. [Botsford]; she resided there with various daughters and grandchildren during her widowhood.

Her will, dated 5 Mar. 1881, bequests: 1) (after all debts be paid) to Sally Smith: all stock, horses, farming tools, hay, grain, beds and household furniture, with the exception of five cows and a certain mortgage against Charity Fuller and Arley Fuller; 2) to Mary Tefft, Betsey Vedder, Adaline Crandall, Philinda Holden, Rachel Vedder's children: the rest of her property; 3) to Richard Conhiser: a house and 7.5 acre lot on the highway from Ash. to Tefft's on condition he stay and work for Sally Smith until the executors are satisfied that he has earned $200. Sally Smith and Charles Holden are appointed executors; witnesses are William Holden of West Valley. Arlie Fuller of E. Ash., and Charity Woodruff of Ash.

Ch (OYER) first 5 b Schuy; last 4 b Ash:

59.	i.	MARY[4], b 1820
60.	ii.	SALLY, b 29 Feb 1822
61.	iii.	BETSEY, b 6 Sept 1824
62.	iv.	ADALINE, b 13 Dec. 1825
63.	v.	HIRAM, b 18 June 1827
64.	vi.	RACHEL, b 1 Jan 1829
65.	vii.	PHILINDA, b Sept 1831
	viii.	CHARITY, b 5 Oct 1833; d Ash, 26 Nov 1848; bur FrktC
66.	ix.	AARON, b ca 1836

[Sources: Botsford; Herk SR; GF DRC; Catt LR, SR; CCHM; LM]

*** THE FRANK FAMILY ***

JOHN H FRANK, Charity's father, was a son of the Frank patriarch, Johann Heinrich Frank (Henry Frank, Sr). He m [rec. GF DRC] 20 Dec. 1795, Anna Margaret Gerlach and resided in Frkf for many years before migrating to Ash, where he farmed in the Frkt area. The children of this large family were: 1) Henry (1804-1876); 2) Peter A (b 1797); 3) a daughter, m _____ Shaffner; 4) Frederick (b 1801); Charity; 6) Abigail; 7) Delana, m George Bridenbecker; 8) Mary Elizabeth (b 29 June 1810) m John Miller; 9) Warner (b 13 Feb 1808); 10) Daniel; and 11) Jeremiah (1811-1866). Most of John H Frank's children and families farmed in the Frkt area.

[For more Frank detail see Chapter 8]

17. JACOB P.[3] OYER (*Peter[2] Frederick[1]*), born Schuy. 14 Mar. 1801; died Van Buren Twp. 4 Nov. 1868, ae. 67 y. 7 m. 20 d.; buried KndmC. He married 15 Aug. 1820 MARY/POLLY REMA/ RIMA, dau. of Peter L. and Maria Catharine (Hochstatter) Rema, b Schuy. 9 Nov. 1802 and bp [rec. Herk. DRC] with sp. Jacob and Margarethe (Bekker) Oyer, died prob. Baldwinsville, Onon. Co. 18 Aug. 1871, ae. 68 y. 9 m. 9 d; buried KndmC.

Jacob made his home first at Frkf. where he was a blacksmith; he was deeded land there 19 Jan. 1821 that was bound on the north by the Mohawk River and on the south by the Erie Canal. He later aquired other parcels in Frkf. On 21 Mar. 1825 Jacob sold his house lot in Frkf., moving to a house on land belonging to his father in Schuy. In 1825 he owned 3 cattle, 2 horses and

7 hogs. Jacob was one of the first trustees of the Methodist Protestant Church, organized in Schuy. in 1835.

On 26 July 1837 Jacob purchased 60 acres in Sandy Creek Twp. (hereafter SC), Oswego Co. and removed there soon after. He purchased 60 more acres 27 Mar. 1839 and added land to his holdings in the 1840's.

In the later 1840's Jacob and family rented a farm in Camillus Twp. (hereafter Cam.), Onon. Co., south of the village of Canton/Memphis. They lived there until early in 1855, going to a farm along Seneca River in Van Buren Twp., Onon., Co., on Lot 16, which he purchased for $12,550 1 Dec. 1855.

[AHA has an account book of Jacob's used during the 1820-30's while he was blacksmithing, showing the extensive work done for many of the relatives and neighbors--so many names allied with the Oyers. Margaret (#74) Auyer Somes used the book to contain clippings and obituaries of family and friends, taking it with her when she moved to Jordan in 1913 and again in 1921 when she went to live with her son, O.A. Somes. It was kept by the family after her death. Hawley gained possesion of it in 1978 after it was found in his grandmother's attic. See Illus p 104-105]

Jacob sold portions of his farm to son Peter; in 1862 he sold some to his son-in-law, Joseph Somes; 3 Oct. 1868 he sold the last portion to Joseph Somes, reserving use of one of the houses for life and reserved until 1 Apr. 1869 enough wheat for himself and his wife and enough firewood for themselves and son Foster. On the same date Jacob wrote his last will and testament, appointing Ira Oyer and Jacob Somes executors. He bequested: 1) all debts and expenses be paid; 2) the executors invest the residue of the estate to provide support for Mary "becoming her wants and circumstances and that all of her wants shall be compiled with and that the expenses thereof with her funeral expenses be a charge on my estate;" 3) after her death the estate be divided equally among the heirs. Witnesses: Henry Daboll and Edwin McDowell, Van Buren. In 1870 Mary is listed living with dau. Harriet in Baldwinsville, presumably dying there.

Ch:

67.	i.	IRA[4] OYER, b Frkf 16 Nov 1820
68.	ii.	PETER J AUYER, b Frkf 25 Oct 1822
69.	iii.	ALMIRA OYER, b Schuy 18 May 1825
70.	iv.	FRANCIS L AUYER, b Schuy 1 June 1827
71.	v.	SIMON AUYER, b Schuy 27 Aug 1829
72.	vi.	VALENTINE AUYER, b Schuy 25 Aug 1831
73.	vii.	HARRIET AUYER, b Schuy 16 Aug 1833
74.	viii.	MARGARET MARY AUYER, b Schuy 24 Oct 1835
75.	ix.	ROMAIN AUYER, b Schuy, 14 July 1837
76.	x.	FOSTER JACOB AUYER, b SC 8 July 1845

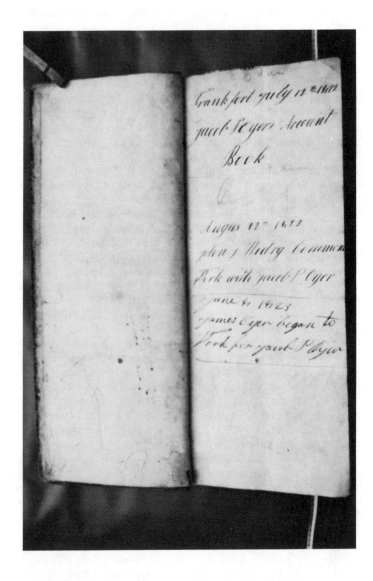

Account book of Jacob P.³ Oyer, 1822. Among his customers were John Finster, Peter Oyer, Michael Widrig, and many other related families.

1822 *From the ol Book*

Jaun 19 th sit one ol Ishoe corkit . 15

1822 22 t sit one ol Ishoe   ...

Jun 11 th to set three ol Ishows corkte 3 ..

March 4 t hoak t littl two ahoak
        to deer his stuft

Abril 6 th put six new lings one   2 5
        swivel t trais chain one
        new long th log chain   5 ..

41   *John Finsler*

Abril 6 to bail litle   15

May 24 to set four new and four
        Ol shoe cork one   5 .

Nov t 1 to upset ax   1 .

Drew 25 t neck yoak   3 15
Jan 4 t iron sloy part his stuft 5 5 0

Abr 12 to sharber two shoes
        new oltwo lewiss   6 5

[Sources: AHA; Auyer; censuses; Onon LR & SR; family rec; cem
rec. For the Rema Family see Chapter 7.]

18.   MARGARET OYER (*Peter² Frederick¹*), born Schuy. Twp.,
Herk. Co., 14 Oct. 1802 died Amboy Twp., Oswego Co., 8 May
1850; buried WmstC. She married 1st _____ CAIN and 2nd
ROSWELL MURRAY ELLIS, son of William Ellis, Sr., born Schuy.
Twp. 7 Dec. 1797; died Amboy Twp. 24 May 1854, ae. 56 yrs, 5
mos, 17 days; buried WmstC.

Her second husband was a farmer, shown in Schuy. Twp. in
1830, residing near the Oyer settlement. By 1840 the family
removed to Rome Twp., Oneida Co. In about 1846 they moved to
Amboy Twp. in southeastern Oswego Co. In 1850 he is shown as
a farmer owning real estate worth $1,800.

Ch (CAIN) from Margaret's 1st m:

　　　　i. PETER⁴ [see Cain/Kane Allied write-up below]
　　　　ii. FRANCIS, identified as of Mich at time of
　　　　　　　grandfather's death
77.　　iii. JOHN F, b Schuy ca 1820

Ch (ELLIS) from Margaret's 2nd m:

78.　　iv. DANIEL C, b 1827
　　　　v. WILLIAM H, b 25 July 1829; d 22 Apr 1904. He m
　　　　　　　CHARLOTTE A NICHOLAS, dau of Garret and
　　　　　　　Nancy Nicholas, b Herk Co ca 1836; both bur
　　　　　　　WmstC. He farmed, res on Lot 98 Amboy Twp; no
　　　　　　　ch.

[For Roswell Ellis's line see Chapter 6.]

*** THE CAIN/KANE FAMILY ***

*While we have data of the Cain/Kane family, we cannot "tie in"
very well. A Peter Kane, b Ilion, Herk Co ca 1820, married Eva
Eliza Vedder, Peter Oyer's (#25) 2nd wife's (Rachel) sister, living
in Ellvl/GrV. There is more data in the Vedder Allied family in
that section. He may be the Peter Cain, Margaret's son shown
above--the dates fit. Eva Eliza m 2nd _____ Frank, as the
guardianship papers for John, Otis H and Ella list their m as Eva
Eliza Frank of GrV (1872), ages 19, 17 and 4. John A, 61; Mary
L, 63; and Vedder R, 34 are in Mansfield 1915 St census. This
then is they in Chamberlin Cem, Ellvl: Mary (Lattin) Kane, b Ellvl
30 Apr 1852; d 2 Jan 1934, wife of John Kane, he b 1854. In GrV
VR is their son Vedder Russell Kane, b GrV 15 May 1881. Luke B
Lattin of Herk Co is Mary's f. Bur in Chamberlin Cem also is
Arthur Kane, b 16 Mar 1848; d 2 June 1923, his wife: Mary Booth;*

f Peter Kane of Ilion, Herk Co.; m is Eve Eliza Vedder. Mary res GrV at time of Arthur's death. This could be the Peter Cain, son of _____ and MARGARET (OYER) CAIN, #18, above.

There was another John Kane of Ellvl who d 15 Sept 1907, from Ireland; bur Ellvl, ae 85; "here 45 yr." His descendants are listed, surr ct rec #237, LV. Honora Kane [surr rec 308] seems to fit with him, a Mary mentioned. Principal shows Margaret Flarety of Carpentersville, Ill with Chas A Case, Ellvl, Adm.

George Cain is listed in Otto in Child. [see Sources]

19. ELIZABETH³ OYER (*Peter², Frederick¹*), born Schuy. Twp., Herk. Co. 29 June 1804; died before 1853. She married FREDERICK REMA, son of Peter L. and Maria Catharine (Hochstatter) Rema, born Schuy. Twp., 14 Aug. 1798; died Waterloo, Seneca Co. 7 Mar. 1879.

Ch: (REMA)

82.   i.   DELANEY⁴, b ca 1821

       ii. MARY L, b Schuy ca 1826; m _____ Bridenbecker. She is listed, apparently widowed, living with her sister Delany Weaver in Frkf in 1850.

     iii. son

     iv. son

[For Rema data see Chapter 7.]

20. JAMES³ AUYER (*Peter², Frederick¹*), born Schuy. Twp. 10 Apr. 1806; died Cam. Twp., Onon. Co. 22 Apr. 1893, ae. 87 yrs, 12 days; buried Fairvale Cem. Cam. He married 1st 13 Sept. 1825/6 MARTHA JANE BURRILL, dau of Jacob and Martha (_____) Burrill, born Herk. Twp., Herk. Co. 21 June 1802 died Cam. 22 July 1875, ae. 73 yrs, 11 mos; buried Fairvale Cem. James married 2nd 7 Mar. 1889 PARTHENA E. LOOMIS, dau of Francis and Maria (Museley) Loomis, born Canton/Memphis, Onon. 1846; died 1916; buried WarC.

James is the first to change to the spelling "Auyer" from "Oyer." On a land record he signed his name that way; his wife signed it "Oyer." No reason for this has change ever surfaced. The Peter Oyer family chart owned by Ralph Auyer (#201) [see Illus p 74] shows the authenticity of the relationship.

James Auyer left his Schuy. home at the age of 17 to work for his older brother Jacob at Frkf., Herk. Co. in his blacksmith's shop. A year later James went to Camillus/Elbridge where his father owned land on Lot 62. James established himself as a

farmer on his father's lands, later purchasing it.   Eventually
James purchased other parcels in the area, becoming one of the
wealthier and more prominent farmers of the Oswego Bitters area.
   Early in 1850 James and his family moved to the nearest village,
Canton, living there for several years. They maintained ownership
of the farm near Oswego Bitters, a mile or two away. James later
made his home in a house in the town of Cam., adjoining his Lot
62 farm, that being his home for the rest of his life.
   The Auyers attended the Elbridge Batist Church early on, moving later to one built in Canton in 1834.
   James' will, dated 4 Mar. 1890, proved 1 June 1893, left his
property: 1) to Sarah Ann Wilson, the house and lot occupied by
her at 605 Taylor Street, Syracuse; 2) to Emily Marlette, the
former Whitney farm occupied by her which James purchased at
foreclosure sale in 1876; 3) after all debts and expenses are paid,
convert the remaining property into money and pay widow Parthena Auyer $2,000, dividing the rest into three parts, paying the
children of Martha Tifft one third, pay the interest of one third
to Sarah Ann Wilson (after her death paying principal to her
heirs) and one third to Emily Marlette (after her death paying the
principal to her heirs).   Joseph Somes was sole executor; witnesses: N.C. Watson of Jordan and Francis Auyer of Cam.

   Ch: (AUYER) all ch from James Auyer's 1st m:

	i.	son--the 1830 Census indicates a male between 5 and 10 yrs of age and the 1840 census indicates a male between the ages of 15 and 20. Perhaps this was a son; there is no further mention.
83.	ii.	MARTHA JANE, b Elb 27 May 1829
84.	iii.	SARAH ANN, b Elb 1830
85.	iv.	MARY E, b Elb 1833
	v.	LETICIA M, b Cam Jan 1842; d Cam 29 July 1842; bur Fairvale Cem. She is bur at the Burrill plot at Fairvale: LETICIA M/ daughter of/ James and Martha/ AUYAR/ DIED July/ 29 1842,/ AE 6 mos.
86.	vi.	EMILY AMELIA, b Cam 9 Nov 1843

••• THE BURRILL FAMILY •••

*JACOB BURRILL, MARTHA JANE's father brought his large
family from Herk to Lot 50 of Camillus/Elbridge Twp (hereafter
Elb) in about 1824. He owned a farm of 46 acres located across
from the James Auyer farm. Many of his sons farmed nearby.
The parents are listed in Elb in 1830 but after that they cannot
be located. A number of unmarried children are bur at Fairvale*

Cem. near Oswego Bitters; others appear to have moved away from the area. Ch: 1) Joshua b ca 1789, m Caroline _____; 2) William b 1 Sept 1791; d Collamer, DeWitt Twp, Onon Co 5 Apr 1862, m Betsey Dodge; 3) Jacob Jr, b ca 1793, m Hannah H _____; 4) Lyman, b ca 1795; d Elb Twp, 11 May 1834, m Electa Campbell; 5) Martha Jane, m JAMES AUYER (#20); 6) Orrin, b ca 1803, d Elb 12 Apr 1823; 7) Ira R, b ca 1806; d 26 Nov 1824 "in his 18th year"; 8) Rawsell, b Aug 1808, d Elb 22 Feb 1835; 9) Marriah L, b 1810, d Elb 21 Mar 1829; 10) Nelson M, b 25 Nov 1811; d Weedsport, Cayuga Co 7 July 1881, m Sophronia M Campbell; 11) Lurania, b Oct 1815, d Elb 2 Nov 1835.

21. SOLOMON[3] OYER (*Peter[2], Frederick[1]*), born Schuy., Herk. Co. 24 Dec. 1808; died 23 Jan. 1858 ae. 50 y. 1 m.; bur Redman Farm Cem., Elb., Onon. Co. He married CHRISTINA REDMAN, dau. David, Jr., and Elizabeth (Millious) Redman, born Elb. 24 Apr 1811; died Elb. 12 Aug. 1844; buried Redman Farm Cem.: "In memory of/ CHRISTIAN,/ wife of/ SOLOMON AUYER/ & daughter of/ David & Elizabeth/ Redman,/ died/ Aug. 12, 1844/ AE. 33."

Solomon is identified as of Schuy. Twp. when he purchased 40 acres on Lot 62 in Elb. Twp., from his father on 28 Jan. 1829. He moved to Onon. Co. soon thereafter, probably staying with his brother James while establishing his own farm next door.

Christina "Auyer" was deeded about 1.5 acres of land from the northwest corner of James' farm from James and Martha Auyer on 4 Apr. 1836. That was where Solomon's farmhouse stood; it later became the O. A. Tifft farm, but burned in the 1920's.

On Mar. 1841, Solomon "Auyeur" deeded his 40 acre farm to James, although he apparently continued to occupy it.

Ch (OYER/AUYER), all b Elb:

87.	i.	JULIA ANN AUYER[4], b Sept 1831
	ii.	ELIZABETH OYER, b ca 1837; m AZARIAH S WHITE, son of Elisha E and Sally White of Van Buren, Onon Co, b 29 Mar 1831 [LR Ft Dodge, Iowa 5 Apr 1858]
	iii.	SEMANTHA OYER, b 22 Apr 1839; d 23 Dec 1841
88.	iv.	CYRUS DAVID AUYER, b ca 1843

[Source: AHA]

Gravestones of Solomon[3] and Christina (Redman) Oyer, located Redman Farm Cemetery, Elbridge Township, Onondaga County, N.Y.

22.   HENRY[3] OYER (*Peter[2], Frederick[1]*), born Schuy. 3 Aug. 1809; died Amboy Twp., Oswego Co. 5 May 1880; buried WmstC. He married CATHERINE CLEMENS, dau Michael and Catharine (Lints) Clemens, born Schuy. 27 June 1817; died Amboy 7 Mar. 1895; buried WmstC.

Ch (OYER):

89.   i.   CAROLINE[4], b 20 Feb 1837
90.   ii.   EMMALINE, b ca 1838
        iii. AMELIA, b ca 1839
        iv. AMANDA, b ca 1840
        v.   EDWIN, b Rome Twp, Oneida Co ca 1841; d Bath, Steu Co 15 Aug 1918, unm
        vi. JUDITH, b Rome 1843; d Amboy, Oswego Co 20 May 1864, unm
91.   vii. EZRA HUGH, b Rome 1844; d 31 Oct 1926
        viii. HORACE, b Rome ca 1845
92.   ix.   ELIZABETH, b 23 Aug 1848
93.   x.   DeWITT, b Mar 1850
        xi.   MALATA, b Rome 1853

94.   xii.   GEORGE HENRY, b 26 Sept 1854
       xiii. ALMEDA, b 1856; d Sept 1929, unm

[Source: AHA; Steu Co SR, VR. For Clemens data see Chapter 6 and p 112]

22.1.   CATHARINE³ OYER (*Peter²*, *Frederick¹*), born Schuy. 29 Aug. 1811; died after 1853. She married HENRY B. WEMPLE, poss. son of Barnabus Wemple. They resided in Rock Co., Wisc. in 1853.

Ch (WEMPLE):

    i.   WILLIAM H⁴, from Otto, was in Civil War; res Mich
         1853
    (There may be other children.)

[Sources: AHA; CCHM]

*** THE WEMPLE FAMILY ***

We do not know Henry's pedigree. However we know that Wemples were early settlers in Mont. Co., with 30 or more referred to in the early history of the towns of Glen and Canajoharie. Col Abraham Wemple commanded a company of cavalry in the Rev. Some others mentioned are John, Andres, Barnet B, Edward, Nicholas, R, Eli, William and William B.
There are many Wemples charted in Edwin Vedder's new edition of The Vedder Family in America, 1657–1985, published in 1987.

[Source: Beers' Mont]

23.   RACHEL³ OYER (*Peter²*, *Frederick¹*), born Schuy. 14 Mar. 1819; died Schuy. 26 July 1889. She married MICHAEL CLEMENS, Jr., son of Michael and Catherine (Lints) Clemens, born Schuy. 14 Feb. 1814; died Schuy. 6 July 1894; both buried MRC.
Michael Clemens farmed and resided in Schuy. all of his life, shown in 1850 next to his father. He's shown as landowner also. He is described as "one of the old and honored residents of Schuy." Rachel, his wife, was "a most estimable lady."

Ch (CLEMENS):

95.   i.   MARY L⁴, b Schuy 1843

*** THE CLEMENS FAMILY ***

Michael Clemens' brother Jacob Clemens m Rachel's sister
HANNAH OYER; their sister Catharine m Rachel's brother HENRY
OYER.

[See also Chapter 6]

24.   DANIEL³ OYER *(Peter², Frederick¹)*, born 27/21 Feb. 1821
[bap. rec. Herk. DRC 28 Mar. 1821 with his parents as sp.]; died
Schuy. 28 Apr. 1883; buried MRC. He married MARY LINTS, dau.
of Peter and Elizabeth (Bowman) Lints, born Schuy. Mar. 1835;
died Schuy. 3 Nov. 1918; buried MRC.

Daniel took over the family homestead farm upon the death of
his father. He was a farmer and also built a cheese factory in
Mar. 1871. He was a trustee of the Union Church oranized from
the old Methodist Protestant Church in 1868. In 1872 he was
elected a trustee of the Miller Rural Cem. Association. In 1870 his
real estate valued at $5,000, with personal property worth $600.
He died intestate. The date of Mary's death links her to the flu
epidemic of 1918. For some detail on that pandemic, see Wallace
Oyer (#162).

Graveplate of Ida Auyer.

Daniel³ and Mary (Lints) Oyer gravestone,
MRC, E. Schuyler, N.Y.

CHAPTER 9

FOURTH GENERATION

25. PETER D.[4] OYER *(David[3], Jacob[2], Frederick[1])*, born Schuy., Herk. Co.; died Franklinville Twp. (hereafter Frklnv.), Catt. Co. 18 Aug. 1896; buried AHC. He married 1st MARY CLARK. She died ca. 1844. Peter married 2nd ca. 1846 RACHEL VEDDER dau of Jacob F. and Margaret P. (Gardinier) Vedder born Fonda, Montgomery Co. (hereafter Mont.) May 1828; died Ellvl. 17 Nov. 1860; buried AHC. Peter married 3rd CATHERINE (ROY) LAWTON, dau. Alexander and Mary (McFarland) Roy, born Aberdeen, Scotland ca. 1825; died Ellvl. 13 Oct. 1907; buried SHC. A Catherine Oyer was a grantor to a William Oyer in Catt. Co. 1863. Catherine died while living on Bryant Hill and is buried in Ellvl. She may have been married to a Vedder also; at the time of her marriage to Peter she had a daughter EMMA who married CHARLES SHEP ARNOLD. They lived in Ellvl. and had no children. Shep was the executor of Peter's estate, along with Catherine.

Peter's LR [Catt Co] of deed with his first wife lists her as "Fanny." Our notes show a Cornelius Clark in Ash. by 1830, perhaps the one who came to Schuy., Herk. Co. from Nine Partners, Dutchess Co. This may be the son Cornelis, who is said to have lived in Wyoming Co. [PSO; Clark Inf 2] We do not know Mary/Fanny's parents--a Cornelius is the father of Elizabeth who married Peter[2], #4.

By 1835 [St. census] Peter was living next door to his father in Ash. It shows him farming with 4 cattle, 2 horses, 10 sheep and 4 hogs.

We learned from Rose (Duhan) Oyer (#162) that her grandfather Duhan's family lived nearby. Peter used to give rides to her father Tom when he was a boy on the stone boat he used. These were horsedrawn sled-like containers that were used to haul the huge stones from the fields that were being readied for either building on or to be cultivated. The family later moved to Ellvl; finally Frklnv.

By 1850 Peter is found with his second wife living on a farm near the hamlet of Plato, Ellvl. In that year his real estate was valued at $1,860. In 1860 he owned real estate worth $1,200 and personal property worth $600, their farm near the E. Otto Twp. border and near various Vedder relatives.

Peter remained in rural Ellvl. for a few years after the death of his second wife. In 1864 he added 30 cows to his holdings. [see illus p 115] By 1865 he is listed with children from both marriages farming there.

By 1870 Peter was married to his third wife and moved to the
village of Ellvl. He had given up farming and was listed in that
year as butcher, owning real estate worth $1,400. Three unmar-
ried sons were living with him, as were his wife's dau. by previous marriage, Emma (Emma married Charles Shep Arnold;
resided Ellvl.; no ch.) and Mary. In 1874 he was listed as butcher
residing on Main St. in Ellvl. An atlas of that day shows his
house on Washington St., near the Roman Catholic Church.

In 1880 Peter, his wife and daughter are listed living in Frklnv.
His occupation is given as farming. Peter is also mentioned as
having had skills as a veterinarian.

Ch (OYER) of 1st m:

97.   i.   CLARK⁵ E, b Frklnv   4 July 1836.

Ch (OYER) of 2nd m, all b Ellvl :

98.   ii.   DAVID SMITH⁵, b 26 Apr 1847
          iii. JACOB BURT, b Aug 1848; 25 Feb 1869
          iv.   CHARLES V., b Sept 1850; d Ellvl 15 June 1864
                ae. "14 yrs, 2 mos"; bur AHC. [See Illus--letter
                signed "niece and cousin, Eliza Nelson"]

[See Clark's text (#97) for additional Civil War era letters.]

99.   v.   FRANKLIN PIERCE, b 25 Jan. 1853
100.   vi.   BYRON EUGENE, b 1855
          vii. infant (twin) d at birth, 17 Nov 1860
          viii. infant (twin) d at birth, 17 Nov 1860

[There is no verification of the twin's birth, but family tradition
states that a wife died giving birth to twins.]

Ch (OYER) of 3rd m:

          ix.   WALTER S, b 1868; d 19 Mar 1869; bur AHC; not
                certain theirs
101.   x.   MARY⁵ E, b 1 Sept 1873

[Sources: CCHM; LM; Ash, Frklnv, Ellvl, GrV VR; Catt Co LR,
SR; family rec; Rose Oyer (#162); military rec; letters]

Camp of the 1.1th N.Y. Vols
Lookout Valley, Tenn.
Dec 15th 1863.

Dear Uncle and Family
Yours came to hand yesterday
I was glad you were in such
good Spirits and have plenty of
eggs and Potatoes but I shall be

East Otto. june 15th /64

Dear Uncle

by request of my mother. I write you
informing you, that of the Death of our cousin
Charlie Oyer. Uncle Peters boy. he is to be buried
to day at Ashford we are a going to the funeral
his death was caused by a hurt which he received
while draging the drag caught in some roots
and he lifted it out and one root struck him in
the bowels which caused his sickness and Death
his Father was gone at the time to buy cows and
did not get home in four or five days after
that he was sick about two weeks. Pa saw him when
he was first sick he did not tell him
about his being hurt. he would have brought
him home with him had he been able to come

Portions of letters: from Clark[5] Oyer when at Lookout Valley, Tenn. 1864 to
Jacob[4] during Civil War; from Eliza Nelson to Uncle Jacob[4] telling of Peter[4]
Oyer's young son Charles' injury and death. Extant are many letters to Jacob, most written by brothers-in-laws while serving in the Civil War and on
a 3-year whaling voyage.

*** THE VEDDER-GARDINIER-TRUAX-VAN DE BOGART-ROY FAMILIES ***

RACHEL VETTER's (Vedder) pedigree comes from HARMEN AL-BERTSE VEDDER who came to America before 1657; likely as early as 1633. He was a trader from Holland in Beverwyck/Schenectady. Through the Vedder line are settlers who worked for the Dutch East India Company. All of the following Dutch allied families came in the 17th century: Abeel, Adams, Bancker, Borsboom, Bratt, Brower, DuTrieux (Traux), DeVos, Evert, Fonda, Gardinier, Glen, Groot, Mebie, Otten, Schermerhorn, Swart, Van der Volgen, Van de Bogart, Van Eps, Veeder, Vischer, Vrooman, Wamp and Winne. Up until 1804 Amsterdam, Mont Co was named "Veddersberg." Interestingly, the vote to change the town's name was a tie, and the President of the Council, a Vedder, had the tie-breaking vote.

Margaret's will is dated 21 Sept 1855, Jacob M, petitioner.

While researching at the historical society in Fonda, Mont Co we located a most interesting note contributed by Frederick Vedder of Amsterdam Feb 20, 1897:

THE NAME OF VEDDER

Tradition has it, as delivered to me by my Grandfather, Frederick Vedder, that his ancestors were originally natives of Scotland and bore the name of McFeather there.

They removed from Scotland to Holland during the religious persecution in Scotland probably in the 14th or 15th century.

After they arrived in Holland the Mc was dropped from their name and Feather, which in the Holland language is spelled Veder, became their name before their removal to America in A.D. 1630.

Vedder families in Catt Co per Concord 1875 St census include: Jacob M, 52, b Mont Co; Harriet, 45, b Erie Co; Ellen M, 12; Clara, 9; Harvey, 6; John N(?), 2 10/12 and Mary, 75, b Mont Co.

A revision of Vedder's The Vedder Family in America 1657-1973 [Edwin Vedder 1974] was published by the author in 1987.

In Ash was a place called Vedder's Corners. In Hume Twp, Allegany Co we find H H Vedder, b 1835 and Simon, b 22 Mar 1809, coming there from Oppenheim, Mont Co.

In LV county miscellaneous records [6:318] we find CORNELIUS VEDDER, late of Erie Co by surr to widow ADELINE (OYER) VEDDER (#62), Bflo 1871, sole exec. Cornelius' parents were Albert and Mary (Seaman), Albert being the son of Johannes

*and Eva (Clute).   Ash 1865 St census shows ch Charity, 17;
Jenette, 13.*

*In 1987 a letter with detailed data from Margaret Vedder of
Auckland, New Zealand was received. Her line stems from Jacob
F Vedder (1814-1867) who m 1st Elinor Visscher.   Their son
Francis Jacob (1838-1910) "jumped ship" in Australia or NZ where
he settled.   He m Anna McPike there and had 8 ch.   Francis'
great-grandson Bruce is Margaret's husband. They are interested
in obtaining details of the family.   [Vedder Inf 1]*

*In 1892 Yorkshire, Catt Co census we find Octavius P Vedder, b
ca 1841 who m Helen _____, b ca 1839, son of Slyvanus and
Emeline (Kent) Vedder; ch: Emma, b ca 1864 and Sylvanus K, b ca
1875.*

*Through the works of Edwin Vedder we have learned that
previous records showing Rachel's mother as Margaret Governeur
have been in error.   It is MARGARET P GARDINIER, as shown in
the records of the DRC, Town of Glen, Mont Co. We were unable
to trace her parentage, although we have substantial Gardinier
detail.   The 1800 census has 2 families in Herk. Co. and 9 in
Mont Co. We know Margaret was b in Fonda. In Concord, Erie
Co, Briggs shows Nichols & Gardinier, merchants   [p 188];
tinsmiths Ferran & Gardinier [p 191].   John and Abram (b 1800)
Gardinier are on Lots 27 & 29 in T6 R7 (Concord) in 1836. John
Gardinier m Juliet Sibley, dau of Benjamin Sibley, they to Wisc.
Abram and Anna (Yates) Gardinier came to Concord from Fultonville, Mont Co, not far from Margaret's birthplace, Fonda. Anna
d 12 Dec 1882. Yates m 1862 Selinda Smith, dau of Calvin Smith;
ch: Stephen A, b 1865; Hattie B, b 1866; Leslie, b 1868. Yates'
bro and sisters do not include Margaret: Thomas, b 1830; Joseph, b
1832 (prob the Jos Y who d St Louis, Mo 7 Feb 1862); Isaiah, b
1837, m _____ Hemstreet; Yates, b 12 Dec 1839; Elias, b 1842;
Robert, b 1844; John, b 1846. Abram's parents were Thomas and
Mary (Hardenburgh) Gardinier who came to E Concord in 1836,
where they owned 240 acres.*

*There are many Gardinier families in Mont and Fulton Co
records, names repeated in later generations in Catt Co above.
SA DRC records show a Margaretha born 30 July 1796 to William
and Maria (Diellebach) Gardinier. The time frame is correct; their
are many other Gardiniers in SA DRC.   We cannot document any
better at this time.*

*The DUTRIEUX/TRUAX line is a most interesting one.   The
pedigree is as follows: Philip DuTrieux b 1585, d ca. 1653, was in
N Amsterdam during Peter Minuit's administration 1624-1629 and
was appointed the court administrator in 1638.   Philip's dau
Rebecca m Simon Simonse Groot.   Rebecca's son Abraham S.*

Groot m 2nd Hestertse Visscher. Their dau HESTER, b 1701, m FRANS VAN DE BOGART (1703-1775); his dau HESTER (1732-1813) m ALBERT VEDDER (1730-1805); their son JOHANNES VEDDER (1757-1818ʳ) m EVE CLUTE (1760-1825); JACOB F VEDDER (1797-1871) m MARGARET GARDINIER (ca 1800-1855). Jacob came from Mont Co with his brother Albert and settled in Ellvl where he was a farmer. After the death of his wife, he lived with his son John; later he was with John's widow Betsey. They are bur at FrktC.

FRANS VAN DE BOGART's pedigree stems from HARMEN MYNDERTSE VAN DER BOGART, b 1612 Netherlands and came to New Netherland in 1631 as surgeon of the ship Eendracht, continuing in the service of the Dutch West India Co until 1633. He then res New Ansterdam until he was apppointed commissary to Fort Orange (Albany). He m JELLISTE CLAESE SCHOUW; d 1648.

Harmen's son FRANS, bp 26 Aug 1640, m ANNTJE TJERKSE, settled Schenec; killed by French & Indians 1690. His son CLAES m BARBARA, dau of TAKEL HEEMSTRAAT of Albany 1699. Claes' son FRANS, b 1703, m HESTER, b 1701, dau of ABRAHAM GROOT in 1726, d 1775. Frans' dau HESTER, b 1732, m ALBERT VEDDER, b 1730, d 1805. Albert & Hester's son JOHANNES VEDDER, b 1757, d 1818, m EVE CLUTE, b 1760, d 1825. Johannes and Eve's son JACOB F VEDDER, b 1797, d 1871 in Catt Co, m MARGARET GARDINIER, b ca 1800 Mont Co, d 1855 Catt Co. Jacob and Margaret's dau is RACHEL, PETER OYER's 1st wife (see #25).

Ch of JACOB F and MARGARET (GARDINIER) VEDDER:

    i.   *JOHN A, b 3 Sept 1818; d Ellvl 7 Apr 1970; m 1st RACHEL OYER (#64), m 2nd BETSEY OYER (#62)*

    ii.   *MARIA, b Glen 27 July 1821; m 1844 Elisha Reynolds, b Savoy, Mass 10 Dec 1816; res Frknvl; then Sala, with son Vedder C Reynolds. Maria d Frknvl 4 Mar 1884; he d Sala 19 May 1893. Vedder was 1 of 6 ch, a teacher and lawyer in S Dayton and Sala. [Adams' Catt]*

    iii. *EVA ELIZA, b Glen 7 Nov 1823; d WV 8 Oct 1898; bur GrV; m PETER KANE/CAIN, b Ilion, Herk Co*
        a) *Arthur, b 16 Mar 1848; d GrV 2 June 1923; m Mary Booth*
        b) *John A, b 23 Jan 1854; d GrV 8 July 1920; m Mary L*
    [Source: GrV VR]

25.   iv. *RACHEL, b May 1828*
        v.   *COMMODORE PERRY, b Ellvl 23 Feb 1838; d New York, 24 Oct 1910. m 1st Betsey E Squire, 2nd*

Genevieve A (Hill) Wheeler. He was a wealthy lawyer and landowner in the Ellvl-GrV area. Commodore's only ch. a son, d y. His home in Ellvl was built by David S Oyer (#98): it is a ski lodge now: Edelweiss Inn.

Peter's 3rd wife, CATHERINE (ROY) LAWTON, was the dau of ALEXANDER and MARY (McFARLAND) ROY. He was b Aberdeen, Scotland ca 1825. GrV VR show a dau June d 26 May 1919, wife of J S Rickard/s. Alex d 10 Aug 1919, showing an uncle John and Ellen Roy: Mrs Julia Roy/Ray of GrV, informant. We have no data regarding Catherine's apparent 1st marriage. While we found Cath- erine bur in SHC, tradition has it she was bur in what is now an abandoned cem in the hamlet of Peth, GrV.

Other [cemetery] informants for GrV VR are a Vedder Kane of GrV and Sarrah Roy of Humphrey, GrV, in 1937.

[Sources: Rose Oyer: Adams Catt: Catt Co surr rec and LR: censuses: CCHM: VR of Ellvl. Frklnv. Ash and GrV: Pearson's Albany: Pearson's Schenec: DR church rec of Albany, Schenectady, Fonda and Caughnaunga. There are many other interesting ancestors, the history of whom could easily be located in Pearson's books. Jacob F has LR 11:245 Catt Co.]

26. JACOB⁴ OYER, *(David³, Jacob², Frederick¹),* born Ash., Catt. Co. 31 Mar. 1823: died Sprvl., Erie Co. 6 Mar. 1909: married 30 June 1847 AMANDA JULIETT SPAULDING, dau. Harvey and Clarissa (Haskins/Hastings) Spaulding, born E. Otto, Catt. Co. 12 May 1827: died Sprvl. 1903: both buried MWC.

Jacob was a farmer and lived for several years in Ash., Catt. Co. He later moved to Erie Co., where he spent the rest of his life. He resided in Sardinia, Cheektowaga, and West Seneca (where he was a Justice of the Peace for 8). He then moved to Sprvl. and operated a saw mill. In 1880 census he is listed as farmer at 144 Mill St. He a member of the Sprvl. Lodge, F. and A.M.

[The second paragraph of this man's obituary is directly respon- sible for the 15 years' research and work culminating in the publi- cation of this book:

After a long, gradually weakening illness, Mr. Oyer last Saturday morning peacefully made the transition from natural-sleep to the sleep that has no earth-awakening. It was a fitting end of a life of devotion to Him whose visible presence he has now entered.

Mr. Oyer was born in Ashford March 31st, 1823, a son of David and Mary Elizabeth Frank Oyer. His grandfather, Jacob Oyer, was captured by the Indians. His great-grandfather was killed at the battle of Oriskany.

Much of Mr. Oyer's life was spent in our town, tho he lived some years in Ashford, Sardinia, Cheektowaga and West Seneca. In the latter town he was for eight years a justice of the peace--an office which he was well-qualified to fill. Much of his life was devoted to agriculture, but for several years after his final return to Springville he was proprietor of the sawmill property near which he has since resided. In 1847 he married Miss Amanda J. Spaulding, a daughter of the late Harvey and Clarissa Spaulding, and they traveled life's journey together more than half a century. She died five years ago. He is survived by three of their six children--Frank E. of Springville, Mrs. Ella Anderson of Buffalo and Harlan Eugene, who is steward of Castle Inn, Buffalo.

Mr. Oyer was a faithful member of the Presbyterian Church. Uniting under the pastorate of Rev. Hiram Eddy, March 29, 1848, his church membership continued nearly sixty-one years.

The funeral at the family residence Monday afternoon, conducted by his pastor, Rev. H. H. Hubbell, assisted by Rev. J. I. Towner, pastor of the F. B. Church, was attended by a large concourse of neighbors and friends, including a delegation from Springville Lodge, F. and A. M., of which he had been a member fifty years.

Among those from away in attendance at the funeral of Mr. Jacob Oyer on Monday were:

H. E. Oyer, Mr. and Mrs. Roland Anderson, Mr. and Mrs. R. E. Oyer and daughter, Mr. and Mrs. B. N. Hadley, Miss Lois J. Oyer, Mrs. Seldon Vaux, of Buffalo; Mr. and Mrs. Smith D. Oyer [#98], Mr. Frank P. Oyer, Great Valley; Mr. and Mrs. Wilbur Nelson, West Valley; Mr. and Mrs. Willis L. Oyer, Mr. and Mrs. Harvey Vedder, Riceville; Mrs. Albert Silliman, Yorkshire; Mrs. Howard Davis, Orchard Park.

Jacob's brother Peter is the author's husband's great-grandfather; therefore Walt would thus be directly related to a revolutionary soldier. The statement that his great-grandfather was killed at Oriskany was the causative factor for a search that eventually led to confirmation, a fact that but one person had previously documented.   In 1908 a descendant had become a member of the DAR, providing substantiating data (although with an error).   Frederick's obscurity, even in his home county, impelled the author to "put him in the books." [Frederick Oyer and His Descendants, 1977] Ralph Auyer (#201) documented him a few years later, and it is his pursued interest that brought all facets together, he apprising me of his and A. Hawley Arnold's work. As more information was promised at the time of the first book, this is the fulfillment of that.

Extant are many letters to Jacob and Amanda, most from relatives while they served during the Civil War. One dates back to 1849, the writer accepting a request to meet with Amanda and friends for the purpose of organizing a Temperance Society.]

Margaret Eve/Eva (Oyer) Nelson Crumb; brother Jacob⁴ and wife Amanda Spaulding; on Crumb Hill, Maples, near E. Otto, N.Y.

Ch (OYER):

      i.   CLARA E.[5], b Sardinia   , Erie Co, 15 May 1848; d

              4 May 1887; m Dr R S HAMBLETON. She is bur
              MWC. She was a teacher and res in Buffalo.

      ii. EDWIN/EDDY J, b Sardinia, Erie Co, 3 Jan 1851;
              d West Seneca 5 Nov 1867; bur MWC

      iii. MARGARET <u>ANN</u>, "Anna M", b Sardinia, 30 Nov
              1852; d 26 Nov 1883; unm; bur MWC; taught
              English at Basel, Switzerland. One source says d
              there.

102. iv. FRANK EMMONS, b 18 Dec 1854
103. v.   ELLADE EMMA, b 1862
104. vi. HARLAN EUGENE, b 1864

*** THE SPAULDING FAMILY ***

*HARVEY SPAULDING was b Middlesbury, Vt 1804. CLARISSA
was b Ft Ann, Washington Co 1805. They were m 1824, moving to
GrV; then in 1826 to Sprvl. Living in different places, they took
up permanent res in Sprvl in 1850.*

*Amanda's bro Harlan Page was b Otto, Catt Co 9 Aug 1839. He
enlisted as a pvt 16 Sept 1861, Co A, 44th Reg't NY Vols. He
participated in the battles of Antietam, Fredericksburg, Chan-
cellorsville, Gettysburg, etc. In 1863 he was commissioned captain in the Seventh Reg't US colored troops. He was sent to
Florida in the spring of 1864; was with the Army of the Potomac
until Lee's surrender. In 1864 he was "breveted by the President,
Major and Lieutenant-Colonel for gallant and meritorious services."
[Briggs' Concord, p 458] He held various commands, being mustered out in 1866 in Baltimore. In 1883 [Briggs] he is shown as a
jeweler in Concord, Erie Co.*

*Another bro Frank P went to sea at ae 19, and was on a whal-
ing voyage of 4 years in the Pacific Ocean. Details of many
years at sea are told in Briggs' Concord, the source of some of
our data. A Frank is listed in Briggs as a carpenter and joiner;
also a collector.*

*Extant are very detailed letters from Amanda's brothers, as well
as other correspondents, written during the Civil War and during
the whaling trips.*

*From Dr. Hadley's letters in 1987 we learn of a Eugene Spauld-
ing in Bflo "some 50 years ago. There were 2 unmarried sisters,
Elizabeth and Eloise... Eloise worked for the BMT subway system
in NYC." They retired to Sprvl; Ruth Ann Hadley (#170) "looked
out for them." Both bur Sprvl.*

We know of no connection with the Spauldings that follow.

There are several in Mont Co early: Jacob, Bleecker Twn Clerk 1833–34; Capt David, in the Civil War; N G of Johnstown and Gloversville; a reverend of Fultonville; and a Samuel of Fish House, Fulton Co.

Jeremiah "Spalding" came to E Otto with wife and several sons May 1823; acquired 400 acres and divided them among his sons. He was an elder in the Presbyterian Church of Otto/First Congregational Church. One son was Tyler Spalding, also of the Pres Church in E Otto, ca 1834. Also a member was Warner Spaulding. Jeremiah d 1836, ae 65.

The Rev Solomon Spaulding, principal of Cherry Valley Academy, was the reputed author of the Book of Mormon. A Eunice Spaulding m Cephas Childs, who had a son Cephas, b Dresden, Yates Co 31 Jan, 1824. Ch of the son Cephas: Eliza, m James Miller; Donald, Minerva, m Joseph Miller; Simon J; James M. Eunice's husb Cephas was killed by a falling tree when his youngest child was 10 days old. She m 2nd Nathan Mason, who brought the family to Crawford Co, Penn. Cephas, Jr m 1848 Mary A Guthrie, b Phelps, Ontario Co; res Humphrey, Catt Co 1852 (in Sala 4 yrs). Ch of Cephas, Jr: Betsey, m Charles Fay; Almon G, m Nettie Wright; John C; Phebe J, m Fred Pierce. All lived on adjoining farms. Cephas Childs enlisted Jan 1862; served 3 yrs in Civil War; fought at Second Bull Run, Fredericksburg, Antietam, and Gettysburg.

Jonathan Spaulding went to Concord, Erie Co at the close of the War of 1812. G W Spaulding owned land in Concord, first settled by Samuel Cooper. Phoebe Spaulding m Tom W Briggs; had 7 ch. Polly Spaulding m Hickok 1875.

In 1850 Ash census is listed Edwin J, ae 24, shoemaker; Emiline, ae 20.

[Beers' Mont; Adams' Catt; Briggs]

27. MARGARET EVE/<u>EVA</u>[4] OYER (*David[3], Jacob[2], Frederick[1]*), born Ash., Catt. Co. 7 Apr. 1827; died Ellvl. 5 July 1909; buried E. Otto Village Cem. Eva had resided Ellvl. 8 years at time of death. She married 1st WILBUR A. NELSON, died Ellvl. 10 Oct. 1850. Eva married 2nd CHAUNCEY S. CRUMB, born Washington (?) Vt. 1 Dec. 1814; died E. Otto 19 Aug. 1890; buried E. Otto Village Cem. He was married previously.

E. Otto's 1870 census lists Chauncey with real estate valued at $17,000; personal estate, $4,000; wife Margarette E., Mary, 16; Franklin, 14; Hannah Crumb, 81, born Mass.; Eliza Nelson, 23; Wilber Nelson, 20; Garrit Smith, 8; Fidelia Drayer, 17; Frederick Drayer, 20, farm laborer; Goetlib Brown, 22, farm laborer, born Mecklenburg; and Lydia Countryman, 19, cheesemaker.

In 1875 St. census, Eliza, Mary E (Nelson), Franklin Crumb, and Garrit Smith are listed, as is Roman Trumiller, 22, servant, born Baden, Germany. In E. Otto 1880 Mary E. Oyer is shown as a boarder. This was Eva's mother, the latter dying while living with her in 1884.

Eva and Chauncey lived on Crumb Hill, Maples, Catt. Co. Payment for her father David's care became a bitter court case (see #98). Chauncey's dau. by his first wife, Emeline L. or S., married Robert A. Wallace, who was the executor of Chauncey's estate. SR 154/6 mentions "the late widow – 1893." He left $800 to Emeline and her husband, Robert A. Wallace; $1,500 to granddaughter Mary "when 21" (13 at the time); one half residue to wife; one half residue to Mary or the General Conference 7th Day Adventists, Battle Creek, Mich. The will was contested because of a 160 acre tract deeded to Chauncey by his wife 30 Dec. 1886, said to be void because of some family arrangement; no title was acquired. This was adjusted amicably. Witnesses: Leonard A. and Lottie E. Wallace. [LV SR 154/6]

Ch (NELSON) from Margaret's 1st m:

  i.   ELIZA ANN⁵, b Erie Co 22 Apr 1847
  ii. WILBUR DAVID, b 19 Dec 1849; bur Mt Hope Cem, Ash in plot with Emeline and Willis Wilbur. Bur there in another plot are Raymond and Mildred.

Ch (CRUMB) from Margaret's 2nd m:

  iii. MARY E, b E Otto ca 1854
  iv. FRANKLIN J, b Ash 18 July 1855; d E Otto July 1877; bur E Otto Village Cem

*** THE NELSON FAMILY ***

WILBUR NELSON's parents were BENJAMIN and ANNE (MORTON) NELSON. They came from Brandon, Vt in 1818 to Concord, Erie Co. Wilbur had many brothers and sisters. While we have many Nelson notes, we are unable to fit them to the families. There is some additional Nelson data in #101.

*** THE CRUMB FAMILY ***

In 1850 HANNAH CRUMB, born Mass., apparently the mother of CHAUNCEY, was with Daniel Bailey whose wife was Deborah, ae 40. With Daniel also were Lewis, 22, born Mass. Hannah J and

*Chauncey Bailey, ae 17 and 7, born New York. Chauncey and a
dau Emeline, listed 9 months old, were with Nathan Larabee nearby, who had 3 daughters who married Larabee brothers. Nathan's
household [1850] also included Roxana Oyer, 19; Fernando F
Leonard, 8; Job Sidney Leonard, 5.*

*There is an old entry of Crumps in Smith's Erie, p 732: Robert
G Crump, b Glenwood (Colden) 1845; owned 400 acres; m 1873
Jennie Williams, b 1855; 4 ch, 3 sons, 1 dau. His parents were
Benjamin and Elizabeth (Lewis) Crump of England who came to
Colden 1832; had 8 children; Eliz d 1879. As the name is
different, there may be no connection.*

28.   MARGARET⁴ LINTS (*Mary³, Jacob², Frederick¹*) born Schuy.
1 Mar. 1831; died Schuy. 1 Mar. 1904; buried MRC. She married
ca. 1851 DUANE E. JACKSON, son of Jacob and Sally (_____)
Jackson, born Herk. Co. 9 Jan. 1823; died Utica, Oneida Co., 5
Sept. 1906; buried MRC.

Duane and Maragaret Jackson farmed in Schuy. on their own
for a number of years. Later they moved in with her parents
and eventually took over operation of the Lints farm. Duane
Jackson died intestate, leaving real estate ($7,000) and personal
property ($2,000) to several nieces and nephews.

Ch (JACKSON) b Schuy :

    i.   CLARINDA E⁵, b 10 Dec 1851; d Schuy 13
          Aug 1897; m LEVI RINKLE, b Schuy 25 Nov 1843;
          d Schuy 14 Aug 1878; both bur MRC
  ii. SEYMOUR W. b Schuy 7 Jan 1863; d Schuy 9 Mar
          1877 bur MRC

29.   JACOB J.⁴ OYER (*John³, Jacob², Frederick¹*), born Ash.,
Catt. Co. Nov. 1824; died Ash. 12 Oct. 1909; buried AHC. He
married ca. 1853 NANCY E. FOLTS, dau. of Peter and Nancy
(Schell) Folts b Jan. 1823; died Ash. 30 Jan. 1909; buried AHC.

Jacob resided in E. Otto. He is listed there as a joiner in
1860, a lumberman in 1870 (with real estate wirth $2,000 and
personal property worth $1,000) and as farmer and sawyer in 1875.
In 1900 Jacob is listed in Ash. as sled maker.

Ch (OYER):

    i.   CAROLINE⁵, b ca 1854
  ii. child--apparently another Caroline
 iii. ALMAN b ca 1865

*** *THE SCHELL FAMILY* ***

*The Folts and Schells had other alliances. Barker has good
Schell records, but no Nancy marrying a Folts. The progenitor
was John Schell, b Nassau-Dilenburg, Germany 1734 d Herk 1 Aug
1802; m SA 16 Feb 1762 Barbara Rasbach. He came to Phila 1752;
to Mohawk V, settled Schell's Bush. For Folts data see Chapt 8.*

30.   **MARGARET E.⁴ OYER** *(John³, Jacob², Frederick¹)*, born
Ash., Catt. Co. 24 June 1826; died E. Otto, Catt. Co. 28 May 1878;
married MAHAMON BOWEN, son of Elias and Lydia (Wellington)
Bowen, born Nelson Twp., Madison Co. 14 Oct. 1815; died E. Otto
16 Feb. 1894; both buried E. Otto Village Cem. Mahamon was a
life-long farmer in E. Otto.

       Ch (BOWEN) all b E Otto:

   i.   MARGARET AUGUSTA⁵, b 18 Nov 1851; d E Otto 21
        Mar 1920; bur E Otto Village Cem. She m CHARLES
        CHASE. She is listed with her parents, apparently
        widowed, as a milliner in E Otto in 1880; no ch.
   ii. LYDIA H, b 17 Apr 1854; d E Otto 27 Aug 1858; bur E
        Otto Village Cem.
105. iii. SNOWEY ANN, b 12 Mar 1856
106. iv. AMY W., b 26 May 1860
   v.   son, d in infancy

*** *THE BOWEN FAMILY* ***

*The Bowen family is of Welsh descent. The American ancestor
of this family is believed to be GRIFFITH BOWEN, who came to
America with wife Margaret in 1638. They had 10 children.
Mahamon Bowen was brought with his sister Alzina (whose dau
Loretta Butler later m Margaret's brother John [#31]) by their
parents in an ox-cart from Madison Co, to Catt Co, settling for a
time in Zoar and later in Whitford Hollow near E Otto. His
parents: Elias b 12 Nov 1792 prob Cheshire, Mass; d 6 Oct 1872.
Elias served in the War of 1812; m Lydia Wellington, b 1799, d E
Otto 2 Mar 1861. They resided in Nelson Twp, Madison Co,
where their first 2 children were born. They later moved to
Catt Co. Mahamon had a brother Elias, b ca 1818; d Ellvl 1903;
he was a res of Erie Co for 84 years. Elias is listed in E Otto
1870 [census] near Mahamon, ae 52; with Lucinda, 54; and Viola,
18. Next door is Levi Bowen, 31; Lydia, 22; Francis, 4. This
seems to conflict with above.*

*In 1892, Ellvl, Walter L Bowen, age 20, son of Clark Bowen, b
Humphrey m Jennie Phillips. He resided in Otto. His mother was
a Butler. Hubert E. Bowen of E Otto had a son Charles W, b ca
1878. On 18 Dec 1900 he was m.*

*Henry Bowen was a member of the First Baptist church in
Sardinia, Erie Co.*

[Sources: LM; CCHM; Briggs; censuses]

31.   JOHN⁴ OYER, Jr. *(John³, Jacob², Frederick¹)*, born Ash. 24
Sept 1828; died E. Otto 24 Dec. 1910 ae 82 y, 3 m; buried AHC.
He married LORETTA BUTLER, dau of Horace and Alzina (Bowen)
Butler, born E Otto 1842; died Ash. 1875; buried AHC. [See Bo-
wen data above]

John helped on his parent's farms until his marriage. He then
resided mostly in E Otto, though for a number of years he lived
in Ash., and in 1880 is listed in the vicinity of Ash. Hollow,
farming.

         Ch (OYER) all b E Otto:

         i.   PHIDELIA⁵, b ca 1862
107.   ii.   CHARLES D, b July 1863
108.   iii. CORA A, b 20 Apr 1870

32.   MARY E.⁴ OYER, *(John³, Jacob², Frederick¹)* born Ash.,
Catt. Co. Mar. 1827; died 15 May 1912; buried AHC. She married
ca. 1850 REUBEN FRANK, son of Jacob H. and Maria Frank, born
Ash. Apr. 1832; died 1912; buried AHC.

Reuben Frank resided for the most part in Ash. In 1850 and
1855 he is listed there as farmer. In 1865 he and his wife with
her parents in E. Otto. In 1870 Reuben is listed working in a
sawmill in Ash. In censuses of 1875, 1880 and 1900 he's shown as
farmer and laborer in Ash.

         Ch (FRANK):

         i.   JOHN J⁵, b Ash Dec 1853; he is listed with his
              parents in Ash in 1900 as day laborer.

          *** *THE FRANK FAMILY* ***

*REUBEN FRANK was one of the large family of JACOB H
FRANK, who came to Catt Co from Frkf in Herk Co at an early*

*date. Jacob H was the son of JOHANN HENRICH FRANK (Henry
Frank Sr). [Further Frank detail in Chapter 8]*

33. **ELIZABETH ANN⁴ OYER,** *(John³, Jacob², Frederick¹)* born
Ash., Catt. Co. 1833; died Ash. 2 Aug 1911; buried AHC. She
married PETER MILLER, son of John and Mary (Frank) Miller,
born 1835; died 1913; buried AHC.
Peter was a farmer. In 1860 he is listed in E. Otto, Catt. Co.,
near the home of brother-in-law Jacob Oyer (#29); other years he
is listed in Ash. where in 1870 he ownes real estate worth $5,565
and personal property worth $1,795.

Ch (MILLER):

    i.   MARY A⁵, b E Otto, ca 1859
   ii.   ELLEN M, b ca 1862
  iii.   FRANCES E, b ca 1865
  iv.   HENRY A, b Ash ca May 1870

*** *THE MILLER FAMILY* ***

*PETER MILLER's mother was MARY FRANK, dau of JOHN H and
MARGARET (GERLACH) FRANK. She was, therefore, a sister of
Charity Frank, wife of John P Oyer (see #16), and Peter Miller
was Charity's nephew. [For additional Miller data see Chapter 6]*

34. **AUGUSTUS V.⁴ OYER** *(John³, Jacob², Frederick¹)*, born E.
Otto Sept 1840. He married HARRIET E. _____, born Onon.
Co. Nov. 1846.
Augustus grew up in E. Otto where he helped on the family
farm. After his father's death, he continued to live there for
several years; in 1870 his farm is listed worth $8,000. Brother
David (invalid) and widowed mother were living with him in that
year. [1870 census]
By 1880 Augustus and family, including his brother and mother,
are listed residing on N. Buffalo Street in Sprvl., Concord,
Erie Co. His occupation is given as farmer. In 1900 and 1910
Augustus, his wife, and son Frank are still in Concord. His occupation is carpenter. 3 of their children had died by 1910.

Ch (OYER):

    i. VAN A⁵, b ca 1875

    ii.   LAURA, b ca 1877

   iii. ANNA, b 1879

   iv. FRANK J, b Concord Apr 1881

    v. child d y

35.   ANDREW J.[4] OYER (*John*[3], *Jacob*[2], *Frederick*[1]), born E. Otto, Catt. Co. 1840; died Ash. 5 Sept. 1890; buried AHC. [Cemetery record states 47 years old, though.] He married 1st LAVINA WIDRIG, dau. of Michael and Sarah (_____) Widrig, born Herk. Co. 1846.

Andrew enlisted in Co. G. 154th Reg't. N.Y. Infantry 1 Sept. 1862. In 1863 he was tried by "Drum Head Court Martial" for "straggling" and sentenced to forfeit one month's pay. In July 1864 he was disabled in the line of duty at Kenesaw Mt. in Ga. He was hospitalized for several months in Louisville, Ky., and was mustered out 11 June, 1865 at Bladensburg, Md.

Lavina was abandoned by her husband in about June 1875; she married 19 Apr. 1881 ABRAM V. HEMSTREET, after having lived with her mother and step-father for a while.

Andrew married 2nd 7 Mar. 1888 at Marshall Co., Iowa LIZZIE GROSS, born ca. 1856. She had been married previously, and married again after Andrew's death. By 1 Jan. 1890 Andrew was back in Ash., apparently without Lizzie. A document dated 19 Mar. 1896 identifies her as of Marshalltown (formerly Gilman), Iowa with a new husband.

He was ill and without money when he returned to Ash., going to live with his sister Mary Frank. Her husband Reuben made a claim for reimbursement to the U.S. government for his having cared for Andrew. In his claim Reuben stated that Andrew continually grew worse and could not be left alone at all. After stating he could not afford to give the time required, he stated that the attending physician charged "ten (10) dollars, and the Undertaker twenty (20) dollars which the claimant must pay."

   Ch (OYER) both b Ash:

    i.   SARAH JENNIE[5], b ca 1869

   ii. IDA M, b 17 Dec 1875

36.   HARRIET CATHARINE[4] OYER (*John*[3], *Jacob*[2], *Frederick*[1]) was born E. Otto, Catt. Co. 24 Apr. 1847. She married CONRAD WIDRIG, son of Michael and Sarah (_____) Widrig, born 1844.

[For Widrig detail see Second Generation Allied Families. We are unable to be certain of Michael's pedigree.]

37.   JOHN H.⁴ OYER *(Frederick³⁻²⁻¹)* born Schuy., Herk. Co. ca. 1816; died New Albion, Catt. Co. 7 Mar. 1876.   He married SARAH ANN (_____), born Oneida Co. ca 1820.

John is listed as farming in Otto in 1840. He is later listed in E. Otto as shoemaker. In 1860 his son Clarence is also listed as shoemaker. By 1868 the family had moved to New Albion, where John is listed as hotel owner. At the time of his mother's death he was in "Catt. Station." A newspaper item states: "John H. Oyer of Otto, whose house was entered by burglars a few weeks ago, has died from the effects of the wounds he received," shot while being burglarized.

Ch (OYER) all b E Otto:

109. i.   CLARENCE D⁵, b ca 1841
      ii. FLORENCE V, b ca 1844; m (_____) WESTCOTT;
           res New Albion in 1876
      iii. EVELINE D, b ca 1848; d before 1860

38.   MARY ANN⁴ OYER, *(Frederick³⁻²⁻¹)* born Schuy. ca. 1819. She married ANDREW HUFSTADER, son of Jacob and Catharine (Rima) Hochstatter, born Frankfort 4 Aug. 1812 and bp (rec. GF DRC) 7 Feb. 1813 (sp. Michael and Elizabeth Hochstatter).   In 1880   the family shows Nelson, 34 still at home; Alzina, 30; Blanche, 9; John Dunson, 26, works on farm; Ambrose H. Fox, farmer; Hester E. Fox, 36; Willie E. Fox, 12, son.

Ch (HUFSTADER) all b E Otto:

110.   i.   LAURA J⁵, b ca 1841; d Ash 22 June 1908; m
             _____ Lang/Long
111.   ii. NELSON, b Feb 1846
        iii. CHARLES A, b ca 1850; d Ash 13 May 1911; listed
             with Geo Hughey family 1880 Ash; m ROSANE, b
             Aug 1850, bur Sprvl, no ch. [Ash 1900]
        iv. LUCY JENNIE, b ca 1854
        v.   SELLE/SELLA, b ca 1857

[For more Hufstader information see Chapter 7]

39.   ROBERT⁴ OYER *(Frederick³⁻²⁻¹)*, born Schuy. ca. 1822; died Ellvl. 12 Apr. 1875. He married PERMELIA COOL, born Mont. Co., ca. 1829. In 1864 he served in the Civil War.

Ch (OYER), all b Ash   :

112.	i.	MARY ALICE[5], b 5 Apr 1847; m MARTIN HENRY WOODRUFF
	ii.	EUGENE, b June 1849, d y
112.1	iii.	MALDEN E, b Apr 1851
112.2	iv.	FREDERICK D, b ca 1853 This may be a different Frederick, as we find records showing him Frederick A, born Lyndon--that is the one we are carrying on.
113.	v.	PERRY R, b Feb 1855
	vi.	ELNORA, b ca 1857, d y
	vii.	CHESTER <u>RICHARD</u>, b ca 1859 He is shown as Richard R, ae 52, working at a last block factory in Frklnv with sister Mary A Woodruff with him. [1915 St census]

40. ANNE[4] OYER *(Frederick[3-2-1])*, born E. Otto 11 Feb. 1828; died Ash. 28 May 1895. She married PETER QUACKENBUSH, son of John Quackenbush, born Catt. Co. 22 May 1827; died 18 Dec. 1895; both buried MtHC.

Ch (QUACKENBUSH):

  i.   LAURA A[5], b Ash   ca 1847

*** *THE QUACKENBUSH FAMILY* ***

PETER QUACKENBUSH was the son of JOHN QUACKENBUSH, who came from Mont Co in 1824, settling in Ash on Lot 54 owned in 1879 by James Neff.
  The first "Quackenboss," Pieter, was a brick layer in 1668 in Albany. The resulting families settled largely in Niskayuna, nearby. In many of the books about the early settlers, descendants have been lost track of when they left the area; they are difficult to match up, especially when given names are repeated.
  "Early in the last century [17th], three brothers named Quackenboss emigrated from Holland to the Colony of New York. One...to New York City; the other two to Albany..." [Beers' Mont]
  Several children were grown when they arrived. One, David, m Ann Scott, dau Lieut John Scott who commanded Fort Hunter. Another was Lieut Abraham D Quackenboss. Andrew Frank (see #5) was another early resident of the town. A Tory sought the scalps of Capt Jacob Gardinier and Abraham because "he knew they would sell at a high price to the British patrons of the

traffic." However, a dau revealed the plan, and Abraham led a
dozen men who located and shot the Tory.

A Peter Quackenboss had the first saw and grist mill in the
Town of Glen, Mont Co; was instrumental in the establishment of
the First Reformed Church there, as well as the transition from
Dutch to English. The first school was in the house of Abraham,
right after the Rev.

The Van Slycks married into the family, and were historically
prominent in Glen also, being among the first settlers of Schenec.
[For more Van Slyck (Van Slyke) data, see John Oyer (#7).]

The earliest connection to the Oyers we are able to make is
with John D (?) Quackenbush, as told above. He had the first
tavern there. A Peter Quackenbush came to Ash from Mont Co in
1819; he was the son of John H, who joined him there in 1821.
Peter's bro David, who as was he was in the Rev, was captured by
the Indians and both made to run the gauntlet, as was his bro
John H. John H's son Peter came from Mont Co to Ash 1819; md
Hannah Prince, dau of Peter Prince of Mont Co; ch: Rebecca (m
Russell A Carter); John, b Mont Co 16 Apr 1818, to Ash, super-
visor 1870; m Mary Bargy, dau of Jacob P and Dorothea (Frank)
Bargy, she being either sister or aunt of Mary Elizabeth (Frank)
Oyer (#5). John and Mary's son Clark P. Quackenbush, 1 of 6 ch,
d Ellvl 1909, the rec showing John of Ellvl, birthplace unknown.
[Ellvl VR] John was another son; he res Eagle, Wyoming Co.
Other sons: Clark P, b 1849, in Ellvl 1833, m Augusta Hinman,
she b Mansfield 1849; and Charles, of Ash.

In Ash 1850 are Peter and Hannah (Prince) Quackenbush, ae 53
and 52; John and Mary Quackenbush, ae 32 and 31, with ch John
J, ae 3 and Clarke P, ae 2. There is John D and Deborah, ae 50
and 47; ch Alex 22, Harriet 18, Edward 16, Christina 13, David 11,
Eliza 8, Daniel 6. They are bur Ash: John D Quackenbush, d 18
Oct 1876, ae 75 y, 9 m, 13 d; wife Deby, d 16 Jul 1884, ae 79 y, 4
m, 28 d.

A John D m Christina West, b 22 June 1838; dau of Rev James
West. Ch: John E, Cora L (m Charles G Dox), and James C.

In Ash 1870: John Quackenbush Jr, 23; Lucinda, 24; Nellie 2;
Pearl 2/12.

In Ash 1880: John Quackenbush, 62; Mary, 61; Bertha A, 10.

In Ash 1880: Charles Quackenbush, 24; Mina E, 20; Sally Multer,
54, mother.

Bur Ash: Daniel Quackenbush, d 10 Apr 1877, ae 38; Alexander
Quackenbush (1828-1870); Eliza Jane (1831-1897), Spencer J (1881-
1958), his w Iola M (1903-19); mother Frederick M (1883-1927);
father John C (1973-1936).

[Sources: Adams' Catt; Everts' Catt; Beers' Herk; CCHM; LV
VR; LM; Ash VR; Ash cem rec; censuses]

41.   SARAH/SALLY⁴ OYER, *(Frederick³⁻²⁻¹)* born E. Otto. 13 Aug. 1831; died Allegany 25 Apr. 1887/90. She married GEORGE ALTENBURG, born 11 Sept. 1935, died 2 Feb. 1869. George was in the lumbering business. Later son Abraham took care of his mother; he moved west after "her death in 1890." [Jones, Geo]

Ch (ALTENBURG):

	i.	EMMA JANE⁵, b 1853
	ii.	EPHRAIM, b 1855, res Granger, Allegany
	iii.	FREDERICK F, b 1856/57, d 1930, res Bradford, McKean Co, Penn
	iv.	THOMAS, b 1858 or 1861, d 23 May 1930, res Dancy, Marathon Co, Wis. He m May 1855 in Wis, ANNA BLACK, b Knowlton, Wis, Feb 1865; d Laurium, Mich, Feb 1940; bur Knowlton, Wis
	v.	CATHARINE, b 1863; in 1888 "whereabouts unknown"
	vi.	HARRIET, b 1865, d 1927, unm
113.1	vii.	ABRAHAM, b 1866
	viii.	MARGARET/MAGGIE, b Allegany 1869, d 1952, m 1) BOONE HALEY; m 2) SAMUEL WADE SIMMONS. Res Allegany 1890 [census]

*** THE ALTENBURG FAMILY ***

GEORGE's grandfather, WILLIAM ALTENBURG, b Germany 1756; d 19 Jan 1821, bur Snell's Bush Cem, Mannheim, Herk Co. William m ELIZABETH MOSHER/MOSHIER, b Dutchess Co 12 June 1765; d 3 June 1845, bur Summit View Cem, Bennington, Wyoming Co. George's father, Daniel Altenburg, was b ca 1788–89 Mont/Saratoga Co. George Altenburg's Uncle John left Allegany in 1854 with his wife and ten children. He settled in Portage Co, Wisc, where they were in the lumbering business.

There was a Charles Aldenburg, b Mecklenburg, Schuy Co in E Otto, ae 24 with wife, ae 22; Analee, 6; Willie, 4 in 1870.

[Sources: Altenburg Inf; Jones, Geo; LM. For more detail see Abraham Altenburg (#113.1)]

42.   JOHN⁴ OYER *(Peter³, Frederick², Frederick¹)*, born Schuy., Herk. Co. 5 May 1815; died Schuy. 26 Sept 1868. He married 28 Feb. 1841 ELIZABETH MOSHER, dau. of George J. Mosher, born 4 Sept 1822; died Schuy. 27 Feb. 1855; both buried MRC. George's father George married Peter Finster's dau. Sophronia.

Ch (OYER) all b Schuy:

114.	i.	ADELINE M⁵, b 6 June 1842
115.	ii.	FRANCES AUGUSTA, b 4 Feb 1844
	iii.	MARY FREDERICA, b 17 Feb 1846; d Schuy 1846
	iv.	CATHERINE ELIZABETH, b 13 Feb 1847
	v.	EDWIN F, b 1 Apr 1850; d Schuy 13 July 1850
116.	vi.	RICHARD HOWARD, b 27 Sept 1851
	vii.	LILA F, b 5 Dec 1854; d Schuy, 19 May 1855

43. MARIA/MARY4 OYER (*Peter³, Frederick²⁻¹*), born Schuy., Herk. Co. 3 Mar. 1817; died Sprvl., Erie Co. 20 Oct. 1890. She married EBENEZER S. CADY, born Chatham, Columbia Co. ca. 1817, son of Arnold and Sarah (Hunt) Cady; died Sprvl. Apr. 1891.

Ebenezer was listed living next door to Peter F. Oyer in 1855; his occupation was given as carpenter. In 1858 he moved to Sprvl., where he was a carpenter and joiner. [Briggs]

Ch (CADY) all b Schuy:

i.	LUCY A⁵, b 1840; d 1872
ii.	SARAH J, b 1844; m NEWEL FRENCH
iii.	MARYETTE, b 1847 d Schuy, 1850
iv.	CASSIUS M, b 1850, d Sprvl, 1871
v.	ELLEN G, b 1853; m GARDNER BERRY, res Reading, Mich
vi.	WILLIAM S (N?), b 1856; res Kalkaska, Mich (A Wm N res Reading, Hillsdale Co, Mich.)

*** THE CADY FAMILY ***

EBENEZER CADY's gr f was EBENEZER who was a Capt in the Revolution, m CHLOE BEEBE, b Ct. This Ebenezer built a home of pine in Chatham, Col Co in 1761-62, which was later taken down and the lumber used to build the Presbyterian meeting house in Spencertown, Col Co. He had 2 sons and 5 daus. His son Arnold, f of Mary Oyer's husband, b Chatham, served as a volunteer of marines in defence of the NY harbor in the War of 1812; m Sarah Hunt, b Washington, Vt.

44. ELIZABETH4 OYER (*Peter³, Frederick²⁻¹*), born Schuy. 25 Feb. 1819, died 25 Apr. 1892. She married 4 Mar. 1844 FRANCIS BROWN, d 29/31 Dec. 1896; resided at Bridgewater, Oneida Co.

Ch (BROWN):

    i.   ADELINE⁵, d 11 Nov 1893; m _____ O'NEAL.

45. ALMIRA⁴ OYER *(Peter³, Frederick²⁻¹)*, born Schuy. 7 May 1829; died Schuy. 27 June 1889 or 1899. She married 13 Apr. 1859 NEHEMIAH RICHARDSON, born 14 Jan. 1828; died Schuy. 8 Aug. 1880; buried E. Schuy.

    Ch (RICHARDSON) all b Schuy:

117.	i.	ANNIAS D⁵, b 24 Dec 1864
118.	ii.	GENEVA CAROLINE, b 2 Dec 1867; d 22 Dec 1943; m GEORGE WADSWORTH; said to have had 1 dau
118.1	iii.	SARAH CATHARINE, b 27 Nov 1869; d Schuy 22 Dec 1869; had dau who m JOHN R JONES

46. LEVI⁴ OYER *(George³, Frederick²⁻¹)*, born Schuy. 5 May 1820; died Ash. 3 Nov. 1851, ae. 31 y, 5 m, 28 d; buried EldC. He married BETSEY OYER (#61), dau. of John Oyer (#16), born Schuy. 6 Sept 1824; died Ellvl. 21 Sept 1908; buried FrktC. Betsey Oyer married 2nd JOHN A. VEDDER.

    Ch (OYER):

119.	i.	GEORGE WASHINGTON⁵, b 2 Jan 1845
	ii.	JOHN L, b 22 Mar 1846/8; d Ellvl 14 Feb 1929. He m 1873 DORA E HANSON, dau of Hudson and Abigail (Vedder) Hanson, b 26 Apr 1854; d Ellvl 22 Jan 1925. Both bur Mt Hope Cem, WV. He was Vice-President of WV Manufacturing; no ch.

47. SIMON⁴ OYER *(George³, Frederick²⁻¹)*, born Ash. 5 Nov. 1831; died E. Otto 1900. He married ca 1861 EMILY J. SACKET, born Dec. 1841; died 1930; both buried MWC., Sprvl. Simon was a shoemaker, carpenter, lumberman and miller. He also farmed and is so listed in 1865 in Ash. He operated mills in Ash. Hollow that were furnished with water power with steam as auxiliary. Lumber, shingles and cheese-boxes were manufactured, and feed was ground. In the 1870 census Simon is listed as dry goods merchant in Ash. Living with him were his nephew, dry goods merchant George W. Oyer as well as his father, George Oyer. In 1880 he is listed as farmer in E. Otto; in 1900 he is listed in Ash. as a retired farmer.

Ch (OYER):

120.   i.   CHARLES A⁵, b 7 July 1863
121.   ii.   EUGENE S, b Mar 1867
       iii. EARL, b 1875; d 1895; bur MWC

48.   ALMEDA⁴ OYER *(Jacob³, Frederick²⁻¹)*, born Herk., Herk.
Co. 1830; died W. Monroe 23 Nov. 1899.   She married 1850
ORSON F. ALLEN, born 1828; died West Monroe 1918; both buried
W. Monroe Cem.
   Orson came to W. Monroe in 1836 with his parents.   He farmed,
eventually taking over the farm of his father−in−law, Jacob Oyer.
In 1860 the family moved to Iowa.   Orson enlisted in the 4th Iowa
Cavalry in 1861, but received a disability discharge ten months
later.   In 1862 the family returned to farming in W. Monroe.

Ch (ALLEN) first 3 b W Monroe:

     i.   FLORRINE F⁵, b 1851; m _____ SEAMAN of
          Parish, Oswego Co
    ii.   ELIZABETH J, b 1854; m _____ SEAMAN of
          Parish
   iii.   CLINTON D, b 1856
    iv.   BURTON C,
     v.   FRED O, b 1872; d 1957 He m MARY E _____,
          b 1869; d 1932; both bur West Monroe Cem.
    vi.   LaPEARL, m _____ McLYMOND of Parish.

49.   WILLIAM H.⁴ OYER *(Jacob³, Frederick²⁻¹)*, born ca. 1832.
He married EUNICE _____, born Oswego Co. ca. 1836.   William was a farmer and farm laborer in W. Monroe.

Ch (OYER):

     i.   ALICE E⁵, b W Monroe, 5 Mar 1858; d W
          Monroe 15 May 1863, ae 5 y, 2 m, 10 d

50.   ROXANNA⁴ OYER *(Michael³, Frederick²⁻¹)*, born E. Otto
ca. 1831; resided Haddam, Kan.; died Wetmore, Kan.   She married
E. Otto NELSON LARABEE, son of Nathan and Delana/Deana (Aldrich) Larabee; died Wetmore, Kan.   Roxanna is the oldest of 3
Oyer sisters who married 3 Larabee brothers.   They appear to
have gone to Wis. and Kan. soon after the Civil War.   [See *The*

Larabee Family after #54.] Otto's 1850 Census shows "Roxanna" in with the family of her in-laws.

51. JOSEPH[4] OYER, *(Michael[3], Frederick[2-1])*, born E Otto 1832; died Ellvl. 9 Oct. 1904.   He married 1863 DELILAH DYE, born 1849; died 1916; both buried SHC.

Joseph enlisted in Co. A, 7th Ill. Vols. in 1861 and served for 3 months.   He returned to E. Otto, where he farmed.   In 1871 he purchased a half-interest in his brother-in-law J.D. Larabee's general store in Ash. Hollow.   In 1875 he is listed as butter dealer living next door to Joseph Larabee, also a butter dealer in Ash. In Feb. 1881 he moved to Ellvl., where he was a horse dealer and ran a livery stable.   1900: listed as a clerk in a drug store.   1910: Delilah is with dau. Olia <sic> and Edward McElroy in Ellvl.

Ch (OYER):

    i.   FRANK[5], b ca 1865; d before 1900

   ii. OLY/OLA B, b 1870, d 1946, m Ellvl 8 Oct 1896 EDWARD H McELROY, son of Bernard and Mary (Demer) McElroy, b 1873; d 1937.   Both bur SHC. Edw worked at a grist mill; no ch.

52.   SARAH JANE[4] OYER *(Michael[3], Frederick[2-1])*, born E. Otto ca. 1834, died Haddam, Kan.   She married George Larabee, son of Nathan and Delana (Aldrich) Larabee, born 1828.   In 1850 Census she is living in Otto with Julius C. Beach and family.

Ch (LARABEE):

    i.   ALBERT
   ii. RUSSELL
  iii. EMMA
  iv. FERNANDO
   v. LESTER

53.   MARY ELIZABETH[4] OYER *(Michael[3], Frederick[2-1])*, born ca. 1833, married MOSES NASH BEACH, son of Moses T. and _____ (Nash) Beach.   Moses T. was born in Mass. before 1800.   [See Beach family--Chapter 10]

Ch (BEACH):

     i.   IDA⁵
121.1   ii. BERTHA, b 14 Apr 1865
    iii. ELMER

54. CATHERINE⁴ OYER *(Michael³, Frederick²⁻¹)*, born E. Otto 1837, died 1887. She married LYMAN LARABEE, son of Nathan and Delana (Aldrich) Larabee, born 1832; both died Pleasant Prairie, Wisc. 1906.

Ch: (LARABEE)

     i. CELIA ELISA⁵, b 1860
    ii. WELBY A, b 1863; d 14 Dec 1938; m BELLE _____

*** *THE LARABEE FAMILY* ***

The Larabee/Larrabee family whose 3 sons m 3 Oyer sisters, daus of Michael⁴ (Jacob³, Frederick²⁻¹) have this ancestry:
ELEAZOR LARABEE⁶ (Eleazor⁵, Willett⁴, Thomas³, Greenfield²⁻¹) b 3 Aug 1756, m MARY GRANT (she b 15 Sept 1767, d 28 May 1835), d E Otto Catt Co 18 Jan 1834(37?); served in the Rev. He brought 5 sons and 4 daus from Hamburg, Erie Co to E Otto, Catt Co in 1824. 4 of the sons were m and had families: Miner, Thomas, NATHAN and Ira. Sidney/Sydney L, the fifth son, b Oneida Co, m Lorinda Scovel later, she b Orwell, Vt 15 Feb 1810, dau of Hezekiah Scovel, who settled in E Otto 1822.
Nathan³'s sons NELSON, GEORGE and LYMAN m MICHAEL³ OYER's daus ROXANNE, SARAH and CATHERINE. Nathan had 1 dau Emeline, b E Otto 23 Jul 1821, m 1st Rev. Job Strong Leonard, m 2nd Andrew Crumb. Her ch Fernando and Job Sidney Leonard by 1st husb were raised by Nathan and wife as Andrew chose not to raise them. She d 18 Sept 1849 E Otto. in 1850 Nathan and Delana Larabee have listed with them Nelson, 26; George, 22; Lyman, 22; Roxana Oyer, 19; Chauncy S Crumb, 25, Fernando F Leonard, 8; Job S Leonard, 5; and Emeline Crumb, 9/12. Job helped to capture Jefferson Davis, president of the Confederacy, during the Civil War. He lived in Pleasant Prairie, Wisc; Haddam, Kan; E Otto; and Ellvl, but d at the home of inf Jessie Buller in LV 1934.
Thomas⁷, b Oneida Co, m Hester Babcock (d 1844). Thomas d Feb 1857. He received a land grant in E Otto for his service in the War of 1812. His son Joseph⁸ Larabee, b 1833, m a fourth Oyer sister, ANGELINE, at Pleasant Prairie, Wisc in 1861. Other

ch: Anson, Albert, Elmira, Thomas G, Sarah, Dolly, Elizabeth, Francis, b 11 Feb 1828, Hiram and Deloss. Thomas d Lake Co, Ill Feb 1857. Francis was a supervisor and justice of the peace in Mansfield, Catt Co.

Pheobe, a dau of Eleazor[5or6], m Caleb Pearce who came to E Otto 1821; a Polly m Solomon Clark.

7 Larabee and 7 Leonard cousins served in the Civil War; only 7 of the 14 returned. There are 17 Larabees bur in E Otto Cem. An Eleazor was justice of the peace in Ellvl ca 1880. There are 2 Eleazors listed in the 1870 Ellvl census, 1 ae 35, 1 ae 61 with wife Mary A, ae 65. At one time there were 40 Larabee voters in E Otto.

Between 1858 and 1869 there were 17 land transfers in Catt Co, with the Larabees selling the land. The land grants procured as a result of the Civil War are no doubt responsible for the migration of these families westward.

[Sources: Adams' Catt; Larabee Inf 1 & 2. #2 has done extensive Larrabee research, his line being Philander Densloe Larrabee, b Catt Co 13 Dec 1832, d Granger, Yakima Co. Wash, m Louisa M Clark 1861, she d 1905 Moscow, Latah Co, Idaho. He believes the f of Philander to be Miner, and has detailed the family. Note he has the 2 "r's" in the spelling.]

55. ANGELINE[4] OYER, (Michael[3], Frederick[2-1]) born Otto/E. Otto, ca. 1840; died Stafford, Kan. She married Pleasant Prairie, Wis. 1861, JOSEPH DELOS LARABEE, son of Thomas and Hester (Babcock) Larabee, born 4 Jan. 1833; died Stafford, Kan. Joseph D. Larabee lived in Ash. where he was in partnership with his brother-in-law Joseph Oyer at Ash. Hollow. In 1865 Joseph is listed as a merchant in Ash.; in 1875 he is listed as a butter dealer living next door to Joseph Oyer. After 16 years in Ash., the family moved to Sprvl where they lived for 5 years. In 1886 they moved to Stafford, Kan. where he was a banker with his sons. [See The Larabee Family and #54 and #56.]

Ch: (LARABEE) both b Ash

    i.   FRANK SHERIDAN[5], b 1864
   ii.   FREDERICK, b ca 1869

[Sources: Larabee Inf 2. Both sons are written up in the Encyc Amer Biog, 19:191 and 20:55-57.]

56.   NELSON[4] OYER *(William[3], Frederick[2-1])*, born E. Otto 28
Feb. 1837/8 [later census indicates 1842/47]; died Sprvl. 9 Mar
1911, ae. 73 y, 9 d.   He married E. Otto 22 Jan. 1865 NANCY
ANN SMITH, dau. of George and Eliza (King) Smith, born Jan.
1841; died E. Otto 24 Mar. 1914, ae. 73 y., 2 m., 3 d.
  Nelson lived with his parents and grandmother in Ash. and E.
Otto, and after his marriage he resided in E. Otto and farmed.
In 1870 he and Nancy res. Frknvl; Nelson was buried E. Otto.

  Ch (OYER):

    i.   CAROLINE[5], b ca 1869
    ii. ALMAN, ca 1865

57.   EZRA[4] HUFSTADER *(Roxanna[3], Frederick[2-1])*, born E. Otto.
1832; died Ash. 11 Sept 1874.   He married MARY _____.

  Ch (HUFSTADER):

    i.   WILLIAM SEWARD[5], res Ash
    ii.   IDA E, m _____ HAMMOND; res Wales, Erie Co
    iii. ELIZABETH/LIBBY, m _____ HILL; res Otto
    iv.   HERMAN L, res Sprvl

58.   JAMES[4] HUFSTADER *(Roxanna[3], Frederick[2-1])*, born E.
Otto Feb. 1838; died Sprvl 1913.   He married HELEN _____,
born ca. 1841.   In 1870 he is listed as a blacksmith with property
worth $6800, personal worth $1500.   Living with them is Eliza
Hawkins, ae 20, housework.   Helen's name is spelled Hellen in that
record.   [A note: in this era many families often took in an
inmate of Father Baker's Home for Orphans in Buffalo to assist in
the home or on the farms.]

  Ch (HUFSTADER):

    i.   Selian, b ca 1864
    ii. Ina B, b ca 1869

59.   MARY[4] OYER *(John[3], Peter[2], Frederick[1])*, born Schuy.
1820; died Sprvl. 1904.   She married SAMUEL TEFFT, son of Alexander and Deborah (Niles) Tefft, born Otsego Co. 1816; died
Sprvl. 1902; both buried MWC., Samuel came from Otsego Co. with
his parents, 3 brothers and 2 sisters in 1827, settling in E. Otto.
Samuel was a farmer and in 1860 had real estate worth $9780;

personal estate worth $1364; by 1874-5 he owned 485 acres. At that time he was also a partner with his son Emmons operating saw, planing, lath, shingle and feed mills. Living with the family were Catherine Conhiser, 23, serving, b Baden; and John Conhiser, 29, farm laborer, b Baden. By 1880 Samuel is listed as a "retired farmer". The family later moved to Sprvl.

Ch (TEFFT):

    i.   EMMONS D⁵, b 1844, d 1925, m MARTHA L _____, b 1848; d 1923 both bur MWC. He resided with his parents, farming with his father. In 1874-5 he is listed as proprietor of a cheese factory in E Otto, as well as partner with his father in the saw and feed mill business. Concord 1910 census shows dau Gretchen, 22.

    ii.   MARY E, b ca 1848

122. iii. IRA O, b June 1851

123. iv. BYRON S, b June 1855.

*** THE TEFFT FAMILY***

SAMUEL's grandparents were OLIVER and DEBORAH (DEWEY) TEFFT were from Conn. of English descent. Oliver's ch included ALEXANDER, Samuel's f, who was b R I 19 July 1784, came by canal to Bflo and by team to E Otto from Richfield, Otsego Co with wife DEBORAH NILES and 6 ch, settling there in 1827, d there 1868. They located on lot 24 with 225 acres. She was the dau of NATHANIEL and DEBORAH (NILES) NILES. [This is not an error.] Nathaniel was a farmer, Freewill Baptist preacher, and author. He also held town offices. Ch of Alexander: Nathaniel Niles, b Richfield 12 Aug 1812; m 1840 Martha Nichols; he was a surveyor, res E Otto (ch: Emory Nathaniel; Emily Amelia [physician]; Anstice J); Alexander, Jr. res E Otto; Samuel (see #59); Dewey, b ca 1818 (minister Free Methodist, E Otto), d 8 Jan 1892, m Harriet _____; Deborah A., Polly (m _____ Donaghue, living in 100th y, 1879); Oliver D; and Olive (m Solomon Steele, preacher Free Methodist, ministering to congregations in several Catt Co towns).

Oliver's other ch were: Samuel, Oliver, Staunton, William Pitt, Deborah and Polly (m Donaghue), she alive in 1879 and in her 100th year.

[There is confusion here, 2 sources differing. Everts' Catt, p 307, says Oliver's ch are Alexander, Samuel, Oliver, Staunton, William Pitt, Deborah and Polly (Donaghue). Adam's list isn't complete; Briggs' data follows.]

*The spring of 1828 the sons Niles, Alex, Samuel and Dewey all
went to Sprvl, Erie Co and brought back 4 bags of apple pumice.
From this were obtained seeds which were planted and a nursery
of 10,000 apple trees were grown. By 1879 over 1,100 were
bearing fruit. Niles began surveying in 1829, "and so great was
the demand upon his time that he made it his principal business."
[Everts' Catt, p 298]*

*In 1877 the apple crop of E Otto realized about $30,000, a vast
amount for that era.*

*Dewey, a minister, N N. and Samuel Teffts and their wives
were organizers and first members of the Free Methodist Church,
E Otto. Prior to 1879 Samuel and Dewey lived about three-
quarters of a mile apart, near the old homestead. They measured
the distance and built a school house just half-way between the 2
houses and hired a lady, graduate of Oberlin College, to teach
their 4 children. She remained about 5 years.*

*Nathaniel Niles Tefft mastered math at a young age. "His love
of study led him to adopt teaching for some years, his success
being remarkable." In addition to this and his surveying, he was
chosen in 1869 to copy the Holland Land Company's field notes
and draw maps for the use of the county offices of Catt. This
was done "to the great satisfaction of the admirers of the useful
and the beautiful. ...a lasting monument to his memory."
[Everts' Catt, p 307]*

*William Pitt Tefft was a musician in the War of 1812, received a
land grant, m 1st Ruth Ann Wheaton; 2nd, her sister Susan.
Stephen E, b Newport, Herk Co 1813, went to Erie Co 1852, father
and mother b Conn, m 20 Mar 1850 Caroline Jenkins, b Herk Co 2
Aug 1828, father b Wales, mother b NJ, ch: Erastus, b Erie Co
1858; Carrie, b Erie Co 1860 (teacher by 1880); Alice M, b Erie Co
1865. These ch not at home at time of census: Ruth Ann, b 30
Sept 1850, d 27 Aug 1863; George E, b 10 Nov 1851, m Alice
Vedder 20 May 1874; Franklin, b 7 June 1853, d 8 Nov 1862; Alma,
b 7 Nov 1854, d 19 Aug 1863.*

*1860 E Otto census lists Dewey Tefft, ae 42; Harriet T, ae 36;
and Harriet Nichols, ae 7.*

*Walter Tefft was an officer in Otto's IOOF Lodge; m Leonora
Botsford, dau of Wiley S, gr dau of Daniel. Wiley, b 3 Mar 1827,
m 9 Nov 1846 Eliza M Ballard, dau of Adam Ballard of Otto.*

Royal Tefft was supervisor of LV, Catt Co 1819-20.

In 1892 St census we find George Tefft, 41; Alice, 41.

*In Ash 1915 St census we find Charles A Tefft, 37; Mary A, 36;
Allice, 14; Stanley, 12.*

[Sources: LM, Adams' Catt, Everts' Catt, Briggs; CCHM]

60.   SALLY⁴ OYER *(John³, Peter², Frederick¹)*, born Schuy., Herk. Co. 29 Feb. 1822; died Ash., 17 Nov. 1897; buried FrktC. She married 1st JACOB FRANK.   Sally married 2nd WILLIAM SMITH, born Orange Co., ca. 1811.

In the Ash. 1880 census, Sally is living with her mother Charity Oyer, as is Charity's grandson Frederick Smith, age 24; Charity Woodruff, age 22, grandaughter and Richard Conhiser, grandson, age 14.

Ch (FRANK) of 1st marriage:

	i.	RICHARD⁵, b 5 Feb 1840, d Ash 26 July 1862, bur FrktC
	ii.	FRANKLIN, b 20 Aug 1843, d 18 Dec 1865, bur FrktC. He enlisted, Sept 1863, for 3 yrs as private in the 64th NY Regt.
	iii.	SARAH, b ca 1844. In 1860 she is listed living with her uncle Hiram Oyer.
124.	iv.	CLARISSA, b 3 Oct 1844
	v.	HIRAM P, b ca 1848
	vi.	ARLIN, b ca 1853; m _____ FULLER.

Ch (SMITH) of 2nd marriage:

	vii.	FREDERICK, b ca 1856
	viii.	CHARITY b ca 1857; m _____ WOODRUFF

61.   BETSEY⁴ OYER *(John³, Peter². Frederick¹)*, born Schuy., Herk. Co. 6 Sept. 1824; died Ellvl. 21 Sept. 1908; buried FrktC. She married 1st LEVI OYER.   [For their children see #47]

She married 2nd JOHN A. VEDDER, son of Jacob F. and Margaret P. (Gardinier) Vedder, born Mont. Co. 3 Sept. 1818; died Ellvl., Catt. Co. 7 Apr. 1870; buried FrktC.

John A. Vedder's first wife was Betsey's sister Rachel Oyer; his sister Rachel married Peter D. Oyer (#25).

Ch (VEDDER):

127.	i.	MARY ELLEN⁵, b 29 Apr 1857

62.   ADELINE⁴ OYER *(John³. Peter². Frederick¹)*, born Schuy., Herk. Co. 13 Dec. 1825; died Ash. 14 Jan. 1885; buried FrktC. She married 1st CORNELIUS VEDDER, son of Albert and Mary/Polly (Seaman) Vedder, born Feb. 1815; died 10 Aug. 1871.   He was a hotel keeper.   He was located in Ellvl [1860]; in Ash [1865].

Adeline married 2nd _____ CRANDALL. In 1880 she was living with her sister Philinda Holden.

Ch (VEDDER):

    i.   CHARLES[5], b ca 1847
    ii. CHARITY, b June 1849; d Ash 20 Nov 1876, ae 27 y, 5 m; bur FrktC, Ash. She m HERBERT EUGENE BALLOU, b E Otto 1848; d 1922; bur SHC. He fought in Co A, 100th NY Vols in the Civil War; later years he was a bee-keeper and taxidermist in Ellvl. He m 2nd MATIE FOX.
    iii. JANETTE, b 2 Oct 1851; d 7 Feb 1880, ae 28 y, 4 m, 5 d; bur FrktC; m WILLIAM J DAY

63.   HIRAM[4] OYER *(John[3], Peter[2], Frederick[1])*, born Schuy., Herk. Co. 18 June 1827; died Ash. 25 Mar 1880, ae. 53 y., 22 d.; buried FrktC. He married Ash. 1 Aug. 1848 MARY FRANK, born Ash. 18 June 1827; died Ash. 25 Mar. 1887; buried FrktC.
Hiram came to Ash. ca. 1828 and spent his life on a farm near that of his father's and near his sisters in Ash. In 1874 he was town assessor owning 114 acres. Franklin Frank, 11 year old nephew, was living with them in Ash. [1855 St. census] Hiram's will was probated 12 Aug. 1880; heirs were sisters and nieces.

Ch:

    i.   JANETTE[5]/JANE A OYER, (adopted), b Erie Co ca 1854; d 1880
    ii. ALBERT WOODRUFF, (adopted), b 1856 or 1862. He is listed in   Ash 1905 St census, ae 45.
    iii. HATTIE, m DUANE LINTS

[For more Woodruff data, see #'s 112, 182, 183.]

64.   RACHEL[4] OYER *(John[3], Peter[2], Frederick[1])*, born Ash., Catt. Co. 1 Jan. 1829; died Ash. 24 July 1854; buried FrktC. She married 2 Mar. 1848 JOHN A. VEDDER, son of Jacob F. and Margaret P. (Gardinier) Vedder, born Mont. Co. 3 Sept. 1818; died Ellvl. 7 Apr. 1870; buried FrktC. He married 2nd Rachel's sister BETSEY, widow of Levi Oyer; his sister Rachel married Peter D. Oyer (#25).

Ch (VEDDER):

125.   i.   ADALIZA E5, b 15 June 1849
126.   ii. ALICE, b 19 Jan 1852
       iii. RACHEL A, b 12 July 1854; m _____ CLARK

65. PHILINDA⁴ OYER *(John³, Peter², Frederick¹)*, born Ash., 7 Sept. 1831; died 1917. She married 4 July 1848 WILLIAM A. HOLDEN, son of Arnold and Patience (Pam_____) Holden (both born in Mass.), born 10 Mar. 1827; died 1912; both buried FrktC.

William is listed as carpenter, residing in Ellvl. in 1850. From 1865 on he is listed as a farmer in Ash. residing near the John P. Oyer homestead. In 1870 he is listed in Ellvl. In 1874–75 William is listed with a WV address, working at the WV Steam Mill Co. In the 1900 and 1910 both William and Flinda ⟨sic⟩ are in Ash.

Ch (HOLDEN):

      i.   BYRON U⁵, b Ash, 19 May 1849; d Ash, 20 Sept 1850; bur FrktC
128.   ii. CHARLES O, b 1850 or 1852
       iii. ELLA P, b 26 Dec 1861; d 30 Sept 1863; bur FrktC.

*** *THE HOLDEN FAMILY* ***

The Holden family descends from GEORGE HOLDEN "of Rev. fame." [Adams' Catt, p 456] A descendant EDWARD had a son ARNOLD who came from N Adams, Jefferson Co; to Aurora, Erie Co; to Ash, Catt Co in 1829. His wife was PATIENCE PAM_____, b Adams, Mass ca 1811, dau of Wm and Martha Pam(_?____). [VR Frklnv] Arnold left Ash i 1865; d intestate Bradford, McKean Co, Penn 26 Mar 1869. Next of kin confirm the ch listed below.

In the census of 1865, widow, age 67, she's res with GEORGE HUGHEY, Jr in Ellvl, part of a large grouping. Such groupings are common in that era as a result of the disruptions of the Civil War. Family members were found living with various related families. It is stated in the gazetteer that 10% of Catt Co's population were casualties in the Civil War. In 1870 she is shown with the Woodruffs. Patience d 25 May 1898 in Frklnv, Catt Co.

Arnold was the supervisor of Ashford in 1831. His children, all living in 1893 were Julia J, m 1845 Allen M Green (his 2nd w), 6 ch, 3 alive in 1893; Jane M, m Noah Pratt, he b 12 June 1832, son of John Pratt. Ch of Jane & Noah: Edwin H, Albert L, Alice B, Edith M; Sarah A, m M Woodworth. Arnold's other ch: John R, b Ash 30 July 1843, enlisted Sept 1861 in Co B, 9th NY Cav, m 18

Jan 1863 Melvina Rush of E Otto, res Frklnv, where he was a director and vice pres of the First National Bank; Amos B of Sparta, Wisc; Martha A, m L C Robbins, Ash; William A, m PHILINDA OYER (#65); Edwin C, Topeka, Kan; Dennison F, Oviatt, Mich; Nelson H, White, S D. Arnold built one of the first framed buildings in Ashford where he had a business of carding wool and dressing cloth, eventually used for manufacturing cloth. It was one of the first of a kind in the county. He held several town offices, and "used his influence to advance the cause of education and the general good of society..." [Adams' Catt, p 456]

A George Holden, 1833-1909, m Betsy Murphy, Sprvl, Erie Co. Ch: May and Robert, b ca 1858 and 1867 resp. [1870 census, Ellvl] He is said to have had 10 bro; one of 2 known is Nelson, who had no children.

George's son Robert is said to be the only one of these Holdens who had children. Robert was b Ash 1866; m 1885 May Ellis. He went to NYC working for the Cunningham carriage firm, moving to Roch about 1895 where he continued working for that early automobile manufacturer. Ch: Helen, Hazel, Lois, Harold, Peter and Ellis. 2 of Robert's sisters were Adelaide and Mary.

Ash VR show a Della Woodruff, b 12 July 1854; d 10 Ja 1919, dau of Leonard and Martha (Holden) Robbins.

Bur in Riceville Cem, Ash are Robert, d 3 Jan 1864, ae 79; Mary, d 28 Dec 1880, ae 80; and Emily, ae 12.

66.   AARON[4] OYER *(John[3], Peter[2], Frederick[1])*, born Ash. ca. 1836. He married ALMIRA _____, born ca. 1842.

Aaron farmed while with his parents. In 1860 he is in a home with his family near the parental homestead. He enlisted in Co. G, 154th Inf. during the Civil War. No record of him is in the wills of either parent; presumably both he and his son died before they did.

Ch (OYER):

i.   JOHN[5], b Ash Aug 1859

[Sources: CCHM; LM; AHA; censuses; Erie Co SR; Everts' Catt; Adams' Catt. For further Ellis detail see Chapter 6.]

67.   IRA[4] OYER *(Jacob[3], Peter[2], Frederick[1])*, born Frkf, Herk. Co. 16 Nov. 1820; died SC, Oswego Co. 28 Feb. 1893. He married 1st 20 Feb. 1851 ELIZABETH HOWE, dau. of Newell and Jane (Snyder) Howe, born SC 19 Aug. 1820; died SC 27 Oct. 1860; both buried WdlnC. Ira married 2nd 12 Apr. 1861 LORETTE/A HOWE,

Elizabeth's sister, born Sandy Creek (hereafter SC), Oswego Co. 20
Apr. 1836; died SC 21 May/June 1885; buried WdlnC.

Ira "started in life for himself at the age of 14 and at his death
owned 336 acres of land." [Churchill's Oswego] As a young man
he worked a farm in Mannsville, Jeff. Co. while living with his
parents. After their move to Onon. Co., Ira retained possession of
the family farm in SC for a number of years. In 1870 he
purchased a farm near the village of Lacona, SC. He was a
prominent farmer in SC, and was a member of Sandy Creek
Masonic Lodge. His death occurred suddenly in the evening.
Walking home from visiting his son Charles he was stricken and
found unconscious after his prolonged absence had caused worry.

Newell Howe was one of the first settlers in the SC area.

Ch (OYER) of 1st m:

129. i. CHARLES H^5, b 7 Oct 1853
      ii. SARAH E, b SC 1855; d SC 5 Dec 1893; bur WdlnC;
           unm; res with her father on his farm north of the
           village of Lacona; member of the SC Baptist Ch

Ch of 2nd m:

130. iii. WILLIAM I AUYER, b Oct 1862
131. iv. LEON J OYER, b 1871
      v. MABEL OYER, b ca 1876; m _____ VAN HORN

68. PETER J.^{4} AUYER (*Jacob^3, Peter^2, Frederick^1*) born Frkf.,
Herk. Co. 25 Oct. 1822; died Jordan, Onon. Co. 12 Aug. 1867;
buried MGC near Jordan (removed from KndmC). He married
BETSEY H. CURTISS, dau. of Wyliss and Betsey (Cline) Curtiss,
born Mt. Washington, Berkshire Co., Mass. 3 Sept. 1825; died
Jordan 1 Aug. 1914; buried MGC. Her brother John K. Curtiss
married his sister Almira Oyer (#69).

Peter was a farmer. He lived in SC for a number of years, but
by 1858 he was living in Van Buren, Onon. Co. On 28 Jan. of
that year his parents deeded him 150 acres of their farm for
$8,000. He later purchased land in the village of Jordan and
moved to a house at 42 N. Main St. shortly before his death. His
will left his property to his wife and daughter, and appoints his
brother-in-law Elisha Curtiss exec. His widow Betsey lived in
Jordan for nearly half a century, renting the Van Buren farm.

Ch (AUYER):

132. i. GERTRUDE ELLA^5, b 18 Sept 1850

Betsy (Curtiss) Auyer; Gertrude (Auyer) Lewis
Edith (Lewis) Craner; Vivus Craner.

69.   ALMIRA⁴ OYER *(Jacob³, Peter², Frederick¹)*, born Schuy.
18 May 1825; died PLymouth, Sheboygan Co., Wis. 1884; buried
Plymouth City Cem.   She married Sept. 1845 JOHN K. CURTISS,
son of Wyliss and Betsey (Cline) Curtiss, born Mt. Washington,
Berkshire Co., Mass., 19 Feb. 1820.   Almira's brother Peter J.
Auyer (#68) married John's sister Betsey. John and Almira lived
in Oswego Co. until Nov. 1860 when they purchased an "extensive
farm" 2 miles south of Plymouth in Wis.

Ch (CURTISS):

i.	JOHN[5]
ii.	JAY
iii.	ROMAINE
iv.	HATTIE
v.	GEORGE
vi.	JEROME

70.   FRANCIS/FRANK L.[4] AUYER *(Jacob[3], Peter[2], Frederick[1])*
born Schuy. 1 June 1827; died Warners, Onon. Co. 20 Feb. 1901;
buried KndmC; married PATIENCE DIADEMA REMINGTON, born
Canada 1831; died Lysander Twp. ca. 8 Mar. 1902; buried WarC.
  Frank Auyer was a farmer and farm laborer. In 1855 he is
found with his wife south of the village of Canton in Cam. Twp.,
Onon. Co. Soon afterward they moved north to the vicinity of SC
in Oswego and Jeff. Counties. They later moved to Wis. for a
few years. In 1880 the family is listed in Elb., Onon. Co. near his
uncle, James Auyer, where he rented a farm. By 1885 he had
moved onto a farm half a mile east of the village of Plainville.
Apparently Frank and his wife divorced. In 1890 Frank was
residing in Cam., presumably with his Uncle James, whose will he
witnessed. After James Auyer's death Frank moved in with his
sister Harriet in Warners. Frank is buried not far from his
parents in KndmC.

Ch (AUYER):

133.	i.	CHARLES JACOB[5], b 26 Aug 1857
	ii.	EDWARD WILLIAM, b Jeff Co 1860; d Meridian, Cayuga Co 1 Mar 1936; bur WarC. Ed Auyer was a farmer and farm laborer all his life; unm; res near the village of Plainville in Lysander Twp, Onon Co during the 1880's. He later resided in Meridian, Ira Twp, Cayuga Co with his sister Nettie (Nellie?). After her death he spent his final months with his nephew Floyd in Meridian.
	iii.	ANNETT G, b 1866; d Meridian 1935; bur WarC
134.	iv.	FRANK A, b Mar 1868
	v.	NELLIE L, b Feb 1880; m _____ TABER; res 309 Portage St, N Canton, Oh in 1931

71.   SIMON[4] AUYER *(Jacob[3], Peter[2], Frederick[1])*, born Schuy.,
Herk. Co. 27 July 1829; died Mannsville, Jeff Co. 14 Aug 1910;

buried WdlnC. He married 1st ROENA B. HANCHETT, dau. of
Daniel G. and Melissa C. (Daniels) Hanchett, born 1831; died
Watertown, Jeff. Co. 1868; buried WdlnC. Simon married 2nd
ANVENETTE BUNCE of Watertown; died Watertown, ae. 72 y.

Simon was engaged in farming in the northern SC area until
around 1865-67, when he moved with his wife to Watertown and
ran a livery stable. In 1885 Simon and his second wife moved to
Ellisburgh Twp., Jeff. Co., where Simon operated a farm of 53
acres 2 miles south of the village of Mannsville.

Ch (AUYER) of 1st m:

i.   LONNIE⁵, d 17 Nov 1859, ae 18 m; bur WdlnC
ii. adopted dau, m J W RICHARDSON of Weedsport,
     Cayuga Co

Ch (AUYER) of 2nd m:

iii. W H, adopted. Anvenette B Auyer's obituary notice
     states: "She brought up W H Auyer, who bears her
     name, although no adoption papers were ever taken
     out."

72. VALENTINE⁴ AUYER *(Jacob³, Peter², Frederick¹)*, born
Schuy., Herk. Co. 25 Aug. 1831. He married 3 July 1851
SOPORONA POTTER, dau. James and Polly (_____) Potter,
born Rodman, Jeff. Co. 1 July 1831; died Evart Twp., Osceola Co.,
Mich. 1 June 1908; buried FHC.

Valentine was a farmer. He and his wife moved from Oswego
Co. to Van Buren Twp., Onon. Co. in 1852, residing on a farm
near his father's. By 1860 the family had moved to SC, where he
was working as a farm laborer. He was living near his brother
Ira Oyer. By 1868 Valentine was back in Onon. Co., leasing 180
acres on Lot 99, Lysander Twp., just north of Jack's Reef. In
1875 the family moved to Hillsdale, Mich.; and in 1884 they moved
to Evart, Mich.

Ch (AUYER):

i.   HELEN⁵, b ca 1857
ii. HARRIET, b ca 1859
iii. KATE A, b ca 1862
iv. FRED, b ca 1865
v.   MARY, b ca 1868; d a few years before her mother;
     m JAMES LAMPHEAR

73.   HARRIET⁴ AUYER *(Jacob³, Peter², Frederick¹),* born Schuy., Herk. Co. 16 Aug. 1833; died Warners, Onon. Co. 12 Oct. 1919; buried WarC. She married 1st Auburn 16 Feb. 1853 HIRAM L. ROE, son of David and Catharine (Van Camp) Roe, born Orleans Co. 2 May 1825; died Elb. 12 May 1861; buried Fairvale Cem., Oswego Bitters.   Harriet married 2nd JAMES H. BUCK, son of Nelson and Sally (_____) Buck, born Cam., Onon. Co. Dec. 1832; died Elb. 5 Mar. 1868, ae. 35 y., 2 m., 13 d.; buried Fairvale Cem.   His son by his 1st wife, DANIEL GOODRICH BUCK, married SUSAN CHRISTINA MCDOWELL.   Harriet married 3rd _____ HALL; no children.

Harriet and her first husband Hiram Roe lived on Lot 50 of Elb., southwest of the village of Canton/Memphis. At first they lived with his parents; later they had their own farm.

James Buck, Harriet's second husband, was raised in the community of Sand Springs (Bangall) in Van Buren Twp., Onon. Co., where his father was a blacksmith and farmer. James tended a bar in a hotel in Canton in 1850. He later farmed in the Sand Springs area. After his marriage to Harriet he resided on the Roe farm. He was a member of the Seneca River Lodge #160, F. & A.M. in Baldwinsville, Onon. Co.

Harriet is listed in 1868 owning 75 acres on Lot 50. In 1870 she is found living in the village of Baldwinsville; her occupation is dressmaker. An 1874 atlas shows her residing in the village of Memphis. She was apparently the widow of Mr. Hall by 1900, when she is listed living (with her brother Francis) in the village of Warners. She made her home there for the rest of her life.

Ch (ROE) of 1st m:

135. i.   ELLA M⁵, b 1856
     ii.   ADA MARY, b Elb Twp, Onon Co 1 Feb 1860; d
             Elb Twp 11 Apr 1868, ae 8 y, 2 m, 11 d; bur
             Fairvale Cem.

Ch (BUCK) of 2nd m, both b Elb:

     iii.   FREDDIE J, b 10 May 1865; d 21 Aug 1865
136. iv.   CORA BELL, b 1 Sept 1866

74.   MARGARET MARY⁴ AUYER *(Jacob³, Peter², Frederick¹),* born 25 Oct. 1835 (apparently originally named Mary Margaret Oyer); died Van Buren 1 June 1922; buried MGC. She married 5 Dec. 1861 JOSEPH HUNTING SOMES, son of Samuel and Mary (Barns) Somes, born Brutus Twp., Cayuga Co. 1 Dec. 1829; died Van Buren Twp. 8 July 1899; buried MGC.

Soon after his marriage, Joseph Somes purchased part of his
father-in-law's farm, purchasing the remainder in 1868. He later
purchased the Edwin McDowell property down the road. He was a
prominent and respected farmer in the area. He was also one of
the principal stock holders of the Jack's Reef Cheese Factory
Association.

After Joseph's death Margaret continued to live in the Somes
house until after the death of her son, H. L. A house was purchased for her on Beaver St. in the village of Jordan and she
moved there for a few years. Her declining health forced her to
move to the home of her son Oren, where she spent her last
years an invalid. She was a devout member of the Memphis
Baptist Church.

Ch (SOMES) both b Van Buren Twp:

137. i.   HENRY LEWIS⁵, b 5 Apr 1863
138. ii.   OREN ALEXIS, b 5 June 1866

75.   ROMAIN/ROMAINE⁴ AUYER *(Jacob³, Peter², Frederick¹),*
born Schuy., Herk. Co. 14 July 1837; died Bath, Steuben Co. 15
Dec. 1907. He married 1860 SYLVIA _____, born ca. 1842-45.

Romain is listed as farm laborer in Elb. Twp. in 1860, living
with married-within-the-year wife, 15 year old Sylvia. During the
Civil War he fought in the 74th Co. L., 9th N.Y. Heavy Artillery.
On 9 Mar. 1866 he purchased a house and lot on Lot 9 of Van
Buren Twp., near his father's farm. In 1892 he and son George
are listed in Elb. Twp. (also in 1892, "Tremaine Auyer" is listed in
Cato Twp.). In 1905 he is found again in Van Buren. His
occupation was either farmer or farm laborer. His last years were
spent at the Soldier's and Sailor's Home at Bath, Steuben Co.,
where he died. Survivng him were his wife Sylvia and son
Adelbert, whose whereabouts were "unknown".

Ch (AUYER):

i.   WILLIS⁵, b ca 1860   A Willis and Flossie Auyer pur-
        chased land at Westbury, Victory Twp, Cayuga Co in
        the 1920's.
                a) LELAND⁶; minister; last address Portland,
                   Ore
139. ii.   ADELBERT, b 1862
     iii.   EMMA, b 1864
     iv.   BURTIE, b 1868
     v.   ELIJAH, b ca 1878, poss the Elijah ae 14 found in
             the 1892 census of Cato Twp, Cayuga Co.

vi.   GEORGE, b 1872 or Sept 1879; d 1961; bur Fair-
mount Cem, Red Creek, Wayne Co. Listed ae 12 y
with father in Elb in 1892 st census; listed as
farm laborer residing with the Jesse Hubbard
family in Lysander Twp in the 1900 Census, employed there 4 months.

76.   FOSTER JACOB⁴ AUYER *(Jacob³, Peter², Frederick¹)*, born
SC Twp., Oswego Co. 8 July 1845; died Van Buren, Onon. Co. 21
Mar. 1899; buried KndmC (no stone). He married 29 Dec. 1864
JOSEPHINE MARVIN, dau. of Asher T. and Elsie (Wilcox) Marvin;
born Van Buren Twp. 3 Mar. 1847; died Van Buren, 17 Feb. 1934;
buried WarC.
In 1868 Foster leased 48 acres from his father on Lot 16, Van
Buren Twp.; in 1870 he is listed in the same house (then owned by
his brother-in-law Joseph Somes) as laborer. In 1880 he is found
near his uncle James Auyer in Elb. By 1888 he was in the
Kingdom District of Van Buren Twp. Foster farmed all his life.
After his death his widow lived on in Van Buren for several years;
her last years were spent with dau. Harriet near Warners.

Ch (AUYER) all but Joseph b Van Buren Twp:

        i.   ELISHA J⁵, b 1866; d Van Buren Twp, 26 June
               1921; bur Riverview Cem, Baldwinsville. Elisha was
               a farm laborer in the Van Buren vicinity.   He
               worked for his brother Peter Auyer for a number of
               years.   He drowned in the Seneca R west of the
               village of Baldwinsville.
140. ii.   PETER J, b 3 Nov 1867
      iii.   MARY E/Matie, b Nov 1868; d Van Buren Twp 10
               Aug 1921; bur WarC. Matie was a domestic servant
               in the family of Cora and Eugene Marvin (her aunt)
               in Warners for a number of years around the turn of
               the century.   She was later a house mother at
               Acacia Fraternity at Syracuse Univ. Her last years
               were spent with bro Peter.
141. iv.   ALONZO L, b 1872
141.1 v.   HARRIET MAY, b 8 Aug 1878
       vi.   JACOB A, b Dec 1879; d Syracuse. Onon Co 21 Oct
               1905; bur WarC.   Jacob was a farmer who lived
               most of his life in Van Buren Twp.   The last 5
               months of his life were spent in Syracuse.
      vii.   JOSEPH W, b Elb Twp July 1883; d Van Buren Twp 30
               Jan 1888. bur KndmC (no stone). Joseph d while his
               parents res in the Kingdom District.

Foster Jacob⁴ Auyer (1845–1899).

77.   JOHN F.⁴ CAIN *(Margaret³, Peter², Frederick¹)*, born
Schuy. ca. 1820. He married 1st MARY JANE _____, born 22
Oct. 1830; died SC, 30 Jan. 1849, ae. 18 y, 3 m, 12 d; buried
WdlnC. He married 2nd HANNAH _____, born ca. 1823. John
lived in SC for a short time.   After his first wife's death he
returned to Schuy. Twp, where he farmed near his grandfather
Peter Oyer's farm. In 1860 he is listed as a farm laborer in SC
near his cousin Ira Oyer.

    Ch (CAIN) all from 2nd m:

i.   HENRY[5], b ca 1852
ii.   MARY J, b ca 1853
iii. LAWYER, b ca 1855

78.   DANIEL C.[4] ELLIS *(Margaret[3], Peter[2], Frederick[1])*, born
Schuy. 1827; died Amboy Twp., Oswego Co., 1876; buried WmstC.
He married LYDIA MARIA FOSTER, dau. of Ardin H. Foster, born
Amboy Twp. ca 1832.
  In 1855 Daniel Ellis, farmer, and his wife are listed living with
the family of his father-in-law Ardin Foster in Amboy Twp. Also
living with them were Daniel's brothers Solomon and Samuel.

Ch (ELLIS) all b Amboy Twp:

i.   ALICE M FOSTER[5], b Nov 1854; d 1886; bur WmstC
ii.   FRANCES IMOGENE, b 1856; d Amboy Twp, 1877;
      bur WmstC
iii. CHARLOTTE E, b ca 1859
iv.   ROSWELL M, b ca 1861
v.   WILLIAM N, b ca 1864
vi.   DANIEL, Jr, b ca 1868

79.   SOLOMON[4] ELLIS *(Margaret[3], Peter[2], Frederick[1])*, born
Schuy. 1832; died Wmst. 1923; buried WmstC. He married MARY E.
_____, born Oswego Co. 1837; died 1926; buried WmstC.
  Solomon accompanied his family from Oneida Co. to Amboy Twp.
in about 1846. He worked as a farm laborer all his life, beginning
with his father and in 1855, after his father's death, he boarded
with his brother Daniel as part of a large family headed by
Daniel's father-in-law, Arlin Foster; later in Amboy; finally to
neighboring Wmst. Twp.

Ch (ELLIS):

i.   SARAH A[5], b Amboy Twp 13 Feb 1859; d Amboy
      Twp 27 Aug 1867, ae 8 y, 6 m, 14 d; bur WmstC
ii.   ELLA G, b Amboy Twp 18 Aug 1861; d Amboy Twp,
      10 Aug 1867, ae 5 y, 11 m, 23 d; bur WmstC
iii. JOHN B, b 1871; d 1921 He m KATHRYN _____,
      b 1872; d 1920. Both bur WmstC
iv.   GEORGE W, b 1873; d 9 Aug 1875, ae 2 y
v.   CORA I, (adopted) m _____ RICE, res Okmulgee,
      Okla 1923

80.   SAMUEL⁴ ELLIS *(Margaret³, Peter², Frederick¹)*, born Schuy. Twp. ca. 1833.   He married 1st HARRIET A. _____, died Amboy Twp. 2 Jan. 1860, ae. 21 y, 2 m; buried WmstC.   He married 2nd MARTHA NICHOLS, dau. of Michael Nichols, born Herk. Co. ca. 1837.

Samuel accompanied his family to Amboy Twp. in about 1846 and worked on his father's farm, later doing so when living with his brother Daniel.   After his marriage he is found farming in Amboy.

Ch (ELLIS) of 2nd m:

   i.   SARAH A⁵, b Amboy Twp Jan 1864

81.   FRANCES SANTONETTE⁴ ELLIS *(Margaret³, Peter²,* *Frederick¹)*, born Schuy. Twp. ca. 1837; died Amboy Twp. 28 Mar. 1863; buried WmstC.   She married DANIEL TOMPKINS VALENTINE, son of Ebenezer and Silvia (Adams) Valentine, born Schuy. 1834; died 10 Dec. 1893, ae. 59 years.

Ch (VALENTINE):

   i.   ORRIN⁵, d y
  ii.   ROSIE, d y

82.   DELANY⁴ REMA *(Elizabeth³, Peter², Frederick¹)*, born ca. 1821.   She married PETER WEAVER, Jr., son of Peter and Charity (_____) Weaver, born ca. 1820.   Peter was a farmer.   In 1850 he is listed residing next to his father (also a farmer) in Frkt. Twp.   He later moved to Waterloo, Seneca Co.

Ch (WEAVER) all b Frkt Twp:

   i.   SIMON P⁵, b ca 1844
  ii.   GEORGE H, b ca 1847
 iii.   LEWIS F, b ca 1849

83.   MARTHA JANE⁴ AUYER *(James³, Peter², Frederick¹)*, born Elb. Twp. 27 May 1829; died Elb. 11 Nov. 1867; buried MGC (removed from Fairvale Cem.).   She married 9 Nov. 1857 ORANGE ANGELL TIFFT, son of Caleb, Jr. and Jane (Alcorn) Dunlap Tifft, born SC, 26 June 1829; died Delmar, Albany Co. 24 Jan. 1923; buried MGC.

Just after their marriage, Orange and Martha made their home with her parents in Cam. They soon moved onto the farm next door (in Elb Twp.), where he farmed for many years. He was a Republican involved in politics, a member of Jordan Masonic Lodge and a long-time member of Memphis Baptist Church. O.A. Tifft died at the home of dau. Carrie Mead at Delmar, Albany Co.

Ch (TIFFT):

142. i.   WILLIAM CARLTON⁵, b 29 Sept 1858
143. ii.   CARRIE LOUISE, b 29 May 1860
152. iii. HENRIETTA MARY, b 9 May 1862
144. iv.   JENNIE BELLE, b 6 Feb 1865

84.   SARAH ANN⁴ AUYER *(James³, Peter², Frederick¹)*, born Elb. Twp. 1830; died DeWitt Twp., Onon. Co. 30 Dec. 1905; buried WdlnC, Syracuse, Onon Co.   She married THEODORE O. WILSON, died Syracuse, 1890.

Theodore lived in Syracuse in a house owned by Sarah's father. He was a paperhanger and interior painter; in later years he is listed as agent.   After his death Sarah lived at various locations in Syracuse, and with her father in Cam. for a time.

Ch (WILSON):

   i.   MARTHA⁵, m GEORGE A MANN, res in 1900 Syracuse
   ii. CHARLES S

85.   MARY E.⁴ AUYER *(James³, Peter², Frederick¹)*, born Elb. Twp. 1833; died Cam. Twp. 11 Oct. 1884, ae. 51 y; buried Fairvale Cem.   She married THEODORE H. BATES, son of Wilson and Margaret (_____) Bates, born Columbia Co., May 1831; died Cam. 13 Oct. 1866, ae. 35 y. 4 m. 16 d.; buried Fairvale Cem.

Theodore was a farmer residing in Cam. south of the village of Canton/Memphis.   After his death his widow moved to that village and later lived with her father.   In 1880 she was listed as having consumption, as tuberculosis was then called.

Ch (BATES):

   i.   HATTIE H⁵, b Cam Twp, 1857; d Cam Twp, 9 Jan 1865, ae 7 y, 5 m; bur Fairvale Cem

86.   EMILY AMELIA⁴ AUYER *(James³, Peter², Frederick¹),* born Cam. Twp. 9 Nov. 1843; died Van Buren Twp. 1933; buried WarC.   She married 1st SULLIVAN WHITNEY, son of Jerome and Catharine (_____) Whitney, born Elb. Twp. ca. 1844; died Elb. Twp. 1 Nov. 1871.   Emily married 2nd at Memphis 18 Sept. 1872 GEORGE MARTIN MARLETTE, son of John and Margaret (Comstock) Marlette, born Fulton, Oswego Co. 20 Jan. 1829; died Memphis 12 Apr. 1921, ae. 90 y, 9 m, 22 d; buried WarC.

Emily and Sullivan made their home on the Whitney farm on Lot 50 of Elb., across the road (Hall Road) from the James Auyer farm.   This farm was purchased by James Auyer and given to his daughter.   She also lived there with her second husband George Marlette, who had served as a private in Co. H of the 2nd Regiment of Wis. Vol. Inf. in the Civil War.   About 1918 they moved to a house in the village of Memphis, where George died. In 1925 Emily was living with her daughter Belle in a house along West Dead Creek Road in Van Buren.

Ch (WHITNEY) of 1st m, all b Elb Twp:

145. i.   ADA L⁵, b 1865
146. ii.   LENA R, b ca 1866
147. iii.   STELLA MAY, b 14 May 1868
148. iv.   JAY J, b 1871

Ch (MARLETTE) of 2nd marriage, both b Elb Twp:

149. v.   HARRY GEORGE, b 24 June 1875
150. vi.   BELLE HATTIE, b 20 June 1884

87.   JULIA ANN⁴ AUYER *(Solomon³, Peter², Frederick¹),* born Elb. Twp. Sept. 1931; died Jack's Reef, Van Buren Twp. 4 Sept. 1905; buried MGC.   She married 26 Feb. 1851 EDWIN MCDOWELL, adopted son of Henry, Jr. and Susan (Marshall) McDowell, born Cam. Twp. 25 Oct. 1828; died Jack's Reef, 27 June 1908; buried MGC.

Edwin was a farmer.   For many years after his marriage he and his wife lived on the Henry McDowell farm southeast of Canton/Memphis in Cam. Twp. along Canal Road.   In 1857 the family, including the elder McDowell and his wife, moved to a farm on Lot 17 of Van Buren at the corner of Daboll and River Roads.   This was later sold to the Somes family.

In 1872 Edwin purchased a farm in Jack's Reef and eventually moved there.   He held several posts with the Van Buren Twp. government, including that of Town Supervisor in 1884-85.   He was secretary of the Jack's Reef Cheese Factory Association and a member of the Christian Church at Memphis.

Julia (Auyer) and Edwin McDowell.

Ch (MCDOWELL) 1st two b Cam., others b Van Buren:

i.   WILLIS G⁵, b 23 Feb 1854; d Syracuse 26 Jan 1908. He m Syracuse 27 Aug 1884 LIBBIE LEROW, b ca 1860; d Indian Castle, Herk Co 19 Nov 1889, ae. 29 y.; both bur WdlnC. Willis was the first graduate of Jordan High School (1872) and also graduated from Cornell Univ (1876). He was appointed to a clerkship in the Onon Co Clerk's Office in 1879 and rose to become Special Deputy Clerk.

ii. FLORA B⁵, b 1 Mar 1856; d Van Buren Twp 10 Jan 1895; m 6 Feb 1879 FRANK REUBEN SPAULDING, son of George Brown and Hannah (Kester) Spaulding, b Van Buren Twp 5 Feb 1856; d Jordan 26 Apr 1929; both bur Elb Rural Cem. Frank was a farmer who res near the community of Ionia in Van Buren Twp. Flora and he made their home with his

parents. After her death Frank m a 2nd time and
moved to the village of Jordan.

[For more Spaulding data see Chapter 9]

151. iii. HENRY AUYER, b 8 Feb 1859
152. iv.   ELMER ELLSWORTH, b 16 Mar 1861
153. v.   SUSAN CHRISTINA, b 12 Apr 1863
     vi.   JENNIE MAY, b 26 Nov 1867; d Van Buren Twp 27
           Sept 1947; m Jordan 12 Dec 1900 HENRY HOBART
           DABOLL, son of Henry and Charlotte (Goodwin)
           Daboll, b Van Buren Twp 5 Apr 1847; d Van Buren
           Twp 25 Aug 1932; both bur MGC. Jennie was
           Hobart Daboll's 2nd wife. He was a very prominent
           and well-to-do farmer in Van Buren, res on a farm
           along Daboll Road in the Pine Hill District. He was
           a member of Christ (Episcopal) Church in Jordan.
           The Daboll's owned land in Lakeland, Fla and spent
           their winters there.
     vii. CORA ELIZABETH, b 10 May 1870; d Van Buren
           Twp 19 Apr 1941; bur MGC, unm. She lived with
           her parents, and after their deaths with her sister
           Jennie Daboll.

88.   CYRUS DAVID⁴ AUYER (*Solomon³, Peter², Frederick¹*),
born Elb. Twp. ca. 1843; died Minn. He married 1st ALICE A.
LYON, dau. of Lewis B. and Susannah (_____) Lyon, born
Ionia, Van Buren Twp. ca. 1849; death n/a.

In 1850 Cyrus is listed living with his father and sisters in Elb.
In 1854 he went to work for his Uncle Daniel Auyer in Schuy.,
Herk Co. as a farm laborer; he was listed there in 1855. He later
returned to Onon. Co. and is identified as of Cam. in 1864 when
he deeded land to his Uncle James. Cyrus lived in the Memphis
area during his short marriage to Alice Lyon; by 1870 they had
separated. Cyrus moved out to Little Falls, Minn. with a woman
from Jordan whom he eventually married. In Minn. he apparently
did quite well, became wealthy. He entered politics. He was also
editor of the Little Falls Gazette.

Alice returned to her father's home in Ionia, Onon. Co. In
1870 she and her dau. are listed there; she is also listed as a
housekeeper for the Orange A. Tifft (recently widowed) family.
She later married (_____) Gorton and lived in Ionia.

Ch (AUYER):

154. i.   JESSIE BELLE⁵, b 15 July 1866

89.   CAROLINE⁴ OYER *(Henry⁸, Peter², Frederick¹)*, born 20
Feb. 1837; died 15 Jan. 1926; buried E. Schuy. She married 26 Jan.
1854 SIMON P. FINSTER, son of Philip and Elizabeth Finster, born
Schuy. 10 Nov. 1829; died Schuy. 6 July 1898; buried E . Schuy.
Caroline Oyer is listed in the 1850 census with her parents in
Rome, Oneida Co. and also with her aunt and uncle, Rachel and
Michael Clemens in Schuy.   After her marriage to Simon they
lived with his parents on their farm in Schuy. where he farmed.

Ch (FINSTER) all b Schuy:

   i.   OSCAR E.⁵, b 1855
  ii.   HERBERT, b ca 1867
 iii.   CORA, b ca 1870

90.   EMMALINE⁴ OYER *(Henry⁸, Peter², Frederick¹)*, born ca.
1838.   She married JOHN H. EDMUNDS, 2nd, son of John H. and
Polly (_____) Edmunds, born ca. 1833. Emmaline and John H.
Edmunds are listed living with his parents in Amboy Twp., Oswego
Co., in 1860. His occupation is given as farm laborer. She later
moved to Manchester, Iowa where she was living in 1918.

Ch (EDMUNDS):

   i.   JOHN⁵, b Amboy Twp, ca 1858

91.   EZRA⁴ OYER *(Henry⁸, Peter², Frederick¹)* We are unable
to sort out the EZRAs. One was born Rome Twp. 1844; one was
born July 1848; one was born Schuy. Mar. 1886 or 18 July 1885;
one died 31 Oct. 1926. For an EZRA D., see #96i. An EZRA was
in Oswego (Co.?) in 1918.

92.   ELIZABETH⁴ OYER *'Henry⁸, Peter², Frederick¹)*, born
Rome Twp. 1844 [1849 per g.s.]; died Schuy. Twp. 1922; buried
MRC. She married JOHN H. HULSER, born 1841; died 7 Apr. 1922;
buried MRC.

Ch (HULSER):

   i.   IRVING E/F⁵, b Schuy Twp, 1877; d Schuy 1944; bur
      MRC
  ii.   EZRA W, b Schuy Twp, 1882; d 1951; bur MRC
 iii.   ADA, d 25 Dec 1898

(Left) John H. and Elizabeth⁴ (Oyer) Hulser family marker. 1841-1922
1849-1922   1877-1944   1882-1951 MRC, E. Schuyler Schuyler, N.Y.
(Right) Oyer monument, MRC.

93. DEWITT⁴ (MILETTE?) OYER (*Henry³, Peter², Frederick¹*),
born Rome, Oneida Co. Mar. 1850; married ca. 1870 MARY _____,
born May 1852. DeWitt is listed [1900 census] with his family in
Rome and Amboy, Oswego Co., a day laborer and owning a house.

Ch (OYER):

   i.   ELLA⁵, b 2873; d 1926; m THOMAS WORDEN
  ii. JANE, b Mar 1877; in 1900 with parents in Schuy,
       indicated as having been m 5 y; no husband listed;
       occupation seamstress

94. GEORGE HENRY⁴ OYER, (*Henry³, Peter², Frederick¹*) born
Rome, Oneida Co. 26 Sept. 1854; died 4 Apr. 1922. He married
SARAH H. BEARDSLEY.

Ch: (OYER)

    i.   EMERY[5]
    ii. CELIA
    iii. BERTHA
    iv. CATHARINE
155. v.   ANSON BEARDSLEY, b 24 Jan 1899

95. MARY L.[4] CLEMENS, *(Rachel[3], Peter[2], Frederick[1])* born
Schuy. 1843; died Schuy. 1922; buried MRC. She married GEORGE
H. STORMES, born 1843; died 1920; buried MRC. George and Mary
are listed in 1870 living with his wife's parents in Schuy. His
occupation is given as railroad brakeman.

    Ch: (STORMES)

    i.   OSCAR E[5], b Schuy ca 1868

96. OSCAR W.[4] OYER, *(Daniel[3], Peter[2], Frederick[1])* born Schuy.
Twp. 8 Dec. 1858/59; died 1934; buried MRC. He married 1st 21
Dec. 1882 ANNA WELDON, born Schuy. Mar. 1835; died Schuy. 3
Nov. 1918 (the flu epidemic again??); buried MRC. Gravestone
shows Anna's birth/death dates as 1860 and 1929?. Oscar married
2nd EMMA HULSER, born 1894; died 1967 buried MRC. Oscar
(O.W.) resided on the old Oyer homestead that had originally
been settled by his great-grandfather Frederick Oyer. He owned
a farm of 158 acres, a cheese factory and saw mill. He was called
"one of the most enterprising and progressive young farmers of
Schuy." George, Oscar and Emma's firstborn, helped with his
brothers as Oscar died when Donald was but 1 year old.

    Ch (OYER) of 1st m, both b Schuy:

    i.   EZRA[5], b Mar 1886.

[This may be the Ezra D who m JULIA A DEELEY of Ostrander
St., Syracuse. Julia d 9 Mar 1987 at the Loretto Geriatric Center
as noted in the Syracuse Post Standard, weekend of 14-15 Mar.
She was 99 y; a native of Oneida; her husb d 1962; surviving are
son Kenneth of Spartanburg, S C; sister Mary Paddock of Baldwinsville; bur Onon Valley Cem. Mary was in a nursing home,
having res 73 E Oneida St, unable to provide data. A Julia,
retired (seamstress?) is in Syracuse city dir; an Ezra listed at 121
Longbeach Circle. In Herk Co LR, 283:78, an Ezra D is shown
with wife of Syracuse, reserving 12 acres for RACHEL OYER. For
other EZRA data see #91]

ii.   EVA, b May 1888 (25 Sept 1887?); m RAY CALHOUN.

Ch (OYER) of 2nd m:

156. iii.   GEORGE, b 10 May 1925
157. iv.   EARL, b 1928
158. v.   LESTER, b 8 Feb 1931
159. vi.   DONALD, b 26 Apr 1933

[Source for #67 through #97: AHA]

Gravestone Oscar[4] and Anna (Weldon) Oyer, MRC; shows date discrepancies.

CHAPTER 10

FIFTH GENERATION

97.   CLARK E.[5] OYER, *(Peter[4], David[3], Jacob[2], Frederick[1])*, born Frklnv., Catt. Co. 4 July 1836; died Los Angeles, Calif. 29 Apr. 1923. He married 1st Alpena, Mich. 26 June 1871 SARAH DAVIS; div'd St. Cloud, Minn. Oct. 1886.   He married 2nd Coeur d'Alene, Idaho 12 July 1909 ELLEN BURCH.

Civil war records describe Clark as 5'7" in height, with a light complexion, blue eyes, and light brown hair. On 18 Aug. 1862 at Jamestown he enlisted as a private in Co. G of the 154th Reg. of N.Y. Volunteers. He was eventually promoted to sergeant, but his military career was filled with hardships. In Jan. 1863 at Fredericksburg, Va. he hurt his back and was excused from duty on and off for the next 6 months. He fought at the Battle of Gettysburg, Penn., and 1 July 1863 was taken prisoner. While being held at Richmond, Va. he became afflicted with the problem of chronic diarrhea; during his 33 day imprisonment he received no treatment for this. From Richmond he was taken to Annapolis, Md., and thence to Camp Row, near Alexandria, Va. He rejoined his regiment at Bridgeport, Ala.

For the next 15 months he was treated for his sickness. While fighting outside of Savannah, Ga. 12 Dec. 1864 he was again taken prisoner and held at Savannah Jail until 4 Mar. 1865. During this period he was subjected to cruel and inhuman treatment, and upon his release was emaciated and unable to return to duty. He was sent to Navy Yard Hospital, Annapolis, for about a month; then received furlough and went home to Ellvl. He returned to Navy Yard Hospital for 15-20 days; then was sent to Wilmington, Del. Hospital until his discharge, which took place at Elmira 6 July 1865.

Returning home to Ellvl. he lived with his father. He was described at this time as thin in flesh, emaciated, and in very poor health and weak. He was unable to perform any sort of heavy farm labor because of his back and illness. Family tradition tells of his having to be fed soup by spoonsful to help him overcome the debilitating effects of starvation.

In Oct. 1871 he went to Stillwater, Washington Co., Minn., living there and in other parts of that state during much of the 1880's. He later resided in Mich., Ark., and Orting, Wash. state. He worked as a lumberman and cooked for the lumber camp, as well as other light work.

We can follow Clark's travels through record of his pension payments, the last finding him in Los Angeles, where he died in

1923. Unfortunately, a 1987 check of the county and surrogate records of that city proved fruitless in locating his children.

We are fortunate to have obtained late in 1987 letters written mostly to Jacob Oyer (#26) from family members, including many from Civil War soldiers. One from Clark, written from the "Camp of the 154th N.Y. Vols., Lookout Valley, Tenn., Dec. 15th, 1863" follows [for portion of it, see Illus p 164]:

Dear Uncle and Family,
Yours came to hand yesterday. I was glad you were in such good spirits and have plenty of eggs and potatoes but I shall be obliged to decline your invitation for the pressent at least. A furlough I would not take if I had the chance and my term of enlistment has not half expired yet.   So you will have a chance to raise potatoes twice yet before you see me unless this cruel war should suddenly come to a terminus.
Well the 23rd of last month we left the Valley and crossed over into Chattanooga and on the 24th made the ground attacks the left centre was [attacked ?] by western troops our right [   ] on their left in line of Battle. We gained a ridge that was not much inferior to old missionary herself. That night we worked making rifle pitts, planting artillery and getting ready for the morning. Well morning came and [   ] Old Joe for he and Genl Thomas took to running the Rebs off Lookout mountain. Something of a job but after 12 hours hard fighting Joe held the mountain.   All this time Genl Sherman was not idle he was on the extreme left and turned their flank in that direction. On the 3 1/2 day our Brigade marched to the extreme left to protect Shermans flank and it was all serene with us. Our Regt did not get the brunt of it in the Battle we only had 9 men wounded in the whole 3 days.   On the fourth we took our line of march in pursuit of the retreating Rebs. Such sights of ammunition and cuisens [   ] corn and corn meal at Chickamunga Station every mud hole chucked full of shell and cuisenter [?], one car load of fixed ammunition [s   ] the truck. Well in we went and had a bully Thanksgiving fresh pork corn meal and molasses coffee and sugar. Well when we got to Talkers ? [   ] two companies of us were detached [dispatched] to [guard ?] prisoners into Chattanooga and then came into our old camp. Remained here untill the 13th of this month then all ordered to guard a waggon train to the corps [confs ?]. I started but had to back out. I have had the Tenn quickstep [diarrhea] so long

that I am pretty weak. If I only had a box of those pills that we used to get I think they would straighten me up again but we dont get any medicine here that is any ac[count] at all.

You asked me how I would like a cemish [commission ?] in a collored Regt. I would accept one for I dont imagine I shall ever get one here our Regt is so small that we cannot muster all the officers that have already got their cemissiens <sic> and have had ever since last July.

The weather has been cloudy and rainy a few days past but now it has cleared again and last night we had a frost.

Good bye write soon
Yours truly
Clark Oyer
Co G 154 N.Y.S. V.
11th A.C. Army
of the Cumberland
Nashville, Tenn.

The "cuisens" apparently refers to food/food supplies.

Ch (OYER), all of 1st m, both alive 10 Mar 1915:

   i.   MATTIE, b Orting, Wash. (?) 31 Mar 1873
  ii. JESSIE, b 22 Jan 1879

98. DAVID SMITH[5] OYER (*Peter[4], David[3], Jacob[2], Frederick[1]*), born Plato, Ellvl. Twp. 26 Apr 1847; died GrV 17 June 1929; buried GrC. He married at the Atlantic House, Sala., Catt. Co., 28 Oct 1876, RUTH ELLEN/ELLA BROWN, dau. of Sheldon P. and Juliaette (Doud) Brown, born Napoli Twp., Catt Co., 2 Feb. 1859; died 175 River St., Salamanca (hereafter Sala.) 10 Apr 1948; buried GrC.

Smith Oyer (as he was known) grew up on his father's farm in Ellvl. As a young man he was a policeman in New York City for a short time; the rest of his life was spent either on his farm in the hamlet of Willoughby, GrV Twp., or in Sala. Smith's father-in-law Sheldon Brown gave him 50 acres of his land in Willoughby, on which he built his house and barn. He later added another 50 acres in Peth, adjoining. This land is still in the family, where Smith's grandson Paul F. Oyer currently lives (see #231).

Smith met his wife Ella while helping to build Sheldon's house. Ella and Smith's elopement at her early age caused Sheldon much anguish, obviously soon overcome by the Oyer magnetism so often found.

He did carpentry work after returning from NYC, boarding at
Sheldon's home as he was building it. After his marriage, he had
a small farm and sold milk from his 8 cows to the cheese factory
in Willoughby.   (Incidentally, this cheese factory was also a
building he built).   His too-early arrival used to annoy the
cheesemaker; he was always the first person there each morning.

When there were carpentry jobs, he fitted them in with his
farmwork. His other buildings include a church and the Ellvl.
home of his uncle, the wealthy land baron Commodore P. Vedder.
Today it is known as Edelweiss Inn, a ski lodge. Smith was noted
for his "gingerbread" trim on houses, as it was known, the orna-
mental wooden trim just below the roofs.

Smith enjoyed children and was not only very helpful, but also
well-liked by everyone. A tape made in 1987 by Rose Oyer, his
daughter-in-law, reveals the warmth of his personality. She grew
close to him from their first meeting. During the early years of
Wallace and Rose's marriage jobs were scarce. They would sometimes go to Smith and Ella's home to stay and help around the
farm. Smith's buggy would be available to them for shopping and
other errands.

Around 1921 Smith and Ella sold their farm and bought a home
on the corner of Summit and Armstrong Streets in Sala.   Ella
liked the location because friends and relatives were nearby.
Smith missed the farm life and spent time at the livery stables
helping out with the horses.

After Smith's death in 1929, Ella lived for alternating periods of
time with her 3 children. Her craftwork consisted of hooked rugs
and pads, knitted mittens, and blankets made from discards from a
paper factory.   She also made many of the grandchildren's
clothes; we can assume she did for her own children as well.
Ella died in 1948 while she was living with her daughter Nellie.

Ch (OYER) all b GrV:

160.   i.   CLARENCE SEYMOUR[6] b 14 Feb 1878
161.   ii.   NELLIE JULIAETTE, b 11 Aug 1880
        iii. GRACE MARY/POLLY, b 20 Mar 1886; d 28 Oct 1918;
              bur GrC; she d in the flu epidemic of 1918. Polly
              had a back deformity, causing the parents to keep
              her from going to school. However Nellie tutored
              her at home, at the expense of her own education.
              Polly was very artistic, a talent found often among
              Oyers. At least 1 picture is extant.
162.   iv.   WALLIS/WALLACE SMITH, b 15 July 1893

Home in Great Valley, N.Y. built by D. Smith[5] Oyer (inset) for future
father-in-law, Sheldon Brown. L to r: Smith Oyer; Juliaette (Doud) Brown;
Sheldon Brown; Ella holding Clarence S.[6] Oyer; James Brown, Ella's brother.
Note the scroll work—"gingerbread" trim on house, for which Smith was
noted.

*** THE BROWN-DOUD-PHILLIPS-SENTER ALLIED FAMILIES ***

According to family tradition, Ruth Ellen/Ella Brown's grandfather DAVID M BROWN, b France 10 Mar 1793, d 1848, bur Napoli, Catt Co [VR; fb], came to America as a French spy at the time of the War of 1812. Tradition further relates that he stopped at the Senter home in N H for a drink while passing by. Fifteen year old Sally was sent to the cellar for a drink of cider for him, and he fell in love with her. He resided in Chester, N H, marrying 7 Dec 1815 [Londonderry TR, 4/548] SALLY/POLLY SENTER of Londonderry, N H. One record states that the Senters were not among the Scotch-Irish first petitioners of the Londonderry area, although they were there by 1719-22, having come from Long Island. John Senter is listed with some additional proprietors of Londonderry in 1722 with the notation, "few if any were Scotch Irish." It add that "The Scotch Irish had their wish fulfilled, the desire for a town to be ruled by their own kith and kin." Listed in that book's appendices are 21 Browns, all having been "Ruling Elders" in Ireland. [Bolton, p265]

Research resulting in much information unfortunately does not confirm parentage of either David or Sally. We believe Caleb Brown who m Sarah to be a brother or uncle. A David and Caleb are listed as petitioners for a highway 9 Dec 1791 in the Chester TR, 2/693.

Sally Senter, b 1 Aug 1799 [fb] or 1800; d 11 Dec 1861 [fb] came from "the Puritan element of New England." [obit] A Senter genealogy states "John Senter¹, one of the Proprietors of Londonderry in 1719, was the ancestor of the Senters of Londonderry, Windham, and Hudson, and representatives of the name in Centre Harbor and other towns in N H and Mass. He was of English descent or birth, and came from Long Island to Londonderry. His home lot was northwest of Beaver Pond. He m Jean _____. They d in Londonderry. Ch b in Londonderry..." [much detail]

Descendants include Samuel, Joseph, Jean, Moses, John, Reuben, Samuel, Samuel, Asa, Abel, Samuel, Issac, William, Allison, Samuel, Fanny, Cynthia, Germain, Delia, Sarah, Sophia, George W, Benjamin-Franklin, and John T. [Morrison's Windham, pp 759-61] Research of Centre Harbor was not able to be done.

David Brown came by ox team with at least his first-born, Lucinda, in a covered wagon to Eagle, Wyoming Co. After a proprietorship of a hotel there, David and his family moved in 1832 to Napoli Twp, Catt Co. Sheldon was b in Eagle. The hotel there was sold. In 1842 while visiting a brother in Maine, David acquired the carcass of a whale 48 feet in length which he had prepared; he then transported it on wagons and canal boats, exhibiting it throughout the country. Illness forced him to give that up; he sold it for $8,000. [Catt Co SR reveal a substantial *portion of that amount was never paid, the carcass eventually going to a museum in Buffalo, where it was displayed as recently as the 1930's.]*

The Browns ran a livery stable in Randolph, Chau Co while residing in Napoli nearby. They also built the Nutting building in E Randolph and the Morrie schoolhouse on old Napoli Rd.

Ella's f. SHELDON P BROWN, was b in Eagle, Pike Twp, Wyoming Co 24 Aug 1818; d 24/26 July 1909; m 15 Aug 1847, 48 or 49; bur GrC. [fb, obits] JULIAETTE/JULIETT DOUD. Juliaette was b Hume Twp, Allegany Co 14 Mar 1826/7, dau of JAMES and MARY/MAY (PHILLIPS) DOUD; d 24 July 1913 at the home of her son, James D Brown; bur GrC.

Sheldon's sister Mary, b 17 Feb 1824 m Charles Fitch, b Columbia Co. He was a merchant, and was in Ill in 1845. Ch: Thaddeus, b Ill ca 1845; Mary R, b Ill; Charles N, Randolph (?). The Fitch home was diagonally across from the Brown livery in E Randolph, Chau Co. They owned several homes in that town.

Sheldon and Juliaette moved to Willoughby, GrV Twp, into their newly-built home (built by or with the help of their dau's future husband, David Smith Over) in 1867. He farmed there, eventually acquiring more acreage, much of which is still in the Over family.

Ch of David and Sally (BROWN):

i. LUCINDA P, b 2 June 1816
ii. SHELDON P, b 24 Aug 1818
iii. SARAH W, b 15 July 1821; d Napoli 15 Apr 1888
iv. MARY, b 17 Feb 1824
v. JOHN QUINCY ADAMS (twin), 1 Dec 1828
  Quincy was mustered in on 16 June 1862 at Randolph at age 32; became a 2nd Lt; disability dischg 13 Jan 1863; comm 1st Lt of Co B 1 Mar 1863; became Capt 23 June 1863. Was at Yellow Tavern, Va 11 Mar 1864; mortally wounded on Pt Lookout, Md 18 June 1864; bur there. Picture extant. (Civil War)
vi. ANDREW JACKSON (twin), b 1 Dec 1828
vii. FRANCES LORANE/LORRAINE, b 18 July 1834, d San Francisco, Calif 29 Aug 1905; husband and she went to Calif (gold rush). He was a photographer. bur "beside my Father in Oakland where Aunt Mary and family are buried." Their dau Hattie, writer of the quoted "letter edged in black" used to inform of deaths. m _____ WITTMAN; res Wash, Ore, and Calif, where she experienced the San Francisco earthquake of 1906. Pictures and letters are extant.

Ch of Sheldon and Juliette (Doud) BROWN:

    i.   *JAMES, b 7 June 1847/49;m ROENA CONGDON 18*
             Dec 1870; a son James d ca 1974; res'd Sala
    ii.   *MARY, b Apr 26 1853/55;d 2 Mar 1922; m ALMOND*
             GUTHRIE 26 Mar 1879; res GrV
98.   iii. *RUTH ELLEN/ELLA, b 2 Feb 1859*

Other SENTERS found in the family Bible are:

    i.   *ELIZABETH, b 10 Jan 1789*
    ii.   *CLARISSA, b 27/9 Aug 1792*
   iii. *ASENATH, b 10 Apr 1794*
   iv. *REUBEN, b 17 Apr ?, 1802; d 12 Dec ?, ae 81*
    v.   *ISREAL, b 27 Apr 1809*

Ella (Brown) Oyer's maternal grandfather, JAMES DOUD, b Hartwick, Otsego Co 13 Jan 1801, descended from EDWARD (G?) DOUD, b 6 Apr 1767 who m 14 Dec 1788 CONTENT FULLER. Edward was a "newcomer to Hume (Alleg Co) in 1815, settling on Lot #31." [Beers' Alleg, pg 306] They came from Otsego Co; they were Whigs, "standard bearers." James m 9 Jan 1823 MAY PHIL-LIPS of New Hartford, Conn, b 20 Jan 1799; d 24 July 1913. He worked at David and Sally (Senter) Brown's tavern in Eagle.

Descendants of EDWARD DOUD include: John Dowd, b 11 Oct 1792; Ebin, b 2 Mar 1793; Orrin Doud, b Hartwick, Otsego Co 30 June 1796; m Sally Phillips of New Hartford, Conn, most likely related to Mary, above; they res Mill's Mills, Hume in 1815; Benjamin, b 2 Dec 1798; James Nelson, a son of James and bro of Juliaette, b 18 Apr 1825; Miles W, b 31 Oct 1826 m 28 Sept 1864 Helen Phillips, res Hume; Seymour L, b 1836 m 1860 Mary J Par-tridge of Pike, Wyoming Co 28 Nov 1860. Seymour was a post-master; William, b 8 Sept 1820 m 9 Sept 1846 Almira E Stone of Milford; Menzer m Lyda Baker 4 Sept 1854; Nelson E m Canelia (sic) Lillabridge 23 Feb 1854; Philo E m Marguerite Flanigan 20 Oct 1853; Monroe W, b 9 Sept 1847; Vermon (sic) W, b 13 Aug 1851; Charles M, b 14 Dec 1853; Willie E, b 25 Feb 1855; Hattie R, b 14 Apr 1860. H Doud was the organizer of the Baptist church in Hume 1835.
   The "Memoranda" page from a family Bible lists the following:
       Miles W Doud b 31 Oct 1826
       Rosan Grover b 8 Dec 1831
            married 14 Sept 1847
       Edward Doud and Content Fuller were m 14 Dec 1788
       Miles W Doudb 31 Oct 1826
       George E Doud b 2 Oct 1823   (elsewhere 24 Oct)

James N Doud   b 18 Apr 1825
Juliaette Doud   b 14 Mar 1827
Maryette Doud   b 27 July 1829
Philo Doud   b 23 Oct 1831
Menzer Doud   b 24 Aug 1833
Seymour L Doud   b 22 Nov 1836
James Doud   b 13 Jan 1801
Mary/May Phillips   b 20 Jan 1799

George E was a lifelong res of Hume. Extant is a picture of a Doud family reunion.

JOHN PHILLIPS settled in Hume, Alleg Co 1824; other Phillips 1828 or 1834. Their pedigree goes back to the first mayor of Boston. Mass. JOHN PHILLIPS (1770-1823) who is bur in Granary Burial Ground, Boston where many of our early patriots are also bur. These include Paul Revere, John Hancock and Benjamin Franklin. We found we believe an error in The Abridged Compendium of American Genealogy, pg 345. It shows John (1701-1768) to be the mayor; it should be 4th generation John (1770-1823). While Boston was a city earlier, the form of government which John was instru-mental in developing took place but a year before he took office in 1822, the city charter being adopted then. Of his short (12 months) rule, it is written, "Mayor Phillips... (helped) organize the new government and put the wheels in motion;...short administration, determined not to fail."

A dispute of interest arose during his tenure, that of whether or not to continue to allow cows to graze on the Boston Common. "...The gentle Phillips, first mayor, being as much a lover of true liberty as his gifted son, let (the cows) alone." The houses bordering the Common were considered so suburban (1804), but it was decided that sun bathing would be forbidden.

The "gifted son" referred to is Wendell Phillips who in 1837 began an anti-slavery movement, becoming the celebrated anti-slavery orator of Boston.

Mayor Phillips m SARAH WALLEY and his pedigree is William[5] (1737-1772), m MARGARET WENDELL; John[4] (1701-1768), m MARY BUTTOLPH (1703-1742); Samuel[3] , m MARY EMERSON; Samuel[2] (1625-1696), m SARAH APPLETON; Rev. George[1] Phillips (1593-1644). He received his A B from Cambridge, Eng 1613; came from Eng on the "Arbella;" to Salem, Mass 1630; founder of Watertown, Mass where he founded the first Congregational Church in America. He m 1st _____ SERGEANT; m 2nd ELIZA-BETH _____. [Comp Amer Gen, p 345; Drake's Boston]

Their route from Mass to Catt Co seems to be through Vermont. It is interesting to note several Douds m Phillips.

      i. *John A Phillips   b 8 Dec 1808*
     ii. *Mary J Phillips   b 3 Oct 1828*
    iii. *Helen R Phillips b 13 May 1832*
     iv. *John A Phillips, Jr b 5 Jan 1837*

The "Deaths" page shows John A d 20 June 1832; his wife Chloe Blossom (b 6 May 1806) d 28 Mar 1837; their dau Mary Jane d 17 May 1845, ae 17.

[Sources: Beers' Alleg; fb; family rec; letters]

   99. FRANKLIN PIERCE⁵ OYER *(Peter⁴, David³, Jacob², Frederick¹),* born Ellvl., Catt. Co. 25 Jan. 1853; died 27 Apr. 1912; buried GrV Cem. Franklin was baptized on 26 Apr. 1912 at the Congregation of Christ's Flock Church, the day before he died. He married JENNIE GRACE GRIERSON, born GrV 30 Nov. 1865; died Dec. 1941; buried GrV Cem. Jennie Grierson's brother was Alex who married Alice _____. They resided in Bflo. before 1935. Franklin Oyer was a farmer in Ellvl. Twp.

      Ch (OYER):

          i.   DANNIE (?), b 12 Aug 1886; d 21 Aug 1886
   163.   ii.   FREDERICK A⁶, b Ellvl 23 Oct 1888/1889
         iii.   GRETCHEN, b 20 Aug 1895; m 1st SAM DENIKE; 2nd
                JAMES MILLER; 3rd MARTIN AHRENS.

   100. BYRON EUGENE⁵ OYER, *(Peter⁴, David³, Jacob², Frederick¹),* born Ash. Twp. 1850. He married JENNIE O'NEILL, born Bflo.; died Jersey City, N.J. 23 Dec. _____, bur there. [obit] Jennie's family moved from Bflo. to Clare Valley, Catt. Co. (many Irish there from Co. Clare, Ireland), settling next door to Peter D. Oyer, whose son she married. The family lived in Ellvl. for several years; undoubtedly the Eugene Oyer who was the town supervisor 1887. He conducted a meat market there. They settled in Jersey City, N.J. prior to 1900.

      Ch (OYER):

   164.   i.   EUGENE⁶, b n/a; d Dec 1966
   164.1   ii.   BARTHOLOMEW/BURT, b ca 1884
   165.   iii.   OLIVE, b n/a
   166.   iv.   KATHERINE/KATHERYN/KITTIE, b 1883
   166.1   v.   WILLIE, b n/a; d ca 1965

vi.   ARTHUR, a probation officer in NYC, resided in
Jersey City, NJ with Olive; unm; d Oct 1952

[Sources: Ruth Oyer; Rose (Duhan) Oyer; Adams' Catt; Ash VR;
CCHM; LM]

101. MARY E.⁵ OYER (Peter⁴, David³, Jacob², Frederick¹), born
prob. Frklnv. 1 Sept. 1873; died 21 Apr. 1953; both buried GrC.
Mary married 23 Feb. 1894 WILLIAM J. NELSON of GrV., son of
John and Lana/Lena B. (Kelly) Nelson, born Machias, Catt. Co. 31
Mar. 1869/71; died 18 Sept 1925; both buried. They resided in
Sommerville Valley and Bryant Hill in Ellvl. Twp.

Ch (NELSON):

167.   i.   CHARLOTTA/LOTTIE⁶, b 20 Dec 1894
168.   ii.   LAURA, b 5 Nov 1897
168.1   iii.   MARGARET, b 7 Jan 1901
168.2   iv.   AGNES, b ca 1906

*** *THE NELSON FAMILY* ***

*John Nelson, William's f, d 28 Dec 1897, ae 59, bur GrC; Lana, b
1848, d 19.hather. In the front yard is a huge mill-
stone, used so well so many years ago. He operated a general
store in Riceville, Ash. Twp., Catt. Co., just 8 miles from Sprvl.
Their son Leon's widow Violet resided in the family homestead
until recently; winters in Fla.*
A Frank J. resided Bflo. St., Sprvl. in 1927.
*Frank's sister Ella Anderson left "1/3 to decedent" 25 Mar. 1909,
including stock shares, bonds and mortgages.*

Ch (OYER) all b Sprvl:

169.	i.	ROBERT EMMONS[6], b 28 Dec 1881
170.	ii.	RUTH ANN, b 15 Jan 1883
	iii.	LOIS JULIETTE, b 26 Dec 1883; d Buffalo 18 Apr 1964; m WILLIS SPAULDING, a lawyer, res Bflo; no ch. Lois had been his housekeeper.
171.	iv.	EDWARD JACOB, b 3 Apr 1885
172.	v.	WILLIS LEVI, b 3 Aug 1887
173.	vi.	AGNES JONES, b 22 May 1890
174.	vii.	HARVEY EUGENE, b 15 Mar 1892
175.	viii.	ESTHER IRENE, b 19 Dec 1894
	ix.	CLARENCE DAVID, b 16 Nov. 1896; d 18 Feb 1920; bur MWC. He played the piano in moviehouses, and res Pasadena, Calif at one time. His death was caused by being crushed by an elevator.
176.	x.	LEON IRVING, b 5 Oct 1899

[Sources: Violet Peterson (Mrs. Leon) Oyer; Elbert Hadley; Charlotte Oyer]

103. ELLADE EMMA[5] OYER (*Jacob[4], David[3], Jacob[2], Frederick[1]*), born ca. 1862; died 1943; married ROLAND ANDERSON. They resided Bflo.

Ch (ANDERSON):

    i. DORIS[6], m 1st _____ VELZY; m 2nd RALPH CUNNINGHAM; res E Aurora; dau VIRGINIA[7]; m _____ VOGT.

104. HARLAN EUGENE[5] OYER (*Jacob[4], David[3], Jacob[2], Frederick[1]*), born ca. 1864; died 1941; married 3 times. Harlan had a drug store in Bflo. Prior to that he was a stewart at the Castle Inn in Bflo. An H. Eugene Oyer is shown in the 1890 Bflo. city directory as a partner in the law firm of Eaton and Oyer, 9 Law Exchange.

Ch (OYER):

    i. FREDERICK CHARLES[6]
       a) HARLAN STANLEY[7], b 5 May 1911

Ch (OYER) of 3rd m:

    ii. ROBERT

We believe there were 5 ch: a dau who m
NORMAN, dec'd; ELEANOR who m _____ BELLES
(div'd); WINIFRED; ROBERT; and JANICE

iii.   CECELIA

105.   SNOWEY ANN⁵ BOWEN, (*Margaret⁴, David³, Jacob², Frederick¹*), born E. Otto Twp. 12 Mar. 1856; died E. Otto Twp. 17 Mar. 1938; buried E. Otto Village Cem. She married HERMAN C. BROOKS, son of Philo and Sally (Boutwell) Brooks, born E. Otto 30 July 1857; died E. Otto 11 Mar. 1933; buried E. Otto Cem. Herman was a farmer in E. Otto.

Ch (BROOKS) all b E Otto:

177.   i.   M DEVER/DEVERE⁶, b 11 June 1889
         ii.   FLOYD D, b 2 Jan 1890; d E Otto 31 Jan 1913; bur E Otto Cem
        iii.   ISA, b 1891; d 4 Feb 1979; m 24 Dec 1912 EVERILL UTLEY, d 29 Jan 1939; res Sprvl

106.   AMY W.⁵ BOWEN (*Margaret⁴, David³, Jacob², Frederick¹*), born E. Otto Twp. 26 May 1860; died E. Otto 8 Aug. 1935. She married FRED BEACH, son of Julius C. and Lucy (Mason) Beach, born 7 Feb. 1858. We believe they farmed in Delevan, Catt. Co.

Ch (BEACH):

178.   i.   DESSIE, m GEORGE HARRISON
178.1   ii.   LUCY, m HENRY RASZMANN, res Bflo

*** THE BEACH FAMILY ***

We have found 2 Overs marrying BEACHES. MICHAEL³'s dau MARY ELIZABETH and AMY BOWEN, above. JULIUS is the son of MOSES T BEACH who came to E Otto with wife, sons and daus from New Ashford, Mass Oct 1821. Moses built a sawmill in 1823; grist mill 1824; they were the first of each, and located on the west branch of Catt Creek. "The grist-mill contained one run of stone, and was capable of grinding 60 bushels of grain per day." [Everts' Catt. p 296] He received the appointment of postmaster from "John Q Adams," built the first frame house, read Wesley sermons. He was town clerk and justice of the peace; d 1879+.

Julius C is listed Otto 1850 b Mass, with real estate valued at $1875, ae 34; Lucy N, 35; Augusta L, 8; Henrietta M, 6; Emma L, 4; and SARAH JANE OYER, 16.

Among the sons is Joseph, who settled on the same lot (11, township 5, range 11). Another, Rev. Augustus, b Mass 1793, grad'd Williams College, anti-slavery activist, d 21 Apr 1878. He is referred to as Deacon Beach. Tyler, settled on lot 12, was a trustee of the First Baptist Church, est. 1831. Nathan Larabee was its clerk, 3 of his sons marrying Oyer sisters!

Another son Henry, d 7 Feb 1847, m Maria Nash, d 14 June 1872 who had 4 sons & 3 daus. His son, Oscar F was b Mass 23 Sept 1818, m 1846 Adeline Hinman, b Catt Co 8 Oct 1827, dau S B and Kesiah Hinman. He & wife both b Vt, S B coming when young with family to NYS, res (1879) Waverly, E Otto Twp, ae 79 & 73. Ch of O F Beach: Edson F, m Laura Eddy of Mansfield 12 Dec 1877; Cornelia, m 8 Dec 1869 A B Rush, E Otto; Addie A, m 7 Oct 1878   L H Northrup, merchant in village of Catt.

A Henry Beach is shown as a farmer in Delevan, Catt Co.

Bertha Beach, dau of Moses Nash and Mary Elizabeth (Oyer—#53.1) Beach is written up, #121.1. The Fox family becomes allied in that section, as does another Clark family.

[Sources: Everts' Catt, LM, LS, Beach Inf 1]

107. CHARLES D.⁵ OYER (*John⁴⁻³, Jacob², Frederick¹*), born E. Otto Twp. July 1863; died Sprvl. 1926; buried MWC. He married ca. 1882 EMMA JANE FRANK, born 25 Jan. 1866; died 13 Dec. 1951 (some say 17 May 1949); buried MWC, Sprvl.

Emma J., widow of Charles, is listed at 49 Lisbon in the 1940 Bflo. directory. In earlier directories we find Emma listed as a nurse, although the family says she was not a nurse.

Listed in 1935 are grandsons Charles H., student, later a salesman; and James D., draftsman, both of whom are now chiropractors, following in their father's footsteps. Their sister Eleanor (#259.1) is also there as a student.

Charles' father John is living with Charles in 1910, E. Otto Census.

Ch (OYER):

    i.   LULU ELEANOR⁶, b E Otto 18 Feb. 1884; d 16 Sept 1972; m E Otto 6 Apr 1907 ERNEST JOHN JAST-ER, son of Theodore and Carrie (Kruse) Jaster, b Sprvl 1879; d 1949; both bur MWC. In 1907 he was an iceman res in Bflo. [The Justin spelling sometimes found is incorrect.]   There was an

Eleanor R, stenographer, N Tonawanda in 1936
directory. In Bflo city directory 1930 Jaster &
Oyer are listed as chiropractors. Ch?

178.2   ii.   ST ELMO C OYER, b Apr 1890

108.   CORA A.⁵ OYER *(John⁴. John³, Jacob², Frederick¹)*, born
E. Otto Twp. 20 Apr 1870. She married FRANK GOODEMOTE, son
of Abraham and Eveline (Fuller) Goodemote, born Ash. 1869.

Ch (GOODEMOTE):

179.   i.   EARL⁶, b 12 May 1892
         ii.   EDNA, b 30 June 1896; m 23 July 1921 ELBERT LINK
180.   iii. ROYDEN, b 9 Dec 1900
181.   iv.   CLARA, b 16 Dec 1904; m ROB W GEORGE

*** *THE GOODEMOTE FAMILY* ***

*An Allen Goodemote is found in Concord, Erie Co early. In
1822 Peter Sampson, who had settled on the north side of Catt
Creek (therefore Erie Co) traded farms with John Goodemote, who
lived on the other side of the creek (Catt Co) on lot 60. (This
"creek" runs through a deep gorge; the bridge Alexander Scoby
built across it in that era was 182 feet in length!)   Baltus and
Philip Goodemote were early members of the Methodist Episcopal
church of Sprvl.*

*James and bro John Goodemote went to Ash 1816 from Kinder-
hook. Columbia Co, where their father Philip was born 1796.*

*Philip served in the War of 1812; ch: James, Elizabeth, Philip Jr.
Ann, John, Sally. David and Sophia. In 1820 the father and their
bro Baltus, Harry and William all went to Ash. A James was b
1821 in Ash; m Maria Wilcox in 1846.*

*John was interested in getting a school building built. Part of a
conversation aconcerning this with Nathan Saunders is quoted in
Adams Catt [p 448]: "Meesder Saunders. ve musd puilt a school
houdst ver de childers! You oppinate me for drusdee. I oppinate
you! Den ve puilt de school houdst and have de monies!" After
trading farms with Sampson. John erected a distillery and made
whisky.*

109.   CLARENCE D.⁵ OYER *(John⁴. Frederick³⁻²⁻¹)*, born E. Otto
1841. We located a Clarence D., yardmaster. Bflo. at 116 E. Eagle
St. in 1880.1 and 2 city directories. In 1890 he is on W. Genesee

St. In 1900 there is a Clarence D. as partner in the law firm of
Patridge and Oyer. In 1917, an attendant at Bflo. State Hosp.
Some of the "unplaced Oyers" found in the Bflo. city directories
may be Clarence's children. [See Chapt 14]

110.   **LAURA J.5 HUFSTADER**, b E. Otto ca. 1841; died Ash. 22
June 1908; married _____ LONG (LANG?). Ch?--no data.

111.   **NELSON⁵ HUFSTADER** (*Mary Ann⁴, Frederick³⁻²⁻¹*), born
E. Otto Feb. 1846, died Ash. 13 Sept. 1905, married ca. 1867
ALZINA _____, born Dec. 1849; died 1926. [Ash. cemetery
rec. shows 1845-1906 for Nelson.] Nelson was an enumerator for
the Ash. 1892 St. census. Ash. 1900 census states he worked in
mill, had 2 ch. Only 1 listed is

    i.   MARSH⁶, b Mar 1881, worked in cheese factory

112.   **MARY ALICE⁵ OYER**, (*Robert⁴, Frederick³⁻²⁻¹*) born Ash.
Twp. 5 Apr 1847; married 5 Apr. 1868, MARTIN HENRY WOOD-
RUFF, son of George Woodruff, born E Otto Twp. 22 Dec. 1843;
died Colony, Kan. 11 Apr. 1914. Mary is listed with a brother,
"Richard R." in Frklnv. 1915 St. census, residing on S. Main St.

    Ch (WOODRUFF):

182.   i.   GEORGE MARTIN⁶, b 15 Aug 1869
183.   ii.   ARCHIE ALVIN, b 5 Apr 1871
        iii. MYRTLE MAY, b Mansfield 3 July 1875; m Sala 31
              Dec 1895 FRANK H MCGUIRE; res Frklnv in 1948.

*** THE WOODRUFF FAMILY ***

*The WOODRUFF family of Catt Co descends from the owners of
the successful Woodruff Seed Company in Farmington, Conn.
The first WOODRUFF in Ash was ISSAC, settling on Lot 53 in
1820 and one of the first assessors, later adding Lots 54 and 62.
He joined David Oyer and Jacob Frank as trustees of the Free-
Will Baptist Society at its formation, the church being begun by
Benjamin Cary with help from Augustus Van Slyke. Meetings were
held in homes and schoolhouses until a church was built in 1852,
receiving their 50-acre "gospel lot" from the HLC.*
 *Issac's connection is unkown. GEORGE WOODRUFF, Martin's f,
has this pedigree: George⁵ (1815-1890); John⁴ (1774-1843); Oliver³*

(1750-1827); Joshua², Capt Fr & Ind War (1708-1776); Mathew¹
(1668/69)-1751). George, a twin of John m one of twin Perkins
girls, Mariett, and had a son Frederick, b 11 May 1851. His son
Elmer b 1884 of Kill Buck m Jennie Tyler; had 2 girls: Alice,
killed in accident 1940 and Jean, b Kill Buck ca 1920, m Robert
Blessing, b Sala ca 1923. He d 1969. Ch: Carol, Sherry, Gary,
Bruce and Jennifer. Jean res Roch. Carol and Sherry res Calif.

George's other ch: Maude, b 1879; Ernest, b 1881; Elmer, b 1884;
Edna, b 1888; Bennie, b 1889; Nellie, b 1891; George W, b 1893;
Jay, b 1895; Earl, b 1899. Jay's descendants include Robert Wood-
ruff of Dansville, Livingston Co, b 1923; m Joyce Stady. Ch:
Mary Beth and Michael Robert (b 1951, 1953). [Woodruff Inf 3;
data rec'd the day before book went to the printer! There is
much more Woodruff information in Abbott.]

Woodruffs also m Holdens, another allied family of the Oyers.

In Ash 1880: Abram Woodruff, 39, and family; with him is Phil-
inda Conhiser, ae 17, servant.

Asher Tyler was agent of the Devereaux lands in Ellvl as of
1836; and was elected to Congress. He later became land agent
for the Erie Railroad, living in Elmira, Chemung Co, dying there
in 1875 ae 77.

There are Woodruffs buried in Frklnv.

[Sources: Woodruff Inf 1,2,3; Everts' Catt; Abbott; LM]

112.1   MALDEN E⁵ OYER (*Robert⁴, Frederick³⁻²⁻¹*), born Ash.
Apr. 1851; married (poss. Ellvl. 9 Feb. 1875) IRENE (PARISH?),
born NYS May 1854 [1900 census]. We find a Melvin Oyer who
married Friem <sic> Parish. As Malden is shown as "Melvin" in
the 1900 Bflo census, this could be he; as the "Friem" was illegible
in the marriage record, it could be "Irene." Malden is listed as a
carpenter at 317 Broadway [1900 Bflo. directory] married 25
years. [1900 census]

   Ch (OYER):

183.1   i.   LOUIS/LEWIS⁶, b 1878

[This then is the father of the LOUIS whose identity escaped us
for so long, whose will was dated 23 Jan. 1958. This "fit" was the
last one made, in Jan. 1988. Eleanor Mullen (#259.1) aided us in
this. There may have been other ch we did not locate, Louis the
only one listed in the census.]

different Frederick from the one shown as son of Robert (#39).
Middle initial variously shown as A., D., and E. The 1915 St.
census shows it looking more like a "D" with him a farmer on
Ischua Rd., Frklnv. Elizabeth Hurlburt was the informant for
Grace's cemetery record.

Ch (OYER):

183.2   i.   LEE EUGENE⁶, b 22 Nov 1887/89/90 [obit; GrV VR;
              1915 census]
        ii.   FLORA, b ca 1902; m _____ DILTZ
       iii.   MILDRED S, b ca 1908; m _____ PULVER,
              Depew, Erie Co
        iv.   FLOYD, b Frklnv ca 1866, d hepatitis 1896; Cadiz

113.   PERRY R.⁵ OYER *(Robert⁴, Frederick³⁻²⁻¹),* born Ash.
Twp. Feb. 1855; died 1920. He married NELLIE E. _____, born
Prussia, Mar. 1861; died 1936; both buried Frklnv. In 1900 census
Perry Oyer is listed as stone mason residing at 21 Church St.,
Sala. In Mansfield, Catt. Co. 1915 St. census, Perry and Nellie are
listed with Earl, and Howard, ae. 16; Donald, ae. 13, grandsons.

Ch (OYER):

        i.   ARTHUR⁶, b Dec 1879
       ii.   CLAUD E, b Dec 1882; d Farmersville 14 Jan 1946
      iii.   EARL C, b Aug 1884
       iv.   BERTHA F, b Apr 1886
        v.   CORA M, b June 1889
       vi.   HORACE C, b Oct 1898

[Sources: Frklnv cem rec; 1900 census]

113.1   ABRAHAM⁵/ABE ALTENBURG *(Sarah⁴, Frederick³⁻²⁻¹),*
born 6 Mar. 1865/66; died Pelican, Oneida Co., Wis.; married NYS
13 Mar. 1888 ADDIE HILLS, dau. of Alphonso and Martha Hills.
    Abe cared for his mother until her death in 1890, after which
he went west to Stevens Point and Dancy, Wis. He there managed
a farm operated by the John Weeks Lumber Co. In 1892 he went
to Rhinelander, Wis. where he was a runner in a lumber camp.
Then for four years he was a driller and tool dresser in southern
Ohio, returning to Rhinelander. He was the manager of a farm
there for 5 years.

In 1911 he settled on his 40-acre farm in the town of Pelican. After erecting a number of buildings, he proceeded to clear the land and develop a "fine agricultural property...furnished with modern farming equipment." General farming and dairying (Holstein cattle) was carried on. "He holds a high place in the esteem of the community. He is a director on the school board..." [Jones, Geo, p 291-2, provided by Altenburg Inf]

Ch (ALTENBURG):

    i.   HOWARD6, b 8 Apr 1889; d 22 Aug 1905

114.   ADELINE M.[5] OYER *(John[4], Peter[3], Frederick[2-1])*, born Schuy. Twp. 6 June 1842; died Schuy. 13 Jan. 1888. She married 11 Sept 1860 DANIEL THOMPSON, born Herk. Co. 1831; died Schuy. 1900. Both are buried MRC. [Source: AHA]

Ch (THOMPSON):

    i.   HOSMER W.[6], b Schuy Twp 1861; d Schuy Twp 1874; bur MRC
   ii.   EDWARD, b Schuy ca 1863
  iii.   NATHAN
   iv.   ADA
    v.   SARAH J
   vi.   MARTHA, b Schuy 1867; d Schuy 1877; bur MRC
  vii.   JESSIE E, b Schuy 1879; d Schuy 1887; bur MRC

115.   FRANCES AUGUSTA[5] OYER *(John[4], Peter[3], Frederick[2-1])*, born Schuy. Twp. 4 Feb. 1844; died Schuy. 19 Mar. 1912; buried MRC. She married 10 Oct. 1866, ALBERT SYLVESTER KNAPP, son of Richardson and Orissa (Burton) Knapp, born 30 Jan. 1843; died 6 Nov. 1881; buried MRC.

Ch (KNAPP) all b Schuy:

118.   i.   NETTIE ORISSA[6], b 24 Jan 1868
      ii.   JOSEPHINE N, b 16 Feb 1872; d Schuy 4 Mar 1872; bur MRC
184. iii.   DELLA ELIZABETH, b 12 Dec 1873
185.   iv.   HARVEY BURTON, b 27 Nov 1875
186.   v.   LIDA FRANCES, b 5 Apr 1880

[Source: Robert Petrie; Clara Van Auken]

116.   RICHARD HOWARD⁵ OYER *(John⁴, Peter³, Frederick²⁻¹)*, born Schuy. Twp. 27 Sept. 1851; died 12 Feb. 1916. He married 29 Sept. 1880 ALICE HULSER, dau. of Jerome and Elizabeth (_____) Hulser, born W. Frkf. 13 May 1857; died 14 Mar. 1916.

Ch (OYER):

187.   i.   HOWARD⁶, b 25 Oct 1892
       ii. LIZZIE, b 8 or 18 Oct 1881; d 21 Dec 1887

[Source: Gertrude Race]

117.   ANNIAS DYER⁵ RICHARDSON *(Almira⁴, Peter³, Frederick²⁻¹)*, born Schuy. 24 Dec. 1864; died Schuy. 30 Nov. 1903; buried MRC; he married 21 Feb. 1894 NETTIE ORISSA KNAPP, dau. of Albert and Frances Augusta (Oyer) Knapp born 24 Jan. 1868; died 6 Oct. 1945; buried Crown Hill Cem., Kirkland Twp., Oneida Co.

Ch (RICHARDSON) all b Schuy:

   i.   EARL⁶, b 7 June 1896; d Schuy 27 July 1896;
   ii. CLARA AUGUSTA, b 4 Mar 1898; d Roch 29 Apr 1972; bur Crown Hill Cem. She m 9 Apr 1949, CHARLES HOWARD VAN AUKEN, b Roch 13 May 1899. Clara was a family historian whose records were used for this family, as well as the foundation of some other families herein. Her husband currently resides with his sister Helen Richardson in Roch.
   iii. SEYMOUR ANNIAS, b Schuy 14 Feb 1900; d Roch 1 Oct 1948; bur Crown Hill Cem; m 29 Mar 1948, HELEN M VAN AUKEN, b 8/9 Apr 1902; res with her bro, C Howard Van Auken in Roch (above).
   iv. ORISSA, b Schuy 15 June 1903; d Utica 14 Dec 1946. She m 18 Nov 1933 EDWARD HERLAN, b 3 Nov 1884; d Utica 27 Apr 1954; both bur Oneida Co; no ch.

[Sources: C Howard Van Auken and the records of wife Clara]

118.   GENEVA C.⁵ RICHARDSON *(Almira⁴, Peter³, Frederick²⁻¹)*, born Schuy. 2 Dec. 1867; died 22 Dec. 1943; married GEORGE WADSWORTH.

Ch (WADSWORTH):

    i.   dau., m JOHN R JONES

[Source: Clara Van Auken; AHA]

119.   GEORGE WASHINGTON⁵ OYER *(Levi⁴, George³, Freder-ick²⁻¹)*, born Ash. 2 Jan. 1845; died GrV 13 Jan. 1920; buried WV Cem.   He married ca. 1873 CLARA A. WEST, dau. of William C. West, born Attica Twp., Wyoming Co. 15 Oct. 1850; died 25 Sept. 1910 [some say born 109 Feb. 1830; died 6 Jan. 1890]; both buried Mt. Hope Cem., WV.

    Ch (OYER):

       i.   LEGRAND L⁶, b Ash Hollow, 19 Feb 1872; d Bflo 7 June 1948; bur West Valley Cem.   He m ca 1894 GERTRUDE WILLIS, dau of Eden and Mary Willis b Apr 1874; d 12 Feb 1944; bur WV Cem.   Le-Grand operated a general store in WV for 30-years and was at one time Ash supervisor. No ch.
      ii.   GLEN/N H, b Ash, Nov 1877; d Bflo 11 July 1940; bur WV Cem; m ALICE NEFF dau of Andrew and Ann (Clary) Neff, b 1879. It is believed they had a dau Ellen or Gertrude.   Ann's father Frederick Clary of Sprvl; her bros Charles C and Andrew B were born 1878 & 1882; her sis Ella 1886.
188. iii.   ROSCOE CONKLIN, b WV 5 Nov 1889

[Sources: Adams' Catt; CCHM; Catt Co VR]

120.   CHARLES A.⁵ OYER *(Simon⁴, George³, Frederick²⁻¹)*, born 1864; married 1894 GRACE _____, born Randolph (?), Catt. Co. 1875; died 1940. He resided in Ash. and died 1935. Res. RFD in Sprvl. 1927; gone by 1931.

    Ch (OYER):

188.1   i.   DeMONT FREDERICK⁶, b 1900

[Sources: Ellis Inf 4; Charles, #188.1i]

121.   EUGENE S.⁵ OYER *(Simon⁴, George³, Frederick²⁻¹)*, born 1867; married LENNORA/NORA L. FOX, dau. of George O. and

Hannah C. Fox, born ca.1869; died 1931. George was born ca.
1837; Hannah was born ca. 1845. Eugene and Nora resided in
Yorkshire, Catt. Co. where he farmed. [1905 St, 1910 census]
George and Hannah's dau. Georgia married Wallace Cheesman.
Georgia died in 1931; Wallace born ca. 1837.

Ch (OYER):

    i.   HAZEL H[6], b 1892
   ii.   THOMAS B, b 1899

This may be the Burton Oyer who is listed on Yorkshire's
Veteran List for WWI who died 1928. He is not found on the
cemetery list or otherwise identified.

*** THE FOX FAMILY ***

*While we have good Fox data, we have not ascertained George's
parentage. See Everts' Catt, especially p 265. Also see Fox
Family after HAROLD CLARK, #188.2.*

121.1   BERTHA BELLE[5] BEACH *(Mary[4], Michael[3], Frederick[2-
1])*, born 14 Apr. 1865; died 30 June 1929. She married 29 Dec
1885 WELLS WALTER CLARK, son of William and Caroline M.
(Stewart) Clark, of Blandford, Mass., born 7 May 1862; died 19
Dec. 1934. (Some state Caroline to be "Helen.") Wells was a
mechanic and farmer in Ellvl. He later owned a clothing store
and was president of the Bank of Ellvl.

Ch (CLARK):

188.2   i.   HAROLD W[6], b 1896

*** THE WILLIAM CLARK FAMILY ***

*WELLS W CLARK's father WILLIAM was b Granville, Mass 28
Aug 1814 and reared in Blandford, Mass. He m 20 Aug 1839
CAROLINE M STEWART of Collinsville, Conn., a native of Blandford on Aug 20 1839, she b 13 June 1816; d Ellvl 30 Nov 1894. In
1840 they came by canal from Albany to Buffalo, and thence "with
a team" (horse carriage) to Ellvl on May 1. He built his home
and farmed on 25 acres, partly cleared. They lived in a deserted
old log house while their home was being built, where "striped
snakes were in possession and would frequently bob up their heads*

through the large cracks in the floor." William added to his land, eventually owning nearly 300 acres. He d Ellvl 6 Apr 1895. William's father was Wells Clark. Williams's other ch were: George and Harlan M, sons who farmed on the family homestead; Charles W, of Mansfield; James O, lawyer in Ellvl; Carrie L, "at home" in 1893; Mary, who d 1889, ae 29. William's sisters: Melissa (1808-1896), m Arch Stewart, bur SHC; and Elizabeth (1821-1892), m Roswell Eddy. All are bur SHC, Ellvl. Wells Walter Clark had brothers and sisters.

[Sources: Everts' Catt; Adams' Catt, p 587-88; Beach Inf 1]

122.   IRA O.[5] **TEFFT** *(Mary*[4]*, John*[3]*, Peter*[2]*, Frederick*[1]*)*, born E. Otto June 1851; died Sprvl. 1902; buried MWC. He married EVA M. _____, born June 1852; died 1932; buried MWC.

Ch (TEFFT):

    i.   JENNIE[6], b ca 1874
    ii.   NELSON, b ca 1876
   iii.   JOHN, b May 1878
   iv.   DEWEY, b Nov 1881

123.   BYRON S.[5] **TEFFT** *(Mary*[4]*, John*[3]*, Peter*[2]*, Frederick*[1]*)*, born E. Otto June 1855; died 1933; buried MWC. He married LUCY C. _____, born Mar. 1853; died 1908; buried MWC.

Ch (TEFFT):

    i.   DAC[6], b Apr 1880
    ii.   ELMER B, b May 1883; d 1936; bur MWC
   iii.   SALLY, b May 1884

[1910 Concord, Erie Co census lists Byron S, ae 54, m 17 yrs, 2 times, and Lucy S, ae 15, dau. Sprvl City Directory for 1927 shows Carrie Tefft at 29 Church St; Chas A, farmer, 106 Bflo St. For some additional TEFFT data see #59.]

124.   CLARISSA[5] **FRANK** *(Sally*[4]*, John*[3]*, Peter*[2]*, Frederick*[1]*)*, born 3 Oct. 1844; died E. Otto 4 Dec. 1896; buried E. Otto Cem. She married JOHN CONHISER, born Germany, 1831.

Ch (CONHISER):

	i.	MARY⁶, b ca 1862
	ii.	PHILINDA, b ca 1864
	iii.	RICHARD, b ca 1866
189.	iv.	ABIGAIL E, b 23 Apr 1868
190.	v.	OYER H, b 1870
	vi.	IDA, b ca 1872
	vii.	ELLA, b ca 1874
	viii.	BLANCHE, b ca 1876
	ix.	ADA, b ca 1879

[Sources: LM; CCHM]

125. ADALIZA E. VEDDER *(Rachel⁴, John³, Peter², Frederick¹),*
born 15 June 1849; died 1924; buried MWC. She married GEORGE
H. HUGHEY, son of George and Mary (McMickle) Hughey, born
Ash. 9 Oct. 1843; died 1929; buried MWC.

George owned the Hughey homestead in Ash., and was a dealer
in live stock, produce and real estate.

Ch (HUGHEY):

	i.	EUGENE G⁶, b 1868; d 1927; bur MWC
	ii.	VEDDER G, b 1881; d 1897; bur MWC

*** *THE HUGHEY FAMILY* ***

*GEORGE HUGHEY was 1 of 11 ch of GEORGE and MARY (Mc-
MICKLE) HUGHEY. The f was b of Scotch parentage in Dublin,
Ire 14 Dec 1803, learned the trade of paper making; to America
(Schenectady) 1824 where he followed that trade and conducted a
grocery and bakery; to Ash 1840. He was highway commissioner,
served on board of supervisors and held other town offices. They
were members of the Baptist church. Ch: James of Ellvl, b Mont
Co ca 1833 who m Louise, b ca 1833 (had ch Edverdo, b ca 1854
who m Sadie Hufstader; Mary E, b ca 1856; and Bradford, b ca
1864); Mary A and Eliza J of Ellvl; John (1st) drowned; John
(2nd), b Ash. m Ida Folts of Mansfield, Catt Co; Matilda, Catherine, Ellen, then "our" GEORGE; Robert; and Rosanie/Roxanne.*

*Ellvl 1870 census shows George, 60, b Ire with real estate worth
$20,000; Mary, 67, b Ire; Roxanne, 18; Robert, 24; John, 22.
George was b 14 Nov 1803; d 9 Mar 1884; Mary was b 25 Dec
1808; d 7 Feb 1879; both bur Ash.*

*Hugheys bur also in Ash: Florence L (1900-1911); Ida M (1851-
1902); John (1847-1900).*

[Sources: Adams' Catt; Everts' Catt; LM; censuses; Ash cem rec]

126. ALICE⁵ VEDDER *(Rachel⁴, John³, Peter², Frederick¹)*, born Ash. 19 Jan. 1852; died Ash. 30 May 1900. She married 20 May 1874 GEORGE N. TEFFT, born ca. 1842; buried MWC.

Ch (TEFFT):

    i.   HARRY VEDDER⁶, b ca 1875
    ii.   MADGE N, b ca 1877
    iii.   CHARLES A, b ca 1878

[For additional Tefft data, see #59]

127. MARY ELLEN⁵ VEDDER *(Betsey⁴, John³, Peter², Frederick¹)*, born 29 Apr. 1857. She married 1st DEXTER CROWELL, son of Martin Crowell of Hamlet, Chau Co.; married 2nd SQUIRE WHITE, son of George and Ellen E. (Pierce) White, born Fredonia, Chau. Co. 11 June 1859.

Ch (WHITE) of 2nd m:

    i.   SQUIRE VEDDER⁶, b Jamestown 10 June 1893

128. CHARLES O.⁵ HOLDEN *(Philinda⁴, John³, Peter², Frederick¹)*, born 1850; died 1900; buried WV Village Cem. He married 1st MELISSA _____, born ca. 1853. He married 2nd CATHARINE E. _____, born 1857; died 1928; buried WV Cem.

Ch (HOLDEN) of 1st m:

    i.   WILLIAM⁶, b Ash Feb 1873
    ii.   JAY C, b Ash Mar 1874

[For additional Holden data see #65]

129. CHARLES H.⁵ OYER *(Ira⁴, Jacob³, Peter², Frederick¹)*, born SC, Oswego Co. 7 Oct. 1853; died SC 26 Oct. 1909 (1905?); buried WdlnC. He married 1881 HARRIET/HATTIE R. WHITE of Adams, Jeff. Co., dau. of Herman and Caroline (Green) White. He was educated at Pulaski Academy; graduated from Watertown Busi-

ness College in 1872. Owning 115 acres, he was a dairy farmer, living near the village of Lacona, SC Twp., near his father's farm.

Ch (OYER):

    i.   CECILE E[6], b SC 29 Jan 1894; m _____ CARTER.

130.   WILLIAM I.[5] AUYER *(Ira[4], Jacob[3], Peter[2], Frederick[1])* born SC Twp. 1863. He married _____ WART, dau. of A. B. Wart. William came from Oswego Co. to the Oswego Bitters area of Cam. Twp., Onon. Co., south of the village of Memphis, where he worked as a tenant farmer. He worked several Memphis area farms in Cam. and Elb. He later moved to Wexford Twp., Mich.

Ch (AUYER):

    i.   HAZEL[6], b Wexford Twp, Wexford Co, Mich 29 Mar 1891. She m 24 Aug 1908 CLIFTON BRIGGS, son of Egbert Briggs of Wexford.

131.   LEON J.[5] OYER *(Ira[4], Jacob[3], Peter[2], Frederick[1])*, born SC Twp. 1871; died SC 13 Dec. 1932; buried WdlnC. He married FLORA F. _____, born 1878; died 1967; buried WdlnC. (She married 2nd 23 Jan. 1935 JOHN PATTERSON of Watertown). Leon resided and farmed on the Ira Oyer farm near the village of Lacona.

Ch (OYER):

191.   i.   ESTHER L[6], b 1901

132.   GERTRUDE ELLA[5] AUYER *(Peter[4], Jacob[3], Peter[2], Frederick[1])*, born SC Sept. 1850; died Jordan, Elb., Onon. Co. 14 Aug. 1943. She married 13 Sept. 1871 ALFRED DENNISON LEWIS, son of Thomas Dennison and Minerva Lewis (Westcott) Lewis, born 1 Sept. 1844; died Jordan 1 Dec. 1924; both bur MGC. Alfred Lewis began as a retail grocer in Jordan, later dealing in coal and insurance. He was supervisor of Elb. 1878-79; res Jordan.

Ch (LEWIS):

192.   i.   EDITH GERTRUDE[6], b 14 Mar 1873

133. CHARLES JACOB⁵ AUYER *(Francis⁴, Jacob³, Peter², Frederick¹)*, born SC 26 Aug. 1857; died Syracuse, Onon. Co. 1 Aug. 1917; buried WarC. He married 1st IDA E. MCINTYRE, born 1852; died Lysander, Onon. Co. 27 Apr. 1885; buried WarC. Charles married 2nd Lysander 10 Mar. 1889 EMMA NOSTRANT, dau. of John Widger and Eunice Caroline (Spencer) Nostrant, born 8 Jan. 1858; died Onon. Co. Home, Onondaga Hill, Syracuse 12 Aug. 1932; buried WarC (Nostrant plot).

In the hotel business, by Sept. 1890 he was proprietor of the "Hotel Auyer" at Little Utica, Lysander Twp. He later lived in Cato, Cayuga Co. (in 1910); then Syracuse where he is listed in 1914 as watchman at Syracuse Institute. Later he tended bar on Magnolia St. His residence in Syracuse was at 740 Otisco St.

Ch (AUYER):

193.   i.   WILLIAM H⁶, b 29 Apr 1878
194.   ii. FLOYD LAVERNE, b 20 Apr 1885

134. FRANK A.⁵ AUYER *(Francis⁴, Jacob³, Peter², Frederick¹)*, born New Lisbon, Juneau Co., Wis. Mar. 1868; died Lysander, Onon. Co. 11 Aug. 1893; buried Jacksonville Cem., Lysander. He married Lysander 26 Dec. 1887 FANNY FIELD, dau. of Thomas L. and Hannah (Somes) Field, born Lysander 4 July 1869. Frank was a tenant farmer in both Lysander and Oswego Bitters, Cam. Twp.

Ch (AUYER):

i.   HAZEL W⁶, m _____ HORTON; res Marshall, Mich
ii.   ETHEL L, m _____ WILERICH; res Tekonsha, Mich
iii. FRANCES W, m _____ SCHOALS; res Marshall, Mich

135. ELLA M.⁵ ROE *(Harriet⁴, Jacob³, Peter², Frederick¹)*, born Elb. 1856; died 22 Mar. 1938. She married WILLIAM ANDREWS, born 1857; died 15 Aug. 1930. William was a dealer in meats, groceries and dry goods; their residence was in Syracuse.

Ch (ANDREWS):

i.   HARRIET LOUISE⁶, d Syracuse, 5 Jan 1980. She was an editorial writer for the Syracuse Post Standard.
ii.   HAZEL E, d Syracuse 19 June 1960; an artist
iii. WILLIAM R, b ca 1890; d 17 Sept 1980. He was a

realtor and managed several farm properties owned
by the family.

136.   CORA BELL⁵ BUCK *(Harriet⁴, Jacob³, Peter², Frederick¹)*,
born Elb. 1 Sept. 1866; died 13 Dec. 1948; buried WarC. She
married 19 Oct. 1886, EUGENE/GENE SHERBURN MARVIN, son of
Henry F. and Esther A. (Hall) Marvin, born Van Buren Center/
Warners, Onon. Co. 14 July 1867; died Syracuse 22 July 1927;
buried WarC. Gene farmed, residing in War. Cora was one of the
best beloved persons of her community, interested in family and
active in the War. Methodist Church. She was fatally burned
when her house caught fire, in spite of attempts by her grandson
to rescue her.

Ch (MARVIN):

195.   i.   HOWARD HUDSON⁶, b 7 Feb 1893

137.   HENRY LEWIS⁵ SOMES *(Margaret Mary⁴, Jacob³,
Peter², Frederick¹)*, born Van Buren 5 Apr. 1863; died Van Buren
15 May 1912; buried MGC. He married 1 Feb 1888, LAURA ANN
BARNETT, dau. of John William and Elizabeth (Hider) Barnett,
born near Peru, Elb. 24 July 1862; died Van Buren 9 Apr. 1942;
buried MGC. Laura had at one time been a domestic servant in
the Somes house. Her sister Sarah Jane Barnett married Harry
Auyer McDowell (#151). H.L. was a farmer and oocupied the farm
which his father purchased from Jacob P. Oyer and resided in the
older farmhouse (later known as the tenant house). After her
husband's death Laura moved into the newer Somes house across
the road, formerly occupied by her mother-in-law.

Ch (SOMES), all b Van Buren:

          i.   RALPH B⁶, b 1 Feb 1890; d Van Buren 16 Oct 1893
196.   ii.   SMITH, b 28 Aug 1892
197.   iii.   FLOYD, b 21 May 1896

138.   OREN ALEXIS⁵ SOMES *(Margaret Mary⁴, Jacob³, Peter²,
Frederick¹)*, born Van Buren 5 June 1866; died 5 May 1941; buried
MGC. He married Lysander 15 Feb 1888 SARAH LILLY SHRUBB,
dau. of John Jr. and Elizabeth (Keys) Shrubb, born Lysander 5
Mar. 1867; died Van Buren 27 Nov. 1950; buried MGC. O.A.

farmed, residing in Lysander for a short time just after his marriage. In Apr. of 1890 he moved to the former Edwin Mc-Dowell farm at Somes Corners and lived there the rest of his life.

He operated "Seneca Acres" dairy farm. After his death his widow continued to live at the farm for several years, but later went to live with her son Kaple in his house across the road.

Ch (SOMES):

	i.	HOWARD WELLINGTON[6], b Lysander 7 Mar 1889; d Van Buren 3 Sept 1957; bur MGC
198.	ii.	KAPLE J, b 23 Oct 1892
199.	iii.	JOSEPH HUNTING, b 7 May 1898

139. ADELBERT[5] AUYER (*Romain[4], Jacob[3], Peter[2], Frederick[1]*), born 1862; died 1915; buried Victory Cem. He married FRANCES H. SMITH, died 1972. Adelbert was a farm laborer, listed as such with Wm. H. Smith in Victory Twp.

Frances married 2nd ADELBERT VAN HORNE and had several children.

Ch (AUYER):

200.	i.	LAVERNE WENDALL[6], b 3 Oct 1912

Ch (VAN HORNE) of Frances' 2nd m:

	ii.	EDITH, d y
	iii.	HERBERT
	iv.	ADELBERT, d 1980
	v.	MILDRED
	vi.	POLLY
	vii.	NINA

140. PETER J.[5] AUYER (*Foster[4], Jacob[3], Peter[2], Frederick[1]*), born Van Buren, Onon. Co. 3 Nov. 1867; died Van Buren 28 Oct. 1952; buried Riverview Cem., Baldwinsville. He married Memphis 12 Nov. 1890 MARY LUCY GATES, dau. of Halbert E. and Sarah Frances (West) Gates, born Van Buren 25 July 1867; died Van Buren 11 Sept. 1942; buried Riverview Cem. Peter farmed. Following his marriage he and his wife moved to a farm about a mile west of the Stone Pile School house on Connors Rd., Van Buren. They later moved about a half mile north of the Kingdom School House, where their two children were born. In about 1901 they moved to the Tilley farm in the Pleasant Valley District of Van Buren at the corner of West Dead Creek and Kingdom Rds.

Peter Auyer worked two farms (totaling about 200 acres) at this location.   In about 1918 he purchased 58 acres from this farm.

Ch (AUYER):

201.   i.   RALPH PETER[6], b 30 July 1899
       ii.   ERWIN WEST, b Van Buren 5 Nov 1901; d Van Buren
             24 July 1984; bur Riverview Cem. Erwin farmed,
             retaining possession of the family farm on Lot 4 of
             Van Buren along W Dead Creek Rd.

141. ALONZO L.[5] AUYER (*Foster[4], Jacob[3], Peter[2], Frederick[1]*), born Van Buren, Onon. Co. 1872; died St. Anthony's Hospital, St. Petersburg, Fla. 21 Jan. 1964; buried WarC. He married 1st SUSAN/SUSIE MARIE SPAULDING, dau. of Harrison H. and Matila A. (Nichols) Spaulding, born Van Buren 15 Oct. 1871; died Van Buren 20 Jan. 1937 buried WarC. Alonza married 2nd JESSIE MARVIN, dau. of Alonzo LeRoy and Emma (Button) Marvin, and widow of Hugh E. Quinn, born Van Buren 22 Aug. 1890. (She was his first cousin).

Alonzo farmed, residing along West Sorrell Hill Rd. in Van Buren, next to his wife's parents. Later he moved to a farm at the corner of Brickyard and Warners Roads just west of Warners.

Ch (AUYER) of 1st m. all b Van Buren:

       i.   MYRNA[6], b 1900; d Calif, 1956; bur WarC. She m
            1st SYDNEY GEORGE (divorced); 2nd _____
            BLACKWELL. She lived in Calif where she was a
            successful author of children's textbooks.
202.   ii.   WARREN H, b 5 Aug 1902
203. iii.   EARL L, b 26 July 1907
204.   iv.   LESLIE F, b 28 Mar 1909

141.1 HARRIET MAY[5] AUYER (*Foster[4], Jacob[3], Peter[2], Frederick[1]*), born Van Buren 8 Aug. 1878; died Van Buren 24 Apr. 1967; buried WarC. She married Memphis 28 Feb. 1894 CHARLES MATTHEW ISBELL, son of Charles and Sarah (Matthews) Isbell, born Onondaga Hill 20 Mar. 1867; died Van Buren 30 Dec. 1950; buried WarC.

Charles farmed, residing on his father's farm, west of the village of Warners.

Ch (ISBELL), all b Van Buren:

    i.   FOSTER C[6], b 18 Aug 1895; d Van Buren 22 Sept 1895; bur WarC

205.   ii. FREDERICK C, b 31 Oct 1896

206. iii. IVA, b 31 Dec 1899

    iv. LAURA, b 6 May 1910. She m 25 Feb 1928 WIATT T WILSON, b Venice, Cayuga Co 1905; d Van Buren 25 Feb 1986; bur WarC. Wiatt farmed, res on the "White Rock Farm" east of Ionia for 28 years.

207.   v. LEAH JUNE, b 4 Oct 1917

142. WILLIAM CARLTON[5] TIFFT (*Martha[4], James[3], Peter[2], Frederick[1]*), born Cam., Onon. Co. 29 Sept. 1858; died home of Mrs. Fred McGowan, Elb., Onon. Co. 26 Aug. 1925; buried Troy, Rensselaer Co. He married in Hamilton HARRIET/HATTIE C. INGALLS, dau. of Fitch H. Ingalls, died 11 Jan. 1942.

Carlton was a schoolteacher, educated at Hamiton College and the Univ. of Roch. He taught school in various places and was principal of the Poultney, Vt. Elementary School. Carlton died while visiting his sister. Hattie taught in the art department of the Troy Conference Academy.

Ch (TIFFT):

208.   i. RACHEL A.[6], b 2 Oct 1893

    ii. WAYNE INGALLS, b 31 July 1896; m 1st 1923 BLANCHE WEVER; m 2nd 14 Aug 1939 BERNICE WETZEL

143. CARRIE LOUISE[5] TIFFT (*Martha[4], James[3], Peter[2], Frederick[1]*), born Elb., Onon. Co. 29 May 1860; died Methodist Home, Fort Edward, Washington Co. 3 Apr. 1956; buried MGC. She married 20 Nov. 1894 GEORGE W. MEAD, born 1864; died Delmar, Albany Co. 26 Apr. 1935.

Ch (TIFFT):

209.   i. MABEL ELLA[6], b Elb 26 Sept 1879

Ch (MEAD) of her marriage:

    ii. GRACE E, (adopted), b 20 Sept 1889; d 22 Aug 1900

  iii. EDNA L, (adopted), b 14 Apr 1900; m EDWARD BAKER

144.   JENNIE BELLE[5] TIFFT *(Martha[4], James[3], Peter[2], Frederick[1])*, born Elb., Onon. Co. 6 Feb 1865; died Jordan, Onon. Co. 30 Dec. 1949; buried Elb. Rural Cem.   She married 27 Dec. 1886 FREDERICK CROSSMAN McGOWAN, son of Cortland D. and Camilla E. (McGowan) Crossman, born Sennett, Cayuga Co. 26 July 1860; died Jordan 10 Oct 1941; buried Elb. Rural Cem.   Fred was raised by his maternal uncle, Charles Grandison McGowan, Jr. in Elb.   He later farmed, renting his uncle's land, subsequently purchasing it. In 1932 he retired, moving in 1941 to a house in Jordan.   Jennie had been a schoolteacher before her marriage.

Ch (McGOWAN) all b Elb:

210.	i.	EDWARD TIFFT[6], b 25 Aug 1888
211.	ii.	ETHEL SARAH, b 9 May 1890
212.	iii.	HAZEL CAMILLA, b 7 Dec 1891
213.	iv.	HELEN LOUISE, b 16 Apr 1895

145.   ADA L.[5] WHITNEY *(Emily[4], James[3], Peter[2], Frederick[1])*, born Elb., Onon. Co. 1865; died Syracuse 14 Apr. 1958.   She married 16 Feb. 1887 CHAUNCY/CHAN J. FOSTER, son of Alfred D. and Abigail M. (_____) Foster, born Van Buren 1865; died Syracuse 25 Feb. 1952.

Chan was a farmer, residing on the Foster homestead in Van Buren near Pine Hill School (along Daboll Road).   In about 1950 they moved to Syracuse to live with their son James.

Ch (FOSTER):

	i.	JAMES R[6], m ANGELINE HEMMER; res in Syracuse.

146.   LENA R.[5] WHITNEY *(Emily[4], James[3], Peter[2], Frederick[1])*, born Elb., Onon. Co. 1866.   She married HENRY BENSON.

Ch (BENSON):

	i.	CLARENCE[6].
214.	ii.	RAYMOND, m FLORENCE _____
215.	iii.	OLIVE, m CLARK STAFFORD

147.   STELLA MAY[5] WHITNEY *(Emily[4], James[3], Peter[2], Frederick[1])*, born Elb., Onon. Co. 14 May 1868; died Elb. 29 May 1946; buried Elb. Rural Cem. (no stone).   She married Memphis, Onon. Co. 2 Feb. 1893 JAMES McCOLLUM PATTERSON, son of Daniel

and Nancy (McCollum) Patterson, born Elb. 25 Aug. 1870; died
Elb. 19 Apr. 1943; buried Elb. Rural Cem. (no stone). James
Patterson was a farmer who resided on a farm (formerly his
parents') along Route 5 between Elb. and Cam. near the town line.

Ch (PATTERSON):

       i.   infant daughter.
      ii.   BERTHA[6], d ae 18 m
216.   iii.   CECIL JAMES, b 26 Oct 1901

148.   JAY J.[5] WHITNEY *(Emily[4], James[3], Peter[2], Frederick[1])*,
born Elb., Onon. Co. 1871; died Elb. 1908; buried MWC. He
married Memphis, Onon. Co. 27 Feb. 1893 EMMA BELLE HESS,
dau. of James M. and F. Louise (Abrams) Hess, born 1874; died
1938; buried MWC.

Ch (WHITNEY) both b Elb:

       i.   HOWARD JAY[6], d Auburn 1978. He m ELIZABETH
          _____; they adopted one dau.
217.   ii.   LUMORA MARVEL, b 24 Jan 1900

149.   HARRY GEORGE[5] MARLETTE *(Emily[4], James[3], Peter[2],
Frederick[1])*, born Elb., Onon. Co. 1876. He married Memphis, Oon.
Co. 25 Oct. 1895, BLANCHE T. THOMAS, dau. of Charles A. and
Rosina A. (Kester) Thomas, born Elb. ca. 1879.

Ch (MARLETTE):

218.   i.   ROSINA A[6], m 14 Aug 1919 WILFRED NEWELL
      ii.   CLAUDE HORACE, b 1897; d ca 6 July 1918; bur Elb
          Rural Cem. He enlisted in June 1917 in the 95th
          Co of the 6th Regiment of the US Marines, Ameri-
          can Expeditionary Forces, one of the first units to
          go into action. While fighting at Chateau Thierry
          on 23 May 1918 he was struck by fragments of a
          high explosives shell and received 3 wounds in the
          leg, a fractured arm and a head wound. He was
          taken to a base hospital where he died.

150.   BELLE HATTIE[5] MARLETTE *(Emily[4], James[3], Peter[2], Frederick[1])*, born Elb. 20 June 1884. She married _____ WILEY.

Ch (MARLETTE) b before her marriage:

219.   i. ERMA E[6], b ca 1893

151.   HARRY AUYER[5] McDOWELL *(Julia[4], Solomon[3], Peter[2], Frederick[1])*, born Van Buren, Onon. Co. 8 Feb. 1859; died Van Buren 14 Jan. 1945, buried WarC. He married 1st Elb. 1 Mar. 1882 SARAH JANE BARNETT, dau. of William and Elizabeth (Hider) Barnett, born near Peru, Elb. 28 Apr. 1861; died Warners 6 Jan. 1909; buried WarC. He married 2nd Baldwinsville 30 Dec. 1916 JESSIE ALICE SEAVER MARTYN, dau. of Richard and Clara Jane (McAmber) Seaver, born Brownville, Jeff. Co. 8 Aug. 1878; died Watertown, Jeff. Co. 5 Apr. 1935.

Harry worked his father's farm at Somes' Corners for several years. After his father sold the farm he moved to Cam. near Warners, moving later to Warners, living in the Marvin house. They later purchased a home on Brickyard Rd. Harry was employed at the Warners brickyard. After his second marriage he moved to Watertown. In about 1941, in failing health, he was brought to live with daughter Flora in Van Buren, where he died.

Ch (McDOWELL) 1st m:

    i.   LAURA BELL[6], b Van Buren 30 Nov 1882; d Warners, 26 Mar 1906; bur WarC
   ii.   unnamed twin infant (stillborn)
  iii.   unnamed twin infant (stillborn)
   iv.   CARL (twin), b 19 Feb 1890; d Cam 5 Mar 1891
    v.   EARL HARRISON (twin), b Van Buren 19 Feb 1890; d Syracuse 12 Nov 1962; bur WarC. He served in France during World War I; later lived in Syracuse where he had several jobs including bartender, clerk, night watchman and factory worker.
198.   vi.   FLORA ELIZABETH, b 21 July 1897

152.   ELMER ELLSWORTH[5] McDOWELL *(Julia[4], Solomon[3], Peter[2], Frederick[1])*, born Van Buren, Onon. Co. 16 Mar. 1861; died Memphis, Onon. Co. 27 Aug. 1936; buried MGC. He married 20 Nov. 1884 HENRIETTA/ETTA MARY TIFFT, dau. of Orange Angell and Martha Jane (Auyer) Tifft, born Elb. 9 May 1862; died Warners 14 Mar. 1946; buried MGC.

Elmer was a schoolteacher, teaching at various places including Lafayette, Taunton, Warners, Fabius and Nunda. In 1911 he was elected superintendent of the Third School District of Onon. Co. At this time he resided on his farm at Jack's Reef. In 1921 he retired and sold the farm. He moved to his father—in—law's farm south of Memphis, later living in the village of Memphis. After his death Etta went to live with her daughter in Warners.

Ch (McDOWELL):

220.   i.   JULIAN HAROLD⁶, b 6 Mar 1891

       ii. MARTHA ELIZABETH, b 4 Apr 1894; d Warners 6 June 1955. She m 4 Sept 1919 GLEN C THOMAS, son of Henry W and Emily (Watters) Thomas, b May 1894; d Warners 1975; both bur WarC.

153. SUSAN CHRISTINA⁵ McDOWELL *(Julia⁴. Solomon³, Peter², Frederick¹),* born Van Buren, Onon. Co. 12 Apr. 1863; died Jordan, Onon. Co. 19 Aug. 1941; buried Riverview Cem. She married Memphis 14 June 1894 DANIEL GOODRICH BUCK, son of James H. and Mary Jane (Goodrich) Buck, born Sand Springs 1859; died Sand Springs, 17 July 1902, ae. 42 y, 10 m, 26 d; buried Riverview Cem.
Susie was a teacher before her marriage. Daniel Buck was a farmer and mail carrier at Sand Springs. He died of appendicitis. After his death Susie moved to a house at 24 Elbridge St., Jordan.

Ch (BUCK) all b Sand Springs:

221.   i.   EDITH ELVIE⁶, b 15 July 1895
222.   ii. WARD EVERETT, b 27 May 1900
      iii. JULIA MAE, b 15 Jan 1902; d Newark 25 Apr 1978; bur Riverview Cem. She was a schoolteacher.

154. JESSIE BELLE⁵ AUYER *(Cyrus⁴. Solomon³. Peter², Frederick¹),* born Memphis 15 July 1866; died Syracuse, Onon. Co. 4 Sept 1955; buried MGC. She married HENRY METTLER, son of Jacob and Mary (Ross) Mettler, born Van Buren 7 Mar. 1858; died Memphis, Onon. Co. 4 June 1938; bur MGC. Henry and Jessie Mettler resided at Memphis. He was employed as a laborer and worked for 15 years as a section hand for the N.Y. Central Railroad (now AMTRAK).

Ch (METTLER):

223.   i.   SATIE ESTELLE⁶, b Nov 1885
       ii. FREDERICK GEORGE, b Van Buren 27 Jan 1890; d Syracuse, Fall <sic> 1966; m 1st MAUDE CREGO, 2nd DOROTHY _____. Fred was a laborer

res 2 Hamilton St, Jordan; he later moved to
Syracuse where he was a dispatcher for NY
Central Railroad (now AMTRAK). He is bur MGC.

224.   iii.   LENA ALICE, b 23 Sept 1892
225.   iv.   MARION AUYER, b 10 Mar 1896
          v.   EDNA DORIS, b 5 Oct 1906; m 1st EARL W
                FLETCHER, son of John W and Minnie A
                (_____) Fletcher, b Cato 1897; d Auburn 11
                Mar 1979; bur MGC (divorced); m 2nd CURTIS
                BUTLER. Earl Fletcher resided at Memphis;
                Curtis Butler was employed as chief clerk for
                the Delaware, Lackawanna and Western Railroad,
                residing in Syracuse and at R D 1, Clay.

[Sources for #'s 129 through 154: AHA; Ralph Auyer.]

155.   ANSON BEARDSLEY⁵ OYER (*George⁴, Henry⁸, Peter², Frederick¹*), born 24 Jan. 1899; died 13 Feb. 1973. He married MARY ROXANNE MILLER, born 2 Feb. 1900; died 4 May 1959.

Ch (OYER):

226.   i.   EZRA HUGH⁶, b Nov 1919
         ii.   JULIA ELIZABETH, b 1921
        iii.   RUTH VERMAY, b 1922
         iv.   VERNA CATHARINE, b 1924
          v.   CELIA MAY, b 1926
         vi.   ANSON B, b 1929
        vii.   GEORGE HENRY, b 1930
       viii.   NORMAN CLIFFORD, b 1931; d 1946; bur
                Williamstown Cem
         ix.   MARY FRANCIS, b 1934
          x.   HUGH MILLER, b 1936

156. GEORGE⁵ OYER (*Oscar⁴, Daniel⁸, Peter², Frederick¹*), 10 May 1925; died 13 Dec. 1977; married MARION YAGER (divorced).

Ch (OYER):

226.1   i.   GEORGE⁶, b Aug 1955
           ii.   MARK, b 1958; to Calif with mother
          iii.   SCOTT, b 1961; to Calif with mother

157. **EARL⁵ OYER** *(Oscar⁴, Daniel³, Peter², Frederick¹),* born 1928; married MARGARET NELSON; died 11 Dec. 1984.

Ch (OYER):

    i.   KAREN⁶, b 1954

158. **LESTER⁵ OYER** *(Oscar⁴, Daniel³, Peter², Frederick¹),* born 8 Feb. 1931; married ARLENE BUSH.

Ch (OYER):

    i.   DENNIS⁶, b Dec 1954
    ii.   DEBRA, b May 1956
    iii. DAVID, b May 1959
    iv. TIMOTHY
    v.   JEFFREY
    vi. WILLIAM, b Aug 1964

159. **DONALD H.⁵ OYER** *(Oscar⁴, Daniel³, Peter², Frederick¹),* born 26 Apr. 1933; married JOANNE NICOLETTE, dau. JOSEPH and ROSE (FRAGALE) NICOLETTE, born 4 May 1936. Don resides in Frkf. and is employed by Mohawk Containers.

Ch (OYER):

    i.   DONALD J⁶, b Frkft 18 Apr 1955; m 27 June 1981 DEBORAH ANDRESKI; res Honolulu, Hawaii
    ii. KENNETH K, b Frkf 26 Apr 1964; res Roch; employed by Sibley's Eastview store.

[We were unable to better update #155 through #159.]

Clarence S.[6] Oyer

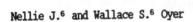

Nellie J.[6] and Wallace S.[6] Oyer

CHAPTER 11

SIXTH GENERATION

160.   CLARENCE SEYMOUR/TANKIE[6] OYER (David[5], Peter[4], David[3], Jacob[2], Frederick[1]), born GrV. Twp., Catt. Co. 14 Feb. 1878; died Delevan, Catt. Co. 9 Apr. 1952; buried SHC, Ellvl. He married 1st 30 Nov. 1898 EDITH MAE CAPRON, born Feb. 1884; died 16 June 1948.   He married 2nd ELIZABETH A./LIZZIE BOW-EN, born Ellvl. 5 Dec. 1879; died Delevan 14 Sept. 1952; buried SHC; no children of 2nd marriage. [Lizzie's 1st husband was Seth Simmons, a banker; they were divorced. He later had a laundry in Gowanda, Catt. Co.]
Clarence raised his family in the David Smith[5] Oyer homestead in GrV.   He was a woodsman and farmer.   For a while he and his son Leland put up billboards in the area, which were much more common in those days.   He resided in Delevan in later years.

Ch (OYER) from 1st m, all b GrV:

227.   i.   BERNICE[7], b 22 June 1901
          ii.   FLORIS, b 26 Nov 1902; d 16 Jan 1929; m Brooks Bennett
228.   iii.   LELAND, b 18 Jan 1905
229.   iv.   LORENE, b 10 Feb 1907
229.1   v.   MARGARET, b 24 Feb 1908

*** *THE CAPRON FAMILY* ***

GrV VR shows Charles Wm Capron d 28 Oct 1937, b 30 Mar 1853, son of Joseph and Mary (Frank) Capron, he b Vt; she Ash. Charles' wife: Gerlder (?) Perryman.   Informant was Mrs Earl Brougham, therefore it may be that Charles would be Clarence's 1st wife's father.

161.   NELLIE JULIAETTE[6] OYER (David[5], Peter[4], David[3], Jacob[2], Frederick[1]), born GrV 11 Aug. 1880; died Sala. 27 Nov. 1967.   She married 1st CHARLES FAY LOUGEE, son of Fred E. and Fannie May (Fay) Lougee, born 27 Dec. 1876; died 1955; both buried GrC. (divorced).   She married 2nd HUGH MORTON.   Nellie was an avid antique collector, traveling throughout the countryside contacting residents.   She had a continuing thriving landscaping business and was actively pursuing this difficult work well into her 80's.

Nellie's handwriting was flawless. The parents kept her sister
Grace from school because of her back deformity, and Nellie often
was enlisted to stay home from her own schooling to tutor her.

Ch (LOUGEE):

230.　　　i.　GEORGIA WINIFRED[7] LOUGEE, b 14 Mar 1901

*** THE LOUGEE FAMILY ***

*Charlie Lougee's ancestors came from Plymouth, N.H. His f was
Frederick; m was Fanny. Fred's brother Frank A paid for niece
Georgia's college education. He lived in the midwest, coming
sometimes to visit. Charlie's family res. in Humphrey, GrV.*

162.　WALLIS/WALLACE SMITH[6] OYER (David[5], Peter[4], David[3],
Jacob[2], Frederick[1]), born GrV. Twp. 15 July 1893; died Sala., Catt
Co., 22 Jan. 1977; buried Calvary Cem., Sala. He married ROSE
JANE DUHAN, dau of Thomas and Sarah (Lynd) Duhan, born GrV.
9 June 1894.

While raising their family, Wallace's work led him to many
fields, nearly all in Catt. Co. Railroading was his main occupation; during the depression of the 1930's he acquired various odd
jobs, including a stint with the Civilian Conservation Corps (CCC)
in Allegany State Park, which he helped to build. [See Illus p
209] For the family it was a vital project, providing badly needed
income. All 3 sons spent time in the CCC's. During all these
years farming for the family needs was essential. Many a neighbor, and in later years, their own children's families, were bene-
factors.

As they had no electricity for over 5 years after their marriage,
the many hardships and adversities overcome are remarkable.
Reminiscing with Rose, who is 93 (in 1987), is impressive.　A
most poignant time was during the pandemic influenza disaster of
1918.

[No one knows where the illness began. Holland, Norway and
Russian Turkestan suffered minor early outbreaks in late 1917. By
"Feb. 1918 it swept over Spain like a tidal wave, afflicting over
eight million Spaniards by June." In March it hovered over the
army trenches; the British called it Flander's Grippe; the Germans,
Blitz Katarrh. Historically it is called the Spanish Flu.

Soon it was in Canada. The first large outbreak in the U.S.
was among thousands of rookies in training at Fort Riley, Kan.
The virus' favorite targets were the young and vigorous.

The influenza reached NYS and the eastern states in Oct. The shortage of doctors and nurses--so many away in the war-- brought about Emergency Nurses Aides, with high school girls unwisely also enlisted to help. Schools, theaters, saloons were closed; any public gathering meant staying as far apart from others as possible.

Trench diggers were called in to cope with the hundreds of graves to be dug.

By the end of Dec., the end was in sight. The final tally: in 4 months over 540,000 Americans had died. Worldwide the total was 22 million--more than twice as many as WWI had claimed in 4 years of war!

Milder outbreaks occurred in 1919 and 1920.]

[Source: Edwin Sayers' "The Great Epidemic," published in the Upstate section of the Roch. Democrat & Chronicle, 8 Nov 1981]

Coping with 2 sick infants and her own sickness, Rose felt that if she could only hang on until Wallace's arrival on Friday from an out-of-town building project for the railroad, she would make out all right. However, watching him coming walking down the road, she knew instinctively that he was worse off than they. (It was a several mile walk from the railroad yards to their home in GrV at that time.)

Her fears were realized; he was gravely ill, not expected to survive. Sickness and death were very prevalent during that epidemic and doctors were badly overworked; coffins could not be made fast enough.

Remember this was war time; men and materials were in short supply. The railroad project, building a sandhouse in Punxsutawney, Pa., was noted for being one of the few buildings erected in that era.

Although ordered to remain in bed, Wallace refused to do so. (As so many developed the complication of lobar pneumonia, as did he, we can look back now to that refusal as perhaps saving his life.) However, at this time his sister Grace, who lived across the creek from them with the parents, did succumb from the influenza. Told not to let Wallace know, Rose had to figure out how to keep him from seeing the funeral, visible from the window she could not keep him from looking out. (Funerals were held from the homes in those days.)

Using the exceptional ingenuity that so characterizes Rose, she found a way. She knew that bon ami, a cleanser available even then, dried to an opaque white after application. She "washed" the windows with it, stating it needed a drying period before removal. Thus she succeeded.

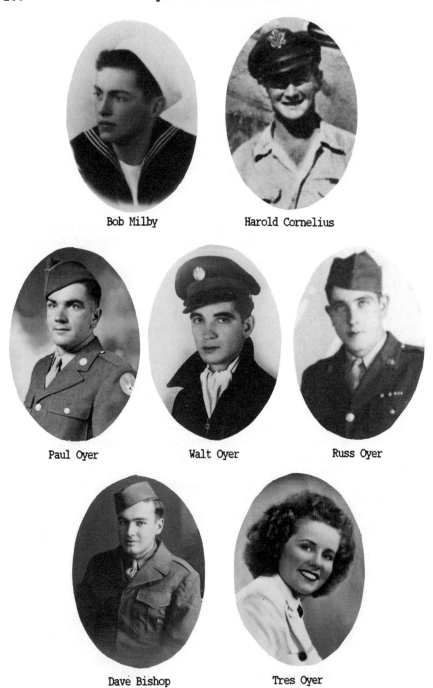

Bob Milby   Harold Cornelius

Paul Oyer   Walt Oyer   Russ Oyer

Dave Bishop   Tres Oyer

Rose Oyer

Wallace Oyer

EDWARD ABERS
PAUL ALBRIGHT
FRANCIS ARNOLD
IRA BABCOCK
LEROY BARGY
JOHN BAXTER
KENNETH BELL
CLEMENT BESS
WILLIAM BIRMINGHAM
JOHN BLACKMAN
GORDON BLENDINGER
JOHN BLENDINGER
RODNEY BLOCK
ROLAND BLOCK
DONALD BLODGETT
FRANK BROWN
SAUL BROWN
WILLIAM BROWN
DUANE BUTLER
CARLYLE CHAMBERLAIN
HAROLD CORNELIUS
ARTHUR CURTIS
SIDNEY CURTIS
VICTOR DOLLARD
FELIX DUHAN
HERMAN FISHER
HOWARD FISHER
RUSSEL GILMAN
ARTHUR GLASKE
BERNARD GRIFFIN
RICHARD GRIFFIN
DONALD GRIFFITH
PAUL HAIGH
CHARLES HARRISON
GUY HARRISON

HAROLD JOHNSON
FRANK KISER
JOHN KISER
HARRY KISER
GILFORD KRAUSE
HAROLD KRAUSE
LLOYD KREAMER
WILBER KREAMER
JAMES KRYNISKI
JOSEPH KRYNISKI
MOXIE KRYNISKI
ROBERT LEWIS
HARRY LIGHT
PAUL LINDELL
SIDNEY LINDELL
CECIL LOUNSBURY
LEO LUBKE
CLIFFORD McDONALD
JAMES McANDREW
JOHN McANDREW JR
DANIEL McNAMARA
ROBERT MESEROLE
JAMES MEYERS
ROBERT MEYERS
HARRY MURPHY
RYAN NORTON
PAUL NYE
CHARLES O'BRIEN
FREDERICK O'HARA
RUSSELL OYER
ALLEN PASSMORE
MALCOLM PELTON
BERNARD PEMBERTON
LELAND PEMBERTON
DANIEL PENNELL

DAVID PENNELL
JOHN PENNELL
MILLARD PERSONS
WILLARD PERSONS
HAWLEY PIERCE JR
GEORGE RAECHER
CLIFFORD REDEYE
FLOYD REDEYE
STANLEY REDEYE
ORMAN RICKEY
MILFORD SANFORD
LEROY SHINE JR
EDWARD SHONESKY
LEO SHONESKY
ROBERT SHONGO
WESLEY SMITH
ARTHUR SNIDER
EARL SNIDER
FRANK SOAMS
RALPH SPRINGER
KENNETH SI CLAIR
EARL TALBOT
ROBERT TAYLOR
DONALD WALBURN
JOHN WARD
JOSEPH WARD
CARLYLE WENRICK
PAUL WHALEN
ERNEST WILSON
GAYLE WOLFORD
MAX YAW
JOHN ZAWATSKI
STANLEY ZAWATSKI
STEPHEN ZAWATSKI
JOHN ZYGLOCKE

WALTER PARTRIDGE
RICHARD BROWN
WALTER BLODGETT
ROBERT MILBY
PAUL OYER
JOHN MURPHY
LAWRENCE SNIDER
IRVING ABERS
CHESTER BROL
LAWRENCE REED
HOWARD REED
J. NEAL BENTLEY
DONALD R BELL
THELMA HARRISON
THERESA OYER
GEORGE LIGHT
RUSSELL TITUS
JOSEPH NICKOLA
DONALD FLAGG
EDWARD CLEVELAND
KENNETH BLISH
ROBERT T. FOLTS
ROBERT TINGUE
GERALD BELL
MALCOLM McMILLAN
CHARLES HUMPHREY
HAROLD COOLE
WALTER OYER
KEITH BLACKMAN
ROBERT A. PEARSON
HAROLD C. JOHNSON
RALPH BOOTH
LESTER HARRIS
LAWRENCE HARRIS
WILLIAM GREY

Honor Roll - Town of Great Valley

In addition to their 5 five children, Wallace and Rose were very
instrumental in helping to raise 2 others.   One, Robert Milby,
born in 1925, son of Guy and Zadie (Cross) Milby, lived next door
to them after their move in 1929 to Kill Buck, GrV. Bob's parents
had died; as a teenager, he was coping alone at home. Despite it
being the depression era and having a full family for whom to
provide, Wallace said one night, "Let's have Bobby come over for
supper" --and he didn't leave. Bob and his wife Helen live in
North Palm Beach, Fla. where he has just retired from 37 years'
service with RCA.   Their daughters: Linda Marie, born Provi-
dence, R.I. 31 July 1949, is married to Samuel Whatley and reside
in Hollywood, Fla. with daughters Claire and Alyson; and Mary
Lucinda/Cindi), born Norwood, Mass. 3 Sept. 1954; resides Royal
Palm Beach, Fla. Bob served in WWII from June, 1943 until May,
1946. He was an Aviation Electronics Technician (AT1), stationed
at Quonset Point, R.I. and Boston, Mass. For 12 years he worked
for RCA as a contract technician at naval bases, aboard ship,
and at the White Sands, N.M. missile testing site.

The second man is Harold "Corny" Cornelius, born 9 July 1922,
also a Kill Bucker who badly needed a home. He and his wife
Cora (Harvey) live in Sala. A retired railroad engineer, he was a
P38 fighter pilot in WWII, retiring with the rank of major after 15
years' service, both active and reserve. His active duty included
New Guinea, Dutch East Indies, and the Philipines. Their ch:
William J., married Judy _____, reside Las Cruces, N.M.;
Shayne, married Charles O'Connell, reside Blairstown, N.J.; and
Cathy, married Donald Pritchard, reside Kill Buck, GrV.

This then brings to 7 the number of service people Wallace and
Rose agonized over during WWII: 3 sons, 1 daughter-in-law, 1
son-in-law, and 2 men they helped raise. While all returned
safely, recent years have shown an untold war chapter--residual
health problems. [See Robert Oyer, #271]

The illustration [p 206-207] includes the Honor Roll of the town
of Great Valley, of which Kill Buck is a part. [Many communities
erected these listing the men as they were drafted to serve their
country; that is why the names are not in strict alphabetical
order. In the 1980's such listings were of those whose lives were
lost; this is not the case and should not be misconstrued.] The
names of 6 of the 7 whom Wallace and Rose supported and agonized over in WWII are there. David Bishop is from LV.

From a community standpoint, Wallace and Rose have left their
mark. Wallace was a moving force in the organization of several
civic groups: a rod and gun club, volunteer fire department, baseball teams, and general fund-raising. He had the fond nickname
of "horse-trader." He was a highly regarded helpful neighbor and
friend to all.

Civilian Conservation Corps camp, Allegany State Park, Cattaraugus Co., N.Y. Wallace[6] Oyer helped in its construction; his sons spent time at it.

Rose, left extremely shy and motherless at the age of 13 was helped largely by the Cattaraugus County Cooperative Extension Service, so vital to the homeakers of the '30's. This brought out the latent leadership, organizational and dexterous abilities she then put to excellent use. Her "credits" include organizing the County Nursing Committee whose loan closet was invaluable; being the prime leader of the highly successful Kill Buck Home Bureau under the auspices of the extension service; being their county leader in teaching upholstering; leading the 4-H club for teen-agers, whose drama group excelled. The skills taught to so many, including her 3 daughters-in-law: home canning, sewing, arts and crafts, repairing--have left an indelible prized mark.

Wallace retired from railroading in 1960. They spent some happy years traveling throughout the country with lengthy stays in Calif. and Fla. before his death in 1977.

As grandmother of 18, great-grandmother of 50, and great-great grandmother of 7 (and counting), her inherent warmth, wisdom, and hospitality have drawn many to her for counsel, reminiscing, and otherwise gaining by an association with her. At 93 she is still vibrantly recalling the valiant struggles through life without indoor plumbing, electricity nor automotive transportation; through poverty, wars, sickness and deaths. She lives alone in her home of over 60 years, and is most grateful for the wonders of life she has lived to experience.

Ch (OYER) all b in Sala:

231.   i.   PAUL FRANCIS[7], b 13 Aug 1916
232.   ii.   RUTH MARIE, b 2 Apr 1918
233.   iii. WALTER CHARLES, b 1 June 1920
234.   iv.   RUSSELL EUGENE, b 1 Apr 1922
235.   v.   BEATRICE JANE, b 15 July 1925

*** THE DUHAN-LYND-BLACKALL FAMILIES ***

All of Rose Duhan Oyer's grandparents arrived from Ireland (hereafter Ire) at the time of the potato famine, which was from 1846-48. What poignant stories and letters we have learned about from relatives! Coming from counties Clare and Cork, they all eventually settled in Catt Co.

Rose's grandfather, JOHN DANIEL DUHAN, b 25 May 1823/25, d Ellvl 6 Jan 1908, bur Holy Cross Cem, came originally to Susquehanna, Penn., said to have arrived in NYC. On the same ship was CATHERINE BLACKALL, who he m 31 Dec 1855 in Cuba, Alleg Co. John D's parents were PATRICK and MARGARET (ROCHE) DUHAN, of Kilmihil, Co. Clare, Ire. John and Catherine

*had 10 children; 5 died in infancy; a 3rd son had no ch. John's
daus: Mary, b Medina, Orleans Co 1857, m John Dineen, d 1909;
Margaret D, b 1862, m Thomas Quinlan, d 1940; a son Michael, b
1865, unm, d 1890.*

*John D worked on the enlarging of the Erie Canal during its
major expansion in the mid-19th century; the building of the
Genesee Valley Canal spur; then on the "competitor" that put the
latter canal out of business, the railroad. [For more canal detail,
so important in this era, see Appendix v.]   John D had a bro
Thomas, b 22 June 1833 who m Ellvl 24 Feb 1868 Bridget O'Connell, b Co Clare, Ireland 17 June 1840, dau of John and Jane
(White) O'Connell.   Their dau Margaret was b 2 June 1881; they
res Ellvl. Another bro Patrick d in Buffalo. The boys were sent
off penniless from their home in Ire.   Can you imagine the
anguish of parents unable to feed their children?*

*John D was a fine singer, his Gaelic songbook a prized pos-
session. His speaking voice was gruff, but he would sing beau-
tifully for hours, in Gaelic. Moving from Lockport, they res
Beaver Meadows, which was near WV, Catt Co. There they settled
on the high ground so coveted by the Irish to avoid the "swamp
fever" so many suffered. (While the canals were worked on, many
contracted a debilitating sickness, the cause of which was not
known. Suspect was the dampness; history shows it to have been
mosquito-borne. The higher land truly was one solution.) He d
Ellvl 6 Jan 1908.*

*John's son THOMAS GEORGE, Rose's f, b Lockport 25 Nov 1855,
m Rexville, Alleg Co SARAH CATHERINE LYND, she b Bryant Hill,
Ellvl Twp, Catt Co 1 Dec 1860, dau of Patrick and Mary
(McKenna) Lynd, d 4 Mar 1908. Tom had to clear the timber from
his 100 acre purchase in Plumbrook, Ellvl Twp, from which he built
his home. The trees had to be burned as there was no way for
him to get them to a mill to be used. Tom had cows and made
and peddled butter to Sala, the closest substantial market for it.
He died 22 Nov 1916 while on a visit to Wallace and Rose's home
in Sala when their home burned. Wallace was able to save Rose
and infant son Paul by breaking a window (cutting his hand
badly), helping them climb out onto the porch roof and jumping to
the ground. Flames prevented Wallace from rescuing his father-
in-law.*

Ch of Thomas and Sarah, all b Ellvl:

*(1) Daniel Patrick, b Ellvl 25 Dec 1884, m 1st 28 Nov 1906 Anna
McKernan, b 18 Sept 1883, dau of Michael and Hannah (Simmons)
McKernan; m 2nd Beatrice (Fee) Kiley, d 5 Mar 1965. Anna d 7
Mar 1923, at time of b of twins, the last of 10 ch: Sarah Loretta
b Jewettville (1907-1970); Thomas Michael, b Ellvl (1909-1938);
Daniel Christopher, b Ellvl (1910-198_); Mary (1912-1963); Alice
(1914-1968); Hubert (1916-1973); Florence (1918-); Jane (1920-*

*ca 1979); Betty and Anna (1923–   ). Beatrice had 3 ch of 1st m
(Kiley): John, Jean and Richard. Dan and Bea had 6 ch: Rose Marie, Helena, Dolores, Catherine, Susanne and William. After several years in Ellvl, the family res Sala.*

*(2) Felix B, b 10 Mar 1887, m 30 Aug 1911 Ethel Harris, dau of
Wooster B and Sarah (Turk) Harris, b Bradford, Penn 16 Apr 1892,
d 8 Feb 1976. Felix worked his f's farm in Plumbrook, Ellvl Twp,
moving to Grv, where he also farmed. He d ca 1968; ch, Bernard
G, b 6 Mar 1915, m 1st 7 Aug 1943 Erna Bachman, m 2nd 1 July
1961 Eleanor (Hinman) Kohler. Erna d 24 Apr 1952. Bernard and
Eleanor res GrV Twp, where he is terminally ill. Bernard and
Erna had 2 sons: Richard David, b 18 Nov 1944, m Shirley Barry
of Churchville, Monroe Co, res Spencerport, Monroe Co; Thomas
Bernard, b 3 Feb 1946; m Karen Kies 14 Aug 1971. Felix' 2nd ch:
Felix, Jr, b 1921; m Marie _____; 6 ch, the oldest, Linda.*

*(3) Marie Philomena, b 4 June 1890, m Leon J Harris, he d 31
Mar 1947. He was Felix, Sr's brother–in–law. They had 1 son,
Edward, b 24 Dec 1913, his m dying 22 Jan 1914. Edward m
Michiko Shabata of Japan.*

(4) Rose (#162)

*John Daniel Duhan's other son John Henry, b Beaver Meadows
23 May 1860, bp Ellvl, m Ellvl 28 Oct 1884 Mary/Mariah Friel, b 2
Feb 1858, dau of Patrick and Mary (Doyle) Friel. John d 1930.
John was a farmer in Somerville Valley, Ellvl Twp. Their ch, all
b Ellvl: Catherine; Mary, b 23 Aug 1887; Clara, b 5 Feb 1889, m 6
Sept 1911 Herman Nannen, ch: Mary Jo, Eleanor, Beatrice, Agatha;
Margaret, b 23 Nov 1893, m Albert Nannen, bro of Herman, d 4
Sept 1985, ch: Genevieve, Mary Katherine, Vincent and Annabelle;
Nellie, b 17 Oct 1895, m Guy Milligan, had dau Josephine, d 1985.
Included in the church rec of the family is James Walsh, listed as
orphan, b NYC 2 June, 1894, having 2 bro, 1 sister, 1 aunt. (It
was a common practice for Catholic families to take in an orphan
from Father Baker's Home ("orphan asylum)" in Buffalo,to raise
and help out.*

*Margaret and Albert died within a span of a few months. Mar-
garet, long crippled with arthritis and aided so compassionately by
her attentive husband, graciously supplied much data in the mid-
1980's, including archives of which we have taken pictures. Her
keen mind, so like her first cousin Rose, could supply every name
for the many people in family groupings, many with "Grandma Duhan" and Father Edward J Rengel prominently shown. Father
Rengel was such a vital participant in these Roman Catholic
families, always ready to play his role as priest and friend.*

*CATHERINE BLACKALL, John Daniel Duhan's wife, was accom-
panied with at least 1 bro (Thomas?, George?) on the journey to
America. She was set off with her only possessions carried in a*

blanket-type holder carried atop her head. Her parents were JOHN and MARY (FALSEY) BLACKALL; Catherine too was b Co Clare, Ire. She was known to still be dancing the Irish jig in her later years. Extant is a candlestick holder that came from Ireland with her; also one of her wood-burned-decorated snuff boxes. Catherine d Ellvl 19 July 1917.

Catherine's sister Nancy/Ann (1828-1891) m Michael Nehill, b 1827; ch: Jack (d in accident); Nellie, m Jack McCadden, res Bflo, Erie Co; Lizzie, res Andover, Catt Co.

Other Blackalls in Ellvl included (1) Patrick, son of John and Johanna (Scanlon) Blackall, b Medina Mar 1857, m Johanna Kelly, dau John and Honora (Roche) Kelly; ch: Mary, b Ellvl 9 Dec 1886; John, b Ellvl 10 Dec 1888, res with them was Jay Sullivan, orphan, b 15 May 1885, d 28 Mar1 1910; they res Somerville Valley; then to Ellvl. (2) Charles Henry, b Ellvl 5 Feb 1865, son of Michael and Bridget (Marven) Blackall, m Ellvl 22 Apr 1890 Julia Driscoll, dau Michael and Johanna (Cunningham) Driscoll, she b Sala 22 Jan 1868, d 11 Feb 1908. Dau: Helena, b Ellvl 6 Dec 1892. Res with them in Ellvl Johanna Driscoll, dau of James and Nellie (McCarthy) Cunningham, b 1825 co Cork, Ire, d 2 July 1911. Rose believes he is the Blackall who ran a general store in Ellvl. (3) Thomas Blackall, m Medina 25 Feb 1858 Mary Kelly, dau John and Johanna (Scanlon) Kelly. He apparently d before 1911. Son: Thomas, b Ellvl 8 May 1868.

One interesting name for a res of a Blackall was "Witch Valley." A Thomas Blackall was a member of Cuba, Alleg Co's RC church, founded in 1853. Our notes show a Thomas (?) b 1790. A George Blackall b co Clare; d 12 June 1893, ae 103 y, 10 m; lived Ellvl 35 yr; 18 ch survived him, 1 m to Timothy Kelly. Early church fires in Ellvl and Cuba destroyed many rec.

Descendant Duhan allied families in America include Cotter, LaCour, Ostrowski, Suto, Call, Woodman, Abers, Bell, Dempsey, Boyd, Pawinski, Feeley. Res include in NY: Sala, Batavia, Bflo, Roch, Spencerport; other states: Md and Fla, plus others unknown.

SARAH LYND's parents, PATRICK and MARY (McKENNA) LYND had 9 other ch: Ann(A), Jane, Wm John, Elizabeth, Margaret, Michael, Julia, Patrick, and Rosana/Rose. Patrick's parents were Michael and Anna/Nancy (Kelly) Lynd of Ballyblagh Townland, co Tyrone, Ire. Pat's bro and sisters: Michael, bp 7 Oct 1825; Elizabeth, bp 25 Mar 1827; John, bp 24 May 1829; Thomas Wm, bp 16 Oct 1831; Mark, bp 24 Aug 1834; and Anna, bp 20 Nov 1836. Patrick was b 19 Sept 1823; Mary his wife b 1831, d 1887 in Ellvl. There are still Lynd and McKenna families in Ire. An Irish research book states that the Lynds in Ire were from a Swedish invasion in the 7th century. Descendant allied families in America

*include McGrath, Friel, McKernan, Murphy, Mueller, Purne, Hay-
den, and Vallely. Places of residence in NY include Roch, Spencerport, Bflo; outside NY; Pittsburgh, Penn; Pawtucket and other
places in RI; Oakland and San Diego, Calif; Burlington, Vt; Frederick, Md.*
   Patrick built cabins on Bryant Hill, Ellvl.
   *Sarah taught school in Andover, Alleg Co. Her early death was
from tuberculosis, the scourge so dreaded for so many years.
Rose was but 13 then, of necessity becoming the housekeeper for
her father.*
   We have no McKenna data.

   *[Sources: Rose Oyer; rec Holy Name of Mary RC Church, Ellvl;
Geo Lynd; Purnell Gen; Charles Simmons (dec'd), Painesville, Oh;
Everts' Catt. Annual Duhan reunions are held in Bflo in mid-
summer; Lynd reunions are held in Roch around Labor Day.*
   *Paddy Waldron of Carrigaholt, Co. Clare (currently studying for
his Ph. D. in Philadelphia, Penn) has much Blackall/McNamara/
Clancy/Durkan, etc data, which he kindly sent to us in 1987.
While he has a Catherine Blackall ancestor, she m George S Clan-
cy. The Blackall family is well documented, and stems from
Thomas Blackall, "descend(ing), as do many of the Cromwellian
landed gentry, from one of those opulent families of the City of
London who supplied the sinews of war to Parliament in its struggle with Charles I, and were recompensed with grants of forfeit-
ed estates in Ireland..." [p 265] "The Blackalls of Killard descend from Thomas Blackall who obtained a lease for lives of Killard and other lands in Co Clare in 1742." [p 267] Quotes are
from an article by the Hon H W B Blackall, Attorney-General,
Gold Coast titled* Abstracts *from* Blackall *Family* Records, *found in
the Irish Genealogist, Vol. 1, No. 9, 1941. The article also
suggests that all Clare Blackalls descended from a known common
ancestor. The name is uncommon now. Mr. Waldron believes it
should be possible to link up the various families. He regards it a
mystery why one branch of the family belonged to the landlord
class while others were forced to emigrate by the famine. He will
be returning to Ireland in 1987 and will contact Blackalls and
research further. Would that we could document this better for
our readers at this time!]*

   163. FREDERICK A.[6] OYER *(Franklin[5], Peter[4], David[3], Jacob[2],
Frederick[1])*, born Ellvl. 23 Oct. 1889; died 21 Sept. 1948. He
married OLGA ROMLER, dau. of Joseph and Elizabeth (Feldman)
Romler, born Hamburg, Erie Co. 16 Aug. 1898/1899; died 24 Feb.
1969. Fred lived in Catt. Co. where he worked on the B.R. & P.

R.R. (later the B & O; then Chessie System); he died before he
could realize his dream of retiring on a farm.

Ch (OYER):

236.   i.   DOLORES[7], b 12 Aug 1920
237.   ii.   JOAN, b 22 Mar 1922
238. iii.   FRED F, b 1 May 1930
       iv.   RACHEL, b 17 Jan 1935; res Jamestown, Chau Co

164.   EUGENE/GENE6 OYER *(Eugene[5], Peter[4], David[3], Jacob[2],
Frederick[1])*, died 23 Dec. 1966.   He married MAY SULLIVAN, d
_____.   Eugene lived in Jersey City, N.J. and later moved
back to Catt. Co., where he lived for some time with Mary (Oyer)
Nelson (#101).

Ch (OYER):

       i.   IRWIN[7]; Irwin and his wife both deceased by 1986
      ii.   OLIVE, b ca 1905; m 1st LaVERNE METZGER,
             div'd; m 2nd _____ _____; res Bflo at one time;
             between Hinsdale and Olean, Catt Co later years.
                  a) JANE
                  b) dau
     iii.   MAY, m CLARENCE CRANDALL.   There are
             Clarence Crandalls living in Buffalo in 1986.
      iv.   EUGENE Jr, sheriff at Waterbury, Conn; d there

164.1   BARTHOLOMEW/BURT6 OYER *(Eugene[5], Peter[4], David[3],
Jacob[2], Frederick[1])*, born ca. 1884; died ca. 1917–1918. He married
27 Apr. 1909 ELIZABETH TEELING, born 10 Aug. 1879; died ca.
1959/60.   They resided in the area around Jersey City and
Milford, N.J.

Ch (OYER):

239.   i.   ANNA[6], b 8 Aug 1911
240.   ii.   JOSEPH ALOYSIUS, b 3 June 1913

[We are most indebted to Ruth (Price) Oyer, Joseph's wife, who
was located by a chance telephone call in 1986 while researching
in the Ringwood area of N. J.   Through her and her relatives we
have been able to document Eugene[5]'s families, unknown up to
that time.]

165.   OLIVE/OLLIE[6] OYER *(Eugene[5], Peter[4], David[3], Jacob[2], Frederick[1])*, born Ellvl.; died Jersey City, N.J. 25 Oct. 1964. She married 1910 JOHN BRADLEY, born ca. 1884; died summer of 1937, ae. 53 y. John was a probation officer in Jersey City, N.J.

    Ch (BRADLEY):

241.   i.   ROBERT E[7], m VERA CUCCI
242.   ii. GENEVIEVE CATHERINE/JANE, m JOSEPH E GREEN

166.   KATHERINE/KITTIE [6] L. OYER *(Eugene[5], Peter[4], David[3], Jacob[2], Frederick[1])*, born Ash., Catt. Co. ca. 1883; died WV Dec. 1938; bur. Mt. Hope Cem., WV 20 Dec. 1938. She married 1st _____ REYNOLDS. Kittie returned to Ash. from N.J. where her parents had settled, widowed with her two small boys where by 1915 [Ash St census] she is found with her brother Arthur Oyer, a 22-year old bookkeeper.

Kittie married 2nd HUGH WAITE, born 6 Jan. 1880/2, son of Andrew J. and Alida Esther (Vosburg) Waite. Hugh is found with Charles Kruse, age 34. [Ash St census] Hugh died 1951; bur. MtHC.

Kittie is said to have had beautiful wavy hair.

    Ch (REYNOLDS) of 1st m, both b Jersey City:

243.   i.   JAMES[7], b 1900
244.   ii. EUGENE, b 25 Jan 1905

    Ch (WAITE) of 2nd m, all b WV:

245.   iii. DOROTHY, b 1918
246.   iv. ALIDA, b 1920
        v.   WELLMAN/BILL, b 1922; res Roch; unm

*** THE REYNOLDS AND WAITE FAMILIES ***

We have no data concerning Kittie's first husband; our con-clusion now is that he was from the N.J. area. There are many Catt. Co. Reynolds well documented; no connection can be made.

There are details concerning both Reynolds and Waites in the Adams' Catt, pages 400 and 1099 for Reynolds; pages 460 and 461 for Waites. In Everts' Catt, see pages 331 for Reynolds; pages 339-340 for Waits. There may be other references.

The Ellvl, Catt Co 1855 St census shows Elisha Reynolds, 38, in town 3 yrs, born Savoy, Mass; wife Maria/Alaia/Mariah (Vedder,

dau of Jacob and Margaret--making her sister of Rachel who mar-
ried Peter Oyer #25), born Mont Co, 32; Mary, 8; Sarah, 7; Alice,
4; and Hiram, 2. They res Frklnv many years; then to Sala with
son Vedder C Reynolds, b 5 Aug 1856. Elisha d there 19 May
1893. Mariah d Frklnv 4 Mar 1884.
Vedder C Reynolds was a teacher and lawyer who served in S
Dayton, Catt Co; Bflo, Erie Co, as well as Sala.

Waites/Waits came from Westchester and Washington counties.
In Ash 1915 St census we find Andrew J Waite, 68, b Ash 1846;
Alida E, 63; and Manley, 43. They also had Maud S, b ca 1883.
Alida was b in Ill. 1852. They were still in Ash in 1915. [Ash St
census]

166.1   WILLIAM/WILLIE[6] OYER *(Eugene[5], Peter[4], David[3],*
Jacob[2], Frederick[1]), died Linden, N.J.   He married LILLIAN
_____; died Hillside, N.J. Willie was a railroad worker in N.J.

Ch (OYER):

    i.   EDWIN[7], dec.   He m LUCILLE _____.   This
          may be the Ed who spent summers with Frederick
          and Olga Oyer (#163)
   ii.   ROBERT
  iii.   VIRGINIA, m CHARLES _____; res Union, NJ
  iv.   JEANETTE, m VINCENT TURHAN; res Summit, NJ

[Sources, #164 through #166.1: Ruth Oyer, #240; Mr. and Mrs.
Graydon Williams of WV; Ash VR and cem rec; censuses]

167.   CHARLOTTA/LOTTIE6 NELSON *(Mary[5], Peter[4], David[3],*
Jacob[2], Frederick[1]) born 20 Dec. 1892; died 15 Jan. 1962; bur
FrktC. (?); married PHILLIE WIDRIG, born 15 Feb. 1892; died 7
Mar. 1950. They resided in Ash; buried Sprvl. Philliie's mother
was CATHERINE/NAN OYER. [not documented]

Ch (WIDRIG):

    i.   ELEANOR[7], b 3 June _____; m MAX HOPKINS; res NC
          and Tallahassee, Fla. Ch (HOPKINS):
          a) FRANK, dec'd; m _____ _____; sons
              JOHN and JAMES res Fla
          b) PHILLIP, m EMMA _____; res Ga; ch
              KEITH and SHANE, the latter m'd, res
              Tallahassee, Fla

168. LAURA⁶ NELSON, (*Mary⁵, Peter⁴, David³, Jacob², Frederick¹*) born 5 Nov. 1897; died 11 Nov. 1965; buried LV, Catt. Co.; married RAYMOND GERWITZ, divorced. Ray died "recently" per informant 1987. They resided Riceville and New Albion, Catt. Co., the first several children born while in Riceville.

Ch (GERWITZ):

    i.   VIOLET⁷, b 3 July 1916; m CARL H BOEHM; d 3 Dec 1966. Carl, b 28 Feb 1909; d 18 Nov 1951; both bur Maple Cem, Sprvl.

    ii.   ALICE m GARY PHILLIPS, dec'd 1977⁻; res Blasdell, Erie Co. Ch (PHILLIPS):
        a) GERALD/CORK8
        b) SANDRA
        c) ANNETTE
        4) HOWARD

    iii.   ALFRED, m DOROTHY _____; have 7 ch; res Bflo
    iv.   BETTY, m twice; no ch (?), res Warren, Penn (?)
    v.   DOROTHY, m LARRY WILLIAMS Ch (WILLIAMS):
        a) DIANE, m, res Sprvl (?)
        b) LARRY LEE, m, res Sprvl (?)

    vi.   LOMAMARIEL/MYRT, m _____ WHITE; 2 m ch, res Bflo
    vii.   RAYMOND, m, res LV

168.1 MARGARET⁶ NELSON (*Mary⁵, Peter⁴, David³, Jacob², Frederick¹*), born 1904; died 30 Oct. 1969; married WALTER DRAYER, born 7 Jan. 1901; died 22 Sept. 1963; resided Kennedy Hill, Machias, Catt. Co. The Regis B., S. K. and William, who are listed in the Machias-area telephone directory, could be related.

Ch (DRAYER):

    i.   WILLIAM⁷, m MARJORIE SCHULENBERG, dau Ray & Cecelia Schulenberg of Bflo; res Ischua Trailer Ct (1978)
        a) WILLIAM⁸
        b) SUSAN

    ii.   NANCY, m RICHARD MAYO; res Willmsvl, Erie Co
        a) RICHARD MAYO
        b) dau

168.2 AGNES⁶ NELSON (*Mary⁵, Peter⁴, David³, Jacob², Frederick¹*), born 1906; married FLOYD WASSON, who died in

1983. They resided Sprvl., where Agnes is still employed by the Robinson Knife Co. She hopes to remain working until April, 1988, when she will retire after having worked there 60 years! Her sister Lottie's daughter Eleanor Hopkins spends weeks with her in the summer, and is like a daughter to Agnes.

Ch (WASSON):

     i. JANE[7], m JAMES PISCATELLI Ch (PISCATELLI):
        a) JAMES F[8], b 1953; m PEGGY VEDDER, dau of Allan and Betty (Jirak) Vedder of Frklnv; have son JAMES ALLEN9
        b) LOIS, b 1954; m JOHN MYERS; res Endicott, Broome Co.
        c) DAVID, b 1957, m THERESA HALL; res Hamburg
        d) MOLLY, b 1961
        e) JACK, b 1964
        f) MARK, b 1965
[Sources, #166.1 through 168.2: Agnes Wasson]

169.   ROBERT EMMONS[6] OYER, *(Frank[5], Jacob[4], David[3], Jacob[2], Frederick[1])* born E. Ash. 28 Dec. 1881. He married 25 Jan. 1906 CECELIA EMMA MINOR, "both of Sprvl." They resided in N. Tonawanda in 1934. Cecelia died Ft. Lauderdale, Fla.

Rob Oyer is described by one relative as "a short roly-poly man." He was a bookkeeper and in later years was employed by his son-in-law Norman Carpenter who owned a bus company in N. Tonawanda. His widow later made her home with her daughter Eleanor in Fla.

Ch (OYER):

247.   i. EUNICE[7], m NORMAN CARPENTER
248.   ii. ELEANOR, m ERNIE BELLAS
       iii. ROBERT, unm and living in Fort Wayne, Ind (as of ca 1978)
       iv. WINIFRED, m HAROLD LUDWIG. Her husband was a teacher, now retired and active in church work, residing in Detroit, Mich. They have several ch.
       v. JANICE, dec'd, m WILLIAM BRUNN. She graduated from Univ of Mich as a lab techinician and m a veterinarian; res Silver Springs, Md; several children.

170. RUTH ANN[6] OYER (*Frank[5], Jacob[4], David[3], Jacob[2], Frederick[1]*), born Riceville, Ash. Twp. 15 Jan. 1883; died 5 Dec. 1964; buried Sprvl. She married 7 Mar. 1906 BERT NELSON HADLEY, son of Henry Hamilton Hadley; he died before 1978. Ruth taught school at one time. Bert was a supreme court reporter for the eighth judicial district located in Bflo. and they resided in Hamburg. Ruth Ann was very much into church work. She spent her last years living with her son Elbert.

Ch (HADLEY):

249.   i.   LAWRENCE STANLEY7, b 5 June 1909
250.   ii. ELBERT HAMILTON, b 10 July 1913
251.   iii. WAYNE NELSON, b 6 May 1919

*** THE HADLEY FAMILY ***

BERT NELSON HALDEY's father HENRY was of the Hadleys who migrated from Brattleboro, Vt. where the first Hadley to come from Wales, Great Britain settled: GEORGE. George was buried there in the early 1700's.

George had at least 2 ch; 1 went south, there being Hadleys in the Carolinas; and 1 went west. "Our" Hadleys were Catt Co pioneers. At the organization of the First Congregational Church in E Ash were Alonzo, Fessenden and NELSON H HADLEY.

Alonzo, b ca 1818 (1870 Ellvl census) and William were sons of JESSE HADLEY, coming from Brattleboro, Vt in 1843, purchasing land in Ash owned by Otis Holland.

Many censuses reveal others, all showing Vt as place of birth. A Betsey E Hadley m Samuel P Arnold of Ellvl, bro of Charles S Arnold, in Ellvl 1836. Nelson H, another son of Jesse, came in 1850, "purchasing the farm where his son Henry H now lives." This then is HENRY HAMILTON, father of our subject. [Adams' Catt, p 456] Nelson m CATHERINE THOMAS; d 6 July 1867; their other son was Willard.

The line of descent then is: EBENEZER[1], b Westford, Mass 16 Apr 1762, m ABIGAIL SPALDING, d 21 Oct 1859, ae 78, bur Riceville Cem, Ash; JESSE[2]; NELSON H[3]; HENRY HAMILTON[4]; BERT NELSON[5]. [This assumes that the Abigail bur in Riceville Cem is Ebenezer's wife.]

A Rev Daniel Hadley went to Leon, Catt. Co. in 1820 from Gerry, Chau. Co. He was a Free-Will Baptist. He followed blazed trees to guide him to that settlement. Cornelius Hadley, b ca 1820, settled Ash 1842. Other heads of families include Charles, b ca 1831; Oscar, b ca 1818 (1870 Ellvl census); and Ebenezer, b ca 1823.

John Hadley of Machias, Catt Co, b ca ca 1818 also; and Rufus Hadley had wills probated 1868 and 1869 respectively. Rufus' heirs include son Charles H, Ash; Lorilla J Wiltsie, Ash; Laura A and Eveline J, Ypsilanti, Mich; Horace W, Winchendon (sic), Mass; Edward L, Whitewater, Wisc.

John's exec was widow Paulina P; heirs: Leverett W, Lockport; Martha M Eastman, Newton, Jasper Co, Iowa; Maria A Peavez, Machias; Caroline/Carrie A Stacy, Yorkshire; Wesley J, Machias; Mary E, Machias; and Nathan L/S of Busti, Chau Co. In 1905 St. census Julia B Hadley, ae 76, is found in Yorkshire, Catt Co.

An A E Hadley went to Concord, Erie Co in 1845; moved to Alexander, Genesee Co 1846; m Ella Wilson; 1 ch: Lottie. [Briggs, p 384]

There are 28 Hadleys bur in Riceville Cem, Ash.

The Hadleys m Rices, after whom Riceville was named. The Rices are said to have descended from Deacon Edmond Rice who settled in Sudbury, Mass. about 1639.

A newspaper clipping of 23 Mar 1956 tells of a 50th wedding anniversary celebration for the Burdette Hadleys of Riceville and lists the following among the guests: the Alvin Hadleys, Mrs Martha Hadley; the Neal Hadleys, and the Alvin Folts. "...married in Bflo...lived most...in this vicinity."

[Sources: Ash cem rec; Everts' Catt; Adams' Catt; W Irving Hadley of Toledo, Ohio letter of 15 Dec 1933; Charlotte Oyer; Elbert Hadley. Dr. Hadley has provided much data on the Hadley families, and kindly supplied us with letters and papers written to Jacob Oyer (#26) during the 19th century. Data from them has been inserted in various places in our text. They are a magnificent addition to our archives.]

171.   EDWARD JACOB[6] **OYER** *(Frank*[5]*, Jacob*[4]*, David*[3]*, Jacob*[2]*, Frederick*[1]*)*, born Sprvl. 3 Apr. 1885; died suddenly 21 Nov. 1913. He married CATHERINE O'BRIEN, whose father was a police officer. He was a pharmacist. This was an instance of a protestant marrying a Roman Catholic causing tremendous family trauma, a shamefully common occurrence, at least in the first half of the twentieth century.

Ch (OYER):

    i.   MARY JANE[7], b ca 1913; she m _____ BARRETT, thought to be a state police officer in Roch.

172.   WILLIS LEVI⁶ OYER *(Frank⁵, Jacob⁴, David³, Jacob², Frederick¹)* , born Sprvl. 2/3 Aug. 1887; died 12 Jan. 1962. He married 9 Sept. 1908 MYRTLE BESSIE WILLIAMS, born Ash. 27 Jan. 1890; died 26 Nov. 1952. Willis was a farmer in WV. He farmed on the Hadley farm there, which was later purchased by niece Ruth (Aul) Stockin (#254) and her husband. He lived in Bflo. and is shown in the 1920 city directory as a carpenter, residing at 89 Greenwood; in 1930 as a sprayer at 159 Lincoln Blvd., Kenmore.

    Ch (OYER):

252.   i.   IONA MARIE⁷, b 26 July 1910
         ii.   DONALD CHARLES, b 6 Nov 1915; d Oct 1928 of
               typhoid fever
253.   iii.   RUSSELL STEWART, b 9 Apr 1927

173.   AGNES JONES⁶ OYER *(Frank⁵, Jacob⁴, David³, Jacob², Frederick¹),* born Sprvl.? 22 May 1890; died Feb. 1978. She married 10 June 1914 CARLTON H. AUL; they resided Bflo.

Agnes was a telephone operator before her marriage. Her husband was an upholsterer and had a good business in Bflo. He retired about 1957, moving to Ft. Lauderdale, Fla. As her husband was in poor health they sold their Fla. home in about 1973 and returned to New York where he died a few weeks later. After his death she lived with her dau. Martha Unger in N.J.

Agnes kept little books with everyone's birth and death dates.

    Ch (AUL):

254.   i.   RUTH⁷, b 9 Apr 1915
255.   ii.   RICHARD, b 4 Aug 1917
256.   iii.   MARTHA, m MELVIN UNGER

174.   HARVEY EUGENE⁶ OYER *(Frank⁵, Jacob⁴, David³, Jacob², Frederick¹),* born Sprvl. 15 Mar. 1892; died 11 Dec. 1975; buried Boynton Beach, Fla.   He married 24 Apr. 1924 Hypoluxo, Fla. LILLIAN FREDERICA/FREDA VOSS. After having gone West twice Harvey settled in Fla. about 1913, purchasing a farm there in 1914 at Boynton/Boynton Beach. He served in WWI from 1917–1919, but returned to Fla. He was a carpenter. His wife's family came to Palm Beach in 1872; her mother had been the first white child born in that area.

Ch (OYER):

257.   i.   HARVEY EUGENE Jr⁷, b 31 Mar 1926

258.   ii.   LOIS PATRICIA, b 17 Nov 1928

       iii. CHARLOTTE ANNE, b 19 June 1930. She is a librarian at Calif State Univ, Northridge, Calif. She is an important informant for the large families of Frank Emmons Oyer (#103).

175. ESTHER IRENE⁶ OYER *(Frank⁵, Jacob⁴, David³, Jacob², Frederick¹),* born Sprvl. 19 Dec. 1893/4; died 13 Feb. 1924. She married Oct. 1919 ROSCOE WALTERS of Bflo. She died of diphtheria; her husband later remarried. It is believed Esther was a teacher. In 1934 they resided Syracuse.

Ch (WALTERS):

     i.   RALPH

176. LEON IRVING⁶ OYER *(Frank⁵, Jacob⁴, David³, Jacob², Frederick¹),* born Sprvl. 5 Oct. 1889; died 17 Nov. 1967. Leon married 1st BETTY _____ (divorced); he married 2nd 15 Mar. 1935 VIOLET PETERSON. Violet resides many months of the year in Fla., having sold the family homestead in Sprvl.

From Dr. Elbert Hadley (#250) we learn that Leon helped him to build his cottage on Lime Lake, Machias, Catt.Co.

Ch (OYER) of 2nd m:

     i.   MARSHA⁷, b Sprvl 7 Aug 1937; m DAVID BYER, b Bflo ca 1935; res Hamburg. Ch (BYER):
          a) BETH ANNE⁸, b ca 1962; m DEAN REINBOLT; res Machias; ch: 1 boy; 1 girl
          b) DAWN, b Nov 1963; m twice; res Penn & N Carolina; ch: boy; girl; boy, b 1987
          c) DAVID, b ca 1964; plays the trumpet
          d) DIANE, b ca 1966
          e) DARLEE, b ca 1967
     ii.   SUSAN, b Sprvl 28 Sept 1943; m DALE WILSON, b Lyndon, Catt Co 11 Nov 1940; res LeRoy, Genesee Co; own Petals & Threads, a flower shop there. Susan is a floral design graduate, and plays the organ. Ch (WILSON):

           a) CYNTHIA HEATHER, b Batavia 15 May
               1968; college student at Johnson &
               Wales, Providence, R I
           b) BRIAN CHRISTOPHER, b Batavia 7 Dec
               1970, student

   iii. ALLAN, b Sprvl 4 Nov 1948; m NANCY WEBSTER,
        b Sprvl 1937. After several years as a machinist
        in Jamestown, Chau Co, they now are in a parts
        production business in Seminole, Fla. They are
        active in church work. Ch (OYER):
           a) MATTHEW, b 1976
           b) NATHAN, b 1978
           c) RACHEL, b 1983

   iv. JACQUELINE, b 5 Oct 1950; m RICHARD BAGWELL
        res S Car; currently Lynchburg, Va where Richard
        is in car sales; Jacqueline is a teacher, studying
        for her masters degree. Ch (BAGWELL):
           a) MICHAEL, b ca 1975
           b) STEPHANIE, b 1984

[Sources for #'s 169 through 176: Susan Wilson; Charlotte Oyer;
Violet Oyer; Erie Co LR, SR.]

177. M. DEVER⁶ BROOKS (*Snowey Ann Bowen⁵, Margaret⁴,
John³, Jacob², Frederick¹*), born E. Otto 11 June 1889; died E.
Otto 1 Nov. 1960. He married E. Otto 27 June 1916 RACHEL G.
SIKES, dau. of Gordon and Rhoda (Torrence) Sikes, born E. Otto
1894; died Sept. 1974. Both buried E. Otto. Dever Brooks resided in E. Otto where his occupation is listed variously as clerk,
farmer, laborer, and later foreman at a gristmill. Last he is listed as manager of James H. Gray Milling Co.

    Ch (BROOKS) all b E Otto:

    i.   TORRANCE (TORRENCE?) BOWEN⁷, b 20 Nov 1918
    ii.   LAURA <u>JEAN</u>, b 4 Oct 1921
    iii. LORA <u>JANE</u>, b 4 Oct 1921; she m 23 Nov 1941
         EDWIN C LECKENSTEIN
    iv. ROBERT SIKES, b 12 Mar 1924; d E Otto 3 Nov
         1933 of polio; bur E Otto
    v.   PHILO JAMES, b E Otto 7 May 1928

178. DESSIE⁶ BEACH (*Amy Bowen⁵, Margaret⁴, John³, Jacob²,
Frederick¹*), married GEORGE HARRISON. They reside Arcade,
Catt. Co. where he was a technician for Borden Milk Co.

Ch (HARRISON):

    i.   FRANCIS[7], b 26 May 1913; m LUELLA BEY; res Arcade.

178.1   LUCY[6] BEACH *(Amy Bowen[5], Margaret[4], John[3], Jacob[2], Frederick[1])*, married HENRY RASZMANN; resided Bflo., Erie Co.

Ch (RASZMANN):

259.   i.   DELEVAN[7], b Mar 1905
        ii. VIVIAN, b ca 1908; d 29 Feb 1916 aged 7 y
      iii. PAULINE, b 13 Aug 1913
      iv. DOROTHY, b 1918

178.2 ST. ELMO CHARLES[6] OYER *(Charles[5], John[4-3], Jacob[2], Frederick[1])*. born E Otto 24 Apr. 1890; d 20 Oct. 1955. He married CLARA BEULAH HENDRIX, born 1889 died 1967. Both are buried MWC.

St. Elmo had a long-standing chiropractic practice in Bflo. At a wedding in Roch. in 1986 was a guest from Ariz. who believed her life was saved by him when medical means failed. She told of what a wonderful reputation Dr. Oyer enjoyed. His two sons have followed in his footsteps.

Ch (OYER):

259.1   i.   ELEANOR MAE[7], b 27 May 1915
260.   ii. CHARLES HENDRIX, b 24 Mar 1917
260.1 iii. JAMES DAVID, b 3 Oct 1919

[Sources: Eleanor Mullen; censuses; Bflo VR]

179. EARL[6] GOODEMOTE *(Cora[5], John[4-3], Jacob[2], Frederick[1])*, born 12 May 1892. He married Paris, France 31 July 1919 AGNES HASCOETT.

Ch (GOODEMOTE):

    i.   EDNA MARIE[7]

180. ROYDEN⁶ GOODEMOTE *(Cora⁵, John⁴⁻³, Jacob², Frederick¹),* born 9 Dec. 1900; he married 1 May 1928, ALDEAN KNIGHT.

Ch (GOODEMOTE):

    i.   CARL⁷
   ii. HELEN

181. CLARA⁶ GOODEMOTE *(Cora⁵, John⁴⁻³, Jacob², Frederick¹),* born 16 Dec. 1904. She married 5 July 1922 ROBERT W. GEORGE.

Ch (GEORGE):

    i.   ROBERT⁷

*** THE GOODEMOTE FAMILY ***

We find a number of Goodemotes, but cannot connect. In Ash 1905 St census are the following: Vedder, 33; Lillian, 31; Eva, 16; and Mirton, 15. Phillip, 79; Katie, 78; Wm, 45; James, 48 head; Dora, 25, wife; Gladis, 7; Violet, 5. Wm H, 67; Ada A, 53; Abram, 62, head. James, 84, f-in-law; Mariah, 80, m-in-law, these with either Bond or Goodemote as head.
In Ash 1915 Emeline, 66 is listed with Vedder. In Yorkshire 1915 is William, 46; Carrie, 45 and Floyd, 18.

[More Goodemote data: Chapter 10]

182. GEORGE MARTIN⁶ WOODRUFF *(Mary Alice⁵, Robert⁴, Frederick³⁻²⁻¹),* was born Ellvl. 15 Aug. 1869; married 1 Sept. 1903 NELLIE BRONDART; in 1948 resided in Frklnv., Catt. Co.

Ch (WOODRUFF):

    i.   FLORENCE A⁷, b Humphrey, Ellvl Twp 9 July 1904
   ii. EULA MAE, b Humphrey 13 Dec 1907, m 25 Aug 1927 WILLIAM ANGIE
  iii. RALPH A, b Machias, Catt Co 21 Dec 1915, m 29 Aug 1939 JESSIE CRAWFORD. No ch as of 1948.
  iv. GERVIS G, b Frklnv 25 Sept 1921, d 17 Nov 1946, m 14 Jan 1945 JEAN E MILLER. Ch: GERVIS G; JANE KATHLEEN

183.   ARCHIE ALVIN⁶ WOODRUFF *(Mary Alice⁵, Robert⁴, Fred-erick⁽³⁻²⁻¹⁾)*, born Ellvl. 5 Apr. 1871; married Lyndon, Catt. Co. 26 Feb 1896 AGNES LITTLE, born Lyndon 6 May 1876, dau John and Mary (Kensie) Little.

Ch: (WOODRUFF):

    i.   GEORGE LAWRENCE⁷, b Lyndon 29 June 1897, m 6 May 1919 LAURA WATKINS. Ch: LAWRENCE⁸, b 1924; HOWARD J, b 1928; HELEN A, b 1930

    ii. DORIS ELIZABETH, b Frklnv 23 Setp 1899, d 19 Aug 1902

    iii. MILDRED GRACE, b 19 Sept 1909, m 16 Nov 1936 CLAUDE HAMMOND; res Frklnv. Ch: JOANNE; MARY JANE

[Sources: Woodruff Inf 1 & 2; Woodruff Genealogy]

183.1   LOUIS/LEWIS⁶ E. OYER *(Malden⁵, Robert4, Freder-ick⁽³⁻²⁻¹⁾)*, born Ash. Apr. 1878; died Bflo; will dated 23 Jan. 1958; married SALINIA E. SHARP, who died 29 Dec. 1961. Both are buried Pine Hill Cem., Bflo. section, as are several of the children.

The Bflo. city directory of 1900 shows Louis with parents, a clerk for a telegraph company, undoubtedly Western Union.

Ch (OYER):

    i.   LEWIS⁷, dec

    ii. MARION E, dec; m WALTER REYNOLDS, res'd Bflo

    iii. WILLIAM C, b Oct ca 1905; shown as "oiler", 1940 Blfo dir; res Bflo

    iv. ETHEL, dec ca 1950

    v.   IRENE, ca 1909; m H PARKER; res Alden, Erie Co

    vi. LAWRENCE E, d ca 1969; bur Pine Hill Cem; shown as a lab worker, 1930 Bflo dir

    vii. MILFORD C, b 5 Aug 1911; m HELEN WATERSON, auto mechanic; res Tonawanda, Erie Co

    viii. MILDRED K, m NORMAN FIERLE; res Hamburg; now Bradenton, Fla

    ix. MILDRED, d y

    x.   ROBERT, d y

[These late additions were achieved with the help of Eleanor Mullen (#259.1), through a phone conversation with Helen, Mil-ford's wife. This family connection eluded us for years; we are most happy to welcome them into the fold. Other sources: Erie Co SR & LR]

183.2 LEE E[6] OYER (*Frederick[5], Robert[4], Frederick[3-2 -1]*), born GrV. 22 Nov. 1887/9; died Frklnv. 2 Mar. 1964; married ETHEL WATKINS of GrV., dau of _____ and ADDIE (SIMONS/ SIMMONS) WATKINS, the father from Ash.; mother from Sugartown, GrV. Lee worked for many years at the Babbitt Funeral Home in Frklnv., dying suddenly at a resturant there. It is believed he had 3 grandchildren.

Lee's sister FLORA OYER DILTZ's last known address was 5550 State St., S.E., Salem, Ore. We were unable to trace.

Ch (OYER):

    i. MARGARET[7], m 1st HAROLD PLACE; m 2nd _____ JACKSON. Mail addressed to 400 Elmwood Av, Bflo returned undeliverable. Margaret is said to have had twins.

[Sources: Frklnv VR; Richard Allen of Babbitt Funeral Home; Rose Oyer]

184. DELLA ELIZABETH[6] KNAPP (*Frances[5], John[4], Peter[3], Frederick[2-1]*), born Schuy. 12 Dec. 1873; died 2 Apr. 1931; married 20 Oct. 1897 ARTHUR WARREN WOOD, b 2 July 1873; died 17 Sept. 1914. Both buried Schuy. Twp.

Ch (WOOD), all b Schuy:

    i. IRA ALBERT[7], b 21 May 1900, d Schuy 23 Mar 1914, bur Schuy

    ii. GLENN CHESTER, b 13 June 1903, d 16 Dec 1913

    iii. KATHRYN FRANCES, b 10 Oct 1905, m 22 July 1944 RICHARD EVAN WILLIAMS, b 2 Apr 1899, d 30 Oct 1970, bur Schuy. She res Utica; no ch.

261. iv. MARGUERITE EMMA, b 1 Sept 1906

261.1 v. RUTH MARION, b 18 Mar 1908

    vi. MILDRED GAYLORD, b 2 June 1909, d N Hartford, Oneida Co 9 Aug 1981, bur W Schuy; m 1st 17 June 1944 CARL CHRIST, b 7 June 1903, d 5 Feb 1957, bur Crown Hill Cem, N Hartford; m 2nd 29 July 1961 GEORGE M BOWMAN, b Utica 30 June 1917, d Utica 19 Mar 1987, bur W Schuy Cem

185. HARVEY BURTON⁶ KNAPP (*Frances⁵, John⁴, Peter³, Frederick²⁻¹*), born Schuy. 27 Nov. 1875, died 7 Oct. 1958, married 19/20 June 1900 MAE HARHAVER, born 10 Aug. 1874, died Ilion 14 June 1947; both buried Ilion.

Ch (KNAPP):

    i.   BURTON MARHAVER⁷, b 4 July 1902, d Roch 17 Sept 1964, bur Ilion; unm

186. LIDA FRANCES⁶ KNAPP (*Frances⁵, John⁴, Peter³, Frederick²⁻¹*), born Schuy., Herk. Co. 5 Apr. 1880; died 9/10 June 1965; married Frkf. 13 June 1900 WILLARD ALVIN DODGE, born 20 Aug. 1880; died Frkf 6 July 1964; both buried Frkf.

Ch (DODGE), all b Schuy:

262.   i.   LOIS MARION⁷, b 7 Dec 1903
        ii. ADRIAN KNAPP, b 3 June 1910, d Ilion 21 Jan 1978, bur Frkf; m 1st JESSIE RUTHERFORD, b 3 Feb 1908, d Frkf 6 Sept 1950, bur Frkf; m 2nd MILDRED C TOONEY, b 8 Oct 1916, d Frkf 9 July 1983; no ch
263. iii. GLADYS LEONA, b 15 Apr 1916

187. HOWARD HULSER⁶ OYER (*Richard⁵, John⁴, Peter³, Frederick²⁻¹*), born Parish, Oswego Co. 25 Oct. 1892; died Utica, Oneida Co. 10 Apr. 1984; married Whitestown, Oneida Co. 13 Jan. 1918 JOHANNA FOPPES, dau John and Gertrude (Vanderlean) Foppes, she born Midway, Wis. 27 May 1898; died N. Hartford 27/28 June 1974; both buried Crown Hill Mem. Pk., Kirkland, Oneida Co.

264.   i.   RICHARD JOHN⁷, b 10 July 1919
265.   ii. RAYMOND HOWARD, b 3 Nov 1922
266. iii. GERTRUDE ALICE, b 7 Apr 1926
267. iv. LUKE HENRY, b 12 Feb 1928
268.   v. ROBERT LEE, b 6 Jan 1936
269. vi. BERNARD GEORGE, b 5 June 1938
270. vii. ELLEN AIMEE, b 30 Nov 1941

[Sources: Gertrude Race, #266; Bernard Oyer, #269]

188.   ROSCOE CONKLIN[6] OYER, (*George[5], Levi[4], George[3], Frederick[2-1]*), born WV., Catt. Co. 5 Nov. 1889; died 15 June 1963. He married BEULAH D FOLTS, dau. E. P. and Carrie (Moore) Folts, born Ash. 6 Feb. 1891; died 8 Mar. 1920 as a result of a maltreated tubular pregnancy.

Ch (OYER):

271.   i.   ROBERT F[7], b 7 July 1918

[Sources: Ash cem rec; Ash VR; Adams' Catt]

188.1   DeMONT FREDERICK[6] OYER (*Charles[5], Simon[4], George[3], Frederick[2-1]*), born Sprvl., Erie Co. 1900; died Wolcott or Richville, Wayne Co. 1960.   He married RUTH LYNN WALKER, born Antwerp, Jeff. Co. 1896; died 1957 Wolcott.   DeMont received his Doctor of Dentistry degree from the Univ. of Bflo., practicing in Wolcott.   Ruth was an accomplished musician, receiving her degree in music from Syracuse Univ.   She was organist for the Wolcott First United Methodist Church.   We are indebted to William Ellis of Sardinia, Erie Co. and Pastor Michael Cremean of the church for "finding" this lost family.   This is their son Charles' reply to our query, finally locating him in Calgary, Canada: "...I was unaware that anyone cared or knew about the history of the Oyers.   In fact, I didn't even know there was anyone else named Oyer 'out there.'   Being the only child of two only children and with no known close relatives, I thought I was the only Oyer existing..."

Ch (OYER), b Wolcott:

i.   CHARLES WALKER[7], b 1936.   He received his BA degree from the Univ of N C; DDS degree from McGill Univ, Montreal, Canada; MS degree from New York Univ., Bellevue Medical Center, NYC. Since 1964 he has res and practiced oral and maxillofacial surgery in Calgary, Canada.   Unm.

[We are indebteded to Ellis Inf 4 for putting us on the trail of this family.]

188.2   HAROLD W[I]LLIAM6 CLARK (*Bertha Beach[5], Mary[4], Michael[3], Frederick[2-1]*), born Ellvl. 25 Aug. 1896; died W. Henrietta, Monroe Co. 15 May 1960; married ELIZABETH FOX, dau. of George Arnold and Emily Ann (Bowen) Fox, and sister of

Charles J. Fox of Ellvl., 99-year old informant who put us in touch with Jeannette (Clark) Popp [Beach Inf 1], who has much Beach, Bowen, Clark, and Fox data. Elizabeth was born 1897; died W. Henrietta 28 Dec. 1980. Both buried SHC.

Harold had a store at 405 Chili Ave., Roch., residing on Burlington Ave. Both were active in civic affairs and in the Genesee Baptist Church.

Ch (CLARK):

271.1 i. JEANNETTE[7], b 1916
       ii. GEORGE FOX, b Painesville, Oh 31 Mar 1921; m 21 Aug 1954 MARION AVERILL, b 24 May 1925. George d Roch 9 Oct 1986. A grad of Bucknell Univ with a BS, he was an ensign in WWII. In Roch he was in urban renewal. Marion is head of nurses at St. John's Home in Roch.
271.2 iii. HAROLD W, b 15 Dec 1922
271.3 iv. ROBERT WELLS, 12 Apr 1925
271.4 v. THOMAS JAMES, b 21 Nov 1926
271.5 vi. EMILY LOUISE, b 8 Mar 1930

*** THE FOX FAMILY ***

ELIZABETH FOX's parents, GEORGE ARNOLd (1862-1912) and EMILY ANN (BOWEN--1867-1941) FOX are descendants of THOMAS II (1603-1693) and ELLEN (GREEN) FOX. The descent is THOMAS II, JABEZ (1647-1702), JABEZ II (1684-_____). THOMAS III (1706-1780), JABEZ III (1745-1780), THOMAS IV (1770-1811), CHAUNCY J (1797-1883), CHAUNCY J, Jr (1832-1895), GEORGE ARNOLD. Elizabeth's other brother was Leslie B. Leslie's eldest son is John W. who resides in Port Dickinson and has much Fox information. Charles, the brother responsible for our reaching Jeannette, our informant, has a family in Ellvl. There is much detail in a book on the Foxes in the possession of Beach Inf 1.

[Sources: Adams' Catt; Everts' Catt; CCHM; LM; Beach Inf 1. For FOX note, see #121.1; for further BOWEN data, see #30]

189.1 ABIGAIL E[6] CONHISER (*Clarissa Frank[5], Sally[4], John[3], Peter[2], Frederick[1]*), born Ash. 23 Apr. 1868; married SHEPHARD COLEMAN HARVEY, born Ellvl.

190.   OYER H[6] CONHISER (*Clarissa Frank[5], Sally[4], John[3], Peter[2], Frederick[1]*), born Ash. 1870; died 1939; married LILLIAN/ LILLIE M. BATES, born E. Otto 1875; died 1939, both buried E. Otto. Living with Oyer [E Otto 1910 census] was ELVA M. WIGHTMAN, ae. 14, step-dau.

Ch that we located (CONHISER), all b E Otto:

i.   GEORGE WILLIAM CONRAD[7], b 17 May 1889
ii. PAUL G, b 29 Jan 1904
iii. MILDRED, b 6 Mar 1905
iv. EARL RICHARD, b 31 Aug 1907
v.   RUTH LOUISE, b 28 Aug 1908

[Conhiser sources: LM; censuses]

191.   ESTHER L[6] OYER, (*Leon[5], Ira[4], Jacob[3], Peter[2], Frederick[1]*), born Sandy Creek Twp. (hereafter SC), Oswego Co. 1901; died Watertown, Jeff. Co. 15 June 1979; married 10 May 1918 DURWOOD W. THOMPSON, son of George and Nettie (Whitman) Thompson, born Wells, Hamilton Co. 11 Jan. 1898.   He died Syracuse 26 Jan. 1980; both buried WdlnC.

Ch (THOMPSON):

i.   OYER[7], m, res Melbourne, Fla

192.   EDITH GERTRUDE[6] LEWIS (*Gertrude[5], Peter[4], Jacob[3], Peter[2], Frederick[1]*), born Jordan, Onon. Co. 14 Mar. 1873; died 22 Sept. 1953.   She married 4 Mar. 1896 LUCIUS JOHNSON FRANCIS CRANER, son of Nicholas and Mary Sophia (Babcock) Craner, born Jordan 10 July 1871; died Auburn, Cayuga Co. 3 Sept. 1969; both buried Maple Grove Cem., Jordan.   Lucius resided in Jordan on N. Main St. where he was at one time a railway clerk for the N.Y. Central Railroad.   He later operated the Craner-Lewis Insurance and Coal Co. Lucius was mayor of Jordan 1927-1937.

Ch (CRANER), b Jordan:

272.   i.   VIVUS LEWIS[7], b 13 Feb 1897

193.   WILLIAM H·6 AUYER (*Charles[5], Francis[4], Jacob[3], Peter[2], Frederick[1]*), born Memphis, Onon. Co. 29 Apr. 1878; married ANNA

FISH. A "Mrs. Anna Auyer, dressmaker" is listed in Syracuse directories 1911 to 1919.

Ch (AUYER):

     i.   LEOTA F[7], b 17 June 1905, m _____ WOOD; res Syracuse 1934

194. FLOYD LAVERNE[6] AUYER (*Charles[5], Francis[4], Jacob[3], Peter[2], Frederick[1]*), born 20 Apr. 1885; died 24 Feb. 1966; married Plainville, Onon. Co. 14 Nov. 1907 MABEL J. CLAPPER, dau. of Judson T. and Josephine (Gorolomon) Clapper, born 1882; died Auburn, 30 Nov. 1975; both buried Meridian Cem., Cato Twp., Cayuga Co. They resided on the south side of Main St. in Meridian.

Ch (AUYER):

     i.   VERA LOUISE[7] AUYER, b 17 May 1911, d Auburn 2 May 1974, bur Meridian

195. HOWARD HUDSON[6] MARVIN (*Cora Buck[5], Harriet[4], Jacob[3], Peter[2], Frederick[1]*), born Warners, Onon. Co. 7 Feb. 1893; died Warners 18 Jan. 1982; married Warners 12 Oct. 1915 CLARA EMMA DENCE, dau Joseph and Ellen (Leppard) Dence, born Lysander, Onon. Co. Howard graduated from St. Lawrence Univ., and was employed by General Electric. He also operated a dairy farm; resided Canton St. Rd., Warners.

Ch (MARVIN):

273.   i.   HOWARD HUDSON[7] Jr, b 11 May 1918
274.   ii. GEORGE ROBERT, b 1920

196. SMITH[6] SOMES (*Henry Somes[5], Margaret Mary[4], Jacob[3], Peter[2], Frederick[1]*), born Van Buren, Onon. Co. 28 Aug. 1891; died Van Buren 13 Sept. 1974. Smith married 23 Oct. 1918 BERTHA ELEANOR PARRY, dau. Alfred Combs and Bertha (Scott) Parry, born Van Buren 4 Oct. 1891; died Van Buren 20 June 1970; both buried Maple Grove Cem., Jordan, Onon. Co.

Howard H.[6] and Johanna (Foppes) Oyer at time of their 50th anniversary.

Clarice Oyer & son Clarence; Clarence & son Ralph.   Identities unknown.

Smith lived his adult life on "Sunset Farm" in Van Buren, which had once been the home of his grandparents, Joseph and Margaret (Auyer) Somes.

Ch (SOMES):

     i.   infant dau, b & d 3 July 1921

     ii. MARGARET ELEANOR[7], b 29 June 1925; m; retired from King Laboratories

275. iii. REBA EVELYN, b 17 May 1927

197. FLOYD[6] SOMES (*Henry Somes[5], Margaret Mary[4], Jacob[3], Peter[2], Frederick[1]*), born Van Buren 21 May 1896; died Syracuse, Onon. Co.; married 29 Mar. 1921 OLIVE BARTON, dau. John and Millicent Barton, born Geddes Twp. 8 Sept. 1893; died Auburn, Cayuga Co. 26 Feb. 1979; both buried Oakwood–Morningside Cem., Syracuse.

Floyd was a dairy farmer who resided at Jack's Reef on the farm once owned by Edwin and Julia (Auyer) McDowell.

Ch (SOMES):

276.   i.   MARTHA LOUISE[7], b 4 Feb 1922

277.   ii. BARTON ROTHWELL, b 14 Dec 1924

198. KAPLE J[6] SOMES (*Oren Somes[5], Margaret Mary[4], Jacob[3], Peter[2], Frederick[1]*), born Van Buren 23 Oct. 1892; died Van Buren 25 Aug. 1962; married Jordan, Onon. Co. 9 Dec. 1918 FLORA ELIZABETH McDOWELL, dau. Harry Auyer (#151) and Sarah Jane (Barnett) McDowell, born Warners, Onon. Co. 21 July 1897; died Auburn, Cayuga Co. 4 Dec. 1982; both buried Maple Grove Cem. Kaple, a lifelong resident of Van Buren, was in partnership with his father and brother: O. A. Somes & Sons dairy farm.

Ch (SOMES):

278.   i.   ELIZABETH JEAN[7], b 23 Aug 1922

199. JOSEPH HUNTING[6] SOMES (*Oren Somes[5], Margaret Mary[4], Jacob[3], Peter[2], Frederick[1]*), born Van Buren, Onon. Co. 7 May 1898; died Syracuse, Onon. Co. 19 Feb. 1971; married MARJORIE LOUISE CLARK, dau. Bertram Grant and Minnie (Reamer) Clark, born Jordan, Onon. Co. 29 June 1899; died Auburn, Cayuga Co. 5 Feb. 1980; both buried Maple Grove Cem., Jordan.

Hunt Somes was employed as an electrician by General Electric, Syracuse, until his retirement in 1963; resided in Jordan.

Ch (SOMES):

279.   i.   ROBERT OREN[7], b 26 Apr 1918
280.   ii.   DOROTHY LEOLA, b 27 Jan 1920

200.   LaVERNE WENDALL[6] AUYER (*Adelbert[5], Romain[4], Jacob[3], Peter[2], Frederick[1]*), born Victory, Cayuga Co. 3 Oct. 1912; married 1st 1937 HAZEL BOUGH, born 1929; married 2nd VIRGINIA (BUSHEY) BRADWAY, born 1923. She had been married to Nelson Bradway; they had a son Owen Richard, born 8 June 1942.

LaVerne worked for Jay McDonald in Plainville; resides now at Phoenix, Oswego Co.

Ch (AUYER), all of 1st m:

281.   i.   RICHARD[7], b 22 Dec 1938
282.   ii.   EMMA JEAN, b 8 Apr 1942
283.   iii. VERNA MAY, b 9 Oct 1947

201.   RALPH PETER[6] AUYER (*Peter[5], Foster[4], Jacob[3], Peter[2], Frederick[1]*), born Van Buren, Onon. Co. 30 July 1899; married 1st ESTHER MARION CLARK, dau. William and Frankie (Foster) Clark, born Pennellville, Oswego Co. 15 Mar. 1898; died Fulton, Oswego Co. 7 Dec. 1971; buried Riverview Cem., Baldwinsville, Onon. Co. Ralph married 2nd 9 Feb. 1974 RUTH (MANCHESTER) CLARK, dau. of Lewis William and Clara May (Hall) Manchester and widow of Leonard Clark; born Syracuse 3 Aug. 1908. Ruth had children by her first marriage. She shares Ralph's interest in genealogy.

Ralph, who shares the dedication of this book, was for many years secretary-treasurer for Mercer Milling Co. in Baldwinsville. He and his second wife reside there, where ill health has curtailed his research in genealogy, but not his avid interest and continued updating. The Peter Oyer (#4) family chart hangs on a wall in their home. We are indebted to him for his years of effort, much of which is contained herein.

Ch (AUYER), all of 1st m:

284.   i.   FOSTER CLARK[7], b 10 Mar 1922
        ii.   BARBARA ELIZABETH, b Van Buren 11 Nov 1924; d
              5 Apr 1925; bur Riverview Cem
285.   iii. WILLIAM RALPH, b 7 Apr 1928

286.   iv.   MARY CAROLYN, b 17 May 1931

202.   WARREN H.[6] **AUYER** (*Alonzo*[5], *Foster*[4], *Jacob*[3], *Peter*[2], *Frederick*[1]), born Van Buren, Onon. Co. 5 Aug. 1902; married Belle Isle, Onon. Co. 28 Dec. 1928 BARBARA WALTER, born 1 Aug. 1901.
Warren was a lineman for the N.Y. Telephone Co., and resides in Baldwinsville, Onon. Co.

Ch (AUYER):

287.   i.   WARREN GERALD[7], b 5 Jan 1930
288.   ii. ARDIS ANN, b 29 Mar 1933
289.   iii. KENNETH WILLIAM, b 3 Oct 1941

203.   EARL L.[6] **AUYER** (*Alonzo*[5], *Foster*[4], *Jacob*[3], *Peter*[2], *Frederick*[1]), born Van Buren, Onon. Co. 26 July 1907; married 26 Aug. 1939 RACHEL HARTER, born Otisco, Onon. Co. 24 Mar. 1912.
A graduate of Syracuse Univ., Earl was an engineer for General Electric in their turbine unit in Mass., now residing at Cincinnati, Ohio.

Ch (AUYER):

290.   i.   STEPHEN E[7], b 13 Sept 1942
291.   ii. DAVID H, b 15 Apr 1948

204.   LESLIE F.[6] **AUYER** (*Alonzo*[5], *Foster*[4], *Jacob*[3], *Peter*[2], *Frederick*[1]), born Van Buren, Onon. Co. 28 Mar. 1909; married 7 June 1929 DORA SPORE, born Elbridge, Onon. Co. 12 Mar. 1912.
Leslie has retained possession of his father's farm just west of Warners, Onon. Co., residing there.

Ch (AUYER), all b Van Buren:

292.   i.   RICHARD ALLEN[7], b 5 Jan 1930
292.1   ii. ANITA JEAN, b 23 Jan 1933
293   iii. WALTER LEON, b 10 Aug 1935

205.   FREDERICK C.[6] **ISBELL** (*Harriet*[5], *Foster*[4], *Jacob*[3], *Peter*[2], *Frederick*[1]), born Van Buren, Onon. Co. 31 Oct. 1896; married 10 July 1920 LILLIAN MAY.

Fred has farmed, owning the Isbell homestead west of Warners, Onon. Co.

Ch (ISBELL):

294.   i.   CHARLES A[7], b 2 Oct 1922
295.   ii. BETTY ANN, b 20 May 1940

206. IVA[6] ISBELL (*Harriet[5], Foster[4], Jacob[3], Peter[2], Frederick[1]*), born Van Buren, Onon. Co. 31 Dec. 1899; married 23 June 1923 EDWARD DELOSH, born 1900; died 10 Dec. 1960; buried Memorial Park, Warners, Onon. Co.

Ch (DeLOSH):

296.   i.   HARRIET SHIRLEY[7], b 25 Nov 1925

207.   LEAH JUNE[6] ISBELL (*Harriet[5], Foster[4], Jacob[3], Peter[2], Frederick[1]*), born Van Buren, Onon. Co. 4 Oct. 1917; married 15 Apr. 1939 EDWARD OLGEATY.

Ch (OLGEATY):

297.   i.   EDWARD[7], b 22 Aug 1940
209.   ii. DIANE, b 14 Oct 1945

208.   RACHAEL A.[6] TIFFT (*Carleton Tifft[5], Martha[4], James[3], Peter[2], Frederick[1]*), born 2 Oct. 1893; died 2 Mar. 1956; buried Oakwood Cem. Troy, Rensselaer Co. She married 21 June 1919 ELMER J THOMAS.

Ch (THOMAS):

299.   i.   RICHARD W[7], b ca 1923
300.   ii. DONALD A, b

209.   MABEL ELLA[6] TIFFT (*Carrie Tifft[5], Martha[4], James[3], Peter[2], Frederick[1]*), born 26 Sept. 1879; married 2 Oct. 1908 LOUIS HEINEMAN, born 6 Feb. 1877.

Ch (HEINEMAN):

        i.   RAYMOND[7], b 8 Nov 1908; m KINDA _____

301.   ii.   VERNA, b 11 Nov 1912

210.   EDWARD TIFFT[6] McGOWAN (*Jennie Tifft[5], Martha[4],
James[3], Peter[2], Frederick[1]*), born Elb., Onon. Co. 25 Aug. 1888;
died Elb. 24 May 1928; buried Elb Rural Cem. He married 16 Aug.
1913 MARGARET M. SMILEY.
Edward lived in the village of Elb., employed by Harold Clarks
Garage. His death occurred as the result of an explosion at work.

Ch (McGOWAN):

302.   i.   LOUISE JANE[7], b 11 Oct 1914
303.   ii.   DORIS ELIZABETH/BETTY, b 12 Feb 1922
304.   iii.   ELLEN TIFFT, b 4 May 1923

211.   ETHEL SARAH[6] McGOWAN (*Jennie Tifft[5], Martha[4],
James[3], Peter[2], Frederick[1]*), born Elb., Onon. Co. 9 May 1890;
married 1st Elb. 19 Feb. 1910 JOHN MARTIN SCHNEIDER, son of
Peter and Barbara Schneider, born 14 Dec. 1884; died 27 Dec. 1943;
buried Highland Cem., Marcellus, Onon. Co. (Divorced) Ethel
married 2nd Tex. 14 Feb. 1930 HERBERT ALBERT MERKLEY, born
Norwood, St. Lawrence Co. 20 Mar. 1906; died Jordan, Onon. Co.
26 Aug. 1970; buried MGC.

Ch (SCHNEIDER), both b Elb:

305.   i.   BEATRICE CAMILLA[7], b 13 July 1913
306.   ii.   JENNIE DORIS, b 15 Aug 1915

212.   HAZEL CAMILLA[6] McGOWAN (*Jennie Tifft[5], Martha[4],
James[3], Peter[2], Frederick[1]*), born Elb., Onon. Co. 7 Dec. 1891; died
Jordan, Onon. Co. 29 Nov. 1936; married 29 Dec. 1914 JACOB
IMBRIE RHODES, born Caylick, Penn. 24 Nov. 1866; died Syra-
cuse, Onon. Co. 7 Apr. 1942; both buried Elb. Rural Cem.
Jacob was a farmer, residing at Mottville, Onon. Co. and
Chamberburg, Penn. before moving to Jordan in 1930.

Ch (RHODES):

307.   i.   JUNIOR IMBRIE[7], b 15 Feb 1919

213.   HELEN LOUISE[6] McGOWAN (*Jennie Tifft[5], Martha[4],
James[3], Peter[2], Frederick[1]*), born Elb. Onon. Co. 16 Apr. 1895;

died Syracuse, Onon. Co. 19 Feb. 1966. Helen married 25 May 1923 STANLEY SARLE KENT, born 25 June 1904; died Jordan 2 Dec. 1975; buried in Canada.

Helen Kent taught school at Jordan and Memphis, both in Onon. Co. Her husband was a mechanic in Jordan. He also worked as a laborer in Syracuse at the Franklin Automobile plant, and other places.

Ch (KENT), both b Jordan:

308.   i.   HARRY STANLEY7, b 3 Oct 1924
309.   ii. JANICE MARILYN, b 13 Sept 1929

214.   RAYMOND6 BENSON (*Lena Whitney5, Emily4, James3, Peter2, Frederick1*), married FLORENCE _____.

Ch (BENSON):

        i.   KENNETH7

215.   OLIVE6 BENSON (*Lena Whitney5, Emily4, James3, Peter2, Frederick1*), married CLARK STAFFORD.

Ch (STAFFORD):

        i.   EDITH7
        ii. LAWRENCE

216.   CECIL JAMES6 PATTERSON (*Stella Whitney5, Emily4, James3, Peter2, Frederick1*), born Elb. 26 Oct. 1901; married Syracuse, Onon. Co. 20 June 1927 LAURA W NEUPERT, daughter of Clifton and Sophia Neupert, born Syracuse 23 May 1909.

Cecil, a retired eletrician, resides on the Patterson homestead where he was born, near Bennett's Corners in eastern Elb. Twp.

Ch (PATTERSON):

310.   i.   CECIL JAMES7, b 11 July 1930
311.   ii. CAROLE ANNE, b 20 July 1926

217.   LUMORA MARVEL6 WHITNEY (*Jay Whitney5, Emily4, James3, Peter2, Frederick1*), born Elb., Onon. Co. 24 Jan. 1900; married 13 Nov. 1917 CHARLES HARTKOPF, born Hoboken, N.J. 31

Aug. 1897; died Cam., Onon. Co. 24 June 1980; buried MWC, Cam.
Charles was an electrician employed by Solvay Process; the
family reside in Cam.

Ch (HARTKOPF), both b Cam:

312.   i.   ELIZABETH[7], b 5 Aug 1919
313.   ii. CHARLES WHITNEY, b 26 Dec 1930

218. ROSINA A.[6] MARLETTE (*Harry Marlette[5], Emily[4], James[3],
Peter[2], Frederick[1]*), married near Memphis, Onon. Co. 14 Aug. 1919
WILFRED W NEWELL.

Ch (NEWELL) include:

       i.   WILFRED WILIET[7], b Shepard Settlement, Rockland
            Co 9 Jan ca 1921

219.   ERMA E·6 MARLETTE (*Belle Marlette[5], Emily[4], James[3],
Peter[2], Frederick[1]*), born ca. 1893.

Ch (MARLETTE):

       i.   LAURA M[7], b ca 1911
       ii. RICHARD H, b 1915

220.   JULIAN HAROLD[6] McDOWELL (*Elmer McDowell[5], Julia[4],
Solomon[3], Peter[2], Frederick[1]*), born Corning, Steu. Co. 6 Mar.
1891; died Auburn, Cayuga Co. 23 Mar. 1970; married Van Buren,
Onon. Co. 6 Mar. 1915 MARIAM ADELLE CLIFTON, dau. Lewis J.
and Anna Louise (Lusk) Clifton, born near Sand Springs 18 Nov.
1893; died 1931+; both buried MGC.
Harold farmed in various locations around the village of Memphis, Onon. Co., moving later to the village of Cato, Cayuga Co.

Ch (McDOWELL):

314.   i.   DONALD ROY[7], b 4 Feb 1916
315.   ii.   MARJORIE RUTH, b 3 Jan. 1918
316.   iii. WALDO GLENN, b 1 Aug 1919
317.   iv.   EUNICE BLANCHE, b 5 July 1922
318.   v.   MARY LOUISE, b 24 Apr 1924
319.   vi.   RALPH EDWIN, b 27 Oct 1926
320.   vii. EARL WAYNE, b 5 May 1931

221.   EDITH ELVIE[6] BUCK (*Susan McDowell[5], Julia[4], Solomon[3], Peter[2], Frederick[1]*), born Sand Springs 15 July 1895; married 16 Sept. 1923 SEWARD PEREZ LERCH, son Anthony and Margaretta J. (Dodsworth) Lerch, born Fayette, Seneca Co. 24 Mar. 1887; died Torrey, Yates Co. 12 Jan. 1955.

Ch (LERCH), all b Waterloo, Seneca Co:

321.	i.	SEWARD JEROME[7], b 9 Nov 1925
322.	ii.	EVERETT ERWIN, b 22 Dec 1926
323.	iii.	BEVERLY SUSAN, b 11 July 1934

222.   WARD EVERETT[6] BUCK (*Susan McDowell[5], Julia[4], Solomon[3], Peter[2], Frederick[1]*), born Sand Springs 27 May 1900; died Auburn, Cayuga Co. 27 July 1976; married Van Buren, Onon. Co. 11 Nov. 1925 PEARL SYLVIA STEVENS, dau. Alfred and Martha (Holway) Stevens, born Cam. Onon. Co. 28 Jan. 1901; died Auburn 19 May 1975; both buried MGC.
Ward Buck was a partner in the firm of Griffin & Buck Insurance Agency in Jordan, where he resided.

Ch (BUCK):

324.	i.	AUREL CHARLENE[7], b 22 July 1930
325.	ii.	RODERICK WARD, b 11 May 1936
	iii.	DONETTA GAY, b Auburn 26 Oct 1943; m 1st Jordan, June 1966 Robert Walker (divorced); m 2nd Crystal Lake, Ill Apr 1970 LAWRENCE BENSON

223.   SATIE ESTELLE[6] METTLER (*Jessie[5], Cyrus[4], Solomon[3], Peter[2], Frederick[1]*), born Van Buren, Onon. Co. Nov. 1885; died Syracuse 12 Apr. 1918; buried MGC, Jordan, Onon. Co.   She married Memphis, Onon. Co. 28 Dec. 1904 MYRON JOSEPH PICKARD, son Lewis and Mina (Fenner) Pickard, born Van Buren 9 Sept. 1880; died Orlando, Fla. 1 Sept. 1979 (after remarrying).
Myron farmed in the Memphis area; the family later moved to Syracuse where Satie died during the influenza epidemic. [See #162 for details of this pandemic.] After her death the children were brought up by the paternal grandparents at Peru, Clinton Co.

Ch (PICKARD):

326.	i.	DOROTHA ROSE[7], b 20 Nov 1905
327.	ii.	KENNETH METTLER, b 1 Oct 1909
328.	iii.	ANITA MARIE, b 2 Sept 1917

224.   LENA ALICE[6] METTLER (*Jessie[5], Cyrus[4], Solomon[3], Peter[2], Frederick[1]*), born Van Buren, Onon. Co. 23 Sept. 1892; married CARL DODSON; divorced. Carl resides in Cam., Onon. Co. where he was employed at the flour mill.

Ch (DODSON):

    i.   CHARLES[7], res Baltimore, Md
   ii.   HELEN, res Puerto Rico

225.   MARION AUYER6 METTLER (*Jessie[5], Cyrus[4], Solomon[3], Peter[2], Frederick[1]*), born Palmyra, Wayne Co. 10 Mar. 1896; married FRANK WILLIAM BRETZER, born Liverpool, Onon. Co. 8 Apr. 1881; died Syracuse 23 Oct. 1965; buried Liverpool.

Ch (BRETZER):

329.   i.   WILLIAM HENRY[7], b 30 July 1921

226.   EZRA HUGH[6] OYER (*Anson[5], George[4], Henry[3], Peter[2], Frederick[1]*), born Nov. 1919; died 1981; married GERALDINE MELVINA ROSER, born July 1918.

Ch (OYER):

    i.   BRENDA[7], b ca 1945

226.1   GEORGE[6] OYER (*George[5], Oscar[4], Daniel[3], Peter[2], Frederick[1]*), born Aug. 1955; married VICKI THAYER, reside Frkf., Herk. Co.

Ch (OYER):

    i.   son[7], b 31 Jan 1983

[Sources for #191 through 226.1: Robert Petrie; AHA; Ralph Auyer; Joanne Oyer (#159)]

Leland C.[7] and Edith (Brougham) Oyer
with son Raymond E.[8] Oyer.

Raymond E.[7] Oyer with one of his
many built and rebuilt vehicles.

CHAPTER 12

SEVENTH GENERATION

227. BERNICE MAE[7] OYER *(Clarence[6], David[5], Peter[4], David[3], Jacob[2], Frederick[1])*, born GrV, Catt. Co. 22 June, 1901; died Ypsilanti, Mich. 5 Oct. 1972, buried Udell Cem. She married 1st EARL BROUGHAM 24 Dec. 1920, div'd. 1941; he born NYS 24 Sept. 1895, died Nov. 1966, buried GrC, GrV Twp. Bernice married 2nd MELVIN WOODROW CAMPBELL, born Detroit, Mich. 28 Feb. 1913; died 3 April 1983, buried Udell Cem., Ypsilanti.

Bernice had undeveloped artistic talents, opting to do craft work: crocheting, knitting and seamstress work. Many of Clarence's line, Bernice's father, have musical and artistic talent. For more detail see Clarence (#160).

Mel and Bernice lived in Kill Buck, GrV. Twp. for several years where Mel had a crate manufactury.

Ch of 1st m (BROUGHAM):

330   i.   DONALD EUGENE[8], b 19 Feb 1925
331   ii. ARLENE JUNE, b 11 Nov 1927
332   iii. RICHARD EARL, b 4 May 1933   1

Ch of 2nd m (CAMPBELL):

333.   iv. JANETTE MARIAN CAMPBELL, b 5 Dec 1941
334.   v. JOANNE ELLEN CAMPBELL, b 9 July 1943

228. LELAND CLARENCE[7] OYER *(Clarence[6], David[5], Peter[4], David[3], Jacob[2], Frederick[1])*, b GrV, Catt. Co. 18 Jan. 1905, married EDITH MAE BROUGHAM, born 1905; she died 8 May 1987 at Livermore, Calif.

Leland and Edith (whose brother Earl married his sister Bernice) lived in many places after leaving Catt. Co.--Fla., Ariz. and Calif., but mainly in Alpena, Mich. Leland has been a builder--from houses to violins, with farming and a trailer hitch business in between. He would build a house in Fla., for instance, live in it while building another and then sell it. For many years every Sept. brought them back to Wallace and Rose Oyer's home in Kill Buck. They were always close, with the latter staying with them for extended visits in later years in Fla. and Ariz.

The Sept. visits to Kill Buck served another purpose--the men picked wild blackberries, with the women waiting to can them. Dozens of quarts would be processed.

Edith became a victim of Alzheimer's disease. After coping in Alpena for some years, Leland and she moved to Calif. about 1985 to be with and/or near their daughter Joyce.

Leland owns a Ford Thunderbird that has taken him over 297,000 miles! In 1986 at the age of 81 he drove from Calif. to Mich. and N.Y. and Fla., visiting friends and relatives along the way. In May 1987 he once again was visiting in the East at Rose Oyer's when his daughter Joyce called to say Edith had passed away. Joyce took care of all the arrangements, with burial in Calif. In 1987 Joyce moved to So. Lake Tahoe, Calif., Leland residing with them.

Ch (OYER), all b GrV:

335. i. RAYMOND ELBERT[8], b 13 Jan 1926
336. ii. ROBERT LEE, b 10 Jan 1928
337. iii. JOYCE, b 15 July 1935

229. LORENE MARIE[7] OYER (*Clarence[6], David[5], Peter[4], David[3], Jacob[2], Frederick[1]*), b GrV 10 Feb 1907, m EDWARD FRANKLIN TREDO; she died Bflo. 1985.

Ch (TREDO):

i. FLORIS EILEEN[8] TREDO, b 12 Jan 1928; m RICHARD
DOBSON. Ch (DOBSON):
  a) RICHARD[9], b 22 Nov 1944
  b) KAREN, b 3 Dec 1946
  c) ROBIN, b 3 Mar 1955
  d) SHAWN, b 26 Dec 1963, res Cowlesville, Erie Co
ii. EDWARD FRANKLIN/MOSIE TREDO, b 25 June 1930; m ELIZABETH/BETTY BURKARD
  a) EDWARD; m; has ch; structural engineer; res Grand Island, Niagara Co
iii. DANIEL CLYDE TREDO, b 10 Jan 1938; m THERESA KWIK

229.1 MARGARET RUTH[7] OYER (*Clarence[6], David[5], Peter[4], David[3], Jacob[2], Frederick[1]*), was born Bflo 23 Feb. 1908; married Ypsilanti, Mich. WILLIAM RICHARD MARSH, born 24 Feb. 1907. She died 1977⁻.

Ch (MARSH):

i. EVELYN JEAN[8] MARSH, b Mich 23 Oct 1930; m 1st
1949 CAROL MCPHERSON, b 17 July 1928; m 2nd
ELMER MATT; res upper Mich; homemaker
   a) RICHARD ALLEN[9] MCPHERSON, b 16 May
      1954; d auto accident 1985; ch: 2 girls; 1 boy
   b) CAROL RUTH MCPHERSON, b 20 Sept 1955
   c) ROBERTA SUE MCPHERSON, b 26 Feb 1958;
      m DAVID THOMAS
         (1) JOSHUA THOMAS[10], b 10 Dec 1978
         (2,3) MALINDA and AMANDA (twins), b
            10 Dec 1980
   d) THOMAS WM MCPHERSON, b 13 Jan 1964
   e,f) DONALD and LARRY MCPHERSON (twins), b
      17 June 1965
   g) ch (MATT) of 2nd m: ROGER b 1 Mar 1967
ii. JOHN WM MARSH, b unknown; last seen in 1964
having moved to Calif. Has ch: MELONY MARSH
iii. MICHAEL ROGER MARSH, b 21 Feb 1941; m 3 July
1964 HELEN ANN FRANCIS. Michael has worked
for the Ypsilanti Maintenance Dept for over 20
years, now pursuing a journeyman electrical
position. Ch (MARSH), all unm:
   a) MICHELE ANN[9], b 10 July 1965
   b) MICHAEL ROGER, Jr, b 28 Sept 1966
   c) SHEILA ANN, b 1 Sept 1967
   d) JASON FRANCIS, b 15 Oct 1968
   e) MILLESSIA ANN, b 12 Feb 1970
   f) BARRY OYER, b 19 Oct 1972
   g) ADRIAN CASE, b 18 Apr 1974
iv. LAUREN THOMAS MARSH, b 20 Apr 1945; m 8 May
1964 KAREN FAITH COTNER. Tom, as the family
has known Lauren, has worked for the Ford Motor
Co. for over 23 years. Karen is a nursing aid and
filing clerk at Ypsilanti's hospital.
   a) MICHAEL ANTHONY MARSH, b 24 Jan 1965
   b) THOMAS DUWAYNE MARSH, b 11 July 1967
   c) DEBRA ANN MARSH, b 23 Feb 1969

The Marsh families are all of Mich. Clarence's (#160) wife Edith
had a sister GLENNA CAPRON who married _____ SNOW. She
was the Director of Women's Physical Education at Eastern Mich.
Univ., then called "Normal College." Clarence and Edith allowed
Margaret to go to Mich. and be raised by Glenna, as she had no
children. This Glenna did from the age of 8, promising her a
college education. That in those days was a highly sought after
attainment, beyond the resources of so many. Margaret became an
LPN (Licensed Practical Nurse) and married JOHN MARSH, the

owner of the profitable Marsh Ice and Coal Co of Ypsilanti. There is a building at Eastern Mich Univ. named for Glenna for her outstanding contributions while at the college.

230.   GEORGIA WINIFRED[7] LOUGEE (*Nellie[6], David[5], Peter[4], David[3], Jacob[2], Frederick[1]*) was born in GrV. 14 Mar. 1901; married GEORGE FRASER WEBSTER, born Chicago, Ill. 30 May 1899, son of George Albert and Jussie A. (Fraser) Webster. Fraser died Washington, D.C. 10 Dec. 1972.

Georgia attended Case-Western Reserve Univ. in Cleveland, Oh., and obtained her bachelor of science degree from Geneseo Normal, now SUNY at Geneseo. Georgia taught math and physical education in a junior high school in Cleveland, teaching later in Roch.

Fraser was in the insurance business in Roch. and the family lived there until 1948. At that time his mother and sister, who were administering the Marjorie Webster Junior College for girls in Washington, D.C., asked for their assistance.

For over twenty years Fraser, Georgia and their sons and wives ran a highly successful junior college. A hard-fought battle with the Accreditation Board of the Middle States Association of Colleges and Secondary Schools, Inc. was won by the Websters, making headline news in *The National Observer*, June 23, 1969. At issue was whether or not Middle States could continue its ban on all profit-making institutions, regardless of quality.

Well-managed financial matters led to financial security for the families. Many adjacent homes were purchased to add facilities and housing for the college, the springboard for a number of prominent women.

After the closing of the college in 1973, the main buildings were sold eventually to the U.S. government to house the national fire academy. However, they never occupied it; the facilities were given to Gallaudet Univ. in 1982 for a preparatory school for the hearing impaired in order for students to improve their skills for entrance into the main college.

Gigi, as she is fondly known, still lives in the home adjacent to the college grounds, where she can still enjoy, among other things, the efforts of her mother Nellie who gardened there until the very last years of her life. Gigi's knowledge and interests cover many areas, and her guidance has been a prominent part of the successes the family has shared.

Ch: (WEBSTER)

338   i. SHERWOOD FRASER[8], b 15 Jan 1929
339   ii. DAVID FRASER, b 16 Oct 1932

*** THE WEBSTER FAMILY ***

Marjorie Webster Junior College originally was a finishing school for girls, founded in 1920 by its namesake with her mother's help as her School of Expression and Physical Education. Marjorie was Fraser's sister. It was licensed as a junior college by the District of Columbia's Board of Education in 1946. It developed a curriculum comparable to that of a good community college. In later years the teacher–pupil ratio was 1 to 11.

[Sources: Karen Chapman; Georgia Webster; David Webster]

Georgia[7] (Lougee) Webster; husband G. Fraser Webster; sons David (left) and Sherwood (right) and wives Marion and Frances.

231. PAUL FRANCIS[7] OYER *(Wallace[6], David[5], Peter[4], David[3], Jacob[2], Frederick[1])*, was born in Sala., Catt. Co. 13 Aug. 1916. He married 24 Apr. 1937, ELLEN EMILY McFEELEY, dau. of John Thomas and Gertrude (Hill) McFeeley, born DuBois, Penn. 25 Oct. 1919. They resided for some years in Kill Buck, GrV. Twp. before building their home on the old Brown/Oyer property in Peth, GrV.

Paul served in the Civilian Conservation Corps during the Depression of the 1930's. [See Illus p 209] He was a navigator and bombardier during World War II and the Korean War, during which he was awarded the Marianna Campaign Medal, Air Medal with two Oak Leaf Clusters, the Asiatic Pacific Campaign Medal, the WWII Victory Medal and the Air Force Reserve Medal. He was liason officer for the Air Force for the Civil Air Patrol and retired as a Lieutenant Colonel from the Air Force Reserve.

Paul worked for the B. R. & P. Railroad (later becoming the B. & O.; then the Chessie System) as a carman, and also was in charge of the wrecking crew. He was very active in community affairs: organizing scout troops and serving as scoutmaster and neighborhood commissioner; organizing and first president of the Kill Buck Fire Dept; school board member during the time of centralization of the Salamanca and area school district. This required approval and funding of the building of a new secondary school as well. His powers of persuasion were put to good use in bringing together the reticent peoples.

Ellen, despite having had 2 heart attacks and having lost a kidney, studied in mid-life to become a Licensed Practical Nurse. She worked for several years at St. Francis Hospital in Olean, for a higher wage than she had earned while an aide at the Salamanca Hospital, where she was paid 19 cents an hour! Ellen was a substitute night supervisor in the Allegany Nursing Home, where her sister-in-law Theresa was the night supervisor, retiring in 1975. She has been active in the B.P.O. Does, a service organization, holding many offices, requiring many trips throughout the country, combined with sightseeing.

She is an avid craft worker. She has made numerous quilts and comforters; knitted, crocheted and sewn innumerable items for all of her family. In one recent month she made six sweater-vests for family members. The Eldercraft organization has been a large beneficiary of her volunteer efforts, and she continues to work blood banks, as she has done for many years.

In 1966 they moved into the home they built on the family property which was purchased by Paul's great-grandfather Brown in 1867. Paul retired from the railroad in 1976. For years he has planted and worked his stands of over 100,000 evergreens, as well as large vegetable gardens, often being forced to re-plant due to frost or flooding. The acreage has for decades been a second home and country recreation spot for the families, with a winding creek providing swimming holes and fishing. Paul acts as caretaker for brother Walt's Hungry Hollow property, which includes mowing many acres and being available for any and all of the jobs that arise. This is another case of the Oyer love of the outdoors. Both Paul and Ellen are most attentive to the care and needs of his mother Rose, who lives about 5 miles from them.

Ch (OYER), both b Sala:

342.   i.   PATRICK JOHN⁸, b 27 Mar 1938
343.   ii. JEROME ALLEN/<u>MIKE</u>, b 9 May 1939

*** THE McFEELEY FAMILY ***

Ellen's father JOHN THOMAS McFEELEY was b 5 June 1880 at Whistletown, Penn; m GERTRUDE HILL, b Steincross, England 18 Nov 1883. John was a railroader, as so many were in the days Sala was a prominent railroad city: the Buffalo, Rochester and Pittsburgh, and the Erie having yards there. John and Gertrude d 11 Dec 1926 and 24 Apr 1968 respectively, both at Sala. Her sister SARAH DOROTHY, b 20 Nov 1910 at DuBois, Penn m EMORY WILBUR, b Orwell, Penn 10 Oct 1911. They live in Sala and have 4 children with families.

232.   RUTH <u>MARIE</u>⁷ OYER, *(Wallace⁶, David⁵, Peter⁴, David³, Jacob², Frederick¹),* born Sala., Catt. Co. 2 Apr. 1918; died Sala. 5 Jan. 1973; buried GrC. She married 10 Mar. 1938 DONALD TERRANCE LEARN, son of Glenn and Kittie (Whitcomb) Learn, born Humphrey, GrV. Twp. 2 Sept. 1912; died there 30 Apr. 1978; buried GrC.

Marie and Don lived in Bflo. a few years while he worked for Houdaille Industries there. They returned to the Learn homestead in Humphrey, town of GrV in 1946. This is where Don's ancestors lived as pioneers, purchasing land in the early 19th century from the Holland Land Company. Don worked as a skilled craftsman at Clark Brothers in Olean for 25 years. Marie's handiwork is seen in the accomplishments of her family, as well as her community.

Their home was open to the many hunters who came to the area.

Ch (LEARN) all except BONITA b Sala:

        i.   DONALD TERRENCE (twin), b & d 6 Sept 1938
344.   ii. DONNA MARIE⁸ (twin), b 6 Sept 1938

345.	iii.	ROSALIE MAE, b 30 Oct 1939
346.	iv.	SANDRA ELAINE, b 24 Apr 1941
347.	v.	BONITA JEAN, b Frklnvl 20 Feb 1943
	vi.	RUSSELL PATRICK, b 25 Apr 1945; unm. Russ has lived in California for a number of years, currently residing in San Diego. He has studied at San Diego College and is active in Little Theater groups. He has been a civilian employee at the San Diego Naval Base. He is an expert window-display craftsman, now traveling to supervise several stores' display functions. He is an avid racquetball tournament player.
348.	vii.	KITTIE FRANCES, b 18 June 1950

*** THE LEARN FAMILY ***

DONALD's ancestor JOHN LEARN was b Northampton Co. Penn, near Easton. (Donald⁶, Glenn⁵, William C⁴, Thomas³, Jacob², John¹) John's father and brother were killed by Indians during the Rev. there near the Poconos Mts. John's sons George and JACOB came to Ischua Twp, Catt Co in 1823 as pioneers. Jacob and his brother George were the first settlers on Dutch Hill.

Jacob's son THOMAS owned 300 acres, purchased from the Holland Land Company for $2 an acre. When they defaulted on payments as so many others did, a long standing civil, military and expeditionary upheaval ensued that constituted "one of the most memorable incidents that ever occurred in Cattaraugus County." [Adam's Catt] Thomas lived in Olean, where he was a merchant and peddler. Thomas peddled glassware, clothing dry goods and silks for 20 years. He served under McClellan in the Civil War during which he lost an arm. After the war he settled in Hinsdale. The son Joseph, bro of WILLIAM⁴ served in the war after his father was disabled.

Thomas³ had 3 brothers: Jacob, Morris and John, all who fought in the Civil War also.

233. WALTER CHARLES⁷ OYER *(Wallace⁶, David⁵, Peter⁴, David³, Jacob², Frederick¹),* ᵇorn Sala., Catt. Co. 1 June 1920. He married GrV. 15 June 1937 PHYLLIS ANN SMITH, dau. of Sydney Lea and Estelle (Palmer) Smith, born Sala. 6 May 1921.

Childhood sweethearts and marriage and business partners, Walt and Phyllis have had an extensive variety of interests and vocations. Walt's persuasive charismatic ways took him from paper boy (an extensive rural route, walked or later sometimes cycled), nursery stock salesman and landscaper to the CCC's.

Both clerked in her parents' combination grocery store/filling station, begun by the Smiths to stem the tide for their family during the depression, excellent training for their future ventures.

Walt was sought after by a college football and 2 major league baseball teams, but life with Phyllis took precedence. His career with the F. W. Woolworth Company, interrupted by one and a half years' service in WWII in the Army Air Corps where he served as a gunnery instructor, brought them and their two young sons to Roch. in 1947.

Choosing not to be promoted to a job that would require traveling, and having moved 13 times because of promotions in 11 years, Walt and Phyllis purchased in 1951 an appliance sales and service business in Roch. It was soon evident that Walt's preference was for servicing rather than selling. In 1954 they formed Oyer's Appliance Service, incorporating a few years later, with Walt as president and vice-president; Phyllis as secretary-treasurer.

The business filled a large need at that time and there followed years of rapid growth, while a family of 4 children were being raised. The children all did a share of the work involved, whether at home or at the business. Many of the bookkeeping/secretarial duties were done at home, where they all helped. With all 4 children involved in both music and athletics, time had to be found to be enthusiastic supporters and spectators.

Employees looked upon Walt and Phyllis as friends and mentors; many a personal problem was solved throughout the years. Some of the employees' children, even spouses, worked for the company.

Walt held the positions of Field Representative and District Service Manager concurrently for the Whirlpool Corp. while operating the business. Duties included holding schools for appliance technicians for Monroe and its surrounding counties, as well as troubleshooting for that brand and several others. An extensive delivery and installation business added employees, peaking at over 40 employees.

In 1969 the business was sold to the Whirlpool Corp. for their entry into company-owned service headquarters. After continuing with them for over 2 years, Walt and Phyllis were finally free to pursue other goals, having had their first week's vacation in 20 years after the sale of the business.

It was then that Phyllis mentioned to her mother-in-law that by the time of the yearly Oyer reunion she would have some genealogical information to present, having been the "keeper of the archives" for both of the families for years.

Soon after, Phyllis read in Jacob Oyer's obituary (#26), "His grandfather, Jacob Oyer, was captured by the Indians. His great-grandfather was killed at the Battle of Oriskany." No one knew

of a Revolutionary War ancestor; and with no name or place to go
by, the search began.

After a great deal of persevering research, in places where even
a retired historian who had set up the card file system had not
heard of him, he, Frederick, was located. He was found in a page
by page search of the 1879 Beer's History of Herk. Co. The first
of many variant spellings thus surfaced. [See Variant Spellings in
the Preface]

A check in Washington, D.C. at the Daughters of the American
Revolution was interesting. There a record was located under the
spelling "Ayer," cross-referenced with "Oyer." Because there were
no living DAR members at that time under that name, they agreed
to open the record for Phyllis. In 1909 a membership was approved for Carrie Folts Butterfield, wife of Horace G. of Cam-
eron, Steub. Co. Her great-grandmother was Margaret Oyer,
daughter of Peter Oyer (#4).

Fifteen years of research are culminating in the publication of
this book.

Let's go back to Walt. He very quickly found he was unable to
not be kept working. Within a span of less than 10 years he sold
real estate; was president of a school board; ran an income tax
service; and became executive secretary of the Rochester Red
Men's Party House, owned by the Improved Order of Red Men of
Roch. This Party House includes 16 bowling alleys and several
banquet rooms, as well as a private clubhouse. Some of these
jobs were done concurrently. In 1987-88 he is "supervising" an
extensive remodeling/addition.

In the meantime Walt's mechanical, gardening, and all-around
"fixing" abilities enabled him to help family, friend and neighbor
alike in a never-ending desire to be challenged and/or helpful. He
currently is still the executive secretary but with an easing of
problems and responsibility as the current (recently retired from
his regular job) president of the Red Men is now able to
participate more in this million dollar business enterprise.

[The Improved Order of Red Men is the oldest national fra-
ternal organization whose first name was Sons of Liberty. They
are the ones who dressed like Indians and dumped the tea in
Boston harbor--the famed Boston Tea Party.]

Phyllis graduated from Jamestown Business College (now
Jamestown Community College) in 1939. In 1940 while she and
Walt were living in Niagara Falls, she began work for the Ford
Motor Company's customer finance company, the Universal Credit
Company. When Walt was transferred to Buffalo she was trans-
ferred to their Kenmore office. When Walt was transferred to
Bradford, Penn. Phyllis was sent to the closest office--Olean.
Shortly after Walt's transfer to Erie, Penn. in 1942 their first

child was born. That ended her employment days until they went into business partnership in 1951.

Phyllis' other interests and pursuits cover several fields: nutrition, prevention, and "unconventional" health practices; tutoring on a one-to-one basis in an elementary school for several years where she also accompanied the school's choir; singing in the Greece Choral Society; volunteering for years for Friends in Service Here (FISH), mainly providing transportation for the elderly. Weekly volleyball begun in 1958 was given up in 1985. She is a member of the Kodak Genealogical Club, having held office several years as well as being a program presenter.

Walt and Phyllis have been square dancers since 1977. Both have had many occasions to deal extensively in service to the elderly or disabled.

Dearest to their hearts, however, is being "available" grandparents. Walt has been known to be providing bait and removing fish from as many as 6 grandchildren's lines at one time! This takes place at Walt and Phyllis' second home on Hungry Hollow Road in GrV, just a few miles from not only the original Brown and Oyer homesteads, and the current Wallace Oyer home where Rose Oyer still lives, but also near the Smith and Palmer homesteads.

For Walt and Phyllis' 40th wedding anniversary, their children arranged through their daughter Diane and her husband's efforts to have 2 of the hills, partly on their property (which consists of nearly 200 acres in the rolling foothills of the Allegheny Mountains), named for a family ancestor. On the west side of the road, just north of the house and two miles from Route 219 on Hungry Hollow Road is Oyer Mountain, fondly called "Tobbogan Hill." On the east side where the pond is located is Smith Mountain. [See Illus Chap 8]

For their 50th anniversary celebration in July 1987 all the family gathered for several days at their beloved Hungry Hollow home, basking in the warmth and love of the companionship of their children and their families. Other highlights of that magnificent week were Stephanie's baptism; the first playing together of a family French horn sextet directed by David; an afternoon at a riding stable; and a reminiscing afternoon at Red House Lake, where the children had camped as youngsters.

Ch (OYER):

350.	i.	DAVID SMITH[8], b Buffalo, 22 July 1942
351.	ii.	WALTER BRIAN, b Buffalo, 26 July 1944
352.	iii.	DIANE ELIZABETH, b Rochester, 27 Apr 1948
353.	iv.	RONALD LEA, b Rochester, 7 May 1957

*** THE SMITH-KING-PALMER-HALE FAMILIES ***

PHYLLIS' SMITH lineage is Sydney[10], Julian[9], Thomas[8], Thomas[7], Daniel[6], Christopher III[5], Daniel II[4], Christopher II[3], Thomas[2], Christopher I[1]. CHRISTOPHER is believed to be the Chris who was b Bodmin, Cornwall, Eng 1600/01, d 1667. He is found in Thomas Godby's muster of 1625 in Elizabeth Cittie, Va. [Jester] We know he was a tobacco planter in Smith's Tribe, Bermuda in 1628; he was a Lt; then Capt; Councillor and Justice for his tribe, a word used to designate land portions in Bermuda. His ch: THOMAS the Elder (will proved 1709); Edward, Maria, Elizabeth, Keturah, Anne, Katherine, Ellen and Seth. [Smith Gen]

To acquire higher education if residing in Bermuda, it was necessary to go to either England or the United States. Phyllis' grandfather JULIAN came to America, studying at the Univ of Penn in Philadelphia, graduating in 1870 as a doctor of medicine. He settled in Sala and was one of the early doctors there. He pio- neered vaccination for small pox.

Phyllis' f SYDNEY LEA, b Sala 11 Dec 1893, d Sala 4 Jan 1975, bur Wildwood Cem, m 1st Edna Jamieson, b Jan 1884, d 1913, dau Thomas A Jamieson; m 2nd ESTELLE/STELLA PALMER, b 11 May 1879, d 26 Oct 1960, dau JONAH DAVIS and EMMA (HALE) PALMER. Sydney was in the carpentering business many years. As a result of odd jobs during the depression of the 1930's, he acquired a house which he had moved to his in-law's property nearby where he began a combination grocery store/gas station/tourist cabin business. It also housed the family.

For nearly 2 years during WWII he res with Walt and Phyllis in Buffalo where he worked for the Bell Aircraft Co. He was proud to be in on the building of the first jet aircraft in the USA, the XP-59 Airacomet. His years in Buffalo were the only years spent out of Sala, and Stella maintained the store and home there while he was away. He returned to the business, which he kept going until about 1970. Keeping a promise made to Stella shortly before her sudden death in 1960, Sydney was the architect/supervisor/ head carpenter of a two-story addition to Phyllis and Walt's Roch. home in 1961, when he was nearing age 78.

His last few years were spent with dau Nea and son-in-law Gleason Corey, who lived next door in the former tourist cabin, which Gleason and his father-in-law added to and converted to their home many years before. For years that has been the gathering place for one and all: family, relatives, or just friends, following in Sydney and Stella's wake, whose store had previously been thus used.

During Hurricane Agnes in 1972, when flood waters forced evacuation, Sydney's comment was, "I never thought I'd live long enough to see the river do this to me," a commentary on the at-

tachment and esteem with which he viewed the Allegany River, upon the banks of which his home/store was for 43 years. He had a powerfully positive influence upon and was a mentor for many people in many walks of life, his grandchildren no exception.

His bro and sisters (Smith), all b Sala; all but Grace and Frederica bur Sala: Cora Helena, b 11 Mar 1875, d 19 Sept 1965, Guy Parkhill; Louise, b 1878, d 1959, m Charles G Vreeland; Frederica Oberlin, b 1880, d 1936, m Erastus Moore; Julian King, b 17 Oct 1881, d 28 June 1960, m Frances Inman; Ida Grace, b 27 June 1891, d 2 Oct 1985, m Franklyn C Herrick; Jesse Edwin, b 18 July 1893, d 14 Nov 1968, m Esther Snyder.

The PALMER lineage is Jonah Davis[7], Rufus[6], Amos[5], Ichobad[4], Solomon[3], Daniel[2], Micah[1].   MICAH/MICHAEL was an original signer of the Plantation Covenant at Branford, Conn, 1668, and thought to be the son of William Palmer, from England to Branford, d 1656. Micah, b ca 1622, d 1681; became a freeman 1669.

Dave, as J Davis was known, came from Lindley, Steuben Co to Sala in in 1869, purchasing an interest in his bro James' grocery store, leaving that to become a clerk in the office of the Railway Express Agency, later becoming messenger. Extant is his 50-year service commendation and medal from the Railway Express Agency, a vital link in those times. It's forerunner was Wells Fargo.

STELLA m at age 35, having been a school teacher. She was very musical; played piano and organ, and sang. Taking over as step-mother to 2 young boys, she and Sydney soon had 3 of their own, Phyllis being b 3 years later. A deep evangelistic feeling for her Episcopal church saw her godmother or sponsor for many; organist and choir director. She, however, converted to a sect that brought her more fulfillment, despite the rift it caused in family and neighbor relationships. Stella and Sydney worked hard raising their family, she cooking and tending store and otherwise providing for them and their children, whose happiness she so fervently sought.

Ch, including Sydney and Edna's, all b Sala: Thomas Lea, b 6 Aug 1907, m Sala Josephine Subject, res Sala; Julian Greenhow, b 13 Sept 1909, m Michigan Center, Mich Ada Locker, res Phoenix, Ariz; Nea Alma, b 1 Oct 1915, m Sala Gleason Corey, res Sala; Palmer King, b 29 Sept 1916, m Helena Vreeland, res Sala; Sydney Lea, Jr, b 2 Apr 1918, m Sala Julia/Jewell Benton, res Sala; Phyllis, b 1921. [See #233]

Stella's bro & sister, all b in Sala: Arthur D, b 1872, d Detroit, Mich 1940's, m 3 times; Ralph H, b 1874, d St. Petersburg, Fla 1942, m Helen Anderson; Alma, b 1881, d Sala 1963, m Frank R Newton.

There are no male Palmer descendants from Rufus[6].

SARAH ESTELLA KING's lineage is DeLancy⁶, Jeremiah⁵, Nath-aniel⁴, Barzilla³, Ebenezer², John¹. She was b Greenwood, Steu Co 1855, d Sala 1903, bur Wildwood Cem.

JOHN¹, d 1753, m BATHSHEBA SNOW. Through the Snows and allied lines we get to STEPHEN HOPKINS, chosen to help with the Mayflower entourage because of his previous American experience (interestingly in the Somers Islands, later called Bermuda!), and the SOUTHWORTHS, which leads to endless English/Norman/Viking/European ancestors.

DeLANCY, the adventuresomeness still there, was an early 1849'er, he and a friend traveling aboard ship around Cape Horn, S America, where storms and strong currents were hazardous, to the gold rush in Calif. Extant is the interesting story of his experiences, including how his expertise as a millwright enabled him to rig up the steering wheel of the ship, badly damaged by a severe storm. There were other '49ers aboard. His proprietorship of the Dudley Hotel in Sala, moving from Steuben Co, begins the Western NY experience.

EMMA FRANCES HALE's pedigree is Daniel⁷⁻⁶⁻⁵, Thomas⁴⁻³, Joseph², Thomas¹. Thomas (Haille)ᵃ, Glover of Watton at Stone, d 1657, bur Hertfordshire, Eng. THOMAS f was THOMAS who m THOMASINE. [Jacobus]

Emma's f DANIEL, b Bennington, Vt, res successively in these NYS towns: Florence, Sackett's Harbor, back to Florence; then on the line of the New York and Erie Railroad: Owego, Barton, Elmira, Watkins (Glen), Hinsdale, finally settling in Olean, where Daniel was in charge of the repair shops for that railroad. [Everts' Catt, p 452]

Emma was a loving, concerned, helpful woman, whose home provided a welcome to many young people. Her and Dave's help in the rearing of dau Stella's fast-growing family knew no bounds.

Like the Palmer's there are no male Hale descendants from Daniel⁷'s line.

[Sources: Jacobus; Adams' Catt; Beers' Alleg; Clayton's Steu; Smith Gen 1; DAR #397729; Donald Hinman; various "Mayflower" books; family rec; Comp Amer Gen; Langston & Buck]

234. RUSSELL EUGENE⁷ OYER, *(Wallace⁶, David⁵, Peter⁴, David³, Jacob², Frederick¹)* born Sala. 1 Apr. 1922, died Dec. 10, 1986, buried Calvary Cem., Sala. He married Sala. 1 Aug. 1942, THERESA WISE, dau. Stanley/Ed and Louise (Skudlarek) Wise (née Bialozynski), born Sala. 6 Jan. 1923, died Sala. 10 Feb. 1982.

When Russ joined the CCC's [see Illus p 209] as a young man, his formal schooling ended. Among the projects on which he worked were the clearing of the land for the building of Shasta Dam in Calif.

Russ served in the US Army during WWII from Sept. 1942 to Dec. 1945. He was in the Corps of Engineers in Iran for over 2 years; he also served in the Army of Occupation in Germany.

He retired from the Baltimore and Ohio Railroad (formerly the Baltimore, Rochester, and Pittsburgh; later the Chessie System) in 1974 after 25 years' service. He and his brother Paul were stalwarts of the wrecking crew, working many long hours under difficult circumstances in all kinds of weather with outmoded equipment.

Russ was so congenial; he spent many hours working with the youth of the area. He was a scoutmaster, football and baseball coach. Earlier he had played organized baseball. He was a member of the American Legion for 41 years, up until his untimely death in 1986.

Theresa joined the WAVES (Women Accepted for Volunteer Emergency Service) early in WWII, serving as a Pharmacist's Mate 3rd Class at Bethesda Naval Hospital in Washington, D.C. She was in charge of x-raying hundreds of men. In those days there was no thought of protection for the technician.

Some years later, she joined her sister-in-law Ellen in studying to become an LPN (licensed practical nurse). She worked several years at St. Francis Hospital in Olean; her later years were spent as night supervisor at the Allegany Nursing Home in Allegany. Tres died of cancer in 1982.

Ch (OYER) b Sala:

354.   i.   EUGENE RUSSELL[8], b 16 Sept 1946
355.   ii. LINDA CAROL, b 2 Jan 1950

*** THE WISE FAMILY ***

THERESA's parents, ED and LOUISE (SKUDLAREK) WISE, spent most of their lives in Sala., where their only other child, Josephine, still res. Her husband, Richard Coombs, d ca 1980; their dau Bonnie is m and res in the Philadelphia/New England area, as her executive husband [IBM?] is often transferred.

235. BEATRICE JANE[7] OYER (*Wallace[6], David[5], Peter[4], David[3], Jacob[2], Frederick[1]*), born Sala., Catt. Co. 15 July 1925. She married 15 May 1945 in Sala. DAVID GEORGE BISHOP, Jr. born LV, Catt. Co. 22 Aug. 1925, son of David George and Margaret (Neiman) Bishop.

Bea is a secretarial graduate of Bryant & Stratton Business Institute of Buffalo, and worked in several offices before becoming the secretary/receptionist for Howard Stoll, M.D. in LV, retiring about 1980. Always an avid reader ("Beatrice, put out that light and go to sleep!"), her interests also include music and round and square dancing. Under her mother's tutelage as a 4-H member, she participated in their prize-winning drama group. During and for some time after her school years Bea sang in groups and played the piano and violin.

Bea and Dave are active members of "Coop's Troops", Gordon Cooper's square dance club in Sala., holding offices and assisting classes for new dancers. They have participated in many a demonstration, being exceptionally graceful dancers.

Many a day would find Bea taking care of the grandchildren; preparing meals; or canning and freezing many quarts of fruits and vegetables.

Dave was a member of the First Cavalry Div. during WWII, 1945-46. He has always been a woodsman--hunting fishing, trapping, woodcutting. They have had sizeable vegetable gardens every year. For many years they raised beagles and were members of the Lake Erie Beagle Club. David retired from his job as automotive mechanic foreman of the Catt. Co. Highway Dept. in LV about 1983.

Beatrice is a devoted daughter who talks with her mother regularly (twice each day) and helps to take care of her needs, including "paper work," no small task, her medical secretarial years being very helpful. One of Rose's joys is seeing them when they stop in on their way to a square dance.

Ch (BISHOP), all b in Sala:

356.   i.   MARY LYNNE[8], b 9 Mar 1948
357.   ii.   DAVID GEORGE III, b 19 Apr 1951
358.   iii. PAUL DOUGLAS, b 2 Oct 1952
        iv.   JANET MARIE, b Sala 12 May 1957
              Janet, unm, has made music more of a career than any of the other Wallace Oyer grandchildren, although many not only are musical, but have participated to quite an extent in both vocal and instrumental groups. For some years she was an avid horsewoman, qualifying as a harness race driver. She won competitions while in high school with the French horn, playing grade six compositions. She was chosen to spend a summer at the Saratoga Performing Arts Center, where she was under the tutelage of Barry Tuckwell of the Philadelphia Orchestra summering there. Janet also

performed in the All-County and All-State bands. She received her Bachelor degree in Music Performance from the Crane School of Music at Potsdam College, Potsdam, NY, the French horn being her main instrument.

During this schooling, she wrote music and lyrics, played guitar, and sang in dance band groups. Her only published work of that time is the lyrics for Professor Arthur Frackenpoles' song, "Morning Star" for piano, optional guitar and string bass, in 1982. Shortly after that Janet began her first band, A-440, with her sister Mary Lynne, playing in the Sala area and in Penn. This propelled her deeper into that arena.

She is assisting with the elderly, her compassion for them serving them well. In 1984 in an effort to move from dance bands to that type of work, she moved from her home and schooling area to where her brother David lives, Cincinnati, Oh. However, music performance again took over; an all-girl band, "ZAMA," based in Cincinnati, traveled and performed extensively in the tri-state area of Oh, Ky and Ind. Janet plays lead guitar, does much of the lead singing, and writes some of the material. She has several copyrighted songs. In late 1987 she gave that up to perform in a house band in Cincinnati.

*** THE BISHOP FAMILY ***

DAVID's father, DAVID G BISHOP, Sr worked for years at the Case Cutlery plant in LV, driving the 20-plus miles each way from their home in LV to Bradford, Penn when the plant moved there from LV in later years. That company has a top reputation for producing fine knives. David, Sr. was b 6 Nov 1880; d 8 Feb 1978. His wife MARGARET was b 22 Apr 1889; d 23 Feb 1978.

[Sources for #231 through #235: family members]

236. DOLORES[7] OYER (*Frederick[6], Franklin5, Peter4, David3, Jacob2, Frederick1*), born WV, Catt. Co. 12 Aug. 1920; married HAROLD RETTBERG, son of Fred and Marguerite (Shearer) Rettberg, born Sala., Catt. Co. 25 Aug. 1918. They reside Sala.

Dolores worked over 30 years in theater management. For many years she was manager of the Seneca Theater in Sala., bad-

ly damaged by Hurricane Agnes in 1972. Dolores then managed
the Castle Cinema in Olean, her husband taking it over in recent
years. They both are involved in church work.

Harold was a conductor on the B & O/Chessie Railroad. Grand-
parenting is a happy part of their lives.

Ch (RETTBERG), all but Mary b Sala:

359.	i.	DIANE M[8], b 19 Mar 1942
360.	ii.	JOAN E, b 20 Mar 1945
361.	iii.	GRETCHEN A, b 9 Nov 1949
	iv.	MARY, b Olean 25 Mar 1964; grad'd RN degree Alfred Univ; employed St. Francis Hosp, Olean

237.   JOAN J.[7] **OYER** (*Frederick*[6], *Franklin*[5], *Peter*[4], *David*[3], *Jacob*[2], *Frederick*[1]), born Ellvl., Catt. Co. 22 March 1922; married DANIEL HODARA, born Sala. 20 Nov. 1916. Joan has retired from her last employment in advertising for the Sala. Press. Dan has retired from his work at the Borden plant in Randolph, Catt. Co. They reside GrV.

Ch (HODARA), both b Sala:

362.	i.	SANDRA[8], b 10 Dec 1943
	ii.	SHARON, b 30 Oct 1946; m ANTHONY PAVIA, b Sala 25 Mar 1931; res Peth Rd, GrV. Tony is disabled; Sharon operates the Ma Cherie Beauty Salon, Sala.

238.   FREDERICK F.[7] **OYER** (*Frederick*[6], *Franklin*[5], *Peter*[4], *David*[3], *Jacob*[2], *Frederick*[1]), born GV, Catt. Co. 1 May 1930; died Sala., Catt. Co. 19 Nov. 1968 in an auto accident. Fred married 10 Nov. 1961 COLLEEN CASE, born 16 Jan. 1929, dau. Jerome Allen and Genevieve M. (Spence) Case.

Ch (OYER):

i.	CASE ANN[8], b Rome, Oneida Co 25 Jan 1952
ii.	FREDERICK JEROME, b Sala 12 June 1956
iii.	RACHEL ANN, b 17 Jan _____, m 1st _____ BARNHART; m 2nd ANTHONY MILATO; res Jamestown, Chau Co

[Source #236 through #238: Dolores Rettberg (#236)]

239.   ANNA⁷ OYER (*Bartholomew⁶, B Eugene⁵, Peter⁴, David³, Jacob², Frederick¹*), born Newark, N.J. 8 Aug. 1911; married 1st HARRY LYNCH ca 1929; he died 1984.   Anna married 2nd LEONARD STEWART (divorced).

Ch (LYNCH):

   i. VIRGINIA ANN⁸, b 31 July 1930; m ROBERT RELLI-
    HEN.   They have 5 dau; res Tall Timber, Md.
    2 of the ch (RELLIHEN):
     a) CHRISTINE⁹, b 12 Oct 1952
     b) SHELLY, b 30 Sept 1954
   ii. JEANNE DOROTHY, b 14 Nov 1934; m Dr SILVIO
    PALETTA; res Hopatcong, NJ   No ch
   iii. GEORGE WILLIAM, b Jersey City NJ 17 July 1937; m
    1st MAUREEN _____, div'd; m 2nd _____
    _____. George has 1 dau; res E Newark, NJ

240.   JOSEPH ALOYSIUS⁷ OYER (*Bartholomew⁶, B Eugene⁵, Peter⁴, David³, Jacob², Frederick¹*), born Newark, N.J. 3 June 1913, died W. Milford, Passaic Co., N.J. 5 June 1982; buried Pequest Union Cem., Pequest, N.J. Joseph married Kearny, N.J. 20 June 1936 RUTH ANNE PRICE, dau. George Hill and Anna (Mishek) Price, born Briarcliff Manor, Westchester Co.

Joseph was an electrician, member IBEW Union Local #102. Ruth was a secretary. Since retiring, she is a volunteer at the Senior Citizens Nutrition Site of W. Milford; and is a member of the Senior Advisory Committee of that place, as well as the Senior Advisory Council of Passaic Co., N.J. Joseph was a member of the Lady Queen of Peace Roman Catholic Church; Ruth is an active member of the Newfoundland Union Methodist Church and Ladies Aid Society. She is treasurer of the AARP Chapter #3849 in W. Mildord, and belongs to other senior clubs. She is a grandmother of 16 and great-grandmother of 2.

We are delighted to have located Ruth in a telephone book the summer of 1986 while again researching the Ringwood area. She has provided us with information on the families of EUGENE and JENNIE (O'NEILL) OYER, as well as other informants. It's her perogative to skip the year of her birth!

Ch (OYER):

363. i. JOAN PATRICIA⁸, b 30 June 1937
364. ii. ROBERT JOSEPH, b 6 May 1941
365. iii. KENNETH ALAN, b 21 Feb 1943
366. iv. RUSSELL JON, b 10 Apr 1950

241.   ROBERT E.[7] BRADLEY (*Olive Bradley[6]*, *B Eugene[5]*, *Peter[4]*, *David[3]*, *Jacob[2]*, *Frederick[1]*), born N.J. ca. 1912; died by 1986 N.J.; married VERA CUCCI.

Ch (BRADLEY):

    i.   JOHN, res Morris Plains, NJ
    ii. ROBERT E, Jr, unm; mugged (murdered) 1962
    iii. GERARD, m JUDITH _____; res Korea??

242.   GENEVIEVE CATHERINE/JANE[7] BRADLEY (Olive Bradley[6], *B Eugene[5]*, *Peter[4]*, *David[3]*, *Jacob[2]*, *Frederick[1]*), born ca. 1915; married JOSEPH E. GREEN.

Ch (GREEN):

    i.   JUDY[8]
        a) NICHOLAS[9], college student
        b) JOSEPH, college student
        c) MINA, college student
    ii. ROBERT E, unm
    iii. JOSEPH, unm
    iv. MARY, m RICHARD PODZIELNY; res Jersey City, NJ
        a) RICHARD[9], b ca 1975
        b) JOSEPH ROBERT, b ca 1980

[Sources #239,240,241,242: Jane Bradley; Ruth Oyer]

243.   JAMES[7] R. REYNOLDS (*Kittie[6]*, *Eugene[5]*, *Peter[4]*, *David[3]*, *Jacob[2]*, *Frederick[1]*), born 1900; died Ash. 12 Apr. 1986; buried MtHC; married FRANCES SCHULTZ. They resided in Jersey City, returning to Catt. Co.; Frances resides Arcade/Frklnv. area.

Ch (REYNOLDS):

    i.   RUTH[8], m _____ SPENCER; res Sprvl
    ii. DORIS
    iii. MARIAN
    iv. RICHARD
    v. KENNETH

244.   EUGENE[7] "HAPPY" REYNOLDS (*Kittie[6]*, *Eugene[5]*, *Peter[4]*, *David[3]*, *Jacob[2]*, *Frederick[1]*), born Jersey City, N.J. 1905; died WV,

Catt. Co. 21/24 July 1975; buried MtHC; married EDITHE ED-
MUNDE, she residing in WV, Catt. Co. with daughter Donna.

"Hap" got this nickname because of his cheery disposition. They
settled in Farmersville Sta., Catt. Co. He was an electrician. He
also worked for Gramco, Inc. in Frklnv.

Ch (REYNOLDS), both b Bflo:

    i.   DONNA MARIE8, b WV 10 Mar 1943, unm, res with
        mother. Donna is an accountant in Bflo.

    ii.   SUZANNE b 15 Mar 1949, m 29 Dec 1973 EARL NYE,
        b Sala 1 Feb 1947; res Sala. Suzanne is a clerk
        for Fanchers; Earl is a bridge foreman for the NYS
        Transportation Dept covering Catt and Chau
        counties. Ch (NYE):

        a) KELLIE SUE9, b Olean, Catt Co 19 Mar
            1974

        b) KARRIE MARIE, b Sala 13 Apr 1976

[Sources #243, 244: Suzanne Nye; Mr & Mrs Graydon Williams;
censuses; cem rec]

245.   **DOROTHY**[7] **WAITE** (*Kittie*[6], *Eugene*[5], *Peter*[4], *David*[3],
Jacob[2], *Frederick*[1]), born 1918, resides Bflo and WV. She married
Dr. WILLIAM F. WHITE, a surgeon in Bflo. who retired in 1978.

Dorothy is a registered nurse who trained at Mercy Hospital
School of Nursing in Bflo., where her husband was a surgeon.
Their beautiful summer home atop a hill overlooking the vast
Oyer-pioneering area of Ashford is known as "The White House,",
where the color white predominates. The welcome mat is there,
where their pleasant personalities are enjoyed by many.

Ch (WHITE):

    i.   WILLIAM F8, b 19 Nov 1942; trained at St John
        Vianney Seminary (now Christ the King) in E
        Aurora, Erie Co, and Catholic Univ in Wash, DC.
        He is serving a residency at St. Louis Parish in
        Bflo (1987).

246.   **ALIDA**[7] **WAITE** (*Kittie*[6], *Eugene*[5], *Peter*[4], *David*[3], *Jacob*[2],
Frederick[1]), orn WV 17 Feb. 1920; married RAYMOND GRAF, son
of William Graf of Clifton, N.J. Lida trained at Mercy Hospital
School of Nursing in Bflo. as did her sister. She was an army
nurse during WWII, during which time she met her husband.

Ray is a retired electrical contractor (Clifton). They reside in Sun City Center, Fla., near Tampa.

Ch (GRAF):

    i.   MICHAEL[8], b Hempstead, L I 1944; m IRENE POLITO. Mike is a Lt Col in the US Marine Corps, a military attache at the American embassy in Senegal, Africa.
       a) MICHAEL[9], student at Duke Univ
       b) SHANNON, senior in high school
       c) CHRISTOPHER, student in London, Eng
       d) KRISTIN, with parents in Africa

[Source #245,246: Dorothy White]

247. EUNICE[7] OYER (*Robert[6], Frank[5], Jacob[4], David[3], Jacob[2], Frederick[1]*), born [n/a]; died before 1979; married NORMAN CARPENTER. Eunice was a nurse, residing in N. Tonawanda.

Ch (CARPENTER):

    i.   NORMAN[8]
   ii.   ROBERT
  iii.   dau, dec'd

248. ELEANOR[7] OYER (*Robert[6], Frank[5], Jacob[4], David[3], Jacob[2], Frederick[1]*), born [n/a]; married ERNIE BELLAS. They are divorced. Eleanor resides in Wauchula, Fla. Eleanor's mother Cecelia, deceased, resided with her.

Ch (BELLAS) living in 1978:

    i.   JERRY[8]
   ii.   TIM
  iii.   son--killed

248.1 WINIFRED[7] OYER (*Robert[6], Frank[5], Jacob[4], David[3], Jacob[2], Frederick[1]*), married HAROLD LUDWIG. Harold was a teacher, becoming principal of a high school in Kenmore, Erie Co. After retirement he became principal of a church school in Detroit. He is a real estate dealer. They reside in S. Lyons, Mich. and have several children. [data n/a]

248.2 JANICE⁷ OYER (*Robert⁶, Frank⁵, Jacob⁴, David³, Jacob²,
Frederick¹*), deceased, married WILLIAM BRUNN; resided Silver
Springs, Md.   Janice graduated from the Univ. of Mich. as a lab
technician.   They have several children.   [data n/a]

249.   LAWRENCE STANLEY⁷ HADLEY (*Ruth⁶, Frank⁵, Jacob⁴,
David³, Jacob², Frederick¹*), born Bflo., Erie Co. 5 June 1909, died
19 Aug. 1987; buried Sprvl. Lawrence married 26 Sept. 1935 MARY
ELIZABETH/BETTY MADISON of Milwaukee, Wisc., she born 1 Feb
1910.   They have an adopted son Peter, believed to be a Dutch
orphan.   Peter was found in a box car along with a number of
other children near the end of WWII.   His father is thought to
have been a German army officer.   Lawrence was a professional
photographer; they resided Hamburg, Erie Co.

250.   ELBERT HAMILTON⁷ HADLEY (*Ruth⁶, Frank⁵, Jacob⁴,
David³, Jacob², Frederick¹*), born Sprvl 10 July 1913; married 26
Dec 1941 EDNA BAKER of Knoxville, Tenn., born Sprvl. 11 Feb.
1916.   Elbert was professor of chemistry and Dean of the College
of Science and now professor emeritus at Southern Ill. Univ. in
Carbondale, Ill.   Elbert and Edna met when he was working for
his Doctor of Philosophy degree in Chemistry at Duke Univ.,
received in 1940.   They were in education in Kenmore, Erie Co.
prior to going to Southern Ill. Univ.

Elbert, whom we reached in late 1987 through Ruth Metzler,
wrote this interesting story regarding his wife:

> ...How did we ever meet???? My grandparents lived in
> Riceville (8 miles from Sprvl.) and the only way my
> mother could attend high school was to go to Sprvl. So
> arrangements were made for my mother and her older
> brother to live with Edna's grandmother during the
> week to attend high school. My mother always kept in
> contact with Edna's gradmother and i 1938 told her that
> I sas at Duke... Edna's grandmother wrote back and
> said that Edna was also at Duke but didn't know many
> people. Soooo--my mother wrote to me and told me to
> go see Edna sometime--which I did and finally married
> her. Some coincidence!!!!

In 1941 Edna received her degree in medical technology from
Duke Univ.   Edna's mother was Clara Jones Baker; her
grandmother was Anna Reed Jones, sister of Susan Jones who
married FRANK OYER (#102).   Elbert and Edna reside in
Carbondale, Ill.

Ch (HADLEY):

   i.   MARILYN RUTH[8], b Bflo 5 Jan 1945; physician's
        ass't at Univ of Mich; res Ann Arbor, Mich. She
        is a foster parent to about a dozen kids each year
        who run away from home because of parental
        abuse, drunkenness, prostitutes, etc. She has them
        until a poermanent place can be found for them.
  ii.   PHYLLIS ELAINE, b Bflo 29 Mar 1947; m BRYCE
        ASHLEY BABCOCK. He is professor of Physics,
        Williams College, Williamstown, Mass. He did his
        research in Geneva, Switz. Ch (BABCOCK):
        a) AMY LYNN9, b Geneva, 15 Sept 1970
        b) DARRYL ASHLEY, b Walnut Creek,
            Calif 11 Feb 1974
        c) EMILY RUTH, b 30 Nov 1982, N Adams,
            Mass

251. WAYNE[7] NELSON HADLEY (Ruth[6], Frank[5], Jacob[4], David[3],
Jacob[2], Frederick[1]), born Bflo. 6 May 1919; married Aug. 1942
VIRGINIA JOMINY, born Detroit, Mich. 13 Oct. 1921. He received
his Bachelor of Science degree in Chemistry from the Univ. of
Mich; a Bachelor of Theology from Eastern Baptist Theological
Seminary. Wayne worked for some time for General Motors in the
Detroit area. He was a First Baptist minister in Somerville, N.J.
for 30 years; now retired and they reside in Toms River, N.J.

Ch (HADLEY):

   i.   LAWRENCE HAMILTON[8], b Detroit 6 June 1945;
        professor of economics at Dayton Univ
  ii.   CHRISTINE[8], b Westmont, NJ 14 Nov 1947; m DAVID
        LAQUINTINO, an associate Episcopal priest in
        Philadelphia, Penn
 iii.   KAREN, b Westmont, NJ 5 Mar 1951; m _____
        DIKE, computer scientist; res near Denver, Colo.
        Karen has a degree in nursing and theology.
  iv.   RONALD, b Somerville, NJ 3 Dec 1955; personnel
        director, Union Carbide

252. IONA MARIE[7] OYER (*Willis[6]*, *Frank[5]*, *Jacob[4]*, *David[3]*,
Jacob[2], *Frederick[1]*), born 26 July 1910; died 1 Jan. 1987; married
22 Aug. 1931 EDWIN J. MOORE, died 12 Nov. 1983. He had a
men's clothing store in Hamburg, Erie Co., where they resided.

Iona had a "cousins" picnic every year at their cottage on Lake Erie at Angola so they could keep in touch and meet one another. This reunion was held later at a number of places.

Ch (MOORE):

    i.   CAROL YVONNE[8], b 11 July 1932; m 1st DONALD BURSON; m 2nd ROBERT BRUDO. Res Bflo area
        Ch (BURSON):
        a) GEOFFREY STEPHEN[9], b 20 Sept 1956; m PENNY STATER
           1) COREY BARTHOLOMEW[10], b 26 Dec1981
        b) LORI ANN, b 6 Sept 1957; m 20 Nov 1980 MICHAEL BUCCINO Ch (BUCCINO):
           1) NICOLE MARIE, b 2 Nov 1981
        c) SUSAN LEIGH, b 16 Oct 1959/60
    ii. DONALD EDWIN, b 1 Mar 1941; m 7 Oct 1965 MERLYN SANDERSON; res Omaha, Neb
        a) DONALD EDWIN· Jr, b 4 July 1968
        b) ANDREW, b 26 Aug 1969
        c) CHRISTOPHER

253. **RUSSELL STEWART[7] OYER** (*Willis[6], Frank[5], Jacob[4], David[3], Jacob[2], Frederick[1]*), born 9 Apr. 1927; died Dec. 1983. He married 28 May 1949 BARBARA MUSE (divorced). Russell is an officer in an insurance company in Birmingham, Ala.

Ch (OYER):

    i.   RUSSELL SCOTT[8], b 22 Oct 1953; m 14 Aug 1976 _____. Ch (OYER):
        a) CHRISTOPHER SCOTT[9], b 2 Oct 1979
        b) MELISSA MUSE
    ii. PATRICIA LYNN, b 13 June 1955; m KEITH CASTLEBERRY. Ch (CASTLEBERRY):
        a) KERRI ANNE (twin), b 13 Feb 1987
        b) ERIN (twin), b 13 Feb 1987

254. **RUTH[7] AUL** (*Agnes[6], Frank[5], Jacob[4], David[3], Jacob[2], Frederick[1]*), born Bflo. 9 Apr. 1915; married DOUGLAS STOCKIN, born 21 Aug. 1918. Ruth and Douglas bought the Hadley farm that Willis and Myrtle had lived on. The farm is now being sold (1987), after having been run for some time by their son David. They reside Pavilion, Genesee Co.

Ch (STOCKIN):

    i.   GAYLE[8], b Bflo 5 Sept 1946; m JOHN LAND; res
        Mannheim, Penn
        a) JEREMY[9], b 13 June 1974
        b) DOUGLAS, b 17 Sept 1981
   ii.   DAVID, b Sprvl 18 June 1948; m MARCELLA
        RICHARDS, b 24 Aug 1951
        a) MELANIE[9], b Sprvl Mar 18 1972
        b) CARY, b 6 Dec 1973
  iii.   GARY, b Sprvl 16 Dec 1950; m LINDA DRAPER, b
        Aug 1952; res Strasburg, Penn
        a) BETH LYNNE[9], b 15 Nov 1977
        b) AUDREY, b 5 Apr 1979
        c) DANIEL JAY, b 20 Oct 1980
        d) MICHAEL DAVID, b 18 Jan 1983
   iv.   CAROL, b Sprvl 3 Oct 1954; m 1976 GARY HOYT, b
        13 Jan 1952; res Pavilion
        a) JARED[9], adopted, b 20 Oct 1986

255.   RICHARD[7] AUL (*Agnes[6], Frank[5], Jacob[4], David[3], Jacob[2], Frederick[1]*), born [n/a]; married PAULINE _____. Richard had an upholstery business in Hamburg, Erie Co.; now retired. All of their children are married; one lives in Atlanta (1978).

Ch (AUL):

    i.   RICHARD[8]
   ii.   VICTORIA
  iii.   EDWARD
   iv.   son

256.   MARTHA[7] AUL (*Agnes[6], Frank[5], Jacob[4], David[3], Jacob[2], Frederick[1]*), born [n/a]; married MELVIN UNGER. They reside in Monroeville, N.J.

Ch (UNGER):

    i.   NANCY[8]
   ii.   TERRY
  iii.   CHARLES
   iv.   DAWN
    v.   LOUANNA

257. HARVEY EUGENE⁷ OYER, Jr. (*Harvey⁶, Frank⁵, Jacob⁴, David³, Jacob², Frederick¹*), born Boynton Beach, Fla. 31 Mar. 1926; married LINDA EVE; divorced. Harvey resides Boynton Beach, and deals in real estate and insurance. He has been mayor of Boynton Beach, and is active in civic and church affairs.

Ch (OYER):

    i.   SUSAN EVE⁸, b 26 June 1966
   ii.   HARVEY III, b 5 Apr 1968
  iii.   LINDA CHRISTIAN, b 2 Aug 1973

258. LOIS PATRICIA⁷ OYER (*Harvey⁶, Frank⁵, Jacob⁴, David³, Jacob², Frederick¹*), born Boynton Beach, Fla. 17 Nov. 1928; married 24 Apr. 1965 FREDERICK P. DOOLEY. Lois is a teacher and Fred is a Certified Public Accountant. They reside in Tucson, Ariz.

Ch (DOOLEY):

    i.   FREDERICK PATRICK⁸, b 9 Jan 1969

259. DELEVAN⁷ RASZMANN (*Lucy Beach⁶, Amy Bowen⁵, Margaret⁴, John³, Jacob², Frederick¹*), born Mar. 1905; married HELEN LOU _____.

[Sources #247-259: Charlotte Oyer; Dean Williams from family rec; WV VR; Violet Oyer; Elbert Hadley; Ruth Stockin]

259.1 ELEANOR MAE⁷ OYER (*St. Elmo⁶, Charles⁵, John⁴⁻³, Jacob², Frederick¹*), born Sprvl., Erie Co. 27 May 1915; married RUSSELL MULLEN, Bflo., Erie Co. 17 Aug. 1939. Russell was born 6 Dec. 1912; died 29 Jan. 1982.

Eleanor is a notable member of the long list of musicians in the Oyer and allied families. She has been a pianist and organist for over 50 years. She has been a director of music for up to 4 choirs and organist in 4 churches in the Bflo. area. Eleanor is a past dean for the Bflo. Chapter of the American Guild of Organists, and is now librarian for that group (1986). She retired in Jan. 1988, and helped us place some of our unplaced Oyers.

In Sept. 1929 as a school project, Eleanor wrote to a woman in Bergen, Norway. In the fall of 1985 she was able to take a Scandinavian tour and to spend a full day in Bergen with Helen and her husband. It was a truly memorable day. "It was as though we had always known each other."

Russell served in WWII, being discharged as a staff sergeant. He received the Purple Heart, awarded for those injured in combat. He was a bus operator in Bflo., and a captain in the Amherst Police Auxiliary. He was a scoutmaster; he enjoyed fishing. He delivered Meals-on-Wheels for a number of years before his death of a cerebral hemorrhage.

Ch (MULLEN), both b Bflo:

367.   i.   KATHY ANN[8], b 9 Nov 1942
368.   ii. BECKY LOU, b 28 Apr 1946

260.   CHARLES HENDRIX[7] OYER, D.C. *(St. Elmo[6], Charles[5], John[4-3], Jacob[2], Frederick[1])*, born Bflo., Erie Co. 24 Mar. 1917; married Bflo. 15 Aug. 1941 FRANCES LORRAINE RUSS, born Bflo. 18 Oct. 1919, dau. John J. and Marie (Grant) Russ. They reside in Ashland, Missouri.

Charles and his brother James (below) are doctors of chiropractic, as was their father.

Ch (OYER), both b Bflo:

    i.   MARY CAROLE[8], b 1 May 1944; res Decatur, Ga
         after having been a school teacher in the Bflo area
         for 20 years
    ii. MICHAEL CHARLES, b 1 May 1949; m JANE ZIER 21
         Oct 1978. Both are reverends and are at the Holy
         Order of Mans in Portland, Ore.

260.1   JAMES DAVID[7] OYER, D.C. *(St. Elmo[6], Charles[5], John[4-3], Jacob[2], Frederick[1])*, born Bflo., Erie Co. 3 Oct. 1919; married ELEANOR HEYWOOD, b Andover, Kans. 16 Dec. 1925; res. in Hamburg, Erie Co.

James is a doctor of chiropractic also, as is his brother Charles. James practices in Bflo. where he is carrying on the fine reputation of healing his father had.

Ch (OYER), all b Bflo:

    i.   G ROBERT[8], b 14 Apr 1952; m PATRICIA PALSBO
         a) JOSH[9], b 13 Nov 1985
    ii. MICHELLE JO, b 18 Apr 1956, musician

iii.   G JAMES, b 19 Nov 1949; m CHERYL JACKSON, b 17
       Nov 1952; no ch

[Sources #259.1, 260, 260.1: family members]

261.   MARGUERITE EMMA[7] WOOD (*Della Knapp[6], Frances[5], John[4], Peter[3], Frederick[2-1]*), born Schuy., Herk. Co. 1 Sept. 1906;
married Utica 14 Sept. 1946 EDWARD O. MIEKAM, born 1910; died
5 Dec. 1972; buried W. Schuy.; Marguerite died Utica 22 Sept.
1982.

Ch (MIEKAM):

   i.   MARTHA JEAN[8], b Utica 1 July 1948; m Utica 18
        May 1974 ROBERT W REALS, b 10 Nov 1948; res
        Mohawk, Herk Co. Ch (REALS):
        a) CHRISTIAN ANDREW9, b Utica 18 Dec 1978
        b) SARAH BETH, b Utica 18 Mar 1982

261.1   RUTH MARION[7] WOOD (*Della Knapp[6], Frances[5], John[4], Peter[3], Frederick[2-1]*), born Schuy., Herk. Co. 18 Mar. 1908;
married 19 Apr. 1932 MILLARD FILLMORE HARRIS II, born 12
Apr. 1906; died 6 Oct. 1976; buried N. Hartford, Oneida Co. Ruth
resides in Utica.

Ch (HARRIS), both b Utica:

   i.   MILLARD FILLMORE III[8], b 4 Dec 1936; m 1st 30
        Sept 1964 AGNES _____, b 31 July _____; div'd;
        m 2nd SHERRY _____, b 26 Mar _____. No ch.
   ii. WAYNE WOOD, b 30May 1941; m Ilion, Herk Co 4
        Apr 1964 ANNE MARIE TILLINGHAST, b 30 July
        1941; res Ilion
        a) STEVEN WAYNE9, b Roch 23 Jan 1965;
            res Ilion
        b) MARK DANIEL, b Roch 12 May 1966;
            res Ilion
        c) ERIC DAVID, b 13 Apr 1967; d 26 Apr
            1967; bur Ilion
        d) KATHLEEN LINDA, b Utica 2 Sept
            1971; res Ilion
        e) CHRISTOPHER JOHN, b Utica 8 Feb
            1973; res Ilion

262. **LOIS MARION[7] DODGE** (*Lida Knapp[6], Frances[5], John[4], Peter[3], Frederick[2-1]*) born Schuy., Herk. Co. 7 Dec. 1903; married Frkf., Herk. Co. 9 Oct. 1926 ALBERT JOHN PETRIE, born 13 Nov. 1904; died N. Hartford, Oneida Co. 7 July 1973; buried Herk. Lois resides Whitesboro, Oneida Co.

Ch (PETRIE):

    i.   ROGER DODGE[8], b Herk 5 Feb 1928; d Herk 14 Apr 1929

    ii.   RICHARD ALBERT, b Herk 24 Mar 1934; res Latham, Albany Co; unm

    iii.   ROBERT WILLARD, b Ilion 16 July 1943; m N Hartford 16 May 1980 MARY VIRGINIA NEVIN, b 24 Aug 1946; res N Hartford, Oneida Co
        a) JENNIFER ANNE, b Charleston SC 14 Oct 1971
        b) BRIAN LELAND, b Ephrata, Penn 20 Dec 1974

263. **GLADYS LEONE[7] DODGE** (*Lida Knapp[6], Frances[5], John[4], Peter[3], Frederick[2]-1*), born Schuy., Herk. Co. 15 Apr. 1916; married 1st CHARLES ELI ROSBROOK, born 10 Apr. 1914; died 11 July 1971; bur Frkf. Gladys married 2nd 1 Sept. 1984 FOSTER BURKE, born 7 Aug _____; died Whitesboro, Oneida Co. 13 Sept. 1984.

Ch (ROSBROOK), all b Ilion, Herk Co:

    i.   ALAN CHARLES[8], b 14 Sept 1939; m Ilion, Herk Co 20 July 1963 BEVERLY SCHONBORG, b 10 Mar 1942; res Victor, Monroe Co. Ch: (ROSBROOK)
        a) GARY ALAN[9], b Ilion 8 Jan 1965
        b) PAMELA LYNNE, b Canandaigua, Ontario Co 4 Aug 1967
        c) ROBERT CHARLES, b Canandaigua 11 Aug 1971

    ii.   DAVID LEE, b 9 Nov 1941; m Ilion 17 Sept 1966 BARBARA JEAN RAYMOND, b 10 Jan 1944; res N Hartford, Oneida Co. Ch: (ROSBROOK)
        a) LAURA ANN[9], b Utica 30 June 1967
        b) CHRISTOPHER SCOTT, b Utica 9 July 1968

    iii.   CYNTHIA JOAN, b 26 Apr 1944; m Whitesboro 31 Dec 1966 KENNETH CLARK BALDWIN, b 28 June 1943;

res Brockport, Monroe Co, Ch (BALDWIN), both b
Roch:
    a)   SHERRI ANN[9], b 27 June 1968
    b)   BRADLEY SCOTT, b 2 June 1970

[Source #261 through #263: Robert Petrie]

264.   **RICHARD JOHN**[7] OYER (*Howard*[6], *Richard*[5], *John*[4],
Peter[3], *Frederick*[2-1]), born Utica, Oneida Co. 10 July 1919;
married BERTHA KIELBASA. They reside Whitesboro, Oneida Co.

Ch (OYER):

    i.   PAUL[8], b Rome 1 Nov 1942, d 19 Nov 1981, bur
        Crown Hill Cem, Kirkland Twp, Oneida Co. He m
        _____, b _____
        a) MICHAEL[9]
   ii.   LYNDA KAY, b Rome 3 July 1948, m RICHARD
        HUTHER, res Ohio in 1976
        a) BRIAN b) KEVIN
  iii.   VICKI SUE, b 18 Oct 1951, m DENNIS DUNGAN,
        div'd; res Mass
        a) JED, b 26 Dec 1971

265.   **RAYMOND HOWARD**[7] OYER (*Howard*[6], *Richard*[5], *John*[4],
Peter[3], *Frederick*[2-1]), born Whitestown 3 Nov. 1922; died 26 Jan.
1976, buried Forest Dale Cem., Holyoke, Mass. He married DORIS
PETERSON.

Ch (OYER):

    i.   DONALD[8], b 12 Nov 1960, unm, res Utica
   ii.   PETER, b 7 Feb 1962, unm, res with mother in
        Holyoke, Mass

266.   **GERTRUDE ALICE**[7] OYER (*Howard*[6], *Richard*[5], *John*[4],
Peter[3], *Frederick*[2-1]), born Whitestown 7 Apr. 1926; married 6 Oct.
1951 EDWARD A. RACE, born 31 Jan. 1926; he died 22 Sept. 1981;
buried Rome Cem. Edward was a civil engineer in refrigeration
and air conditioning at Griffiss Air Force Base, Rome. Gertrude is
employed by the Oneida Co. Dept. of Social Services, residing in
Rome.

Ch (RACE):

  i. NANCY JEAN[8], b _____24 Nov 1952; m DAVID
P MORRISON 24 Sept, 1977. He was b 25 Sept
1953, and has served in the U S Coast Guard in
Alaska and Maine. Dave is currently employed by
NYS Power Authority, Marcy. Ch (MORRISON):
    a) MICHAEL D[9], b Portland, Me 13 Apr 1980
    b) STEVEN P, b Utica, 20 Aug 1982
  ii. JANET ELIZABETH, b _____ 27 Jan 1955; m 29
Jan 1977 LARRY D KOON, b 2 Oct 1948. The
family is stationed at Pease Air Force Base,
Portsmouth, NH. Ch (KOON):
    a) JASON DEAN[9], b Denver, Colo 7 June 1978
    b) SARAH E, b Plattsburgh 26 Jan 1981

267. LUKE HENRY[7] OYER (*Howard[6], Richard[5], John[4], Peter[3], Frederick[2-1]*), born Whitestown Twp. 12 Feb. 1928; married 30 June 1951 BARBARA COLEMAN, born 30 Aug. 1932. Luke works at Revere Copper and Brass in Rome. Barbara operates the B & L Ceramic Shop at their home on Stone Rd., Whitesboro. They also have an interest in Village Ceramics in Utica.

Ch (OYER):

  i. LARRY WILLIAM[7], b 25 Aug 1953, res Utica, unm
  ii. DIANE HELEN, b 8 Oct 1955; m 6 Oct 1979 MARC A
CANGELLO; employed by Faxton Sunset Nursing
Home in Utica. Ch (CANGELLO):
    a) DANA LYNN[8], b Utica 23 Nov 1980
  iii. KATHLEEN ANN, b 28 Dec 1962, unm, licensed
practical nurse in nursing homes, currently Cayuga
Co Nursing Home, Auburn, Onon Co; res Auburn

268. ROBERT LEE[7] OYER (*Howard[6], Richard[5], John[4], Peter[3], Frederick[2-1]*), born Whitestown Twp. 6 Jan. 1936; married DIANN SAYERS, born 7 June 1946, now divorced. Robert is a long-time employee of the Chicago Pneumatic Company in Utica.

Ch (OYER):

  i. TINA MARIE[8], b 13 July 1965; attends SUNY
Fredonia, Chau Co, doing student teaching there
  ii. MARY BETH, b 5 July 1971, is a student, living with
her mother in Utica

269.   BERNARD GEORGE[7] OYER *(Howard[6], Richard[5], John[4], Peter[3], Frederick[2-1])*, born Whitestown Twp. 5 June 1938; married 5 Sept 1964 HELEN ROSE WINNIE, born 24 June 1942, dau. of George and Helen (Heim) Winnie, born Utica 19 June 1902 and 30 July 1904 respectively.   George died Utica 20 Feb 1976, buried Forest Cem there.   His ancestors came from Germany.   Bernard is a sergeant in the New York State Dept. of Correction, assigned to the Auburn Correctional Facility.   Helen is a registered nurse; administrative supervisor employed at Auburn Memorial Hospital. Bernard has been most cooperative, with offers of assistance.

Ch (OYER):

i.   JoANNE[8], b Elmira, Chemung Co 8 June 1965; is a secretary in a department store in Auburn

ii.   JENNIFER, b Utica, Oneida Co 15 Sept 1967; a student of marine biology at Riverhead, LI

iii.   SUSAN ROSE, b Auburn, Cayuga Co 9 June 1969; student SUNY Canton College of Technology, Canton

iv.   JEFFREY, b Watertown, Jefferson Co 4 May 1970; student

270.   ELLEN AIMEE[7] OYER, *(Howard[6], Richard[5], John[4], Peter[3], Frederick[2-1])*, born Whitestown Twp. 30 Nov. 1940; married 9 Dec. 1961 DAVID G. FORDER.   They reside in Clark Mills.

Ch (FORDER):

i.   COLLEEN[8], b 23 June 1962; m 12 July 1986 JAMES A'HEARNE

ii.   NOREEN, b 16 Aug 1965; employed Liberty Travel, N Hartford

iii.   NORMAN HOWARD, b 15 Mar 1971; student

iv.   DAVID GORDON Jr, b 25 Jan 1976; student

[Sources #264 through #270: Gertrude Race; Bernard Oyer]

271.   ROBERT FOLTS[7] OYER *(Roscoe[6], George[5], Levi[4], George[3], Frederick[2-1])*, born 7 July 1918; married BEULAH WINIFRED (BAY) LOUNSBURY, born 28 Oct. 1921, dau. Arthur and Pearl Bay. Robert served in the First Infantry Div. during WWII, suffering chronic mental problems as a result.   He is hospitalized at the veterans' hospital in Canandaigua, Ontario Co.

We here quote from a 1987 AMVETS brochure regarding our war veterans:

Although our Nation has been *at peace* since 1975, thousands of American veterans still fight an unseen enemy in the confines of their hearts and minds.

For these veterans, the aftermath of battlefield exposure manifests itself in anxiety, depression, nightmares and a heightened sense of alienation from their fellow human beings.

...it wasn't until 1980 that a condition known as *posttraumatic stress disorder* (PTSD) was officially diagnosed and categorized.

PTSD is not new. It has existed for years, known in World War I as "shell shock" and in World War II as "combat fatigue." Yet, America is only at the bare brink of understanding this perplexing emotional bankruptcy.

Veterans of battle, upon returning home, often completely immerse themselves in the responsibility of education, careers or raising a family, thereby disrupting the normal recovery and grieving process by numbing and blocking out traumatic memories and feelings of the wartime atrocities they witnessed and endured.

It is not until years later...that latent PTSD finally surfaces.

...prolonged silent anguish...can eventually bring even the most steadfast persons to their knees...

Regretfully, we can never fully repay their devotion, but we can send our messages of genuine concern...

Ch (OYER):

340.   i.   WILSON MARK[8], b 9 Mar 1941
341.   ii. CAROL PEARL, b 19May 1942

271.1   JEANNETTE[7] CLARK (*Harold Clark[6], Bertha Beach[5], Mary[4], Michael[3], Frederick[2-1]*), born 1916; married 1 July 1942 ROBERT POPP, born Roch., Monroe Co. 8 June 1918. They reside in Walton, Delaware Co. Jeannette taught social studies and Bob taught math and physical education there and coached. He was the principal at Walton Central High School, from which they retired in 1979. In 1987 she and her husband spent a month in Scotland pursuing genealogy. Their granddaughter is a much-celebrated liver transplant patient, operations performed in Chicago, Ill. in 1986 at Wyler Children's Hosp. Christina is now a completely normal girl, even involved in sports.

Ch (POPP):

i. BARBARA JEAN[8], b Roch 13 Apr 1944; m 2 Aug 1968 Mt View, Calif CALVIN BAKER, b 5 July 1942;res Conyers, Ga, suburb of Atlanta. Barbara is a dietitian at Decataur General Hosp in Atlanta; Calvin is an accountant in Atlanta. Ch (BAKER):
   a) MARK RYAN[9], b Grand Junction, Colo 24 Sept 1973
   b) TYLER CHAD, b Grand Junction 15 July 1975

ii. JAMES ALAN, b Walton 8 Jan 1947; m 1st Hamburg, Erie Co 27 June 1970 BARBARA NOONAN, b 21 Feb 1947; div'd; m 2nd Albuquerque 18 June 1983 GABRIELLA KEMENES who was m 1st to Dr Fiber. Their ch: Antonia, b 3 Nov 1977. James res Cedar Crest, NM. James and Gabi are teachers in the Albuquerque public schools, he a reading specialist; she works with the mentally and physically handicapped children. Ch (POPP), of 1st m:
   a) JESS ANDREW, b Albuquerque, NM 12 Mar 1975
   b) BENJAMIN JAMES, b Albuquerque 23 Sept 1978

iii. MARY ELIZABETH, b Walton 20 Dec 1949; m Walton 15 Sept 1970 ROBERT WILSON, b 16 Apr 1949; res W Henrietta, Monroe Co. in the Clark homestead, Windy Knoll on E River Rd. Mary received her RN from Monroe Community College, and was a head nurse at St. John's Home, Roch. Bob has a general store in W Henrietta called the Cornor Store. He also has a construction company: B & L. Ch (WILSON), all adopted, all brothers and sisters:
   a) KEITH DOUGLAS, b 19 Jan 1975
   b) TIMOTHY JACOB, b 25 May 1976
   c) JENNIFER FRANCES, b 15 Apr 1977
   d) CHRISTINA ANN, b 12 Jan 1979

iv. ROBERT WILLIAM, b Walton 5 Apr 1953; m 1st Chicago, Ill MATIE ELERY, b 1953; m 2nd Destin, Fla 27 June 1983 ROSEMARY CELESTE HODGIN, b Brownsville, Tex 19 Aug 1953; res Roswell, Ga, suburb of Atlanta. Bob graduated with BS from Plattsburgh State Univ; his MBA 1984 from Nova Univ, Ga. He is a computer specialist with Digital Equipment as of 1987. Rosemary is a dentist; graduated with a DDS degree from Emory Univ May 1986.

v. PATRICIA LOUISE, b Walton 18 Jan 1957; m Walton 3 Sept 1983 KERRY T LOUGHMAN, b New Rochelle,

Westchester Co 19 June 1957; res Castleton, Rensselaer Co. Patti received a BA in social work from SUNY at Plattsburgh in 1980 and works at Medical Fiscal Management in Albany. Kerry graduated from St. Michael's College, Winooski, Vt and is a claims manager for Metropolitan Life Insurance Co in Albany.

271.2 HAROLD W[6] CLARK (*Bertha[5], Mary[4], Michael[3], Frederick[2-1]*), born 15 Dec. 1922; m 7 May 1946 BONNIE GEER, b 10 Feb 1923. Harold graduated from Wooster Univ. in 1947; from the Univ. of Roch. 1950 with a Ph.D. degree. He served as a biochemist with the Arthritis Institute for 35 years.
There are 2 grandchildren.

Ch (CLARK):

    i.   LINDA C7, m DAVID JAMIE
    ii. STEWART
    iii. MARGERY
    iv. JANET
    v.   JOHN
    vi. LORI

271.3 ROBERT WELLS[6] CLARK (*Bertha Beach[5], Mary[4], Michael[3], Frederick[2-1]*), born 12 April 1925; married Dec. 30 1947 MARY KAYE FRITZ; died Akron Hosp., resided Hudson, Oh. 8 May 1964. Bob graduated from Syracuse Univ. in 1950. He was a lieut. in the Air Corps in WWII. Mary Kay graduated from Mt. Vernon College in 1947.

Ch (CLARK):

    i.   ROBERT TODD[7], b 1949
    ii. MARK TANNER, b 1950
    iii. CHRISTOPHER WELLS, b 1951

271.4 THOMAS JAMES[6] CLARK (*Bertha Beach[5], Mary[4], Michael[3], Frederick[2-1]*), born 21 Nov. 1926; married 19 Sept. 1949 DELORES WETZEL. Tom served in the US Navy in WWII and owns the Thomas Clark Insurance Agency in W. Henrietta, Monroe Co.

Ch (CLARK):

    i.   LESLIE ANN[7], m STEPHEN KLEIN
   ii. THOMAS JAMES
  iii. CYNTHIA DEEANE, m RONALD HOWLETT
  iv. PAMELA JEAN

271.5   EMILY LOUISE[6] CLARK (*Bertha Beach[5], Mary[4], Michael[3], Frederick[2-1]*), born 8 May 1930; married 31 Aug. 1949 WILLIAM R. YOUNG.
William served in the US Navy in WWII; graduated from the Univ. of Roch. and Cornell Univ. His doctorate is in etymology. He worked for the Rockefeller Foundation in Mexico, India, Thailand and Indonesia. He retired circa 1987 and resides in Staunton and Springfield, Va.

  Ch (YOUNG):

    i.   GEORGE CLARK[7]
   ii. DOUGLAS ALLEN
  iii. KENNETH HAROLD

[Source for #271's: Beach Inf 1]

272.   VIVUS/VEVUS LEWIS PETE[7] CRANER (*Edith Lewis[6], Gertrude[5], Peter[4], Jacob[3], Peter[2], Frederick[1]*), born Jordan, Onon. Co. 13 Feb. 1897; died Moravia, Cayuga Co. 1 June 1980; married 12 June 1922 RESA LOUISE BALDWIN, dau. of James Elmer and Edith Estella (Tracy) Baldwin of Baldwinsville, Onon. Co., she born 28 Sept. 1899; died Moravia 8 Aug. 1986.
Vivus was educated at Jordan, and the military school at Manlius. He was a member of Jordan Lodge #386, F. & A. M., initiated 18 Nov. 1918; raised 20 Jan. 1919. He was also a member of the Salem Town Commandery Knight Templars, the Tigris Temple Shrine, the Jordan Old Boys, and the Jordan Fire Dept.
He was the proprietor of Craner Insurance Co., and an inspector for ALCO Power Co., Auburn. They left the Lewis homestead in 1948, moving to an apartment in the Craner home on N. Main St., Jordan. Vivus died in a nursing home.

  Ch (CRANER), b Syracuse:

369.   i. ALFRED JAMES[8], b 19 Mar 1924

[Sources: Marge Craner; obituaries]

273.   HOWARD HUDSON/<u>DEKE</u>7 MARVIN, Jr. (*Howard Marvin*[6], *Cora Buck*[5], *Harriet*[4], *Jacob*[3], *Peter*[2], *Frederick*[1]), born 11 May 1918; died 3 June 1974; buried Riverview Cem., Baldwinsville, Onon. Co. Deke married 1943 MAE MERRIFIELD, born 1920. He graduated from Warners High School, Onon. Co.; served in the U.S. Navy. He was a Mason.

Ch (MARVIN):

    i.   CYNTHIA[8], b 1948
    ii. SHARON, b 1950; m STEVE NELSON

[Source: Howard Marvin to Ralph Auyer]

274.   GEORGE ROBERT7 MARVIN (*Howard Marvin*[6], *Cora Buck*[5], *Harriet*[4], *Jacob*[3], *Peter*[2], *Frederick*[1]), born Van Buren Twp. 1920; married SYLVIA WADE.

Ch (MARVIN):

    i.   WADE[8], b 14 Dec 1947
    ii.   MELLONIE, b 27 Dec 1948; m 1971 RENE du LOPEZ
        a) JULIANNA[9], b 1971
        b) RAQUEL, b 1974
    iii. DAVID, b 18 Feb 1951
    iv.   STEPHEN GEORGE, b 2 May 1952; m 1978 CATHERINE PARSON; res Puerto Rico
    v.   GEORGE <u>ROBERT</u>, b 6 Apr 1955

[Source: Howard Marvin to Ralph Auyer.]

275.   REBA EVELYN7 SOMES (*Smith Somes*[6], *Henry Somes*[5], *Margaret Mary*[4], *Jacob*[3], *Peter*[2], *Frederick*[1]), born 17 May 1921; married 23 June 1951 MICHAEL EDWARD BATTAGLIA, son of Russell and Jennie Battaglia of Bflo., Erie Co.

Ch (BATTAGLIA):

    i.   MICHAEL EDWARD[8], Jr, b Ridley, Penn 20 Mar 1952; m 24 June 1972 CARIN BENNETT, b 18 Sept 1952
        a) NATHAN MICHAEL[9], b 8 Aug 1975
        b) KIMBERLY JENNIE, b 18 Jan 1978
    ii. JOHN <u>MARK</u>, b Drexal Hill, Delaware Co, Penn 6 Oct 1953; m 30 June 1978 ELLEN PAYNE, b 30 July 1959

iii. PETER SOMES, b Drexal Hill, Penn 10 Nov 1954; m
      22 Oct 1977 LEAH BATHURST, b 22 Mar 1955
iv.   RUTH LYNN, b Kingston, Ulster Co 27 Nov 1956; m
      18 Dec 1976 WILLIAM J WILLIAMS, b 4 May 1955
      a) JOSHUA⁹, b 12 May 1979
v.   JOEL DAVID, b Kingston 9 Jan 1960
vi.   DEBORAH ANN, b Kingston 1 Apr 1963

[Source: Margaret E Somes]

276. MARTHA LOUISE⁷ SOMES *(Floyd Somes⁶, Henry Somes⁵, Margaret Mary⁴, Jacob³, Peter², Frederick¹)*, born at the Floyd Somes farmhouse, Jack's Reef, Van Buren Twp., Onon. Co. 4 Feb. 1922; married at home 23 Aug. 1943 HUBERT E RETCHLESS, son of Ralph B. Retchless, born 4 Apr. 1923. They reside Lysander Twp., Onon. Co.

Ch (RETCHLESS), both b Syracuse, Onon Co:

i.   PATRICIA LOUISE⁸, b 5 Mar 1946; m ED HORNING
     a) KATIE, b 8 Aug 1976
ii. JEAN SUZANNE, b 9 Nov 1950; m 7 Mar 1976 PARRY
     WILL KITCHNER, son of Wilbur Norman and Doris
     Amelia (Parry) Kitchner, b Syracuse 8 Dec 1950

[Sources: Floyd Somes; Mrs. Barton Somes; Mrs. Wilbur Kitchner.]

277. BARTON ROTHWELL⁷ SOMES *(Floyd Somes⁶, Henry Somes⁵, Margaret Mary⁴, Jacob³, Peter², Frederick¹)*, born at the Floyd Somes farmhouse at Jack's Reef, Van Buren Twp., Onon. Co. 14 Dec. 1924; married 17 Feb. 1944 SHIRLEY LOUISE/HONEY BENTLEY, dau. of Claude and Viola (Gibbs) Bentley, born Solvay, Onon. Co. 5 Dec. 1923.
Barton farms, having purchased the old Voorhees farm (poss. the same as that farmed by Valentine Auyer in the 1870's). Members of the Jordan United Methodist Church, Barton and Honey reside in Lysander Twp.

Ch (SOMES), both b Syracuse, Onon Co:

i.   GARY BARTON⁸, b 12 Apr 1945; m 25 Feb 1967
     LINDA McCHESNEY, b Penn 1 Mar 1946. Gary
     farms and res near his parents. Ch (SOMES), all b
     Auburn, Cayuga Co:

        a)   BRENT BARTON[9] (twin), b 6 Aug 1968
        b)   BRUCE DAVID[9], (twin), b 6 Aug 1968
        c)   SUZANNE CAROL, b 13 June 1973
   ii. BARBARA ANN, b 14 June 1949; m 10 May 1969
        GERALD RAY SWEET, of Massena, St Lawrence
        Co, b 14 Aug 1948. Ch (SWEET), all b Auburn:
        a)   JULIE ANN[9], b 19 Sept 1970
        b)   SCOTT MICHAEL, b 23 Sept 1972
        c)   MATHEW RAY, b 3 July 1977

[Source: Mrs. Barton Somes]

278. ELIZABETH JEAN[7] SOMES (*Kaple Somes[6], Oren Somes[5],
Margaret Mary[4], Jacob[3], Peter[2], Frederick[1]*), born at the Oren A.
Somes farmhouse, Van Buren Twp., Onon. Co. 23 Aug. 1922;
married 23 Aug. 1943 ALBERT HEPPENSTALL ARNOLD, son James
Irza and Anna Caroline (Mundlein) Arnold, born Flushing 11 Dec.
1919; reside Cooper Rd., near Jordan.
Elizabeth attended the Pine Hill District Schol, Jordan High
School, and had nurses training at Memorial Hospital, Syracuse,
Onon. Co.
Albert is a semi-retired architect; he and Betty are the
proprietors of Studio Antiques in Elb., Onon. Co.

   Ch (ARNOLD), all b Syracuse:

    i. DAVID MITCHELL[8], b 12 July 1951; m 12 May 1973
        SUSAN CAROL McCOY, dau of William and Ellen
        McCoy of Altamont, Albany Co, b 27 July 1952
        a)   EMILIE SIOBHAN[9], 15 Sept 1982
   ii. JAMES KAPLE, b 24 May 1953; m Dillon, SC 6 May
        1973 DOREEN ELIZABETH PROULX, dau of Louis
        Robert and Marilyn Elizabeth (Quinn) Proulx, b
        Cortland, Cortland Co 21 Sept 1954 (div'd) Ch
        (ARNOLD), b Syracuse:
        a)   BENJAMIN LOUIS[9], b 20 Dec 1973
  iii. ALBERT HAWLEY, b 22 Oct 1958; graduated from
        Onondaga Community College and Syracuse
        University, receiving an AB degree in Visual and
        Performing Arts and Education. He has taught in
        Jordan, Baldwinsville and W Genesee High Schools;
        is Assistant Director of Elbridge-Jordan Marching
        Band, which has won high honors statewide. Haw-
        ley is organist at the Jordan Methodist Church,
        and composes and plays music for silent movies.
        In addition he builds, tunes, and repairs pipe

organs, and has had much to do throughout central NY in this field.

His interest in family history stems from when he was a student in high school and came into possession of Jacob Oyer's (#17) account book. Hawley's book on the brothers, Jacob, James and Solomon Oyer/Auyer required three years of research, correspondence and interviewing. Much of this was done in conjunction with Ralph Auyer (#201). Ralph's introduction of Hawley to the author is responsible for the collaboration that produced this book. As cited previously, only the over-committment of his time necessitated his withdrawal from the project in early 1987.

[Sources: AHA, Ralph Auyer]

279. ROBERT OREN[7] SOMES (*Hunting Somes[6], Oren Somes[5], Margaret Mary[4], Jacob[3], Peter[2], Frederick[1]*), born Syracuse, Onon. Co. 26 Apr. 1918; married Jordan 24 Sept 1948 ALLURA JUNE PLANTZ, dau. of Frank M. and Catherine Mae (McCloud) Plantz, born Syracuse 30 June 1924.

Bob is employed by the N.Y. Telephone Co. They reside near Jordan and are members of the Jordan United Methodist Church.

Ch (SOMES), all b Syracuse:

    i.   KATHLEEN GAIL[8], b 21 June 1949
    ii. BEVERLY JUNE, b 22 Apr 1951; m 23 Jan 1971 DONALD EUGENE GREEN, son of Harold Eugene and Elizabeth Irene (Cuff) Green, b Auburn, Cayuga Co. 11 Feb 1951. Ch (GREEN), all b Auburn:
        a) CRAIG MICHAEL[9], b 7 Nov 1971
        b) COREY MATTHEW, b 28 July 1975
        c) CHRISTOPHER MARK, b 31 Dec 1980
    iii. JANET CAROL, b 24 Apr 1959

[Source: Mrs. Robert O. Somes]

280. DOROTHY LEOLA[7] SOMES (*Hunting Somes[6], Oren Somes[5], Margaret Mary[4], Jacob[3], Peter[2], Frederick[1]*), born Jordan, Onon. Co. 27 Jan. 1920; married at home 30 July 1939 JUDSON KENNETH/PETE FREER, son of Claude Freer, born Conquest, Cayuga Co. 29 Jan 1916; reside Albany, Albany Co.

Ch (FREER):

    i.   CYNTHIA LEE[8], b Syracuse 19 Apr 1940; m 24 Aug 1958 WILLIAM EDWARD FULLER, b 8 Feb 1932. Ch (FULLER):
        a) SHERYL ANN[9], b Pittsfield, Penn 31 Jan 1961
        b) ROBERT WILLIAM, b Pittsfield 6 Nov 1963
        c) SCOTT STEPHEN, b Daytona Beach, Fla 17 May 1968
   ii. DOUGLAS ROBERT, b Auburn, Cayuga Co 1 Feb 1944; m 8 Feb 1965 BARBARA LOUISE PRICE. Ch (FREER):
        a) DOUGLAS ROBERT[9], Jr, b Schenectady, Saratoga Co 10 Aug 1965
        b) KENNETH EVAN, b 26 Aug 1967

[Sources: Mrs Robert O Somes and Mrs Judson K Freer]

281. RICHARD[7] AUYER (*LaVerne[6], Adelbert[5], Romain[4], Jacob[3], Peter[2], Frederick[1]*), born 22 Dec. 1938; married 6 June 1959 M. CAROLYN BOND; died 11 Oct. 1986. Carolyn is residing in Oswego, Jeff. Co.

   Ch (AUYER):

      i.   CRAIG RICHARD[8], b 6 June 1960; m 28 June 1986 KATHY BARTELO
     ii. KENNETH GEORGE, b 6 Jan 1962
    iii. MICHAEL LaVERNE, b 24 Jan 1964
    iv. JULIE ANNE (twin), b 13 June 1972
     v. JEFFREY ALLEN (twin), b 13 June 1972

282. EMMA JEAN[7] AUYER (*LaVerne[6], Adelbert[5], Romain[4], Jacob[3], Peter[2], Frederick[1]*), born 8 Apr. 1942; married 20 Aug. 1960 ROBERT TETRAULT.

   Ch (TETRAULT):

      i.   TERRI LYNNE[8], b 18 Aug 1961; m July 1982 TIMOTHY SCHELL. Ch (SCHELL):
        a) MELISSA ANNE[9], b Nov 1981
        b) CONNIE LEE, b Oct 1986

    ii. ROBERT CHARLES, b 4 Mar 1964; m Aug 1986
         JESSICA PATTERSON
   iii. KURT LaVERNE, b 5 Aug 1965
   iv. BRIAN KEITH, b 5 Sept 1966

283. VERNA MAE[7] AUYER (*LaVerne[6], Adelbert[5], Romain[4], Jacob[3], Peter[2], Frederick[1]*), born 9 Oct. 1947; married 10 Nov. 1967 JACK ZAHN.

  Ch (ZAHN):

    i. TODD JOSEPH[8], 25 Dec 1971
    ii. MATTHEW TIMOTHY, b 25 Apr 1974

[Sources: LaVerne and Virginia Auyer, Ralph Auyer]

284. FOSTER CLARK[7] AUYER (*Ralph[6], Peter[5], Foster[4], Jacob[3], Peter[2], Frederick[1]*), born Syracuse, Onon. Co. 10 Mar. 1922; married 14 Oct. 1945 ELIZABETH JANE NORTHRUP, dau. of Rufus and Martha (Jones) Northrup, born 16 Feb. 1924.

Foster was a member of the U.S. Army Air Corps during WWII, flying 75 missions in the air cover for the Normandy invasion June 1944. He continued to serve in the AAC Reserve.

Foster is retired from the N.Y. Telephone Co. and they reside in Baldwinsville, Onon. Co.

  Ch (AUYER):

    i. BARBARA OLA[8], b 16 Jan 1947; m 1st M ROBERT GRADY; div'd. He is the managing editor of the Plattsburg <u>Press-Rebpulican.</u> Barbara m 2nd 16 Dec 1984 EDW JACOB SCHOLEN. Barbara uses the surname Grady. She grad'd from Paul Smith College, SUNY Plattsburg; teaches Newport, Vt schools. Ch (GRADY):
        a) JILL[9], b 1973
        b) PAMELA NANCY, b 19 Mar 1976
        c) CHRISTINE BETH, b 1977
    ii. MARTHA ELIZABETH, b 23 Jan 1955; m TIMOTHY NUSS. Ch (NUSS):
        a) MATHEW, b 1924

285. WILLIAM RALPH7 AUYER (*Ralph⁶, Peter⁵, Foster⁴, Jacob³, Peter², Frederick¹*), born Van Buren, Onon. Co. 7 Apr. 1928; married 2 Sept. 1950 YVONNE RUSS, dau. of Frank and Bert Russ.
William in employed by the N.Y. Telephone Co. and resides in Fairhaven, Cayuga Co.

Ch (AUYER):

    i.   WILLIAM⁸, b 14 Feb 1952; m 18 Apr 1981 LORI LYNN HITT.   Ch (AUYER):
        a) MICHELE⁹, b 29 July 1983
        From Lori's prev m: AMY, b 21 Jan 1977
    ii.   PETER, b 9 Sept 1955; m Aug 1977 REBECCA WRIGHT of Savannah, Wayne Co. Res Kent, Oh; later Roch, Monroe Co.; currently Memphis, Tenn. Ch (AUYER):
    iii. JONATHAN, b 20 Oct 1981
        b) JASON, b 5 Oct 1983
        c) DIANA, b 4 July 1985
        d) JEREMY, b 2 June 1987
    iii. VALERIE, b 9 Dec 1956; m 2 Sept 1979 THOMAS E WILSON
    iv. KIM MARIE, b 20 Mar 1960
    v.   KRISTA B, b 14 May 1961; m 21 Mar 1987 KENNETH CAYEA.   Krista grad'd Syracuse Univ; taught Boiceville Schools; currently on sabbatical leave at Ithaca College

286. MARY CAROLYN7 AUYER (*Ralph⁶, Peter⁵, Foster⁴, Jacob³, Peter², Frederick¹*), born Syracuse, Onon. Co. 17 May 1931; married 1st 2 June 1951 JOHN PECKHAM (divorced); married 2nd 21 Nov. 1984 JOSEPH WELCH.
Carolyn is a bookkeeper in an insurance office in Port Chester, Westchester Co.

Ch (PECKHAM):

    i.   PETER ALLAN⁸, b 18 Sept 1952 m 1st SUSAN THORPE (div'd); m 2nd New Greenwich, Conn 20 May 1979 CYNTHIA ANN WULHAM, dau of Ronald and Molly Wulham (div'd); m 3rd LYCE COWARC, b 5 Dec 1955. Ch (PECKHAM) of 1st m:
        a) KRISTINA, b 1972
    Ch (PECKHAM) of 3rd m:
        b) MELISSA, b 4 July 1987

ii.   PERRY DEAN, b 11 Aug 1956; m 9 Oct 1982 DEBRA
      IRENE JOHNSON; grad'd Univ of Penn; employed
      city of NY Trans Dept
iii. THOMAS CRAIG, b 27 July 1959

287.   WARREN GERALD[7] AUYER (*Warren[6], Alonzo[5], Foster[4], Jacob[3], Peter[2], Frederick[1]*), born 5 Jan. 1930; married 10 Oct. 1968 ZADEAN PEARSON, born 25 July 1934. They own a weekly newspaper in Idaho and reside there.

Ch (AUYER):

i.   KELLI[8], b 25 Mar 1972

288.   ARDIS ANN[7] AUYER (*Warren[6], Alonzo[5], Foster[4], Jacob[3], Peter[2], Frederick[1]*), born 29 Mar. 1933; married 1952 DONALD EGAN.
Ardis is in charge of Canton Woods Senior Citizen Center, Baldwinsville.

Ch (EGAN):

i.   DONALD J[8], b 5 Jan 1953

289.   KENNETH WILLIAM[7] AUYER (*Alonzo[5], Foster[4], Jacob[3], Peter[2], Frederick[1]*), born 3 Oct. 1941; married 26 June 1966 MARSHA LEE ROGERS born 14 May 1945.
Ken is a teacher in Lafayette High School, south of Syracuse. They reside along River Rd., north of Jack's Reefs, not far from his great–great–grandfather Jacob P. Oyer's farm in Van Buren Twp., Onon. Co. Ken and Marsha operated the Kenmara Farm there until 1979, when they sold their stock and purchased the C. W. McIntyre & Sons General Store at Peru, Onon. Co.

Ch (AUYER):

i.   SANDRA LEE[8], b 18 June 1967
ii.   ROBERT WARREN, b 5 Nov 1969
iii. KEVIN AVERY, b 10 Aug 1971

[Sources: Ralph P. Auyer and Miss Sandy Auyer]

290.   STEPHEN E.[7] **AUYER** (*Earl*[6], *Alonzo*[5], *Foster*[4], *Jacob*[3], *Peter*[2], *Frederick*[1]), born Lynn, Mass. 13 Sept. 1942 – data n/a.

291.   DAVID H.[7] **AUYER** (*Earl*[6], *Alonzo*[5], *Foster*[4], *Jacob*[3], *Peter*[2], *Frederick*[1]), born Salem, Mass. 15 Apr. 1948; married 20 June 1970 DONNA EMMERT, born Cincinnati, Oh. (divorced).

Ch (AUYER):

    i.   JILL NICOLE[8], b Valdosta, Ga 24 Aug 1978

292.   RICHARD ALLEN[7] **AUYER** (*Leslie*[6], *Alonzo*[5], *Foster*[4], *Jacob*[3], *Peter*[2], *Frederick*[1]), born Van Buren, Onon. Co. 5 Jan. 1930; married 1 Oct. 1960 BETTY JEAN NENSEN. They reside Troy, Rensselaer Co.

Ch (AUYER):

    i.   LANCE LESLIE[8], b Detroit, Mich 14 Nov 1962
    ii. MARIE AGNES, b Detroit, Mich 21 Aug 1965

292.1   ANITA JEAN[7] **AUYER** (*Leslie*[6], *Alonzo*[5], *Foster*[4], *Jacob*[3], *Peter*[2], *Frederick*[1]), born Van Buren, Onon. Co. 23 Jan. 1933; married 9 May 1953 WILLIAM DALY. They reside Watertown, Mass.

Ch (DALY), both b Oneida, Madison Co:

    i.   ERIC WILLIAM[8], b 5 Nov 1954; m 3 Sept 1977 CHRISTINE O'BRIAN; res Waltham, Mass
    ii. NAN IRENE, b 5 Nov 1956; res Long Beach, Calif

293.   WALTER LEON[7] **AUYER** (*Leslie*[6], *Alonzo*[5], *Foster*[4], *Jacob*[3], *Peter*[2], *Frederick*[1]), born Van Buren, Onon. Co. 10 Aug. 1935; married Indiana, Penn. MARY FRANCES LYNPH. They reside Fort Collins, Colo.

Ch (AUYER):

    i.   LYNN ANN[8], b Pomona, Calif 20 May 1966
    ii. PATRICIA JEAN, b Phoenix, Ariz 4 June 1968
    iii. SUSAN MARIE, b Phoenix, Ariz 22 July 1969

iv.   ANDREA JANE, b Ft Collins, Colo 7 Sept 1971

[Source for data #284 through #293: Ralph P Auyer]

294. CHARLES A.[7] **ISBELL** (*Frederick Isbell*[6], *Harriet*[5], *Foster*[4], *Jacob*[3], *Peter*[2], *Frederick*[1]), born 2 Oct. 1922; married 1 Apr. 1959 JEANNE PAQUETTE. They reside San Bimas, Calif.

Ch (ISBELL):

   i.   CHARLES FREDERICK[8], b 1959

295. BETTY ANN[7] **ISBELL** (*Frederick Isbell*[6], *Harriet*[5], *Foster*[4], *Jacob*[3], *Peter*[2], *Frederick*[1]), born 20 May 1940; married 3 Sept. JAMES GREENE.

Ch (GREENE):

   i.   CYNTHIA A[8], b 25 Nov 1961
  ii.   DEBORAH L, b 28 Apr 1963
 iii.   PEGGY MARIE, b 4 Dec 1964
  iv.   CHRISTINA, b 20 Aug 1969

296. HARRIET SHIRLEY[7] **DELOSH** (*Iva Isbell*[6], *Harriet*[5], *Foster*[4], *Jacob*[3], *Peter*[2], *Frederick*[1]), born 25 Nov. 1925; died 19 Feb. 1971; married 8 Dec. 1943 ELWYN McINTYRE, son on Lyman and Jennie (Burns) McIntyre. Elwyn died 15 Oct. 1964.

Ch (McINTYRE):

   i.   VALERIE M[8], b 9 Oct 1944; m 15 Apr 1968 JOHN
        PAUL CYR; res Avon, Ontario, Canada. Ch (CYR):
        a) RACHELLE MARIE, b 7 Aug 1973

297.   EDWARD[7] **OLGEATY** (*June Isbell*[6], *Harriet*[5], *Foster*[4], *Jacob*[3], *Peter*[2], *Frederick*[1]), born 22 Aug. 1940; married 18 June 1960 BARBARA HORTON. They reside Bellville, Ill.

Ch (OLGEATY):

   i.   VICTORIA ANN[8], b 19 May 1961
  ii.   SCOTT EDWARD, b 22 Dec 1964
 iii.   SANDRA LYN, b 31 Aug 1969

298. DIANE⁷ OLGEATY (*June Isbel⁶, Harriet⁵, Foster⁴, Jacob³, Peter², Frederick¹*), born 14 Oct. 1945; married 18 July 1973 MICHAEL MOSS. They reside Lyons, Ill.

Ch (MOSS):

    i.   CATHERINE MARGUERITE⁸, b 16 Sept 1977

[Source for #294 thru #298: Ralph P. Auyer, information supplied to him by the families of Foster J. Auyer.]

299. RICHARD W.⁷ THOMAS (*Rachael Tifft⁶, Carleton Tifft⁵, Martha⁴, James³, Peter², Frederick¹*), married 8 Mar. 1947 ANN COMSTOCK. Richard died in 1952, enroute to Florida, before the birth of his last child.

Ch (THOMAS):

    i.   RICHARD PAUL⁸, b 29 July 1948
    ii. MARTIN JAMES, b 14 Aug 1949
    iii. DEBORAH ANN, b 2 Oct 1952

[Sources: Mrs. J. H. McDowell; Tifft FB]

300. DONALD THOMAS – data n/a

301. VERNA⁷ HEINEMAN (*Mabel Tifft⁶, Carrie Tifft⁵, Martha⁴, James³, Peter², Frederick¹*), born 11 Nov. 1912; married 11 Feb. 1929 RICHARD ROSS, born 24 Sept. 1906.

Ch (ROSS):

    i.   LEE R⁸, b 15 Aug 1930
    ii. LOUIS R, b 17 Feb 1933
    iii. LAWRENCE E, b 29 Dec 1936

[Source: Tifft FB]

302. LOUISE JANE⁷ McGOWAN (*Edw McGowan⁶, Jennie Tifft⁵, Martha⁴, James³, Peter², Frederick¹*), born 12 Feb. 1922 (Sun. 2 p.m.); married 1st 12 Dec. 1939 DONALD COYNE; married 2nd 16 June 1951 RAYMOND JOSEPH MATERA.

Ch (COYNE) of 1st m:

    i.   MELINDA LOU[8], b 2 Feb 1941
   ii. MICHAEL PHILLIP, b 4 Feb 1943

Ch (MATERA) of 2nd m:

  iii. MARY ELLEN

[Sources: Carolyn Zelias and Tifft FB]

304.   ELLEN TIFFT[7] McGOWAN (*Edward McGowan[6], Jennie Tifft[5], Martha[4], James[3], Peter[2], Frederick[1]*), born 4 May 1923 (3 p.m.); married 1st 4 Sept. 1941 JOHN F HACKBARTH; married 2nd DANIEL MAIERHOFER.

Ch (HACKBARTH):

     i.   JOHN[8], b 23 June 1942
    ii. RONALD, b 11 Sept 1944
   iii. BONITA, b 7 Sept 1946
   iv. SCOTT, b 29 July 1949
    v. RICKIE ELLEN, b 28 Aug 1952
   vi. KEVIN

[Sources: Carolyn Zelias and Tifft FB]

305.   BEATRICE CAMILLA[7] SCHNEIDER (*Ethel McGowan[6], Jennie Tifft[5], Martha[4], James[3], Peter[2], Frederick[1]*), born near Elb., Onon. Co. 13 July 1913; married 24 Dec. 1929 CHARLES WALDORF CRYSLER, son of Charles Davis and Florence Eliza (Cole) Crysler, born 15 July 1908. They reside Marcellus Falls, Onon. Co.

Ch (CRYSLER):

    i.   JOHN/JACK CHARLES[8], b 25 July 1930; m 16 May 1958 RUTH MARY FARNSWORTH, b 24 Aug 1934; res Ga.
   ii. FLORENCE ELIZABETH, b 8 Jan 1932; m 1st 21 Oct 1950 FRANCIS CARLETON NEGUS, b 10 May 1926; div'd. M 2nd 12 Sept 1970 JACK MICHAEL ANTAL, b 18 Jan 1916; d 1 Aug 1975. Florence res Fairfield Heights, Oh

a) NANCY ANN[9] NEGUS, b 19 Nov 1951;
m 8 Aug 1970 KEVIN CHARLES FICHTER,
b 26 Feb 1950; res near Elb, Onon Co. Ch
(FICHTER):
1) CASEY JOHN[10], b 25 Nov 1971
2) TINA ELIZABETH, b 19 Dec 1973
3) CRYSTAL ANN, b 11 May 1975
b) STEVEN JOHN NEGUS, b 29 Apr 1954;
m 24 Aug 1973 JODYNE McLAUGHLIN, dau
of Paul and Marilyn McLaughlin, b 24 Nov
1953; div'd. M 2nd 19 Jan 1980 NANCY
ANN NOTARPOLE, b 27 Sept 1956
1) MELISSA LYNN[10] NEGUS, b 11 June
1980
c) ROBERT EDWARD/EDDIE CRYSLER, b 6
Dec 1939;1 m 18 Feb 1961 NORMA MARIE
FOSTER, dau of Warren and Grace Foster, b
16 Feb 1940. Ch (CRYSLER):
1) SCOTT EDWARD[10], b 20 Jan 1962
2) DAWN MARIE, b 26 Aug 1965
3) ANGELICIA SARAH, b & d 21 Oct 1967
4) STACEY SCHARLENE, b 20 Nov 1979

306. **JENNIE DORIS[7] SCHNEIDER** (*Ethel McGowan[6]*, *Jennie Tifft[5]*, *Martha[4]*, *James[3]*, *Peter[2]*, *Frederick[1]*), born near Elb., Onon. Co. 15 Aug. 1915; married at her mother's home in San Antonio, Tex. 5 May 1935 CHARLES LOYT SEALES, son of James Daniel and Martha Lucinda (Brown) Seales, born at Moody's Crossroads, near Leeds, Ala. 31 Jan. 1911. Charles died at Veterans' Hospital, Syracuse, Onon. Co. 25 June 1977; buried MGC. Doris resides Jordan, Onon. Co.

Ch (SEALES):

i. CAROLYN BELLE[8], b Ft Sam Houston Army Hosp,
San Antonio, Tex 26 Nov 1937; m 22 Oct 1955
ROBERT JOSEPH ZELIAS, son of Walter and Mary
Zelias, b 13 Oct 1936; res near Jordan, Onon Co.
Ch (ZELIAS), b Auburn, Cayuga Co:
a) SUSAN MARIE[9], b 15 Nov 1956
b) ROBERT JOSEPH, b 13 Nov 1959
c) LAURA LYNN, b 14 Sept 1965
ii. ROBERT LOYT, b Ft Sam Houston Army Hosp, San
Antonio, Tex 1 Jan 1942; m 25 Sept 1965
ROSEMARY HOWELL, dau of Kenneth and Marion
Howell of Cato, Cayuga Co, b 7 Apr 1947.
Ch (SEALES):

    a)   JOSEPH/JODY KENT[9], b 24 Aug 1966
    b)   HOPE MICHELLE, b 23 Oct 1967
    c)   TODD MITCHELL, b 28 Oct 1971
iii. DAVID MARTIN, Ph D, b Auburn, Cayuga Co 27 Dec
      1947; m Los Angeles, Calif 8 July 1972 SUSAN
      BETH FREEDMAN, dau of Harold and Faye (Rosen-
      thal) Freedman, b Los Angeles 11 May 1949
        a)   ALAN DELOS[9] MARTIN, b 18 Oct 1980

307.   JUNIOR IMBRIE[7] RHODES (*Hazel McGowan[6], Jenie Tifft[5], Martha[4], James[3], Peter[2], Frederick[1]*), born 15 Feb. 1919; married 16 May 1942 EUNICE VERA RANDALL of Jordan, born 11 Feb. 1921. They reside Lynchburg, Va.

Ch (RHODES):

    i.   LINDA ANNE[8], b 9 July 1943; m 1st 31 Jan 1963
         FRANK F EUBANKE, div'd; m 2nd RICHARD C
         OMOHUNDRO, b 5 Jan 1936. Ch (OMOHUNDRO):
           a)   ERIC MICHAEL[9], b 25 Nov 1979
    ii. BARBARA JEAN, b 21 July 1945; m 10 Oct 196_
         ROBERT ELIZAH HATCHELL, b 22 May 1945. Ch
         (HATCHELL):
           a)   AMY MARIE[9], b 26 Feb 1966
           b)   JAMES THEODORE, b 6 Oct 1968
           c)   JOY BELINDA, b 7 Jan 1975
    iii. CAMILLA VERA, b 13 July 1956

308.   HARRY STANLEY[7] KENT (*Helen McGowan[6], Jennie Tifft[5], Martha[4], James[3], Peter[2], Frederick[1]*), born Jordan 3 Oct 1924 (7 a.m.); married 1st 3 July 1947 JANET FRANCES GRUCELSKI, born Syracuse, Onon. Co. 20 July 1927. Janet died of leukemia while in Long Island, N.Y. 25 Oct. 1975. Harry married 2nd Dallas, Tex. 28 May 1976 BARBARA MITCHELL, born Ft. Worth, Tex. 13 July 1937. They reside Arlington, Tex.

Ch (KENT):

    i.   ROBERT STEVEN[8], b 18 Apr 1949;; m 23 July 1971
         SUE DELL BALDRIDGE, b 5 Oct 1947
           a)   JUSTIN SARLE, b 23 Dec 1977
    ii. DEBORAH CAROL, b 21 Dec 1952
    iii. SUSAN GAYLE, b 5 Oct 1964

[Source: Carolyn Zelias]

309. JANICE MARILYN[7] KENT (*Helen McGowan[6], Jennie Tifft[5], Martha[4], James[3], Peter[2], Frederick[1]*), born Jordan, Onon. Co. 13 Sept. 1929; married 24 June 1950 ROBERT CULVER.

Ch (CULVER):

    i.   CHRISTINE LOUISE[8], b Fulton, Oswego Co, 13 Apr 1956; m 19 Aug 1974 ROBERT LEVINS
         a) TIMOTHY ERIC[9] LEVINS, b 4 Jan 1975
    ii. ROBERT WILSON, b 11 June 1959; m 12 Aug 1978 CHRISTINE L BOSSELER

[Source: Carolyn Zelias]

310. CECIL JAMES[7] PATTERSON, Jr. (*Cecil Patterson[6], Stella Whitney[5], Emily[4], James[3], Peter[2], Frederick[1]*), born Bennett's Corners, Cam. Twp., Onon. Co. 11 July 1930; married 1st MARTHA DOANE; married 2nd KATHRYN JEANETTE HORNER. They reside Elb. Twp.

Ch (PATTERSON) by 1st m:

    i.   LINDA LEE[8], b Auburn, Cayuga Co 3 Feb 1954
    ii. CECIL/BUTCH JAMES, III, b Syracuse, Onon Co 11 June 1957
    iii. CYNTHIA ANNE, b Syracuse 11 Feb 1962

[Source: Cecil J Patterson, Sr]

311. CAROLE ANNE[7] PATTERSON (*Cecil Patterson[6], Stella Whitney[5], Emily[4], James[3], Peter[2], Frederick[1]*), born Elb. near Bennett's Corners, Onon. Co. 20 July 1936; married 28 June 1960 JOHN ABBOTT, born 3 July 1930. They reside in Cam., Onon. Co.

Ch (ABBOTT):

    i.   KAREN MARIE[8], b Syracuse, Onon Co 31 Aug 1963

[Source: Cecil J Patterson, Sr]

312. ELIZABETH LORRAINE[7] HARTKOPF (*Lumore Whitney[6], Jay Whitney[5], Emily[4], James[3], Peter[2], Frederick[1]*), born Cam., Onon. Co. 5 Aug. 1919; married 21 Oct. 1944 HAROLD FRITZ McDUFFIE, born Atlanta, Ga. 20 Apr. 1917. They reside Tenn.

Ch (McDUFFIE):

   i. KURT CHARLES[8], b Syracuse, Onon Co 4 Sept 1946;
      m 11 June 1972 ANDREA SWEETMAN. Ch
      (McDUFFIE), both b Knoxville, Tenn:
        a) JOSHUA ALEX[9], b 28 July 1975
        b) ELISSA BROOKE, b 27 May 1979
  ii. DAVID FERGUSON, b Oak Ridge, Tenn 13 Sept 1950
 iii. MARK WHITNEY, b Oak Ridge, Tenn 11 Apr 1952
 iv. GREGORY PHILLIPS, b Oak Ridge, Tenn 8 May 1958;
      m 10 Feb 1979 TAMMY HAMPTON

[Source: Mrs Fritz McDuffie]

313. CHARLES WHITNEY[7] HARTKOPF (*Lumora Whitney[6], Jay Whitney[5], Emily[4], James[3], Peter[2], Frederick[1]*), born Cam., Onon. Co. 26 Dec. 1930; married 1958 BARBARA CUNNINGHAM, dau. of Burt and Winnie Cunningham; divorced. Charles resides in Fla.

Ch (HARTKOPF), both b Auburn, Cayuga Co:

   i. JILL BARBARA[8], b 5 Nov 1961
  ii. JACQUELINE LEE, b 31 Dec 1963

[Source: Charles W Hartkopf]

314. DONALD ROY[7] McDOWELL (*Harold McDowell[6], Elmer McDowell[5], Julia[4], Solomon[3], Peter[2], Frederick[1]*), born Van Buren Twp., Onon. Co., near Ionia 4 Feb. 1916; married 1st EUNICE HUNTLEY of Ticonderoga, Essex Co., born 7 July 1908. Eunice died 8 Feb. 1975; buried MGC. Donald married 2nd 11 Dec. 1976 HAZEL EVA (HOUSE) LIPPERT, born 31 Mar. 1910. He farms in Elb. Twp., near Jack's Reefs.

Ch (McDOWELL), all b Auburn, Cayuga Co:

   i. DAVID ELMER[8], b 29 Apr 1944; m 2 Aug 1975
      CHARLENE RUTH TANNER, b 1 July 1944
        a) TIMOTHY DAVID[9], b 27 May 1976
        b) TAMARA RUTH, b 7 Apr 1978
        c) THOMAS ROY, b 30 Oct 1979
        d) TODD MICHAEL, b 31 Jan 1981

[Source: Donald R McDowell]

315.   MARJORIE RUTH[7] McDOWELL (*Harold McDowell[6], Elmer McDowell[5], Julia[4], Solomon[3], Peter[2], Frederick[1]*), born Van Buren Twp., Onon. Co. near Jack's Reefs 3 Jan. 1918; married LAWRENCE LEYBURN, born 26 Sept. 1914.

Ch (LEYBURN):

   i.   EARL J[8], b 6 Mar 1948; m 26 June 19__ JOYCE HUNTER. Ch (LEYBURN):
      a) BRIAN EARL[9], b 11 Apr 1971
      b) BRADLEY WILLIAM, b 10 May 1975
  ii. BRUCE, b 9 Apr 1951; m 27 Aug 1976 JANICE CLAYCOMB McCANN. Ch (LEYBURN):
      a) DALE JAMES[9], b 8 Jan 1978
      b) NATHAN JAY, b 4 July 1979
 iii. CINDY, b 19 Feb 1957; m 26 June 1976 TIMOTHY PERRAULT; div'd; m 2nd EUGENE MYERS

[Source: Mrs J H McDowell]

316.   WALDO GLENN[7] McDOWELL (*Harold McDowell[6], Elmer McDowell[5], Julia[4], Solomon[3], Peter[2], Frederick[1]*), born Cam. Twp., Onon. Co., north of Bennett's Corners 1 Aug. 1919; married THELMA SMITH, born 9 Apr. 1919 (divorced).

Ch (McDOWELL):

   i.   FREDERICK JOHN[8], b 17 Oct 1942; m 27 Apr 1962 PATRICIA LOVELESS. Ch (McDOWELL):
      a) PAMELA KAYE, b 25 Oct 1962
      b) JOHN JEFFREY, b 30 July 1966
      c) SCOTT ROBERT, b 14 Mar 1968
      d) MICHAEL GLENN, b 12 Dec 1972
  ii. KAY ELAINE, b 6 June 1946; m C JAMES WHEATON
 iii. JUDY ANNE, b 6 Sept 1948; m 1969 JEFFREY McCULTY

[Sources: Mrs J H McDowell; Waldo G McDowell]

317.   EUNICE BLANCHE[7] McDOWELL (*Harold McDowell[6], Elmer McDowell[5], Julia[4], Solomon[3], Peter[2], Frederick[1]*), born Cam. Twp. near Memphis, Onon. Co. 5 July 1922; died 4 May 1952. Eunice married LESLIE LONGYEAR, born 8 Aug. 1921.

Ch (LONGYEAR):

    i.   VIRGINIA JUNE[8], b 5 July 1943; m 23 Nov 19__
        WILLIAM BOYCE. Ch (BOYCE):
        a) TIMOTHY WILLIAM[9], b 26 Nov 1965
        b) DANIEL EDWARD, b 10 May 1968
    ii. STANLEY CHARLES (twin), b 24 May 1946; m
        CHERYL DENMAN. Ch (LONGYEAR):
        a) CHARLES LESLIE[9], b 15 Jan 1971
        b) JEFFREY TODD, b 4 Dec 1973
    iii. STEPHEN JOHN (twin), b 24 May 1946; m KATHIE
        LAPP. Ch (LONGYEAR):
        a) DAWN MARIE[9], b 9 Nov 1969
        b) STEPHEN JOHN, b 22 Sept 1967
        c) JOSEPH BYRON, b 28 Sept 1972

[Source: Mrs J H McDowell]

318. MARY LOUISE[7] McDOWELL (*Harold McDowell[6], Elmer McDowell[5], Julia[4], Solomon[3], Peter[2], Frederick[1]*), born Cam. Twp. near Memphis, Onon. Co. 24 Apr. 1924; married ELWYN FRENCH, born 10 Oct. ____.

Ch (FRENCH):

    i.   JAMES ELWYN[8], b 4 Mar 1949; m 8 Feb 1969 LINDA
        KIPPEL. Ch (FRENCH):
        a) DAWN MARIE[9], b 15 Feb 1971
        b) ANDREA MARIE (twin), b 13 Oct 1973
        c) HEATHER ANN (twin), b 13 Oct 1973
    ii. DEBORAH JEAN, b 10 Feb 1952; m 29 May 1976
        DARYL NITKOWSKI. Ch (NITKOWSKI):
        a) DOUGLAS[9], b 10 Feb 1978
    iii. DOUGLAS, b 10 Feb 1958

[Source: Mrs J H McDowell]

319. RALPH EDWIN[7] McDOWELL (*Harold McDowell[6], Elmer McDowell[5], Julia[4], Solomon[3], Peter[2], Frederick[1]*), born Cam. near Memphis, Onon. Co. 27 Oct. 1926; married JUNE HORR, born 11 Sept. 1927.

Ch (McDOWELL):

    i.   GARY CARL[8], b 5 Feb 1949; m ELLEN MERRIT.   Ch
        (McDOWELL):
        a) MATTHEW MARK[9], b 20 July 1971
        b) LESLIE MICHELLE, b 4 July 1973
   ii. PAULETTE ADELE, b 7 Feb 1950; m 23 June 1979
        KARL P. FALZGRAF
  iii. LESTER DALE, b 27 Mar 1951
   iv. RORY HAROLD b 7 Mar 1960

[Source: Mrs J H McDowell]

320.   EARL WAYNE[7] McDOWELL (*Harold McDowell[6], Elmer Mc-Dowel[5], Julia[4], Solomon[3], Peter[2], Frederick[1]*) born Cam. near Memphis, Onon. Co. 5 May 1931; married LOIS PURDY, born 2 June 1934.

Ch (McDOWELL):

    i.   ROSEMARIE[8], b 19 Aug 1954
   ii. KATHLEEN ANN, b 31 Mar 1957
  iii. SANDRA LEE, b 28 July 1958; m JAMES ACOME. Ch
        (ACOME):
        a) ROBERT MICHAEL[9], b 1 Nov 1977
   iv. JEFFREY, b 2 Dec 1962
    v. BARBARA LYNN, b 5 Feb 1965
   vi. LAURA, b 7 Feb 1966

[Source: Mrs J H McDowell]

321.   SEWARD JEROME[7] LERCH (*Elvie Buck[6], Susan McDowell[5], Julia[4], Solomon[3], Peter[2], Frederick[1]*), born Waterloo, Seneca Co. 9 Nov. 1925; married 1st Dresden, Yates Co. 1 June 1950 BEVERLY DUNSHIE; married 2nd Penn Yan, Yates Co. 19 July 1963 ELEANOR PARMELEE.

Ch (LERCH), all b Penn Yan, by 1st m:

    i.   DANIEL JEROME[8], b 7 Nov 1950

Ch (LERCH), by 2nd m:

   ii. MATHEW ALLEN, b 2 Feb 1966
  iii. VALERIE LOUISE, b 31 May 1967
   iv. MARSHA ELLEN, b 25 Nov 1970

[Source: Mrs E R Hunt]

322.   EVERETT ERWIN[7] **LERCH** (*Elvie Buck*[6], *Susan McDowell*[5], *Julia*[4], *Solomon*[3], *Peter*[2], *Frederick*[1]), born Waterloo, Seneca Co. 22 Dec. 1926; married St. Petersburg, Fla. 9 Jan. 1948 HELEN STEVENS.

Ch (LERCH), b Penn Yan, Yates Co:

    i.   STEVEN DALE[8] (twin), b 18 Feb 1954
   ii. VANESSA GAIL (twin), b 18 Feb 1954; m Penn Yan 2 Apr 1977 WILLIAM SHEPARD.   Ch (SHEPARD), b Canandaigua:
        a) BRAD WILLIAM[9], b 12 June 1978
  iii. DIANE MARIE (adopted Dec 1950)
   iv. CAROL LEA (adopted Dec 1950)

[Source: Mrs E R Hunt]

323. BEVERLY SUSAN[7] **LERCH** (*Elvie Buck*[6], *Susan McDowell*[5], *Julia*[4], *Solomon*[3], *Peter*[2], *Frederick*[1]), born Waterloo, Seneca Co. 11 July 1934; married Dresden, Yates Co. 6 Oct. 1956 ELWYN R. HUNT.

Ch (HUNT), all b Penn Yan, Yates Co:

    i.   RUSSELL SCOTT[8], b 13 Feb 1958
   ii. NANCY SUSAN, b 24 Apr 1960
  iii. RONALD ELWYN, b 23 Dec 1962

[Source: Mrs E R Hunt]

324.   AUREL CHARLENE[7] **BUCK** (Ward *Buck*[6], *Susan McDowell*[5], *Julia*[4], *Solomon*[3], *Peter*[2], *Frederick*[1]), born Syracuse, Onon. Co. 22 July 1930; married 16 June 1951 DAVID DERALD ROBEDEE, son of Floyd Anson and Twila Katherine (Harber) Robedee, born Auburn, Cayuga Co. 29 June 1929.   They reside near Jordan, Onon. Co.

Ch (ROBEDEE), both b Auburn:

    i.   BARBARA JAYNE[8], b 14 Mar 1958
   ii. JULIE ANN, b 23 Oct 1962

[Source: Mrs D Robedee]

325.   RODERICK WARD[7] **BUCK** (*Ward Buck*[6], *Susan McDowell*[5], *Julia*[4], *Solomon*[3], *Peter*[2], *Frederick*[1]), born Jordan, Onon. Co. 11 May 1936; married 1st 14 June 1958 MARY MARGARET CUMMINGS (divorced); married 2nd MRS MARGARET WILLIAMS.

Ch (BUCK):

    i.   JAMES WARD[8], b Aug 1959
    ii. KRISTIN MARY, b Nov 1963
   iii. HEATHER, b 26 Feb 1969

[Source: Mrs D Robedee]

326.   DOROTHA ROSE[7] **PICKARD** (*Satie Mettler*[6], *Jessie*[5], *Cyrus*[4], *Solomon*[3], *Peter*[2], *Frederick*[1]), born at the Halstead house in Memphis, Onon. Co. 20 Dec. 1905; married 25 Nov. 1927 HUGO VANSELOW, son of Otto and Mary (Grudman) Vanselow, born Grand Rapids, Mich. 11 Oct. 1905. They resided Syracuse, Onon. Co. for several years before removing to Mich. Hugo died at Bloomfield Hills, Mich. 25 Sept. 1972.

Ch (VANSELOW):

    i.   CLARENCE HUGO[8], b Syracuse 30 Sept 1928; m 30 June 1951 LEOLA DAWN RANDALL, dau of Rev Leon Randall, Methodist clergyman at Elmira, Chemung Co at the time of their m. Leola was b 27 Nov 1929. Ch (VANSELOW):
       a) NEAL RANDALL[9]/RANDY, b Syracuse 16 Apr 1952; m Nov 1973 JULIE BRYSON. Ch (VANSELOW):
          1) JENNIFER ERIN BRYSON[10], b Hendersonville, N C 10 Feb 1975
       b) LAURIE NANCY, b Syracuse 15 Dec 1953; m 1st RAY INGRAM (div'd); m 2nd at Maui, Hawaii 1 Dec 1977 KURT JOHNSON
       c) JUDY ANITA, b Slocum Heights, Syracuse 4 Apr 1955; m 25 Aug 1974 DAVID HARRY
       d) RONALD GEORGE, b Greenville, Penn 26 June 1957; m Oct 1978 JOYCE _____
       e) DANIEL RICHARD, b Greenville, Penn 18 May 1959
       f) KATHLEEN/KATHY MARY, b Greenville, Penn 16 Dec 1960; m Riparius, Warren Co 11 Aug 1979 KENNY BRZOZOWSKI

g) REBECCA ANN/BECKY, b Greenvile, Penn 27 Aug 1963

[Source: Mrs H Vanselow]

327. KENNETH METTLER[7] PICKARD (*Satie Mettler[6], Jessie[5], Cyrus[4], Solomon[3], Peter[2], Frederick[1]*), born Van Buren, Onon. Co., near Peru 1 Oct. 1909; married 1st 30 June 1936 FLORENCE PINCKNEY, dau. of Jake and Anna Pinckney, born Jordan 13 Feb 1912. She died Jordan 7 Jan. 1956. Ken married 2nd Elb., Onon. Co. 1 Oct. 1960 HELEN (McCOLLUM) CHAMBERLIN, dau. of John McCollum, born Elb. 12 Apr. 1915. Helen and Ken are fifth cousins through the Redman family. They reside Jordan.

Ch (PICKARD), b Syracuse, Onon Co:

    i.   SUSANNE MARIE[8], b 2 Nov 1943; m 1963 ROBERT FIELD; res Weedsport, Cayuga Co. Ch (FIELD), all b Auburn, Cayuga Co:
       a) ROBERT CHARLES[9], b 2 Feb 1964
       b) JOHN KENNETH, b 15 Feb 1966
       c) MICHAEL JOSEPH, b 6 Jan 1970
       d) DAVID WILLIS, b 17 Aug 1971

[Sources: Mrs H Vanselow, Mrs F Mittins, Mrs H Pickard]

328. ANITA MARIE[7] PICKARD (*Satie Mettler[6], Jessie[5], Cyrus[4], Solomon[3], Peter[2], Frederick[1]*), born Syracuse, Onon. Co. 2 Sept. 1917; married 1 June 1937 FRANK WILLIAM MITTINS, son of Arthur Frank and Elsie Martha (Clark) Mittins, born Swindon, Wiltshire, Eng. 15 Sept. 1909.

Ch (MITTINS), both b Syracuse:

    i.   SHARON ELAINE[8], b 16 Feb 1941; m 26 Apr 1964 ANTHONY TARDIO, b 15 Jan 1943. Ch (TARDIO), both b Syracuse:
       a) DEBORAH LYNN[9], b 17 Dec 1967
       b) KATHY ANN, b 14 Oct 1969
   ii.   RONALD ARTHUR, b 23 July 1943; m Los Angeles, Calif 21 July 1979 PATRICIA K LOMMEN, dau of Leonard H Lommen, b 7 Feb 1951

[Source: Mrs F Mittins]

329.   WILLIAM HENRY⁷ BRETZER (Marion *Mettler⁶*, *Jessie⁵*, *Cyrus⁴*, *Solomon³*, *Peter²*, *Frederick¹*), born Syracuse, Onon. Co. 30 July 1921; married FRANCES WILSON; they reside Orlando, Fla.

Ch (BRETZER):

   i.   BENITA LOUISE⁸, m JAMES COX
  ii.   JOANNA
 iii.   FREDERICK WILLIAM, killed Fairbanks, Alaska
         Easter Sunday, 18 Apr 1976
  iv.   JACQUELINE
   v.   JEFFREY

[Source: AHA]

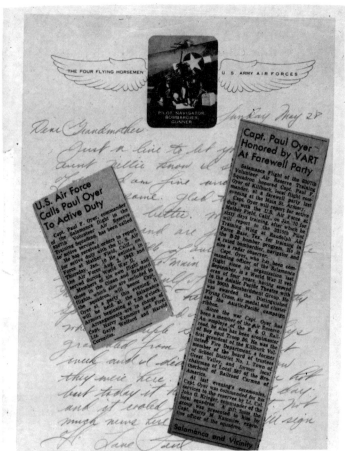

Background: letter from Paul F. Oyer to grandmother, Ella Brown.
Foreground: newsclippings—Paul's military service.

330. DONALD EUGENE⁸ BROUGHAM *(Bernice⁷, Clarence⁶, Da-vid⁵, Peter⁴, David³, Jacob², Frederick¹)*, was born 19 Feb. 1925, married 1st 1947 BETTY _____, married 2nd 1951 MARGARET _____. They reside in Brookland, Ark. Don has been a truck driver most of his life.

Ch (BROUGHAM):

    i. DONNA JEAN⁹ BROUGHAM, b 26 Feb 1950, m THUR-MON(D) BYRD, div'd. Donna resides northern Mich; is a Director of Occupational Therapy, having earned her degree from Eastern Mich Univ.
        Ch (BYRD):
        a) MATTHEW
        b) MARK

331. ARLENE JUNE⁸ BROUGHAM, *(Bernice⁷, Clarence⁶, David⁵, Peter⁴, David³, Jacob², Frederick¹)*, was born 11 Nov 1927. She married 2 July 1948 ALFRED EUGENE HIVELEY, b 19 Nov 1928; reside Wayne, Mich.
Arlene works at a nursing home; Alfred has been a semi truck driver most of his life. They have large gardens, as well as fruit trees and strawberries.

Ch (HIVELEY):

    i. BRUCE EARL⁹, b 21 Mar 1949, unm'd. Bruce is an electronic robotic technician.
    ii. ELLEN MARIE, b 19 Feb 1953, m JAMES ELIJAH CHATHAM, b 14 Mar 1953. Ellen is a medical technician. Her husband James has a bachelor's degree in Math and Computers from Eastern Mich Univ. Ch (CHATHAM):
        a) MEGHAN MARIE¹⁰, b 13 May 1979
    iii. VICKI LYN HIVELEY, b 17 Jan 1961, m 21 May 1982 MICHAEL JAMES TENNANT, b 13 Oct 1954. Vicki is a radiographer; her husband Michael has worked at General Motors for 11 years. Ch (TENNANT):
        a) LINDSEY RENEE, b 11 Nov 1982
        b) LEEA, b 8 Dec 1987

332. RICHARD EARL⁸ BROUGHAM *(Bernice⁷, Clarence⁶, David⁵, Peter⁴, David³, Jacob², Frederick¹)*, born 4 May 1933, married ROBERTA _____, resides in Limestone, Catt. Co.

Ch (BROUGHAM):

    i.   SANDRA KAY⁹, b 1955
         a) ROSIE¹⁰
   ii. DEAN EARL, b 1971

333. JANETTE MARIAN⁸ CAMPBELL *(Bernice⁷, Clarence⁶, David⁵, Peter⁴, David³, Jacob², Frederick¹)*, born 5 Dec 1941 Brighton, Mich. married in Fla. 26 April 1961 GEORGE ARTHUR FERGUSON, born Dunedin, Fla. 14 June 1940. They reside Ypsilanti, Mich.

Janette is our family informant and like so many was reluctant to write of their accomplishments. However she has kept in touch with her Aunt Rose, and her biographical letter to her on the occasion of Rose (Duhan) Oyer's 90th birthday cele- bration is being quoted. Janette attended college in Fla. where she met her husband. She has a degree in Commercial Art, and for some years had her own business of decorating halls for weddings and special occasion parties. She is a floral designer and artist. George is a Master Electrician, having worked for Janette's father while completing his electrical training. George has also been a percussionist for a country western band, and Janette has filled in for him, too!

Janette's father Mel Campbell lived with them his last 2 years. An electrical contracting business in 1987 has given way to George becoming an electrician foreman for a busy contractor. Their sons David, James, and Michael had helped in that business.

Ch (FERGUSON):

    i.   DAVID GLEN⁹, b Tampa, Fl 4 Aug 1961
         a) CHRISTOPHER ALLEN¹⁰ MORRISON-FERGUSON, b Ypsilanti 15 Aug 1984
   ii. MICHAEL MEL ORENE, b Pontiac Mich 26 Mar 1965, m 12 May 1984 GERALDINE RAYMOND, b Ypsilanti 24 May 1965
  iii. JAMES CHARLES LLOYD, b 17 Oct 1968
  iv. STEVEN DUWAYNE, b 26 Jan 1973

334. JOANNE ELLEN⁸ CAMPBELL *(Bernice⁷, Clarence⁶, David⁵, Peter⁴, David³, Jacob², Frederick¹)*, born 9 July 1943. She married 1st 18 June 1961 LEROY ELMER HUMBARGER, div'd; married 2nd 22 Dec 1970 ALBERT BERT HUMBARGER, LeRoy's uncle. They reside in Ypsilanti, Mich.

Joanne has been a transmission assembly worker for General Motors for over 10 years, with nearly perfect attendance; she is also a seamstress.   Albert is a retired excavation contractor. They reside less than a mile from Joanne's sister Janette.

In 1955 while the Campbell family lived in Kill Buck, GrV. Twp. JoAnne saved the life of a 7-year old neighbor boy, Kevin Prey, from the icy waters of GrV. Creek.   After he had fallen into the water, instead of panicking and running for help, she waited for him to resurface and told him to grab her hand.   She was awarded a medal for her heroism.

Ch (HUMBARGER) of 1st m:

  i. BRENDA LEE[9], b 18 Oct 1962, m MARK OLIVER BURNS, b 31 Jan 1963; they are "expecting"
  ii. LEROY ELMER II, b 24 July 1965
 iii. SANDRA DEE, b 29 April 1968

Ch (HUMBARGER) of 2nd m:

  iv. ROBERT b 2 Nov 1971
  v. ALBERT/BERT, b 10 Dec 1974

335.   RAYMOND ELBERT[8] OYER (*Leland[7], Clarence[6], David[5], Peter[4], David[3], Jacob[2], Frederick[1]*), was born Catt. Co. 13 Jan. 1926; married Ypsilanti, Mich 28 June 1948 VERA ALICE BOYD, b 17 Oct 1929; she died Victorville, Calif June 1983.   Raymond supplied us with a fascinating account of his life.   While we are condensing it here, we are putting it in its entirety in Appendix iv as it exemplifies some Oyer traits.   As he says, "...perhaps others...will read...and recognize a tie to what and who they are."

Raymond's chronicle shows the family emigrated to Mich. in 1932.   This was because his father Leland had been told there was work in the auto industry there that paid more than twice what he was earning a week in N.Y.S.--instead of $2 he could earn $5. His mother Edith who by then was married to HARRY TURNER went to Mich next. Then after hearing from Leland, his sister Bernice and her first husband Earl Brougham moved to Mich. Bernice took in boarders while Earl worked on a dairy farm. After returning to N.Y.S. on a hunting trip, he did not choose to return.   After divorcing, Bernice married one of her boarders, Melvin Campbell.

Ray has resided in Mich., Fla., Ariz. and Calif. at times, before settling in Victorville, Calif. permanently. In various businesses with his father and on his own, he found his calling working with cars and other automotive vehicles--racing, building, rebuilding. He has been a professional automotive paint and body man for many years. Ray delivers Meals on Wheels for the elderly and resides with son Donald in Victorville where Don is the manager of a Radio Shack store.

Ch (OYER):

    i.   DONALD GARY[9], b Ypsilanti 13 Dec 1963

336.   ROBERT LEE[8] OYER (*Leland[7], Clarence[6], David[5], Peter[4], David[3], Jacob[2], Frederick[1]*), was born in Buffalo 10 Jan. 1928; married 1st Mich. BETTY JANE SHULTZ, born 22 Jan 1923, div'd; married 2nd JEAN _____. They reside Ypsilanti, Mich. Betty moved to Fla. where she met with an unfortunate accident, creating chronic mental problems.

Ch (OYER), all of 1st m:

    i.   LELAND[9]
    ii. ROBERT
Leland and Robert reside in Fla.
    iii. DEBRA ANN, b Ypsilanti, Mich 12 May 1955; m 1st 22 June 1973 ROBERT JOHN CUNNINGHAM, div'd Mar 1982; m 2nd 28 May 1982 RICHARD LAURENCE HARRELL, Sr. Debra has always had a love for art. After doing commercial art and being an art instructor, she is now doing free lance art work in various media: oil, water color, acrylics, pen and ink, air brush, pastels, landscapes, architecture, animals, and portraits. More recently she is also into computer work. After having been a legal secretary in the State Attorney's office in Tampa, she currently is a general office manager for a parking lot company, handling the payroll, daily reports, etc. for eighteen lots. Ch of 1st m (CUNNINGHAM):
        a) JOSEPH MICHAEL[10], b 13 May 1976

[Sources: Debra Ann Harrell; Janette Ferguson; JoAnne Humbarger]

337.   JOYCE[8] **OYER** (*Leland*[7], *Clarence*[6], *David*[5], *Peter*[4], *David*[3], *Jacob*[2], *Frederick*[1]), was born Ypsilanti, Mich. 15 July 1935. She married 1st Dec. 1953 WILLIAM HERBERT BAXLEY, Jr., born Jacksonville, Fla. 1933, div'd 1964 Ariz.;   married 2nd LARRY D. KING, born 8 Dec. 1938   Phoenix, Ariz; reside S. Lake Tahoe, Calif., having left Livermore in 1987.

Joyce and Larry run a thriving furniture store and flea market, which is being turned over to their children. They took over the care of her father and mother about 1985 when Edith's bout with Alzheimer's disease was too much for Leland to cope with. Leland resides with them, Edith having died in a nursing home in 1987.

Ch (BAXLEY) of 1st m:

  i.   LESLIE[9], b Inglewood, Calif 17 July 1956; m
       JOHN MAY; res Columbus, Ga
       a) KIMBERLY MAY
       b) JASON MAY
 ii.   KATHRYN, b Inglewood, 26 July 1958; m 2 Dec
       1983 JEFF LYNCH; res Antioch, Calif
       a) JESSICA LYNCH
iii.   WILLIAM, b Inglewood 18 Dec 1959, m GENA
       _____, res Wilson, Wyo
 iv.   SANDRA, b Phoenix, Ariz 1 Oct 1961; res Livermore,
       Calif

Ch (KING) of 2nd m:

  v.   POLLY LEANN, b San Bernardino, Calif 5 Feb 1969

[Sources: Joyce King; Rose Oyer; Leland Oyer]

338.   SHERWOOD FRASER[8] **WEBSTER** (*Georgia Lougee*[7], *Nellie*[6], *David*[5], *Peter*[4], *David*[3], *Jacob2*, *Frederick1*),was born Roch. 15 Jan 1929; married 1st Washington 1952 FRANCES TEWES, born San Antonio, Tex. 7 Sept. 1931, dau. of Charles and Adelaide (Tewes) Harding of San Antonio; divorced 1974. He married 2nd SARAH LITTLE, living in Scottsdale, Ariz.; divorced 1987.

Sherwood grew up in Roch., moving with his parents to Washington as a young man. He graduated with a degree in Business from the American Univ., Washington, D.C. He was recruited by the CIA while attending college. He served in the U.S. Coast Guard; worked for an investment firm, Merrill Lynch; and was a salesman. Sherwood joined the family college project, becoming a Vice-president and Dean of Admissions at Marjorie Webster Junior College.

During the accreditation proceedings (see #230) Sherwood was most active in pursuing that successful venture.

After the college was closed, Sherwood worked with and helped to fund work on automotive air pollutant control devices. This has been with the support, both moral and financial, of family and investors. While such devices have met with varied achievements, the political struggle to bring about some very successful inventions has unavoidably consumed years of battling the "establishment" and the corporate world. (Unavoidable in the sense that Sherwood's determination won't allow him to give up the quest.) Litigation has ensued; the final results are still pending. Customers such as General Motors and several countries are ensuring eventual success.

As an adjunct to this Sherwood has interests in other political issues, law, and environmental policies. He resides with his mother at the family home in Washington.

Frances, Sherwood's first wife, was born in San Antonio, Tex., where her mother, ADELAIDE (TEWES) HARDING, still lives, and where Frances spends time each summer. Frances is a graduate of the Marjorie Webster Junior College in 1951, where Sherwood later became vice-president. She has taught pre-schoolers and kindergarteners for years, currently teaching at the Wash. Episcopal School since 1976. She was a great asset to the family during the years of operating the college, recognition for which was noted in the school's publication in 1969. She resides in Bethesda, Md.

Ch (WEBSTER):

    i.   DAVID SHERWOOD[9], b New Orleans, La 26 May 1954 while his father served in the Coast Guard. He has been a salesman in Reston, Va and shares the family interest in current events; res Bethesda.

    ii. KAREN LEE, b 8 Mar 1958; m Ithaca 1985 DANIEL ROBERT CHAPMAN, b Ithaca 18 Sept 1959, son of John and Shirley (Beach) Chapman of Ithaca. Karen graduated from Northern Ariz Univ, Flagstaff, Ariz with a BS in Sociology in 1981. After working for the Divi Hotels Corp in Ithaca 2 yrs they moved to Roch where she is now employed by the Univ of Roch, currently assisting in one of their clinics. Her hobbies and activities show a keen interest in active sports, religion and antiques. Dan, after 4 years as a Federal Express courier has become their customer service representative, training on computers as well as being a sales coordinator in Rochester. Dan is responsible for their active participation in fundamentalist

Christianity; his guitar playing and composition are religion-oriented. They are "expecting" in May 1988; they moved into their home near Lake Ontario in Irondequoit Twp, Monroe Co in 1987.

iii.   KATHERINE LEE, b Washington, DC 28 Sept 1960. Katherine graduated from Hood College, Frederick, Md in 1984 with a BA in English/communications. She is employed by the National Georgraphic Society as a Customer Service Representative in Gaithersburg, Md.   She resides in a renovated barn in Shephardstown, W Va and is interested in gardening and walking. Kathy is to be married in Sept 1988.

339.   DAVID FRASER[8] WEBSTER (*Georgia Lougee[7], Nellie[6], David[5], Peter[4], David[3], Jacob[2], Frederick[1]*) was born Roch. 16 Oct. 1932.   He married 1956 MARION CLARK McCORMACK, born Washington, D.C. 12 April 1934, dau of John Carnegie and Thelma (Clark) McCormack.

David grew up in Roch., moving to Washington, D.C. in 1948 with his family.   He graduated from the Univ. of Maryland in 1955 with a B.S. degree in business and a commission as a lieutenant in the U.S. Air Force.   In 1959 his father, G. Fraser Webster, asked David to join him and his aunt, Marjorie Webster, as the Business Manager of Marjorie Webster Junior College.   Three years later he became the Vice President.   In 1968 he became the acting president, replacing his ailing father.   As such, he held things together at the school during the time others were embroiled in the accreditation litigation.

David successfully negotiated the sale of the college in 1971 (see #230).   This sale was foreclosed, and resold to the U.S. government in 1976.   He then was involved in convention management, arranging nationwide educational seminars.

He currently is the Vice President of the Employee Benefits Underwriters, a firm involved in marketing voluntary employee benefit programs.   He is also involved with crippled children under the auspices of the Kiwanis Club.   He serves on the board of Stronghold, Inc.

Marion has been an integral part of the pursuits of the Websters.   She graduated from Penn. Hall Junior College in 1954; attended the Univ. of Maryland, leaving at the end of her junior year to marry.   In 1960 Marion began in an administrative capacity.   Quoting from the college paper, "Mrs. David Webster has done more than her share to add variety to the college life... (they) entertained the faculty and staff in a regal manner...It was also she who responded in the early hours of February 17th

(1969), the day of the college fire. Her calm manner and quiet but efficient way of handling matters of crises were certainly noted by all."

Since the closing of the college she has been actively engaged as a realtor. She has been involved in civic affairs in her association with the Junior League of Washington and the Women's Board of the Washington Heart Assoc. Other activities include tennis, jogging and gardening.

Ch (WEBSTER), both b in Washington, DC:

    i.   CHRISTIE ADAIR[9], b 22 Mar 1957; has an AA degree from Centenary College for Women 1978; BS degree from Univ of Maryland 1980. She is a Recreation Specialist for the Dept of Recreation in Ocean City, Md. Her other interests are golf, jogging and softball. Christie is currently res with her parents and is in the process of pursuing a change of career.

   ii.   JOHN FRASER, b 29 Apr 1959; AA degree from Montgomery College; has studied oilfield training at Eastern N Mex Univ. After working for 3 years in the computer management field, he is currently pursuing a BS degree in Business Admin.

[Sources: Karen Chapman; David Webster; school publication]

340. WILSON MARK[8] OYER (*Robert7, Roscoe6, George5, Levi4, George3, Frederick2, Frederick1*), born Sala., Catt. Co. 9 Mar. 1941; married 16 July 1962 SUZANNE TRAYLOR, born Richmond, Va. 19 July 1940. They reside in Humphrey, GrV, Catt. Co.

Mark is a science teacher in the Sala. Central District High School, where his courses include Physical Science, Earth Science and Biology. Suzanne is an elementary teacher in Sala. Their children, both adopted, are excellent students.

Mark has in his possession two things passed on from the earliest Oyer family. One, thought all these years to be a bible, is actually a Lutheran hymn book, as identified by Dr. Delbert Gratz of Bluffton College, Bluffton, Ohio. He states it "turns up rather frequently among Lutheran families," adding that it is possible that Reformed churches or other church persons used this hymnal as well. It was printed in Marburg, Germany in 1745.

[See Illus p 24. The note accompanying the ownership of this, written by LeGrand L. Oyer, son of George W. (#120), provides confirmation of the account in Beers' Herk., p. 141, of John

Finster's experience with the loom, saved from the Indian raid.
See Chapter 6.]

Ch (OYER) b Olean:

    i.   SETH AARON[9], (adopted) b 11 Feb 1975
   ii. AMY LYNN, (adopted) b 13 Mar 1979

341. CAROL PEARL[8] OYER (*Robert7, Roscoe6, George5, Levi4, George3, Frederick2, Frederick1*), born 19 May 1942 GrV., Catt. Co.;
married JOSEPH PAUL ADAMCZAK, born 2 Jan. 1936, Sala. Carol
teaches Kindergarten in Sala. Her husband is a barber there.

Ch (ADAMCZAK):

    i.   MARY ANN[9], b 15 Aug 1965, college student
   ii. MICHAEL JOSEPH, b 17 Sept 1967, college student
  iii. JANET DEBORAH, b 13 Jun 1974

[Source #340, 341: Mark Oyer]

342. PATRICK JOHN[8] OYER, (*Paul7, Wallace6,, David5, Peter4, David3, Jacob2, Frederick1*), born Sala. 27 Mar 1938, married
CARMALETTA WHITMER, born Ellvl. 23 Aug. 1945; divorced.
Patrick, after a short tour of duty in the air force spent mostly
in England, has been active in the administration of various furniture plants, in Williamsport, Penn.; Jamestown, Falconer and Sala.
in N.Y. At one time he was responsible for the complete interiors
of such stores as Adam Meldrum & Anderson Company in Olean
and Sibleys in Rochester. Pat resides in Randolph, Catt Co.

Ch (OYER):

    i.   PAUL KEVIN[9], b Sala 26 Oct 1964. He has worked
        in a furniture plant in Falconer.
   ii. PATRICK JOHN, Jr, b Sala 6 May 1966; m 25 July
        1987 in Randolph DARLENE JEAN McELWAIN, dau
        of Donald D and _____ McElwain, Sr. Pat has
        chosen farming as a career. They are "expecting"
        in 1988.
  iii. JEFFREY ALLEN, b Williamsport, Penn 28 Nov 1967
   iv. CHRISTOPHER JAMES, b Williamsport, 2 Sept 1970
    v. MICHELLE ELLEN, b Williamsport 16 Feb 1973; res
        Cookville, Tenn

Pat's sons Paul and Jeff are employed in the Randolph and Jamestown area. Chris hopes to join an armed service. Michelle, a student, lives with her mother and her second husband, _____ Griffin, in Cookeville, Tenn.

343. JEROME ALLEN/MIKE[8] OYER (*Paul[7], Wallace[6],David[5], Peter[4], David[3], Jacob[2], Frederick[1]*), was born Sala. 9 May 1939. He married in Carrollton Twp. 13 Feb 1960 CAROL WITMER, born Doylestown, Penn. 5 Aug. 1941. Although Paul and Ellen's second son was named Jerome, Ellen fought a losing battle trying to prevent him from being known as "Mike." Both Pat and Mike were football players as was their father, with resultant chronic injuries.

Mike spent 10 years in the US Navy as an electronics technician, based for 8 years in Jacksonville, Fla. He left the service in 1968 from Andrews Air Force base in Washington, D. C. with the rank of AE 1.

After learning the appliance servicing business at his Uncle Walt's business in Roch., he and Carol began a successful sales and service business with a partner in Geneva, Ontario Co. Their knowledge thus experienced led them to be asked to join an ex-service friend and wife's highly lucrative business in Jacksonville, Fla. He began as service manager to over 40 men, while Carol joined the office force. Their current positions include Operations\Service Manager and Payroll Administrator in the multi-million dollar businesses, Consumers Warehouse, E-Z Appliance Rental and their associated stores, with branches in Fla. and Ga. In 1987 they expanded, eliminating retail appliance sales, opting for furniture and carpeting retailing.

Ch (OYER):

i. MICHAEL ALLEN[9], b Quonset Point, RI 14 Aug 1960, m VALERIE VALENTINO of Geneva. Michael is a "seal" (elite frogmen) in the US Navy, based in San Diego, Calif. Both had worked for his parents' business in Geneva. Valerie has also been a medical receptionist. Ch (OYER):
  a) JOSHUA MICHAEL[10], b San Diego 26 May 1987
ii. JONATHON PAUL, b Jacksonville, Fla 28 Jan 1962; m ROBIN LEE of Rossville, Ga. They met while they were in the medical service at Ft. Sam Houston, Tex. and were medical corpsmen in the US Army based in Augsburg, West Germany, from where they

returned Nov 1987. They expect to settle in Rossville, helping Robin's father in his business.
   a) JONATHAN, PAUL Jr, b Augsburg, W Germany 24 Jan 1986
   b) JUSTIN PHILLIP, b Augsburg 21 June 1987

iii.   TIMOTHY JAMES, b Jacksonville 16 July 1963. After completing his tour of service duty as an electronics technician in 1986 in the US Marines, Tim became his parents' top service technician. He served carrier based planes while in the Marines. Enlisting in the US Army in 1987, Tim required surgery. While recuperating he went back to his childhood town, Geneva, Ontario Co. and m 6 Nov 1987 his childhood sweetheart, Mary Margaret Sollenne. He is in electronics school Ft Sill, Okla.

iv.   CARRIE ANN, b Washington, DC 30 Nov 1964. Carrie, who excels in swimming, works with her parents in their busines as a computer programmer. While in high school in Geneva she held the record for the back stroke; their free style team was number one in the section. In 1987 she went to be with bro Michael in San Diego; employed there.

344.   DONNA MARIE[8] LEARN, *(Marie[7], Wallace[6], David[5], Peter[4], David[3], Jacob[2], Frederick[1]),* born Sala. 6 Sept. 1938. She married Little Valley 30 Nov. 1957 DONALD RICHARD DECHOW, Sr. born Sala., 1 Dec. 1934 (separated). Donna is the night supervisor at a group home for the mentally disabled in Sala. An avid interest that she and her husband have had in horses has been carried on extensively with their children. Donna lives in Sala.

Ch (DECHOW):

i.   STEVEN ALAN[9], b Sala 18 May 1959. He m Downsville 28 June 1986 MARIE CHRISTINE EGLIN, b Bethpage, Long Island 20 May 1959, dau of Ernest and Jane Eglin of Bethpage b 20 May 1959. They reside Downsville. Steven is a wrangler at a dude ranch in that area.

ii.   SCOTT EDWARD, b Trenton, NJ, 22 July 1960. He m 26 June 1986 RENEE MARTINEZ, b 24 July 1962 Scott is a professional rodeo clown and bull rider in Houston, Tex. They reside Conroe, Tex.
   a)   COBY DECHOW, b ca 1982, stepson

iii.   DONALD RICHARD Jr, b Jamestown, Chau Co 31 Aug 1966; m 18 Dec 1987 ELLYN MARIE

BERKBIGLER, dau of Wayne and _____ Berkbigler of Perryville, Mo. Don has won national
recognition in horsemanship and horse show
judging, although still a college student. He has
won an ROTC (Reserve Officers Training Corps)
scholarship and is to graduate from Murray State
University, Ky. in 1988. He has completed his
ROTC Advanced Camp at Ft Lewis, Washington
and Ft Knox, Ky.

[Source: Donna Learn]

345.   ROSALIE MAE[8] LEARN, (*Marie[7], Wallace[6], David[5], Peter[4], David[3], Jacob[2], Frederick[1]*), born Sala. 30 Oct. 1939. She married 15 May 1965 WALTER NOSAL, born Sala. 24 June 1920 (separated).

Rosalie's family has had a keen interest in horses also, but has been limited to 4-H horsecamp counseling/management with participation of Christie and Marlene in area horse shows.

Her husband Walt is a retired skilled woodworker, having worked in Sala. and Jamestown furniture plants. Rosie's main job is as a school bus driver for Salamanca Central, where she has taken an active role in the bus drivers' union. She has helped in food management and waitressing in various businesses; currently she is employed part time at the Allegany State Park restaurant in the administration building. In 1987 a knee injury while driving her bus route has caused problems, resulting in surgery. She has returned to the bus driving job.

Ch (NOSAL):

i.   LYNNORE MARIE[9], b Bflo, 18 June 1958, m 15 May
      1978, EUGENE K DRUGG, b 10 May 1956; div 1985.
      Lynnore is active in real estate sales and is a
      secretary for the Board of Realtors in Elmira.
      a) JARED EUGENE[10] DRUGG, b Olean 14 1979
ii.   CHRISTIE ANN, b Olean, Catt Co 8 July 1966.
      Christie was very ctive in the award-winning Sala
      High School Marching Band. She was the drum
      major and did much to train her successors. She
      currently is a secretary at the administrative
      offices of Allegany State Park, Catt Co, having
      graduated from Syracuse Univ with an associates
      degree in business.
iii. MARLENE KAY, b Olean, 7 Apr 1970. Marlene has
      won over 80 awards in horsemanship, receiving a

great deal of assistance not only from her parents
but her sister Christie also. Among her honors
were grand champion western ponyrider in Catt.
Co.; placing 3rd in 1982 at the NYS Fair in
bareback equitation and 5th in junior fitting and
showmanship, pony class. She earned 7 grand
champion awards. She graduates from Sala Central
School in 1988.

346.   SANDRA ELAINE[8] LEARN (*Marie[7], Wallace[6], David[5],
Peter[4], David[3], Jacob[2], Frederick[1]*), born Sala, 24 Apr 1941. She
married Ellvl, 30 Jan 1960, DAVID ANTHONY STARR, b Sala 7 Aug
1941. They reside in St. Charles, Mo.

Sandra and Dave's life has had the variety of a multi-year
career in the armed services. Her jobs have included variety
store clerking, while her husband's duties have taken him from
ROTC (Reserve Officer's Training Corps) supervision to extensive
service duties, retiring in 1985 as a Command Sergeant Major (E-9)
with over 26 years' duty.

A partial listing of his accomplishments is interesting:

mountaineering instructor
assistant/advisor, adoption agency, South Korea
army personnel management specialist (included responsibility
    for policy and procedure at times for over 30,000 soldiers)
participated in deployment of troops during Cuban crisis
managed next-of-kin notification/survivor reporting, Vietnam
    casualties
senior military science enlisted instructor
participated in air lifts during Belgium Congo crisis
deployed and participated in teams in defense of French
    President De Gaulle during attempts by Algerian paratroopers
    to overthrow the French Government in Paris
Command Sergeant Major of the Army's only active replacement
    battalion, early 1980's
senior enlisted advisor to the Commander-In-Chief of US Army
    Europe at Rhein Main Air Force Base and the German Flug-
    hafen (Frankfurt Airport)
responsible for managing the assignment and movement of more
    than 100,000 soldiers and family members annually
supervised and participated in the movement and identification
    of remains of U.S. Marine Corps Beirut bombing casualties,
    1984
assisted in the recovery process of Brigadier General Dozier
    from the Red Brigade, 1984
provided protocol for all arriving and departing civilian and

military dignitaries transiting The Federal Republic of Germany.
Command Sergeant Major and senior enlisted supervisor of a quad–service enlisted and officer medical training facility in Texas

In 1987 David is in charge of security guards at a large plant while taking college courses to acquire a degree in management and/or sociology. They may establish a home back in Catt. Co.

Ch (STARR):

    i.   BRENDA ELAINE[9], b France, 18 Dec 1960, m Williamsport, Penn 22 Nov 1986 JOHN E. JONES, b Williamsport 11 May 1960. Brenda served several years in the US Army from 1979, graduating from The Defense Language Institute at Presidio, Monterey, Calif, and was stationed in Fulda, Germany, as an Electronic Warfare Signal Intelligence Voice Interceptor. She also served a short time in the Army Band. She is currently employed by General Motors, St Louis, Mo; res O'Fallon, Mo.
    ii. MARILYNN JEAN, b France 22 Jan 1962, m 31 July 1982, IAN P MEAGHER, b Regensburg, W Germany 13 June 1960. Marilynn (Missy) had a short armed services career in the Army Band. Missy did extensive work with the Junior Army ROTC before that. Her husband is still a band member, as well as an instructor at Fort Carson, Colo. Ch (MEAGHER):
        a) SEAN[10], b Landstuhl, W Germany, 8 June 1984
        b) JOHN DAVID, b Ft Carson, Colo 27 Aug 1987
    iii. WALTER JOSEPH, b Ft Mead, Md 21 Apr 1966, graduated from High school in Frankfort, W Germany in June 1984. Wally is a professional clown, sought after by community groups, and has worked as a security officer under his father. He is pursuing a public relations career as well.
    iv. THOMAS ANTHONY, b Olean, 24 Feb 1971, a student with musical interests as well as woodworking and auto mechanics.

[Source: Sandra and David Starr]

347.   **BONITA JEAN[8] LEARN** *(Marie[7], Wallace[6], David[5], Peter[4], David[3], Jacob[2], Frederick[1])*, born Frklnv. 20 Feb 1943. She married Kill Buck (by J.P. Donald Learn, her father) 31 Dec 1968, RALPH LEE SKAGGS, born 25 Feb 1939. They reside in Bradford, Penn. Bonnie and Ralph have been successful contractors in the vicinities around Bradford; building, remodeling and repairing homes. Bonnie works right along with her husband.

They both are very active in Little League baseball and high school sports involving their children.

Ch (SKAGGS) b Bradford, Pa:

    i.   BRADLEY JOSEPH[9], b 22 Mar 1971
    ii. DERRICK LEE, b 7 Nov 1978

348.   **RUSSELL PATRICK[8] LEARN** *(Marie[7], Wallace[6], David[5], Peter[4], David[3], Jacob[2], Frederick[1])*, born Sala. 25 Apr. 1945. Unmarried; see Marie, #232 for biographical data.

349.   **KITTIE FRANCES[8] LEARN** *(Marie[7], Wallace[6], David[5], Peter[4], David[3], Jacob[2], Frederick[1])*, born Sala. 18 June 1950. She married Apr. 1973, ROY OSGOOD, born Humphrey, GrV. Twp. 4 June 1948. Kittie and Roy live in the Learn family homestead. A serious hand injury prevents Roy from employment. He helps in the home to free Kittie for her work as an aide at the Sala. Nursing Home.

Ch (OSGOOD) b Olean:

    i.   BERDETTE EDWARD[9], b 26 June 1974
    ii. WAYNE DOUGLAS, b 16 Aug 1977

350.   **DAVID SMITH[8] OYER** *(Walter[7], Wallace[6], David[5], Peter[4], David[3], Jacob[2], Frederick[1])*, was born Bflo., 22 July 1942. He married 1st 28 Aug. 1966 ALISON LAUTER, born Ill. 20 Oct. 1945, dau. of Robert and Evelyn Lauter (divorced 1976). He married 2nd 26 June 1982 MARCELLA (WHITE) YAHN, born Chicago, Ill. 20 Sept. 1954, dau. of Arthur and Marcella (Theusch) White. Arthur was born in Iowa; the mother Marcella was born in Geneseo, N.D.

David's insatiable appetite for knowledge and accomplishment have brought him many honors and achievements. His interests encompass art, history, literature, music, science and sports, in addition to his career in medicine. In the interest of brevity, we shall just list some of his awards, honors, and degrees, et cetera.

SECONDARY SCHOOL

Bausch and Lomb Science Award
The Harvard Book for high achievement citizenship/scholarship
Rochester City mile champ
President - Student Council
National Merit & Regents Scholarship
Standard Bearer (comparable to valdictorian)

COLLEGE

honor societies
chemistry award
3.75 cumulative average
chosen 1 of 4 members nationwide - outstanding TKE (fraternity)
co-captain track team
held 2-mile record 2 years
co-chairman Freshman Orientation
BS in chemistry

MEDICAL TRAINING

graduated Magna Cum Laude with Thesis - Harvard Medical
   School
2 years at National Institutes of Health (National Cancer
   Institute) for US Public Health Service while serving also as
   instructor of medicine at Georgetown University. Left with
   rank of Lt. Col.; served USN Reserves 7 years
fellowship - Massachusetts General in endocrinology while
   serving as instructor at Harvard Medical School

HONORS, SOCIETIES, TEACHING AND PUBLICATIONS

Phi Beta Kappa
Executive committees--several hospitals
Diplomate, American Board of Internal Medicine
Diplomate, Endocrinology and Metabolism
Teaching: V.A. Hospital; Northwestern Memorial Hospital;
Endocrine Journal Club; Symposiums
Publications: Hormone Research, 1968
                Advances in the Biosciences, 1973
                Cancer, 1979
                Archives of Dermatology, 1982

CAREERS

Director of Ambulatory Services - Evanston Hospital, Evanston,
   Ill.
Currently:
   for 9 years in group practice: Associates in Internal Medicine
      associated with Northwestern Memorial Hospital - downtown
      Chicago
   director - Northern Ill. Affiliate of the American Diabetes
      Association
   assistant professor, clinical medicine, Northwestern Memorial
      Hospital
   chairman program committee - ADA annual seminar 1987
   listed - "Who's Who in Medicine"

David has continued his interest in running and tennis,
competing regularly. He and his wife Marcella are avid music
listeners rather than performers, although he played violin and
percussion during his school years. Marcella played the violin.
Marcella has an Associate of Science degree as a Medical
Laboratory Technician (MLT [ASCP]) from Loyola University in
Chicago. She has been a laboratory manager for a rheumatolo-
gist, a position that involved drug study research; and has been
office manager for a plastic surgeon.
Marcella shares David's interest in sports, and was captain of
her tennis club, and is still competing in the YMCA league. She
was involved in music, dance and gymnastics for many years and
taught aerobics in 1986 and 1987 in the North Suburban YMCA in
Northbrook, Ill. She has served on the board of the Chicago
Opera Theater, having been very active in fund-raising.
The children of the first marriage, Andrew and Whitney, live
with their mother Alison (Lauter) and her second husband, Edward
Kitch, in Charlottesville, Va.
Three year old Nicole and infant Stephanie bring extraordinary
fulfillment to their lives.
David's dedication to his profession has brought him many ac-
colades; he is held in high regard by his patients, students and
colleagues alike. As we have found in so many Oyer marriages,
strong spousal support has been a prime motivating and moving
force in aiding and abetting David's successes.

   Ch (OYER) of 1st m:

      i.   ANDREW ROBERT[9], b Boston, Mass 23 June 1969.
           He graduated from Charlottesville, Va High School
           in 1987. Andrew was the solo trumpeter in his
           school band. Baseball is his chief athletic

interest.   He is attending UCLA, Los Angeles, Calif.

ii.   WHITNEY CATHERINE, b Washington, DC, 11 Sept 1971. Whitney although still a student is pursuing an active interest in art, attending summer camps for art.

Ch (OYER) of 2nd m, both b Chicago, Ill:

iii.   NICOLE MARIE⁹, b 9 Aug 1984
iv.   STEPHANIE ANNE, b 10 Mar 1987

351.   WALTER BRIAN⁸ OYER, *(Walter⁷, Wallace⁶, David⁵, Peter⁴, David³, Jacob², Frederick¹)*, born Bflo. 26 July 1944.   He married 28 Aug 1965 MARJORIE LEE FISCHER, dau. Howard and Lydia (Murray) Fischer, born Roch. 6 Sept. 1944.

Brian graduated from Roch.'s Charlotte High School in 1962. A French horn player (the first of 3 in his family), he was active in instrumental music throughout his schooling, including the Roch. City School District's noteworthy Inter-High Program of the past. He was Standard Bearer of his school; winner of the Harvard Book (given to a male senior of high academic standing and citizenship); and was chosen for the National Honor Society. Brian was also active in athletics, as a member of the cross country, basketball and track teams. He tied the school record for the pole vault.

Brian received his B.A. and M.A. in Geology from the University of Roch., where he served as president of the Concert Band, warden of the Canterbury Club, co-chairman of the World University Service fund drive, and co-chairman of the Freshman Orientation Committee.   He was also co-captain of the Division III state champion track team in 1966. He set a Fauver Stadium record at the University of Rochester and was state champion in the pole vault in 1965.

Brian has taught Earth Science and Introductory Science in the Greece Central School District since 1968. His teaching style is unobtrusive, a typical Oyer trait. He has been an excellent mentor and motivator; several of his students have attained responsible positions in the fields of astronomy and earth science. Brian has also taught classes in geology and astronomy at the Roch. Museum and Science Center and the Strasenburgh Planetarium.

Among Brian's several hobbies are gardening, photography (winning a local award in a Kodak annual snapshot contest), model trains, and woodworking.

He has continued active volunteering, serving on committees at his church; acting as a consultant and sound engineer for a local radio station; and serving as sound engineer for his school's music department.   As such, he is happily able to participate in his children's many musical performances.

Margie and Brian were high school sweethearts. She went on to Hartwick College, where she earned her B.A. in German. After graduation and marriage, Margie taught high school German for 2 1/2 years while Brian was in graduate school. She elected to put her promising career on hold when their first child was born in 1969.

Margie remained an active volunteer in the community, however, serving as publicity chairman and teacher assistant for the Childbirth Education Association of Rochester. Margie has served as a volunteer coordinator, bazaar co-chairman as well as other positions as a member of the Parent-School Association; secretary of the Worship Committee, teacher, coordinator of a refugee project, and member of several other committees for churches they have attended. Margie taught German in the Continuing Education program in the Greece Central School District. In 1980 she returned to school, earning her Masters in Education from the Univ. of Roch., and certification in Spanish at SUNY Brockport. She has taught secondary school German and is currently teaching Spanish and German on the junior high level for the Greece Central School District.

Margie is a member of the New York State Association of Foreign Language Teachers; treasurer of the Rochester Chapter of the American Association of Teachers of German; and has served as a foreign language curriculum consultant for the development of the Secondary Library and Information Skills Curriculum for the New York State Education Department.

Margie too has been deeply involved in aiding Athena High School's music department productions, serving on various committees.

All 3 children are involved in music, having had piano instruction from an early age. None has ever missed being on the honor roll throughout their schooling. Currently Mark and Anne are at Athena Junior-Senior High School where their father teaches.

The home has had its fill of various pets: hamsters, gerbils, fish, cats, and the one and only Orbit, their dog.

Beth and Mark have had the unique opportunity of having had their father as their earth science teacher, a situation happily experienced by all concerned. Anne is looking forward to doing that also.

Ch (OYER), all b Roch:

    i.   ELIZABETH ANNE[9], b 5 June 1969. Beth, graduating in 1987 ranking second in her class of 320, sings, plays the piano and French horn, and performed in Athena's noted show choir for 3 years and their musical productions; is a member of the National Honor Society; took dancing and piano lessons over 10 years; has been an assistant piano teacher. She worked many hours at the computer on this book-- a huge help. She is attending Bucknell Univ with a possible major in Elementary Ed.

ii.   MARK ALAN, b 5 Apr 1971. Mark has found his "mark" in percussion, and is currently studying at the Eastman School of Music's Community Education Department. Being chosen while a sophomore to be the school's show choir's percussionist was an honor; he is in the pit orchestras and jazz band, as well as the other school bands. In 1987 he became a member of the prestigious Roch Philharmonic Youth Orchestra.

iii. ANNE MARIE, b 20 Jan 1974. Anne, although a French hornist in the junior high groups, leans heavily towards athletics; especially soccer, basketball and volley ball. She has a keen interest in animals, horses in particular, and had achieved award-winning performances in both English and Western riding as a very young rider.

352.   DIANE ELIZABETH[8] OYER (*Walter[7], Wallace[6], David[5], Peter[4], David[3], Jacob[2], Frederick[1]*), born Roch. 27 Ap.r 1948; married 27 June 1970 PETER CHARLES QUAGLIANA, son of Edwin and Anne Quagliana, born Roch. 30 Nov. 1949. Peter divorced Diane in 1987.

Music and sports have been an important part of Diane's life. She has played French horn and sung throughout her life, participating in not only school and Rochester's inter-high programs but pit orchestras, college bands and church festivals, the latter usually along with her brother Brian. She is a member of the National Honor Society.

Diane is a tennis, canoeing, racquetball, and hiking enthusiast, and is currently a soccer coach for many of the young boys in Naperville, Ill. who participate in the Parks District program.

Diane and Peter are both graduates of Rensselaer Polytechnic Institute, where she received her B.S. degree in biology; he received his B.S. in mathematics. Diane worked both there and at the Univ. of Pittsburgh in microbiology research. Pete received his masters degree in business administration at Carnegie Mellon's Graduate School of Industrial Administration.

Peter's transfers by employer Rockwell International took them from Pittsburg to Columbus, Ohio and then to Naperville, Ill. He was a personnel administrator in the latter two places. He is currently with the Hendrickson Company as Director of Human Resources in Burr Ridge, Ill.

Diane in 1986-7 was the district president of the Home and School Association of Naperville, which encompasses 11 elementary, 4 junior and 2 senior high schools, and has been instrumental in achieving several accomplishments from an educational and administrative standpoint. (This corresponds to the Parent Teacher Associations.) She has taught and studied the bible extensively, and has sung with the noted West Suburban Choral Union based in Wheaton, Ill. She has been involved in community concerns in that rapidly growing area. She entered the job field once more in 1987, and in October began as an Information Systems Associate with AT&T Corp. in Naperville.

Peter's musical involvements are what brought them together. He played the string bass and sousaphone; toured with his school's award-winning marching band; was drum major of his college band; and played in pit orchestras at his schools.

Both boys are following their parents' musical footsteps, studying piano and singing. David, just turned ten, auditioned for and was accepted in the senior choir of the Young Naperville Singers, joining junior and senior high school students. He was a soloist in their junior choir, and is a soloist in the senior choir, as well as his church choir. He plays the French horn too; in 1987 he became first chair hornist in the Naperville community band. Eight year old Dan has already shown unusual artistic talent, sculpting scenes of clay.

Ch (QUAGLIANA):

    i.   DAVID PETER[9], b Pittsburgh, Penn 4 Jan 1977
   ii.   DANIEL LEA, b Columbus, Oh 22 May 1979

353.   RONALD LEA[8] OYER (*Walter[7], Wallace[6], David[5], Peter[4], David[3], Jacob[2], Frederick[1]*), born Roch. 7 May 1957; married 6 May 1978 JULIE MARIE WILSON, born Roch. 30 Oct 1957, dau. of David and Nancy (Cook) Wilson.

Ron, like so many other Oyers, has an extensive musical background--in Roch.'s inter-high band and orchestra; as an eighth grader a member of the first Roch. Philharmonic Youth Orchestra as first chair French horn. He switched to the trumpet later, and played in his school's pit orchestras. Ron was all-scholastic in soccer in Roch. for 3 years, earning a stipend for it at the Univ. of Pittsburg. He is a member of the National Honor Society.

Julie, a vocal soloist from grade school days, had leading roles in a number of her high school's musicals. She and Ron met while participating in the Cadets of Greece Drum and Bugle Corps in 1974. With Julie as drum major and Ron on horn, their corps went on to be the international Class A champion in 1975.

They spent several more years deeply involved with a senior drum and bugle corps in Roch. Both began work at Eastman Kodak in the late 1970's, Julie leaving her job when Robbie was born.

Ron's electronic knowledge and his positive and practical approach to tasks has led to significant accomplishments, both on and off the job.

Ron and Julie are very active in church work where their organizational and musical skills are put to good use. They are members of the Youth and Worship Commissions. They have been vocal soloists in the musicals their church has performed, both there and on tour. Julie directs the youth choir and often the bell choir. In 1987 she and Ron organized the Praise Choir, which she also directs.

Their impact on the young people with whom they deal has proven to be highly inspirational and rewarding to all. Campouts for 20 to 30 are yearly occurrences at the Hungry Hollow home. Sports are a big part of their activities, in which they enjoy participating.

Their home next door to Ron's parents has proved to be of inestimable value for all concerned. Having lost her mother before the children were born, Julie is happy to have Phyllis and Walt so close and so willing to help. Sharing Robbie and Rickey is a delight for them and helps to make up for the "lost time" when their own children were growing up.

Projects jointly planned and executed have improved both homes and grounds. One of Ron's latest accomplishments has been to patiently tutor Phyllis in the use of her computer, without which these pages could not have been written!

    Ch (OYER), both b Roch:

    i.   ROBERT EDWARD[9], b 30 May 1983
   ii.   RICHARD LEA, b 8 Sept 1985

354.   EUGENE RUSSELL[8] OYER *(Russell[7], Wallace[6], David[5], Peter[4], David[3], Jacob[2], Frederick[1])* born Sala. 16 Sept. 1946; married Sala. 21 Nov. 1970 MARY AGNES WUJASTYK, dau. of Stanley and Rose Wujastyk, born Sala. 6 Jan. 1946. Gene has worked for the National Fuel Company for 23 years, in Gowanda for several years before returning to Sala. in 1976. He is a foreman for the company.

Gene has worked with the youth in baseball and football. For his efforts he was awarded an honorary plaque by the Junior Chamber of Commerce. Currently he is the governor of the Moose Club in Sala.

His wife Mary Agnes has worked at the Sala. District Hospital as a bookkeeper/payroll clerk since 1977. In recent years, Gene and Mary's help with his ailing parents had been invaluable.

Their boys are very active sports participants, including football, baseball, bowling, golf, soccer, basketball and track. Gene placed fifth in the shot put in an international track meet. He also competed in the AAU/USA (Amateur Athletic Union) Junior Olympics national meet in Utah in 1987, where he placed 9th in the discus and 20th in the shot put, having qualified previously by placing first in both events in the Eastern Regionals.

Ch (OYER):

  i.   MICHAEL SCOTT[9], b Gowanda, 5 Sept 1971
  ii. EUGENE RUSSELL, b Gowanda, 18 Feb 1973
  iii. LUANNE MARIE, b Olean, 6 Feb 1985

355. LINDA CAROL[8] OYER, (*Russell[7], Wallace[6], David[5], Peter[4], David[3], Jacob[2], Frederick[1]*), born Sala. 2 Jan 1950. She married 3 Mar. 1975 OWEN STEVEN McLARNEY, born Sala. 24 Feb. 1950 (divorced 1982). Linda has taught at the Seneca School in Sala. for 16 years. Helping out with her parents while raising her 3 girls proved a challenge she handled well. Russ, although quite crippled, had helped a great deal. This was very meaningful to him-- how he enjoyed those little girls!

Linda has been a cheerleading coach (Pee Wee, in which all her girls have been active), and on the county group's board of directors. She composed a kit and manual for the Human Growth and Development Committee for her school; served on the committee for their enrichment program for excellent students; and helped examine computer software for use in their K-3 building. She served four years on a Curriculum Committee that meets, advises, revises and works on any curriculum problems in K-3 grades; compiled and rewrote New York State's Social Studies curriculum for the second grade for their district's use. Linda is the Clinical Supervisor of a program designed to help teachers improve their teaching skills and recognize their strengths and weaknesses, requiring lesson observations. This and attending English-as-a-Second Language workshop is done along with her regular teaching duties.

All 3 girls are active in gymnastics, dancing, and piano lessons, as well as the cheerleading. Amber is also taking flute lessons.

Ch (McLARNEY) all b Olean:

    i.   AMBER RENEE[9], b 3 Sept 1976
    ii. ERIN LEIGH, b 23 May 1979
    iii. MEGGAN THERESE, b 15 June 1981

356.   MARY LYNN[E]8 BISHOP (*Beatrice[7], Wallace[6], David[5], Peter[4], David[3], Jacob[2], Frederick[1]*) was born Sala. 9 Mar. 1948 and married 12 Oct 1968 THOMAS MICHAEL HALTERMAN, born Sala., son of James and Helen (Thompson) Halterman. (Divorced 1976.)

Mary Lynne performed in vocal groups and was a percussionist during her school years, singing in a church choir, school assemblies and dances and at weddings. She was a moving force with the soft-rock group, "A-440," along with her sister Janet. Mary plays rhythm guitar, and writes and plays original material, currently performing for church services.

Mary is a graduate of the Jamestown Business Institute (now Jamestown Community College) and worked in the library of the Univ. of Pittsburgh's Bradford campus until her marriage. Her husband's work took them from Bradford to Fair Haven, Cayuga Co., where they spent several years.

With a divorce coming within 6 months after the birth of her youngest, Mary supported her children working as a nurse's aide at the Sala. Hospital. She soon was assisting the purchasing agent, who had a terminal illness, and was permanently promoted to that position in 1979. She has other duties at the hospital as Safety Director, where long hours without commensurate wages has been difficult while at the same time raising her 3 boys. Her parents have been extremely supportive.

In 1986 she moved into her newly-purchased home in LV.

Michael has been a NYS Park Ranger, currently patrolling in Allegany State Park where he has been for 14 years.

Ch (HALTERMAN), the 1st 2 b in Bradford, Penn:

    i.   THOMAS MICHAEL[9], Jr, b 25 July 1969; attends college in Wyoming
    ii. TIMOTHY MICHAEL, b 14 Dec 1971
    iii. TODD MICHAEL, b Oswego 24 Nov 1975

357.   DAVID GEORGE8 BISHOP, III, (*Beatrice[7], Wallace[6], David[5], Peter[4], David[3], Jacob[2], Frederick[1]*) was born Sala. 19 Apr. 1951.

He married 5 Jan. 1977 MARSHA BRAMSON, dau. of Seymour and Sally Bramson of Ohio whom he met while attending the University of Rochester, from where he graduated with a bachelor's degree in geology.

He began work as a chemist for the American Chemical Co. in Philadelphia, Penn. After his marriage he began with the Inmont Chemical Co. in Cincinnati, Oh., now United Technologies, where he was second in command in a laboratory. When UT was sold and a move to another city was required, David resigned. He is currently attending Xavier College to obtain a masters degree in business administration.

David's wife Marsha received her Doctor of Medicine degree at the Univ. of Penn., Philadelphia, Penn. In Cincinnati she has combined working for the city and a clinic with a private practice. They purchased their new home there in 1985.

Ch (BISHOP) all b Cincinnati, Oh:

    i.   MICHAEL RICHARD[9], b 7 Feb 1978
   ii.   SARAH ROSE, b 18 Sept 1980
  iii.   SAMUEL DAVID, 30 Apr 1983

358.   **PAUL DOUGLAS**[7] **BISHOP,** *(Beatrice*[7]*, Wallace*[6]*, David*[5]*, Peter*[4]*, David*[3]*, Jacob*[2]*, Frederick*[1]*)* born Sala. 2 Oct. 1952. He married 26 June 1971, SHERRY BROOKS, dau. of William and Odette Brooks. After many years in Bradford, they now reside in New Port Richey, Fla.

Paul played drums in his high school band and started his own band at the age of 13. His band performed at school dances and recreational areas, with Paul playing both drums and guitar, doing back-up singing. He eventually started playing bass guitar and through the years he has played all types of music for dances, weddings and in-house bands.

Paul's training was in auto-body repair. He worked many different jobs, the longest for Haliburton, oil riggers at Bradford, for whom he drove the huge trucks. In July 1982 while they were living in Bradford, their 5 year old son drowned during an outing at the Bishop family camp on Conewango Creek, which feeds Lake Chautauqua in Chau. Co.

As work with Haliburton was sporadic, they moved to Florida in 1985, with the hope of a new beginning. Paul worked for a paving company, shortly becoming the foreman with his own truck. He recently began driving refuse haulers for International Waste Systems. Sherry started work as a cook in a fast-food restaurant, soon becoming the head cook. She now manages one.

Sherry's father, blown up while in a tank in Normandy during WWII, wandered across a field to a farmhouse for help, and there met the girl he married, Odette.

Shawn and Jason, although students, have parttime jobs--all in all the move to Fla. was a good one for the family.

Ch (BISHOP):

    i.   SHAWN DOUGLAS[9], b Bradford, Penn 17 Jan 1972
    ii. JASON BENJAMIN, b Olean 22 Mar 1973
    iii. PAUL PATRICK, b Bradford, 30 Sept 1976; d 13 July 1982

[Sources: family members]

359.   DIANE M.[8] RETTBERG (*Dolores[7], Frederick[6], Franklin[5], Peter[4], David[3], Jacob[2], Frederick[1]*), born Sala., Catt. Co. 19 Mar. 1942; married JAMES R. PIERCE, born 30 July 1940 (divorced).

Ch (PIERCE):

    i.   BRYAN J[9], b Sala 15 Feb 1962; m TINA CHURCH, b Bradford, McKean Co, Penn 9 Sept 1964; res Eldred, McKean Co, Penn
    ii. LORRAINE D, b Sala 6 May 1964; m JOSEPH McCASLIN; res Bentwatton, Eng where he is serving in the US Air Force. They are "expecting."
    iii. TODD A, b Sala 1 May 1966; m KIM BELL, b Olean 16 Jan 1966; res Pordione, Italy
          a) BRANDON A, b Olean, Catt Co 29 July 1984
          b) DOROTHY N, b Vichenza, Italy

360.   JOAN E.[8] RETTBERG (*Dolores[7], Frederick[6], Franklin[5], Peter[4], David[3], Jacob[2], Frederick[1]*), born Sala. 20 Mar. 1945; married DOUGLAS SAMPSON, born Sala. 3 Sept. 1946; reside Sala.

Ch (SAMPSON), both b Sala:

    i. MARIE KAY[9], b 6 Aug 1974
    ii. HAROLD DOUGLAS, b 10 Aug 1977

361.   GRETCHEN A.[8] RETTBERG (*Dolores[7], Frederick[6], Franklin[5], Peter[4], David[3], Jacob[2], Frederick[1]*), born Sala., Catt.

Co. 9 Nov. 1949; married MICHAEL ANDERSON, born Sala. 22 Apr. 1948. Gretchen is the head nurse in Obstetrics and Gynecology at St. Francis Hospital in Olean, Catt. Co.

Ch (ANDERSON):

  i.   JENNIFER L⁹ (twin), b 12 June 1972
  ii. JEREMY M (twin), b 12 June 1972
  iii. JESSICA A, b 24 Aug 1976
  iv. MAUREEN A, b 23 June 1981

362.   SANDRA⁸ HODARA (*Joan⁷, Frederick⁶, Franklin⁵, Peter⁴, David³, Jacob², Frederick¹*), born Sala., Catt. Co. 10 Dec. 1943; married WILLIAM JOHN ALTMAN, born Franklin, Penn. 5 Feb. 1931. They reside GrV., Catt. Co.

Ch (ALTMAN), both b Bflo:

  i.   JOAN⁹, b 3 Aug 1966
  ii. SUSAN, b 16 Dec 1969

[Source #359 through 362: Dolores Rettberg]

363.   JOAN PATRICIA⁸ OYER (*Joseph⁷, Bartholomew⁶, B Eugene⁵, Peter⁴, David³, Jacob², Frederick¹*), born Jersey City, N.J. 30 June 1937; married Kearny, N.J. 7 Oct. 1956 RAYMOND ZUJUS. They reside with 2 daughters and 3 sons in Uncasville, Conn.

364.   ROBERT JOSEPH⁸ OYER (*Joseph⁷, Bartholomew⁶, B Eugene⁵, Peter⁴, David³, Jacob², Frederick¹*), born Kearny, N.J. 6 May 1941; married in Mass. 6 Dec. 1963 JANICE PARSONS. They reside with 1 dau. and 2 sons in Portsmouth, R.I.

365.   KENNETH ALAN⁸ OYER (*Joseph⁷, Bartholomew⁶, B Eugene⁵, Peter⁴, David³, Jacob², Frederick¹*), born Kearny, N.J. 21 Feb. 1943; married W. Milford, N.J. 5 Feb. 1966 THERESA RHINESMITH. They reside with 2 daus. and 4 sons in Newton, N.J.

366.   RUSSELL JON⁸ OYER (*Joseph⁷, Bartholomew⁶, B Eugene⁵, Peter⁴, David³, Jacob², Frederick¹*), born Kearny, N.J. 10 Apr.

1950; married Stony Point, Rockland Co. 14 Sept. 1985 BARBARA CUMMINGS; reside Stony Point.

Ch (OYER):

    i.   stepson
   ii. JONATHAN RUSSELL[9], b 10 Mar 1987

[Sources #363 through 366: Ruth Oyer; Jane Bradley]

367.   KATHY ANN[8] MULLEN (*Eleanor[7], St. Elmo[6], Charles D[5], John[4-3], Jacob[2], Frederick[1]*), born Bflo., Erie Co. 9 Nov. 1942; married 27 Dec.1961 GARY LEE DAVIES, born Minneapolis, Minn. 19 June 1937.

Ch (DAVIES):

    i.   TRACY VICTORIA[9], b Bflo 21 July 1962; m 15 Aug 1986 LEONARD SIWICKI
         a) KARA MAE[10], b 4 Nov 1983
   ii. MICHAEL RUSSELL, b Bflo 2 Nov 1963
  iii. JAMES FREDERICK, b N Tonawanda 1 Aug 1965
   iv. PAUL ALLEN, b Blfo 21 Jan 1968
    v. RICHARD GARY, b Bflo 23 July 1968, adopted

368.   BECKY LOU[8] MULLEN (*Eleanor[7], St. Elmo[6], Charles D[5], John[4-3], Jacob[2], Frederick[1]*), born Bflo., Erie Co. 28 Apr. 1946; married 18 Apr. 1967 SALVATORE LaGRECA, born Sicily 12 Feb. 1949.

Ch (LaGRECA):

    i.   SALVATORE[9], b Bflo 10 Apr 1969
   ii. MARK ANTHONY, b Lockport, Niagara Co 14 Sept 1971
  iii. SHAUN DAVID, b Amherst, Erie Co 19 Dec 1977

[Source #367,368: Eleanor Mullen]

369.   ALFRED JAMES[8] CRANER (*Vivus Lewis[7], Edith Lewis[6], Gertrude[5], Peter[4], Jacob[3], Peter[2], Frederick[1]*), born Syracuse 19 Mar. 1924; died Columbus, Oh. 27 Mar. 1979. He married 21 June 1959 DORIS MARGUERITE/MARGE McKAIG, dau. of F. Burton and Marguerite (Manning) McKaig, born Syracuse 7 Mar. 1929.

Alfred, schooled in Jordan, Onon. Co., entered the Coast Guard Prep. School at Washington, D.C., and in 1943, the Coast Guard Academy. In 1944 he joined the U.S. Navy, serving in WWII. He was discharged in 1946; graduated with a degree in Business Administration from Syracuse Univ. in 1950. He reeived his masters degree from SUNY Oswego, and taught in the schools of north central N.Y.

In 1973 he went to Columbus, Oh. where he was a guidance counselor.

Ch (CRANER):

i. MARTHA BALDWIN[9], b Fulton, Schoharie Co 21 Oct 1961
ii. ALFRED JAMES, II, b Watertown, Jefferson Co 24 June 1963
iii. CYNTHIA RUTH, b Watertown 13 April 1965

[Sources: Marge Craner; obit]

I THINK THAT I SHALL NEVER SEE
A FINISHED GENEALOGY

CHAPTER 14

UNPLACED OYERS

*** OYERS IN BUFFALO CITY DIRECTORIES ***

YEAR	NAME	OCCUPATION	ADDRESS
1861-65	NO OYERS		
1875	NO OYERS		
1888,9	NO OYERS		
1890	H Eugene (Harlan Eugene, son of Jacob?)		Eaton & Oyer 9 Law Exch
1910	Edward (son of Jacob?)	310 Franklin	clerk
	Harry E	Am Rest	603 Mai
1915	Catherine	milliner	7th
	Guy	stockbroker	202 Eagle
	Harry	barber	20 Eagle
1917	C O	insurance	10032 Morgan Bldg
	Cath (wid Edw)		7th
1918	G N (Glenn N?)	treasurer	Sprvl
	Gretchen G		72 Days Pk
	Guy		14 Camp
	Harry L		Division
	Robert E		"
	This is same res St Elmo is shown at (#178.2)		
1900	[all now placed]		
1920	Glenn N	mgr Cascade Cider	292 Linden
	Guy		
	Harry L		
	Rob't E	cashier Wire Wheel Corp	
1930	Guy R (Vera)		50 Kehr
	Harry L (Cecelia)		255 Stntn
1932	(several) plus:		
	Robert	auditor	Hypochlorite Prod
	(no Charles)		
	Elizabeth	maid	789 Potomac
	Glenn N (Tessie)		
1936	(several) plus:		
	Elizabeth M	stenog	189 Box
	Eleanor R	stenog	N Tonawanda
1940	Guy R (Vera)	swch	422 Moselle
	Harry L (Cecelia M)	blk op	189 Box
	Tessie (wid Glenn)		837 Main, Apt 15

APPENDIX 1

ADDITIONAL HASENCLEVER DATA

Our visit to the Ringwood area in 1986 reveals continued attempts to restore the Ringwood Ironworks where the Hasenclever men first worked. Ringwood and others in the area supplied George Washington with not only ammunition, but supplies, such as army kettles, stoves, tools, and many other items. There too was forged the chain that prevented the British fleet from sailing up the Hudson River during the Revolution.

The rapidity with which the workmen got the decayed ironworks producing again, as well as providing housing, roads, dams, and necessities, is noteworthy. At Ringwood still stands one of the original houses, although badly burned in the mid-1980's. [See Illus pp 15,16]

We were told by Ernest Krauss that our Frederick is shown on a list of the workmen as "Freiderich Ayrer." We do not know where this list is, although we know his widow, Martha Krauss, had Hasenclever papers that were to be translated. It may be among the collection of Krauss' now at Ringwood.

A director of Ringwood Manor (restored) has suggested that our Frederick could be one of those chosen to be sent to the Mohawk Valley because homes and other structures were to be built, thereby theorizing he could have been a carpenter.

The arrival in the Mohawk Valley in March 1766 of some of the workmen is told in the correspondence between Sir William Johnson and William Darlington, as found in the Sir William Johnson volumes.

We quote now from Hasenclever's own words in his book. [Hasen Case] The book was originally published by Hasenclever himself in 1773 in his own defense. This rare book has thus been preserved for us, our copy a gift from Ernest Krauss in June 1974.

Among the many problems he wrote about in addition to those quoted [Chapter 5, p 36] were the flooding – "spring freshets," which washed out structures and seed. Continuing his text:

I chose this plantation [Mohawk River] at such a distance, because I could not get fertile land near New York, for the purpose of planting Hemp, Flax, and Madder.

...fickleness of the people...[I] departed 13 Nov 1766...returned Aug 1767...found nothing accomplished ...but, on the contrary, a furnace had been ruined; forges and houses burnt; a Potash manufacture neglected and that fine settlement adjoining to the fertile German Flats on the Mohawk river, begun for the cultivation of Hemp, Flax and Madder, entirely abandoned.

There is perhaps, no better Iron in the world than this cinder-iron, particularly for the use of waggon-tire, plough-shares and implements for husbandry; it is tough, and almost as hard as steel.

This method making bar-iron was not known before my arrival in America, nor in England, 'till a year ago... By introducing this method of working, some thousand tons of Iron may be extracted from the old furnace cinders, and, with the addition of the rejected old forge cinders, may make good bar-iron.

In Germany they use only 400 bushels of coal to make 3 ton of pig-iron, and in America they consume 855 bushels to make the same quantity...

[weakness of the wood]...that the Savages formerly
fired the woods to hunt the Deer, by which the roots
of the trees were damaged; but he had found by experience, that the woods which had been cut 18 years, and
now grown up again, were much stronger as to require
1/4 to 1/3 [?] less coal than the old wood...when the
country is more populous, and the wages cheaper, that
then they will make Iron as cheap in America as they
do now in Europe.
　　...expensive produce of a Pearl-ash Manufactory on
the Mohawk River... month of October 1767...Three men
for a week at 3 s. [shillings] per day but as they plant
India corn, it very seldom happens that both crops fail,
and generally have one good crop either of wheat or
India corn ...plowing; harrowing; pulling flax, watering
and drying; breaking and swindling; transport...exorbitant
high American wages...prodigious impoverishers of land,
...farmers have not yet cattle enough to make manure,
and when once the land is exhausted, it will bear no
grain...spring draughts...hard labour...in want of
hands...clearing of new land takes up much of their
time--a business not known in England.

Hasenclever became involved in bankruptcy proceedings and
endless lawsuits and delays. In 1769 he left for London in the
hope and expectation of clearing his name and reestablshing his
position, lost by his partners' actions. He never returned to
America; in 1773 he left London for Landshut, Silesia (Prussia)
where "Frederick the Great" assigned him to reorganize and
improve the linen industry. In this he was successful.
　　In a poignant letter to the Prussian minister in London he
declared his innocence and requested assistance in the long-
standing lawsuits.
　　In Jack Chard's introduction to the book reprinting, he sums it
up:

　　He had the vision and energy of a great industrialist,
and was apparently well-liked and respected by his
contemporaries in the New World. He died on June
13th, 1793. Seven months after his death the long
drawn out court proceedings in England were decided in
favor of Hasenclever....But the American Company was
in bankruptcy. Hasenclever had been vindicated, but he
did not live to see it.

OTHER OYERS IN AMERICA

We will now look at information available regarding Oyers who have been successful in locating their roots. Bear in mind an eventual "linkage" with the New York Oyers is a strong possibility.

In our listing of sources and references there are a number of books that have been written concerning Eyers/Oyers. [We have noted so many instances where these spellings are interchangeable that we completely accept this popular variant spelling.] There is a most informative detailed book by the Reverend Frederick S. Weiser [Weiser].

This book tells of the arrival of a "Mardin Eyer" on the ship Ann at Philadelphia, Penn. 28 Sept. 1749. Thus we see Johan Martin Eyer's arrival in America is one that predates our Frederick (1764). The only other one we know of is Hans (John) Eyer, 1744. Our informant, David Eyer of Ligonier, Penn. does not know what their relationship was, but feels they were likely brothers or cousins. We feel knowledge of their history is relevant and of interest.

Johann (John) Martin Eyer was born in Kutzenhausen–Feltbach, which is in Lower Alsace, Germany in 1729, according to his baptismal record in France; and his parents were Johann Jacob and Anne Barbara (Lowenstein) Eyer. He died 28 March 1804 in Hamilton Twp., Monroe Co., (formed from Northampton Co., Penn. in 1835).

Details regarding church records of Martin (as he is next refereed to) and his wife Anna Dorothea Beuscher follow. Martin was naturalized in 1765 at Bedminster Twp., Penn. He owned land in Haycock Twp., Bucks Co., Penn.

David Eyer (noted above) traces his ancestry to Martin, and succeeded in backing up 2 more generations. Martin's grandparents are Peter and Anna Maria (Schweigler or Schweizer) Eyer; Anna born in 1651; died in Kutzenhousen in 1729. Peter was born in Switzerland in 1646. He died in Kutzenhausen in 1719.

Martin and Dorothea had at least 10 children, dating from 1755 to 1778. There is a wealth of information in Rev. Weiser's book concerning the first born, Johan Adam, who never married. He was born 27 July 1755 and died 29 Dec. 1837. He was very well educated and had a love of learning. He was a master penman and knew both the German and English language and script.

It is thought his teacher or teachers might have been Mennonite and/or Schwenkfelder members. [The latter is a religion similar to the Mennonite's, whose persecuted members also found refuge in Penn.]

John Adam Eyer described himself as a Schuldiener, which is a Swiss and south German term. A booklet of texts which was written by him to be an example for the student was similar to one used in various sections of Switzerland.

John Adam Eyer was a noted Fraktur and Vorschrift artist. The earliest booklet, of 1780, contains a city skyline reminiscent of Zurich, Switzerland. Extant are numerous examples of Fraktur and Vorschrift art. Some may be seen in the Fraktur Room at the Winterthur Museum and Gardens, Winterthur, Del., which is about 6 miles from Wilmington.

John Adam was also a noted musician, whose impact in music upon the community and through it on the entire Penn. Dutch folk culture was most noteworthy.

This watercolor and ink Vorschrift drawing reproduced on stationery which states it is attributed to Johann Adam Eyer of Bucks County, Penn., and was probably done sometime between 1800 and 1820. The soldiers and couples possibly represent a military wedding. The original drawing, 12 3/8 by 15 1/2 inches, is displayed in the Fraktur Room, Winterthur Museum and Gardens, Winterthur, Del.

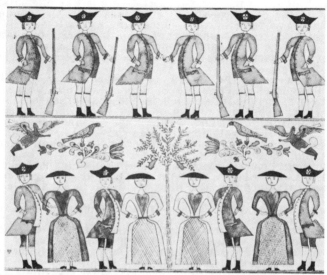

Only the melodies of the favorite hymn tunes of that time were written out. The Marburg hymnal had both Lutheran and Reformed editions. In 1786 the Lutherans replaced it with an American collection; in 1797 the Reformed did the same, as did 2 Mennonite conferences, one in 1803 and one in 1804. However many of the same melodies were retained. Rev. Weiser makes the interesting statement that "...hymnody has always been a leveling factor in Christian sectarianism; and the Pietistic movement had greatly increased that tendency in late eighteenth and early 19th century Pennsylvania Germandom. One is hard put to find hymn texts popular in this period which delineate doctrinal differences between the 3 church groups mentioned above." [Weiser, p. 462]

John Frederick Eyer, John Adam's brother, was also a teacher, artist and musician. His son Henry C. Eyer was a musician whose The Union Choral Harmony, Consisting of Sacred Music , with German and English words to each tune, adapted to the use of Christian Churches of every Denomination, became not only one of the most popular German–English tune books in the 19th century, but extensively propelled the Eyer influence into the singing of the Penn. Germans. This he published at Harrisburg in 1833; reworked and republished in Philadelphia in 1839.

John Adam Eyer was a lifelong Lutheran, although he served in a Mennonite school. He disagreed with the Mennonite prohibition of military service. The military emphasis (in other Frakturs) is due in part no doubt because at least two of the other brothers were in the Revolution.

It is believed that Eyer's decorated flyleaves contributed to the popularity of fancy penmanship as found on bookplates. Rev.

Weiser relates that this custom is alive today in Mennonite and Amish communities in Montgomery and Bucks Counties in Penn.

John Adam Eyer's leadership abilities are apparent in the fact that he was chosen by both Lutherans and Reformed to be the bookkeeper and treasurer of the fund established for a new church building at Christ-Hamilton Square, Monroe Co, Penn. in 1829. Extensive minutes, both in German and English, as well as the charter, were made by Eyer.

The next pages of Rev. Weiser's book show that "Eyer" changed to "Oyer" in the generation that followed; he states that Johann Adam Eyer's name was pronounced and frequently spelled Oyer.

Many more accomplishments are cited. The family history continues details of land records, and the establishment of Bloomsburg, variously known as Eyersburg, Oyersburg, Oyersschdeddel, or Eyerstaedtel. Information from Gordon Oyer states that this was originally known as "Oyertown" or "Oyersburg." Oyer Avenue still runs through it. Nearby "Eyer's Grove" was named for a descendant of Ludwig Eyer, John Adam's brother. Gordon has done much research, and has maps showing Oyer locations in Penn.

There is a great deal of additional genealogical data in the Weiser book. However, here we shall leave this line of so many Penn.-rooted Oyer families.

The other early Oyer families that we have referred to are the "New Orleans Oyers," a name we originated for our purposes. Our data comes largely from Verle and Margaret Oyer of Gibson City, Ill. who have done so much research on these families. Their son Gordon is carrying on for them; we are deeply indebted to them for their encouragement and interest as well as their data.

In our preface we have told of the arrival of 23 Oyers on the ship Superior at New Orleans in 1830. They sailed from Le Havre, France. All show their country of origin as "Suisse" (Switzerland), though they had lived in France. Hermann and Gertrud Guth through their research for Verle and Margaret Oyer have learned that these ancestors lived at Hemersbergerhof in the Palatinate in Germany in 1777. These were the families of Johannes Oyer, Senior and Johannes Oyer, Junior.

Johannes Oyer, Junior had sons Joseph Oyer I, born in 1777, and Jacob Oyer. The family lived from 1807 to 1830 at Neiderhof, Lorraine, France. This is several miles from the city of Saarburg. The 12 oldest children of Joseph Oyer I are listed as being born there. His first wife was Katharine Schrag (Schrock). After her death he married Magdalena Litwiller, the daughter of John and Francoise Serre (Zehr) Litwiller.

Joseph's brother Jacob married Barbara Schertz. Two of their girls died before the families came to America. Jacob apparently later married a Barbara N_____.

This then is the listing of these families as shown on the ship's list:

1. Johannes Oyer	85 years	12. Joseph Oyer II	16
2. Anna Oyer	36	13. Magdalena	23
3. Catherine Oyer	33	14. Catherine	21
4. Joseph Oyer	7	15. Anna	17
5. Jacob Oyer	49	16. Hans	13
6. Barbara Oyer	35	17. Peter	11
7. Infant Oyer	10 days	18. Christian	10
(#7 was born at sea and named Joseph)		19. Maria	9
8. Susanna Oyer	22	20. Barbara	8
9. Anna Oyer	16	21. Andrew	6
10. Joseph Oyer I	54	22. Elizabeth	3
11. Magdalena	45	23. David	1

Joseph I, Magdalena and their family lived in Butler Co., Ohio near Hamilton until 1838. They moved to Tazewell County, Ill., traveling the Ohio, Mississippi and Illinois Rivers.

Verle and Margaret have found no further record of 85 year old Johannes, nor of Joseph I; he is not listed in the 1850 census. All of the above list have been traced except #2, #3, and #4.

Further research by the Guths has shown the following regarding the the New Orleans Oyers' earliest ancestors in Europe. Jean Oyer, Senior is shown on a list of the subjects of the Duke of Zweibrucken, living in Hermersbergerhof in 1776 and 1777. A son Jean was born in 1745, who later lived in Neiderhoff and married Jacobe Regle. She died 25 March 1820 at the age of 71. Their children were Jean (1768 supposedly), Joseph (1774) and Jacob (1781) as well as daughters. These Jean Oyers are the same as noted above, this being the French spelling.

Of the other early Oyers, Christian and George, Christian is shown in the 1790 census in Dauphin Co., Penn. and is listed under the "Pa. Heads of Families." [For George, see Chap 5]

Gordon Oyer has supplied this information: "Christian Eyer was probably the son of an older Hans (John) Eyer of Lancaster Co., Penn. who arrived in America in 1744. The elder Hans (with wife Barbara) first appears in 1750 land records where he bought 300 acres in Lebanon Twp. from the Penn. family. He died in 1782. His will lists the following children (all indications are that they are listed in order of birth): Jacob (eldest), Mary, Abraham (b 1748), Barbara (b 1750), Christian, Catherina, Elizabeth, and John (the last 3 were by another wife, Catherina). I had estimated Christian's birth to be between 1751 and 1755 based on available information...In subsequent genealogies, the elder John and his daughter Barbara are referred to as 'Oyer.'"

Dr. Gratz has recently supplied this data which seems to correlate with Christian, above. He located Christian Eyer who d 1812, age 55, putting his b 1757. His wife was Verena Jordi; ch Daniel, d 1811, age 20 yr 8 mo; Elisabeth, d 1812, age 29 yr 1 mo 14 d; Johannes, d 1864, age 62 yr minus 17 da; Jacobina, m Jacob Egli in 1818; Catharina, d 1848, age 61 yr 2 mo minus 2 da; Catharina, m Christian Wolber. One of Catharina's children (born from 1815 through 1829), married a Peter Muller.

He found a Johannes Eyer who m Jacobina Rediger; their son Jacob d y in 1840 and had no ch. A Johanes Kempf, son of Johannes Kempf and Maria Scheef (?) d 1819; m Barbara Eyer; had ch Barbara, d 1812 and Elisabeth, b 1799. [Dr. Gratz' data comes from the Konigsbach Mennoniten Register.]

Informants tell us that the Amish have a custom of naming the first 2 children of both sexes after the grandparents. Among the many given names that all the Oyer families share, regardless of their roots, are Christian, Joseph, Jacob, Peter, David, Frederick, Magdalena, John, Catherine, Andrew and Elizabeth.

May future researchers may find this information useful.

[Sources: Oyer Gen 1,2,3,4,5; Weiser; Gratz]

COATS OF ARMS DETAILS

We are including coats of arms information even though we have
been told that Switzerland assigns no official status to them.
This comes from the book we quoted in Chapter I concerning Historical Oyer Information. [Valaisan WB]

1. In blue a golden trademark, (growing out of a green
"three-topped" hill, called a Dreiberg,) composed of a lily stem
supported by two buttresses surmounted by a gold initial M
and accompanied on the left and right each by two six-
pointed golden stars one above the other.

On an oven in Mund, with the initials S.E. and the year
1596, appears the oldest well-known coat of arms of the Eyer
family, a capstan (or winch) (that is a pole on a lowered
chevron) as trademark. On a [plain/plateau] (Tessel) from one
of the Simplon Alps appears the same trademark, on the right
of a globe accompanied by the inscription Joh. Eyer of year
1713 and on another Tessel of the same alp again the same
trademark, above the globe with the inscription John Eyer of
Termen 1881. The trademark is also the dominant part of a
coat of arms accompanied by the initials A.M.E. on an altar
painting of approximately 1810 in the chapel of Rosswald in
Termen: in blue on the black Three-topped hill, the capstan
formed silver trademark surmounted by two six-pointed silver
stars.

A different aspect of the coat of arms is shown on an oven
at the former parsonage of Glis (the same coat of arms as
described under No. 1, but without color indication.) This
with the initial M surmounted lily could be supposed to honor
the Virgin Mary. The coat of arms is accompanied by the
letters I.M.E. and the year 1783. In the book of Heraldry in
Wallis 1946 the bottom part of the trademark has erroneously
been translated as Cocksfoot. The colors of the coat of arms
have been reported by J. Lauber. Information by P. Heldner,
Glis, 1972 and 1973.

2. In blue, on a three-topped hill, a similar trademark.
Here we recognize the trademark of the first coat of arms,
but, overturned, supplemented with two diagonal buttresses
and without the lily.

This coat of arms, which is used by the Eyer family in
Baltschieder, together with the initials H.A. (Hans Aier) and
the year 1696, can be seen on an oven in the former Eyer
House in Birgisch. Likewise without diagonal buttresses, on a
post of 1697 in Mund with the initials HE. MA, and the same
on a post of 1758.

Information supplied by P. Heldner, Glis, 1973. Compare also
from the aforementioned: History and Chronicles of Baltschieder, Visp 1971, page 43 and 50.

This coat of arms has later been surrendered in favor of a
so-called "expressive" coat of arms, thereby following a newer
general explanation of the family name, taking Eier into the
escutcheon.

3. In blue, over the green three-topped hill two silver eggs
side by side, surmounted with two six-pointed gold stars.
Woodcarvings of J.Jergen (Jerjern) Reckingen, approximately
1935, are in possession of the famiy of Dr. J. Eyer-Gross in
Saint-Maurice and R. Loretan-Imbiederland in Sitten. Compare
Book of Heraldry of Wallis, 1946, volume 7. (The heraldic
assertions on page 90 are here corrected.)

Variations: l) with three eggs side by side, indicated on an oven of 1749 in Mund as III. 2) Between the two eggs are two flowers with stem and leaves growing on the three-topped hill.   This is found on an oven in Mund with the initials WMICE (Eyer) and AMIA with the year 1755. 3) Three eggs, placed 2. l., with the three-topped hill, but without the stars or the flowers. (Collection Ismael Furrer, 1911.) 4) Coat of arms III with gold field (notes from Fr. Lager); 5) Three eggs, placed 2. l. without further decorations, found on the alps Gredetschtal on a discarded Tessel, with the name Peter Eyer, from Birgisch, 1857 (Collection P. Heldner.)
4.   Divided, upper in blue with two 5 pointed gold stars, bottom in black with three silver eggs, side by side. Seal in the collection of Dr. Victor Bovet (1853-1922). Information from J. Marclay, Monthey, 1955.

Our translator, Jackie Smith of Chatham, Ontario, Canada, has these notes concerning the above:

Grosskastlan is a title--president and judge
Landratsbote is a deputy, delegate
Dreiberg is translated as 3-topped hill for lack of a better
    description. Drei means 3, berg means mountain or hill.
Tessel is a dialect word, perhaps a stake such as surveyors
    use. The ovens are probably stone coal and wood stoves.

These Eyer coats-of-arms are explained in the text. Switzerland does not assign any official status to coats-of-arms.

[Sources: Gratz; Schweiz FN; Schweiz HB; Valaisan WB]

AUTOBIOGRAPHY OF RAYMOND ELBERT OYER

On Jan. 13, 1926 I became the first born of my parents, Lee and Edith Brougham Oyer and grew up to be a 6', brown haired, brown eyed, oval faced man. My birth took place in our home in [the town of Great Valley], Cattaraugus [County], New York. Other children of the family included a younger brother Bob, born two years later, and a sister Joyce, born some ten years later. The family lived in New York until I was age 6. Then the family moved to Denton, Michigan. At age 7, we moved to Ypsilanti, Michigan, where I remained until I went into the army at age 18.

Basic training was the first of many activities to lure me west. Camp Roberts, located in the northern half of California, became my training ground and home for the next two years. World War II was the "current event" of that time and I was soon to be shipped to Yokohama, Japan. Fortunately for me, I was not a part of the heavy fighting. After a short time in Yokohama I was sent to the Island of Hokkaido where I spent my last year in the Army before being discharged.

Upon my return to the states, I went back home to Ypsilanti. On June 28, 1948, I married Vera Alice Boyd Oyer, my most treasured friend and sweetheart for the next thirty-five years. Vera died of cancer in June, 1983.

For the first two years of our marriage, we lived in Sumpter, Michigan, then moved to a lake in Belleville. The next fourteen years were spent in a little green house in Ypsilanti, Rosenville Township, across the street from the church where we were married. Donald Gary Oyer, our son, was born in Ypsilanti, December 13, 1963.

Though not all our lives have been spent in Michigan, we did have a real yo-yo effect going on for some time. We moved from Michigan to Florida, Florida to Michigan, Michigan to Phoenix, Phoenix to Michigan, back to Phoenix, then back to Michigan, out to California, back to Michigan, and finally back to California where I think I have finally "settled in". While living in Phoenix and in California I frequently teamed with my father in business ventures. In Florida I built homes for a living; in Arizona I worked with my dad in his trailer hitch shop. At one time I opened a shop of my own--a welding shop in California. The business was thriving, but I found out I was not cut out to be a businessman. Demands of the public were too confining. What I needed and went back to was the work that seemed to remain constant in my life--my work with cars.

My life has been a fluid one. I was blessed with the skills that have enabled me to be an independent, self-sufficient person. I have done masonry, carpentry and welding; for more than 35 years I have been a professional paint and body man (I do my own custom painting on my vehicles), and I have built and driven race cars. Racing has been a special love to me, as a profession and as a hobby. There's nothing that excites me more than the roar of the engines and the power they symbolize. I have a true appreciation for the work and technology that goes into the finished product. My automotive "tinkering" has taken me into a variety of phases with cars. I have built custom cars, raced cars, motorcycles and twin-engine go-carts. Races have included short track racing, enduros (some as long as 500 miles), off-road single seat competition as a driver and builder, modified and old model stock car racing, NASCAR new stock cars (some races 250 miles long), scramble, the Baja 500, Mint 500 and a number of 250 milers. I doubt the day will come when you'll see a mere one or two vehicles parked around my home.

To list all the cars I have built, rebuilt, revived and put to rest would add volumes to this. I wouldn't subject you to that. A sampling, however, might be what I now have: four VW's (one is rebuilt '57 red convertible, a rebuilt '63 Baja bug, my "everyday" VW vehicle and one '57 oval window VW being built with a chopped top, a '47 Plymouth I restored, a Mercury my son drives and pick-up camper with a camper shell, newly painted and finely tuned. I had several others a few short months ago, but have sold them to make room for other restorations and making of custom cars. If you haven't already guessed, VW's are one of my specialties, though I have worked on a great many other makes and models.

In the June 1976 publication of Off Road magazine, a feature article was done on a car I rebuilt for Malcolm Smith, noted motorcycle racer from Riverside. That was a real thrill for me. I have won a number of racing trophies too, that have added an equal amount of pleasure. These trophies may not be too meaningful to others, but they're icing on the cake for me, after putting in so much work to get there.

I'm not sure how extensive the inborn talents and skills are throughout the family. My father and grandfather were quite adept with their hands and their carpentry work, and there are traces throughout of artistic genes. My father played a guitar. I spend a good deal of time learning music (I'm self taught) and a few years ago, I decided to try painting landscape pictures (also self-taught). Both Bob and Joyce can draw, too. For me, the music and drawing are indoor hobbies that fill my time meaningfully when I can't be outdoors working on cars.

When I was younger, I was active in the sport of archery and won a number of trophies in state tournament competitions.

The real highs, though, are still the ones to be found behind the wheel in an automobile. Whether it's trekking through the desert in a Dune buggy discovering new terrain, or watching a major racing event, it keeps my adrenalin flowing.

As a child I was always working with my hands. I dreamed of someday building and flying my own airplane. Today, I'm more trusting of transportation on the ground and have traded that dream for my work with cars. It affords me a freedom I always seem to need. I never did like being closed up in a room, including school. I wanted to be able to explore and investigate--things I do daily in my life. I'm a loner, of choice. I like the solitude of my own world and don't conform easily to the choices of others. I'm a nature lover and find a deep sense of serenity in nature, especially in trees.

Though this is only a thumbnail sketch of my life, perhaps others in my family will read this and recognize a tie to what and who they are. It's been pleasurable to offer a glimpse to anyone who cares to read this. I'm looking forward to reading about the rest of you.

The Holland Purchase and its range and town layouts, Western New York.

Courtesy of Rochester Public Library

THE HOLLAND LAND COMPANY AND THE ERIE CANAL

Courtesy of Rochester Public Library

Lockport's 10 locks.

The Holland Land Company was a Dutch enterprise that greatly influenced the settlement of much of Western New York, and thence points west. The land was purchased from Robert Morris by the HLC with funds of money from Holland held in trust by grantees for their benefit because they were aliens and couldn't purchase and hold real estate in their names. Changes by trustees and transfers sanctioned by the Legislature, the whole tract was conveyed by trustees by three separate deeds to HLC, or rather to the individuals, composing three branches of the company. They chose this land as it was "nearest Philadelphia," the residence of their general agent.

It was organized by Dutch bankers in 1796 and they obtained an area covering the entire western part of NYS. Their names included Wilhelm Willink, Nicholas Van Staphorst, Pieter Van Eeghen, Hendrick Vollenhaven, Rutger Jan Schimmelpenninck, and Jan, Wilhelm, Jr and Jan, Jr Willink; Hendrick Seye, and Pieter Stadnitzki. "...conveyances of the land purchased of Mass. by Robert Morris were conveyed to him by four separate deeds." [Briggs, p 32]

In the 1770's, the Province of Massachusetts extended to Lake Erie on the west. The area of Western New York had been held by the Seneca Indians, of the Iroquois Tribes, holding it by virtue of their conquests over other tribes--the Mohicans, Hurons, Eries and Ottawas. The area then was obtained through dealings with the Indians involving money and other things they desired by the provincial government of Massachusetts. Nathaniel Gorham was a member of the governor's council of Massachusetts. He and Oliver Phelps along with wealthy friends bought 6 million acres, all of current New Yrok State west of the Pre-emption Line, for $1 million in Massachusetts securities, the equivalent of $175,000 cash or 3 cents an acre.   The Pre-emption Line ran from the Pennsylvania border north to Sodus Bay.

In July 1788, through the Buffalo Creek treaty, title was cleared.   Financial problems complicated things, finally being settled by selling the western portion to Robert Morris of Philadelphia in 1791.   Morris was a merchant who helped to finance the Revolution.   The land bordered the Phelps-Gorham purchase on the east, and even extended into NW Pennsylvania.   Known as the Holland Purchase, they developed the holdings, planned town sites, and sold the lands on liberal terms directly to settlers.

The HLC opened its main office in Batavia, Genesee Co. in 1801. They began with 300,000 acres; two years later they added about a million more.   Some land was in central New York.   It all was managed by the same agent in Philadelphia, Robert Morris.

Morris also purchased a huge tract that includes Rochester for $75,000, reselling it to a group of London capitalists headed by Sir William Pulteney for $275,000.

Joseph Ellicott was the principal surveyor.   The land was divided first into ranges 6 miles wide from Pennsylvania to Lake Ontario, numbered from east to west.   This line was known as Transit Line.   Secondly the land was divided into townships, 6 miles square, numbered from north to south.   Thirdly, the land was divided into lots, three-fourths mile square, equalling 360 acres, then sold in parcels.   They were often divided into thirds so that each parcel was 120 acres.   (The surveyors for several reasons frequently had variations in the accuracy of their plotting.)

In 1823 the price for an acre of land was $2.   The HLC offered land for the first church in each area, calling them the Gospel lots.   The company was taken over by the Farmers Loan and Trust by 1846.

How important the HLC was for our families can be seen in this list of those who were either agents or purchasers, as found in the HLC index of records found at the Olin Library, Manuscripts and Archives at Cornell Univ.: Arnold, Clark (27), Crumb, Crary (4), Finster (5), Fox (4), Frank (9), Hammond, adley, Hinman, Hurlburt, Miller, Pratt, Reynolds (10), Spaulding, Vedder (4), Waite (many) and White.   Oyers included David, Frederick, George, John, Jacob, John P, Peter D., and William.

[Lack of time prevented a complete check; details of these indexes and HLC records are now located at SUNY Fredonia, Chautauqua Co.]

Development of corduroy roads helped in the difficult travel of that era.   These were roads made of planks, using milled timber, 4 x 4, laid on 4 x 4 joists, with a slight slope for drainage.   No nails or spikes were used, yet they could carry double the weight of an unimproved road.

The pebble ridge that ran parallel to Lake Ontario seemed a natural place to build a "turnpike."   By 1818 Ridge Road was "the best in the United States," running from Sodus, between Rochester and Syracuse, to Lewiston, on the Niagara River.

LeRoy, Genesee Co., situated at the crossroads of two major wagon trails, was one of the first boom towns in the country.

In addition to the inns, hotels and taverns that blossomed were hostelries.   Some of these buildings still are in use today; some were not that reliable.   Log huts provided many a traveler with crude quarters.

Of great importance in the development and settlement of Western New York and furthering the success of the fledgling Holland Land Co. was the renowned Erie Canal. It was from WNY that the first demands for a canal originated. Joseph Ellicott, agent of the HLC at Batavia, nurtured the project with invaluable support, stating that the projected canal would be "an object of vast importance to the United States." (letter to Simeon De Witt, 30 July 1808, *HLC-WNY Canal Documents, p 3*) The canal would connect the Hudson River (and thus the Atlantic Ocean) to Lake Erie (and thus the Great Lakes, eliminating the bottleneck of Niagara Falls).

There were other supporters, as well as detractors. However, it was DeWitt Clinton, a staunch supporter for such a canal who, with unceasing efforts, eventually brought it to fulfillment. He was the governor of New York from 1817 to 1823.

Joining him in a canal commission were Gouverneur Morris, Stephen van Renssalaer and others. Known as "Clinton's Ditch," the political battle was eventually won and New York State's legislature agreed to fund the enterprise in 1811, after being turned down by the federal government. Work was carried on by gangs of workers, numbering in the thousands, many of them European immigrants. "Swamp fever" took a heavy toll among the workmen.

In the debate over the location of the western terminus of the Erie Canal where it would empty into Lake Erie and hence all of the Great Lakes, proponents for the villages of both Buffalo and Black Rock argued their case. The canal commissioners chose Buffalo, which later merged with Black Rock. Thus the explosive growth of that area was born. Nearby Lockport grew from 3 families in 1821 to 337 families by Jan. 1822.

When the surveyors came to Monroe Co. in 1819 to lay out the route through the fledgling community of Rochester, it was found to be necessary to carry water over water, as the Genesee R. intersected the route. The aqueduct thus engineered was a marvel, it being 802 feet long with nine "great, beautiful arches." It is still to be seen in Rochester, located where the river flows under the Broad St. bridge, whose arches are the same. Broad St. was built along the bed of the former canal.

Various sections opened as they were completed. By 1820, Syracuse saw 73 boats at its section.

The canal was 40 feet wide and 4 feet deep. Eighty-three locks, including 5 with a rise of 66 feet in Lockport, overcame the 571-foot difference in the levels of the bodies of water. Various sections were completed in 1820 and 1823 and the canal was opened with elaborate celebrations in 1825--an engineering marvel of its time at a cost of $7 million. Beginning at Buffalo, the *Seneca Chief* left for Albany. Soon a flotilla joined it, and a week later it floated into the Albany basin where a 24-gun salute and many speeches greeted the ships. As it then continued down the Hudson, the banks of the river became alive with bonfires, cannon salutes, and cheers. Eventually steaming up the East R., on 4 Nov. DeWitt Clinton slowly poured the keg of water from Lake Erie into the Atlantic Ocean--the "Wedding of the Waters."

The canal cut travel time by one-third and shipping costs nine-tenths. Originally built for freight transport, passenger carriers soon developed, paving the way for the flood of immigrants that soon followed.

Packet boats first offered canal travel to the public in 1820, the Erie Canal Navigation Company being organized then. They were drawn by horses or mules, with fresh ones stabled about every 14 miles along the route. An average trip cost 4 cents a mile, this making the cost of a trip from Utica to Rochester in 1823 requiring 2 days and 2 nights $6.25. This price included meals and lodging on the boat; it was 3 cents a mile without the meals! Some traveled in large numbers at a penny a mile. Of an overnight trip to Rochester and back to Buffalo a traveler wrote "...it is altogether cheaper than staying at home."

Packet boat and passengers. Note team on the towpath on the right.

Aqueduct carrying the Erie Canal over the Genesee River, Rochester, N.Y.; may still be seen. Broad St. runs over its top.

Competition soon arose. After bitter feuding, opponents decided that merging was more profitable than competing. Packet boats multiplied, and prices dropped. By 1827 there were 6 lines of boats operating between Buffalo and New York, using 160 boats boats towed by 882 horses, and employing several hundred.

Canal boats' size was originally limited by the 90 by 15 foot size of the locks. Although there were disadvantages to canal boat travel, it was much less difficult than the hardships of stagecoach travel. The shallow depth of the canal lessened sinking worries, and gliding along was comfortable. Low bridges were problems, requiring passengers to prostate themselves to prevent being swept overboard!

The smaller packets carried 40 to 50 passengers; the later larger ones 100. The long cabins were lined with cushioned benches; in the center were tables for eating. There was also a small library and a writing desk supplied with ink. The benches folded out into beds.

Line boats stowed passengers in with the freight. They traveled 3 miles an hour rather than 4; they were more comfortable as well as cheaper. Travel on the canal "became an interesting and often convivial social unit. Frequent additions and departures from crowded wharves brought continual variety... Whist, draughts, and backgammon were popular diversions. The passengers joined in song, and somtimes one would read aloud for the edification of the company. The packet cabin became a ready forum for debate on any subject from temperance to politics..." [Shaw, pp 210, 211]

By 1836 there were 3,000 boats on the canal; by 1826 Albany had had nearly 7,000 boats arrive from the West.

> I've got a mule, her name is Sal,
> Fifteen years on the Erie Canal!
> She's a good old worker and a good old pal!
> Fifteen years on the Erie Canal!
> We've hauled some barges in our day,
> Filled with lumber, coal and hay,
> And ev'ry inch of the way we know
> From Albany to Buffalo.
>
> Low bridge, ev'rybody down,
> Low bridge, for we're goin' thru a town!
> And you'll always know your neighbor,
> You'll always know your pal,
> If you've ever navigated on the Erie Canal.
>
> We'd better get along, old gal,
> Fifteen years on the Erie Canal!
> 'Cause you bet your life I'd never part with Sal!
> Fifteen years on the Erie Canal!
> Giddap there, Sal, here comes a lock,
> We'll make Rome 'bout six o'clock,
> Just one more trip and then we'll go
> Right back home to Buffalo.
>
> [Repeat chorus]

This song, The Erie Canal ,was the popular American Work Song of its day. [Author apparently unknown]

Work that took several years beginning in 1836 deepened and widened the canal 70 feet wide and 7 feet deep, with double locks of 110 by 18 feet. A number of branches, several becoming important, were built. WNY demanded a waterway to connect the

Erie Canal with the Allegany River, but the eventual Genesee Valley feeder was doomed to failure soon after completion by the advent of the railroad. However, it is the building of it that brought Rose (Duhan) Oyer's grandfather to Cuba, Catt. Co. in the 1860's (after having worked on the enlarging, including in the Lockport area where Rose's father was born). Where would this story be without that having taken place?!

By 1838 approximately one-half of all the stock in the transportation lines on the waterway were owned or controlled by citizens of Rochester.

The Erie Canal's accomplishments were many: it contributed to New York City's financial development, opening the way for New York City to become the chief Atlantic port; opened the eastern markets to the farm products of the midwest after having been responsible for the immigration into that area; and it helped to create a number of large cities, as well as the peopling of the countryside. As an example of the country's growth because of the canal, growth of Rochester was aided by the arrival of furniture, sugar, molasses, rum; canal-side docks, wharves and warehouses. High quality grain, milled in Rochester, was to be shipped principally by canal. By 1838 Rochester was known the world over as the greatest producer of flour! All in all, the canal and its consequences became a huge financial success for many.

Many of the settlers from the East who went West to pioneer land in such states as Ohio, Ill., Mich. and Ind. traveled the canal to help get there.

With the advent of railroads in the 1850's, some branches' usefulness was destroyed, as well as the canal's long-haul profitability. In the early twentieth century, a complete renovation, rerouting, and conversion brought about the Barge Canal, used commercially profitably for many years. In further need of extensive work and being unsuitable for today's larger boats, it is now being developed as a recreational "gem" for New York State instead, with tow paths becoming bike/hiking paths. However, it continues to be used commercially to some extent mainly by barges. In winter, the water level is lowered and the canal is closed down.

[Sources: HLC rec at Olin Library, Cornell Univ.; Rundel Library, Rochester; Smith; Shaw; Hosmer; Erie Canal Museum, Syracuse; Col Ency.]

ABBREVIATIONS, ABBREVIATED FORMS AND SOURCES
Does Not Include Oyer Family Informants

Adams' Catt - Adams, William. History Gazetteer & Biographical
 Memorial of Cattaraugus County. Syracuse, N.Y.:1893.
adm - administrator
AHA - A. Hawley Arnold (#278iii), collaborating researcher and
 author; his initials supplant identity of his sources.
ae - aged
AHC - Ashford Hollow Cemetery, Cattaraugus County
Altenburg Inf - Alice Altenburg, Allegany, N.Y.
Amish/Mennon -"Amish", World Book Encyclopedia (1976) Vol I, p
 408. "Mennonites", World Book Encyclopedia (1976) Vol XIII,
 pp 325-326.
Ash - Ashford
b - born
Barker - Barker, William V. H. Early Families of Herkimer
 County, New York. Baltimore: Genealogical Publishing:1986
Barzun and Graff - Barzun, Jacques and Henry F. Graff, The
 Modern Researcher. New York: Harcourt, Brace and World, Inc.,
 1970.
Beach Inf 1 - Mrs. Robert (Jean) Popp, Walton, N.Y.
Beers' Alleg - Beers, F.W. History of Allegany County, New York.
 New York: 1879.
Beers' Herk - Beers, F.W. History of Herkimer County, New York.
 New York: 1879.
Beers' Mont - Beers, F.W. History of Montgomery and Fulton
 Counties, New York. New York: 1878.
betw - between
Bflo - Buffalo, Erie County, N.Y.
Blackall Inf 1 - Margaret Nannen, Ellicottville, N.Y. (deceased)
Blackall Inf 2 - Paddy Waldron, 39 Park Dr., Dublin 6, Ireland.
Blackall-Duhan-Lynd church records - Holy Name of Mary Roman
 Catholic Church, Ellicottville, N.Y., courtesy of Father
 McCarthy.
Bolton-ScotchIrish - Bolton, Charles K, Scotch Irish Pioneers in
 Ulster and America, Boston: Bacon and Brown, 1910.
Botsford - Botsford, Cattaraugus County Gazetteer, 1874-75 [n/a]
Botsford Gen - author n/a, Botsford Family Genealogy. Balti-
 more: Gateway Press, revised edition of Vol. II, 1983.
bp - baptized
Briggs - Briggs, Erasmus, History of the Original Town of
 Concord, Erie Co., N.Y. Rochester: Union & Advertiser
 Company, 1883.
bro -brother
Brown Gen - Gregory Schwarz, Enfield Center, N.H.
Brumbaugh & Faust- Brumbaugh and Faust. Lists of Swiss
 Emigrants in the Eighteenth Century to the American Colonies,
 Vols I and II. Washington D.C.: National Genealogical Society,
 1925.
Buck and McDermott - Buck, Clifford and William McDermott
 (editor). Eighteenth Century Documents of the Nine Partners
 Patent, Dutchess County, New York, Vol X. Baltimore: Gateway
 Press, 1979.
bur - buried
ca - circa (about)
Cam - Camillus, Onondaga County, N.Y.
Catt - Cattaraugus County, N.Y.
CCC - Civilian Conservation Corps, active during the 1930's.
CCHM - Cattaraugus County Historical Museum, Little Valley, N.Y.
cem - cemetery
ch - children

Chau - Chautauqua County, N.Y.
Churchill's Oswego - Churchill, John C. (editor). Landmarks of
   Oswego County Syracuse, N.Y.: D. Mason & Co, 1895.
Child - Child, Hamilton. Gazetteer and Business Directory of
   Cattaraugus County, N.Y. 1874-75. Syracuse: Printed at the
   Journal office, 1874
Clark Inf 1 - Mrs. Jean Popp, Walton, N.Y.
Clark Inf 2 - Clark Steinhardt, Two Rivers, Wis.
Clayton - Clayton, W. Woodford. History of Steuben County,
   Philadelphia: 1879
Clinton Papers - The Public Papers of George Clinton, First
   Governor of New York New York State, 1902.
Comp Amer Gen - Virkus, Frederick Adams. The Abridged
   Compendium of American Genealogy, 7 v. A. N. Marquis, 1925-
   42.
Col Ency - The New Columbia Encyclopedia, edited by Harris and
   Levey, New York & London: Columbia University Press, 1975.
Ct/ct - court
d - died
dec - deceased
d y - died young
dau - daughter
Drake's Boston - Drake, Samuel A. Landmarks of Boston, Boston,
   Mass.: Little, Brown, 1972, c 1960
DRC - Dutch Reformed Church
Duhan Inf - Margaret Nannen, Ellicottville, N.Y. (deceased)
ed - edited/editor
Elb - Elbridge Township, Onondaga County, N.Y.
EldC - Elderkin Cemetery, Cattaraugus County, N.Y.
Ellis Inf 1 - Mrs. Sally Dwyer, Victor, N.Y.
Ellis Inf 2 - Mrs. Jane Morris, Pittsford, N.Y.
Ellis Inf 3 - Mrs. Faith Finster Ellis, Springville, N.Y.
Ellis Inf 4 - William Ellis, Sardinia, Erie Co., N.Y.
Ellvl - Ellicottville
Everts' Catt - Everts, L.H., History of Cattaraugus County, New
   York. New York: 1879.
exec - executed/executor
Faesch Gen - "Johann Jacob Faesch, Morris County Iron Master."
   The North Jersey Highlander. Vol 3, Issue 56 (Fall 1979).
FB - family bible
Fauchner - Fauchner, Henen Botsford. Botsford Family Genealogy
   - The Line of Joseph, Revised Edition, Vol. II. Fauchner, 1983
Fed - federal
FHC - Forest Hill Cemetery   [location n/a]
Frank Inf 1 - Sterling Kimball, Burton, Mich.
French - French, J H LL.D. Gazetteer of the State of New York.
   Syracuse: R.P. Smith, 1860.
Frkf - Frankfort, Herkimer County, N.Y.
Frklnv - Franklinville, Cattaraugus County, N.Y.
FrktC - Franktown Cemetery, Ashford Township, Cattaraugus
   County
Frothingham - Frothingham, Washington. History of Fulton
   County, Syracuse: D. Mason & Co., 1892
g s - gravestone
GF - German Flat(t)s, Herkimer County, N.Y.
Gratz - Dr. Delbert Gratz, Mennonite Historical Librarian-
   Genealogist, Bluffton College, Bluffton, Ohio
GrC - Green Cemetery, Great Valley Twp., Cattaraugus County
grdau - granddaughter
grson - grandson
GrV - Great Valley, Cattaraugus County, N.Y.

Hart and Kreider - Hart, Simon and Harry Kreider. Lutheran
  Church in New York and New Jersey 1722-1760. New York and
  New England: United Lutheran Synod of New York. 1920.
Hasen Case - North Jersey Highlands Historical Society. The
  Remarkable Case of Peter Hasenclever. New Jersey: North
  New Jersey Highlands Historical Society, 1970.
Hasen Notice - Homes/Holmes, Henry A. LL.D. Notice of Peter
  Hasenclever, an Early Iron Manufacturer. 1874/5; reprinted in
  Transactions, Albany Institute, vol VIII, 1876.
Herk - Herkimer Township or County, N.Y.
Hosmer - Hosmer, Howard C. Monroe Country (1821-1971).
  Rochester, N.Y.: Flower City Printing, 1971.
Hostetler - Hostetler, Rev Harvey. Descendants of Jacob
  Hochstetler, Elgin, Ill.: Brethren Publishing Co., 1912. Also
  Descendants of Barbara Hochstetler and Christian Stutzman ,
  Elgin, Ill.: Brethren Publishing Co. 1912.
inf - informant
inv - inventory
Ire - Ireland
Jacobus - Jacobus, Donald L. and Waterman, Edgar F. Hale,
  House and Related Families. Hartford, Conn: Conn. Historical
  Soc., 1952.
Jeff - Jefferson County, N.Y.
Jester - Jester, Annie Lash and Hiden, Martha Woodroof.
  Adventurers of Purse and Person, Virginia, 1607-1625. Princeton
  University Press: 1956
Johnson - Volumes of Sir William Johnson Vol V. Prepared by the
  Div. of Archives and History, Albany, N.Y.: Univ. of State of
  New York, 1927.
Jones, Geo - Jones, Geo. O. et. al. History of Lincoln, Oneida and
  Vilas Counties, Wis. Minneapolis-Winona, Minn.: 1964
Jones - Jones, Henry Z. Jr. The Palatine Families of New York
  1710 Vol I & II. Pub. by the author, Universal City, Calif.:
  1985.
KB - Kill Buck, Great Valley Twp., Cattaraugus County, N.Y.
Klock - Klock, Col. Jacob. History of the Town Of Schuyler
  Manuscript at Herkimer Co. Historical Society: 1930
KndmC - Kingdom Cemetery, Van Buren, Onondaga County, N.Y.
Knittle - Knittle, Walter A. Early 18th Century Palatine
  Emigration. Philadelphia: Dorrance & Co., 1937.
Kreider - Dern, John, Harry J. Kreider et. al. The Albany Proto-
  col, Wilhelm Christoph Berkenmeyer's Chronicle of Lutheran
  Affairs in New York Colony, 1731-1750. Ann Arbor, Mich.:
  United Lutheran Synod of New York and New England, 1971.
Langston & Buck - Langston, A. L. and Buck, J. O. Pedigrees of
  Some of the Emperor Charlemagne's Descendants, Vol. II, n.p.
  USA: 1974
Larabee Inf1 - Mrs. Jessie Buller, Taft, Calif.
Larabee Inf2 - Fred Rathbun, Littleton, Colo.
LM - Lorraine Marvin, Historian, Gowanda, N.Y.
LR - land records
LS - Lorna Spencer, Historian, Cattaraugus County Historical
  Museum, Little Valley, N.Y.
LV - Little Valley, Cattaraugus County Seat, N.Y.
Lynd Inf 1 - George Lynd, Rochester, N.Y.
Lynd Inf 2 - Lorraine Purnell, Salem, Ore.
m - married
MacWethy - MacWethy, Lou D. The Book of Names Especially
  relating to the Early Palatines and the First Settlers in the
  Mohawk Valley. Boston: Genealogical Pub. Co., 1969.
McGill - McGill, Ralph. "There is Time Yet." Atlantic Monthly,
  Sept. 1944.

Merrill - Merrill, Mrs. George Drew. History of Allegany County-
    A Centennial Memorial. Alfred, NY: Ferguson Pub., Ed 1896.
MGC - Maple Grove Cemetery, Onondaga County, N.Y.
Miller - Miller, J.C. Origins of the American Revolution. Stan-
    ford, Calif: Stanford University Press, 1843-1959.
MK - Mohawk River, Valley, N.Y.
Mon - Monroe County, N.Y.
Mont - Montgomery County, N.Y.
Morrison's Windham - Morrison, Leonard A., The History of
    Windham in New Hampshire 1719 - 1883. Boston, Mass.:
    Cupples, Upham & Co., 1883.
MRC - Miller Rural Cemetery, Schuyler, Herkimer Co.
ms(s) - manuscript(s)
MWC - Maplewood Cemetery, Springville, Erie County, N.Y.
MtHC - Mt. Hope Cemetery, Ashford Twp., Cattaraugus County
n/a - not available
Nellis - Nellis, Milo. "Col. Jacob Klock, Patriot." Enterprise and
    News, May 23 1928.
NJ extracts - Nelson, William, ED. Documents Relating to the
    Colonial History of New Jersey. Vol XXV. Paterson, NJ: The
    Call Printing and Publishing Co, 1903. pp 344-345.
NO - New Orleans, Louisiana
NP - New Petersburg, Herkimer County, N.Y.
obit - obituary
Onon - Onondaga County, N.Y.
Osw - Oswego County, N.Y.
Oyer Gen 1 - Verle and Margaret Oyer, Gibson City, Ill.
Oyer Gen 2 - Oyer, Darrell. Oyers in America, 1982; Descendants
    of Christian Oyer and Katherine Zehr, March, 1982. Alexandria,
    Va.
Oyer Gen 3 - Dr. and Mrs. Hermann Guth, Saarbrucken,
    W.Germany
Oyer Gen 4 - Gordon Oyer, Champaign, Ill.
Oyer Gen 5 - David Eyer, Ligonier, Penn.
Oyer Gen 6 - Dr. Hermann, Ministerialrat, Saarbrucken, W.
    Germany
Oyer Gen 7 - Paul Anthon Nielson, Interlaken, Switz.
Oyer Gen 8 - Hubert Eyer, Naters, Switz.
p/pp - page/pages
Palmer Gen - Donald Hinman, Endicott, N.Y.
Pearson's Alb - Pearson, Jonathan. First Settlers of Albany Co.,
    N.Y. Baltimore: Genealogical Publishing Co (reprint), 1976,
    1978, 1984. Material from: J. Munsell, 1872.
Pearson's Schenec - Pearson, Jonathan. Genealogies of the
    Descendants of the First Settlers of Schenectady 1662-1800.
    Baltimore: Genealogical Publishing Co (reprint), 1976, 1982.
poss - possibly
PR - probate records
prob - probably
PSO - unsourced research notes or conclusion of Phyllis Oyer
pub - publisher
rec - recorded at/records
Reid - Reid, W. Max. The Mohawk Valley: Its Legends and its
    History 1609-1780. Harrison, NY: Harbor Hill Books, 1979
    (reprint).
res - reside
Reynolds - Reynolds, Cuyler. Hudson Mohawk Genealogical and
    Family Memoirs. 4 Volumes. n.p.: Lewis Historical Publishing Co.
    1911.
Roch - Rochester, Monroe County, N.Y.
SA - Stone Arabia, Herkimer County, N.Y.
Sala - Salamanca, Cattaraugus County, N.Y.

SC - Sandy Creek, Oswego County, N.Y.
Schuy - Schuyler Township, Herkimer County, N.Y.
Schweiz FN - Familiennamenbuch der Schweiz (The Book of Family
   Names of Switzerland).AG Zurich: Polygraphischer Verlag,
   1969.
Schweiz HB - Historisch-Biographisches Lexikon der Schweiz
   Dritter Band. Neuenburg: Egolf-Guttingen [n/a]
Shaw - Shaw, Ronald E. Erie Water West - A History of the Erie
   Canal 1792-1854. n.p.: Univ. of Ky. Press, 1966
SHC - Sunset Hill Cemetery, Ellicottville Township, Cattaraugus
   County, N.Y.
sic - copied correctly--quoted exactly
Smith - Smith, H. Perry. History of Erie County, Volume I.
   Syracuse, N.Y.: 1884.
Smith Gen - Smith, Brian; Chatham, Ontario, Canada
Snell - Snell, Ada. Palatines Along the Mohawk. South Hadley,
   Mass.: Snell, 1948.
sp - sponsor
Spieler - Spieler, Gerhard. Peter Hasenclever, Industrialist.
   Linden, NJ: New Jersey Historical Society, Vol 59 No 4, Oct.
   1941.
Sprvl - Springville, Erie County, N.Y.
SR - surrogate records
st - state
Steu - Steuben County, N.Y.
Strassburger - Strassburger, Ralph LL.D. Pennsylvania German
   Society Vol XLII. Birdsboro, Penn: The Penn. German Society,
   1934.
SUNY - State University of New York, located in various cities
TCC - Thomas Corners Cemetery, Ashford Township, Cattaraugus
   County, N.Y.
TR - town records
twp - township
unm - unmarried
Valaisan WB - Nouvel Armorial Valaisan--Neues Walliser
   Wappenbuch (New Wallis Coats-of-Arms Book). Saint-Maurice:
   Editions Du Scex, 1974.
Van Slyke Gen - Judith Rutherford, Silver Springs, N.Y.
Vedder Gen - Vedder, Edwin Henry. The Vedder Family in America
   1657-1985. n.p.: Henry Edwin Vedder, 1987.
Vedder Inf I - Margaret (Mrs. Bruce) Vedder, Auckland, New
   Zealand
VM Oyer Gen - Oyer, Verle and Margaret. Joseph Oyer 1814-1866
   Pioneer Immigrant. Gibson City, Ill: Verle and Margaret Oyer,
   1963, 1984.
Vosburgh CR - Vosburgh, Royden Woodward. Early NY Church
   Records Transcribed and Edited by the NY Genealogical and
   Biographical Society. New York: New York Genealogical and
   Biographical Society, 1913-1917.
VR - vital records
WarC - Warners Cemetery, Onondaga County, N.Y.
Watson - Watson, Estelle Clark. Loyalist Clarks, Badgleys and
   Allied Families. Rutland, Vt: Tuttle Pub., 1954.
WdlnC - Woodlawn Cemetery, Sandy Creek, Oswego County, N.Y.
Weiser - Weiser, The Rev Frederick S. Ebbes fur Alles-Ebber;
   Ebbes fur Dich Something For Everyone; Something For You.
   Breinigsville, Penn: The Penn. German Society, 1980.
Widrig Inf - Mrs. Lois Blotner, Amarillo, Tex.
wit - witness
Wmst/WmstC - Williamstown & Williamstown Cemetery, Oswego
   County, N.Y.
Woodruff Inf 1 - Jean Blessing, Rochester, N.Y.

Woodruff Inf 2 – Mildred Hammond, Franklinville, N.Y.
Woodruff Inf 3 – Robert Woodruff, Dansville, N.Y.
WWI,WWII – World Wars I and II
WV – West Valley, Cattaraugus County, N.Y.
y-m-d – years, months, days
Young – Young, Owen D. The Palatines of New York State.
    Johnstown, NY: The Palatine Society of the United Evangelical
    Lutheran Church of New York and New England Inc., 1953.
Young's CHAU – Young, Andrew H. The History of Chautauqua
    County, N.Y. Buffalo: Matthews & Warren, 1875.
yr/yrs – year/years

use of decimal point in person's number, i.e. 112, 112.1 – insertion
    made after numbering completed, done to eliminate need for
    renumbering; has no pedigree significance
/ – used to denote original/subsequent names, i.e. Theobald/David;
    Ruth Ellen/Ella, the latter being the name used
underlining of a name indicates name known by, i.e. Johan Jacob

**ALL PLACES IN TEXT ARE IN NEW YORK STATE UNLESS
OTHERWISE NOTED**

INDEX

This index has features designed to aid the researcher.

1. A number affixed at the end of a given name indicates the generation from the progenitor (the first in America). With rare exception, this refers to Frederick Oyer[1].
2. The "&" between male and female represents man and wife.
3. Listing of names with commas but no spaces between names shows they are listed from census records.
4. Pre-20th century churches/religions are indexed, as are references to military units. All wars are indexed.
5. Non-capitalized surnames usually indicate non-allied. There is no other significance of capitalization.
6. Numbers refer to the page number, not the ancestral number.

JOSEPH 264
MINA 264
NICHOLAS 264
ROSIE 306
_____, CHARLES 217
_____, Floyd 149
100th NY Vols 144
154th Inf 146
154th Reg't NY Vols . . . 165
2nd Reg't Wisc Vol Inf . . 158
44th Reg't NY Vols 122
4th Iowa Cavalry 136
64th NY Regt 143
95th Co 6th Reg Marines . 197
9th NY Cavalry 145
9th NY Heavy Art 152
A'HEARNE
  COLLEEN 277
ABBOTT
  CAROLE 296
  JOHN 296
  KAREN MARIE8 296
Abeel 116
Abers 213
Abrams
  F LOUISE 197
ACOME
  JAMES 300
  ROBERT MICHAEL9 300
  SANDRA 300
ADAMCZAK
  CAROL 313
  JANET DEBORAH 313
  JOSEPH PAUL 313
  MARY ANN9 313
  MICHAEL JOSEPH 313

Adams 58, 116
  John Quincy 177
ADDIE
  SIMMONS 228
AHRENS
  GRETCHEN 174
  MARTIN 174
Aiyer . . . . v, 31
Aldenburg
  Analee,Willie 133
  Charles 133
Aldrich
  Delana 137
  Delana/Deana 136
ALLEN
  ALMEDA 136
  BURTON C 136
  CLINTON D 136
  ELIZABETH J 136
  FLORRINE F5 136
  FRED O 136
  LaPEARL 136
  MARY 136
  MARY E (_____) 136
  ORSON F 136
ALTENBURG v
  ABRAHAM 133, 182
  ADDIE 182
  ANNA 133
  CATHARINE 133
  Daniel 133
  ELIZABETH 133
  EMMA JANE5 133
  EPHRAIM 133
  FREDERICK F 133
  GEORGE 133
  HARRIET 133

ALTENBURG (cont'd)

HOWARD6 183
John 133
MARGARET/MAGGIE 133
Sarah 92
SARAH/SALLY 133
THOMAS 133
WILLIAM 133
ALTENBURG families 133
ALTMAN
JOAN9 331
SANDRA 331
SUSAN 331
WILLIAM JOHN 331
American Baptists 28
American Company 337
American Lutheran 29
Ames
Stanley ii
Amish 9, 26, 339, 341
Amish-Mennonite 9
Ammann
Jacob 7
Anabaptists 8, 9
Anderson
DORIS6 176
Ella 120
Ella (Oyer) 175, 176
ELLADE 176
GRETCHEN 330
Helen 257
JENNIFER L9 331
JEREMY M 331
JESSICA A 331
MAUREEN A 331
MICHAEL 330
Ralph 28
Roland 120, 176
ANDRESKI
DEBORAH 201
ANDREWS
ELLA M.5 191
HARRIET LOUISE6 191
HAZEL E 191
WILLIAM 191
ANGIE
EULA MAE 226
WILLIAM 226
Anglicans 27
ANTAL
FLORENCE 293
JACK MICHAEL 293
Appleton
SARAH 173
ARMSTRONG
Marion 58
Marion & _____ 58
Mrs H K 68
ARNOLD
ALBERT HAWLEY . . i, 103, 121, 284
ALBERT HEPPENSTALL 284
Benedict 45
BENJAMIN LOUIS9 284

Betsey 220
Charles 220
CHARLES SHEP 113, 114
DAVID MITCHELL8 284
DOREEN 284
ELIZABETH 284
EMILIE SIOBHAN9 284
EMMA 113, 114
JAMES KAPLE 284
Jas I & Anna C (Mundlein) . . . 284
Samuel P 220
SUSAN 284
Wayne i
Assembly of God 28, 29
Auer . . . . vi, 8
AUL
AGNES JONES6 222
CARLTON H 222
EDWARD 270
MARTHA 222, 270
PAULINE (_____) 270
RICHARD 222, 270
RUTH7 . . . . 222, 269
VICTORIA 270
AUYER v
(Wart) 190
ADELBERT 152, 193
ALICE 160
ALONZO L 153, 194
ANDREA JANE 291
ANITA JEAN 237, 290
ANNA 232, 233
ANNETT G 149
ANVENETTE 150
ARDIS ANN 237, 289
BARBARA 236, 237
BARBARA OLA8 287
BETSEY H 147
BETTY JEAN 290
BURTIE 152
CAROLYN 286
CHARLES JACOB5 . . . . . . 149, 191
CHRISTIAN 109
Christina 109
CRAIG RICHARD8 286
CYRUS DAVID 109, 160
Daniel 75, 76, 93, 160
DAVID H 237, 290
DIANA 288
DONNA 290
DORA 237
EARL L 194, 237
EDWARD WILLIAM 149
ELIJAH 152
ELISHA J5 153
ELIZABETH 287
EMILY AMELIA 108, 158
EMMA 152, 191
EMMA JEAN 236, 286
ERWIN WEST 194
ESTHER 236
ETHEL L 191

AUYER (cont'd)

FANNY	191
Flossie	152
FLOYD LAVERNE	191,233
FOSTER CLARK7	236, 287
FOSTER JACOB	103, 153
FRANCES	193
FRANCES W	191
Francis/Frank	103, 108, 149, 151
FRANK A	149,191
FRED	150
GEORGE	153
GERTRUDE ELLA5	147, 190
HARRIET	103, 149, 150-1, 153, 194
HAZEL	190, 191, 236
HELEN5	150
IDA	191
JACOB A	153
James	31, 76, 108, 109, 149, 153, 158
James & Martha	109
JAMES3	107, 109
JASON	288
JEFFREY ALLEN	286
JEREMY	288
JESSIE	160, 194, 199
JILL NICOLE8	290
JONATHAN	288
JOSEPH W	153
JOSEPHINE	153
JULIA ANN	109, 158
JULIE ANNE	286
KATE A	150
KATHY	286
KELLI8	289
KENNETH GEORGE	286
KENNETH WILLIAM	237, 289
KEVIN AVERY	289
KIM MARIE	288
KRISTA B	288
LANCE LESLIE8	290
LAVERNE WENDALL6	193, 236
LELAND6	152
LEOTA F7	233
LESLIE F	194, 237
LETICIA M	108
LONNIE5	150
LORI	288
LYNN ANN8	290
MABEL	233
MARGARET MARY	103, 151
MARIE AGNES	290
MARSHA	289
Martha	109, 287
MARTHA JANE	107, 108, 156, 198
MARY	150
MARY CAROLYN	237, 288
MARY E	108, 157
MARY E/Matie	153
MARY FRANCES	290
MARY LUCY	193
MICHAEL LaVERNE	286
MICHELE9	288

MYRNA6	194
NELLIE L	149
Parthena	108
PATIENCE	149
PATRICIA JEAN	290
Peter	194, 288
PETER J	103, 147, 148, 153, 193
RACHEL	237
Ralph	107, 121
RALPH PETER6	194, 236
REBECCA	288
RICHARD7	236, 237, 286, 290
ROBERT WARREN	289
ROENA	150
ROMAIN/ROMAINE	103, 152
RUTH	236
SANDRA LEE8	289
SARAH ANN	108, 157
SIMON	103, 149
SOLOMON	109
SOPORONA	150
STEPHEN E7	237, 290
SUSAN/SUSIE	194, 290
Sylvia	152
Tremaine	152
VALENTINE	103, 150, 283
VALERIE	288
VERA LOUISE7	233
VERNA MAY	236, 287
VIRGINIA	236
WALTER LEON	237, 290
WARREN GERALD7	237, 289
WARREN H	194, 237
WILLIAM H.6	191, 232
WILLIAM I	147, 190
WILLIAM RALPH	236, 288
WILLIAM8	288
WILLIS5	152
YVONNE	288
ZADEAN	289
Auyer—Oyer explanation	107

Auyter

W H	150

AVERILL

MARION	231
Ayarer	vi
Ayer	vi
FREDERICK	254
Hans	3
Ayre	vi

AYRER

	v, vi
Elizabeth	47
Fredrick	38
Freiderich	335
Friederik	35
George	60
Jacob	60

BABCOCK

AMY LYNN9	268
BRYCE ASHLEY	268
DARRYL ASHLEY	268
EMILY RUTH	268

BABCOCK (cont'd)
Hester 138, 139
Mary Sophia 232
PHYLLIS 268
BACHMAN
Erna 212
Bacon
Francis 29
BAGWELL
JACQUELINE 224
MICHAEL 224
RICHARD 224
STEPHANIE 224
Bailey
Chauncey 125
Daniel 124
Deborah 124
Hannah J 124
Lewis 124
Baker
B 94
BARBARA 279
CALVIN 279
Clara Jones 267
David 63
EDNA 195, 267
EDWARD 195
Ellen 94
Lyda 172
MARK RYAN9 279
TYLER CHAD 279
BALDRIDGE
SUE DELL 295
BALDWIN
BRADLEY SCOTT 275
CYNTHIA 274
Jas E & Edith E (Tracy) . . . 281
KENNETH CLARK 274
RESA LOUISE 281
SHERRI ANN9 275
Ballard
Adam 142
Eliza M 142
BALLOU
CHARITY 58, 144
Charles 58
David (Blue) 58
Eliza 58
Eunice 58
Herbert Eugene 58, 144
James M 58
John 58
Mary 58
Matie 58
Polly 62
Sophia 98
Spencer 58
William 58
Ballou (Blue)
DAVID 53
Bancker 116
Baptist 26, 172
Baptists 27

BARBER
Ira 72
Sanford 72
BARGY v
Barbara 72
Catherine 71, 72, 85
Dorothea/Dorothy 71, 85
Dorothy Ann 71
Elizabeth 71
Garrett 71
Jacob 71, 85
Jacob & Dorothea (Frank) . . 132
Jacob P 85
James J 72
Lawrence 71
Maria/Polly 67
Mary 71, 132
Michael 71
Nancy 71, 72, 89
Peter 67, 71, 89
Peter & Eliz 89
Polly 71, 72
BARGY/BIRCHI/BIRKEY families 4, 65, 70
Barker 55, 71, 72
BARNES
Helen 328
BARNETT
John Wm & Eliz (Hider) . . . 192
LAURA ANN 192
Sarah Jane 192, 198
Wm & Elizabeth (Hider) . . . 198
BARNHART
RACHEL 262
BARNHART, _____ 262
Barrett
Eliza 53, 58
MARY JANE7 221
BARRETT, _____ 221
BARRY
Shirley 212
BARTELO
KATHY 286
BARTON
John & Millicent 235
OLIVE 235
Barzun and Graff 26
BATES
HATTIE H5 157
LILLIE M 232
MARY E.4 157
THEODORE H 157
Wilson & Margaret (_____) . . 157
BATHURST
LEAH 283
BATTAGLIA
CARIN 282
DEBORAH ANN 283
ELLEN 282
JOEL DAVID 283
JOHN MARK 282
KIMBERLY JENNIE 282
LEAH 283

BATTAGLIA (cont'd)

MICHAEL EDWARD8 282
NATHAN MICHAEL9 282
PETER SOMES 283
REBA 282
Russell & Jennie 282
RUTH LYNN 283
Battle of Oriskany 85, 87
Bauman 90
BAXLEY
  GENA (_____) 309
  JOYCE 309
  KATHRYN 309
  LESLIE9 309
  SANDRA 309
  WILLIAM 309
  WILLIAM HERBERT 309
Baxter
  Annie Scott 91
BAY
  BEULAH WINIFRED 278
BEACH
  Addie A 178
  Adeline 178
  AMY (BOWEN) 177
  Augusta,Henrietta,Emma . . . 178
  Augustus 178
  BERTHA 138, 178, 186
  Cornelia 178
  DESSIE 177, 224
  Edson F 178
  ELMER 138
  FRED 177
  Henry 178
  IDA5 138
  Joseph 178
  JULIUS 137, 177, 178
  Julius & Lucy (Mason) 177
  Laura 178
  LUCY 177, 178, 225
  Maria 178
  MARY ELIZABETH 137, 177
  Moses & Mary Eliz (Oyer) . . 178
  MOSES NASH 137
  MOSES T 177
  Moses T & _____ (Nash) . . . 137
  Oscar F 178
  Tyler 178
BEACH families 177
Beardsley
  SARAH H 162
BECKER
  Conrad; Friederich; sister Anna
    Elizabeth; Jacob, ... 11
  Jan Jurrianse 63
  Johann Jacob, wife Maria
    Elizabeth 11
  Peter, wife Elizabeth 11
  Tibalt 60
BEEBE
  CHLOE 134
Beers 46
BEKKER . . . . v, 26, 40, 55

Catherine 63
Dabold/Diebold 35, 63, 73
Dabold & Eliz 59
Elizabeth 63
Henrich 66
Johan 11
MARGARETHA/E 51, 59, 73
Maria 72, 73
Michel, Simon, Mighel, Antony and
  Johan Peter 11
BEKKER family 65
BEKKER/BECKER family 63
BELL 213
  Andrew 90
  KIM 330
BELLAS
  ELEANOR 266
  ELEANOR (OYER) 219
  ERNIE 219, 266
  JERRY8 266
  TIM 266
BELLES, _____ 177
[Benninger's] Reg't 60
Bellinger, Peter. . . . 39, 40, 45,
  46
Bellinger's Reg't . 53, 55, 65, 71, 72
  85, 86, 88, 89
Bender
  Elizabeth 89
BENNETT
  Betsy 56
  CARIN 282
  FLORIS 203
  Helen & Vincent 56
  Helen May 56
  Jane Stewart 56
  John Lansing 56
  Robert H 56
  Vincent 56
Bensley
  Agnes 94
  Sophia 94
Bensley Bros 94
BENSON
  CLARENCE6 196
  DONETTA 242
  FLORENCE (_____) 196, 240
  HENRY 196
  KENNETH7 240
  LAWRENCE 242
  LENA 196
  OLIVE 196, 240
  RAYMOND 196
  RAYMOND6 240
BENTLEY
  Claude & Viola (Gibbs) . . . 283
  SHIRLEY LOUISE/HONEY 283
BENTON
  Julia/Jewell 257
Bercki - see also Bargy . . . 40
BERKBIGLER
  ELLYN MARIE 316

BERKBIGLER (cont'd)
Wayne & _____ 316
Berkenmeyer
  Wilhelm C 24
BERRY
  ELLEN 134
  GARDNER 134
Beuscher
  Anna Dorothea 338
BEY
  LUELLA 225
Beyer
  Marg(aret?) 53
Bialozynski
  see also WISE 258
BICKFORD
  Hazel 56
  Jack 56
  Lawrence 56
  Mary Jane 56
Biggs
  Thankful 77
Birchi/Bargy 9
Bircky/Birkey - see also Bargy
  Peter 71
BISHOP
  BEATRICE 259
  D Geo & Marg (Neiman) . . . 259
  DAVID GEORGE . .208, 259-261, 328
  JANET MARIE 260
  JASON BENJAMIN 330
  MARGARET (NEIMAN) 261
  MARSHA 328
  MARY LYNNE8 . . . . . 260, 328
  MICHAEL RICHARD9 329
  PAUL DOUGLAS7 . . . . 260, 329
  PAUL PATRICK 330
  SAMUEL DAVID 329
  SARAH ROSE 329
  SHAWN DOUGLAS9 330
  SHERRY 329
BISHOP families 261
Black
  ANNA 133
BLACKALL
  CATHERINE 210, 212
  Charles Henry 213
  George 212, 213
  Helena 213
  Jack 213
  Johanna 213
  John 213
  John & Johanna (Scanlon) . . 213
  JOHN & MARY (FALSEY) 213
  Julia 213
  Lizzie 213
  Mary 213
  Mich & Bridget (Marven) . . . 213
  Nancy/Ann 213
  Nellie 213
  Patrick 213
  Thomas 212, 213
BLACKWELL, _____ 194

MYRNA 194
Bleeckers 38
BLESSING
  Bruce 181
  Carol 181
  Gary 181
  Jean 181
  Jennifer 181
  Robert 181
  Sherry 181
BLOSSOM
  Chloe 174
BLOTNER
  Lois 69
  Lyle 69
  Michael 69
BOEHM
  CARL H 218
  VIOLET 218
BOND 226
  98
  M. CAROLYN 286
Book of Mormon 123
BOOTH
  Mary 106, 118
BORK
  Inge iii
BORSBOOM 116
BOSS
  David 101
  Serepta 93
BOSSELER
  CHRISTINE L 296
Boston Tea Party 254
BOTSFORD
  Daniel 142
  Leonora 142
  Wiley S 142
BOUGH
  HAZEL 236
Bouquet, Col. 66
Bovet
  Victor 342
BOWEN 231
  Alzina 126, 127
  AMY 177
  AMY W 126, 177
  Charles W 127
  Clark 127
  Elias 126
  Elias & Lydia (Wellington) . . 126
  ELIZABETH A./LIZZIE 203
  Emily Ann 230
  Francis 126
  GRIFFITH 126
  Henry 127
  Horace & Alzina (Bowen) . . 127
  Hubert E 127
  Levi 126
  Lucinda (_____) 126
  Lydia 126
  MAHAMON 126

BOWEN (cont'd)
MARGARET AUGUSTA5 126
MARGARET E.4 126
SNOWEY ANN5 . . . . . . 126, 177
Viola 126
Walter L 127
BOWEN families 126
BOWMAN
Elizabeth 112
GEORGE M 228
MILDRED 228
BOYCE
DANIEL EDWARD 299
TIMOTHY WILLIAM9 299
VIRGINIA 299
WILLIAM 299
BOYD 213
VERA ALICE 307
BRADLEY
GENEVIEVE CATH/JANE7 . . 216, 264
GERARD 264
JOHN 216, 264
JUDITH (_____) 264
OLIVE/OLLIE6 216
ROBERT E.7 . . . . . . 216, 264
VERA 216, 264
BRADWAY
Nelson 236
Owen Richard 236
VIRGINIA 236
BRAMSON
MARSHA 328
Seymour & Sally 328
BRAMSON-BISHOP
MARSHA 328
Brant
Joseph 40, 45
Bratt 116
Bratts/Pratts 91
Breitenbacher 90
Margaret 72
BREITENBACHER family 65
BRETZER
BENITA LOUISE8 304
FRANCES 304
FRANK WILLIAM 243
FREDERICK WM 304
JACQUELINE 304
JEFFREY 304
JOANNA 304
MARION 243
WILLIAM HENRY7 . . . . . 243, 304
BRIDENBECKER
_____ 107
Delana 102
George 102
MARY 107
BRIGGS
CLIFTON 190
Egbert 190
HAZEL 190
Phoebe 123
Tom W 123

British . 10, 39, 40, 45, 47, 48, 59,
                                 63, 204
British-Iroquois 47
Brockway
Reuben M 55
BRONDART
NELLIE 226
BROOKS
Dever 224
FLOYD D 177
HERMAN C 177
ISA 177
LAURA JEAN 224
LORA JANE 224
M DEVER/DEVERE6 . . . . . 177, 224
Philo & Sally (Boutwell) . . . 177
PHILO JAMES 224
RACHEL 224
ROBERT SIKES 224
SHERRY 329
SNOWEY ANN5 177
TORRANCE BOWEN7 224
William & Odette 329
BROUGHAM
ARLENE JUNE8 . . . . . . 245, 305
BERNICE 245
BETTY (_____) 305
DEAN EARL 306
DONALD EUGENE8 . . . . . 245, 305
DONNA JEAN9 305
EARL 245, 307
EDITH MAE 245
MARGARET (_____) 305
Mrs Earl 203
RICHARD EARL8 . . . . . . 245, 306
ROBERTA (_____) 306
SANDRA KAY9 306
Brower 116
BROWN 255
ADELINE5 135
ANDREW JACKSON 171
Caleb 170
David & Sally (Senter) . . . 172
DAVID M 170
ELIZABETH4 134
Ella 170
FRANCES LORANE/LORRAINE . . . 171
FRANCIS 134
Goetlib 123
JAMES 172
James D 171
JOHN QUINCY ADAMS 171
JULIAETTE/JULIETT 171
LUCINDA P 170, 171
Margareth 47
Marsha A 94
Martha Lucinda 294
Mary 171, 172
ROENA 172
RUTH ELLEN/ELLA 167, 172
SALLY/POLLY 170
Sarah (_____) 170

BROWN (cont'd)

SARAH W 171
Sheldon & Julia'te (Doud) 109, 171
SHELDON P . . . 167, 168, 170, 171
BROWN families 170
BRUDO
  CAROL 269
  ROBERT 269
Brumbaugh & Faust 8, 9
BRUNN
  JANICE 219, 267
  WILLIAM 219, 267
BRYSON
  JULIE 302
BRZOZOWSKI
  KATHLEEN/KATHY 302
  KENNY 302
BUCCINO
  LORI ANN 269
  MICHAEL 269
  NICOLE MARIE 269
BUCK
  AUREL CHARLENE7 . . . . . 242, 301
  CORA BELL5 . . . . . 151, 192
  DANIEL GOODRICH 151, 199
  DONETTA GAY 242
  EDITH ELVIE6 . . . . . . 199, 242
  FREDDIE J 151
  HARRIET (AUYER) ROE 151
  HEATHER 302
  JAMES H 151
  JAMES WARD8 302
  Jas H & Mary Jane (Goodrich) 199
  JULIA MAE 199
  KRISTIN MARY 302
  MARGARET WILLIAMS 302
  Nelson & Sally (_____) . . 151
  PEARL 242
  RODERICK WARD7 . . . . . 242, 302
  SUSAN 199
  WARD EVERETT6 . . . . . 199, 242
Bull Run, Battle of 98
BULLER
  Jessie 138
BULLIS
  Catherine 98
BULTER (sp?)
  Russell 69
  Mary 69
BUNCE
  ANVENETTE 150
BURACH
  ELLEN 165
Burghy/Birkey/Bargy/Birchi
  see also Bargy 17
Burgi 8
Burgoyne 45
  (Gen. John) 48
BURKARD
  ELIZABETH/BETTY 246
BURKARDT
  April 57
  Kris 57

BURKE
  FOSTER 274
  GLADYS 274
Burnetsfield Patent 25
BURNS
  BRENDA 307
  Jennie 291
  MARK OLIVER 307
BURRILL 108
  Betsey 109
  Caroline _____ 109
  Electa 109
  Hannah 109
  Ira R 109
  JACOB 108, 109
  Jacob & Martha (_____) . . 107
  Joshua 109
  Lurania 109
  Lyman 109
  Marriah L 109
  MARTHA JANE 107-109
  Nelson M 109
  Rawsell 109
  Sophronia 109
  William 109
BURRILL families 108
BURSON
  CAROL 269
  COREY BARTHOLOMEW10 269
  DONALD 269
  GEOFFREY STEPHEN9 269
  LORI ANN 269
  PENNY 269
  SUSAN LEIGH 269
BUSH
  ARLENE 201
BUSHEY
  VIRGINIA 236
BUTLER
  CURTIS 200
  EDNA 200
  Loretta 126, 127
BUTTERFIELD
  Carrie (Folts) 254
  Horace G 254
BUTTOLPH
  MARY 173
BUTTON
  Emma 194
BYER
  BETH ANNE8 223
  DARLEE 223
  DAVID 223
  DAWN 223
  DIANE 223
  MARSHA 223
BYRD
  DONNA 305
  MARK 305
  MATTHEW 305
  THURMON(D) 305

CADY
  Arnold 134
  Arnold & Sarah (Hunt) 134
  CASSIUS M 134
  CHLOE 134
  Ebenezer 92, 134
  ELLEN G 134
  LUCY A5 134
  MARIA/MARY 134
  MARYETTE 134
  SARAH J 134
  WILLIAM S (N?) 134
CADY families 134
Cadys v
CAIN v
                                106
  _____ & MARGARET (OYER) . . 107
  FRANCIS 106
  George 107
  HANNAH (_____) 154
  HENRY5 155
  John F 73, 106, 154
  LAWYER 155
  Margaret 106
  MARY J 154, 155
  Peter 106, 107
  PETER4 106
CAIN/KANE families 106
CALDWELL
  Abbis 54
CALHOUN
  EVA 164
  RAY 164
Call 213
Calvin
  John 25
CAMPBELL
  BERNICE 245
  Electa 109
  JANETTE MARIAN8 . . . . . 245, 306
  JOANNE ELLEN8 . . . . . . 245, 306
  MELVIN WOODROW . . 245, 306, 307
  Sophronia M 109
CANGELLO
  DANA LYNN8 276
  DIANE 276
  MARC A 276
CAPRON
  Charles Wm 203
  Edith (OYER) 247
  EDITH MAE 203
  Gerlder (?) 203
  GLENNA 247
  Joseph & Mary (Frank) 203
CAPRON families 203
Carlton, Major 59
CARPENTER
  EUNICE 219, 266
  Norman 219, 266
  NORMAN8 266
  ROBERT 266
CARTER

CECILE 190
  Russell A 132
Cary
  Benjamin 180
Casar
  Carl 14
Case
  Chas A 107
  COLLEEN 262
  Jerome & Genevieve (Spence) . . 262
Castelli
  Jim 29
CASTLEBERRY
  KEITH 269
  KERRI ANNE 269
  PATRICIA 269
Catholics 13
CAYEA
  KENNETH 288
  KRISTA 288
CELESTE
  ROSEMARY 279
CHAMBERLIN
  HELEN (McCOLLUM) 303
CHAPMAN
  DANIEL ROBERT 310
  Henry 69
  KAREN 310
  Nancy 69
  Phoebe Ann 69
Chard
  Jack . . . . i, 19, 337
Charles II 10
Chart, Peter Oyer 107
Chase
  CHARLES 126
  Eunice 98
  Frank 98
  MARGARET AUGUSTA5 126
CHATHAM
  ELLEN 305
  JAMES ELIJAH 305
CHEESMAN
  Georgia (Fox) 186
  Wallace 186
CHILD
  Marsha 94
  Mary Ann 94
CHILDS
  CATHARINE 94
  Cephas 123
  Charles 94
  Ellen 94
  Eunice 123
  Isaac B 94
  Lewis & Deborah (Starks) 94
CHILDS family 94
CHRIST
  CARL 228
  MILDRED 228
Christ (Epis) Ch 160
Christian 27

Christian & Missionary Alliance . 29
Christian Church 159
Christian Church (Disciples of
  Christ) 27
Christianity 26, 29
Christians 27, 28, 39, 66
CHURCH
  TINA 330
Church of the Nazarene 29
Church of the Reformation . . . 21
Civil War . 98, 114, 123, 136, 138,
  139, 144-146, 152, 158, 166, 252
CLAPPER
  Judson & Jos'ine (Gorolomon) 233
  MABEL J 233
CLAPSADDLE 45
  Wilhelm & Maria 79
CLAPSATTLE 40
  Andreas 86
  Andrew 85, 86
  Augustinus/Tinus 86, 88
  Catherine 86
  Elisabeth/Betsy 86, 87
  Gertraud 85, 86
  Jacob 86
  Maria 86
  MARY 88
  Mary/Polly 85
  Phoebe 86
  William 86
  Wm & Mariae (Haener) 86
CLAPSATTLE families 86
CLARK . . . . v, 279
  Alexander 77
  Andrew 77
  Augusta 77
  Benjamin 77
  Bert & Minnie (Reamer) . . . 235
  BERTHA 186
  BONNIE 280
  Caroline 77, 186
  Carrie L 187
  Charles W 187
  CHRISTOPHER WELLS 280
  Corinna_____ 77
  Cornelis_____ 113
  Cornelius . . . 73, 76, 77, 113
  CYNTHIA DEEANE 281
  David 77
  DELORES 280
  ELIZABETH 73, 76, 77, 113, 187,230
  ELIZABETH (FOX) 231
  EMILY LOUISE 231, 281
  ESTHER MARION 236
  Francis G 77
  Frederick 77
  George 187, 231
  Harlan M 187
  HAROLD W . . . 186, 230, 231, 280
  Henry S 77
  Hiram 77
  Homer 77

J T 77
James O 187
JANET 280
JEANNETTE7 . . . . 231, 278
Jeremy 77
JOHN 280
Leonard 236
LESLIE ANN7 281
LINDA C7 280
LORI 280
Malinda_____ 77
Margaret_____ 73
MARGERY 280
MARION 231
MARJORIE LOUISE 235
MARK TANNER 280
Martha 303
Mary 77, 113, 187
MARY KAYE 280
Matthew 28
Melissa 187
PAMELA JEAN 281
Polly 139
RACHEL A 145
ROBERT TODD7 280
ROBERT WELLS6 . . . . . . 231, 280
Sanford 77
Simon 77
Solomon 139
STEWART 280
Thelma 311
THOMAS JAMES . . . 231, 280, 281
WELLS WALTER 77, 186, 187
William 77, 186, 187
Wm & Caroline (Stewart) . . . 186
Wm & Frankie (Foster) . . . 236
CLARK families 76
CLARK, ... 145
CLARK, WILLIAM families . . . 186
CLARY
  Andrew B 185
  Ann 185
  Charles C 185
  Ella 185
  Frederick 185
CLARY families 185
CLEMENS . . . . . . v, 4, 40, 71
  Abram 54
  Catharina/e 54, 76, 110 112
  David 62
  Gerhart 54
  Hannah 73, 112
  HANNAH/NANCY 76
  Jacob . 53, 54, 61, 62, 73, 76, 112
  Mary 53
  MARY L.4 . . . . 111, 163
  MARY MARGARET 53, 54
  Michael 54, 76, 111, 112
  Michael & Cath (Lints) . 76, 110, 111
  NANCY 54
  Philip 54
  RACHEL 54, 111

CLEMENS (cont'd)
Rachel & Michael 161
CLEMENS families 54, 112
CLEMENTZ
  Margareth 47
CLEMONS 21
CLIFTON
  Lewis & Anna L (Lusk) 241
  MARIAM ADELLE 241
Clinton
  DeWitt 59, 349
Clinton Papers 59
Clinton's Ditch 349
CLUTE
  EVE 118
Co A, 7th Ill Vols 137
Co G 154th Reg't NY Inf 129
COLE
  Florence Eliza 293
COLEMAN
  BARBARA 276
COLSH
  Anna 47
COMSTOCK
  ANN 292
  Margaret 158
Confederacy 138
CONGDON
  ROENA 172
Congreg - Christ's Flock Church .174
Congregational Church 173
CONHISER
  ABIGAIL E6 . . . . 188, 231
  ADA 188
  BLANCHE 188
  Catherine 141
  CLARISSA 187
  EARL RICHARD 232
  ELLA 188
  GEO WM CONRAD7 232
  IDA 188
  John 141, 187
  LILLIE 232
  MARY6 188
  MILDRED 232
  OYER H6 . . . . 188, 232
  PAUL G 232
  Philinda 181, 188
  Richard 101, 143, 188
  RUTH LOUISE 232
CONRAD
  Roy 79
COOK
  100
  Eunice 58
  LAMANTHA 100
  Nancy 325
  Wm 58
Cook, Mrs.. 100
COOL
  PERMELIA 130
COOPER
  Samuel 123

COREY
  Gleason 256, 257
  Nea Alma 256, 257
CORNELIUS
  Cathy 208
  Cora 208
  Harold "Corny" 208
  Judy (____) 208
  Shayne 208
  William J 208
Cornwallis 45
Corps of Engineers 259
COTNER
  KAREN FAITH 247
Cotter 213
Countryman
  Lydia 123
COWARC
  LYCE 288
COYNE
  DONALD 292
  LOUISE 292
  MELINDA LOU8 293
  MICHAEL PHILLIP 293
Crandall
  Adaline 101
  CLARENCE 215
  MAY 215
  Norman 98
  Ursula 98
CRANDALL, _____ 144
CRANER
  ALFRED JAMES8 . . . . .281, 332, 333
  CYNTHIA RUTH 333
  DORIS 332
  EDITH GERTRUDE6 232
  LUCIUS J F 232
  MARTHA BALDWIN9 333
  Nich & Mary S (Babcock) . . . 232
  RESA 281
  VEVUS/VIVUS LEWIS PETE7 . . 232, 281
CRAWFORD
  JESSIE 226
CREGO
  MAUDE 199
Crossman
  Cortland & Camilla (McGowan) . 196
Crowell
  DEXTER 189
  Martin 189
  MARY ELLEN5 189
CRUMB
  Andrew 138
  CHAUNCEY S . . 81, 123-125, 147-149
  Emeline 124, 125, 138
  Eva 124
  Franklin 123, 124
  Hannah 123, 124
  MARGARET EVE/EVA4 . . . . . 123, 124
  Mary 123, 124
  MARY E 124
CRUMB families 124

Crump
  Ben & Elizabeth (Lewis) . . . 125
  Carol 56
  Robert G 125
Crumps 125
CRYSLER
  ANGELICIA SARAH 294
  BEATRICE 293
  CHARLES WALDORF 293
  Chas D & Florence E (Cole) . 293
  DAWN MARIE 294
  FLORENCE ELIZABETH 293
  JOHN/JACK CHARLES8 293
  NORMA 294
  ROB'T EDWARD/EDDIE 294
  RUTH 293
  SCOTT EDWARD10 294
  STACEY SCHARLENE 294
CUCCI
  VERA 216, 264
CULVER
  CHRISTINE 296
  CHRISTINE LOUISE8 296
  JANICE 296
  ROBERT 296
  ROBERT WILSON 296
CUMMINGS
  BARBARA 331
  MARY MARGARET 302
CUNNINGHAM
  BARBARA 297
  Burt & Winnie 297
  DEBRA 308
  DORIS 176
  Jas & Nellie (McCarthy) . . . 213
  JOHANNA 213
  JOSEPH MICHAEL10 308
  RALPH 176
  ROBERT JOHN 308
CUNNINGHAM (?)
  VIRGINIA7 176
CURTISS
  ALMIRA 148
  Betsey 147, 148
  Elisha 147
  GEORGE 149
  HATTIE 149
  JAY 149
  JEROME 149
  John K 147, 148
  JOHN5 149
  ROMAINE 149
  Wyliss & Betsey (Cline) . 147, 148
CYR
  JOHN PAUL 291
  VALERIE 291
DABOLL
  Henry 103, 160
  Henry & Charlotte (Goodwin) . .
JENNIE 160
DALY
  ANITA 290

CHRISTINE 290
ERIC WILLIAM8 290
NAN IRENE 290
WILLIAM 290
DAMOOT
  Margaret 85
Darlington
  William 336
Dash
  John 27, 28
DAVID
  Mrs Howard 120
DAVIES
  GARY LEE 332
  JAMES FREDERICK 332
  KATHY 332
  MICHAEL RUSSELL 332
  PAUL ALLEN 332
  RICHARD GARY 332
  TRACY VICTORIA9 332
Davis
  Jefferson 138
  SARAH 165
DAY
  JANETTE 144
  WILLIAM J 144
de Graffenried
  Thomas 10
DECHOW
  COBY 315
  DONALD RICHARD 315
  DONNA 315
  ELLYN 315
  MARIE 315
  RENEE 315
  SCOTT EDWARD 315
  STEVEN ALAN9 315
Declaration of Independence 26
DEELEY
  JULIA A 163
DEET
  Henry 98
  Josephine 98
DELOSH
  EDWARD 238
  HARRIET SHIRLEY7 . . . . . 238, 291
  IVA 238
Demood
  Catharine 47
Dempsey 213
DENCE
  CLARA EMMA 233
  Jos & Ellen (Leppard) 233
DENIKE
  GRETCHEN 174
  SAM 174
DENMAN
  CHERYL 299
Devereaux 181
DEVOS 116
DEWEY
  Deborah 141

DIELLENBACH
  Maria 117
DIKE
  KAREN 268
DIKE, _____ 268
DILTZ
  FLORA (OYER) 228
DILTZ, _____ 182
DINEEN
  John 211
  Mary 211
DINIS
  Sybila 47
DOANE
  MARTHA 296
DOBSON
  FLORIS 246
  KAREN 246
  RICHARD 246
  ROBIN 246
  SHAWN 246
DODGE
  ADRIAN KNAPP 229
  Betsey 109
  GLADYS LEONA 229, 274
  JESSIE 229
  LIDA 229
  LOIS MARION7 . . . . . 229, 274
  MILDRED 229
  WILLARD ALVIN 229
DODSON
  CARL 243
  CHARLES7 243
  HELEN 243
  LENA 243
DODSWORTH
  Margaretta 242
DONAGHUE
  Polly 141
Donaghue, _____ 141
DOOLEY
  FREDERICK PATRICK8 271
  LOIS 271
DOUD
  Almira 172
  Benjamin 172
  Canelia 172
  Charles M 172
  CONTENT 172
  Ebin 172
  EDWARD 172
  George E 173
  Hattie R 172
  Helen 172
  JAMES & MAY (PHILLIPS) . . 171
  James Nelson 172
  Juliaette 167, 172
  JULIAETTE/JULIETT 171
  Lyda 172
  Marguerite 172
  Mary 172
  MAY 172

  Menzer 172
  Miles W 172
  Monroe W 172
  Nelson E 172
  Orrin 172
  Philo E 172
  Sally 172
  Seymour L 172
  Vernon <sic> W 172
  William 172
  Willie E 172
Doud bible listings 172
DOWD
  John 172
DOX
  Charles G 132
  Cora 132
DOYLE
  Mary 212
DRAPER
  LINDA 270
DRAYER
  Fidelia 123
  Frederick 123
  MARGARET 218
  MARJORIE 218
  NANCY 218
  Regis B 218
  S. K. 218
  SUSAN 218
  William 218
DRISCOLL
  Johanna 213
  Julia 213
  Mich & Johanna (Cun'ham) . . . 213
DRUGG
  EUGENE K 316
  JARED EUGENE10 316
  LYNNORE 316
du LOPEZ
  JULIANNA9 282
  MELLONIE 282
  RAQUEL 282
  RENE 282
DUHAN
  Alice 211
  Anna 212
  Anna (McKERNAN) 211
  Beatrice (Fee) Kiley 211
  Bernard 212
  Betty 212
  Bridget 211
  CATHERINE 210, 212, 213
  Clara 212
  Daniel Christopher 211
  Daniel Patrick 211
  Dolores 212
  Eleanor (Hinman) Kohler 212
  Erna 212
  Ethel 212
  Felix B 212
  Felix, Jr 212

DUHAN (cont'd)

Florence 211
Helena 212
Hubert 211
Jane 211
John 211
JOHN DANIEL 210
John Henry 212
Karen 212
Linda 212
Margaret 211, 212
Marie ( ) 212
Marie Philomena 212
Mary 211, 212
Mary/Mariah (Friel) 212
Michael 211
Nellie 212
PAT & MARGARET (ROCHE) . . . 210
Patrick 211
Richard David 212
ROSE JANE . . . 204, 210, 212, 214
Rose Marie 212
Sarah 214
SARAH (LYND) 211, 213
Sarah Loretta 211
Shirley 212
Susanne 212
Thom & Sarah (Lynd) 204
Thomas 211
Thomas Bernard 212
THOMAS GEORGE 211
Thomas Michael 211
William 212
DUHAN families 210
Duke of Zweibrucken 340
DUNGAN
   DENNIS 275
   JED 275
   VICKI 275
DUNSHIE
   BEVERLY 300
DUNSON
   John 130
Dutch . . 11, 21, 24, 25, 132, 267,
                               347
Dutch (Deutsch) 38
Dutch East India Co 116
Dutch Mennonites 9
Dutch Reformed 26
Dutch Reformed Church . . . 21, 25
Dutch West India Co 21, 118
DU TRIEUX/TRUAX
   Philip 117
   Rebecca 117
DUTRIEUX/TRUAX families . . 116, 117
DWYER
   James Patrick 57
   John Joseph 57
   Marisa 57
   Nicole Lauren 57
   Robert John 57
   Sally 57
   Thomas Edward 57

DYE
   DELILAH 137
DYGERT 55
   Abraham 67
   Abram 67
   Anna 87
   Dorothy 87
   Hannah 67
   Lucretia 67
   Margaret 86
   Maria 86
   Mary 67
   Sadie/Sally Ann 67
   Warner & Magdalena (Herkimer) . . 87
   Wm & Maria Elis (Ecker) . . 86
Eacher 26
Earthcare: Lessons - Love Canal . 28
EASEMAN
   Stephen 60
EASTMAN
   Martha 221
Eaton and Oyer 176
Ecumenical Task Force 28
ecumenism 27
EDDY
   Frances 94
   Hiram 120
   Laura 178
   Roswell 187
Edic
   CATHERINE 88
EDMUNDE
   EDITHE 265
EDMUNDS
   EMMALINE 161
   JOHN 161
   John H & Polly ( ) . . 161
EEISEMANN 40
Eendracht 118
EGAN
   ARDIS 289
   DONALD 289
Egger 8
EGLI
   Jacob 341
EGLIN
   Ernest & Jane 315
   MARIE CHRISTINE 315
Eier (Oyer)
   Peter 53
Eierer vi
Eigher vi
EIRER vi
   Johann Dieterich 79
ELERY
   MATIE 279
Ellicott
   Joseph 348, 349
ELLIS 38
   Albert E 56
   ALICE M FOSTER5 155
   Carol 56

ELLIS (cont'd)

Carolyn 57
CHARLOTTE 106, 155
Claude 57
Clayton J 56
CORA I 155
Cornelia 56
Daniel 106, 155, 156
David 57
Edward 91
Eliza 57
ELLA G 155
Faith Finster 57
FRANCES IMOGENE 155
FRANCES SANTONETTE4 156
Geraldine 56
HARRIET 156
Inez L 56
James 57
JOHN 56, 57, 101, 155
Katherine V 57
KATHRYN (_____) 155
Lorinia/Vinny/Beatrice 57
Lorraine 57
LYDIA 155
Madge 56
Margaret 57
MARGARETT 106
MARTHA 156
Mary 55-58, 155
May 56, 146
Murray 57
Nancy A 55
PETER 55
Phoebe 57
Polly 57
Richard C 56
Richard James 56
Robert Clayton 56
Robert J 56
Robert Misner 56
ROSWELL MURRAY . . . 57, 106, 155
SALLY 55
Sally Misner 57
Samuel 57, 155
SAMUEL4 156
SANTONETTE 156
Sarah 57, 155, 156
Solomon 155
Stephen L 57
Sylvia 56
WILLIAM . 53, 55-57, 95, 106, 155
Ellises v
Emerson
  MARY 173
EMMERT
  DONNA 290
English 11, 20, 24, 132, 338
English/Norman/Viking 258
Episcopal 28, 29
Episcopalian 28
Episcopalians 26-28
Erasmus 7

ESSIG
  Sylvia 56
EUBANKE
  FRANK F 295
  LINDA 295
EUER vi
  Peter—see also Oyer 73
EVANS 100
  LAMARTHA 100
EVE
  LINDA 271
EVERHART
  ADA 100
Evert 116
Everts 64
EYER vi
  Barbara 341
  Christian 341
  Daniel 341
  David . . . . i, 2, 4, 338
  Elisabeth 341
  Fritz 3
  Hans (John) 338
  Henry C 339
  Hubert i
  Jacobina 341
  Joh Jacob & Anne (Lowenstein) . .338
  Johan Adam 338
  Johan/John Martin 2, 337
  Johannes/John 341, 342
  John Adam 338, 339
  John Frederick 339
  Ludwig 340
  Mardin/Martin 337, 338
  Peter 342
  Peter & Anna M (Schweigler or
    Schweizer) 338
  Verena (Jordi) 341
Eyer family 342
Eyer-Gross
  J, Dr. 342
EYERER vi
  JOHANN FRIEDERICH1 . . . . .iii, 31
Eyers/Oyers 337
EYGNER
  Anna Margaretha 11
  Peter 11
Eyre vi
EYRE (Oyer)
  Elisabetha 49
FAESCH
  Johann Jacob . . ii, 13, 14, 17-20
  Madame 18
FALSEY
  MARY 213
FALZGRAF
  KARL P 300
  PAULETTE 300
FARMER
  Lydia 73
Farmers Loan & Trust 348

FARNSWORTH
RUTH MARY 293
Father Baker's Home - Orphans . .140
FAY
Betsey 123
Charles 123
Fee
Beatrice 211
Feeley 213
FELDMAN
ELIZABETH 214
FENNER
Mina 242
Fenster, Finsterer, Finsterle,
Finsterbach, and Finsterwald
see Finster 8
FERGUSON
CHRIS A MORRISON 306
DAVID GLEN9 306
GEORGE ARTHUR 306
GERALDINE 306
JAMES CHAS LLOYD 306
JANETTE 306
MICHAEL MEL ORENE 306
STEVEN DUWAYNE 306
FERNCROOK
Elizabeth 86
Ferran & Gardinier 117
FIBER
Antonia 279
FICHTER
CASEY JOHN10 294
CRYSTAL ANN 294
KEVIN CHARLES 294
NANCY 294
TINA ELIZABETH 294
FIELD
DAVID WILLIS 303
FANNY 191
JOHN KENNETH 303
MICHAEL JOSEPH 303
ROBERT 303
SUSANNE 303
Thom L & Hannah (Somes) . . . 191
FIERLE
MILDRED 227
NORMAN 227
FINSTER 8, 26, 71
ABRAM B 53
CAROLINE 161
Catharine 53, 72, 92
CORA 161
Elisabeth/Elizabeth 55, 72
GEORGE 54
HERBERT 161
Hiram 55, 71
Huldah 55
JACOB 53-55
Johannes/John 17, 31, 220
Johannes/John - see John
John . 38-40, 45, 46, 48, 51, 53,
55, 57, 62, 63, 71, 73, 312

John & Maria Freder'ke (Schnek) . 92
John & Mary (Schneck) 60
John & Margarethe 92
JOHN2 53
MARGARET 62
Mary Margaret 54
MARY/MARIA F (SCHNECK) 51
MARY/POLLY 53, 55
OSCAR E.5 161
Peter 53, 72, 100, 133
Philinda 55
Philip 53, 62, 72
Philip & Elizabeth 161
Polly 57
SIMON P 161
Sophronia 133
WILHELM (WILLIAM) 54
Finster(s) 55
First Baptist Church 178
First Cavalry Div 260
First Congreg Church 220
First Infantry Div 278
First Reformed Ch 132
FISCHER 26
Howard & Lydia (Murray) . . . 322
MARJORIE LEE 322
Fischer/Visscher 91
FISH
ANNA 232
FITCH
Charles 171
Charles N 171
Mary 171
Mary R 171
Thaddeus 171
FLANIGAN
Marguerite 172
FLARETY
Margaret 107
FLETCHER
EARL W 200
EDNA 200
John W & Minnie (_____) . . . 200
FOLTS . . . . v, 40, 91
Abraham 87
Allen 88
Alvin 221
Ann Margret 87
Anna 87
Anna Catherine 87
Anna Eva _____ 87
Anna Maria _____ 87
BEULAH D 230
Caroline 87
Catharina/e 87, 89
Charles 71, 88
Conrad 87, 89
D V 88
Daniel 87
David H 88
Delia 87
Dorothea/Dorothy 87

FOLTS (cont'd)

E P & Carrie (Moore)	230
Elisabeth/Elizabeth/Betsy .	86-88
Ernest	88
Frank	88
George Luman	88
Harriette	88
Henry	88
Hiram 87,	88
Ida 88,	188
JACOB	87
Jacob C	87
JACOB MELCHIOR	87
Johannes	87
Joseph 87,	88
Joseph Conrad	86
Luke	88
Margaret	88
Margaretha ____	87
Maria	88
Mariette	88
Mary 87, 88,	98
Matthew	88
Melchior	87
Metchum	87
Morris	88
NANCY E	125
Newton	88
Oliver 87,	88
Peter	68
Peter & Nancy (Schell) . . .	125
Polly	71
Sally	87
Sarah	88
Severenus/Sylvanus . . . 88,	247
Sylvanus	88
Timothy 87,	88
Warner 71,	87
William 87,	88
Wm H	88
Folts families 87,	126
Fonda	116

FOPPES

JOHANNA	229
John & Gertr (Vanderlean) .	229

FORDER

COLLEEN8	277
DAVID G	277
DAVID GORDON	277
ELLEN	277
NOREEN	277
NORMAN HOWARD	277

FOSTER

ABIGAIL M (____)	196
ADA	196
Alfred & Abigail (_____) .	196
ANGELINE	196
Ardin H	155
Arlin	155
CHAUNCY/CHAN J	196
Frankie	236
James	196
LYDIA MARIA	155

NORMA MARIE	294
Warren & Grace	294

FOX

Ambrose H	130
Charles	231
CHAUNCY	231
ELIZABETH	230
ELLEN	231
EMILY	231
Geo A & Emily Ann (Bowen) . . .	230
Geo O & Hannah C	186
GEORGE 67,	231
Georgia	186
Hester E	130
J	101
JABEZ	231
John W	231
LENNORA/NORA	186
Leslie B	231
Matie 58,	144
THOMAS	231
Willie E	130

FOX (FUCHS?)

Hannah	67
FOX families 186,	231

FRACKENPOLE

Arthur	261

FRAGALE

Rose	201

FRANCIS

HELEN ANN	247
Franck	10
FRANK . . . . v, 26, 40,	87
	106
Abigail	102
Andrew/Andries9, 84, 85, 86, 88,	131
Anna	87
Anna Margaret 85,	102
Anna/Nancy/Eve/Eva . . . 85,	91
Annie M	86
ARLIN	143
Catharine 84,	85
CHARITY 85, 100, 102,	128
Christopher	84
Clarissa 101, 143,	187
Conrad 84,	87
Daniel 86,	102
Delana	102
Dorothea/Dorothy Ann . . . 71,	85
Elisabeth 66,	85
Elizabeth 84,	86
EMMA JANE	178
Ernest	86
Eva 84,	86
FRANKLIN 143,	144
Frederick 85, 86, 101,	102
Frederick F	86
Gertraut	85
Helen E	86
HENRICH/HENRY	84
Henry 67, 79, 81, 84-86, 89, 100-102, 128	

FRANK (cont'd)

Henry & Gertr (Claps'le) 71, 79, 91
Hiram 101, 143
Hiram & Arley 101
Jacob . . 79, 81, 85, 86, 143, 180
Jacob & Maria 127
Jacob H 85, 86, 127
Jeremiah 86, 102
Johann/John Stephen 84
John 60, 86, 87
John & Margaret (Gerlach) . . 100, 128
John H 85, 102
JOHN J5 127
John L 84
Joseph 84
Julia M 86
Lawrence 60, 84, 86
Lawrence & Liddy (Multer) . . . 86
Lyman B 86
Manley J 86
Margaret 84, 85
Maria 84
Maria Cath/Eliz 85
Maria Catharina 79
Mary . . . 55, 84, 128, 129, 144
Mary (Maria?) _____ 86
Mary E 87, 127
Mary Elizabeth . 71, 79, 84, 102
Mary/Polly 85
Matthew 84
Michael 84
Mrs Betsy 86
Nancy Eva 90
Olive 101
Peter 84, 86
Peter & Elizabeth (Ferncrook) . 86
Peter A 86, 102
Phebe 85
Reuben 86, 127, 129
RICHARD5 143
Robert 86
Sally 101
SARAH 143
Stephen 84
Timothy 87
Warner 102
Welthy 86
FRANK families . . 65, 84, 102, 127
Franklin
Benjamin 173
FRASER
Jussie A 248
Frederick the Great 337
Frederick, Count, of Wied . . 13
Free Methodist 26, 141, 142
Free-Will Baptist Society . . . 180
Free-Will Baptists 26
Freedman
Harold & Faye (Rosenthal) . . 295
SUSAN BETH 295
FREER
BARBARA 286

Claude 285
CYNTHIA LEE8 286
DOROTHY 285
DOUGLAS ROBERT9 286
JUDSON KENNETH/PETE 285
KENNETH EVAN 286
Freewill Baptist 141
FRENCH 25, 48, 170
ANDREA MARIE 299
DAWN MARIE9 299
DEBORAH JEAN 299
DOUGLAS 299
ELWYN 299
HEATHER ANN 299
JAMES ELWYN8 299
LINDA 299
MARY LOUISE 299
SARAH 134
French & Indians 118
French and Indian War 84, 87
FRIEL 214
Mary/Mariah 212
Pat & Mary (Doyle) 212
FRITZ
MARY KAYE 280
Froelke
Ruth iii
FULLER
Arley 101
ARLIN 143
Charity 101
CONTENT 172
CYNTHIA 286
ROBERT WILLIAM 286
SCOTT STEPHEN 286
SHERYL ANN9 286
WILLIAM EDWARD 286
FULLER,
fundamentalist 29
FURRER
Ismael 342
Gannett News Service 29
Gansevoort
(Peter) 40, 59
GARDINIER . . . . . . v, 26, 116
_____ (Hemstreet) 117
Abram 117
Abram & Anna (Yates) 117
Elias 117
Hattie B 117
Isaiah 117
Jacob 131
John 117
Jos Y 117
Joseph 117
Juliet 117
Leslie 117
MARGARET 117, 118, 143
Margaretha 117
Robert 117
Stephen A 117
Thom & Mary (Hardenburgh) . . . 117

GARDINIER (cont'd)
Thomas 117
Wm & Maria (Diellebach) . . . 117
Yates 117
Gates
(Gen. Horatio) 47
Halbert & Sarah F (West) . . 193
MARY LUCY 193
GEER
BONNIE 280
Genesee Baptist Church. . . . 231
Genl Conf 7th Day Adventists . 124
GEORGE
CLARA 179
CLARA6 226
MYRNA 194
ROBERT W 179, 226
SYDNEY 194
George Ritter Company 10
GERLACK
Anna Margaret 85, 102
Margaret 100, 128
German 13, 14, 19, 24, 25, 32, 39,
46, 267, 323, 338
German Lutherans 69
Germans . . . 11, 24, 25, 38, 204
GERWITZ
ALFRED 218
ALICE 218
BETTY 218
DOROTHY 218
LAURA6 218
LOMAMARIEL/MYRT 218
RAYMOND 218
VIOLET7 218
GIBBS
Viola 283
GIVEN
Ruth 56
Glen 116
GODBY
Thomas 256
GONGAL
April 57
Joseph 57
GOODEMOTE
Abraham & Eveline (Fuller) . 179
Abram 226
AGNES 225
ALDEAN 226
Allen 179
Ann 179
Baltus 179
CARL7 226
CLARA 179, 226
CORA 179
David 179
EARL6 . . . . 179, 225
EDNA 179, 225
Elizabeth 179
Emeline 226
Eva,Mirton 226
Floyd 226

FRANK 179
Gladis,Violet 226
Harry 179
HELEN 226
James 179
James & Dora 226
James & Mariah 226
John 179
Maria 179
Philip 179
Phillip & Katie 226
ROYDEN 17, 225
Sally 179
Sophia 179
Vedder & Lillian 226
William 179
Wm 226
Wm & Carrie 226
Wm H & Ada 226
GOODEMOTE families 179, 226
GOODWIn
Charlotte 160
Gorham
Nathaniel 348
GOROLOMON
Josephine 233
GORTON
Alice (Lyon) Auyer 160
Gorton, _____ 160
GOSS
Charles 88
Elizabeth 88
Governeur
Margaret 117
GRADY
BARBARA 287
CHRISTINE BETH 287
JILL9 287
M ROBERT 287
PAMELA NANCY 287
GRAF
ALIDA 265
CHRISTOPHER 266
IRENE 266
KRISTIN 266
MICHAEL 266
RAYMOND 265, 266
SHANNON 266
William 265
GRANT
Marie 272
MARY 138
GRATZ
Delbert . . . . . i, 3, 6, 312, 341
Great Britian 48
Greek Orthodox 27
GREEN
Allen M 145
BEVERLY 285
Case 68
CHRISTOPHER MARK 285
COREY MATTHEW 285

GREEN (cont'd)

CRAIG MICHAEL9 285
DONALD EUGENE 285
ELLEN 231
GENEVIEVE CATH/JANE 216
Harold & Elizabeth I (Cuff) . 285
JANE 264
JOSEPH 216, 264
JUDY8 264
Julia 145
Lillian 68
MARY 264
ROBERT E 264

GREENE
BETTY 291
CHRISTINA 291
CYNTHIA A8 291
DEBORAH L 291
JAMES 291
PEGGY MARIE 291

GRIERSON
Alex & Alice (_____) 174
JENNIE GRACE 174

GRIFFIN
CARMALETTA 313

GROOT 116
ABRAHAM 118
Abraham S 117
HESTER 118
Simon Simonse 117

GROSS
LIZZIE 129

GRUCELSKI
JANET FRANCES 295

GRUDMAN
Mary 302

Guillot
Alex 10

Guth
Hermann . . . . i, 2
Hermann & Gertrud 340

GUTHRIE
ALMON(D) 172
MARY 172
Mary A 123

Habsburg 7

HACKBARTH
BONITA 293
ELLEN 293
JOHN 293
KEVIN 293
RICKIE ELLEN 293
RONALD 293
SCOTT 293

HADLEY 222
A E 221
Abigail 220
Alonzo 220
Alvin 221
B N 120
BERT 220
Betsey E 220
BETTY 267

Burdette 221
CATHERINE 220
Charles 220, 221
CHRISTINE8 268
Cornelius 220
Daniel 220
Ebenezer 220
EDNA 267
Edward 221
Elbert . . . . ii, 122, 223
ELBERT HAMILTON 220, 267
Ella 221
Eveline 221
Fessenden 220
GEORGE 220
HENRY 220
Henry Hamilton 220
Horace 221
JESSE 220
John 221
Julia 221
KAREN 268
Laura 221
LAWRENCE HAMILTON8 268
LAWRENCE STANLEY7 . . . . 220, 267
Leverett 221
Lottie 221
MARILYN RUTH8 268
Mary 221
Mrs Martha 221
Nathan 221
Neal 221
NELSON H 220
Newton 221
Oscar 220
Paulina 221
Peter 267
PHYLLIS ELAINE 268
RONALD 268
Rufus 221
Ruth Ann 122, 220
VIRGINIA 268
WAYNE NELSON 220, 268
Wesley 221
Willard 220

HADLEY families 220

Haener
Mariae 86

HAILLE(A)
Thomas 258

Haldeman
(Gov) 59

HALE v
Daniel 258
EMMA FRANCES 256, 258
Joseph 258
Thomas 258
THOMASINE 258

HALE generational 258

HALEY
BOONE 133
MARGARET/MAGGIE 133

HALL
. . . . 151
Clara May 236
HARRIET 151
THERESA 219
HALTERMAN
James & Helen (Thomspon) . . 328
MARY LYNNE 328
THOMAS MICHAEL 328
TIMOTHY MICHAEL 328
TODD MICHAEL 328
HAMBLETON
CLARA 122
R S 122
HAMMOND
Abram 97, 98
Agnes 98
BETSEY 97
Betsy 97
CLAUDE 227
Clinton 97, 98
Cordelia 97
David 98
Electa 98
Ella 98
Eunice 98
Frederick 98
Henry C 98
IDA 140
JOANNE 227
John 97, 98
Joseph 97, 98
Joseph & Sarah (Middaugh) . . 97
Josephine 98
Louise 97
Lovinia 98
Mary 98
MARY JANE 227
MILDRED GRACE 227
Napoleon 97
Robert 97
Samuel 97, 98
Sarah E 98
Sophia 98
Ursula 98
Washington 97
William 98
HAMMOND families 97
HAMMOND, _____ 140
HAMPTON
TAMMY 297
Hanchett
ROENA B 150
Hancock
John 173
HANSON
DORA E 135
Hudson & Abigail (Vedder) . . 135
HARBER
Twila Katherine 301
HARDING
ADELAIDE (TEWES) 310

Chas & Adelaide (Tewes) . . . 309
HARHAVER
MAE 229
HARRELL
DEBRA 308
RICHARD LAURENCE 308
HARRIS
AGNES (_____) 273
ANNE MARIE 273
CHRISTOPHER JOHN 273
Edward 212
ERIC DAVID 273
Ethel 212
KATHLEEN LINDA 273
Leon J 212
MARK DANIEL 273
Michiko 212
MILLARD FILLMORE 273
RUTH 273
SHERRY (_____) 273
STEVEN WAYNE9 273
WAYNE WOOD 273
Wooster & Sarah (Turk) . . . 212
HARRISON
DESSIE 177
DESSIE6 (BEACH) 224
FRANCIS7 225
GEORGE 177, 224
LUELLA 225
HARRY
DAVID 302
JUDY 302
Hart and Kreider 24
HARTER
RACHEL 237
HARTKOPF
BARBARA 297
CHARLES 240
CHARLES WHITNEY 241
CHARLES WHITNEY7 297
ELIZABETH LORRAINE7 296
ELIZABETH7 241
JACQUELINE LEE 297
JILL BARBARA8 297
LUMORA 240
HARVEY
ABIGAIL 231
Charles 96
Cora 208
Elijah 96
Elijah & Betsey _____ . . . 95
Elijah & Delilah 96
ELIZABETH 95
Gates (Erastus) 96
IDA ALNORE7 231
Isaac H 96
SHEPHARD COLEMAN 231
HARVEY families 96
HASCOETT
AGNES 225
Hasenclever 31, 32
Franz/Francis Caspar 14

HASENCLEVER (cont'd)
Peter . . ii, iii, 10, 12, 14, 17,
         19, 21, 31, 32, 38
Hasenclever workmen . . 63, 65, 68,
              70-72, 89, 335
Hasenclever, Peter 31,32,54, 55, 337
Haskins/Hastings
  Clarissa 119
Hassenclever
  Peter 32, 34, 35
  Peter - see Hasenclever 34
HATCHELL
  AMY MARIE9 295
  BARBARA 295
  JAMES THEODORE 295
  JOY BELINDA 295
  ROBERT ELIZAH 295
Hawkins
  Eliza 140
Hayden 214
Heemstraat
  BARBARA 118
  TAKEL 118
Hegeman 18
Heim
  Helen 277
HEINEMAN
  KINDA (_____) 238
  LOUIS 238
  MABEL 238
  RAYMOND7 238
  VERNA 239
  VERNA7 292
Heinrich
  Elizabeth 59
Heldner
  P(aul) 342
  Paul . . . . i, 2
Helmer
  71
HEMMER
  ANGELINE 196
Hemstreet
  ABRAM V 129
HENDRIX
  CLARA BEULAH 225
Herk. Co. Historical Society . . 26
Herkimer 40
  George 39
  John Jost 40
  Nicholas 39, 40, 45-47
Herlan
  EDWARD 184
  ORISSA 184
Hermann i
HERRICK
  Franklyn C 257
  Grace 257
Herricks v
HESS . . . . v, 40
  Augustinus 88
  CATHERINE 88
  Elias Hanen 88

  Elizabeth 88
  EMMA BELLE 197
  George 88
  George W 88
  Honyost 88
  HONYOST H 88
  James F & Louise (Abrams) . . . 197
  Johannes 88
  JOHN 88
  Joseph 88
  Margaret 88
  MARY 88
  Mary E 88
  Michael E 88
  Nancy 88
  Polly 88
Hess families 88
Hessians 20
HEYWOOD
  ELEANOR 272
HICKOK 123
  Polly 123
HIDER
  Elizabeth 192, 198
HILL
  ELIZABETH/LIBBY 140
  Gertrude 250, 251
HILL, _____ 140
HILLER
  Elisabeth 72
  Jacob 72
HILLS
  ADDIE 182
  Alphonso & Martha 182
HINMAN
  Adeline 178
  Augusta 132
  Eleanor 212
  S B & Kesiah 178
HITT
  LORI LYNN 288
HIVELEY
  ALFRED EUGENE 305
  ARLENE 305
  BRUCE EARL9 305
  ELLEN MARIE 305
  VICKI LYN 305
HLC landholders, list 348
Hochstadter/Hufstatter
  see also variant spellings . . . 17
HOCHSTATTER 64
  Catharine N 66
  Christian 59, 62, 65-67
  Christian & Maria Cath (Widrig) . 63
  David 65
  ELIZABETH 63, 65, 66
  Jacob 66
  Jacob & Cath (Rima/Rema) . .99, 130
  Johann George 67
  Johann Heinrich 66
  Margaret 67
  Maria Catherine . . . 65, 66, 67, 72

HOCHSTATTER (cont'd)

Maria/Polly	67
Michael	67
Michael & Elizabeth	130
Polly	71
Theobald/David	67
Hochstatters	17
Hochsteder	
Alan R	21
Hochstetler	4, 65
Alan	17
Christian	65
Jacob	65
Wm F	65
Hochstetler Massacre	65
Hochstetter	v, 21, 40, 71
Hockstedter	26
HODARA	
DANIEL	262
JOAN	262
SANDRA8	262, 331
SHARON	262
HOFFMAN	
Margreen	28
HOFSTADER	
David	89
HOLDEN	
Adelaide	146
Amos B	146
ARNOLD	145
Arnold & Patience (Pam___)	145
Betsy	146
BYRON U5	145
CATHARINE	189
Charles	101, 145, 189
Dennison F	146
Douglas	56
EDWARD	145
Edwin C	146
ELLA P	145
Ellis	146
Ellis/Pete	56
Emily	146
GEORGE	145, 146
Grant	56
Harold	56, 146
Hazel	56, 146
Helen	146
Helen May	56
James	56
Jane M	145
JAY C	189
John R	145
Julia J	145
Lois	56, 146
Martha	146
Mary	146
May	56, 146
MELISSA	189
Melvina	146
Nelson	146
PATIENCE	145
Peter	146

Philinda	101, 144-146
R G	56
Robert	146
Ruth	56
William	101, 145, 146, 189
HOLDEN families	145
Holdens	181
HOLLAND	
Bert & Maude	56
John	67
Mary	67
Otis	220
Holland Land Co	79, 142, 251, 252, 347
Holland Purchase	348
HOLWAY	
Martha	242
Homes	
Henry A	19
HOPKINS	
ELEANOR	217, 219
EMMA (___)	217
FRANK	217
JAMES	217
JOHN	217
KEITH	217
MAX	217
PHILLIP	217
SHANE	217
STEPHEN	258
HORNER	
KATHRYN JEANETTE	296
HORNING	
ED	283
KATIE	283
PATRICIA	283
HORR	
JUNE	299
HORTON	
	191
BARBARA	291
HOSTETLER	
Harvey	65
Hostetler Gen	21
HOUSE	
HAZEL EVA	297
HOWE	
ELIZABETH	146, 147
LORETTE/A	146
Newell	147
Newell & Jane (Snyder)	146
HOWELL	
Kenneth & Marion	294
ROSEMARY	294
HOWLETT	
CYNTHIA	281
RONALD	281
HOYT	
CAROL	270
GARY	270
JARED9	270
HUBBARD	
Jesse	153

HUBBELL
  H. H 120
HUFSTADER
  Abraham 68
  Ada 99, 100
  Alace 68
  Alzina 130, 180
  ANDREW 130
  Blanche 130
  Catharine 100
  Charles 68, 130
  ELIZABETH/LIBBY 140
  Ezra 99, 100, 140
  HELEN (   ) 140
  HENRY HARRISON 100
  HERMAN L 140
  IDA E 140
  INA B 140
  JACOB 99, 100
  James 99, 100, 140
  Jane 68
  LAMANTHA 100
  LAMARTHA 100
  LAURA J.5 . . . . 130, 180
  Lottie,Matie 68
  LUCY JENNIE 130
  MARSH6 180
  Mary 68, 130,140
  Michael 64, 68
  Nelson 130, 180
  ROSANE 130
  ROXANNA 99, 100
  Sadie 188
  SELIAN 140
  SELLE/SELLA 130
  Seneca 68
  William 99, 100, 140
HUFSTATER
  Abraham 67
  Abram 67
  Alace/Alice 67
  Alson 67
  Amos E 68
  Andrew 67, 68
  Charles 68
  Christian 67
  Cornelius,Edna 67
  David 68
  Edwin 67
  Eliza 68
  ELIZABETH 67
  Ezra 68
  Ferdinand 67
  Ferdinand,Edwin,Alon 67
  Francis,Almira,Charles,Oscar . 68
  Fred 67, 68
  Hannah 67
  Hellen 68
  Henry Arrison 67
  Jacob 67, 81, 85, 99
  James 67, 68
  Jennie 67

  Jeremiah 95
  Jeremiah,Ella,Esther,Emma,Ab-
    ba,Clara,Henry H 67
  Jeremiah,Jane,Peter,Geo
    Ward,Esther 66
  MARY 67, 68
  Mary,Walter,Herbert 68
  Michael 67, 81, 97
  Ophelia 68
  Rufus 68
  Sadie/Sally 67
  Sally Ann 68
  Temperance 68
  Vida M 68
  Willard 67
  Willard,Hannah,Mary E 68
HUFSTATERS
  Francis 68
HUGHEY
  ADALIZA E.5 188
  Bradford 188
  Catherine 188
  Edverdo 67, 68, 188
  Eliza J 188
  Ellen 188
  EUGENE G6 188
  Florence L 188
  Geo 130
  Geo & Mary (McMickle) . . . 188
  GEORGE 145, 188
  Ida 88, 188
  James 67, 188
  John 88, 188
  Louise 188
  Mary 188
  Matilda 188
  Robert 188
  Rosanie/Roxanne 188
  Sadie 67, 188
  VEDDER G 188
HUGHEY families 188
Huguenots 8, 25
HULSER
  ADA 161
  ALICE 184
  ELIZABETH 161
  EMMA 163
  EZRA W 161
  IRVING E/F5 161
  Jerome & Eliz (   ) . . . 184
  JOHN H 161
HUMBARGER
  ALBERT/BERT 307
  BRENDA LEE9 307
  JOANNE 306
  LEROY ELMER 307
  ROBERT 307
  SANDRA DEE 307
HUNT
  BEVERLY 301
  ELWYN R 301
  NANCY SUSAN 301

HUNT (cont')
RONALD ELWYN 301
RUSSELL SCOTT8 301
Sarah 134
HUNTER
JOYCE 298
Robert 25
HUNTLEY
EUNICE 297
HUFLBURT
Elizabeth 182
HUTHER
BRIAN 275
KEVIN 275
LYNDA 275
RICHARD 275
Indian 39, 60, 66, 313
Indians . . 11, 25, 38-40, 45, 46,
49, 51, 54, 65, 66, 70, 85,
132, 254, 347
INGALLS
Fitch H 195
HARRIET/HATTIE C. 195
INGRAM
LAURIE 302
RAY 302
INMAN
Frances 257
Interchurch Council 27
IRER . . . . vi, 31
Frederick 46
Irish 25, 211
ISBELL
BETTY ANN 238
BETTY ANN7 291
CHARLES A.7 . . . . . 185, 291
CHARLES FREDERICK8 291
CHARLES MATTHEW 194
Chas & Sarah (Matthews) . . 194
FOSTER C6 195
Fred 238
FREDERICK C 94, 195
HARRIET 194
IVA 195, 175, 238
JEANNE 291
LAURA 195
LEAH JUNE 195, 238
LILLIAN 237
Iser vi
Isler 10
Iver vi
JACKSON
CHERYL 273
CLARINDA E5 125
Duane 89
DUANE E 125
Jacob & Sally (_____) . . . 125
MARGARET 228
MARGARET4 125
SEYMOUR W 125
JACKSON, _____ 228
JAMIE
DAVID 280

LINDA 280
JAMIESON
Edna 256
Thomas A 256
JASTER
ERNEST JOHN 178
LULU 178
Theodore & Carrie (Kruse) . . . 178
Jaster & Oyer 179
Jehovah's Witnesses 29
JENKINS
Caroline 142
Jews 13, 27, 28
JIRAK
Betty 219
John S
Oyer 6
JOHNSON
Alexis Lockling 53
DEBRA IRENE 289
Frederica M (Mrs Widrig) . . . 53
Hiram 53
Horace M 53
KURT 302
LAURIE 302
Paul 29
Seymour P 53
William 336
JOMINY
VIRGINIA 268
JONES
_____ (Wadsworth) 185
Anna Reed 267
Henry Z. 13
JOHN E 318
JOHN R 135, 185
Martha 287
Mary Ann 94
Susan 175, 267
Jordan Masonic Lodge 157
JORDI
Verena 341
JOSLIN
Lorraine 57
JUKKER
Catherine 70
Johannes 70
Justin 178
KANE
Arthur 106, 107, 118
Ella 106
Eva Eliza 106, 118
Honora 107
John 106, 107, 118
Mary (Booth) 107
Mary (Lattin) 106
Mary L 106, 118
Otis H 106
Peter 106, 107
Vedder 106, 119
KANE/CAIN
PETER 118

Keeler
    Eva 47
Kellenbenz
    Hermann 14
KELLY
        (BLACKALL) 213
    ANNA/NANCY 213
    Johanna 213
    John & Honora (Roche) 213
    John & Johanna (Scanlon) . . 213
    Lana/Lena B 175
    Mary 213
    Timothy 213
KEMENES
    GABRIELLA 279
KEMPF
    Johanes 341
KENSIE
    Mary 227
KENT
    BARBARA 295
    DEBORAH CAROL 295
    Emeline 117
    HARRY STANLEY7 . . . . . 240, 295
    HELEN 239
    JANET 295
    JANICE MARILYN . . 229, 240, 296
    JUSTIN SARLE 295
    ROBERT STEVEN8 295
    STANLEY SARLE 240
    SUE 295
    SUSAN GAYLE 295
KESTER
    Hannah 159
    Rosina A 197
KEYS
    Elizabeth 192
KIELBASA
    BERTHA 275
KIES
    Karen 212
KILEY
    Beatrice. 211
    Jean 212
    John 212
    Richard 212
KING v
    Barzilla 258
    BATHSHEBA 258
    DeLANCY 258
    Ebenezer 258
    Eliza 140
    Jeremiah 257
    JOHN 258
    JOYCE 309
    LARRY D. 309
    Nathaniel 257
    POLLY LEANN 309
    SARAH ESTELLA 257
KING generational 257
King of England 48, 87
KIPPEL

LINDA 299
Kitch
    Alison 321
    Edward 321
KITCHNER
    JEAN 283
    PARRY WILL 283
    Wilbur N & Doris A (Parry) . . 283
KLEIN
    LESLIE 281
    STEPHEN 281
KLOCK 36, 54, 63, 69, 70
    Catherine 87
    Daniel 72
    Eve 72
    John 87
KNAPP
    Al & Frances Augusta (Oyer) . . 184
    ALBERT SYLVESTER 183
    BURTON MARHAVER7 229
    DELLA ELIZABETH 183, 228
    FRANCES 183
    HARVEY BURTON 183, 229
    JOSEPHINE N 183
    LIDA FRANCES 184, 229
    MAE 229
    NETTIE ORISSA 183, 184
    Rich'dson & Orissa (Burton) . . 183
KNIGHT
    ALDEAN 226
Knittle 9, 10, 24, 25
Knoll, Pastor 25
KOHLER
    Eleanor 212
Konigsbach Menn Register 341
KONRAD
    Marisa Suzanne 57
KOON
    JANET 276
    JASON DEAN9 276
    LARRY D 276
    SARAH E 276
Korean War 250
KRAUSS
    Ernest . . . i, 13, 14, 17-19, 335
    Martha 336
Kreider 25
KRUSE
    Charles 216
KWIK
    THERESA 246
LaCour 213
LaGRECA
    BECKY 332
    MARK ANTHONY 332
    SALVATORE 332
    SALVATORE9 332
    SHAUN DAVID 332
LAMPHEAR
    JAMES 150
    MARY 150

LAND
  DOUGLAS 270
  GAYLE 270
  JEREMY9 270
  JOHN 270
LANG/LONG
  LAURA 130
  Lang/Long, _____ 130
LAPP
  KATHIE 299
LAQUINTINO
  CHRISTINE 268
  DAVID 268
LARABEE v
  ALBERT 137
  ANGELINE 138, 139
  Anson,Albert,Elmira,Thom,Sa-
    rah,Dolly,Eliz, Francis . . 139
  BELLE 138
  CATHERINE4 138
  CELIA ELISA5 138
  Delana 138
  ELEAZOR 138, 139
  Emeline 138
  EMMA 137
  FERNANDO 137
  Francis 139
  FRANK SHERIDAN5 139
  FREDERICK 139
  George 137, 138
  Hester 138
  Hiram,Deloss 139
  Ira 138
  J.D. 137
  Joseph 137-139
  LESTER 137
  Lorinda 138
  LYMAN 138
  MARY 138, 139
  Miner 138
  Nathan 125, 138, 178
  Nathan & Delana (Aldrich) 136-138
  NELSON 136, 138
  Nelson,Geo,Lyman 138
  Pheobe 139
  Polly 139
  ROXANNA 136
  RUSSELL 137
  SARAH JANE4 137
  Sidney/Sydney 138
  Thom & Hester (Babcock) . . . 139
  Thomas 138, 139
  WELBY A 138
  Larabee brothers 125, 136
LARABEE families 138, 139
LARABEE generational 138
Larrabee
  Philander Densloe 139
LATTIn
  Luke B 106
LAUBER
  J 342

LAUTER
  ALISON 319
  Robert & Evelyn 319
LAWTON
  CATHERINE (ROY) 113, 119
LEARN
  BONITA JEAN8 . . . . . . 252, 318
  DONALD 251, 252, 319
  DONNA MARIE8 . . . . . . 251, 315
  George 252
  Glenn 252
  Glenn & Kittie (Whitcomb) . . . 251
  Jacob 252
  JOHN 252
  Joseph 252
  KITTIE FRANCES8 . . . . . 252, 319
  MARIE 251
  Morris 252
  ROSALIE MAE8 . . . . . . 252, 316
  RUSSELL PATRICK8 . . . . 252, 319
  SANDRA ELAINE8 . . . . . 252, 317
  Thomas 252
  William 252
LEARN families 252
LECKENSTEIN
  EDWIN C 224
  LORA JANE 224
LEE
  ROBIN 314
  Lee (Robert E) 122
LENTS 45
  Anna 47
LENTZ 40
  Anna 47, 71
  Joanne 76
  Margaret 72
  Maria 70
  Michael & Catherine 69
  Peter 72
  Philip 70
LEONARD
  Emeline 138
  Fernando 138
  Fernando F 125, 138
  Job Sidney 125, 138
  Job Strong 138
  Leonard families 139
Leppard
  Ellen 233
LERCH
  Anthony & Marg (Dodsworth) . . 242
  BEVERLY 300
  BEVERLY SUSAN 242, 301
  CAROL LEA 301
  DANIEL JEROME8 300
  DIANE MARIE 301
  ELEANOR 300
  ELVIE 242
  EVERETT ERWIN7 . . . . . . 242, 301
  HELEN 301
  MARSHA ELLEN 300
  MATHEW ALLEN 300

LERCH (cont'd)

SEWARD JEROME7 . . . . . 242, 300
SEWARD PEREZ 242
STEVEN DALE8 301
VALERIE LOUISE 300
VANESSA GAIL 301

LEROW

LIBBIE 159

LEVINS

CHRISTINE 296
ROBERT 296
TIMOTHY ERIC9 296

LEWIS

ALFRED DENNISON 190
EDITH GERTRUDE6 . . . . . 190, 232
GERTRUDE ELLA5 190
Thom & Minerva Lewis (Westcott) . 190

LEYBURN

BRADLEY WILLIAM 298
BRIAN EARL9 298
BRUCE 298
CINDY 298
DALE JAMES9 298
EARL J8 298
JANICE 298
JOYCE 298
LAWRENCE 298
MARJORIE 298
NATHAN JAY 298

LILLABRIDGE

Canelia <sic> 172

LINCOLN

Louisa 94
Mrs Geo 68
W F 94

LINK

EDNA 179
ELBERT 179

LINTS

ANNA v
ANNA 89
Catharine/Catherine 54, 89
DUANE 144
Duane,Jane A 90
Elizabeth 89
Harry 90
HATTIE 144
Jacob 89
JOHN 88-90
John & Anna 71
John & Mary 90
John & Mary (Oyer) 89
Lister 90
Margaret 89, 125
Maria 89
Martha,Catherine,Jane,Philip . 90
MARY/POLLY 88, 112
NANCY 54, 71, 89
Peter 54, 89
Peter & Eliz (Bowman) . . . 112
Philip 89, 90
Philip & Mary (Rinckle) . . . 88
Polly 90

Sarah 89
LINTS families 89

LIPPERT

HAZEL EVA (HOUSE) 297

LITTLE

AGNES 227
John & Mary (Kensie) 227
SARAH 309

LITWILLER

John & Francoise (Serre) . . . 340
Magdalena 340

LOCKER

Ada 257

LOMMEN

Leonard H 303
PATRICIA K 303

LONES

George 69
Susanna 69

LONG (Lang?) 180
LONG/LANG (?), LAURA 180

LONGYEAR

CHARLES LESLIE9 299
CHERYL 299
DAWN MARIE9 299
EUNICE 298
JEFFREY TODD 299
JOSEPH BYRON 299
KATHIE 299
LESLIE 298
STANLEY CHARLES 299
STEPHEN JOHN 299
VIRGINIA JUNE8 299

Loomis

Francis & Maria (Museley) . . . 107
PARTHENA E 107

LOUGEE

CHARLES FAY 203
Charlie 204
Fanny 204
Frank A 204
Fred & Fannie May (Fay) . . . 203
Frederick 204
GEORGIA WINIFRED7 . . . . 204, 248
NELLIE JULIAETTE6 203
LOUGEE families 204

LOUGHMAN

KERRY T 279
PATRICIA 279

LOUNSBURY

BEULAH (BAY) 278
Loveland & Daggets 94

LOVELESS

PATRICIA 298

LOWENSTEIN

Anne Barbara 338
Loyalists 77

LUDWIG

HAROLD 219, 266
WINIFRED 219, 266

LUSK

Anna Louise 241

Lutheran 11, 21, 24-26, 28, 29, 51, 312, 339
Lutheran Church of the Incarnate
   Word 28
Lutheran Church—Missouri Synod . 29
Lutheran Trinity Church 26
Lutheranism 24
Lutherans 21, 26, 27, 339
LYNCH
   _____ (_____) 263
   ANNA 263
   Edward 96
   GEORGE WILLIAM 263
   HARRY 263
   JEANNE DOROTHY 263
   JEFF 309
   JESSICA 309
   KATHRYN 309
   MAUREEN (_____) 263
   VIRGINIA ANN8 263
LYND
   Ann(A) 213
   Elizabeth 213
   Jane 213
   John 213
   Julia 213
   Margaret 213
   Mark 213
   Mich & Nancy (Kelly) 213
   Michael 213
   Pat & Mary (McKenna) . . 211, 213
   Patrick 213
   Rosana/Rose 213
   SARAH 211, 213
   Thomas Wm 213
   Wm John 213
LYNPH
   MARY FRANCES 290
LYON
   ALICE A 160
   Lewis & Susannah (_____) . . 160
   Susannah (_____) 160
MacWethy 71
MADISON
   MARY ELIZ/BETTY 267
MAIERHOFER
   DANIEL 293
   ELLEN 293
MANCHESTER
   Lewis W & Clara (Hall) . . . 236
   RUTH AMELIA 236
MANN
   GEORGE A 157
   MARTHA 157
MANNING
   Marguerite 332
Marclay
   J 342
MARLETTE
   BELLE HATTIE5 . . . . . 158, 197
   BLANCHE 197
   CLAUDE HORACE 197

   Emily 108, 158
   ERMA E.6 . . . . 198, 241
   GEORGE MARTIN 158
   HARRY GEORGE5 . . . . . 158, 197
   John & Margaret (Comstock) . . 158
   LAURA M7 241
   RICHARD H 241
   ROSINA A.6 . . . . 197, 241
MARSH
   ADRIAN CASE 247
   BARRY OYER 247
   DEBRA ANN 247
   EVELYN JEAN8 247
   HELEN 247
   JASON FRANCIS 247
   JOHN 247
   JOHN WM 247
   KAREN 247
   LAUREN THOMAS 247
   MARGARET 246
   MELONY 247
   MICHAEL ANTHONY 247
   MICHAEL ROGER 247
   MICHELE ANN9 247
   MILLESSIA ANN 247
   SHEILA ANN 247
   THOMAS DUWAYNE 247
   WILLIAM RICHARD 246
MARSHALL
   Susan 158
Martin
   Hans (John) 8
MARTINEZ
   RENEE 315
MARTYN
   JESSIE ALICE SEAVER 198
MARVEN
   BRIDGET 213
MARVIN
   Alonzo & Emma (Button) . . . 194
   Asher & Elsie (Wilcox) . . . 153
   CATHERINE 282
   CLARA 233
   Cora & Eugene 153
   CORA BELL5 192
   CYNTHIA8 282
   DAVID 282
   EUGENE/GENE SHERBURN 192
   GEORGE ROBERT7 . . . . . 233, 282
   Henry F & Esther (Hall) . . . 192
   HOWARD HUDSON/DEKE7 . .192, 233, 282
   HOWARD HUDSON7 233
   JESSIE 194
   JOSEPHINE 153
   MAE 282
   MELLONIE 282
   SHARON 282
   STEPHEN GEORGE 282
   SYLVIA 282
   WADE8 282
MASON
   Eunice 123

MASON (cont'd)

Nathan 123
MATERA
  LOUISE 292
  MARY ELLEN 293
  RAYMOND JOSEPH 292
MATT

  ELLEN 293
MANCHESTER
  Lewis W & Clara (Hall) . . . 236
  RUTH AMELIA 236
  Sarah 194
MAY
  JASON 309
  JOHN 309
  LESLIE 309
  LILLIAN 237
MAYO
  NANCY 218
  RICHARD 218
McAMBER
  Clara Jane 198
McCADDEN
  Jack 213
  Nellie 213
McCANN
  JANICE CLAYCOMB 298
McCARTHY
  NELLIE 213
McCASLIN
  JOSEPH 330
  LORRAINE 330
McCHESNEY
  LINDA 283
McClellan, Gen George 252
McCLOUD
  Catherine Mae 285
McCOLLUM
  HELEN 303
McCORMACK
  John C & Thelma (Clark) . . . 311
  MARION CLARK 311
McCOY
  SUSAN CAROL 284
  Wm & Ellen 284
McCULTY
  JEFFREY 298
  JUDY 298
McDOWELL
  BARBARA LYNN 300
  CARL 198
  CHARLENE 297
  CORA ELIZABETH 160
  DAVID ELMER8 297
  DONALD ROY7 . . . . . . 241, 297
  EARL HARRISON 198
  EARL WAYNE7 . . . . . 241, 300
  Edw & Julia (Auyer) 235
  Edwin 103, 152, 158, 193
  ELLEN 300
  ELMER ELLSWORTH5 . . . . 160, 198
  Etta (TIFFT) 199
  EUNICE 297

EUNICE BLANCHE7 . . . . . . 241, 298
FLORA B5 . . . . 159, 198
FLORA ELIZABETH 198, 235
FREDERICK JOHN8 298
GARY CARL8 300
Harold 241

EUGENE/GENE SHERBURN 192
GEORGE ROBERT7 . . . . . . 233, 282
Henry F & Esther (Hall) 192
HOWARD HUDSON/DEKE7 . .
Henry 158, 160
Henry & Susan (Marshall) . . . 158
JEFFREY 300
JENNIE MAY 160
JESSIE 198
JOHN JEFFREY 298
JUDY ANNE 298
JULIA ANN4 158
JULIAN HAROLD6 . . . . . . 199, 241
JUNE 299
KATHLEEN ANN 300
KAY ELAINE 298
LAURA 198, 300
LESLIE MICHELLE 300
LESTER DALE 300
LIBBIE 159
LOIS 300
MARIAM 241
MARJORIE RUTH 241
MARJORIE RUTH7 . . . . . . 241, 298
MARTHA ELIZABETH 199
MARY LOUISE7 . . . . . . 241, 299
MATTHEW MARK9 300
MICHAEL GLENN 298
PAMELA KAYE9 298
PATRICIA 298
PAULETTE ADELE 300
RALPH EDWIN7 . . . . . . 241, 299
RORY HAROLD 300
ROSEMARIE8 300
SANDRA LEE 300
SARAH 198
SCOTT ROBERT 298
SUSAN CHRISTINA5 . . . .151, 160, 199
TAMARA RUTH 297
THELMA 298
THOMAS ROY 297
TIMOTHY DAVID9 297
TODD MICHAEL 297
WALDO GLENN7 . . . . . . 241, 298
WILLIS G5 159
McDUFFIE
  ANDREA 297
  DAVID FERGUSON 297
  ELISSA BROOKE 297
  ELIZABETH 296
  GREGORY PHILLIPS 297
  HAROLD FRITZ 296
  JOSHUA ALEX9 297
  KURT CHARLES8 297
  MARK WHITNEY 297
  TAMMY 297

McELROY
  Bernard & Mary (Demer) . . . 137
  Edward 137
  OLY/OLA 137
McELWAIN
  DARLENE JEAN 313
  Donald D & _____ 313
McFARLAND
  Mary 119
McFeather 116
McFEELEY
  DOROTHY 251
  ELLEN EMILY 250
  GERTRUDE 251
  John & Gertrude (Hill) . . . 250
  JOHN THOMAS 251
McFEELEY families 251
McGnot
  Clem & Elis Barbara . . . 79
McGowan
  Charles Grandison 196
  DORIS ELIZ/BETTY 239
  EDWARD TIFFT6 . . . . . 196, 239
  ELLEN TIFFT7 . . . . . 239, 293
  ETHEL SARAH6 . . . . . 196, 239
  FREDERICK CROSSMAN 196
  HAZEL CAMILLA6 . . . . . 196, 239
  HELEN LOUISE6 . . . . . 196, 239
  JENNIE 196
  LOUISE JANE7 . . . . . 239, 292
  MARGARET 239
  Mrs. Fred 195
McGRATH 214
McGUIRE
  FRANK H 180
  MYRTLE MAY 180
McINTYRE
  ELWYN 291
  HARRIET 291
  IDA E 191
  Lyman & Jennie (Burns) . . . 291
  RACHELLE MARIE 291
  VALERIE M8 291
McKAIG
  DORIS MARGUERITE/MARGE . . . 332
  F. Burton & Marg'ite (Manning) .
                                332
McKENNA 214
  MARY 211, 213
McKERNAN 214
  ANNA 211
  Michael & Hannah (Simmons) . 211
McLARNEY
  AMBER RENEE9 328
  ERIN LEIGH 328
  LINDA 327
  MEGGAN THERESE 328
  OWEN STEVEN 327
McLAUGHLIN
  JODYNE 294
McLYMOND
  LaPEARL 136

McLYMOND, _____ 136
McMickle
  Mary 188
McPHERSON
  CAROL 247
  CAROL RUTH 247
  DONALD 247
  EVELYN 247
  LARRY 247
  RICHARD ALLEN9 247
  ROBERTA SUE 247
  THOMAS WM 247
McPike
  Anna 117
Mead
  Carrie 157, 195
  EDNA L 195
  GEORGE W 195
  GRACE E 195
MEAGHER
  IAN P 318
  JOHN DAVID 318
  MARILYNN 318
  Missy 318
  SEAN10 318
Mebie 116
Memphis Baptist Church . . . 152, 157
Memphis Christian Church 159
Mengins
  Leicester 56
  Lois 56
Mennonite 9, 26, 338, 339
Mennonites 7-9, 25
MERKLEY
  ETHEL 239
  HERBERT ALBERT 239
MERRIFIELD
  MAE 282
MERRIT
  ELLEN 300
Methodist Episcopal church . . . 179
Methodist Protestant 26
Methodists 26-28
METTLER
  DOROTHY 199
  DOROTHY (_____) 199
  EDNA DORIS 200
  FREDERICK GEORGE 199
  HENRY 199
  Jacob & Mary (Ross) 199
  JESSIE 199
  LENA ALICE 200
  LENA ALICE6 243
  MARION AUYER 200
  MARION AUYER6 243
  MAUDE 199
  SATIE ESTELLE6 . . . . . 199, 242
METZGER
  JANE 215
  LaVERNE 215
  OLIVE 215

Metzler, Ruth . . . . ii, 267
MEYER 90
  Catherine 86
  Joseph 86
Michael 10
  Franz Louis 9
Middaugh
  Sarah 97
MIEKAM
  EDWARD O 273
  MARGUERITE 273
  MARTHA JEAN8 273
MILATO
  ANTHONY 262
  RACHEL 262
MILBY
  Guy & Zadie (Cross) 208
  Helen 208
  Linda Marie 208
  Mary Lucinda/Cindi) 208
  Robert 208
MILLER . . . . . v, 11, 26, 40, 71
  ANNA CATHERINE 63
  C G 88
  Elizabeth/Eliza . 54, 55, 72, 123
  ELIZABETH ANN4 . . . . . .55, 128
  ELLEN M 128
  FRANCES E 128
  George M & Catherine (Bekker) . 55
  GEORGE MATTHEW 63
  GRETCHEN 174
  HENRY A 128
  Huldah 55
  James 123, 174
  JEAN E 226
  John 102
  John & Mary 55, 128
  Joseph 123
  MARY A5 128
  Mary Elizabeth 102
  MARY ROXANNE 55, 200
  MARY/POLLY 55, 95
  Michael 55
  Minerva 123
  PETER 55, 128
  Valentine 55, 60
  Valentine & Sarah (Witrig) . . 55
MILLER families 128
MILLIGAN
  Guy 212
  Josephine 212
  Nellie 212
ministerium 24
MINOR
  CECELIA EMMA 219
Minuit
  Peter 117
MISHEK
  Anna 263
MISNER
  Geraldine (Holland) 56
  Virginia 56

MITCHELL
  BARBARA 295
MITTINS
  ANITA 303
  Art F & Elsie M (Clark) 303
  FRANK WILLIAM 303
  PATRICIA 303
  RONALD ARTHUR 303
  SHARON ELAINE8 303
MONTGOMERY
  Richard 48
MOORE
  ANDREW 269
  CAROL YVONNE8 269
  Carrie 230
  CHRISTOPHER 269
  DONALD EDWIN 269
  EDWIN J 268
  Erastus 257
  Frederica 257
  IONA 268
  MERLYN 269
Mormons 28
MORRIS
  Betsy Holden 56
  Jane 56
  John Bennett 56
  Richard Bennett 56
  Robert 347, 348
  Robert H 56
  Robert T 56
Morris, Gouverneur 349
MORRISON
  DAVID P 276
  MICHAEL D9 276
  NANCY 276
  STEVEN P 276
MORRISON-FERGUSON
  CHRISTOPHER ALLEN10 306
MORROW
  AVA 98
  Betsy (Oyer) 98
  EUDORA 98
  James 98
  Jenette 98
  John G 97, 98
  Lafayette 98
  Mary 98
MORROW families
  MORROW 98
MORTON
  HUGH 203
MOSHER/MOSHIER
  ELIZABETH 133
  George J 133
Mosimann 8
Moslems 28
MOSS
  CATHERINE MARGUERITE8 292
  DIANE 292
  MICHAEL 292
Mueller 214

MULLEN
  BECKY LOU8 . . . . 272, 332
  ELEANOR 271
  KATHY ANN8 . . . . 272, 332
  RUSSELL 271
MULLER
  Andreas & Eva 55
  Peter 341
  see also variant spellings . . 4
Muller/Miller 8
MULTER . . . . v, 40, 87
  55
  SALLY 55, 132
MUNDLEIN
  Caroline 284
MUNGER
  Elizabeth 87
  Justin 87
Murphy 214
  Betsy 146
Murray
  Lydia 322
MUSE
  BARBARA 269
MYER(S)
  John 84
  Maria 84
MYERS
  CINDY 298
  EUGENE 298
  John 84, 219
  LOIS 219
  Mary 84
NANNEN
  Agatha 212
  Annabelle 212
  Beatrice 212
  Clara 212
  Eleanor 212
  Genevieve 212
  Herman 212
  Margaret 212
  Mary Jo 212
  Mary Katherine 212
  Vincent 212
NASH
  Maria 178
NASH, _____ 137
NEFF v
  ALICE 185
  Andrew & Ann (Clary) 185
  James 131
NEGUS
  FLORENCE 293
  FRANCIS CARLETON 293
  JODYNE 294
  MELISSA LYNN 294
  NANCY 294
  NANCY ANN9 294
  STEVEN JOHN 294
NEHILL
  Michael 213

Nancy/Ann 213
NEIMAN
  Margaret 259
NELSON
  AGNES6 . . . . 175, 218
  BEN & ANNE (MORTON) 124
  CHARLOTTA/LOTTIE6 . . . . 175, 217
  Eliza 114, 123, 124
  John & Lena B (Kelly) 175
  LAURA6 . . . . 175, 218
  Lottie 219
  MARGARET 175, 201, 218
  MARGARET EVE/EVA4 123
  Mary E 124, 175
  SHARON 282
  STEVE 282
  Wilbur 120, 123, 124
  WILBUR A 123
  WILBUR DAVID 124
  WILLIAM J 175
NELSON families 124, 175
NENSEN
  BETTY JEAN 290
NEUPERT
  Clifton & Sophia 240
  LAURA W 240
NEVIN
  MARY VIRGINIA 274
New Orleans Oyers . 4, 9, 17, 21, 70,
  340
New York Oyers 21, 70, 337
New York Reg't 85
NEWELL
  ROSINA 197, 241
  WILFRED 197
  WILFRED WILIET7 241
NEWTON
  Alma 257
  Frank R 257
NICHOLAS
  CHARLOTTE A 106
  Garret & Nancy 106
NICHOLS
  Martha 141, 156
  Matila A 194
  Michael 156
Nichols & Gardinier 117
NICOLETTE
  JOANNE 201
  Joseph & Rose (Fragale) . . . 201
Nielson
  Paul Anthon i
NILES
  Deborah 140, 141
  NATHAN & DEBORAH (NILES) . . . 141
NITKOWSKI
  DARYL 299
  DEBORAH 299
NOONAN
  BARBARA 279
NORDSTROM
  Li 57

NORMAN, _____ 177
North Jersey Highlander 13
NORTHRUP
  Addie 178
  ELIZABETH JANE 287
  L H 178
  Rufus & Martha (Jones) . . . 287
NOSAL
  CHRISTIE ANN 316
  LYNNORE MARIE9 316
  MARLENE KAY 316
  ROSALIE 316
  WALTER 316
NOSTRANT
  Emma 191
  John W & Eunice C (Spencer) . 191
NOTARPOLE
  NANCY ANN 294
NUSS
  MARTHA 287
  MATHEW 287
  TIMOTHY 287
NUTT
  James W 60
NYE
  EARL 265
  KARRIE MARIE 265
  KELLIE SUE9 265
  SUZANNE 265
O'BRIAN
  CHRISTINE 290
O'BRIEN
  CATHERINE 221
O'CONNELL
  Bridget 211
  Charles 208
  John & Jane (White) 211
  Shayne 208
O'NEAL
  ADELINE 135
O'NEAL, _____ 135
O'Neill
  JENNIE 174
Odell
  Charles 98
  Ella 98
OLGEATY
  BARBARA 291
  DIANE 238, 292
  EDWARD 238
  EDWARD7 . . . . 138, 238, 291
  JUNE 238
  SANDRA LYN 291
  SCOTT EDWARD 291
  VICTORIA ANN8 291
OMOHUNDRO
  ERIC MICHAEL9 295
  LINDA 295
  RICHARD C 295
Oneidas 45
OSGOOD
  BERDETTE EDWARD9 319

KITTIE 319
ROY 319
WAYNE DOUGLAS 319
OSTROWSKI 213
OTTEN 116
OUDERKIRK
  Lyman B 73
  Philinda 73
Our vii
OWEN
  Martin & Thankful 96
OYD
  Susan 47
OYER . . vii, 11, 25, 26, 32, 64, 68,
          71, 84, 87, 100, 132, 181
  _____ (Carter) 190
  Aaron 101, 102, 146
  Abraham 341
  ADALINE 94, 102
  ADAM4 95
  ADELIA4 92
  Adeline . . . 116, 134, 143, 144 183
  AGNES JONES6 . . . . . . 176, 222
  ALBERT4 93
  ALICE (HULSER) 184
  ALICE (NEFF) 185
  ALICE E5 136
  ALISON 319
  ALLAN 224
  ALMAN 125, 140
  Almeda 96, 111
  ALMEDA L4 96
  ALMEDA4 136
  Almira . 93, 94, 103, 135, 146-148
  AMANDA 110, 119
  AMELIA 110
  AMY LYNN 313
  ANDREW J 90, 129
  ANDREW ROBERT9 321
  ANGELINE4 . . . . . 97, 138, 139
  ANN4 92
  ANNA 129
  ANNA (WELDON) 163
  ANNA CATHERINE 63
  ANNA6 215
  ANNA7 263
  ANNE MARIE 324
  ANNE4 131
  ANSON 55, 163, 200
  ARLENE 201
  ARTHUR 175, 182, 216
  AUGUSTUS V.4 . . . . . . .95, 128
  AUGUSTUS/GUST 90
  BARBARA 269, 276, 331, 341
  Barbara N 340
  BARTHOLOMEW/BURT6 . . . . 174, 215
  BEATRICE JANE7 . . . . . 210, 259
  BERNARD GEORGE7 . . . . . ,229 277
  BERNICE 203, 245, 307
  BERTHA 163, 182, 275
  BETSEY . . . 97, 102, 118, 135, 144
  BETSEY (OYER) 135, 143

OYER (cont'd)

BETSEY4	143
BETTY	308
BETTY (_____)	223
BEULAH	230
BEULAH (BAY) LOUNSBURY . . .	278
Bob 343,	344
BRENDA7	243
Brian 255, 322-3
Burton	186
BYRON EUGENE	114
BYRON EUGENE5 114,	174
C O	334
CARMALETTA	313
CAROL	314
CAROL PEARL8 278,	313
CAROLINE . . 110, 125, 140,	161
CARRIE ANN	315
CASE ANN8	262
Cath (wid Edw)	334
CATH ELIZABETH4	96
CATHARINA/CATHERINA . . . 49,	341
CATHARINE . . 76, 93, 99, 112,	163
CATHARINE3	111
CATHARINE4 . . . . 94, 97,	308
CATHERINE . . . 54, 96, 110, 113,
	138, 221, 334
CATHERINE (ROY)	119
CATHERINE ELIZABETH	134
CATHERINE/NAN	217
CECELIA . 177, 190, 219, 266,	334
CELIA	163
CELIA MAY	200
CHARITY 85, 100-102,	143
Charity (FRANK)	128
CHARLES A.5 136,	185
CHARLES D.5 127,	178
CHARLES H.5 . . . . .147, 178,	189
CHARLES HENDRIX7 225,	272
CHARLES V	114
CHARLES WALKER7	230
CHARLOTTE ANNE	223
CHERYL	273
CHESTER RICHARD	131
Christian 9, 62,	341
CHRISTINA	109
CHRISTOPHER JAMES	313
CHRISTOPHER SCOTT9	269
CLARA	185
CLARA BEULAH	225
CLARA E.5	122
Clarence 130,	247
CLARENCE D.5 . 130, 176, 179,	180
CLARENCE SEYMOUR/TANKIE6 168,	203
CLARK E.5 114,	165
CLAUD E	182
COLLEEN	262
CORA A	127
CORA A.5 127,	179
CORA M	182
Daniel 49,	73
DANIEL3	112
DARLENE	313

Darrell . . . . i, 3,	25
David 93, 128,	201
David & Mary Eliz (Frank) . . .	120
DAVID SMITH5 . . 114, 119, 167,	203
DAVID SMITH8 255,	319
DAVID3 . . 71, 79-82, 85, 90, 100,
	124, 180
DAVID4 90,	93
DAVIS4 95,	98
DEBORAH	201
DEBRA 201,	308
DELILAH	137
DeMONT FREDERICK6 185,	230
DENNIS6	201
DEWITT4 (MILETTE?) 110,	162
DIANE ELIZABETH8 255,	324
DIANE HELEN	276
DIANN	276
Dilect	92
DOLORES7 215,	261
Donald 163, 164,	182
DONALD CHARLES	222
DONALD GARY9 308,	343
DONALD H.5	201
DONALD J6	201
DONALD8	275
DORA	135
DORIS	275
EARL 136, 164,	182
EARL C	182
EARL5	201
EDITH 203, 245,	307
Edward	334
EDWARD JACOB6 176,	221
EDWIN 110,	217
EDWIN/EDDY J	122
ELEANOR . . . 177, 178, 219,	272
ELEANOR MAE7 225,	271
Eleanor R 179,	334
ELEANOR7	266
ELIJAH4	96
Elisabeth	49
ELISABETHA . . . 31, 46, 48, 49,	51
ELIZABETH . 63, 66, 67, 72, 73, 76,
	77, 83, 95, 107, 110, 334, 341
Elizabeth (Harvey)	96
ELIZABETH (HOWE)	146
ELIZABETH (MOSHER)	133
ELIZABETH (TEELING)	215
ELIZABETH A./LIZZIE	203
ELIZABETH ANN 55, 90,	128
ELIZABETH ANNE9	323
Elizabeth M	334
ELIZABETH/ELIZA	62
ELIZABETH3	107
ELIZABETH4 . . . 93, 109, 134,	161
Ella (Brown)	167
ELLA5	162
ELLADE EMMA5 122,	176
Ellen 185, 250,	259
ELLEN (BURCH)	165
ELLEN AIMEE 229,	277

OYER (cont'd)

ELLEN/ELLA (Brown) . . . 167, 172	GERTRUDE (WILLIS) 185
ELNORA 131	GERTRUDE ALICE7 . . . . . . 229, 275
EMERY5 163	GLEN/N H 185
EMILY 135	Glenn N 334
EMMA 93, 163, 178	Gordon . . . . i, 2, 340
EMMALINE 110, 161	Grace 168, 204, 205
ERIN 269	GRACE (_____) 185
ESTHER 176, 190, 223, 232	GRACE L 182
ETHEL 227, 228	GRETCHEN 174
EUGENE 131, 174, 215	Gretchen G 334
EUGENE & JENNIE (O'NEILL) . . 263	Guy 334
EUGENE RUSSELL8 . . 259, 326, 327	H Eugene 176, 334
EUGENE S.5 . . . . 136, 186	HANNAH 112
EUNICE 136	HANNAH/NANCY 76
EUNICE (_____) 136	Hans 1, 2
EUNICE7 . . . . 219, 266	HARLAN EUGENE5 . . . .120, 122, 176
EVA 164	HARLAN STANLEY7 176
EVE 76	HARRIET 98, 128, 189
EVELINE D 130	HARRIET CATHARINE4 . . . . .90, 129
Ezra D (5?) 163	Harry 334
EZRA HUGH6 . . . .110, 200, 243	HARVEY EUGENE . . 176, 222, 223, 271
EZRA4 161	HARVEY III 271
Fanny 113	HATTIE 144
FLORA 182, 190	HAZEL H6 186
FLORENCE V 130	HELEN 227, 277
FLORIS 203	HENRY 54, 76, 110, 112
FLOYD 182	Hildebrand 1
FRANCES 99, 272	Hiram 101, 102, 143
FRANCES AUGUSTA5 183	HIRAM4 144
FRANK 137, 267	HORACE 110, 182
FRANK EMMONS5 . 120, 122, 175, 223	Howard 182
FRANK J 129, 175	HOWARD HULSER6 229
Frank P 120	HOWARD6 184
FRANKLIN PIERCE5 . . . . 114, 174	HUGH MILLER 200
Fred & Olga 217	IDA M 129
FRED F 215	IONA MARIE7 . . . . 222, 268
Frederick . vii, 2, 4, 8, 11, 17,	Ira 31, 150, 154, 190
19, 24, 26, 31, 32, 45, 48, 51,	IRA4 . . . . 103, 146, 147
71, 121, 163, 254, 337	IRENE 181, 227
FREDERICK A.6 . . . .131, 174, 214	IRENE (PARISH?) 181
FREDERICK CHARLES6 176	IRWIN7 215
FREDERICK D 131	Jacob 2, 51, 53, 61, 62, 87,
FREDERICK F.7 262	96, 128, 253, 340
FREDERICK JEROME 262	Jacob & Amanda 121
Frederick2 48, 53, 63–66, 73, 97	Jacob & Margaret (Bekker) . . . 102
Frederick3 . . . . 64, 91, 95, 97	JACOB BURT 114
FREDERICK5 182	JACOB J 62, 90, 125
Friederich/Frederick 17	Jacob M 116
G JAMES 273	JACOB P . 72,73,76,102–3,107,192,289
G N 334	Jacob2 . . . . . . 59, 60, 73, 120
G ROBERT8 272	JACOB3 . . . . . . 64, 73, 95, 136
GEORGE WASHINGTON5 . . . 135, 185	Jacob4 . . . . 80, 81, 83, 119, 166
George . 45, 55, 163, 164, 341	JACQUELINE 224
GEORGE HENRY4 . . . .111, 162, 200	Jakob 1
George J 49	James 73
George W 135, 312	JAMES DAVID7 . . . . . .178, 225, 272
George3 . . . 64, 91, 95, 97, 135	JANE 162, 272
George4 98	JANETTE5/JANE 144
GEORGE5 200	JANICE 177, 219, 267, 331
GEORGE6 . . . . 200, 243	Jean 340
GERALDINE 243	JEANETTE 217
Gertrude 185	JEFFREY 201, 277, 313

OYER (cont'd)

Jennie (O'Neill) 174
JENNIFER 277
JEROME ALLEN/MIKE8 . . . 251, 314
JERUSHA 99
JESSIE 167
JOAN 215, 262
JOAN PATRICIA8 . . . . . 263, 331
JOANNE (NICOLETTE) 201
JoANNE8 277
Johann 1
JOHANN FRIEDRICH (FREDERICK) Sr .
                                49
JOHANN GEORGE 49
Johann Jacob-see also Jacob 32, 45
JOHANN JACOB2 . . . . . . 49, 59
JOHANNA 229
Johannes 340
John 4, 61, 85, 126
John & Charity 101
JOHN F.3 98
JOHN H.4 . . . . .92, 130
JOHN L 135
John Martin 9
JOHN P³ . .76, 85, 100, 128, 145
John S i
JOHN3 . . 90, . 62, 90, 132, 135
JOHN4 . 90, 93, 101, 127, 133, 178
JOHN5 146
JONATHAN PAUL 314, 315
JONATHAN RUSSELL9 332
Joseph 2, 98, 139, 340
JOSEPH ALOYSIUS7 . . . . 215, 263
Joseph I 340
JOSEPH4 . . . . 97, 137
JOSHUA MICHAEL10 314
JOYCE 246, 309, 343, 344
JUDITH 110
JULIA 163, 200
Julia (Deeley) 163
JULIE 325
JULIUS C4 99
JUSTIN PHILLIP 315
KAREN6 201
Kastlan 1
KATHERINE/KITTIE 6 . . . 174, 216
KATHLEEN ANN 276
Kenneth 163
KENNETH ALAN8 . . . . . . 263, 331
KENNETH K 201
LARRY WILLIAM7 276
LAURA 129
Lavina 129
LAWRENCE E 227
Lee & Edith Brougham . . 309, 343
LEE EUGENE6 . . . . 182, 228
LeGrand L 312
LEGRAND L6 185
LELAND CLARENCE7 . .203, 245, 307
LELAND9 308
LENNORA/NORA 186
LEON IRVING 175, 176
LEON IRVING6 223

LEON J.5 . . . . 147, 190
LESTER5 . . . . 164, 201
LEVI 95, 135, 143, 144
LEWIS7 227
LILLIAN (   ) 217
LILLIAN FRED'ICA/FREDA . . . 222
LINDA 271
LINDA CAROL8 . . . . . . 259, 327
LINDA CHRISTIAN 271
LIZZIE 129, 184
Lois J 120, 176
LOIS PATRICIA7 . . . . . 223, 271
LORENE MARIE7 . . . . . . 203, 246
LORENZ/Lorentz 49
Lorette(a) . . . 126, 127, 146
LOUIS/LEWIS6 . . . . . . 181, 227
LUANNE MARIE 327
LUCILLE, (____) 217
LUKE HENRY7 . . . . 229, 276
LULU ELEANOR6 178
LYNDA KAY 275
MABEL 147
Magdalena 93, 340
MALATA 110
MALDEN E5 . . . . 131, 181
MARCELLA (WHITE) YAHN 319
Marcus 25
Margaret . . . 57, 61, 76, 81, 126,
                        201, 203, 254
Margaret (Crumb) 82
Margaret (Vedder) 116
MARGARET ANN, "Anna M" . . . 122
MARGARET E 90, 123, 126
MARGARET EVE/EVA4 123
MARGARET RUTH7 246
MARGARET3 106
MARGARET7 228
MARGARET(HA) (BEKKER) 51, 53, 59, 62
MARGARETHE2 63
MARIA/MARY 63, 93, 134
Maria Cath/Eliz 85
MARION 200, 227
MARJORIE 322
MARK 200, 312
MARK ALAN 324
MARSHA7 223
Martin 1
Mary 61, 68, 72, 92, 102-3, 112, 114
                    134, 140, 162, 341
MARY (CLARK) 113
MARY (FRANK) 144
MARY AGNES 326
MARY ALICE5 . . . . 131, 180
MARY ANN/POLLY 67, 90, 130
MARY BETH 276
MARY CAROLE8 272
MARY E . 71,79,81,82,90,124,127,132
MARY E.5 175
Mary Elizabeth 177
Mary Elizabeth (Frank) . . . 132
MARY ELIZABETH4 . . . . . . 97, 137
MARY FRANCIS 200

OYER (cont'd)

MARY FREDERICA 134
MARY JANE7 221
Mary Margaret 151, 315
MARY ROXANNE 55, 200
MARY/POLLY . 55, 62, 88, 95, 102
MATTHEW 224
MATTIE6 167
MAY 215
MELISSA MUSE 269
Melvin 181
MICHAEL ALLEN9 314
MICHAEL CHARLES 272
MICHAEL SCOTT9 327
Michael3 . . . 64, 97, 138, 177
Michael4 . . . . 98, 138
MICHAEL9 275
MICHELLE ELLEN 313
MICHELLE JO 272
MIKE (see also Jerome). . . . 314
MILDRED K 227
MILDRED S 182
MILFORD C 227
MYRTLE 222
NANCY . 54, 91, 92, 125, 140, 224
NATHAN 224
NELLIE E (____) 182
NELLIE JULIAETTE6 . .168, 203, 204
NELSON4 . . . . .99, 140
NICOLE MARIE9 322
NORMAN CLIFFORD 200
OLGA 214
OLIVE 174, 175, 215, 216
OLY/OLA B 137
OSCAR W.4 163
PATRICIA 272
PATRICIA LYNN 269
PATRICK JOHN, Jr 313
PATRICK JOHN8 . . . 251, 313, 314
Paul F 167
PAUL FRANCIS7 . 210, 211, 250, 259
PAUL KEVIN9 313
PAUL8 275
PERRY R.5 . . . . 131, 182
Peter . . . vii, 1, 4, 31, 46, 48,
          49, 61, 75, 95, 254, 275
PETER & ELIZABETH 54
PETER D4 . 77, 83, 106, 113,120,
          143, 144, 174, 217
PETER F3 . 53, 64, 89, 92, 93, 134
Peter F. & Catharine 92
Peter J4 103
Peter2 . 53, 57, 60, 73, 76, 77,
          90, 113, 154
Peter3 93
PHIDELIA5 127
PHILINDA4 . . . . . .102, 145, 146
PHYLLIS (Smith). . . 82, 252, 257
R. E 120
RACHEL . . 54, 76, 102, 112, 113,
          143, 163, 215, 224
RACHEL ANN 262
RACHEL3 111

RACHEL4 144
RAYMOND ELBERT8 . 246, 307, 308, 343
RAYMOND HOWARD7 . . . . . . 229, 275
REUBEN4 92
RICHARD HOWARD5 . . . . . . 134, 184
RICHARD JOHN7 . . . . 229, 275
RICHARD LEA 326
Richard R 180
ROBERT . 92, 130,176, 177, 182, 208,
          217, 219, 334
ROBERT EDWARD9 326
ROBERT EMMONS6 . . . . . . 176, 219
ROBERT FOLTS7 . . . . 230, 278
ROBERT JOSEPH8 . . . . . . 263, 331
ROBERT LEE . . . 229, 246, 276, 308
ROBIN 314
RONALD LEA8 . . . . . ii, 255, 325
ROSCOE CONKLIN6 . . . . . 185, 230
Rose (Duhan) 251, 255, 306
Rose (Duhan) 11, 113, 168, 204, 354
ROXANNA/ROXANA/ROXANNE 64, 99, 125
ROXANN(E)A 97, 136, 138
RUSSELL EUGENE7 . . . . . . 210, 258
RUSSELL JON8 . . . . 263, 331
RUSSELL SCOTT8 269
RUSSELL STEWART7 . . . . . 222, 269
RUTH 176, 220, 230, 263
RUTH MARIE7 . . . . 210, 251
RUTH VERMAY 200
SALINIA E 227
SALLY/SARAH . 92, 102, 133, 138, 143
SARAH 130, 138, 147
SARAH (Davis) 165
SARAH H (BEARDSLEY) 162
SARAH JANE 96, 97, 137, 178
SARAH JENNIE5 129
SCOTT 200
SEMANTHA 109
SETH AARON9 313
SIMON4 . . . . 95, 135
Smith D (see David S5). .120,167,171
Smith & Ella 168
Solomon 73, 76, 109
ST ELMO CHAS6 . . . . . . 179, 225
STEPHANIE ANNE 322
SUSAN 175, 223
SUSAN EVE8 271
SUSAN ROSE 277
SUZANNE 312
Tessie 334
THEOBALD/DAVID3 . . . . . . 61, 62
Theresa 250, 258, 259
THERESA (Rhinesmith) 331
THOMAS B 186
TIMOTHY 201, 315
TINA MARIE8 276
VALERIE 314
VAN A5 128
Vera Alice Boyd 307, 343
Verle 2
Verle & Margaret . . . . .i, 4, 340
VERNA CATHARINE 200

OYER (cont'd)

VICKI 243, 275
Violet 175, 223
VIRGINIA 217
W. Mark - see Wallis 51
Wallace - see Wallis
Wallace & Rose . . . 168, 245
WALLIS/WALLACE SMITH6 . . . 168,
204, 211, 255, 260
Walt & Phyllis 82, 256
WALTER BRIAN8 - see Brian 255, 322
WALTER CHARLES7 . .11, 25, 82, 120
210, 251, 252, 314
WALTER S 114
WHITNEY CATHERINE 322
WILLIAM 64, 113, 201
WILLIAM C 227
WILLIAM H.4 . . . . . .96, 136
WILLIAM/WILLIE6 217
WILLIAM3 99
Willis & Myrtle 269
WILLIS LEVI6 . 120, 174, 176, 222
WILSON MARK8 - see Mark . 278, 312
WINIFRED 177, 219, 266
Oyer Mountain 82
Oyer sisters 138
Oyer, ship list 340
Oyers 26

PADDOCK

Mary 163
Palatinate 340
Palatine . . . 10, 11, 25, 39, 88
Swiss 10

PALETTA

JEANNE 263
SILVIO 263

PALMER

. . . . v, 255
Alma 257
Amos 257
Arthur D 257
Daniel 257
Dave 257
EMMA 258
ESTELLE/STELLA . . .252, 256, 257
Helen 257
Ichobad 257
JONAH DAVIS & EMMA (HALE) 256, 257
James 257
MICAH/MICHAEL 257
Ralph H 257
Rufus 257
Solomon 257
STELLA 257
William 257
PALMER families 257
PALMER generational 257

PALSBO

PATRICIA 272

PAM

PATIENCE 145
Wm and Martha 145

PAQUETTE

JEANNE 291

PARKER

H 227
IRENE 227

PARKHILL

Cora 257
Guy 257

PARMELEE

ELEANOR 300

PARMENTER

. . . . 100
LAMARTHA 100
Martha 99

PARMETER

Jerusha 99

PARRY

Amelia 283
BERTHA ELEANOR 233

PARSON

CATHERINE 282

PARSONS

JANICE 331

PARTRIDGE

Mary J 172
Patridge and Oyer 180

PATTERSON

BERTHA6 197
CAROLE ANNE7 . . . . . 240, 296
CECIL JAMES6 . . . . . 197, 240
CECIL JAMES7 . . . . . 240, 296
CYNTHIA ANNE 296
Dan & Nancy (McCollum) . . 197
JAMES McCOLLUM 196
JESSICA 287
JOHN 190
KATHRYN 296
LAURA 240
LINDA LEE8 296
MARTHA 296
STELLA 196

PAVIA

ANTHONY 262
SHARON 262
PAWINSKI. 213

PAYNE

ELLEN 282
PEABODY 94

PEARCE

Caleb 139
Pheobe 139

PEARSON

ZADEAN 289

PEAVEZ

Maria 221

PECKHAM

CAROLYN 288
CYNTHIA 288
DEBRA 289
JOHN 288
KRISTINA 288
LYCE 288
MELISSA 288
PERRY DEAN 289

PECKHAM (cont'd)

PETER ALLAN8 288
SUSAN 288
THOMAS CRAIG 289
Penn
  William 9
Penn. Dutch 9, 338
Pennsylvania Gazette 66
PERKINS
  Mariett 181
PERRAULT
  CINDY 298
  TIMOTHY 298
PERRYMAN
  Gerlder (?) 203
PETERSON
  DORIS 275
  VIOLET 223
PETRIE . . . . v, 40
  ALBERT JOHN 274
  Anna Catherine 87
  BRIAN LELAND 274
  JENNIFER ANNE 274
  Jost & Cordelis (Demuth) . . . 87
  LOIS 274
  MARY 274
  RICHARD ALBERT 274
  ROBERT WILLARD 274
  ROGER DODGE8 274
PETRY 45
  Marx 35, 39, 63
  Marx – see Petrie 35
Phelps
  Oliver 348
Phelps-Gorham 79, 348
PHILLIPS
        Sergeant 173
  ALICE 218
  ANNETTE 218
  ELIZA (____) 173
  ELIZABETH 173
  GARY 218
  George1 173
  GERALD/CORK8 218
  Helen 172
  HOWARD 218
  Jennie 127
  JOHN 173
  MARGARET 173
  MARY/MAY 171–173
  Sally 172
  Samuel 173
  SANDRA 218
  SARAH 173
  Wendell 173
  William5 173
Phillips bible listings 174
PICKARD
  ANITA MARIE 242
  ANITA MARIE7 303
  DOROTHA ROSE7 . . . . . 242, 302
  FLORENCE 303
  HELEN 303

  KENNETH METTLER 242
  Lewis & Mina (Fenner) 242
  MYRON JOSEPH 242
  SATIE 242
  SUSANNE MARIE8 303
PIERCE
  BRANDON A 330
  BRYAN J9 330
  DIANE 330
  DOROTHY N 330
  Fred 123
  JAMES R 330
  KIM 330
  LORRAINE D 330
  Phebe 123
  Thomas 94
  TINA 330
  TODD A 330
Pilgrims 8
PINCKNEY
  FLORENCE 303
PISCATELLI
  DAVID 219
  JACK 219
  JAMES 219
  JANE 219
  LOIS 219
  MARK 219
  MOLLY 219
  PEGGY 219
  THERESA 219
PLACE
  MARGARET 228
PLANTZ
  ALLURA JUNE 285
  Frank M & Cath (McCloud) . . . 285
PODZIELNY
  JOSEPH ROBERT 264
  MARY 264
  RICHARD 264
POLITO
  IRENE 266
Pompton Plains Reformed Church . . 21
Pope Pius II 7
POPP
  BARBARA 279
  BARBARA JEAN8 279
  BENJAMIN JAMES 279
  GABRIELLA 279
  JAMES ALAN 279
  JEANNETTE 278
  JESS ANDREW 279
  MARY ELIZABETH 279
  MATIE 279
  PATRICIA LOUISE 279
  ROBERT 278 279
  ROSEMARY 279
POTTER
  James & Polly (____) 150
  SOPORONA 150
PRATT
  Albert L 145

PRATT (cont'd)

Alice B 145
Edith M 145
Edwin H 145
Jane 145
John 145
MAGDALENA 93
Noah 145
Peter & Olive (Short) 93
Peter W S 93
Sarah A 145
Presbyterian 21, 26
Presbyterians 26-28
Prey
  Kevin 307
PRICE
  BARBARA LOUISE 286
  Geo H & Anna (Mishek) . . . 263
  RUTH ANNE 263
PRINCE
  _____ 98
  Hannah 132
  Peter 132
PRIOR
  Ruby 57
PRITCHARD
  Cathy 208
  Donald 208
Prol
  C. E. i
  Elbert i
Protestants 13, 21
PROULX
  DOREEN ELIZABETH 284
  Louis R & Marilyn (Quinn) . . 284
PRUYN
  William P 93
PRYNE
  Francis 64
PULTENEY
  William 348
PULVER
  MILDRED 182
PULVER, _____ 182
PURDY
  LOIS 300
PURNE 214
PUTNAM
  Tare 85
QUACKENBOSS
  Abraham 131, 132
  Pieter/Peter 131, 132
Quackenbosses
  see also Quackenbush v
QUACKENBUSH 26, 87
  Alex,Harriet,Edw,Chris-
    tina,David,Eliza,Dan . . . 132
  Alexander 132
  Ann 92
  ANNE4 131
  Augusta 132
  Charles 132
  Charles & Mina 132

Christina 132
Clark P 132
Cora L 132
Daniel 132
David 131, 132
Deby 132
Eliza Jane 132
Frederick M 132
Hannah 132
Iola 132
James C 132
John 71, 92, 131, 132
John & Deborah 132
John & Lucinda;Nellie,Pearl . . 132
John & Mary; Bertha 132
John J,Clarke P 132
LAURA A5 131
Mary 71, 92, 132
PETER 131, 132
Peter & Hannah (Prince) . . . 132
Rebecca 132
Spencer J 132
QUACKENBUSH families 131
QUAGLIANA
  DANIEL LEA 325
  DAVID PETER9 325
  DIANE (OYER) 82, 324
  Edwin & Anne 324
  PETER 324
QUINLAN
  Margaret D 211
  Thomas 211
QUINN
  Hugh E 194
RACE
  EDWARD A 275
  GERTRUDE 275
  JANET ELIZABETH 276
  NANCY JEAN8 276
Ramseier 6
RANDALL
  EUNICE VERA 295
  LEOLA DAWN 302
  Leon 302
RASBACH
  Barbara 126
Rasselstein Mill 13
RASZMANN
  DELEVAN7 . . . . 225, 271
  DOROTHY 225
  HELEN LOU (_____) 271
  HENRY 177, 225
  LUCY 177, 225
  PAULINE 225
  VIVIAN 225
RAYMOND
  BARBARA JEAN 274
  GERALDINE 306
Reader's Digest 29
REALS
  CHRISTIAN ANDREW9 273
  MARTHA 273

REALS (cont'd)

ROBERT W 273
SARAH BETH 273
REAMER
  Minnie 235
RECKINGEN
  J Jergen (Jerjern) 342
REDIGER
  Jacobina 341
REDMAN v
  CHRISTINA 109
  David & Elizabeth (Millious) 109
Reformation 26
Reformed Church .11,21,24,26,312,339
REGLE
  Jacobe 341
  Susanna 2
REIFF
  Anna 54
REIGEL
  Catharine 47
REINBOLT
  BETH ANNE8 223
  DEAN 223
RELLIHEN
  CHRISTINE9 263
  ROBERT 263
  SHELLY 263
  VIRGINIA 263
REMA 70
  Anna 73
  Catharine 66, 72, 100
  Christian 72, 89
  David 72
  DELANEY/DELANY4 . . . . 107, 156
  Elizabeth 72, 89
  Eve 72
  Frederick . . . 72, 73, 107
  George 72
  Jacob 72, 89
  JOHANNES/JOHN 35, 72, 100
  Lany 72
  Lydia 73
  Margaret 72, 89
  Maria 66, 72, 73
  Mary 72, 73, 102, 107
  Peter 72, 73
  Peter & Maria Cath (Hochstabler) 107
  Peter L 66
  Philinda 73
  Sarah 89
  Sophronia 72
REMA families 72
REMINGTON
  PATIENCE DIADEMA 149
REMY
  Jacob 13
  Johan Heinrich 13, 14
RENCKEL 40, 45
  Laurence - see Rinckle . . . 33
RENEKEL
  Laurence 32
RENGEL

Edward J 212
RETCHLESS
  HUBERT E 283
  JEAN SUZANNE 283
  LOUISE 283
  PATRICIA LOUISE8 283
  Ralph B 283
RETTBERG
  DIANE M.8 . . . . . . 262, 330
  DOLORES·7 261
  Fred & Marg (Shearer) . . . 261
  GRETCHEN A.8 . . . . . 262, 330
  HAROLD 261
  JOAN E.8 . . . . 262, 330
  MARY 262
Revere
  Paul 173
Revolution . . 27, 47, 60, 73, 77, 85
  88,89,111,132,134,138,145,339,348
Revolutionary 51, 253
REYNOLDS
  Alice 67
  Cuyler 63
  DONNA MARIE8 265
  DORIS 264
  EDITHE 265
  Elisha 118, 216, 217
  EUGENE 216
  EUGENE7 "HAPPY" 264
  FRANCES 264
  JAMES7 216
  JAMES7 R 264
  KATHERINE/KITTIE 6 216
  KENNETH 264
  MARIA 118
  Maria/Mariah 216
  Mariah 217
  MARIAN 264
  MARION 227
  Mary,Sarah,Alice,Hiram . . 217
  RICHARD 264
  RUTH8 264
  SUZANNE 265
  Vedder C 118, 217
  WALTER 227
REYNOLDS families 216
REYNOLDS,_____ 216
REYNOLDSHap
  Hap 265
RHINESMITH
  THERESA 331
RHODES
  BARBARA JEAN 295
  CAMILLA VERA 295
  HAZEL 239
  JACOB IMBRIE 239
  JUNIOR IMBRIE7 . . . . 239, 295
  LINDA ANNE8 295
  VERA 295
RICE
  CORA 155
  Edmond 221

RICE families 221
RICE,_____ 155
RICHARDS
  MARCELLA 270
RICHARDSON
  ALMIRA 135
  ANNIAS DYER5 . . . . . . 135, 184
  CLARA AUGUSTA 184
  EARL6 184
  GENEVA CAROLINE.5 . . . . 135, 185
  Helen 184
  J W 150
  Mrs. Duane 46
  NEHEMIAH 135
  NETTIE 184
  ORISSA 184
  SARAH CATHARINE 135
  SEYMOUR ANNIAS 184
RICKARD/S
  J S 119
RIDDLE
  Caroline 87
Riema 40
RIMA - see also REMA
  BETSEY 53
  JOHANN FRIEDRICH 63
  Katy 53
  MARIA 63
  Peter 46, 60
RIMA family 65
Rima(h) v
RIN[C]KLE
  Lawrence, Jr 60
RINCKEL
  Lorenz/Laurence . . . 32, 34, 35
  Lorentz, Catharina 49
RINCKLE
  Catherine 68, 70, 71
  Lorentz 70
  Maria 70, 89
Rinckle families 70
Ringwood Iron Works . . 19, 31, 335
RINKILL
  Catharine 47
RINKLE
  CLARINDA 125
  LEVI 125
ROBBINS
  L C 146
  Leonard & Martha (Holden) . . 146
  Martha 146
  Mary 53
ROBEDEE
  AUREL 301
  BARBARA JAYNE8 301
  DAVID DERALD 301
  Floyd & Twila (Harber) . . . 301
  JULIE ANN 301
ROBERT 308
ROCHE 11
  HONORA 213
  MARGARET 210

Roch Democrat & Chronicle . . . 28, 29
Roch Institute of Technology . . . 27
ROE
  ADA MARY 151
  David & Cath (Van Camp) . . . 151
  ELLA M.5 . . . . 151, 191
  HARRIET 151
  HIRAM 151
ROGERS
  MARSHA LEE 289
ROJAS
  Rosa 57
ROLLIn
  Phoebe 86
Roman Catholic 10, 26-29
Roman Catholic Franciscan 28
ROMAR
  Elisabeth 72
ROMLER
  Jos & Eliz (Feldman) 214
  OLGA 214
ROSBROOK
  ALAN CHARLES8 274
  BARBARA 274
  BEVERLY 274
  CHARLES ELI 274
  CHRISTOPHER SCOTT 274
  CYNTHIA JOAN 274
  DAVID LEE 274
  GARY ALAN9 274
  GLADYS 274
  LAURA ANN9 274
  PAMELA LYNNE 274
  ROBERT CHARLES 274
Rosencrantz
  (Pastor) Abraham 25, 49
ROSENTHAL
  Faye 295
ROSER
  GERALDINE MELVINA 243
ROSS
  LAWRENCE E 292
  LEE R8 292
  LOUIS R 292
  Mary 199
  RICHARD 292
  VERNA 292
Ross and Butler 45
ROUGEAUX
  Virginia 56
ROWLAND
  Anderson 92
  Polly 68
ROY
  Alex & Mary (McFarland) . . 113, 119
  John & Ellen 119
  Sarrah 119
ROY/Ray
  Julia 119
RUSH
  A B 178
  Cornelia 178

RUSH (cont'd)
Melvina 146
RUSS
  FRANCES LORRAINE 272
  Frank & Bert 288
  John J & Marie (Grant) . . . 272
  YVONNE 288
Russian 27
RUTHERFORD
  JESSIE 229
SACKET
  EMILY J 135
  Mrs Geo 68
SAMPSON
  DOUGLAS 330
  HAROLD DOUGLAS 330
  JOAN 330
  MARIE KAY9 330
  Peter 179
SANDERSON
  MERLYN 269
SAUNDERS
  Nathan 179
SAYERS
  DIANN 276
SCANLON
  JOHANNA 213
SCHEEF (?)
  Maria 341
SCHELL
  Barbara 126
  CONNIE LEE 286
  John 126
  MELISSA ANNE9 286
  Nancy 125, 126
  TERRI 286
  TIMOTHY 286
SCHELL families
  SCHELL 126
Schenck 26
SCHENK
  Trudy iii
SCHERMERHORN 116
SCHERTZ
  Barbara 340
SCHIMMELPENNINCK
  Rutger Jan 347
SCHNECK
  George & Barbara . 51, 55, 59, 63
  George & Lena 55
  MARY (MARIA) FREDERICKA . . . 51
  MARY FREDERICKA 55
SCHNEIDER
  BEATRICE CAMILLA7 . . . 239, 293
  ETHEL 239
  JENNIE DORIS 239
  JENNIE DORIS7 294
  JOHN MARTIN 239
  Peter & Barbara 239
SCHOALS, ____ 191
SCHOLEN
  BARBARA 287
  EDW JACOB 287

SCHONBORG
  BEVERLY 274
SCHOUW
  JELLISTE CLAESE 118
SCHRAG/SCHROCK
  Katharine 340
Schuldiener 338
SCHULENBERG
  MARJORIE 218
  Ray & Cecelia 218
SCHULTZ
  BETTY JANE 308
  FRANCES 264
Schumacher
  Cecelia 79
Schuyler
  Philip J 48
Schuylers v
Schwenkfelder 338
SCOBY
  Adaline L 94
  Addella 94
  Agnes 94
  Alex & Serepta (Boss) 93
  Alexander 94, 179
  Emeline E 94
  EMMA JANE 93
  Frances 94
  Herbert D 94
  Louisa A 94
  Madison 94
  Marshall D 94
  Maryette 94
  Sam 94
  Sophia 94
  Wm G 94
SCOBY families 94
Scotch-Irish 170
SCOTT
  Ann 131
  John 131
  Justus & Catherine (Bullis) . 98
  Mary E 98
SCOVEL
  Hezekiah 138
  Lorinda 138
SEALES
  ALAN DELOS9 MARTIN 295
  CAROLYN BELLE8 294
  CHARLES LOYT 294
  DAVID MARTIN 295
  HOPE MICHELLE 295
  Jas D & Martha L (Brown) . . 294
  JENNIE 294
  JOSEPH/JODY KENT9 295
  ROBERT LOYT 294
  ROSEMARY 294
  SUSAN 295
  TODD MITCHELL 295
SEAMAN
  ELIZABETH 136
  FLORRINE 136

SEAMAN, _____ 136
Secretariat for Christian Unity . 27
Senecas 45
SENTER
  [list of descandants] 170
  Jean (_____) 170
  John 170
  Sally 170
SENTERS, bible list 172
Seventh Reg't 122
Seventh-day Adventists 29
SEYE
  Hendrick 347
SHABATA
  Michiko 212
SHAFFNER
  _____ 102
SHARP
  SALINIA E 227
Shawnee 66
SHEAD
  Nancy 53
SHEARER
  Marguerite 261
SHEPARD
  BRAD WILLIAM9 301
  VANESSA 301
  WILLIAM 301
Sherman, General 166
SHIFFNER
  Mary 69
SHORT
  Olive 93
SHRUBB
  John & Eliz (Keys) 192
  SARAH LILLY 192
SIBLEY
  Benjamin 117
  Juliet 117
SIKES
  Gordon & Rhoda (Torrence) . . 224
  RACHEL G 224
SILLIMAN
  Mrs. Albert 120
SIMMONS
  Hannah 211
  MARGARET/MAGGIE 133
  SAMUEL WADE 133
  Seth 203
Simons
  Menno 7
SIWICKI
  KARA MAE10 332
  LEONARD 332
  TRACY 332
SKAGGS
  BONITA 318
  BRADLEY JOSEPH9 319
  DERRICK LEE 319
  RALPH LEE 319
SKIFF
  Maria 47

SKUDLAREK
  Louise 258
SMILEY
  MARGARET M 239
SMITH 255, 256
  Ada 257
  Anne 256
  Calvin 117
  CHARITY 143
  CHRISTOPHER 256
  Cora Helena 257
  Daniel 256
  E 94
  Edna 256
  Edward 256
  Edwin 257
  Elizabeth 256
  Ellen 256
  Emeline 94
  ESTELLE/STELLA 256
  Esther 257
  Frances 257
  FRANCES H 193
  Fred & Charity 101
  Frederica Oberlin 257
  FREDERICK 143
  Garrit 123, 124
  Geo & Eliza (King) 140
  Grace 257
  Helena 257
  Ida Grace 257
  Jackie 6, 342
  Jewell 257
  Josephine 257
  Julian Greenhow 82, 256, 257
  Julian King 257
  Katherine 256
  Keturah 256
  Louise 257
  Malcolm 344
  Maria 256
  NANCY ANN 140
  Nea Alma 257
  Palmer King 257
  Phyllis Ann 252, 256, 257
  Sally 101
  Selinda 117
  Seth 256
  Stella 257
  Sydney & Edna 257
  Sydney & Estelle/Stella (Palmer) 252
  SYDNEY LEA 256
  Sydney Lea, Jr 257
  THELMA 298
  THOMAS 256
  Thomas Lea 257
  WILLIAM 143
  Wm H 193
SMITH families 256
SMITH generational 256
Smith Mountain 82
SNECK 40

SNEK
  Magdalen 47
SNOW
  BATHSHEBA 258
  GLENNA 247
SNOW,_____ 247
SNYDER
  Esther 257
  Jane 146
SOLLENNE
  MARY MARGARET 315
SOMES 158, 192
  BARBARA ANN 284
  BARTON ROTHWELL7 . . . . 235, 283
  BERTHA (PARRY) 233
  BEVERLY JUNE 285
  BRENT BARTON9 284
  BRUCE DAVID9 284
  DOROTHY LEOLA7 . . . . . 236, 285
  ELIZABETH JEAN7 . . . . . 235, 284
  FLORA 235
  FLOYD6 . . . . 192, 235
  GARY BARTON8 283
  HENRY LEWIS5 . . . . . . 152, 192
  HOWARD WELLINGTON6 193
  Hunt 236
  Jacob 103
  JANET CAROL 285
  Jos & Marg (Auyer) 235
  Joseph 103, 108, 152, 153
  JOSEPH HUNTING6 . . .151, 193, 235
  JUNE 285
  KAPLE J.6 . . . . 193, 235
  KATHLEEN GAIL8 285
  LAURA 192
  LINDA 283
  MARGARET . . 103, 151, 152, 235
  MARJORIE 235
  MARTHA LOUISE7 . . . . . 235, 283
  OLIVE 235
  OREN ALEXIS 103, 152, 235
  OREN ALEXIS5 192
  RALPH B6 192
  REBA EVELYN7 . . . . . 235, 282
  ROBERT OREN7 . . . . . 236, 285
  Samuel & Mary (Barns) 151
  SARAH 192
  SMITH 192, 233, 235
  SUZANNE CAROL 284
SOMES
  HONEY 283
Sons of Liberty 254
Southern Baptist 29
SOUTHWORTHS 258
SPALDING
  ABIGAIL 220
  Jeremiah 123
  Tyler 123
Spanish Flu 204
SPAS
  Andy 57
  Claudette 57

Edward 57
Faith 57
Li 57
Rosa 57
SPAULDING
  Almon G 123
  AMANDA JULIETT 119, 120
  Betsey 123
  CLARISSA 122
  David 123
  Donald 123
  Edwin J 123
  Eliza 123
  Elizabeth 122
  Eloise 122
  Emiline 123
  Eugene 122
  Eunice 123
  FLORA 159
  Frank P 122
  FRANK REUBEN 159
  G W 123
  George B & Hannah (Kester) . . 159
  Harlan Page 122
  Harrison & Matila (Nichols) . . 194
  HARVEY 122
  Harvey & Clarissa (Hastings)119, 120
  Jacob 123
  James M 123
  John C 123
  Jonathan 123
  LOIS 176
  Mary A 123
  Minerva 123
  N G 123
  Nettie 123
  Phebe J 123
  Phoebe 123
  Samuel 123
  Simon J 123
  Solomon 123
  SUSAN/SUSIE MARIE 194
  Warner 123
  WILLIS 176
SPAULDING families 122
SPENCE
  Genevieve M 262
SPENCER
  Eunice Caroline 191
  RUTH 264
SPORE
  DORA 237
Squire
  Betsey E 118
St. Leger 40, 45, 48
St. Paul's Church 28
STACY
  Caroline/Carrie 221
Stadnitzki
  Pieter 347
STADY
  Joyce 181

INDEX (cont'd)

STAFFORD
  CLARK 196, 240
  EDITH7 240
  LAWRENCE 240
  OLIVE 240
STAHRING
  Elizabeth 84
  Frederick Philip 84
STARKS
  _____ 98
  Deborah 94
  Jedediah 94
STARR
  BRENDA ELAINE9 318
  DAVID ANTHONY 317
  MARILYNN JEAN 318
  SANDRA 317
  THOMAS ANTHONY 318
  WALTER/Wally JOSEPH . . . 318
STATER
  PENNY 269
STAUFFER
  Hans 54
STEELE
  George 69
  Maria 68
  Nicholas 68
  Olive 141
  Solomon 141
STEINWAX 71
  Arnold & Gertraud 54
  Eva Catherine 54
  Tibalt 60
STEINWAY
  Gertraud. 47
STEVENS
  Al & Martha (Holway) 242
  GRACE L 182
  HELEN 301
  PEARL SYLVIA 242
STEWART
  ANNA 263
  Arch 187
  Caroline M 186
  Helen 186
  LEONARD 263
STOCKIN
  AUDREY 270
  BETH LYNNE9 270
  CAROL 270
  CARY 270
  DANIEL JAY 270
  DAVID 270
  DOUGLAS 269
  GARY 270
  GAYLE8 270
  LINDA 270
  MARCELLA 270
  MELANIE9 270
  MICHAEL DAVID 270
  RUTH 222, 269

Stoll, Howard 260
STONE
  Almira E 172
STORMES
  GEORGE H 163
  MARY 163
  OSCAR E5 163
SUBJECT
  Josephine 257
Suisse (Switzerland) 340
SULLIVAN
  Jay 213
  MAY 215
Suto 213
Swart 116
SWEET
  BARBARA 284
  GERALD RAY 284
  JULIE ANN9 284
  MATHEW RAY 284
  SCOTT MICHAEL 284
SWEETMAN
  ANDREA 297
Swiss 10, 17, 71, 338
Swiss Mennonites 9
Swiss Mercenary 13
Switzers 10, 25
TABER
  NELLIE 149
TABER, _____ 149
TANNER
  CHARLENE RUTH 297
TARDIO
  ANTHONY 303
  DEBORAH LYNN9 303
  KATHY ANN 303
  SHARON 303
TEELING
  ELIZABETH 215
TEFFT v
  Alex & Deborah (Niles) . . . 140
  ALEXANDER 141, 142
  Alice 142, 189
  Alma 142
  Anstice J 141
  BYRON S 141
  Franklin. 142
  Nathaniel Niles 141, 142
  NELSON 187
  Niles 142
  Olive 141
  Oliver 141
  OLIVER & DEBORAH (DEWEY) . . 141
  Polly 141
  Royal 142
  Ruth Ann 142
  SALLY 187
  SAMUEL 140-142
  Staunton 141
  Stephen E 142
  Susan 142
  Walter 142

TEFFT (cont'd)
William Pitt 141, 142
TEFFT families 141, 187
Temperance Society 121
TENNANT
  LEEA 305
  LINDSEY RENEE 305
  MICHAEL JAMES 305
  VICKI 305
TETRAULT
  BRIAN KEITH 287
  EMMA 286
  JESSICA 287
  KURT LaVERNE 287
  ROBERT 286
  ROBERT CHARLES 287
  TERRI LYNNE8 286
TEWES
  Adelaide 309
  FRANCES 309
THAYER
  VICKI 243
THEUSCH
  Marcella M 319
Thirty Years' War 13
THOMAS
  Addella 94
  AMANDA 247
  ANN 292
  BLANCHE T 197
  CATHERINE 220
  Chas A & Rosina (Kester) . . 197
  DAVID 247
  DEBORAH ANN 292
  DONALD 238, 292
  ELMER J 238
  GLEN C 199
  Henry W & Emily (Watters) . . 199
  JOSHUA 247
  MALINDA 247
  MARTHA 199
  MARTIN JAMES 292
  RACHAEL 238
  RICHARD PAUL8 292
  RICHARD W.7 . . . . . 238, 292
  ROBERTA 247
Thomas, General 166
THOMPSON
  ADA 183
  ADELINE 183
  DANIEL 183
  DURWOOD W 232
  EDWARD 183
  ESTHER L6 232
  Geo & Nettie (Whitman) . . . 232
  HOSMER W.6 183
  JESSIE E 183
  MARTHA 183
  NATHAN 183
  OYER7 232
  SARAH J 183
THORPE
  SUSAN 288

Tifft
  CARRIE LOUISE 195
  BERNICE 195
  BLANCHE 195
  Caleb & Jane (Alcorn) Dunlap . . 156
  CARRIE LOUISE 157
  HARRIET/HATTIE 195
  HENRIETTA/ETTA MARY . . . 157, 198
  JENNIE BELLE5 . . . . . 157, 196
  MABEL ELLA6 . . . . . 195, 238
  MARTHA JANE4 . . . . . 108, 156
  O A & Martha Jane (Auyer) . . 198
  ORANGE ANGELL (OA)109, 156, 157, 160
  RACHAEL A.6 . . . . . 195, 238
  WAYNE INGALLS 195
  WILLIAM CARLTON5 . . . . 157, 195
TILLINGHAST
  ANNE MARIE 273
TINKCOM
  Geo 88
TJERKSE
  ANNTJE 118
TOONEY
  MILDRED 229
Tories 11, 38, 40
TORRENCE
  Rhoda 224
Tory 45, 131, 132
TOWNER
  J. I 120
TRACY
  Estella 281
TRAVERS
  Eugene 68
TRAVIS
  Earl 68
TRAYLOR
  SUZANNE 312
TREDO
  DANIEL CLYDE 246
  EDWARD/MOSIE 246
  ELIZABETH/BETTY 246
  FLORIS EILEEN8 246
  LORENE 246
  THERESA 246
TREVETT
  Madge 56
TRUMILLER
  Roman 124
Tryon
  William 48
Tryon Co Committee of Safety . . . 39
Tryon Co Militia 39, 86, 88
TURHAN
  JEANETTE 217
  VINCENT 217
TURK
  SARAH 212
TURNER
  HARRY 307

TYGERT
  Peter 46, 47
TYLER
  Asher 181
  Jennie 181
UNGER
  CHARLES 270
  DAWN 270
  LOUANNA 270
  MARTHA 222, 270
  MELVIN 222, 270
  NANCY8 270
  TERRY 270
United Church of Christ . . . 27
United Methodists . . . 26, 28, 29
Upstate NY Synod of the
  Evangelical Luth Ch in Amer . 28
UTLEY
  EVERILL 177
  ISA 177
VAESCH/FAESCH
  see also Faesch 13
Vail-Ballou Press 10
VALENTINE
  DANIEL TOMPKINS 156
  Ebenezer & Silvia (Adams) . . 156
  FRANCES SANTONETTE4 156
  Nancy/Nancey 72
  ORRIN 156
  ROSIE 156
  SIDNEY. 72
VALENTINO
  VALERIE 314
VALLELY 214
VAN AUKEN
  C Howard 184
  CHARLES HOWARD 184
  CLARA 184
  HELEN M 184
VAN CAMP
  Catharine 151
VAN DE BOGART 116
  FRANS 118
  HESTER 118
VAN DER BOGART
  CLAES 118
  FRANS 118
  HARMEN MYNDERTSE 118
VAN DER BOGART families . . . 118
VAN DER VOLGEN 116
Van Eeghen
  Pieter 347
VAN EPS 116
VAN HORN
RAYMOND 331
  MABEL 147
VAN HORN, _____ 147
VAN HORNE
  ADELBERT 193
  HERBERT 193
  MILDRED 193
  NINA 193

POLLY 193
VAN RENSSALAER
  Stephen 349
VAN SLYCK 40
  Gerard 60
  Jacob 60
Van Slycks 132
VAN SLYKE 87, 132
  Anna Eva/Nancy Eve 85
  Augustus 81, 85, 91, 180
  Augustus & Nancy Eva (Frank) . . 90
  John 87, 91
  MARY ANN/POLLY 90, 91
  Morris 91
VAN SLYKE families 91
Van Staphorst
  Nicholas 347
VANDERLEAN
  Gertrude 229
VANSELOW
  CLARENCE HUGO8 302
  DANIEL RICHARD 302
  DOROTHA 302
  HUGO 302
  JENNIFER ERIN BRYSON10 . . . 302
  JOYCE (_____) 302
  JUDY ANITA 302
  JULIE 302
  KATHLEEN/KATHY MARY 302
  LAURIE NANCY 302
  LEOLA 302
  NEAL RANDALL9/RANDY 302
  Otto & Mary (Grudman) 302
  REBECCA ANN/BECKY 303
  RONALD GEORGE 302
Vatican 27
Vatican II 27
VAUX
  Mrs. Seldon 120
VEDDER 25, 26, 91
  Adaline 101
  ADALIZA E.5 . . . . 145, 188
  ADELINE 143
  ADELINE (OYER) 116
  ALBERT 118
  Albert & Mary (Seaman) . . . 116
  Albert & Polly (Seaman) . . . 143
  Alice 142, 145, 189
  Allan & Betty (Jirak) 219
  Anna 117
  Betsey 101, 118
  BETSEY (OYER) 118
  Betsey (Oyer) Oyer 135, 143
  Bruce 117
  CHARITY 58, 144
  Charity,Jenette 117
  CHARLES 144
  COMMODORE PERRY 118, 168
  CORNELIUS 116, 143
  CORNELIUS & ADELINE (OYER) . . 58
  Edwin 111
  Elinor 117

VEDDER (cont'd)

Ellen M,Clara,Harvey,John . . 116
Emma 117
Eva Eliza 106, 107, 118
Francis Jacob 117
Frederick 116
Genevieve 119
H H 116
HARMEN ALBERTSE 116
Harriet 116
Harvey 120
Helen 117
Jacob & Marg (Gardinier) . . 113,
                      143, 144, 217
Jacob F 117, 118
Jacob M 116
JANETTE 144
JOHANNES 118
Johannes & Eva (Clute) . . . 117
JOHN 118, 135, 143, 144
MARGARET 117
MARIA 118
Maria/Mariah 216
Mary 116
MARY ELLEN5 . . . . . . 143, 189
Octavius P 117
PEGGY 219
Rachel . 101, 106, 113, 118, 143,
                      144, 217
RACHEL (OYER) 118, 144
RACHEL A 145
Selinda 117
Simon 116
Slyvanus & Emeline (Kent) . . 117
Sylvanus K 117
Vedders v
Veder 116
VEEDER 91, 116
Veeders v
VELZY
  DORIS 176
VELZY, _____ 176
VETTER
  RACHEL [VEDDER] 116, 117
Vischer/Fischer 116
VISSCHER
  Elinor 117
  Hestertse 118
VOGT, _____ 176
Vollenhaven
  Hendrick 347
Von Graffenried
  Christoph 10
VOSBURG
  ALIDA 216
Vosburgh's CR 63
VOSS
  LILLIAN FRED'ICA/FREDA . . . 222
VREELAND
  Charles G 257
  Helena 257
  Louise 257
Vrooman 26, 91, 116

WADE
  SYLVIA 282
WADSWORTH
  GENEVA 135, 185
  GEORGE 135, 185
Wainwright
  Robert 28
WAITE
  ALIDA 216
  Alida E 217
  ALIDA7 265
  Andrew & Alida (Vosburg) . . 216
  Andrew J 217
  DOROTHY 216
  DOROTHY7 265
  HUGH 216
  Kittie 216
  Manley 217
  Maud S 217
  WELLMAN/BILL 216
WAITE families 216
WALKER
  DONETTA 242
  Jedediah 88
  Robert 242
  RUTH LYNN 230
WALLACE
  Emeline 124
  Leonard A 124
  Lottie E 124
  Robert A 124
Walley
  SARAH 173
WALSH
  James 212
WALTER
  BARBARA 237
WALTERS
  ESTHER IRENE6 223
  RALPH 223
  ROSCOE 223
WAMP 116
War - 1812 92, 134, 138, 142, 170, 179
WARNER
  Adaline 94
  Wm H 94
WART
  A. B. 190
Washington
  George 335
WASSON
  AGNES6 218
  FLOYD 218
  JANE7 219
WATERSON
  HELEN 227
WATKINS
  _____ & ADDIE (SIMMONS) . . . 228
  ETHEL 228
  LAURA 227
WATSON
  N.C. 108

WATTERS
  Emily 199
WEAVER
  Delany 107, 156
  GEORGE H 156
  Gertraut 85
  LEWIS F 156
  Michael 85
  PETER 156
  Peter & Charity (_____) . . 156
  SIMON P5 156
WEBER
  Inez 56
  James B 56
  Margaret (Maria?) 85
WEBSTER
  CHRISTIE ADAIR9 312
  DAVID FRASER8 . . . . . 248, 311
  DAVID SHERWOOD9 310
  FRANCES 309
  Geo A & Jussie (Fraser) . . . 248
  GEORGE FRASER 248, 311
  GEORGIA/GIGI 248
  JOHN FRASER 312
  KAREN LEE 310
  KATHERINE LEE 311
  Marjorie 249, 311
  NANCY 224
  SARAH 309
  SHERWOOD FRASER8 . . . . 248, 309
WEBSTER families 249
WEGNER
  Erich 2
Weiser
  Frederick 26, 337, 339
  Frederick S 3
  John Conrad 24
WELCH
  CAROLYN 288
  JOSEPH 288
WELDON
  ANNA 163
  BYRON S.5 187
  Caroline 142
  Carrie 142
  CHARLES A 189
  Chas & Mary 95
  Chas & Mary; Allice,Stanley . 142
  DAC6 187
  Deborah A 141
  Dewey 141, 142, 187
  Dewey & Harriet; Harriet . . 142
  Eliza 142
  ELMER B 187
  Emily Amelia 141
  EMMONS D5 141
  Emory Nathaniel 141
  Erastus 142
  EVA 187
  EVA M (_____) 187
  George & Alice 142
  George E 142, 189

Gretchen 141
Harriet 141
HARRY VEDDER6 189
IRA O.5 . . . . 141, 187
JENNIE6 187
JOHN 187
Leonora 142
LUCY 187
MADGE N 189
MARTHA 141
Mary 101, 140, 141
Wellington
  Lydia 126
WELLS
  Claudette 57
  J 57
WEMPLE 91
  Abraham 111
  Andres 111
  Barnabus 111
  Barnet B 111
  CATHARINE 111
  Edward 111
  Eli 111
  HENRY B 111
  John 111
  Nicholas 111
  R 111
  William 111
WEMPLE families 111
Wemples v
WENDELL
  MARGARET 173
WENTS 40
Wesley
  John 25
WEST
  Christina 132
  CLARA A 185
  George 80
  James 132
  Sarah Frances 193
  William C 185
WESTCOTT
  FLORENCE V 130
 130
WETZEL
  BERNICE 195
  DELORES 280
Wever
  BLANCHE 195
WHATLEY
  Alyson 208
  Claire 208
  Linda Marie 208
WHEATON
  C JAMES 298
  KAY 298
  Ruth Ann 142
  Susan 142
WHEELER
  Genevieve A (Hill) 119

Whigs 11, 172
WHITCOMB
  Kittie 251
WHITE
  Art & Marcella (Theusch) . . 319
  AZARIAH S 109
  Cordelia 97
  DOROTHY 265
  Elisha & Sally 109
  ELIZABETH 109
  George & Ellen (Pierce) . . . 189
  HARRIET/HATTIE R 189
  Herm & Caroline (Green) . . . 189
  JANE 211
  LOMAMARIEL/MYRT 218
  MARCELLA 319
  MARY ELLEN5 189
  SQUIRE VEDDER6 189
  WILLIAM F8 265
  Wm 97
WHITE, _____ 218
WHITMAN
  Nettie 232
WHITMER
  CARMALETTA 313
WHITNEY 108
  ADA L.5 . . . . 158, 196
  ELIZABETH 197
  EMILY 158
  EMMA 197
  HOWARD JAY6 197
  JAY J.5 . . . . 158, 197
  Jerome & Cath (_____) . . . 158
  LENA R.5 . . . . . . 158, 196
  LUMORA MARVEL6 . . . . . 197, 240
  STELLA MAY5 . . . . . 158, 196
  SULLIVAN 158
WIDRICK
  Barbara 72
  Polly 72
WIDRIG . . . . v, 40, 55, 71
  Catherine 68, 69
  CHARLOTTA/LOTTIE6 217
  Conrad 68, 69, 72, 129
  ELEANOR 217
  Elizabeth 68, 89
  Eva Catherine 68
  George 68, 69
  George & Maria Elisabeth . . . 68
  Hannah 69
  HARRIET CATHARINE4 129
  Jacob . . . 45, 60, 69, 70, 72, 95
  Jacob & Cath Elis 89
  Jacob & Catherine (Rinckle) . . 72
  Jacob W 68
  James 72
  John Simon 69
  Lavina 69, 129
  Lawrence 72
  Louise 69
  Maria 65, 68
  Mary/Mary Margaret . . . 69, 72

  Maytie 69
  Michael . . . 35, 45, 68, 69, 89
  MICHAEL & MAGDALENA 65
  Michael & Sarah (_____) . . . 129
  Nancy 69
  Philinda 55
  Philip 68
  PHILLIE 217
  Sarah _____ 69
  Sophronia 72
  Susanna 69
  William 69
Widrig families 70
Widrig family 68
Widrig generational 69
Wied
  Count of 13
WIGHTMAN
  ELVA M 232
WILBUR
  DOROTHY 251
  EMORY 251
WILCOX
  Elsie 153
  Maria 179
WILERICH, _____ 191
WILEY
  BELLE 197
  _____ 197
Willebrands
  Johannes, Cardinal 27
Willet
  Marinus, Col. 45, 85
WILLIAMS
  DIANE 218
  DOROTHY 218
  Elmer D 98
  Jennie 125
  JOSHUA9 283
  KATHRYN 228
  LARRY 218
  LARRY LEE 218
  MARGARET 302
  MYRTLE 222
  RICHARD EVAN 228
  RUTH 283
  Sarah 98
  WILLIAM J 283
Willink
  Jan 347
  Wilhelm 347
WILLIS
  Eden & Mary 185
  GERTRUDE 185
WILSON
  BRIAN CHRISTOPHER 224
  CHARLES S 157
  CHRISTINA ANN 279
  CYNTHIA HEATHER 224
  DALE 223
  David & Nancy (Cook) 325
  Ella 221

WILSON (cont'd)

FRANCES 304
Jennifer 278
JENNIFER FRANCES 279
JULIE MARIE 325
KEITH DOUGLAS 279
LAURA 195
MARTHA5 157
MARY 279
ROBERT 279
SARAH ANN4 . . . . . . 108, 157
SUSAN 223
THEODORE O 157
THOMAS E 288
TIMOTHY JACOB 279
VALERIE 288
WIATT T 195
WILTSIE
Lorilla J 221
Winne 116
WINNIE
George & Helen (Heim) 277
HELEN ROSE 277
WISE
Ed & Louise (Skudlarek) . . . 258
THERESA 258
WISE families 259
WITMER
CAROL 314
WITRIG
Catherine 70
Michael & Elizabeth 55
WITRIG family 65
Witterich/Wuttrich/Widrig
see also Widrig . . .4, 17, 21, 26
WITTMAN
FRANCES LORANE/LORRAINE . . . 171
Hattie 171
Lorraine 171
WOLBER
Christian 341
WOOD
ARTHUR WARREN 228
DELLA ELIZABETH6 228
GLENN CHESTER 228
IRA ALBERT7 228
KATHRYN FRANCES 228
LEOTA 233
Lillian F. 10
MARGUERITE EMMA7 . . . 228, 273
MILDRED GAYLORD 228
RUTH MARION7 . . . . . 228, 273
WOOD, _____ 233
Woodman 213
WOODRUFF
_____ 143
Abram & family 181
AGNES 227
ALBERT 144
Alice 181
ARCHIE ALVIN6 . . . . . 180, 227
Bennie 181
Charity 101, 143

Della 146
DORIS 227
Earl 181
Edna 181
Elmer 181
Ernest 181
EULA MAE 226
FLORENCE A7 226
Frederick 181
GEORGE 180, 181, 226, 227
GERVIS G 226
HELEN 227
HOWARD 227
ISSAC 180
JANE KATHLEEN 227
Jay 181
Jean 181
JEAN E 226
Jennie 181
JESSIE 226
John 181
Joyce 181
LAURA 227
LAWRENCE 227
Mariett 181
MARTIN HENRY 131, 180
MARY ALICE5 . . . . . . 131, 180
Mary Beth 181
Maude 181
Michael Robert 181
MILDRED GRACE 227
MYRTLE MAY 180
Nellie 181, 226
RALPH A 226
Robert 181
WOODRUFF families 180
Woodruff generational 180
WOODWORTH
M 145
Sarah 145
WORDEN
ELLA 162
THOMAS 162
WRIGHT
Nettie 123
REBECCA 288
WUJASTYK
Stanley & Rose 326
WULHAM
CYNTHIA ANN 288
Ronald & Molly 288
WWII . 250, 253, 256, 259, 260, 265,
267, 272, 278, 280, 281, 287,
329, 343
Wydrig 60
YAGER
MARION 200
YAHN
MARCELLA 319
YATES
Anna 117

Yohn
  Frederick C 45
YOUCKER
  Catherine 70
YOUNG
  DOUGLAS ALLEN 281
  EMILY 281
  GEORGE CLARK7 281
  KENNETH HAROLD 281
  WILLIAM R 281
YOUNG/JUNG
  Elizabeth 71
ZAHN
  JACK 287
  MATTHEW TIMOTHY 287
  TODD JOSEPH8 287
  VERNA 287
ZEHR (Serre)
  Francoise 340
ZELIAS
  CAROLYN 294
  LAURA LYNN 294
  ROBERT JOSEPH 294
  SUSAN MARIE9 294
  Walter & Mary 294
ZIER
  JANE 272
ZUJUS
  JOAN 331

This 1920's horse drawn bus was Kill Buck, N.Y.'s first school bus.
(Photo courtesy of Wilma Tyler)

CERTIFICATE OF MARRIAGE.

This Certifies

That on the *Fourteenth* day of *September* in the year of our Lord one thousand eight hundred and sixty *five*, at the Town of *Persia Cattaraugus* County, and State of New York, I

United in Marriage

Andrew Ozer of the Town of *Otto*

and *Livina Widrick* of the Town of *Ashford*

that I am satisfied they are respectively of sufficient age to contract marriage; and are personally known by me, or satisfactorily proven, to be the persons above named. And also that after due inquiry made, there appeared no impediment to such marriage.

I do further certify the *James Shaffner* and *Mahala Shaffner* were present at such marriage as attesting witnesses.

James Shaffner

Mahala Shaffner
Witnesses.

Frank A Newell
Justice of the Peace

Printed and Sold by Benton & Andrews, Rochester, N.Y.

review appeared in the January

The New York Genealogical and

Record (Vol. 121, page 57).

Book Reviews [January

LIES, *Their History and Genealogy*, by Phyllis Smith Oyer. 1988. Cloth, 6×9,
2. Price: $30. plus $3.50 p&h from Mrs. Oyer, 263 Bakerdale Rd., Roch-
376]

er, also known as Frederick Oyer, emigrated in 1764 probably from Ger-
w Herkimer County, New York, and died at the Battle of Oriskany in
een collecting data on his descendants since before 1977, when she issued
he genealogy (Rec. 109:179). In this new edition she has assembled her
: and cited sources at the end of each entry, included biographical infor-
ds, outlined the historical background for the early generations, and added
amilies. Our review copy also contains three pages of additions and cor-
the impression that much research, careful organization and planning
of this attractive book.

Steuben Echoes

Genealogy Comments:
Ruth Magill has submitted the
following review of a book give
to our Library.

Oyer and Allied Families
by Phyllis Smith Oyer

This book is far more than a
genealogy of Johann Friedrich
EYERER (Frederick Oyer). It de-
scribes the historical and reli
background of families who came
from Germany, through France,
Holland, and England to New York
and New Jersey. The greatest
emphasis is on the families who
eventually settled in the Mohawk
Valley - not only the Oyers, but
also Folts, Clarks, Hammonds,
Vedders, Gardiners, Truaxes, Fox
and many, many other lines- eigh
generations of them as they move
on to Western New York and to ot
States.
There are detailed maps of small
areas, reproductions of wills,
plaques at historical sites,
pictures of homes and churches,
and portraits of family members,
and finally, an index of over 50
pages.
The research and documentation m
this one of the most valuable bo
in our collection. We are indebt
to Phyllis Smith Oyer for this
volume which will prove helpful
many of our members.

I Remember Grandma

Grandma, with Grandpa's support, gradually assumed the responsibility for my sister and myself when we were toddlers. She was teaching school in Humphrey. It was a one-room school with built-in outhouses. Grandma made the wood and coal fires. She supervised our taking out the ashes and bringing in the wood and coal. We also ran out to the pump and brought in two pails of water to fill our water crock which had a little fountain on it. Grandma was only teaching kindergarten through grade six them with about 25 students. Her rest period for the day was monitoring our play period. Grandma often had a kettle of hot water on the stove. Students brought jars of food in their lunch pails to heat for hot lunches.

I remember Grandma who got up for morning milking of the dairy cows, some years at 4 a.m., then helped with the feeding and cleaning of the animals.

Next was hurry to the house for breakfast, help get two children ready for school, and rush all three of us one mile to her teaching site. Sometimes we walked. After the school day, which included sweeping the building, it was back home for supper. Then rush to the barn for evening milking and other chores. Bedtime was often as early as we could get there with Grandma reading stories in a voice loud enough for all of us to hear from our pre-nocturnal slumber spots.

Carol and I left for college. Grandpa retired and went to Florida winters. Grandma continued to teach in Ellicottville, with modern facilities at last, but at home alone with our winters. She did it to pay for our college educations It was very rewarding. She glimpsed us occasionally on weekends and paid large bills. Grandma only did that until she was 73.

As a bride, Grandma went to the state of Washington to spend a couple of years in the shack helping Grandpa complete his five years of occupancy to become a homestead owner of 160 acres of semi-desert. During that interval, they spent a winter cooking for a logging crew in the mountains but didn't get paid because the company went bankrupt.

Can I possibly put a Grandma like that to rest with a born yesterday, died today, and survived by me?

W. Mark Oyer
Grandson of Pearl Starks Bay

May her new adventures be her best yet.

Tribute to grandmother written by W. Mark Oyer.

Former Residents Appliance Service Wins High Honor

ROCHESTER—Oyer's Appliance Service, Inc. at 189 North Water St., operated by Mr. and Mrs. Walter C. Oyer, formerly of Salamanca and Killbuck, has been judged the leading RCA Whirlpool service department in the nation.

The honor is the result of a nationwide audit in which 300 customers were interviewed in the Rochester area and Oyer's scored 99.4 per cent satisfaction.

Other fields covered were the parts department, warranties, training service literature and administration. The Oyers have been in the business for eleven years and recently moved to a new warehouse. They have twenty-nine employes.

Mrs. Oyer does all the firm's bookkeeping and much of the detail work at their home at 263 Bakerdale Rd. Mr. Oyer trains his own employes and servicemen and dealers in the Rochester area.

Albany State Barracks Oct 6 no
Brother Jacob   I recd your letter
in due time and now take
the oportunity to answer
this sunday morning we had
to pack our knapsacks for
g inspection paraded and
inspected then we went to church
on Broad way 4th presbytiran- Prof
J Wool leads the singing and such
singing I never heard before I
was at his house by invitation

REMEMBER ELLSWORTH!

Page

Mr Jacob Oyer
Buffalo
N.Y